The Land
of
Seasons and Songs

Sayed Athar Husain Naqvi

Grosvenor House
Publishing Limited

This book is published by
Grosvenor House Publishing Ltd
Link House
140 The Broadway, Tolworth, Surrey, KT6 7HT.
www.grosvenorhousepublishing.co.uk

A CIP record for this book
is available from the British Library

ISBN 978-1-83975-560-6

بہ اسمِ سُبحا نہو

Be – Isme Subhanahoo

With the name of God, the glorified

In memory of my parents, their parents
and the parents of their parents

And

To the great peoples of the lands of the subcontinent
of India - the Land of Seasons and Songs.

ہندوستان کے لوگ شاستری، پنڈت اور گپتا

سہروردی، سیّد، پرویزی اور مرزا

عجب شانِ خلقت دکھائیں یہ ہر انداز سے

نبوّت نہ آئی انکے ڈر ضرورت نہ تھی انکو آج نہ فردا

Hindostan Kay Loag Shastri, Pandit Aur Gupta
Suharwardi, Sayed, Parwezi Aur Mirza
Ajab Shan-e Khilqat Dekhaein Yeh Her Andaz Say
Nbuat Na Aaee Inkay Dar Zaroorat Na Thhi Inko Aaj Nah Farda

People of India; Shastri, Pundit and Gupta
Suharwardi, Sayed, Parwezi and Mirza
All show unique grandeur of creation from every angle
Prophethood did not come to their door, they had no need today
neither tomorrow

ACCOLADE

I have read the book and found it engaging,
well written and very enjoyable.
Corinna Holmes – Fourth Estate Ltd. London

I have not seen writing like this in my eighteen years of work
Gul Afshan – Ferozsons Publishers. Karachi

There are nuggets in it
Linda Stevens - Pinner Philosophy Group. London

It is going to be book of the year
Alan Johnston - Pinner Philosophy Group. London

Biblical in style and it has all that
Harrow Reading Group. London

It is Magic
Librarian Pinner Philosophy Group. London

CONTENTS

ACKNOWLEDGEMENTS

The glimpses of the glorious rules of the Nawabs of Awadh and their style of living presented in the passages of the Land of Seasons and Songs have their sources of information in the authenticity of the words of my venerated elders. And for that they have found their place in the book. I am immensely thankful to these venerated souls for describing bits of these essentials of important cultural values in sketches that inspired my imagination to form a picture of the glorious Awadh as drawn in the book. The book then is filled by my cultural affinity with the Shia Muslims life and its associated values and my personal observations using vision and insight in the capacity of a writer.

I am very thankful to my late wife Begum Najma Husain, for her consistent support, her restraint comments and timely information she provided to me on so many topics. She was Master of Arts in Psychology, MA Previous in Islamic History and Bachelor of Art in Education and had twenty-three years of teaching experience and I am very greatly obliged to her for her contributions and help in writing this book. I am also very thankful to my sons, particularly to Sayed Asad Husain and then to my nephew Syed Adnan Hussain for their valuable assistance in all computer related works. And I am thankful to my parents for such pious life they led where from satisfaction and serenity flew that I absorbed to turn to write.

I further, profoundly thank the honoured Khateebs, the Imams of the mosques, *Waez* – the sermon givers and to the Swamis for their valuable speeches, in particular I am thankful to Allama Rashid Turabi Marhoom (Pakistan), Allama Talib Jauhari (Pakistan), Imam Juma, Maulana Taufiq Najfi Moosvi (Pakistan), Imam Juma Maulana Farazdaq Razavi (London), Imam Juma, Maulana Mohammad Hasan Maroofi (London), Maulana Urujul Hasan Meesam (India), Aayet Ullah Aqeel al Gharvi (India), Allama Abbas Kumaili (Pakistan), Hafiz Tasadduq Husain (Pakistan) Maulana Ghazanfar Abbas (India), Masoud Davoudi (Iran),

Shree Kirtit Bhai Jee (India), Shree H.G. Devakinandan Das (India), Gurudev Shree Chitrabhanu (USA), many a pieces of their speeches have had revelations and have been placed in the book.

I am then thankful to other Ulema and Swami, whose names have not been mentioned here but whose teachings and style, have stayed in the subconscious of my mind and have influenced my writing. To the performances of the Ram Lila, the resplendent narrates of Ram Katha and to the Krishna Darsh; to all of these I owe my profound thanks.

My thanks are due to Begum Razia Arshad Aas for her compilation of the book Al Manaqib, quoting the poetic verses of great saints in eulogy of Hazrat Ali AS., some of which I have quoted in the book. Thanks, are also due to Maulana Mohammad Shareef Noori for his Baarah Taqreerein, from which interesting anecdotes have been taken for the book. I have special thanks to professor Al Hajj Zainul Abedeen for his booklet Bara Imam and to Dr Mohammad Tejani Samavi for his series of very valued books. And I am thankful to many, many other valued writers whose thoughts illuminate my mind and this book.

I profusely thank next the Public Libraries in London for their immense ready help they render. And I am thankful to the internet which has been such an immense help with historical data and pertinent information and I am indebted to the Pinner Philosophy Group London for the philosophy talks there that have been so contributory to the book.

I am then so very thankful to that Unseen Force that renders help that I come across every now and then during the writing of this book; the undefined source substantiating the data and helping in the narration of the events that I was writing. It is all God's *Maslehat* – the design, and the order is wholly miraculous, they happen and come walking on their feet.

In the end I thank God of all creation for His Aayat 29: 69:

And those who strive in Our (cause) – we will certainly guide them to Our Paths: for verily God is with those who do right.

And I acknowledge the capacity of the word 'and' in the English language, without which I would not know, how I could write the book.

In the end, I thank God of all creation for His Aayat 91. 1-15: *Wash – Shamsi Wa Zuhaa-haa. Wal-Qamari Iza Talaa-ha. Wan-Nahari Iza Jallaa-ha. Wal-Layli Iza Yaghshaa-ha...,* for the God's style that I humbly borrow with His consenting and try copy and express thoughts in the ways of His surprises and wonders.

-: . :-

Synopsis

The Land of Seasons and Songs is a flower basket of humour, poetry and is an acquainting with the cultures and the traditions indigenous to the land, and presenting logical discourses. It is recollection of the yesteryears, with observations of happenings. It is a book of criticism, punches and reformative doses. The book reviews the present-day society and describes the culture de-grand of the subcontinent of India. It describes of its Kings, feudalism, genius of the peoples, and it sheds light on the world divisive politics as and when it deviates from the path of peace. It draws attention to the excellences of poetry that is a naturally flourishing trait in the subcontinent of India. The book presents the picture of India under the British rule and remembers of British with affection. The book is written in vivid English and the profession of the book is eulogy of the pious and pleasing the soul of the reader. This edition is republished with enhanced charm.

The central character of the book is Bachchu Yarwah the Aekkewan – the horse and cart driver. His peculiarities of commands he generates to control his horse on the road, creating a world of phenomena and his life he leads in his village gives an insight into the Indian-ology, the Indian colloquialism of the region he lives in. The thoughts put in the book are from the observations, as factual as the fall of snow:

Snow

It is snowing outside
Grass and ground are white
Birds have only branches to peg on
Or fly across to unknown bites
This is nature, it has made everything quiet
The men don't walk, dogs not out to stride
Unless you are secure in shelter will die
End of world but will not come, time will continue to ride

Sayed Athar Husain

INTRODUCTION

The book, The Land of Seasons and Songs is a Kashkole – a bowl of the mendicant in which assortment of thoughts and events have been poured as they come waiving their flag and join in the collection and there after give their specific fragrance. The book mentions of the kings and the paupers with alike profoundness. The book's asset is its humour that revolves round the country horse and cart driver for his peculiarities he displays and his slang he brings out and through his innocence he spells the heritage of the village life in India.

The English used in the book is translation of the thought flow of the Urdu bred mind, expressed in the English language. And in processing simplistic explanations through interaction with my religious tendencies produce expressions of some uniqueness here and there. The book discourses current politics, religion of the pious and describes of the Takfiris – the fallacious and of the life of the chaste. The events mentioned are trimmed to give flower fragrance and bare the tragedy they shed. And looking from a place in the cosmos, the world presents itself is a place of remorse and tragedy, since most of the great personalities in the end meet world behaviour with them of disarray.

The book follows the guide line of the Prophet of God Hazrat Mohammad Mustafa SAWW:

Mizahul Momin Aebada

"The most favoured act near God is to please the heart of the Momin[1]."

---

[1] Generally, any gold hearted person who considers other's good is better than his, is like a Momin. Imam Jafar Sadiq AS. said, 'The believers are servants of each other'. Asked, 'How are they servants of each other?' The Imam replied, 'By being of benefit to each other.'

The book is poised to please the pious and the good people of the world. It in all its humility is composed to please the solemn souls – the purity full people world over, who follow humanitarianism – the way of peace in the world. It takes one to the yesteryears of the simple days and draws a picture of the past. The Indianology is a world of its own specific, and the culture is brought to the fore, by the book. The book is vividly written and the thoughts and expressions in it are in the mould of humour.

The glimpses of the glorious rule of the Nawabs of Awadh and their style of life presented in the passages of The Land of Seasons and Songs have their sources of information taking origin from the respectability of the words of my venerated elders. And for that the information in the book carries inadmissible error and its worthiness is sound as the capital of India standing with its history and for this have found their place in multiplicity, in the book as their right. And I am immensely thankful to these venerated souls for describing bits of facts that inspired my imagination to form a picture of the glorious Awadh as drawn in the book and write it. But the book has been mainly filled by my observation of faith and trait of the people and my experience as designate of the society. My background with my association and affinity with my Brahman friends in my growing school days and my breathing and growing in my village has many memories to be narrated that have appeared in the book indirectly. Then it has been enriched by my personal observations and the insight into the cultures of the peoples of the subcontinent of India and my vision in the capacity as a writer. In the wake of it, I am prompted to write this couplet:

The definition of the Momin given by the 11th Imam, Imam Hasan Askari AS. is: 'In the Kalima the Momin includes the declaration of Aliyun Wali Ullah, in 24 hours he offers 51 Rakats of Namaz, he prostrates on earth, he recites Bismillahir-Rahmanir-Rahim (the Aayet of mercy) loudly in prayer, he wears ring in the right hand and he recites Doay Qunoot – the supplication in the 2nd Rakat before prostration.' The definition of Momin in the dictionary is trustworthy, of perfect faith, a dutiful man.

لطفِ الفت قائم ہے حسنِ اخلاق و وضع داری سے
ملحوظاتِ مرتبہ ، نفس کی سادگی ، شانِ دستر خوانی سے

سید اطہار حسین

Lutf-e Ulfat Qaem Haai Husn-e Aekhlaq-o Waza Dari Say
Malhoozat-e Martaba, Nafs Ki Sadgi, Shan-e Dastar khwani Say

Charm of love is in vogue with beauty of mannerism and
formalism
By observing level of distinction, simplicity in self, dignity of food
table

Awadh has been the land of the *Momineen* - the esteemed learned,
pious, thriving by the richness of their self-knowledge and their purity
filled living. Many bits of their culture have been made evident in the
book and are decorative of the book. Then there is my fondness of
England, which flares its deliberations in expressions and bursts out
here and there its lop-sidedness in the book.

The book: The Land of Seasons and Songs has been in my hand for
twenty-five years and all these years I could never get ready to take it
to the press though it was complete in its themes and layouts. It took
so long, since I began to write other books and articles and the book
was put on hold. But in its nascent life it picked up many notable
events that took place in the world, especially in Pakistan, and the
glimpses of these are presented to the reader as these are important
developments in politics and in the justice domain in the world.

The profession of the book is to please the soul of the reader.

Part I

The Soul and the Man

کرشمہ سازی و نوازش اللّٰہُمَّ کی

Karishma Sazi Wa Nawazish Alla Humma Ki

Marvel making and bestowing favour on the call of 'O God'

God Almighty is *Rabbul Samawat-e Wal Arz.* (Sustainer of the skies and the earth). He SWT has given man power, but only to the extent of his deliberations. So, we begin with the definition of the power of man and his limitations:

خدا نے ایسی بنائی طریقت آ دمی کی
رکھی قدرت کی ساکھ پر نہیں مقدوری کی

قہر و الفت سے بھری عقل اوج و توانائی دی
دشت و دریا کو فتح کرنے کی لِلہی دی

رات دی تبّدُ لِ وقت دیا دن کی رعنائی دی
فصلِ مربوط صفت سوز لاجوردی دی

حق و باطل میں فرق کرنے کو گویائی دی
حق میں حق گھول دیا آدمی کو تَرّابی دی

یہ سب کرشمہ سازی ہے نوازش الم نشرح کی
آدمی اب کیو ں نہ کرے آمادگی خدا پرستی کی

سیّد اطہار حسین

Khuda Nay Aaisi Bana-ee Tareeqat Aadmi Ki
Rakhi Qudrat Ki Saakh Per Naheen Maqdoori Ki

Qahr-o Ulfat Say Bhari Aql, Auj-o Tawana-ee Dee
Dasht-o Darya Ko Fateh Karnay Ki Lillahi Dee

Raat Dee Tabbadul-e Waqt Diya Din Ki Rana-ee Dee
Fasl-e Marboot, Sifat Soaz Lajwardi Dee

Haque-o Batil Mein Farq Karnay Ko Goya-ee Dee
Haque Mein Haque Ghoal Diya Aadmi Ko Tauwabi Dee

Yeh Sub Karishma Sazi Haai, Nawazish Alum Nashrah Ki
Aadmi Ub Kewn Na Karay Aamadgi Khuda Parasti Ki

Translation

God so made the way of spiritual evolution of man
Kept in him foundation of power, but not of absoluteness of
    power

Filled the intellect with anger and affection, gave height and
    strength
To conquer the desert and river gave power for God closeness

Gave night, gave change of time, gave glamour of the day
Gave harvest one after the other, gave burning with quality
    azure

For making difference in right and wrong gave ability to talk
Diffused the righteousness in righteousness gave man right of
    penitence

This is all the wonder making and the kindness of Alam Nashra
    (the manifest of opening the way)
How not man will do consolidation to readiness to God worship

-: . :-

I

THE LAND OF TWO RIVERS

I

One phenomenon not very understandable but one that is in common observation of many is that when providence smiles on someone, some peculiarity of that person turns into unseen advantage for him and good fortune is alerted and put on its tiptoe pursuit of the individual to seek out the feeblest of the excuse and locate suitable occasion and shower favours on him. Very pertinent to this phenomenon was the case of the *Aekkewan* – the horse and cart driver, Bachchu Yarwah who lived in a rudimentary village in the Land of Seasons and Songs with certain of his peculiarities. And the good fortune was put on alert by the providence to follow the Aekkewan and deliver the dividend allocated for him for his select discourse issued off him. And the good fortune started its probe to seek out suitable occasion to shower discreet favours on the Aekkewan.

The Aekkewan, Bachchu Yarwah was born in the heart of the part of the country where two rivers met. It was a country of charm and liveliness all through its length and breadth. The people lived there a life of majesty sufficed in their needs by reasonable wealth and some lived there in apt poverty and all instances of moral move in that country were the outcome of the variety of the people's graciousness in manners, skills, mellowness and the seriousness in life. And the country stood heightened, enlivened with its grace and distinction and with its individuality. And in all the things that happened there in this country of grace and beatitude was due to the manifestation of the sweet nature of this country that was an endowment to its people the heritage of peace transferred it to its people. And this wonderful country was synonymous to its people to the name of: 'The Land of Seasons and Songs' and it was so endeared by its people that they were ready to lay their lives on its dignity and for its accommodative spirit.

The country for all its charm that pervaded it, and for all the excellences that livened it, heightening its grace and distingué in its individuality that typified its attractiveness, had bought for it from its people their unbounded devotion and their unwavering love for it and the country was the jealous Amanat, the keepsake for its people and it was deeply loved by them. And each one protected it as more precious an object than their lives and they felt proud for it, for they loved its soil that smelled of love and peace.

The country had given to the horse and cart driver all that he could want and this was in spite of his prickly talk and his unwieldy expression that he hurled in the air without applying any restriction on him for using them, without taking into account discretionary preferences for the suitability of place and time to use them and without showing any leniency in the stinginess of the words he selected to convey what meaning he wanted to convey in dealing with the situation arising during the performance of the zestful discharge of his mare's duty - that was the routine carriage of the load of the passengers by her horse and cart to and fro to places.

The expressions the horse and cart driver used, though they formed the core of the command to the horse and were his professional requirement, but they obliquely wrapped in them hidden meanings found aggressive by some as these hit them squarely and the insinuations in them appeared deliberately flung at them and this brought a rumpus unseen by the horse and cart driver. And this was wholly due to the vastness of the meanings hidden in the expressions carried in the expanse of the words and was unintended. And in some respects, the interpretations that were derivable from the extraction in the meaning of the words spoken by the horse and cart driver were found by some totally unacceptable and outrageous, and by some outright slanderous, who happened to fall in the audible range of the trail of the hard-hitting sequence of the ravelling of these words. Since the meaning extruded off them at length by them invariably touched their vulnerability to intense anger and uncontrolled fury.

The country of the Aekkewan had Its history 130 - 120 million years old when its land separated from Antarctica and came floating from the south to the north and stood at its place in Asia. This land collided with the high land to join the north and it raised a huge crust of earth to form the Himalayas of which its countrymen have ever been proud of. And the country reciprocated and gave to its people delicacies and delights, herbs and trees and gradual transformation to modernity and to the horse and cart driver what substantial blessings in his recognitions that was not imaginably possible.

But Bachchu's phenomenon of originating commands of uniqueness in wording was unsettling for others, doing their nerve-wracking and jolting them to draw conclusion averse against the horse and cart driver's observed audaciousness, and for that his proprietary to what he wanted, and exactly that he got was something not understandable by others for the ease with which these showered their entailing beneficences on him with their largesse of the endowments. It was completely a stunning surprise for many for all what he was favoured with. And it was despite the denigration he caused to others, albeit from the overlapping meanings of the words he spoke, which all said about these; were unintentional irruption, nevertheless were anguishedly hurtful phenomenon to the others the words vulnerability was hitting.

And it was suspected that all that endowment to the horse and cart driver that was, was due to the unspecified favour of the country he was born in, to make his unconstrained rise to prosper. And in all that endowment he was recipient of, when looked at it, he was as much a lopsided part and parcel of favours showered on him by the country's hospitability, as the country was a lopsided design and presentation of marvels in its formations and its topography and its vast spaces and the legendry scheme of things in the shaping and the beautifying of its spectaculars, which were the nature's approbation to it.

The country where the horse and cart driver lived was all-pervading of the unquestionable magnanimity of vastness that made it claim of the highest and the holiest and to have the pleasantest of things around and about it. It had high mountains standing to rise high to sky height, with their unchallengeable claims of being unmatched monuments of divinity on divine preferences, symbolic of God's authorisation for presenting their magnificence with His 'Be there' command – *Kun Fayakun,* with their placement at the places of their stationing, from times unmemorable and bygone, ten and even twenty million years ago, jutting their peaks to the highest of the heights that man claimed.

It had wide long rivers with their holy waters taking their preferred course of flow in three cardinal directions in its land, and proudly telling of the legends that bred in their bosom and spread their waters over the country's courts and planes in their span and flow and told of their longevities with their brimming fullness. It was a country that courted vast sprawling planes, stretching from one end to the other of the country and filling the country with the lush green forests and dunes of golden sand.

It was endowed with four seasons of distinct characteristics with which each one in the country was familiar with. And each one of the country men knew of their natures and as to when they came to visit them, and they counted their sequential occurrences on the pores of their fingers and very much cherished them and their names for what they brought, and what they brought was a vigour of culture and extravagance in the life of the people.

The exclusivity of the climatic change these seasons brought was from one peak to the other, recurrent and vastly different in nature to each other, with their spectaculars of overwhelms and their extravagance. And to know their nature and experience their rule and tamper was one dictate in life not to be missed to, and one had to be in their environs to go through it. They filled life with their hue and colour and made all lost in the abounding of their apportioning pleasure and the entirety of the rationale of their characteristics they imbued in men swept everyone in the waves of joy and merriment of cute effect, each of a different flavour.

The experience of the seasons one went through was beyond description. It was as subtle as one wanted to be. The sooth seeking spirit encaged in one's being was ever seeking elation and it was prong lifted by the seasons. This was the occasion in the progression of life that these seasons came with each of their visits at the appointed times as ever, and that was one surety the people of the Land of Seasons and Songs had in composure that repeated again and again. And the pleasantries associated with them were so commodiously provided to the people with their festivities that it was the unique award from them to the country and to its people and it was one gift to this wonderful country that was cherished by its peoples and the people were thankful to the country to what they were and where they were, in this wonderful Land of the Seasons and Songs.

-: . :-

I

THE BASANT AND THE HOLI

II

Of all the seasons in the Land of Seasons and Songs, there was one, without which the joy and the fun would not have reached to the larger number of the peoples of the land and the spirit of the communality would not have emerged in this land of blessing. This season so rolled out fun and joy, dragging the multitude to jump on its wagon train of pleasantries whose wheels it chugged and there was no one left aloof of its benedictions. It vibrant and dedicated to deliver goodness, decapitated all miseries venturing nearing the people. This was season, when people turned ecstatic and became all jubilant and exhibited them with unlimited bursts of zest. People dressed in pleasant yellow dresses, and with all a lightened heart, filled with the air of the season, wished to touch the heights of the skies.

There was zest in the people, and trailing the season of the Basant came the festival of the two days of celebration of the Holi and people in their unbound ecstasy, a vast number of them started to throw coloured water and coloured powders on each other, colouring each other in a rainbow of colour and celebrating the Holi, celebrating with an unpretentious joy. Singing Holi songs and creating moments of visionary art through dancing, pooling in their talents and making the season festive.

Holi is a celebration of triumph of good over evil. A bonfire is raised on the previous night of the Holi to remind of the evil that will perish and the good that will triumph, and the Holi celebration is plain thanksgiving for the triumph of good over the evil.

Hiranyakashipu was King of Demons. He was granted a boon by Brahma for his penance he carried out, steadfastly cleansing him of all traces of blame on his person. It was the rendering of the boon

10

granted to him that opened a lid to his finding any demand he could make; it would be granted. He demanded:

"He will not be killed during day or night, neither inside home nor outside, not on earth nor on sky, neither by man nor by an animal, and neither by Astra (super weapon) nor by Shastra (sacred scripture)." And that he was granted.

With this bejewelling of him - the seeming impossible granted to him, he grew arrogant and attacked Heavens and Earth. He demanded that people stop worshipping gods and start worshipping him - start praying to him. He had a son Prahlada. The son refused to pray to him. He was a devout of god Vishnu. Hiranyakashipu therefore became wildly angry with him and ordered him killed and Prahlada prayed to Vishnu to save him.

Hiranyakashipu's order was carried out. Prahlada was poisoned, but the poison turned into nectar in his mouth. He was then ordered to be trampled by elephants, but the elephants turned docile to him. He was then ordered that he be put in a room with hungry poisonous snakes. He was left there to die, but the snakes turned pets and friendly and he survived among them. Hiranyakashipu's attempt to kill his son failed. Then he ordered Prahlada be taken to a pyre in the lap of his demoness sister Holika. This sister of Hiranyakashipu had a boon that protected her from getting burned in the fire. The demoness Holika carried Prahlada in the fire tied to her lap. But everyone watched with amazed eyes, the demoness Holika was burnt to death and Prahlada survived unharmed. He was unhurt, because he was a devotee of Vishnu, while she was an evil soul and she was burnt.

So, the Holi is a celebration of triumph of Prahlada over the demoness Holika, symbolising; 'good triumphing over the evil'. Or was it the triumph of Holy Rama over Ravan! Or was it the triumph of Prophet Ibrahim AS. over King Nero (Namrood)!

Lord Rama had returned to Ajodhya after vanquishing Ravan - the ten heads devil. Then the Prophet Ibrahim AS. was thrown in the fire by Namrood, but the Prophet had come out of the fire unharmed and he defeated Namrood's large army with the help of the gnats who came in defence of his faith. So, fire was symbolic of victory and an ominous good event must be backed and supported.

There was no record when the Holi started; save by a vague incident recorded in the 7th century Sanskrit drama throwing some light on the tradition of the Holi. But the festival has an older history linked with the Vedic culture of some 4000 years BC.

Hiranyakashipu continued to live an unending life because of the boon in his pocket. And he continued to terrorise God's creation on its strength. Then one day Lord Vishnu came in the form of Narsimha. This spirit was half-man - half- lion, and strong as mountain. He killed Hiranyakashipu at dusk – neither day nor night, on the steps of the porch – neither inside nor outside, by restraining him on his lap – neither on earth nor on sky and mauling him with his claws – neither by weapon nor by scripture and the boon was not violated and Hiranyakashipu was killed.

Holi is celebrated in September; it is a folk festival and it develops kinship among folks and is more a cultural festival than a religious event but has a religious tone. It is completely acceptable to classes outside Hinduism for its spirit of good for creating folk gaiety. The joyous Holi song Hori says:

Aaj Viraj Mein Holi Re Rasiya

Today there is Holy in the bright land, O fond

The folks sing the song and exude joy. This festival permits ladies looked at by men with pleasure, however the ladies show reserved aloofness, but in the end to extenuate their passes, ease their rigidity and accept folk's advances, permitting a chequered liberty to them.

The Provost of the State Army of Banaras State in Ramnagar, the capital of the Maharaja of Banaras had his own ideas and carried the liberty of freedom of expression as he construed imagination a bit far. He sent one battalion of the army detachment, marching the length of two miles, singing folk songs on the tarmac road to the fort of the Maharaja. His men smeared in colour powder, and some in oil film coated on their muscular body did the most bizarre display. The man's organ made from some black wood was tied on the groins of the leading muscular soldier from the battalion and he jerked it in front and sides on the *Dholak Ki Thap* - the beat - the *Taal* of the Dholak.

12

And the Dholak was slung from the neck of one of the soldiers in the middle row. And all men in the troop formation with their bodies glistening were marching towards the fort, showing their strong manly body. They went to the fort of the Maharaja to congratulate on the coming of the Holi festival and the felicitations were conveyed to the Rani – the queen, and they were appropriately rewarded by the Rani.

For the Holi celebration, *Pichkari* – the spray gun, buckets full of dry colour powder and buckets of coloured water were the sources to throw colour water on each other. Troupes of folks went to the houses and were welcomed with Gujia – the knitted flour filled with Helwa and fillings of nuts, shaped ship shape and fried, offered with platefuls of cardamoms with delicately dressed Paan(s) by the house owners to whom they offered their felicitations. The Paan was of rose fragrance and carried the placid cachou that filled the mouth with pleasantness and everyone became cheery, very special and very privileged.

When the Paan was lifted to be eaten after a settlement of a controversy, it was dressed in Chandi Ka Waraq – thin silver leaf. It was used as symbol of taking up the vow by the folk concluding the agreement in the negotiation, which was carried out with terms set. And taking of Paan folded with three corners, or as a Glory, conically tugged shape and lifted up as vow to vouch that commitment will be honoured, the Paan glory held a significant importance.

-: . :-

I

THE NAUROZE

III

Nauroze is a festival of appeal to God to remove scarcity and oblige with gift of abundance. Naurose is celebrated in thankfulness to God for the harvests He bestowed to the mankind and man presented the best of its sort in thanksgiving for the variety of crops, God gave to man. The first, world celebration of Nauroze was held in the capital of Iran on 27 March 2010 to tell its celebration was in keeping with fine manners. The timing of the celebration of the Nauroze in Asia Minor, Middle East countries, and the Far East countries is 21 March to April in the spring. The Aryan people had migrated to India from the central Asia where the Naurose - the New Year was celebrated in the spring equinox by the polytheists before the influence of Zoroastrianism in the early first millennium BCE. However, Nauroze is believed to have been introduced by Zoroaster himself and hence the Zoroastrians celebrate Nauroze on the 26 of March. It is a festival mentioned in the Avesta, written by Zoroaster himself.

In the Shia Muslim houses in India, the table is laid with the varieties of the organically grown fruits in thanksgiving for the Nazar or offering. The offering is made on articles of sweet and greenery, and water is sprinkled on each other in the subcontinent of India. This tradition has a relevance with the God's command to the Prophet Hazrat Hizqeel AS. to sprinkle water on the dead he prayed for – ref. Aayet 2:243. He sprayed water taking in his palm and the dead one by one became alive – this occurred on the Nauroze.

On the day of the vernal equinox - 21 March, the sun is directly over the equator and there is an equal distribution of sunlight over the two hemispheres from north to the south. Following the vernal equinox day, the days gradually get longer and nights shorter. There is an exact moment in time and space on earth between the north and the south pole when the sunlight reaching to the either poles is exactly equal and there is a perceiving that it is the moment of *Tahveel* or change, the auspicious moment appears at this time, and it is indicated by the turning of a rose placed in a bowl of water on the table. The rose starts to rotate. This is the moment when appellations are made, and it is when prayers are accepted, and blessings descend.

The water of the bowl is sprinkled in the four corners of the house for *Khaair* - the blessing. The water is sprinkled on the faces and on the persons of the household for Khaair – good omen, to liven life. Coloured water spraying is also used with sanctity to be cheerful.

The vernal equinox on 21st March 656 AD coincided with Hazrat Ali AS. ascending to take the seat of the Khilafat. This was the apparent ascension, he was Wasi – the legatee and Khalifa even in the times when he was not Caliph for 25 years. This was by dint of the word of the Prophet of God Hazrat Mohammad Mustafa SAWW at the feast of the Zul-Ashira. Aayet 26:214 said: "and warn thy nearest relations".

The first act in the Tableegh – proselyting of Islam by the Prophet SAWW was in the 4th year of the Prophethood to invite his family members of Banu Hashim to accept Islam. About forty of the tribe's people came to the feast of Zul-Asheera. There the guests noticed the food is never short, despite their large consumption. The guests left after eating and drinking without giving an occasion to the Prophet to speak. So, the Prophet invited them again on the second day. Now after dinner the Prophet spoke, 'I have message of God who ever will support me he will be, my brother, Wasi – successor and Caliph' and there when Ali three times stood up with his Labbaik Ya Rasool Allah (I am present O Messenger of God), and no one else had responded, he was declared Wasi – the legatee of the Prophet by the Prophet.

And this position and status of the Ameerul Momineen Hazrat Ali Ibn Abi Talib AS. of legatee could not be denied, even if the post of the Khalifa was taken from him. He was in all factuality all the time the real Khalifa. Further to that, God called him Wali and he was declared

Maula[2] at the Ghadeer-e Khum. And when the apparent Khilafat came to him, he glorified the Khilafat.

'Justice to the measure of the morsel of an ant was done if the morsel was snatched of someone and mercy in justice to specs was included in his rule by Hazrat Ali.' The offender guilty, if he was fortunate possessing memorization of a fair number of Quranic Aayat in his mind, Ali's mercy forgave him to suffer no punishment. So, justice in its span has so many intricacies in its span to be kind and benevolent and was a dictate of the level of the knowledge and spirituality of the Qazi – the Judge, and no possibility was left not to give benefit to the guilty by the divine knowledge holder of authority. But the Qazi giving judgement by the constitutional laws made by man was slave to these laws and had no mandate nor authority to deviate from it existed. And this is the flaw of the man-made rule. When the Khilafat had returned to the rightful place to Hazrat Ali AS., the multitude overjoyed ran with voluntary allegiance to Hazrat Ali and that of such strength that it was never seen like of it before happening to any Caliph in Madina.

Therefore, on this day of the ascending of Hazrat Ali AS. on the *Mansab-e Khilafat* – office of the Khilafat falling on the Nauroze, the Shian-e Ali offer Nazar to Maula Ali. Fruits of seven colours and sweets of a colour matching the stellar background - the constellation in which the sun rises on the vernal equinox, are placed on the table. In the present times the sun rises in the background of Pisces and each of the ten planets are representing ten distinct basic human urges, man experiences. And because of precession the earth's north pole faces different starfield – the sky colour over the 2600 years of the period of the completion of the orbit of precession, producing different era.

The earth's precession takes about 25,800 years for one complete cycle. Since there are in total twelve constellations for the sun to make

---

[2] In a sermon, the Prophet of Islam, Hazrat Mohammad Mustafa SAWW, when returning after the historical Hajj under his patronage and guidance called the Hajjis and delivered on the 18th of Hajj 632 AD in Ghadeer-e Khum, Mun Kunto Maula Fa Haza Aliyun Maula, declaring Hazrat Ali, Maula and the consequent right of the Wilayet – his lordship over the world of Islam.

its journey through, it means sun stays in every constellation for about 2150 years on the days of vernal equinoxes. And there is one era of one consequence for this period. And in the cosmos the creation created by God has two elements, the soul and the matter. The soul is to experience, and the matter is to influence the experience. In the cosmos, each stellar system will have its own Nauroze. This will be the law of the universe and since the universe is vast and unimaginably vast, there will be a Nauroze every split moment of the existence of the God's creation in His creation.

-: . :-

I

THE BASANT AND THE KITES

IV

The scintillating effect of the season of the spring arouses good-naturedness, affection and infuses body with flare for creativity. The fun of light - heartedness and nature's gift of merriment last throughout the season and there is celebration all-round. The Basant season brought more in pleasantness than one could tell, when people with newness filled in their hearts found their spirit rise to elation. They were winged and wanted to fly. People wanted to be air borne and do impossible, and everything beyond them seemed possible. And one sport which found a resurging appeal with the greater number of people, was the kite flying. People strung their kites in the sky in the breeze of the season and saw it swing and run and race in all four directions. The weather was clear of dust and free of storm and carried a pleasant fragrance. The kites fluttered in the wind, whizzing in the sky, and went rushing round in successive rush competing with each other, and a trail of joy trailed with them in succession.

And a chorus of spirited cheers was raised by the enthusiasts, those bucking the kites and those doing flying. They presented spiritedness and frequentative burst of pleasure, and no gauge could measure the intensity of pleasure. Its moments of exhilarations were recorded in the memory recesses, which imprinted themselves there on the canvass of the recollection of memory for a later day reviving. The kites filled the sky and the kite fliers filled the open roof-tops, patios and fields for celebrating the Basant. The *Pepeeri, Baja* and *Bhoan-poo* – the clarinets, trumpets and bugles – blared and shrilled. And the kites, each of a distinct colour and of two genders; the *Gudda(s)* and the *Guddi(s),* the boy dolls and the girl dolls filled the sky. These challenged one another, competing with each other in the air. And this simple sport of kite flying provided fun and joy.

A little planning in the manipulation of the string, heaving, tugging, pulling and slackening and using diligence and deploying alertness for pouncing on a dosing kite and ducking an escape from the sudden attack of a daring kite floating in the near sky, trying to make a surprising attack on its nearby prey when found a moment of its in-alertness, were the fun of the kite flying. If a kite was slackening and drooping, exhibiting no life, there at these moments, the attacking kite charged with its attack.

The strings were made of two parts; the front part was made sharp with glass-dust covering. The string was drawn wet through glue and glass-dust, it sharply cut the string of the other kite. The rest of the string was kept plain for safe handling and all strings were selected from the fine strong twine.

The kites rushed at each other, chasing and clashing and entangling and toppling each other for establishing supremacy in the sky. The kites scanned the space around, manoeuvring them and establishing their oneness of supremacy over the other. Some enthusiasts flew their kites so high in the air that it could not be seen and only the pull of the string told the kite flier that the kite was flying still connected at the other end of the string with the reel of the kite flier. This was the sustained joy and excitement, which lasted all through this fun filled season of the Bahar.

The link of the Basant with the land of Punjab was that on the second Sunday of the Februarys, yellow dress was worn by the trees in the fields. The mustard trees and the mustard fields made so by the land of yellow flowers were synonymous to the season of Bahar or Basant. The flowers blossomed and covered the land. And people became thrilled by this yellow of the fields, and yellow dress was worn by people to unionise with the nature. And it is the boon of spring that yellow flowers blossom and trees transform themselves to lush green looks and kites are slung in the air to rise in the sky to reciprocate nature and the kite fliers declare their successes with each 'Woh Kata' – there I have cut. And the rival's kite falling lurching from above in the air, falling to the ground to the waiting bunch of youngsters, or sometimes it was the surprised gift to someone to collect it as loot to take away the falling kite running after it and catching hold of its string, chasing it.

The kites when they were cut and had fallen to the ground, they became anyone's property whoever caught it by its string. And the kite flier losing his kite was busy winding up his string still floating in the air and falling from the sky fast and these were the funs of the sport of kite flying. Kite flying costs little and offers so much in simple pleasure. And the discipline the kite flier infuses is heroic. It is rejection of penny pinching.

-: . :-

I

POLITICS AND THE
POLITICAL FALLACIES

V

Kite-flying was one sport which required no club to join to enjoy the fun. The vast open sky was the club and the open arena for the activity of the kite flying. The open sky and the free-flowing air to lift the kite were providing the space and the propellant for the kite to fly. And everything was *Mubah* – permissible in it. But in politics, the first conditions were to be in Kaaif – in the state of involvement, free of laziness, affluent and next join a club that dealt in politics. Then the politician had to show that he was educated, a degree holder, but the kite flier only needed enthusiasm and a cheery nature. The kite flier was seasonal and Kaif appeared in the season of Bahar and he was relaxed. Unlike him, the politician was all the year round on his toes, a full-time bound slave committed to politics, they are assumed to be good, but they are with inundations of harassing information to mob at the public. They try to convince that they are never in the wrong and these are the characteristics of a politician good or bad.

But there are worst examples of politicians also to be found in Punjab, who have given a bad name to the sweet land of the five rivers. Their scorns, sleek methods, tongue lashing, outright illegalities and nepotism are as common as dressing up and going to five times for prayer in the day. The Law Minister of Punjab Government, Rana Sana Ullah is guising him a purist, but he is away from Islamic principles. He is the vertebra of the PML-N and he is not only abusive but aggressive, ready to mar others' cheeriness, and scuttle Basant activity. He snubbed the spirited PPP Governor of Punjab, Salman Taseer, threatening to arrest him, because he wanted to fly kite and inaugurate the Basant festivities.

The PML-N Punjab parliament under the hard-brandishing Law Minister, Rana Sana Ullah banned the kite-flying in Punjab in disregard to the public sentiments who wanted to enjoy the innocent pastime. This obnoxious minister and his Chief Minister Shabaz Sharif banned the Mubah – that was allowed by the Shariah and both of them are tongue lashing and of refutation to God's sanction. But Rana Sana Ullah went further, he appeared with the terrorist organisation – with the chief of the Sipah-e Shaba – a banned organisation, inviting him to a public-address meeting and standing with him behind the rostrum. This was done to remove hurdles for his government in the coming election in Punjab to win majority seats in election 2013, using the support of the terrorists and mixing with terrorist is anti-Islam.

Then he created such an atmosphere against the Governor Salman Taseer in Punjab that he was assassinated by the Punjab police constable Malik Mumtaz Qadri. This misguided of a Muslim for this act of sin was declared a hero by the incarcerated of fallacy and he was continuously protected from his execution sentence passed on him.

The Chief Minister of Punjab, Shahbaz Sharif is the first line supporter of Jamaat-e Dawah the political arm of the Lashkar-e Taiba, a banned organisation and Shahbaz Sharif's party cadre is supporter of the Lashakar-e Jhangvi - the terrorists. In the murder of Governor Salman Taseer, though Constable Mumtaz Qadri is from the Barelvi sect, but when it comes to extremism, he like-minded pro-Taliban Deobandi. And because the Taliban ideology appeals to all, the Hanafi, the Gilani and the Barelvi factions have joined hands to support the murderer Constable Mumtaz Qadri and have given pledge to each other to get him released from jail and honour him. So, the values of Islam are openly flouted for political cause. And all moral teachings of Islam are cast aside by declaring a murderer a *Ghazi*[3] – the conqueror. This is going against the command of the Sharia and Aayet 47:22 says:

---

[3] Constable Mumtaz Qadri was placed on guard duty of Governor Salman Taseer by the Punjab Police and given live bullets in his belt, of which twenty-seven bullets he sprayed on the governor in broad-day light when he was entering in his car. The assassin was sentenced to two death sentences and fined, but he was called Ghazi by the wicked Muslims. The Punjab Police repeated its record of murder, on 17th June 2014 on pretext to demolish barriers erected on court order, They went to hold Dr Tahirul Qadri's political momentum against the government of the PMLN. Punjab

(Hypocrites) is it far from you that if you become ruler start spreading mischief on earth and snapping relation and connections from your close ones.

But those supporting a murderer are stinging their soul, they will be denied receiving the good news from the Prophet SAWW. The Holy Quran says in Aayet 7:188: *(O Prophet) say...I am but a warner and the giver of good news (of paradise) to the people who believe.*

In the territorial limits of the Punjab Government, its governor is slighted by the low cadre law minister, the prayer houses of the minority Shia mosques and Imam Baargah are attacked and bombed, by the terrorists, who are protected by the PMLN, and the mishap with a motor cycle rider due to kite flying was magnified beyond all proportion to score a political point. The kite strings in the past have wounded folks and the kite fliers have fallen from the roof tops, but the banning of the kite-flying was killing a tradition and squandering the freedom of people. And it was against the law of nature.

The Law Minister openly said with covert intention: 'Anyone who violated the ban will be arrested'. This slant was meant for the Governor of Punjab, who wanted to use the efficacy of his office to pamper kite flying and he had said he will inaugurate the Basant. This slighting of a liberal governor was undemocratic and his humiliation emboldened the murderer to murder the governor. The sitting government was against the governor and the murderer was put on duty when it was not his turn to be there on duty. And politics was veered to murder.

The banning of the kite flying was for egoism and arrogance and although it had court order to support it, but that was again in suppression of human rights and the judges have been known in Punjab to toe the line of the ruler and take order, asking on phone who to convict and how severe. The justice Malik Mohammad Qayyum asked Nawaz Sharif who phoned him to convict Benazir. The Punjab Government of the PML-N scuttled the kite flying, stunning the economic activity. Their mind could not capacitate itself to think that the kite-flying was an innocent pastime and a sport that should not be harmed and left to thrive, only laws should have been made to fly kite

---

police there murdered 12 citizens and injured sixty in Lahore Model Town residential area. The Punjab Police is said to have had instructions from the chief minister.

from safe area. The Law Minister also said. 'He - the governor can run on the street tearing off and throwing his clothes but he will not be given the car[4] he asks for'. Now look at this blighting gall ruining the culture of decency represented by the people of Pakistan, such degrading talk in colour, race and language are murder of culture.

This was scandalous politics, sinisterness interfacing with uncouth assault. This rude slant made for the highest functionary of the province by a lower cadre party politician was extreme in the disruption of decency and normalcy and there was nothing like it in the entire slate of politics, past or present. This demonstration of wreck lessness was done because the governor was criticising the Punjab Government, which was showing poor performance. The governor was from the PPP, whose government was at the centre and was PML-N's bitter rival. But the 18th amendment had given the provinces extended independence and power. And the PMLN was rude, lawbreaking and slandering and refusing to welcome even prime minister of PPP in Punjab. This party used politics as a catapult to sling volleys of disrespect and arrogance. One of their politicians from Faisalabad, Abid Sher Ali used the word *Budtameez* – nasty mannered (abusive word in the Urdu language) for a sitting PPP Federal Minister on the TV talk show programme and I am witness to it. Aayet 2:205 from the Holy Quran says:

Wallaahu laa yuhibbul- fasad.

Allah does not love mischief-making.

Decency ought to be the yardstick of goodness implementing adequacies in a politician. The political parties are enrolling party men and not looking in whether they have aptitude to lead and help, and whether they come from a background that has a pleasing record of decency. They must allow entry to only those who will create elegance

---

[4] The Governor had asked for a bulletproof car. There were 14 – 15 bulletproof cars with the provincial government. These were deployed mostly on the duty of the Khadim-e Aala – the Chief Minister and his entourage and for the duty of the PML-N politicians, but not one was allowed to be used by the Honourable Governor.

in the society. The Chief Minister of Punjab Shahbaz Sharif says to the President of Pakistan Asif Ali Zardari:

'I will drag Zardari on the streets of Karachi, Larkana, Peshawar and Lahore after election and if I don't do that my name is not Shahbaz Sharif.'

In 2011 he says: 'O Zardari what do you know, what honour of the races...is.'

This was not politics but straight slander. It was perhaps the repercussion to the abusing of the PPP politicians that their young chairman of the party, Bilawal Bhutto Zardari charged his party workers on 18 October 2013, to hunt down the Sher or the lion, meaning the PML-N. He called Imran Khan – Buzdil Khan for appeasing the Taliban. When the Taliban bombed the Church, and made blasts in Peshawar, killing MPAs and attacking Imam Bargarh, Imran khan was all sweet to them and did not say one disparaging word against them. Imran Khan will say he was under threat, and so Bilawal used the word Buzdil for him, because he is also threatened, but has shown a different mantle.

Bilawal Bhutto Zardari went full steam ahead in politics starting from October 2013. His speech was full of zeal in the style of his grandfather Z.A. Bhutto and mother Benazir Bhutto. He says, he sacrificed his childhood so that his mother may defend the party, and he promises to fight for the people. He says, 'Today the parties taking refuge behind the terrorism of the terrorists are celebrating in its mayhem. They think they have defeated the PPP (in the 2013 election); I have this to say to them,' and then he reads the following couplets:

مرے تن کے زخم نہ گن ابھی، مری آنکھ میں نور ہے
مرے بازوؤں پر نگاہ کر، جو غرور تھا وہ غرور ہے

ابھی دیکھ قبضہء تیغ پر، مرےکف کی سخت گرفت ہے
بڑا منتقم ہے مرا لہو، یہ مرے نصب کی سرشت ہے

Meray Tan Kay Zakhm Na Gin Abhi, Meri Aankh Mein Noor Haai
Meary Bazoo-oan Per Nigah Kar, Jo Ghuroor Tha Woh Ghuroor Haai

25

Abhi Dekh Qabza-ay Tegh Per, Meray Kuff Ki Sakht Giraft Haai
Barda Muntaqim Haai Mera Lahoo, Yeh Meray Nasab Ki Sarisht
Haai

Don't count the wounds on my body, still there is light in my eyes
Look at my arms the pride that was that pride is

Look at the hilt of the sword, the grip of my hand is strong
Very avenging is my blood; this is from the writing of my descent.

The style of delivery of the verses and the wording of the couplets was
not market place announcement, it was genuine political slogan - a
social contract to deal with firm politics with reason and art. The force
behind it was of a knight charging on a high horse with sword drawn.
The Greek poet Archilochus says:

'The fox knows many things, but the hedgehog knows one big
thing.' (Ref. Tolstoy and History by Isaiah Berlin).

There are different interpretations of these words, but it mainly
means that the fox, for all its cunning is defeated by the hedgehog's
one defence.

Let's hope the young blood is going to be the hedgehog and he
defeats the fox for a better Pakistan. Definitely the years to come are
going to see an interesting Pakistan.

When the PPP was in power, from March 2008 - March 2013, the
PML-N as opposition party opposed all taxes the PPP would levy to
generate money to increase economic activity and achieve a better tax
turnover in the country. The PML-N opposed the introduction of the
GST, VAT and tax amnesty or tax exemption on money brought into
Pakistan to generate additional revenues. But as soon as the PMLN
entered in power in 2013, they immediately adopted this policy as the
first thing after their take over in the very first few days. Now if this is
not foxy cunningness then what else is?

Now they are daily printing money and at such a fast rate that just
after five months of their take over the inflation rate has gone up from
5.9 in June, to 10.9 in November. In his election campaign, Mian
Nawaz Sharif had declared with tantrum to break the Kashkole or the
beggar's bowl, and not go to borrow as it made the nation slave of the
lender, but within the first month the party was at the IMF's door with

their bowl and indebted the country by 5.3 billion dollars, indebting each citizen of Pakistan – new born and old with 80,000 rupees each, which in the next five months increased to 96,000 rupees per person in Pakistan indebted to IMF.

This brought such inflation in the country that the dollar which was at rupees 95 jumped to rupees 107 in inflation. What they said in election they are doing all opposite of it. The slogan in their election campaign was of a good guy, it was hailed by the people, but it was one for stealing the election and not out of any sincerity towards the nation. Now they are in power and their governance has no will to contain terrorism. And because they are a bully party with terrorists at their back, they frighten the critics.

The media journalist serving as spokesmen of the Taliban, consider them their soul mate and do not speak against them. No one, except Senator Sayed Faisal Raza Abedi speaks against the PMLN, PTI and the Jamiat-e Ulema-e Pakistan for no allocation of budget to complete the construction and the laying of Iran-Pakistan gas pipeline, which he considers is a mega project, yet costing to Pakistan only one third the cost of the Pakistan's share of cost and that too through the sale of wheat to Iran.

It was so advantageous a project that it was to enable Pakistan to distribute Gas from the country to North, to the South-East Asia and to India. But the PML-N's love for Saudi Arabia and a convincing will full distancing from Iran generates the disbalance not to take up this project. The dictate of Saudi Arabia, Gulf States and the USA is clung to at the cost of the Pakistani people's interest. This is the trait of the nature of the prejudicial politics from the PMLN. And the history of the PMLN is, there is no critical authoritarian politician of literary, intellectual background in their row and file. Intriguers and circuitous yes, and they smarten, brag and fling abuse and insult. Pakistani Taliban, Lashkar-e Jhangvi, Jundullah, Sipah-e Sahaba and these terrorists are on the rise, buoyed by the PMLN.

'The kingdom can still run of Kufr – the paganism, but not of tyranny', says Hazrat Ali.

Kufr Ki Hukoomat to Chal Sakti Haai Laikin Zulm Ki Naheen

The terrorists need a helping hand of reform and a rational methodical government to put them on the right road. But there is a show of passivity in the character and a slump in the ethical values in the politician and hence in the government. Rather than setting an example for them, presenting a role model of the prime minister, Nawaz Sharif is seen involved in extruding pomp for the family and for himself. He takes with him his entire family on his visit to China from 4th to 9th of July 2013, even his son who is in England and has nothing to do with politics is taken along there as a baggage.

This exploitation of politics and unethical trait is no pride of profession and that from the Prime Ministerial seat. But this is of least bother to the PML-N party. They suppress all opposition, and their highhandedness is such that they see to it that they are clapped for it. Such is the result of the trait of *Baradk* - the bombastic talk in Punjab. And they say; 'Sir, one should earn by fair means, and if that is not possible, he should earn by foul means.' And what is austerity and Islamic way does not concern them. Nawaz Sharif has expensive flats in London but cannot tell how he purchased this property and says addressing the court, 'what to them, if I have.'

The abuse of power and the trampling of morality is the hallmark of the PMLN's Chief. In Pakistan, there is no pillar of the state like the supreme leader in Iran – Vilayet-e Faqih to check slide in morality and keep the ship of the state on the steady course of righteousness through following precept. The tendency to break law is for egoistic reason and is a point of honour and a fashion in Punjab. In the recent jail break on the 30th of July 2013, 100 Taliban terrorists passed through established check post in the city of D.I. Khan. They went in a procession of 60 vehicles to the central jail and freed 250 hard criminals in a four-and-a-half-hour operation, and safely went back to the northern territory with the prisoners, they freed.

It is anticipated the prisoners freed will be dispatched to fight against the Bashar al Asad's regime in Syria. In this attack on the jail, they slaughtered five Shia Muslims in the jail and abducted five women – four inmates and one-woman police constable. And in two days not one statement of condemnation was issued by the government against the Taliban, let alone taking any action to establish the writ of the law. It reminded one of the theoretic Banana states. Pakistan, if it is not one, it is behaving one under PMLN.

The government is only interested in establishing their hold on power - on the administrative structure of the country to rule. They stoop and make pilgrimage to the 90 MQM headquarters to get support for them in the National Assembly for the Presidential election of July 30, 2013 and promise to them to include them in the Federal Ministerial slot. And if this is not bribery, what else is. This is the same MQM whom they branded terrorists and included a clause in the charter of democracy to exclude them from being included in any government. This is reckless axing of ethics. This is outlandish display of greed to satiate their hunger for power and it is scandalous PMLN doing. And no person and party of such credentials should lead a respectful nation.

When the PML-N planned to build the motorway in 1997, their blue-eyed select party member politicians knew of the plan from before election in 1990. They went buying land at cheap price from the poor farmers whose land fell en route the motorway. And when the project needed these lands, they sold it at exorbitant price to the motorway authority, drawing their reward from the public exchequer. This way fooling the poor farmer and filling their coffers and the worst in this was; the length of the motorway increased because of deviations by 79 kilometres between Lahore and Islamabad, permanently costing the nation the penalty of a pony tax of fuel and time, which was a drain not returnable. The fairest practice should be to investigate this swindle and bring to book the culprits.

Charles de Gaulle founded the French Fifth Republic. He made France a major power in the world. He was a General and a visionary. Charles de Gaulle says:

'I have come to the conclusion the politics are too serious a matter to be left to the politicians.'

In other words, this visionary is saying, the politician needs a guiding hand of the pious to keep him on the path of morality.

This saying of General De Gaulle leaves no room to elect conscious less or anyone with dubious record. A parson should not be put in charge where a bishop is needed. Persons like Rana Sana Ullah and Shahbaz Shareef, the mouthy insidious of Punjab, exhibit crude behaviour showing no respect to other human being. Their language and unethical remarks are flattening the culture of decency, but Punjab as a whole province is comfortable with it. They vote and elect them again and again. But their victory pattern is not a guide of their sound leadership. Justice is a force and it will show up one day. Meanwhile the voter must educate them to know of their responsibility to vote righteous character.

The politician's work will be service to humanity if he is learned and pious and follows Islamic values. Mahmood Ahmad Dinijad of Iran is an example of a selfless politician; the world will remember him for long. And if the politician is an aspirant for quick gain from politics, like the umpteen of them, working for the propensity of self-grandeur, scrounging expenses - like claimed by some British MPs from the British Treasury for buying duck houses, or for their moat cleaning or for bee removing, in spite of their handsome salary of £74,000 a year as British MP, and getting around ten week's paid holiday a year, he is an extra baggage for the nation.

However, using legitimate means to get rich was a fair industry and there was no inhibition to accumulating wealth through moralistic means even in politics. If fair accumulation of wealth was made by fair means; even if using the fame and the trappings of the office the politician sat in, to pedal him forward was fair. It was not an unethical acquiescing or wading into money making, provided his conscious was satisfied that what he was doing was right ethically.

Supposing a politician obtained a 10% commission for his celestial and honest effort in a work and the emergent deal was due to his extraordinary expertise in a field, it should be deemed legitimate. No one should question him on this account as his wealth generated was genuine, provided it was not contrary to the ethics or jeopardised public interest. He should declare his earning and pay tax on it. And this wealth should be considered as incentive wealth.

It was the same as the doctor did his private practice and the professor wrote book on the side of his lesson giving to the students, or the school teacher made additional income through private teaching, or the prince raked money by engaging himself in some commercial activity besides his princely duties, which was paid for as state allowance. It was all permitted and legal. The fair utilisation of talent was fair, said the moralist. And any scrutiny into such activity categorising it as corruption was invasion of privacy and was misunderstanding. If the earning was sought through fair and ethical pursuit, it was Halal. This however does not mean entering in side employment, as then it is violating loyalty.

But still if the talent was used entirely for accumulating wealth, it was the lowest form in the pursuit of earning or *Risq* i.e., the winning of bread. The talent has to be invested to generating Risq and balance it by paying Zakat and Khums. Putting in good work irreproachable and free from blame deed is the highest honour and satisfaction to soul, without it the earning has no credibility.

The PML-N Chief, Mian Nawaz Sharif of Punjab made an empire of industry using the office and the trappings of the political power. During his first tenure in 1990 as Prime Minister, the Ittefaq Foundry flourished under him since the scrap of non-ferrous metal and iron from the Gadani ship-breaking yard was reduced in price and the scrap was bought by Nawaz Sharif's foundry. It was carried day and night by the railway wagons reserved for it to the foundry from Karachi to Lahore. The scrap price was lowered at the cost of ruining the ship-breaking industry[5]. The small businessmen- ship -breakers were ruined. Once the scrap was converted into iron bars and billets made, the price of iron was increased for the benefit of the Ittifaq Foundry, thus doubly providing it profit venue. This method was not Halal. The entire operation was unethical, based on theft. It financially ruined a sector of the community.

Distinctions in life the nature does not give as donation, but this award is earned. Nawaz Sharif tried to introduce a bill in the parliament to declare him through law 'Ameerul Momineen' – Lord of the faithful. He wanted to saddle him in the chair like of the Taliban ruler Mulla Umar in Afghanistan. The Ameerul Momineen is the title of Hazrat Ali AS. The rest who took this title did Jabr – excess on them and

---

[5] Obsolete and redundant ships used to come from Southern Europe for their breakg up at the Gaddani beach. Small businessmen ship breakers found it no more feasible to continue with the breaking of ships since the price of the scrap was decreased, reducing their earnings, for living. The industry in 1990 was ruined, many ship breakers' assets sank.

committed hypocrisy. Nawaz Sharif ventured to aspire that appellation, not knowing what it was and events proved he was ignoramus. The Ameerul Momineen will not be involved to receive 35 Lacs from the stolen 24 Crore Rupees (240 million US $) from the Mehran Bank[6]. Such incredulous things happen in Pakistan – a Muslim state.

عجب خلق امّت میں کچھ آدمی ہیں
سیاست میں بھونڈے فراست میں بودے ہیں
ارادہ مومنوں کے امیر بننے کا ہے
مومن کے مُعارض امیرالمومنی کےطالب ہیں

Ajab Khalq Ummat Mein Kuchh Aadmi Haain
Siyasat Mein Bhonday Ferasat Mein Boday Haain
Aerada Mominoan Kay Ameer Bannay Ka Haai
Momin Kay Moaariz, Ameerul Momeni Kay Talab Haain

Strange among the Ummat are created some people
In politics awkward in intellect dim
Intention is to become lord of the believers
Quarrel with Momin desirous of becoming chief of Momineen

Sayed Athar Husain

This desirous of becoming Ameerul Momeneen - Nawaz Sharif, when he was Prime Minister of Pakistan visited United States of America on unofficial or semi-official visit from 20th to 23rd October 2013. On 23rd of October after three days of wait, he met President Obama. The Facebook friends put posts showing his sheepish posture in front of

---

[6] A most unusual case in the history of politics was that the ISI (Inter-Services Intelligence) was illegally provided an outlandish sum of 24 crore Rupees on the contrivance of the politician President Ghulam Ishaque Khan 1988 – 1993 to distribute among the political parties to strengthen their hands to stop the PPP from coming back in power in 1990. The money was loaned by the owner of the Mehran Bank - Yunus Habib for this operation. The ISI kept half, siphoned off, and distributed half to 39 fictitious and non-fictitious parties. This was historic corroborative scandal and the judiciary of the country kept quiet about it, although there was an Asghar Khan Petition in November 2012, but no concrete action was taken by the court. Nawaz Sharif had received 35 Lacs, Jamat-e Islami 50 Lacs, and similarly amounts to other parties (See Wikipedia and other journalistic sources for greater details).

President Obama with their slighting comments. He called Mrs Obama - Mr Obama when referring to her with no pick of right words; he asked President Obama to visit Pakistan and taste his Dal Qeema. He read his address to the President shown by press from folded pieces of paper pulling them out from his pocket. He was such an embarrassment to Pakistan. He was so muddled that Obama was tickled with uncontrollable laughter.

That was not joy for Pakistan. It needed leaders of stature, not poorly educated activists to represent the country. How he ever has climbed to that high post to be prime minister, sheds light on General Gilani and Ziaul Haque's poor vision. Also, the entire voting coterie bringing him to be prime minister is guilty in front of the people and the country of Pakistan. In contradiction to his dismal performance, when Z.A. Bhutto met President Kennedy in 1963 in Washington, after a day of talks, Kennedy looked at Bhutto in admiration and said: 'If you were American you would be in my cabinet.' Bhutto retorted, 'Be careful Mr President, if I were an American you would be in my cabinet.' This is the level of leadership Pakistan needs, not immature upstarts ruling over 20 billion people.

The kindness, ease and benevolence accorded by God in return to the service of approved and virtuous deed is an earning called Sawab and its accreditation to the recipient is not possible to be seen but only perceived and so is the phenomenon of the retribution – the Saza or the punishment for smearing others with acrimony and derogatory remarks. The appropriation of reward and punishment for either of these is in the hand of the providence. All this cannot be accounted for by any corporeal Aehtesab - accountability formed of a motivated force given birth to, by Nawaz Sharif-led bureau. During the first tenure of office, Nawaz Sharif appointed a one Mr Saifur Rahman – the ill-famed bureaucrat. He embarked on fabricating cases against Asif Ali Zardari, to catch him and put him in jail. He put him in Jail without much ado for twelve years, with trumpeted nick name of Mr 10%, but nothing came of it, only apology from Saifur Rahman.

Never a politician finds a place of distinction unless he has mastered literature, philosophy, ethics, delivery of thought and has read the letter of Hazrat Ali to his governor Malik Ashtar for his spiritual and administrative guidance. The accountability bureau formed by Nawaz Sharif was charged to do trial and persecution of the rival party's political stalwarts. Saifur Rahman acting a human without conscious was so enthusiastic about this lifetime chance of skinning alive his ideological and corporeal enemy that he spent millions of nation's monies to entrap the PPP stalwart Asif Ali Zardari, but he failed. There was no substance or if there was it did not surface to be seen by others. But his personal hate for the PPP made Pakistan suffer. Only Asif Ali Zardari was given a thorough bad name, but his luck and talent could not be separated from him that stood by him and he kept rising in stature.

And this Zardari bashing, created a culture which caught up with the press and the public and it did a great disservice to the nation, it made the nation temperamentally bitter and prejudicial. The media was caught in propaganda galore and the whole scenario turned sickening. All designed to deviate the attention of the public and focus it away from the corrupt practices of Nawaz Sharif. Asif Ali Zardari's victimisation by Saifur Rahman was a black spot on the slate of morality, but such is the propaganda campaign by the political parties that nothing bad is remembered about them, and the PML-N were returned to power in May 2013 aided by the rigging of votes.

The scandal of 'thirty-five punctures' (see comments on Zem TV – Pakistani Talk Shows of February 2014) code named – rigging in election by the care taker chief minister of Punjab Najam Sethi, speaks of the trend of well-versed way of law breaking as if a God certified Halal act. His crescendo was arranging the election win for the PMLN through rigging, and other means, but he was unfortunate, his talk on phone was caught and recorded. Nevertheless again, for five years the entrustment of God i.e., the nation of Pakistan was grabbed by impiety, arrogance and chicanery forces and Nawaz Sharif ruled from the throne in Islamabad from May 2013 – July 2017. Its abrupt end came as he was disqualified to hold office.

-: . :-

I

INDRA GANDHI, Z.A. BHUTTO AND THE ASSASSIN

VI

Democracy is cut to create personalities of excellence. Indra Gandhi was called Goongi Gurdya (the dumb doll) by the media and by the Congress party bosses who had elected her. But soon she so centralised power under her that the phrase was coined for her: Indra is India and India is Indira. And she was named woman of the Millennium in the on-line poll by the BBC. Rabindra Nath Tagore named her Priyadarshani in his interview with her and her full name had become Indra Priyadarshani Gandhi. And truly she became Empress of India. She was called Goddess Durga for winning the war against Pakistan by Atal Bihari Vajpayee. But winning the war with Pakistan for the separation of its East wing from its West wing was easy. All the injustices played by West Pakistan against its Eastern wing had snowballed together to score victory for India. It was not the army that surrendered, it was the politicians' fault for which the army surrendered. Mohammad Ali Chaudhari as Finance Minister would not let a penny go to East Pakistan in development. General Ayyub Khan said there are no stones in East Pakistan to build road, General Iskandar Mirza the President asked the army sent to East Pakistan to suppress ruthlessly the dissidents.

So, victory for Indra Gandhi was easy with the East Pakistan population grievances unattended and India ready to exploit the situation. But Indira was a humanitarian she agreed without preconditions to send the prisoners to their home. And why not, Zulfequar Ali Bhutto was on the table opposite her with his incorruptible nature and his awareness of world affairs with his literariness aiding him. Bhutto was Indira's collegue at Oxford University and that was the tool he used to soften the heart of Indra Gandhi. But there emerged in Pakistan a General thankless and as a bat, and as ruthless as a mongoose and he hanged this preserver of the dignity of the nation, despite world appeal to spare his life. And Indra and Bhutto both were assassinated by their guards, Bhutto by his General and Indra by her body guard.

The General with his organised display of extremism hanged Z.A. Bhutto on the pretext that he committed felony[7] to hatch his murder. Z.A. Bhutto was the General's mentor, master and benefactor, who had decorated him with four stars – of whom he was once a devout obedient servant but he wrapped his loyalty in one go once he made the coup and initiated scheme to hang Z.A. Bhutto for his precautionary self-preservation not to be sent to the grave hole and this was height in individual criminal act. He manipulated the outcome of the judgement from the court for the poise of the hold of power and that despotism was all right for the General.

Such thanklessness and blind heartedness as not to see that the Life Filled Bhutto had done greater things for the people and taken up greater projects of greater values for the happiness of the people, and if there was slip on the file and the executives and the politicians used it as tool to eliminate him, the General's mould shaped it in death. A maxim evolved out of his goodness and good character and obedience to God was: People asked the Life Filled, "Where the money will come from, for the projects you have undertaken." The Life Filled had announced of massive projects. His reply was *Qalandari* (saintly); he said: "The money will come; God will send it."

Besides nation building and enhancing its image in the international arena, Bhutto did greater things for the army, guided by his inborn subtleties and supported by the largesse of the enemy he

---

[7] Nawab Mohammad Ahmad Khan Kasuri had broken away from Z.A. Bhutto and had made daily norm such confrontation in the parliament that had made working impossible. Vexed one day Bhutto wrote on the file to the FSF, 'Put him right' or some such disciplinary sentence. They misunderstood and murdered Mohammad Ahmad Khan Kasuri. They one night woke up Z.A. Bhutto at 11PM and the director informed him that Kasuri was murdered.

was dealing with. The enemy in her comfortable *Aivan* - the fortress, was the sophisticated Indra Gandhi; she believed in moral values and was generous. When Zulfiqar Ali Bhutto was expired of all logic to present to Indira at the Shimla conference, he took aid of the rhetoric, but with the art of politics quietly mumbled and said to her, "Remember you always obtained less marks in tutorials than me at Oxford." And she allowed the dignity of the 92, 000 to prevail, and dignity of the vanquished not trampled. She let that prevail what was good and idealistic tendency of human nature and the guise of her inbred sophistication of her family and its assets she represented, and she set a precept in diplomacy to be friendly to be followed by others.

But the celestial connection claiming General Ziaul Haque disgraceful and aloof of any exhibit of kindness, hanged Z.A. Bhutto, because he did not carry these finer values, shown by Indira Gandhi. This human, in its form only showed that recognition to reciprocity of return of good by greater goodness did not brush past him, and he kept the Life Filled Bhutto in a solitary miserable cell and publicized him to be, "*Aasteen ka Sanp*"- snake in the grass - a certain someone in inner circle who is ready to bite and pour poison. And this foul speaking was in spite of his awareness that the Life Filled shed convincing fragrance.

The similitude of the *Aasteen Ka Sanp*, he drew for the Life Bearing Bhutto was in fear for his life that had prompted the beast in him turn into abuse and to beguiling aggressiveness. And aided by his inborn malice and apportioned bad blood in him and supported by the secondary help extended to him by the wild analysis of the seasoned *Kohistani Siyasatdan* – the rugged mountainous politician, Khan Abdul Wali Khan, he entered in the domains where he subjected him to commit despicable brutality.

The dead body of the Life Filled was not allowed a public decent burial. The Kohistani Politician's ungracious cutting remark was the propellent to murder, topping up the General's intangibility to justice. The Kohistani Siyasatdan (the hilly politician) was of the same calibre as the Life Filled – the *Raygistani Siyasatdan* – politician coming from the hot dry desert, still the Kohistani was will full tool of betrayal of his class and whispered into the General's ears, "There were one grave and two corpses." And the Kaan Ka Kachcha – too credulous, a gullible General, amputated the honour of all fair Generals.

This pettish paradigm of the Kohistani Politician helped the General take the road he had put his foot on and he boxed him from danger and selected the essence of life of the nation, the Life Filled to make a corpse. And the logic of the gory Kohistani Politician was simple, his party was disbanded by the Life Filled, his coalition government was dismissed by him in the higher interest of the country and the Kohistani with it had lost two governments of two provinces in 1974 and the cause of it was betrayal of the cause of Pakistan. This book finds it imperative that his great misconduct be accounted for, as these were not ignorable. Wali Khan and his colleagues and friends were arrested, and some escaped and went in exile and freedom of operation to them was disallowed by the Life Filled.

The reason was the Kohistani Politician had veered away politics from the central cause of Pakistan to the molehill of nationalism and to ethnic bind to embrace his clans from the outer boundaries of the nation spread into Afghanistan and he threw his and his people's fate, fame and fortune in the lap of his neighbour, the Pashtun Afghanistan. And his record was, he called Quad-e Azam; 'Agent of English' and his party activists bombed and blew bridges and his party's Awami National Party's Secretary General, Ajmal Khatak deserted the country for Kabul and said he will return riding on the tank.

The Life Filled whom Ziaul Haque sent to gallows was locked in a miserable cell of Adiala jail, with an open, effusive and unclean toilet, which was intentionally left to stink, and a secondary General sent to kick him. The court had helped the acrid General to choose the Life Filled as corpse. But the constitution had made the despot General the corpse, and the constitution was standing as symbol of power of the country, which posed a deeper risk to the acrid General. The constitution had a stronger vertebra, which though the acrid General himself had amended and sinisterly disabled it not to harm him but in the ultimate feared its weight and hold on the nation if the Life Filled lived.

The compelling action, driving him doing as he will, whipping and breaking lashes at the back of the countrymen who were registering protest against him for inhumane act to murder the Life Filled, was driven by his fear and sinisterness of his evident inherent lack of intellectualism and overestimating his own tin pot wisdom. Exploiting the nation and using the muscle power of the army he was put to lead by mistake, selected by the Life Filled to advance his agenda of military actions and support of civil policies. In betrayal he shed the innocent blood and dented morality, and he was that callous and conscious less that he was not going to be bothered about its consequences in the hereafter. And the intellectual, Oxford educated the Life Filled was not allowed the last wish he was entitled to, to meet his friends and family, and the tactician in the general turned to dilute his responsibility of hanging this Adi Kavi – the original poet of diplomacy and decency, by putting the subject for debating and consultation to the umpteen numbers of Generals of his army.

He announced his plan of execution of the Life Filled to the Generals, calling their meeting. The Generals supporting him were ready to say aye. They bowed their heads with a largess of nod, denying legitimacy of power as it ought to be used. And some of those who tried to look into the eyes of the acrid General were cowed down to submission, and the overcautious fearful acrid General of classified controversial religious bend of mind made him float in the sin of hanging the Life Filled – i.e., the odorous Prime Minister Zulfequar Ali Bhutto was hanged and this was sin, God did not like and made punishment evident in the world. The acrid General fell from the sky in flame and nothing was left of him save his jaws.

But before that the acrid General in his life caused problem to precipitate. He made the army opportunity seekers by overruling the settled question of not initiating a war. He led them into initiators of war, making their trait and motto - Jihad Fi Sabeel Allah – initiating a war for the service of God, and he opened the army's doors to infiltrators. And minds were so infected with heresies that later Core Commander of Karachi Muzaffar Usmani numerously interceded to get the arrested Taliban released from the IG police. And this dictator General so wanted to display his grasp on power in the style of Rashid Caliphs that he asked the Ummah - the nation of the Prophet SAWW, to pray Namaz-elstesqa - rain prayer for the country and then obsession took command of him, and he repeated the order again for it. And he left no opportunity unexploited not to capitalize on the tender feelings of the Muslim Ummah, seeking out a 'yes' from them through camouflaged referendum, relying on an affirmative from them for their affinity to faith and exploiting their religious bend of mind and conveying to them, it was in love and service of religion that he ruled.

The General played a simple-minded soldier, but he was repressive, and he held the country in the palm of his hand and he was called by the evaluating a dictator, but by the *Takfiri* – the infidelity charged, called him the saviour. He hanged one Prime Minister – the Life Filled, Party Chief and Chairman of the biggest political party in the country and tried to undo his party and dramatically dismissed another Prime Minister. And he created fear and unsettled those qualified to be saddled in the seat of power, pulling them down, not to take the helm and guide in the affairs of the nation. Only one entrenched in notional superiority, a vague, wistful and potentially corrupt man, all along a rogue and misfit for the nation - the renowned delirious Nawaz Sharif, who sees Khala-ee Makhlooq – space creatures due to the deluge of his defect in wisdom was pushed to hop in the prime chair of the ministers.

Further, the General's adaptation of the slogan 'Don't abandon your belief and don't be prodding into others belief' – Apna Aqeeda Chhordo Naheen Ayr Doosray Ka Aqeeda Chherdo Naheen, ignored the ethics of who was right and who was wrong, and this was dehumanising people. This General sent this guide line to the nation in the Iran - Iraq war by saying, '*Meri Manein toe Iss Maamlay say Bilkul alug Rahein*,' – if you take to my advice, stay aloof of this matter. This was not Islamic character. The motto of the religion he followed was, 'go by what was truth and uphold it.' And the action of the head of the state should be to guide the Ummat to conform to the guide line of the faith and not that he introduces his own fallacious philosophy. Islam is a religion that has total ban on open fallacious Qyas – the foment of wrong opinion

While he made this unholy analysis and sat making a nation hostage, and aloof of the neighbour's sufferings, by 1988 nearing to the end of war, 400,000 Iranis were killed by the invasion of Saddam Husain - his own forces' casualties not so small. Saddam Husain had invaded Iran on 22 September 1980 without formal warning, but the General rejected such observations and made the nation lame, not siding with truth. He confused the nation, 'help them (Iran and Iraq)' in his impassionate speech, 'help if nothing else with, then by prayer only'. This appeal from him was cosmetic, because all the factions, Wahabi, Alqa-e-da, Taliban, Sipah-e Sahaba, each were out supporting Saddam Husain and were musical cord of disruption, collectively weakening the mechanism of bond of the Muslim Nation.

This detached idealism and distancing from Islamic principle and realism was despite the number of stars put on his shoulders by the Life Filled to upgrade his relevancy to Islam. It was the correct Aqeeda - the faith content that ruled the right approach to problems, not the stars on the shoulder, and the general sunk him further. General Ziaul Haque had evolved an oppositely charged philosophy, it said, 'let no harmony of views prevail', and there were consequential harsh feelings between the groups of the faith holders and factions at variance pouring out prolixity harming and denting composure of each. Ziaul Haque also not capacitated him either to investigate the philosophic wisdom of sage Lao Tzu and derive lesson from his maxim that the old sage had coined two thousand five hundred years back:

> *When the country is ruled with a light hand*
> *the people are simple.*
> *When the country is ruled with severity*
> *the people are cunning*

Lao Tzu - the Old Master is said to have lived for one hundred years in the beginning of the fifth century BC in China. The sage practiced Tao and Te (Way and Virtue). Lao Tzu says:

> *Act with non-action*
> *Work without doing*
> *Taste the tasteless*
> *Consider small great, increase the few*
> *Reward bitterness with kindness.*

Philosopher Confucius (K'ung Fu-Tzu) 551- 479 BC had no wishes and material desire. He was a philosopher of ethics and moral, full of wisdom in the behavioural sciences and worldly philosophy; he went to Lao Tzu, to Chou and asked him to tutor him in the rites. Lao Tzu sent him away and only said 'not to be arrogant'. Was this a censure on him? But Confucius spoke of Lao Tzu:

'Things that run can be trapped, what can swim can be caught in traps. Those that fly can be shot down with arrows. But what to do with the dragon I do not know. It rises on the clouds and sails on the winds. Today I have met Lao Tzu and he is like dragon.'

The philosophy of Lao Tzu was beyond the grasp of the General. Also, his handicap in intellectualism could not have allowed him reach out to look into the advanced talk of Blaise Pascal, who lived about 1656, who says:

"A good citizen is one who doesn't always keep his mouth shut."

The General was unconcerned with these sublime wisdoms. He took out his lash in response to the people's protest and lashed the citizens when they opened their mouth. People immolated them in his time and little the General knew of these discredits that fell in his lap. The rising Shia Aalim, Shaheed Ariful Husain Al Husaini was ruthlessly sprayed with bullet by the Sipah-e Sahaba at the twilight of this terrifying General's rule. This Aalim was symbol of Shia political power and a uniting voice to bring the Muslim Ummah close to each other. And it was the silent Ah – cry of pain that the general within days met his end. This Alim was educated at the Najaf Schools of religious learning in Iraq in Fiqah, Hadith and Philosophy and was a link, representing the Ummah with the Ulema, but his life was cut short. The understanding of the philosophy of Islam was beyond the Takfiris and the faulty cognition of the General.

Ziaul Haque's ideological unionizing was with the famous Saddam Husain. He had exiled Ariful Husain from Iraq for his revolutionary thinking in 1973 and then in 1974 the Shah of Persia exiled him from Qum for his association with Aayetullah Khomeini, and in the end he became a victim of General Ziaul Haque in Shia containment policy. He was killed for pursuing Shia cause. The General's flag officer was blamed for involvement in this killing and the only fault of the Aalim was he organized Shia strength. He was martyred on 15th August 1988, in collusion with the General's free roving Intelligence and the Sipah-e

Sahaba party, who fired bullets at him in ambush of his motorcade. The Sipah-e Sahaba enjoyed the patronage of the General, coupled with the helping hand of the external powers in Saudi Arabia. The assassination was made two days before the General's plane crash and his demise.

The Holy Quran said. 'Killing of one human being was killing the entire human race'. And the killing of an Aalim was killing the birth of an idea. The command of God abhorred all this despicable act. And the best that emerged to decree against the murder of the Life Filled was: 'Had the prodigious judgement been allowed to be passed by the original constituent number of nine judges[8] of the bench, the judgement given would be the verdict 'not guilty' in the ratio 5:4 in favour of the Life Filled.'

The verdict of death sentence from the court was obtained after manipulation through delay in hearing, waiting initiating hearing till the retirement of one judge who favoured acquittal. Then one in favour of acquittal, fell ill or was declared ill. In spite of that, still there was only a slim majority in the ratio of 4:3, and Anwarul Haque sentence verdict of Lahore High Court was upheld. Anwarul Haque was of the same *Berardi* – the clan as Ziaul Haque. And the Lahore High Court Chief Justice Molvi Mushtaq Hussein who had passed the death sentence was known to openly hate Z.A. Bhutto and is known to have said, 'if he is not going to give him death sentence who else will give'.

Here we see an innate phenomenon occurring. When Molvi Mushtaq died his funeral procession was attacked by the honeybees – thousands of them bunched on his corpse and people ran for safety. In these men running Ghulam Mustafa Khar was there, they ran and left Molvi Mushtaq's dead body and the bees clung on to the corpse of Molvi Mushtaq. One or two deaths occurred among the mourners and

---

[8] The four judges who upheld death sentence to Zulfequar Ali Bhutto were all from Punjab. The General doing the murder was from Punjab. The petition was dismissed on 24th March 1979 and Bhutto was hanged hurriedly on 4th April 1979 in small hours in Punjab. The Life Filled was trapped in the net of death by the mean General whose army men Bhutto got back from prison in India, they raised no voice for him and they were all from Punjab. But wrath of God was so severe that the General burnt for 2 hours in the wreckage and nothing was left of him but his Jaw. That was buried by his politician son and then the sentencing to death judge's corpse was bitten by furious bees. In Aayet 5:44 Allah says, ... whoso judges not by that which Allah has revealed is Kafir.

the bees stung so hard that their heads pierced inside the body and had to be pulled out from the flesh. The reckoning of his life's doing in the hereafter had started very early that people saw happening in this world. This was the Providence's way of establishing justice through the exhibit of Azaab (torment), and reminder to humanity to do justice.

The justice system of the Creator - the Indubitable Power was not to let bygones be bygones and the doings of other judges will certainly be dealt as per merit. And to the zealot who said. "My blood boils when I see someone belonging to Bhutto's political party," and raised the petty sloganeering of 'Jaag Punjabi Jaag' – wake up Punjabi, wake up, the Nawab of Ralah, the ruler with ethics and morality said, "The emotionality showing hate is a trend unbecoming of a leader. He is scuttling freedom of choice of man and dragging down fate." So, the dictator General Ziaul Haque said for this adopted apprentice Nawaz Sharif; 'his own life may be added to his'.

The PPP was carrying the party symbol 'Al-Zulfequar; - sword of Hazrat Ali AS. The symbol was picked up in Najaf-e Ashraf, and Ziaul Haque who had initiated intense persecution of the Pakistan People's Party needed a flag bearer to keep this viciousness going on and Nawaz Sharif was his voice in politics, who spoke the language of his mentor and was Zia's ideal flag bearer to establish a Sunni alone Pakistan of such group as detached from the culture of Urfa – recognising righteousness, thinkers and contended class. Ziaul Haque had hatched a big conspiracy in the country to scuttle the faith into the narrow lane of prejudice. And because we see Nawaz Sharif lacked intellectualism, so he had to use brute force, like raid on the supreme court of Sajjad Ali Shah.

Idealistically the PPP of the Life Filled Z.A. Bhutto is the most suited party to lead Pakistan, with Z.A. Bhutto's idealism in Wilayet of Ali. Its base is Sindh, the most tolerant of all the provinces in Pakistan. And let this relevancy of approach to life change Pakistan to God principles. Imran Khan has potential, but is untested and unfortunately has inclination to some form of Talibanization in Pakistan, then Imran Khan has no command on Urdu.

Nawaz Sharif was under trial for contempt of court, but he did not hear his sentence, he sent an unruly mob, with Tariq Aziz, the popular TV host and one MNA together with a cabinet member to attack the chief justice. The mob pelted at the Supreme Court, and the Chief Justice Sajjad Ali Shah had to hide after he was bashed repeatedly with a briefcase on the head. So, Nawaz Sharif is an offender. The judgement that was not allowed passed by the court of Sajjad Ali Shah makes him disqualified. So, he was disqualified long ago and it would have been better for him if he had listened to the judgement of Justice Sajjad Ali Shah, rather than later be tried in Panama leak case and be totally stripped of honour. And God was going to be kind to him but he behaved apostate and refused His kindness.

The entire nation became conspiratorial and shirked responsibility and bore the guilt. The press and the media did not heave a sigh louder than a hiss not to be heard at the onerous of the crime that took place. The soul of the father of the nation, became drenched in remorse but the General was cheery his life was saved. The press hid the offer of Z.A. Bhutto to Sheikh Mujibur Rahman after he took over as prime minister following the defeat of the army in East Pakistan to come and take over as prime minister, to which the Sheikh refused and said, 'He cannot rule Pakistan from West Pakistan'. He wanted all along the capital shifted to Dacca, and new coin minted. And they suppressed the news of the far sight of this prime minister - he started work on creating a federation of Afghanistan, Pakistan and Bangladesh. And if ever anyone could do it, it was the genius of this prime minister Z.A. Bhutto, whom the wicked general hanged and terminated his life to save his neck. The politician from the north had whispered in his ears 'there was one grave and two corpses'.

General Ziaul Haque wanted to prove he was a greater God loving Muslim than all the Ayetullahs and the celestial priests. He changed the character of the army to become a monk. He forced commandos to discard Ya Ali and adopt Ya Allah. He appointed Mullas to lead Salat to the regiments. He made the commandos mellow that did not suit to their nature of warfare. The wingless angle Fitrus who had committed Turk-e Oola – shedding the imperative of the highest in submission and the wings were fallen and he dropped to an island, when hosts of angels were going for congratulation to the Prophet SAWW at the birth of Imam Husain AS., they saw him and took him for cure to the Imam. And Fitrus rubbed him with the cot of the new born Imam and he was cured and flew singing, 'I am slave of Husain I am freed by

Husain'. And this hotchpotch of a General, did not know of the power of the Aehlebaait and he created that havoc that will take umpteen numbers of generals to clear it.

This low in faith General made the army opportunity seekers, overruling the settled question of not initiating a war. He led them into initiation war by making their trait and motto - *Jihad Fi Sabeel Allah* – initiating a war in the service of God, and he opened the army's doors to the infiltrators. The minds were so infected with the heretic thoughts generated by him that later Core Commanders of Karachi Muzaffar Usmani numerously interceded to get the arrested Taliban released from the IG police. And this General so wanted to display his grasp on power in the style of the first Caliphs that he asked the *Ummah* - the nation of the Prophet SAWW, to pray *Namaz-e Istesqa* (استسقا)- rain prayer for the country and obsession took hold of him, and he repeated the order again for it.

This menace thrusting him on the nation left no opportunity unexploited not to capitalize on the tender feelings of the Ummah, seeking out a 'yes' from them through a camouflaged referendum, ensuring through the design of the questionnaire that he obtained an affirmative from them. They were responsive in affinity for boosting faith and put the stamp on yes and he exploiting their wasf – the quality to adhere to religion had achieved the command to stick around and he ruled for ten years and had come for three months. He cast his image in the mould of one simple minded, but he was called by the evaluating - a cunning dictator but by the *Takfiri* – the infidelity charged – a saviour. He hanged the Prime Minister; Party Chief and Chairman of the biggest political party in the country and tried to undo his party and dramatically dismissed another Prime Minister. And he arrested Poet Ahmad Faraz for writing the poem 'Muhaasra', who was compared with Poet Sheikh Mohammad Iqbal for he recited poem against his military rule and the poet had to take refuge by exiling him. And he created fear and unsettled those qualified to be saddled in the seat of power, devastating them not to be able to take the helm and guide the masses in the affairs of the nation, and what a ruin he was!

Mir Shah Nawaz Bhutto was killed in mysterious circumstances in Syria; he had entered in international campaign to save his father's life and had raised a group called Al Zulfequar to overthrow the Zia regime. Shah Nawaz Bhutto resorted to arms to target Ziaul Haque's demise. Al Zulfequar high jacked a PIA plane on flight from Karachi to Kabul and killed a military person taking him to be the son of Ziaul Haque. The Aayet 2:178 says: O of faith, those murdered unjustifiably in retaliation you are commanded to take life in revenge of life. As this Shariat was operative Ziaul Haque should have been long executed, even before he met his fate.

Ziaul Haque was jittery of condemnation in the world press and for the support Al Zulfequar received. Sensing danger for him, he called Al Zulfequar and the entire Bhutto family terrorists - recall his outlandish talk to the nation. Mohammad Javad Zarif says Iran was begging for a single missile from places to places. But Ziaul Haque even sold a few Stinger missiles to the warring for some monetary benefits – not known where the money he used, but called Bhutto and family illegitimate sons.

And he shut the cross-fertilization of ideas and the talk of love to open hearts and pulled down the nation's ethical standing already hitting the rock bottom in excelling qualities, turning it to isolationism by yelling Gali – the swear words for the Bhuttos on the radio. Simultaneous with discord to help extinguish the fire of hate between Saddam and Iran, he put across the negative slogan, 'Apna Aqeeda Chordo Naheen, Doosray ka Aqeeda Chehrdo Naheen'- do not abandon your belief and do not prod in other's belief. This was encouraging Firqah Wariat – a sectarian divide slogan, against which Hazrat Ali AS. says:

Narul Forqat-e Aharro Min Nar-e Jahannum

The fire of the sectarian divide is hotter than the fire of Hell.

The divide was due to the denial of the authority of God appointed Imams under the notion that the Masoom – the free of vices and free of sins Imams stopped coming after the death of the Prophet SAWW and they ignored the Hadith-e Saqlaain, the spoken directive of the Prophet SAWW:

I am leaving behind two weighty things with you, one; Quran and the other my Aehlebaait (Itrati), as long as you will stick to them both, you will not be lost (go astray).

Not submitting to the divine nurtured progenies, the Aehlebaait' nationhood was the cause of the extremism. It was not scarcity of commodity or lack of education or the paralysing poverty, but it was due to the state of mind and the deficiency of the application of *Adl* – the justice, in the faith fundamental. And it was strongly evidenced by Usman Farouk Abdul Muttalib, a Mechanical Engineer from the UCL, president of the Islamic Society (ISCO) at the UCL. He was son of a rich Nigerian father who on 25th of December 2009 tried to blow up the plane over Detroit by lighting up explosive on his body. He was all ready to blow him and the 278 innocent passengers, but miracles happen, and the plane and passengers were safe and he was unarmed.

Now look at the vast gulf of the objectivity. The Shia Mujtahid, Mufti Jafar Husain for the sake of Sunni Shia unity says, "The difference between the Shia and the Sunni is only to the extent of difference prevailing between Shia thought and the four schools of thought of Aehl-e Sunnah", to this, the Sunni response was, 'It was said by one in *Taqiyya* - dissimilation to win favours from the Sunnis.' And the Sunni extremists said, 'there was a very grave difference between the faith of the Shias and the Sunnis. The Shias are conspirators; they quoted the names of Mir Jafar and Mir Sadiq'. The comment on this jibe is: The Sunnis prefer disunity between Shia and Sunni. They are afraid unity means they will become one of the Shias, because stronger ideology wins.

Because of this bickering the extremism is showing its face everywhere; the fair eye of President Pervez Musharraf saw in National Reconciliation Ordinance (NRO) Oct. 2007 an escape route to bring back eventual harmony by giving amnesty to the politicians against all politically motivated cases falling between January 1, 1986 and October 12, 1999 and 8000 cases were closed to bring back Benazir from self-exile and strengthen democracy, as the NRO was against the politically motivated cases. But the irony is for the sake of opposition the Chief Justice Iftikhar Mohammad Chaudhari flattened the NRO as unconstitutional in 2009. There then the anchors and media becoming hyper, beaming, scheming and conspiring to pull down the President of the Islamic Republic of Pakistan A.A. Zardari and crumble the democratic government.

The high-power bench of the 17 judges constituted by the Chief Justice Iftekhar Mohammad Chaudhari passed order on 16 December 2009 that all orders and all acquittals and amnesties allowed under the NRO were illegal and those orders were as if never existed. The judges after this predicament turned out to be predators, exuberant with excessiveness. They brought in biased articles bracketed in their order for provisioning further future actions to establish their imperialistic authority and there was a further slippage in the standard of justice. The Muslim league and far right parties - the Islamist parties were out to humiliate the government and pep up the judiciary, backing it up to the hilt to target the government of A.A. Zardari and this was second rate and third-rate politics and science of logic buried. It all led by the judiciary of Chief Justice Iftekhar Mohammad Chaudhari.

On 17th February 2010 a wrong was made right and right made wrong on the orders of the CJ. A junior judge was given a senior chair, not on merit but for politics. The ethics was violated, the right of rule was of the government and there was to be no dictating by the judiciary. It was the way of Hazrat Ali AS. as Caliph for absolute justice, he admonished the Qaziul Qazat for making distinction between him as appellant and the Jew the defendant in reception in his court. The Qazi(s) were the appointees of the Caliphs not a Qazi appointing a Qazi of his choice, for playing game not inherent in the Islamic vision of:

Mun Tora Haji Bagoyam tu Mara Haji Bago

I call you a Haaji and you call me a Haaji

Iftikhar Mohammad Chaudhary has been controversial in the following matters:

1. He allowed bail to the Lal Masjid extremist Maulana Abdul Aziz, who immediately started anti-state activity.
2. He acquitted Nawaz Sharif in the case of state terrorism and conspiracy. Nawaz Sharif had not allowed the landing of the PIA plane carrying the C-in-C of the country and putting the full load of civilian passengers' life in jeopardy.

3. He dragged in clauses not in context with the articles of constitution in the judgement on the NRO, making it contiguous to indict the President of the country, opening a closed case and politicising the judgement.

4. He took Suo motu notice on matters not of grave concern, but that which will embarrass the government and will take it towards destabilisation and ignored serious cases all for political reasons.

5. He issued orders to fix the price of the commodities and ordered to make appointments and transfers of executive personnel to have a finger in the pie of the administration.

6. He appointed a lower seniority judge to the higher post bypassing the courts own standing ruling to appoint only a senior and not a junior of him.

Never has a judiciary brought its name to such a disrepute as the judiciary of his 17 judges' bench of the Supreme Court, headed by Iftikhar Mohammad Chaudhari. It was labelled as the politicised judiciary, trying to defame, disqualify and dethrone the sitting President A.A. Zardari from the seat of Presidency. For its deed the bench of the judges earned the name of; the Imperialist Judiciary, Overactive Judiciary, Biased Judiciary, glorified clerks. And the President Asif Ali Zardari said in Chakwal, 'This was using trick of a conspiratorial pen, to oust a running government.' And he came out to be more moralistic than the imposing panel of the 17 judges, sparing no possibility in not exploring articles 62 - 63 of the constitution for applicability in their judgement to scuttle the government.

It was all an expression of hidden dismay for not being able to hold back A.A. Zardari. He triumphantly demolished the use of the law of necessity – holding back the military from taking over the civil power and created a paved corridor for him to march on, attired in stateliness, and subduing difficulties, keeping him in the seat of the presidency as President.

The hate against A.A. Zardari was from the time he married the talented brain of politics – the gem of the country, Benazir Bhutto when he was a non-entity, save that he was wearing a Balochi Paggard – turban on his head. But hold! The hatred for him was also because he was a Shia Muslim or a Shia ideology assimilating Muslim. But one would like to use proposition; if three times he offers prayer in public with his hands folded, then ten times he should offer prayer with hand dropped with prostration on earth and not on the carpet. And for any President of Pakistan, it was necessary to respect the Muslims brightening and shining Islam than the mere numbers as the count heads.

Pakistan was secular as was the proclamation of the Quad-e Azam due to the composition of its different precept of the citizens in the religion of Islam. Pakistan is not a unitary client of one faith, it has Sunnis, Shias, Christians, Hindus, Ahmadis and Zoroastrians, they all have their statutory right and should be nourished with love just as much as allocated to the Sunni faith man. This ethical law was binding on all the Governors and on all the heads of the commissioned bodies of the state to treat each individual as creation of God and not one belonging to an ism.

A.A. Zardari to appease Nawaz Sharif, marred his name by his speech in in Gardhi Khuda Bukhsh, where he said: 'Billa aa Gaya haai na Janay Dena.' (The male cat has come don't let him go). This derogatory phrase was used for General Pervez Musharraf who had given him NRO, brought him in the country and inhabited him. This referred Billa had held a fair election and thereby Zardari could form his government and become president. That speech was totally ungracious and was from a sick mind.

None of the civilian ruler ever is known to have held a fair election. It was only the aristocratic General Yahya Khan and then General Musharraf who both had clean character to ingress the philosophy of fair election that comes with honesty in nature.

About three thousand years before Christ, Shamans in China were the body of people who poured out wisdom and taught the art of ruling and their recognition in the land was equivalent to the infallible Imams of the House of the Prophet SAWW. The first of them was Fu Hsi in 3000 BC. The book Tao Te Ching carries forward their influence in China. Lao Tzu wrote Tao Te Ching in two parts, Tao the main theme and Te the supporting sayings. And Kung Fu-Tzu or Confucius writes of Lao Tzu:

The Master said: 'Riches and honours are what people want. If these cannot be gained in the right way [Tao], they should not be kept (from it). Poverty and meanness are what people dislike. If it had been obtained in the right way [Tao]then I would not try to avoid them.' (The Analects, Book 4:5). And the book Tao Te Ching has influenced Chinese thought for over two thousand years.

A parallel to that (right way) in Tao was the gift of Fidak from God to the Prophet of Islam SAWW. When the Prophet SAWW was returning after conquering Khyber, the Jews presented the orchard of Fidak to the Prophet to be on the right side of the Prophet and the Prophet accepted that and used its income to finance war, and on needy poor and destitute families. Any *Faa* in Islam was the Prophet's property and he gifted it to Bibi Fatimah Zehra SUA. He even wrote a paper of her right on it. This land was taken away by the Khalifa-e Rashid I after the death of the Prophet SAWW and made state property.

Bibi Fatimah Zehra SUA claimed that it was her heritage and asked the Khalifa to return it to her, saying it was her *Miras* – the inheritance, but the Khalifa refused to give it back to her and quoted from somewhere, 'the prophets leave no heritage' and indulged him in acrimony with the descendant of the Prophet SAWW. That pillar of his faith he passed on to his followers, who among them extremists lose their control on them if anyone talks of the infallibility of the Aimma-e Aehlebaait.

The claim of Fidak by the infallible Bibi Fatimah Zehra SUA, for its ownership by the Prophet SAWW and now her heritage, sheds light on the fundamental principle that anything given in some consideration to someone was acceptable and legitimate to possess it.

But near Khalifa-e Rashid II, it had no legitimacy without firm proof. When he heard his governor in Bahrain Hazrat Abu Huraira had amassed wealth in Bahrain, he called him back and asked for an explanation that how he became so rich. Abu Huraira said he was presented with some horses and thereof he bought and sold and bred and made his wealth. The Khalifa did not find that an acceptable explanation of turning from pauper to being affluently rich. Abu Huraira was awarded punishment of lashes and removed from the governorship and ten thousand Dirham out of the twenty thousand Dirham which he confessed he had accumulated were confiscated. But it is said Abu Huraira had made 400,000 Dirham.

The point is, generating money i.e., accumulating wealth is not forbidden if it is by honest means. Legalised earning in exchange for selling talent and expertise, even when using public office was Halal[9] if pursuing Halal trade, contributory to aiding the country financially. These ethical subtleties must be studied before the Anchors launch them to take the platform as critic and visionaries.

The Life Filled Z.A. Bhutto chose the symbol of his party, the sword of Hazrat Ali, Al Zulfequar in *Najaf-e Ashraf.* Al Zulfequar was the sword in whose eulogy the angel sang *La Fata Illa Ali La Saaif Illa Zulfequar* – 'there is no youth but Ali, and no sword except Zulfequar'. And Zulfequar Ali Bhutto had vision to bring that relic to the nation that was banned abstractly by Ziaul Haque, and replaced by a hypothetical arrow. All this is imbalanced politics. The sword of Ali is ever eulogised, and the arrow has a relation with it. But the state of Pakistan is boycotting this gift by the divine.

But he could not boycott the explosive slogan of *Roti, Kaprda aur Makan* – bread clothe and shelter that was so powerful and attractive to the people that it ever-kindled hope in their hearts. There was simplicity in it with vastness of activity in front of it. The Holy Quran talks of attiring in purified clothes in Aayet 74:4 and the motto of the PPP were in conformity with the Quranic call of the basic needs of man. The righteous Islamic movement means the Alzulfequar its owner and his practices were also the basic need of the man and the masses, which the prejudicial mind of the general did not accept. But the Ayetullahs consultative association evolved conformation with Quran and the symbol Alzulfequar - the weapon enforcing righteousness.

The exoneration of Zulfequar Ali Bhutto from the blame of dismemberment of the country was to be derived from, after three times Prime Minister of Bangladesh Sheikh Hasina Wajid said, 'on the 7th of March 1971, the separation from Pakistan was based on the truth of the Agratala conspiracy.' She said, 'after being released on 22 April 1969 Sheikh Mujibur Rahman Went to London and finalised separation with exact dates of separation.' This statement should

---

[9] This topic has also been dealt with to an extent under the sub-chapter 'Fallacies and Politics' p.12.

remove Buhtan (slander) and Gheebat (backbiting) against Bhutto as these are great sins in Islam. And adopting a policy of tolerance truth will add laurel to the status of the Muslim, of which let the entire Pakistan share it.

And if one wants to be fair, he ought to recall that Zulfequar Ali Bhutto called Sheikh Mujibur Rahman after the surrender of East Pakistan to come and take charge of the nation in 1972. But Sheikh Mujeeb found it impossible to rule Pakistan with the seat of power in the West Wing. The issue was, shifting the capital to East Pakistan. There was a six - point agenda: minting new rupee, reforms, language issue, giving priority to the Bengali language. This though, their right was a plateful, and then when Sheikh Mujibur Rahman did not come to West Pakistan as offered, the Life Filled said, *Idhar Hum Udhar Tum* - Here me and there you, let's build the nations. And he started on the ragtag formation of a federation of Afghanistan, Pakistan and Bangladesh. Also, he started on the inevitability need of the country to produce a nuclear bomb, sorting out its teething problems and preparing bed for its birth.

It was second determined effort to exploit the country's potential to making the bomb. A survey of the engineers and scientists was made in the country and the talented were herded up in a secret city Koheta. His predecessor Hussein Shaheed Suharwardi was the first festooned thinker of the nation to build the bomb, but his period of rule was short and he was not extended cordiality by the Punjab.

Zulfiqar Ali Bhutto embarked on removing all hurdles confronting the realisation of possessing the bomb and he put many stalwarts in prison under the press and publication ordinance, all under the rule as chequered and advanced by the press themselves. Then he imprisoned some dubious, trying breaking affiliation of the federation, and there was harshness and excessiveness in the measures taken to the extent the democracy permitted, and unending and excessive accusations from the uncompromising politicians started taking their toll at him, but the aim was the bomb.

Z.A. Bhutto was devising. He said, 'let's make a pool of Islamic scientists and engineers' and he generated the concept of Islamic bomb. He said he will fight a thousand years of war over Kashmir, and his policy was two pronged: he was talking of the federation of the near Muslim states and discreetly working towards reversion of the East Wing to reverting to embracing the West Wing suited to the demands of the two wings.

Science was perfect but not the scientist and politics was Aebadat - the worship but certainly not by the circuitous politician and he ought to be an *Aalim Bil Amal* – the learned conducting within the bounds of the set parameters of the God's Laws. The socialism of the Life-Filled leading to nationalisation of the industries and banks hurt the nation as this was detached from the natural law. Then his reform into the land holding limits, inclusive of his own 16000 acres, he gave away to the poor *Haris* – the Sindhi land tillers, hurt him and his family interest, but all he did that to volunteer and set precept. But neither it was effective; nor necessary. If the privileged owning the land masses stayed within the bounds set by the God's law to distribute from the proceeds in taxes, Zakat and Khums, it was not necessary to distribute the land, only what needed was making it more productive. But these were the days of governing activities by the philosophy of socialism and there was confusion. The fast runners were the losers and Dr Mubashshir Hasan was his communist think tank, responsible for the debacle.

Of the scientists, even Albert Einstein seems to have had difficulty passing the preliminary. He was born in Germany in 1879. He was agnostic and just before publishing the theory of the general relativity in 1917, Albert Einstein asked a number of astronomers whether the universe was expanding. Einstein's equation showed the universe was either growing or shrinking. The astronomers said it was stable. So, Einstein introduced in the equations a cosmological constant that held the universe steady. A decade later Edwin Hubble discovered the universe was expanding. On that Einstein said the insertion of the constant was his "biggest blunder".

But then the constant was later found to be necessary to match theory and observation. And Zulfiqar Ali Bhutto was a constant for stability, but the bickering fearful for his life General sent him to gallows and be buried in Larkana. The sincerity he poured in, in building infrastructure and all he did for the country was rewarded to him by the brute by squeezing his life out of him, but he turned Shaheed! And a nation must arrive at the truth; the crude looking, ill-educated of no decent family - a bigoted extremist must never be allowed to rise to the top echelon in position as the Chief of the Army, no matter how senior in length of service the rogue is.

Again, to be fair no one made as many solid friends in the arena of world diplomacy as Zulfiqar Ali Bhutto did, and the friends he picked were pick of the time; Moammar Gaddafi, Chou En Lai, Ahmad Seokarno, Indra Gandhi, Sheikh Mujibur Rahman, Yasir Arafat, United Arab Emirates Sheikh Al Nahyan and Saudi Arabia's King Faisal and he even extended his hand beyond the Durand Line to the autocratic but honoured Sardar Mohammad Dawood. And in all this diplomacy, who felt most annoyed was the Secretary of State Henry Alfred Kissinger. He said, 'he will make such an example of him that the world will remember.' And true the Life Filled was hanged on 3 April 1979 against all appeals from the world leaders for clemency, such brute cannot be a Muslim at heart. Bhutto Shaheed's frail body was buried after his Namaz-e Janaza was said by the village Imam in Gardhi Khuda Bukhsh. This reminded people of Abu Zar Ghaffari RA who died in isolation after the Caliph Usman bin Affan banished him from the city For Abu Zar Ghaffari criticise Caliph Usman. A passing caravan of Hazrat Malik Ashtar gave him the burial. But his magnanimity will be remembered in all times to come.

The British parliamentarian George Galloway said about Kissinger; 'He is the biggest war criminal in the world today, with blood of millions of people in Vietnam and Cambodia and Laos and Chile and East Timor on his hands. He will never appear behind a court or be behind bars.' And true as Kissinger had said, despite all appeals of clemency to spare his life Ziaul Haque hanged the Life Filled and bought wrath for him of justice loving Pakistanis and of the world.

General Ziaul Haque had done another grave disservice to the nation. He had sabotaged the signing of the pact between the Life Filled and Sardar Mohammad Dawood. Sardar Dawood had committed to recognise the Durand Line, if the Kohistani Politician along with his party men was released. But the General advanced the theory that 'it was likely the army cadre will show displeasure' and he opposed the signing and stopped the settlement between the two countries. This was wickedest disloyalty to the nation and Ziaul Haque must be tried for it even after his demise and burial. This was due to the traitor element in him to hold back the Prime Minister not getting the laurels on his forehead and glory for the nation. But later, once he was in power, he released the Kohistani Politician, less Durand Line settlement. And what he did was irreparable damage through his betrayal of the nation. In effect he let live the line of friction that was going to be erased all for his personal glory which he found not. He let left a permanent tension sizzling on the Pak-Afghan border. And Ziaul Haque was a traitor, he has proved many times so.

Ziaul Haque had no remorse he had sabotaged the Islamic norm of good neighbourly relations, but had his selfish and wicked deprivation stop the political one up Manship of Zulfiqar Ali Bhutto. For him it was a greater success than the interest of Pakistan, such was the nature of the beast of politics in Ziaul Haque, and the propogandists call him Mard-e Momin – man of deepest right faith.

The self-centred politics in these times was such that the accreditations of the Memorandum of Understandings obtained by Asif Ali Zardari with the foreign corporations – Korea and others in the first stint of the government of Benazir Bhutto, even when favourable to the country were not allowed their implementation in the country by the press critiques. And the farmer's lands purchased cheap before the election for the planned motorway and sold at exuberant price after the election by the Pakistan Muslim League (N) politicians to the government were not questioned by anyone. Such sinister planning to think of a project to skin the government and cheat the poor, speaks of gangsterism in the PMLN.

When Z.A. Bhutto was handed over the presidency, the nuclear programme was at standstill. In 1972 it was activated, and in 1974 the nation was wading into advanced field of nuclear physics and mastering in quantum mechanics and from 1976 on, the country went full steam ahead making bomb grade uranium, even when it was cut in two halves due to previous political and military failure.

Pakistan Civilian Nuclear Programme was started by Prime Minister Hussein Shaheed Suharwardi. It was locked up and put in the cold storage by General Mohammad Ayyub Khan and remained so till 1972. Ayyub Khan said, if he will ever need the bomb, he will buy it off the shelf. The 150 million Dollar nuclear programme was too expensive for him. Ayyub Khan instead went for space research programme and started the activity under the aegis of Pakistan Space and Upper Atmosphere Research Committee. His concern was more ethical than the military strategy and as it would appear, he was right, the Islamic Republic of Iran says, 'any weapon causing blanket destruction and loss of life of innocent is un-Islamic.' However, Aayet 8:60 says:

'And as far as you can with your strength and with your horses tethered to the stake prepare (with battle ready hardware) against infidels, with this you will dismay enemy of God and your enemy and besides that others as well, whom you do not know but God knows, and whatever you spend in the way of God you will have met it fully and no oppression will be subjected on you be repaid.'

Thus, making and keeping a powerful nuclear bomb as deterrent was passable. It enhanced the state of preparedness to keep one in readiness to a connect to infallibility. Only the observation was, 'using the bomb to kill was Haram', but it was not outside the law of God to punish with earthquake and cease them, see Aayet 7:78. They were deniers and they challenged.

General Pervez Musharraf,[10] is a consolatory prize for the nation. The General was presiding with an air of assurance and stability, and each dawn of the day, saw nabbing of the misconceived involved in religious extremism, and he in spite of his infatuation for secularism was still more suited to the service of the religion, than those considering them licensed Islamists, but not knowing the spirit of Islam.

---

[10] General Musharraf was in power for nine years till 18 August 2008, when A.A. Zardari took over as President on September 6, 2008. The General has since taken up voluntary ambassadorial work for Pakistan in the world arena, giving talk and getting paid for it. But he is haunted by the revenge thirsty in Pakistan, inclusive of the Islamists parties of Jamat Islami and the Tahreek-e Insaf Party of Imran Khan and the Pakistan Muslim League - N. The greatest virtue Gen. Musharraf possessed was, he stood against the terrorist and the extremist. Then he had put under house arrest a host of the politicised judiciary with tendencies of sympathy for the terrorists. The extremism pervades in their cadre; the Abbottabad court rules on October 30th 2009; Musharraf is a proclaimed offender. They compel take away any feeling of pride heart harbours for our judiciary.

They had only notions of knowledge with infirmness in faith and all misguided by their prejudices with precepts in Sharia creating unrest with their detached Fiqah to the one followed by the followers of the Twelve Imams who had no extremism and the model state was Iran, which not only produced pistachios, carpets and poetry but also did justice, vice crushed and virtue spread, and did faster research backed by logic and reasoning and bold decisions with results produced.

Philosopher Reverend Frank Julian Gelli's voice is frequently heard in defense of the Shia faith and he calls him 'an Anglican Shia'. He defends clergy rule in Iran, and says, 'he defends it, because it is a fellow clergy rule.' Frank Julian Gelli says: "The trend in the West is; they now rely on religion and thanks to the revolution in Iran of Imam Khomeini, there is a revival of religion in the West."

And it was clear no one wanted an irreligious state; most of all certainly not the Lincoln educated Great Leader founding the nation of Pakistan, but only just an equal opportunity nation. And the Watchful Religion of Efficacy - Islam said, 'Its bastion is state', and the state is a phenomenon not aloof of the practice of religion. And the Watchful Religion is the kicking force driving faith and practice in the heart of the living soul and it carries him to esteem. And it was in the practice of the Watchful Religion that when a soul of esteem, like the Head of the State departed, the state sent him away on his journey with dignity, with funeral prayer led by an Aalim. And though the soul had departed, yet it had done the pivotal last service to the state, it had fixed the direction of the state. The soul had married the state and the religion.

So, a central authority of piety and virtue - a symbol ruling the mind of the human beings as a whole and as individual and reminding of 'God's existence' was necessary in a state. And where interpretation into the very essence of the conveyances in the Aayet 4:1 was needed it was to be done with positivism not of *Attaqoo Rabbakum - Daro* (fear) from God, but of 'observe Taqwa - piety and fear from the bad result of negligence towards God.' And God was not someone to be feared from but one to be loved.

This trend of lack of positivism is seen in the Aalim Dr Israr Ahmad to criticise the *Khalifatullah* Imam Husain AS. – the vicegerent of God. On the 9th of Moharram year 2006, he downgrades the status of the

Imam that is higher than the *Nabiyan-e Salaf wa Salabat* status (the past great formidable Prophet's status) by his antagonistic talk: "The Imam was not a martyr but only a slain person". This is due to the offshoot of the misinterpretation of the Aayet 4:59 (Ati Allah, Ati Rasool Wa Ulil Amr) – obey Allah and the Messenger and those in authority among you. But by those in authority is meant God appointed and not Yazid like, which the Aalim Dr Israr Ahmad interprets and thereby fallaciously categorises God appointed Imam Husain AS., something a rebellion and Halak. And this is because he does not understand of God's justice that is one of the pillars of Islamic faith, because it is not in his Fiqah.

Imam Husain AS. was Masoom - infallible, God appointed Imam, who set the firmament of honour for the world's 5 billion of the God's creation, guiding them to stand by righteousness, also guiding an unknown number of jinns – the God's creation from the smokeless fire. But Dr Israr Ahmad spreads malice against the Imam of the Ummah that he is not Shaheed. Not only that in a Manazra – dialectic with Aayet Ullah Gharvi he says: *Shion Kay Aqeeda-ay Asmat Nein Islam Ko Bahut Nuqsan Pahunchaya* - the faith of the Shias of sinlessness did deliver to Islam lots of damage. In other words, he says that the Aimma-ay Athaar were not Masoom. And this faith injected in the Sunni mind is the bone of contention between the Shias and the Sunnis.

This has led the Sunni world to berate the Aimma with the appellation of Rahmatullah Alaih (RA), whereas the Shia's appellation is Alaihissalam (AS.). And truly there is no ambiguity about the Masoom status of the Aimma-ay Athaar. Aayet 33:33, says the Aehlebaait are free of fallacy – and in the Aehlebaait, the wives of the Prophet SAWW are not included. Poet Zamir Jaferi finds it an argument of the ignoramus that the Aimma are not innocent and says:

Arzoo Mein Chaukas Hum Justujoo Mein Kahil Hum
Aalimoan Ki Dunya Mein Behtareen Jahil Hum

In longings, ahead of cleverness we, in deliberations lethargic we
We the finest ignorant in the world of the learned

The problem with the majority of the Muslims – of faith Sunnat Wal Jamaat in accepting the Aimma-e Aehlebaait Masoom or infallible is in that event this Muslim will have to condemn Yazid and Muawiya or for that matter anyone standing to confront the Aimma-e Aehlebaait and their traditional loyalty to the ruler on the seat of the Caliphate as interpreted by him from the Quran keeps the Sunni faith bound in loyalty to Yazid and Muawiya. And in this the Shia and the Sunni can never align their thought, unless they become of one view - what God intends. This is tragedy arising out of politics and the affairs of the world.

This Aalim, Dr Israr Ahmad did not end his talk on the PTV just on that note; he said the word Shaheed is not in Quran. Dr Kalb-e Sadiq was also a guest of the TV anchor, he replied, 'yes, there is.' The word Shaheed is present in Aayet 41:53 and although he regularly gives lessons on Quran on the TV, he apparently did not know of it that the word existed in the Quran. And the criteria set by Aayet Ulla Aqeel al Gharvi for the status of Shaheed and Halak is; those with Hazrat Ali and with Aehlebaait are Shaheed and those opposing them are Halak.

In view of the foregoing beliefs of Dr Israr Ahmad, speaking for Yazid and challenging the martyrdom of Imam Husain AS., it is little wonder if he criticises Quaid-e Azam for his 11th of August 1947 speech before the first Constituent Assembly. Dr Israr says, 'I wish he had not made that speech'. The Quaid-e Azam was reminding the nation, whether you are Hindu, Muslim, Christian, Jew, you are free in Pakistan to go to your temples, church, synagogue; you are free. Your cast and creed were not the business of the state. Quaed-e Azam was leading 180 million people of the nation and in importance he was father of the nation and the rightest person to set the direction of the nation and not a Maslaki – belonging to a school of thought – opinionated, a controversial Aalim like Dr Israr Ahmad. And when his interference exceeds unchecked and circumvents law and the Shariat, this Maslaki Aalim speaks - refer to Jang Newspaper of August 20, 2009:

"Mujhay uun loagoan say Shadeed Aekhtelaf haai jo Shiyoun ko Alal Itlaq Ghaair Muslim Qarar detay haain."

I hold severe difference of opinion with those who freely declare Shias non-Muslims.

(He is saying that Shias are non-Muslims, only he favours not to beat the drum about it.)

He says call them Kafir but with reservation. Such Aalim have created disunity among the Muslims. Islam calls a man a Muslim if he claims he is a Muslim. It is a quote from the saying of Imam Jafar Sadiq AS. and he is the undisputed Imam of the Sunni as well as of the Shia and look at the demeaning of Dr Israr Ahmad. He likes to impose grim orthodoxy from the books of the last thousand years since Muawiya's rule that the Shia is not Muslim. Such Aalim are problem for the Muslims, they have their own religion not governed by the edicts and commands of Allah.

The method of prayer of the Kafirs was not approved by God, but the Kafir in the unapproved in worship of God did a lesser disapproval than the Munafiq who performed God's approved prayer but his heart carried hidden ills. The Munafiq was worse than the Kafir and worse than the pagan. The non-Muslims, Christians, Jews and the Hindus, were better than those who were hypocrites.

The lament is, the Majlis-e Aamla - the working body of the Wafaqul Madaris, who are teaching 2000,000 Muslim students, instructs the 125,000 Madrassas: 'Make Khatam-e Bokhari Shareef – reading from the beginning to the end, your daily routine'- reports Daily Ausaf of London, January 23, 2010. Whereas in this book were such Ahadiths as:

The Prophet SAWW sometimes in forgetfulness used to conduct two Rakats of Namaz as four Rakats and that the Prophet SAWW once forgot to take bath of purification after his sexual gratification – Ghusl-e Janabat and led the Namaz in the mosque. So, this the level of Eman taught by Sahi Bukhari. Then this book of status: 'Sahi Bukhari Baad Uz Kalaam-e Baari' – 'the truthful book Bukhari is next to the word of God, the Quran,' it has Hadith: The Surah Q, Aayet 50:30 says God will ask Jahannam – the hell, 'Are you filled' 'The fire of hell will say, 'Send more (my stomach is empty) and God will send more sinners and the hell will ask for more and God will send more sinners and then it will say its stomach is still empty and God will put His left leg in it and its stomach will be filled – the hell will say I am satisfied.'

This narration in the Sahi Bukhari may have been accommodated in support of the belief that God is entirely responsible for the actions of His creatures. After the sinners could not fill the hell, God puts His leg as He was responsible for the sinners to meet their end and for hell to be satisfied. But the conception of God given is that God has body, but He is that Who cannot be contained in any bodily form nor in imagination.

The need was, Majlis-e Aamla instructed the Madrassas to adhere to the 'Hadiths-e Saqlain (Hadiths of two weighty things.)' The Hadiths says:

"I am leaving behind two weighty things, Quran and my Itratee – my progenies – the Aehlebaait – the offspring of Fatima Zehra SUA and Hazrat Ali AS. As long as you will hold on to them, you will not be lost (destroyed)."

But even in this day with the availability of the facility of analysis, laptop and data, the Hadiths-e Saqlain is not lionised by the fashionable society. It is considered it is discriminatory, since it is ignoring the Shaba, true but this is command to emphasise the love for the Aehlebaait. There are no race and people except the Shia Muslims who act upon this Hadith. And critic Aalim like Dr Israr Ahmad and Dr Zakir Naek appear set to mislead the Ummah. Dr Naek calls himself Muballigh (propagator of religion). Now the word Muballigh has been used by God in Quran only once for the Prophet Hazrat Mohammad Mustafa SAWW when God asked him to do the *Tableegh* that was to convey the message to the Ummah at the Ghadeer-e Khum of the Lordship of Ali. The Prophet was asked to make the announcement of the Wilayet of Hazrat Ali AS. in that painful heat, surely this was a matter of extreme urgency. This was a matter of the administration of the universe and the administrator had to be introduced and identified. And so systematic and scientific is the religion of Islam.

And this announcement was the finale and the gist of the Message God had been waiting to be completed. And this was the final work of the Messenger ship, which the Prophet SAWW completed in emergency under the burning sun in front of the Ummah. A show was staged with the performance of the Nabi raising the arm of the Wali, so that the Ummah may see who. So, the word Tableegh in meaning has that far reaching message, which is freely abused by Dr Zakir. He through his Tableegh calls Yazid - imprecated, *Razi Allah Unho* – i.e.,

God agrees with him, which was impossible for God to show that gesture to him, since God was just.

Yazid's urge for power demanded the head of Imam Husain AS. He knew the status of Imam Husain AS. and yet his disparaging of the Imam and his arrogance was due to his and his ancestors' ignominiousness and he ruined him through his rebellion to God and slaughter of Imam. No single man has caused that hurt and loss to mankind as Yazid did by killing the whole house of Imam Husain AS. A thousand lessons in love and humanism, issued from them were stopped. Yazid's black deed has left a permanent wound, shame and remorse in the world. Yazid was a tyrannical assassin, he took wine, did gambling and openly said, 'No Angel came to the Prophet of God SAWW bringing *Wahi* – the revelations.' Whereas the angels came every day at the shrines of the Prophet SAWW.

Yazid sought allegiance from Imam Husain AS. to strengthen him. Imam Husain AS. was Imam of the Ummah. God's rule aside even worldly etiquette did not allow it that a subservient ask the master to bow his head before him. He did not want to know that the Imam carried virtue like of the past Prophets. And that a Imam did not submit his allegiance to the like of Yazid. And the best Yazid could do was incursion of tyranny and kill, which he did and killed the Imam, his pious and brave brother and beautiful sons and angel like companions all these exemplary humans, he killed. And deprived humanity of the finest virtue it had on the surface of earth, which was to eliminate imperfection from the humanity.

Yazid's army attacked and took captive all the holy family of the Imam and marched them from Karbala to Kufa, then Kufa to Damascus taking them through the market places of Damascus and the only surviving male of the house, Imam Zainul Abedeen AS. was chained and fettered and the pious ladies of the House of the Prophet made to appear without head cover. And how could Zakir Naek call this perpetrator of sin Razi Allah? By calling Yazid, Razi Allah Unho, Zakir Naek was at war with God. The divine justice will not stop not to reach Zakir Naek to hold him responsible to spread injustice and his fate in the hereafter will be tied with Yazid.

In the degrees of faith attainment, there was first *Adab* – the obedience generated in the self to the utmost, then there was *Eman*

– the deep conviction in faith, then *Yaqeen* – the unshakable belief, and there were degrees in Yaqeen, bringing one's extent to closeness to Islam. The companions of the Prophet SAWW reached up to 10 degrees in Yaqeen and some to the 9th degree and some to the 8th and this was an arduous achievement and Razi Allah Unho was used for such higher souls who had attained Yaqeen beyond the ordinary degrees and after one was certain they had attained the approval and consent of God through their perseverance and their affairs were clean, seen within them and without them: then they were called RA.

For example, Hazrat Salman Farsi was at the 10th degree of Eeman, Hazrat Abu Zar Ghaffari at the 9th degree of Eeman and Hazrat Miqdad at the 8th degree and they were RA. But Yazid was an outright condemned junk, and yet the religious seminaries tried to confuse the innocent Muslims to call him Razi Allah Unho to bring a crack in the Yaqeen - the faith of the Muslims and make Islam look deviant of firm principles and unbalanced and without justice. And those like of Zakir Naek who implanted such views in the citizens of the nations of the world, did great damage to the community of the world.

-: . :-

I

FIVE GENERALS AND
THE NAWAB OF RALAH

VII

There were five Generals who placed them as President of the country and there was Nawab of Ralah with his morale ascendancies who ruled over the sovereignty of the Generals and the Generals were of various talents in the pyramid of the military hierarchy of Pakistan, all still donning the uniform of the state of Pakistan and appearing in the guise of wise; wearing the cap of distinction on their heads and carrying invasive brain, capable of assuming lots of responsibility. Of these one was Major General Sahibzada Iskandar Ali Mirza, the most experienced politician also, an accomplished doctrinaire administrator, an ICS, a bureaucrat, first President of Pakistan who brought his demise by installing his trusted General Ayyub Khan as Martial Law Administrator. Ayyub Khan gobbled up his presidency, and soon exiled him to the penniless state of oblivion to live in London, accusing him of conspiracy.

This was tyranny, Iskandar Mirza was not an ambitious man, but of the aristocratic class, he called the Punjab politicians – peasant. Major General Sahibzada Iskandar Ali Mirza was a man of self-respect, and he could not be accused of corruption because he did not know that word and neither was the disease rampant in the country when he was at the helm of governance. And at least he deserved respectable living with remuneration and not left to be penniless and live like a poor of no means but Ayyub reduced him to that. The citizens of Pakistan pay tax to see dignified acts done on their behalf and they abhor ungentlemanly behaviour dished out to a gentleman. Ayub Khan installed himself as President in 1958 and spoke. "The Quaed was a sick man." And that: "People wanted blood to flow in the street, but I did not approve of it."

This terrifying and estranged speech the General made with language revolutionary and foreign to the ears in the Royal Albert Hall Auditorium in London in 1960. Royal Albert Hall was a building of repute where only concerts of orchestral music were held to ignite idealist flame to fire the subconscious to dynamism. It was a different force to Doa (the supplication) which took the soul to ascendency with the ripples of tranquillity. Albert Hall was where, the prayer was music and it was music that soothed the ears, but that was where the talk of blood on the streets was made by the terrifying General Ayyub Khan and that was the product of the mind of a General.

When Queen Victoria went to see the Royal Albert Hall Auditorium, it was almost nearing its completion in 1870, she saw it and spoke. "It looks like British Constitution." I went to this British Constitution to listen to the speech of General Ayyub Khan in 1960 when he came to address the British Pakistanis after his coup. And what I heard from the Autocrat President was a fearful explosion of revelation of military take over. Insidiousness, emerging from the mouth of the General. It shook the listeners' constitution. This was General Mohammad Ayyub Khan speaking, totally an estranged man. He surely had a note of finality in his voice and the atmosphere was of a hushed-up audience, who felt they had been caged by military power. There was a bitter taste in the mouth, after that speech. The worst was he had called Quaed-e Azam – 'he was a sick man'. Though after several years of bickering in the country, in his person, hope had emerged, and he had national admiration and soon scored worldwide acceptance for his macho - the he-man-ship bearings he carried.

In 1953 Ayyub Khan was Chief of the Army Staff, Commander-in-Chief of the Royal Pakistan Army. He was invited to take breakfast at the dining Hall with the Pre-cadets at the Joint Services Pre-cadets Training School at its 11th JSPCTS course in Quetta. I was there, House Prefect of the Tochi House. Ayyub Khan had agreed to take breakfast only of mango slices, and that he was served. Mangoes, peeled and sliced and no one dare put anything else in front of him. He had a smiling face with impressive moustache of an awesome authority that placed its front to the opposite, who felt subdued. He did not eat outside to show how much or how little he ate and left he slices.

67

Ayyub Khan's sons were in JSPCTS course, one was Gauhar Ayub, Prefect of the Bolan House and I was then Prefect of the Tochi House, and we would walk together to the Hall. Gauhar Ayub's elder brother Altaf Ayub was also in the same course, but he was more of a bully than a cadet and was ready to thump someone, behaving like an adjutant and everyone else was just a pre-cadet before him. But Gauhar Ayub was always a polished, deep man of exuberance, in cleverness I found him bred and brought up. He kept aloof and alone and authoritative, and he behaved so. He would choose me to converse and we got along well, but I have memory as if he toyed with me, and would throw remarks to make me look for escape. He later retired as Captain and entered in Parliament and was elected Speaker of the Parliament.

Field Marshal Ayyub Khan made a diversion from the peaceful course he was following. Just when Pakistan was progressing under him; it is painful to say he brought looming dark clouds engulfing the skies of the nation. He opened war front with India, and he only won some recognition when he resigned, saying, "I cannot preside over the destruction of my country". Only a few handful party workers of the People's Party had started breaking the window panes, but his nature was so sophisticated that he couldn't take it, and he said, he would rather go than play trickeries.

President Ayyub Khan was an old Aligarhian and he cared for the founder of Pakistan Mohammad Ali Jinnah. He used to come to Karachi from the newly shifted capitol in Islamabad, every two months. And this time he came to Karachi he said he wants to go to the grave of the Quaed-e Azam to pay respect to him. He was told he cannot go there to that hill, there are a cluster of huts there and no passage to go to the grave. Ayub was shocked and he said he must go, and a track was made in emergency, whereby he went and presented him to the leader - the creator of the nation.

And Ayyub Khan was shocked the way the grave looked isolated and did one stint of marvel, Ayyub Khan floated an international tender and appointed the best Turkish architects[11] to conceive, design

---

[11] It is said on the insistence of Fatimah Jinnah, Architect Yahya Merchant of Bombay built the tomb as copy of the structure in Bhendi Bazar, South Bambai, of Raudat

and erect a building long due as Mausoleum of the Quad-e Azam - a debt on the conscious of the nation. The Quaed-e Azam`s Grand Mausoleum emerged in 1968 on a high plinth from white slate of marble. He conceived of it, provided fund, and his will built the Mausoleum. And these visionary feelings were natural, there was not a single soul in the Land of Seasons and Songs who had not admiration for the Quaed-e Azam. A unique personality of principle, embalmed in honesty, and presenting a groomed look for the absorption of sophistication by the nation. Quad-e Azam gave the motto to the nation: Tanzim, Eeman, Yaqeen-e Mohkam - (Unity, Faith, Discipline). And what a beautiful summarised way of life he gave. But the people of Pakistan soon forgot this Imami slogan.

By far the most authoritative ruler if there was one in Pakistan it was Ayyub Khan. At the pinnacle of his power, he was admired as saviour. His friend was General Mohammad Musa Khan, he appointed him Commander in Chief when he took over Presidency, superseding him over two Generals and General Mohammad Musa shew his mantle. He blocked Indian General J.N. Chaudhari who had done surprise attack on Lahore. J.N. Chaudhari had said, 'by the evening of 6th September I will drink a peg of whisky in the Lahore Gymkhana' but he could not cross 100-yard-wide BRB canal at the outskirt of Lahore where General Mohammad Musa stood with his chest thrust at General J.N. Chaudhri. He could not go to drink whisky neither he got to take a sip of water in Lahore Gymkhana.

Field Marshal Mohammad Ayyub Khan now appointed General Mohammad Musa Khan Governor General of West Pakistan 1967 – 1969, a post that has no virtual existence anymore now and General Musa Khan was the biggest and the most authoritative governor in Pakistan, no one can dream of that anymore, ruling such a vast land. And Ayyub Khan's friendship with Governor Musa took him to Quetta where General Mohammad Musa Khan used to hold the *Lajam* – the reign of the Zuljenah in the Moharram procession and Field Marshal Mohammad Ayyub Khan held one reign, and General Mohammad Musa Khan leading, holding the other reign so was proceeding the

---

Tahera – the Mausolium of late Sayedna Tahir Saifuddin the spiritual leader of Bohri Muslim.

69

Moharram procession. These were the best times in the history of Pakistan. General Mohammad Musa Khan has written the book 'My Version' and his biography 'Jawan to General'.

A time came in the life of General Ayyub Khan when he was remembered with derogatory slogan of Ayyub Kutta Ha-ay. – Ayyub dog Ha-ay, but when his bier was lifted for his last journey from this world, people had wet eyes and showed their love they had for this aesthetic and literary General, educated at the Aligarh University. People were crying. The only honest opportunity to let the nation led to secure security he missed was denying power to Mohtarma Fatimah Jinnah and she had legitimacy for it. She was symbol of unity of Pakistan and she was shredded to hypothetical misnomers and virulency by him.

The third General's non-tactical show of the fling of disdain of 'that woman' for the lady who was considered 'Empress of India', caused the national disaster of the dismembering of the country. His Hazara Aagha-ee slash, boomeranged hovering on his head. He had said that before also but repeated that and that too at the bi-millennium of the empire longevity celebration of Cyrus the Great of 550 BC, staged by the Shah of Persia - Emperor Raza Shah Pahlavi at the ruins of the imperial capital Persepolis in October 1971. And the President of Pakistan Agha Yahya Khan was an important guest

That disdain dispatched to the Empress of India, Indra Gandhi from the dictatorial slights of the President of Pakistan General Agha Yahya Khan Qizalbash in the presence of the Russian President Leonid Brezhnev was in the same vein as of Harry Truman venting his feeling for General Charles de Gaulle; 'That nose will be chopped off' over his differences with the USA, Also the same as of the French President Jacques Chirac for the Iron Lady of England, Margaret Thatcher: "But what more does she want from me, this housewife my balls on a plate."

As answer to that deliberate disdain from Harry S. Truman to Charles de Gaulle, there was the controlled expression from Charles de Gaulle:

'The better I get to know men, the more I find myself loving dogs.'

70

And Charles De Gaulle was a man so upright that when his car in Paris was heading for office it was sprayed with bullets and despite his bodyguard pleading, 'Duck Sir please, Duck Sir please,' De Gaulle did not. He kept his head high. De Gaulle was made of that material, which was stronger than steel, he was a Godly man and he did not like to bow his head. And as of that Iron Lady of Great Britain, she may have forgiven Jacque Chirac of France, but it was not like so from the Empress of India, Indra Gandhi. She unleashed her anger on the 3rd of December 1971 and men and Aagha(s) of Pakistan fell flat on their face at the borders of the East Wing of the nation (now Bangladesh), and she beat the drum of triumph: "We have drowned the two-nation theory in the Bay of Bengal."

But Indira in her Aivan (the palace) knew her drowning of the two-nation theory was only a tall claim. It was only a rearrangement of the destined course that had emerged. The writer's guild said there were 3000 words of Arabic, Persian and Urdu languages that were common between East's and the West's languages and there was the binding love and the cohesion of religion and the binding force of the common history, and the net outcome of all that incursion of Indian army and the thrusting of bayonets was not entirely that what Indra Gandhi's claim was.

All that feverish disdain and the plucky challenge to Indira from the Hazara Aagha was due to his *Khassa* – the speciality of his bred of Hazara aristocracy and the Qizalbash princely couth, and Indra replied to him that was loud and clear, but sad he was never heard, to allow him to speak what happened and why his strength failed, and he was largely condemned. And his was the old-world-sophisticated of mannerism, old values and polished ways with which he is resting in peace under the sprouts of blessings. One thing is certain, never he could be equated with grabbers and confounders and he will be remembered for giving the nation the taste of first free election, with the implementation of the maxim; *Haque Ba Haquedar Raseed* – the right of ownership reached to the rightful. He gave birth to the most democratically elected government to rule.

General Agha Yahiya Khan's services were of such value that he brought literalists from Russia and China by dint of which literalists and translators were created of these foreign languages in Pakistan and they began translating literature from each other's archives and the Russian Friendship House is an extension of that event in Karachi holding regular *Sha-e-ree Nashisht* – gathering of the poets and literalists at the Russian Centre of Science and Culture.

But the episode of the Generals implanting them in the saddle of power in Pakistan with the force of infantry and bayonet behind them was reversion from growth to decline - a divestiture from democracy and an advance towards anarchism. And the cult of these hops started when the early bureaucrat Governor General Malik Ghulam Mohammad wanted all concentration of power in his hand, whose mind was conditioned by the imperial ways of the British viceroyalty power. Malik Ghulam Mohammad, despite his paralysis and a tongue that could not pronounce words, ruled as Governor General for four years 1951 -1955.

Malik Ghulam Mohammad as Governor General had founded an Establishment of Bureaucrats in the Army, it worked separate of the government with him to smooth out riddles for continuation of his rule, and on its strength, he could dismiss Prime Minister Khwaja Nazim Uddin and even declare the Lion of Bengal Molvi A. K. Fazalul Haque in 1954 a traitor and put him in jail for his liberal foreign policy towards India. Such were the neglects of justice and adaptations of brute politics.

Molvi A.K. Fazalul Haque was that distinguished Muslim Leaguer and Chief Minister of undivided Bengal who was pioneer of Pakistan and that freedom fighter who had presented the resolution of Pakistan in 1940 and who stood to protect Pakistan. But he was valued for his determinism and solution for a riddle free Pakistan. And no less involved in this polluted politics were the later star politicians humiliating East Wing. To start with, one who assumed the authority of the President was the secretary defence with his only ability of being administrator and of awe and style, Major General Iskander Mirza. He took over as President and then the Sandhurst trained General Ayyub Khan and then the Princely General Yahya Khan and the slide had begun to creating the Bangladesh Nation, and the talent and the binding force to cohesion and unity, Mohtarma Fatimah Jinnah was numbed, squandered and held back determinedly.

Mohtarma Fatimah Jinnah was given the title of Mather-e Millat – mother of the nation and Khatoon-e Pakistan – lady of Pakistan she was one elegant and of known services to have been co-companion of the father of the nation his sister to create Pakistan. And now in the election of 1965 she was called traitor and conspirator – agent of USA, when she stood for presidential election against Ayub Khan, whom she called dictator. She won from Dhaka and Karachi and virtually she won the election but because it was the Basic Democracy system, she was defeated by a narrow margin through the bought votes of the B.D. members, who were rewarded with jeeps and money. The tragedy was she was never allowed to write her biography and it was censured before it went to press. And the phenomenon had continued from the time of Liaqut Ali Khan. And the nation was deprived of this valuable book. And the possession of the state progressed and this time she was found dead at night 9 July 1967. Begum Shaista Ikram Ullah gave her Ghusl-e Maiyat – wash of the dead body. She found there were marks of torture on her neck.

And the corpse was placed in a vehicle with roofless back. Under escort of police and city deputy commissioner it was taken for burial to where the grave of her brother, the Father of the nation Mohammad Ali Jinnah was. Over a Lac people gathered and nearing to the grave they wanted to lift the Mayyat -the dead body on their shoulders from the vehicle to lay in the grave, but there was the cavalry charge on them to disperse them and when that failed the police baton charged and next the tear shells were fired. And people in anger resorted to stoning the police. Such was the respect and love for Mohtarma Fatimah Jinnah.

All this distancing of people was for what, save to save something sinister from the sight of the people. Mohtarma Fatimah Jinnah did not die a natural death in the massive palace of the Mohatta Palace. She was murdered. And Pakistan lost a dear soul who was mother and sister of the nation. She had stayed with her brother - the father of the nation and prolonged his life till he won Pakistan, when he was suffering from TB. She stood by him day and night, and the nation of Pakistan did not pay her back in love and honour and lost its opportunity to show graciousness. And these things God does not like.

She was nation's benefactor and was not treated in equivalence to it, and this is a knot of thanklessness in the destiny of Pakistan.

If Mohtarma Fatimah Jinnah had been allowed to serve as the elected President of Pakistan, East Pakistan would not have fallen. Pakistan would still be one nation and perhaps Kashmir would be another independent country or part of Pakistan. But good that a Bangladesh emerged for Pakistan to know of its behavioural standing. Mohtarma Fatimah Jinnah's popularity during election in East Pakistan was so great that train carrying her from Dacca to Chittagong was 22 hours late, people were continuously pulling the chain and asking her to speak on the way. And if Bangladesh would have been with Pakistan the loot staged in Pakistan in the times of Nawaz Sharif would not have dared peep its head out.

Summing up the activity of General Agha Yahya Khan was the saying of Hakeem Luqman: Surah Luqman, Aayet 31:12 says:

"And verily We bestowed wisdom upon Luqman (and had enjoined upon him) to be grateful to Allah and one that is grateful to Allah (it is for his own good) and one who took to be ungrateful (he did his own deprivation), because God after all is untouched (by these) and worthy of praise."

Hazrat Luqman Hakeem AS. was bestowed wisdom by God and he was identified as wise by Quran and many parables originate from him. There are some 3000 *Nasayeh* - the counsels of Hazrat Luqman AS., which are the gems of wise sayings, found outside Quran. Hazrat Luqman Hakeem AS's. ancestry five generations back through his father Aud, and grandfather Aus, went to the Prophet Hazrat Noah AS. The brother of Hazrat Luqman was Prophet Hazrat Aziz AS. and Hazrat Luqman was so wise and accomplished that God gave him the status of a *Nabi* - a Prophet. And by profession he was said to be a carpenter. No one lived in his times for less than four hundred years and Hazrat Luqman is said to have lived for 1000 years.

Hazrat Luqman was once in the service of a nobleman, working for him as a valet. He was a very good cook. The nobleman asked him to cook something good. Hazrat Luqman said, 'Very well Sire', and he cooked tongue and brought it to him. The noble man said, 'is that what you call very good?' Hazrat Luqman said, 'Sire, it is that good that with it you can win a kingdom.' The nobleman after some time said to Hazrat Luqman, 'all right, now cook something bad.' Hazrat Luqman said, 'Very well Sire' and he cooked tongue again and brought it to him. The nobleman said, 'what again tongue?' Hazrat Luqman said, 'Sire, it is that bad that through it you can lose one whole kingdom'. And the bitter tongue in Pakistan lost the whole country we called East Pakistan.

Of the Generals, the fourth of them imbued him with tendencies not exhibited by Generals. He unmasked his face of a scheming murderer and turned down world request of sparing life and justice not nabbed. This General was Ziaul Haque the baddy of Pakistan, ruining the good name of the judiciary by dragging them in to be part of the murder. There were as good Chief Justices as Rana Bhagwandas Prithiani 1942 – 2015 or Chief Justice, Alvin Robert Cornelius or Chief Justice Sir Abdul Rashid, all these names he dragged to mud by precipitating judicial murder. His relation Ameer-e Jamaat Mohammad Mian Tufail called him: 'He was Salahaddin Ayyub' and whether it was a fair comparison the accounts of his doings will tell.

Salahaddin Ayyub was distinguished for his knowledge in the Sunni Shafi faith; he was driven by its zeal. He removed the name of the Fatemeh Caliph from the *Khutbas* - the addresses of the Friday prayers in Egypt. Mian Tufail's Salahaddin – Ziaul Haque also pursued the course of the bit of Shia Muslim extermination. This bit of the atrocity against the Shias was in common and in unison with Salahaddin Ayyub and was comparable in its sprawl. But where Salah addin Ayyub will earn a name for him in history Ziaul Haque will not reach near to the pass mark to it. When Salah addin Ayyub died, he did not leave behind any gold coins, not even enough to buy a piece of land for his burial. But what disparity! When this 4th General died, the tactician in him left behind a gorgeous sum for his son, Ijazul Haque to boast of millions.

General Ziaul Haque chopped and chiselled the constitution to fit to the analogy drawn for him of Salahaddin Ayyub by Mian Tufail and he all along boosted him wearing the boots of the army with his full hold on power manoeuvring to stay put him in power. He postponed election date after date and went on planning to rule forever, but he smeared his name for spreading fear, treachery and dismay and spread bickering about and around and fell like a ball of fire from the sky with his aeroplane. And his death reminded one of the nature's silent retribution – (Makafat-e Amal) an example of justice in action for the life taken of the Life Filled which though ten times more precious than his, but the principle of retribution was made evident by God. The only thing that could be said about Z.A. Bhutto was that he considered his policies and work that exemplary and necessary that an element of Hitlaranium had born in him. That had caused him loss of many good friends and had led him to refuse compromise with Ziaul Haque and his Hitlaranium preferred laying down his life and going to grave than submitting his ego to a person like Ziaul Haque.

There was no comparison between the disrepute of the riotous General Ziaul Haque and the learned and ethical Life Filled Zulfiqar Ali Bhutto's idealism. Bhutto was an outstanding person of his time, loved as well as given bad press. He was a learned politician and his subtle and off the cough accurate high judgement voluntarily produced hard hitting phraseology and philosophic axioms of literalistic value and were creation of a consummate mind. He says:

"War is not a game and a game are not war."

This axiom he coined when the Pakistan hockey team returned from their world hockey championship competition. They had lost the championship. So, they threatened, treating the medal awarders, referees and the ladies garlanding them, by waving shoes in front of their nose on the victory podium they stood on. This appalling act was done by them since the referees had placed them in the second position. And their superiority claims to be at first position was the same as of Hitler, who said the Arian race were the superior most, but when the black John Wood Roft of America from African descent won the race in Germany in the Olympics, Hitler was all agitated and furious.

The maxim of war and game was also chastising the army, cutting in at their debacle of their humiliating defeat and surrender in the East Pakistan, losing one whole country and it was very fresh in the memory of everyone. It was an abomination not acceptable.

Z.A. Bhutto writes in his book, The Third World, using metaphors showing his literary ability. Describing of peace which required infusion of energy to overcome deficiencies, he writes:

"We have been associated in CENTO and RCD. To speak metaphorically, ours has been a chariot drawn by three horses and moving on two wheels, on the political- strategic and economic terrain of the last quarter of the twentieth century. Neither of the two wheels can move with speed. Each is ante-diluvian. This is apparent if we examine the intrinsic strength of these organisations."

And the 5th General Sayed Pervez Musharraf, stayed in Wazu-ablution ready to do good. He used the darkness to covering up the dangers and would advance in the enemy territory regardless of any backing of adequate army, free of fear and gallantry was his shield. Only when accusation of ball tampering was hurled at his cricket team, his balance of faculties turned to disadvantage of full eccentricity. At the verdict at Lords, he was frantic defending his accused lads. And went to blame the referee and the management for ignoring his team not awarding the first place. His intensity of judgement and vision were folded up here by the sentinel in him parrying any misnomer coming to the team.

And by nature, with his commando instinct guiding him, and he presiding as guardian and standing in the sentry box for the nation, he put his nose in each major and minor issue and launched the slogan of *Roshan Khyali* – enlightenment, by which he quietly meant that people use reason and sense. But the clergy claiming to speak for Islam took it as anti-Islam, since it nailed down their extremism. The slogan was meant to bring reform, but the media and the Maslaki Aalim, broke lose all assent to jeopardy and distorted its meaning and intention.

The General brought the cult of free discussion and checked extremism and forced hate to make compromise and brought hopes and jogtrots of certain glimmer but could not pacify critics and do to slash sluggishness and infuse efficiency and spiritedness and arouse abatement in imperfections and standardise standards. And the General not pushed them with military iron hand to work for God and not stopped them make umpteen numbers of sleazy, now rising and now falling political parties. But during the term of his office, he had time to write 'In the Line of Fire' - his memoirs or the *Sarguzasht* - what had passed. The book needs purging its weak premise and removing quirk. The General says:

"... Foreign universities, which have mostly produced political leaders disconnected from Pakistan's culture and history, leaders who have damaged the country, not only with their corruption but also with their alien political and economic philosophies."

This was an accusation on the foreign universities, they turning out qualified in the field as educated for Pakistan, sending them there for leadership. But the foreign universities were not the cause of the prevailing defects in the country's pool of leadership, the deficiency arrowed at the fundamentals of faith they followed. And the accusation is removed and detached from the tradition in Islam which asks to go to learn even to China. The Hadiths says:

'Go to learn to foreign lands even to as far as to China.'

But where the General's catastrophic failure emerged was the violent death of Mohtarma Benazir Bhutto. It was duty of the state to protect her. The assassins charged at her from all directions like bees that charged on the corpse of the discredited Molvi Mushtaq the chief justice of Lahore High Court for fallaciously sentencing to death Zulfequar Ali Bhutto. It was opportunity galore for the killers of Mohtarma Benazir Bhutto. She was exposed. And they had to kill her, a sharp shooter telescopically aided gun took life of this gem of the country - a laser guided bullet shot her.

The assassins were from the Taliban terrorists and they succeeded with their frontal attack. Then there was backing to them from the uniformed men. So many men in uniform are Taliban. One Brigadier level went to the hospital and dictated what report will be written about the death cause. The Taliban have infiltrated in the army, thanks to Ziaul Haque. In fact, they are everywhere, and now there is no easy solution save the refurbishing and the reform of the *Deen* of the people. Their way of life should be changed with *Adl* placed as the fundamental of faith in the style of their Shia counterparts in their country and the faith content refurbished, borrowing the principles from the Shia Fiqah. And they should be taught to go for quality rather than the quantity of payer. Hazrat Ali AS. has said:

One hour's deep thought is better than one year's rigorous prayer.

But the prayer the Taliban know of is to whip Islam in everyone's brain of their traditional approach and what they have understood and interpreted of it. The Taliban are all the time on the express road to murder those who do not follow them and they never are in the library to assimilate Ilmiat – the learning, they are in the murder field and churn out dead bodies. They are ruining peace and claim Jannat is their backyard. And the judiciary is all the time making fallacious judgement to favour them and the media and the commentators putting lame excuses for the judiciary and say that everyone makes mistakes. This immoral practice in the God's world in the religion of Islam must stop. Particularly so in the realm of judiciary; the judge is taken that perfect of faith person, who does not indulge in emotionalism and gives judgement strictly on the ethics of justice, not dictated by his affiliation to a particular faith.

The Taliban terrorists have systematised killing and issue a systematic list of people to be assassinated by them in order of their efficacy who are likely to hinder the Taliban agenda. They judge their worth and their reform potential and the good they might bring in the world. Professor Sibt-e Haider was put the 9th on the hit list but he was gunned down earlier than promised in the declared list on the 18th of March 2013 and his few more days, months, years of life was snatched away from him unannounced.

Benazir's murder was open for all to see. The secret hands washed away all the forensic evidence from the road. The fire brigade was ordered to wash off the road which they did within next two hours of the murder. The state machinery did not move and no effort was made to catch the murderers and nothing happened. It was a big unified conspiracy.

Benazir was precious lady of Pakistan, but like her Mohtarma Fatimah Jinnah was also murdered and Nusrat Bhutto was hit on the head to bleed. It is the duty of a citizen to raise voice on murder and brutality, to be honest and not hold back other's credits. Benazir Bhutto spent 11 years sifting the gravel and sand and the gems of education and learning in the USA and then in England and then did five years of prime minister ship in two stints in Pakistan. She says her four years were the happiest at the Radcliffe college Harvard in the USA where she did her undergraduate and shifted to Oxford for four years study of philosophy, politics and economics. So, she spent 11 years of her short life on education, five years as ruler of the country, assassinated on 27 December 2007, born 21 June 1953.

For 39 years as the suffering lady of Pakistan she bore the hardships. The Punjabi of Punjab so squarely hated that she ever knew she was not one of them. And the Sindhi of Sindh so squarely loved her because she was one of them. She wanted to be loved by all and she loved all, but still assassinated. After the venom was spread against Z.A. Bhutto in Punjab in the time of Ziaul Haque the mind of Punjab had changed and to ensure it stayed that way this humped shoulder general brought Nawaz Sharif to sit at the apex of the government. And though Benazir was born of distinctions, Nawaz Sharif called her on the floor of the Assembly *Peeli Taxi* – yellow taxi. Benazir must have been shocked to have ever been made overtures to his kind of utterance and she retorted: Nawaz Sharif a time will come when women of your house will be Zaleel - rebuked in 'Gali Koochay' - streets and corners.

Benazir Bhutto was right Nawaz Sharif and his family has seen those days. Benazir was granddaughter of Sir Shah Nawaz Bhutto, a politician, landowner, Khan Bahadur – born 8 March 1888 – died 19 November 1957, son of aristocrat family of Sindh. Sir Shahnawaz was prime minister of Junagadh at the time of independence. He passed on the paper of accession of Junagadh to Pakistan to Quad-e Azam Mohammad Ali Jinnah. In 1930 -31 he was delegate to Round Table Conference, London for the question of Sindh separation from the Bombay province; in all 16 Muslim delegates were invited from India. Sir Shah Nawaz did his role as one of the prime of the country.

Shaheed Benazir's life time was short she was dedicated to her father and to his zeal for the people. She wrote book Reconciliation – Islam Democracy and the West. She writes on page 217:

"Chief Justice Iftekhar was removed from office on charges of corruption. When the first hearing of the court case came up, the President of the Islamabad Bar Association ... made a protest. This was joined by other political parties and civil societies".

And see how Pakistan hugs sentimentalities and not realities and reasonings. The removal of the corrupt Chief Justice became the catalyst to trigger pent up fury against general Musharraf's regime as he was anti terrorists.

Air Marshal Asghar Khan writes in his book, 'We've Learnt Nothing from History': Ziaul Haque actively encouraged the group of Sunni delegation calling at him from Para Chinar Area in the North who expressed their fear that lots of people were converting to Shia faith. He advised the Sunni delegation to take care of it themselves, and not to expect help from the government to sort out such things. They had complained that the Shia Ulema in Chilas and Gilgit area were converting people to their way of Islam. He gave them the impression that his government will not interfere if they took strong-arm measures.

Ziaul Haque's advice led to wide spread religious riots in Kohistan and in the adjoining areas of Chilas and Gilgit. Many people mostly Shias were killed and their houses burnt. 'A foreign diplomat who happened to be travelling by road from Skardu to Islamabad a couple of days after it started, told me that he saw en route houses burning and that the route presented a spectacle of war and destruction.' Ziaul Haque's outrageous power was through terror he had instilled in people. His one wink to the Taliban had stacked the dead bodies of the Shia Muslims from Skardu to Karachi, and he was a removed unconventional dictator. Asghar Khan further writes:

"The unchecked sermons in the mosques and the Madrassas of Pakistan and the absence of a government policy of restraint, increased this malady manifold. Even normal prayers in mosques were not free of danger, and police guards to protect the faithful whilst in prayer became a common sight. In Karachi alone, one hundred doctors, mostly Shias, were murdered in one year, many of whom had left lucrative practice abroad and had returned to their native land in order to serve their people."

In making a fair evaluation of the fifth General, Pervez Musharraf, it was his therapeutic move, all credit to him, this General unsheathed the sword to demolish the Shurr – the evil. It was rising from the bellows of the Lal Masjid. They had risen there to reject the constitution, wrap up democracy and the rule of law in Pakistan, stampeding decency. There women in all black Abaya were lined up on the rooftops with sticks in hand, they called it 'true Islam.' And they vowed to spread their version of Islamic Sharia all over Pakistan. He demolished this notional Islam which was being incubated in the Lal Masjid incubator, which was spreading fast in the country. They were attacking video shops and giving dates by when they will see the Sharia is implemented. It was horrifying to see the beeline of hooded women in black gown with stick in their hands demonstrating their belligerence and projecting frightening sinisterism through which they wanted to mould Islam to the Mulla's fancies.

General Musharraf ought to have been thanked for this transformation bringing back rule of law to normalcy and for the service he rendered to Islam, but the coterie of the conservative lawyers and the Islamist political parties overtaken by their personal vendetta and their religious cult were bent on writing history otherwise. Hype was created against General Pervez Musharraf, airing the frenzy that he had committed tyranny of breaking up the Lal Masjid power, where were self-immolating bombers and weapons and this supposed to be tyranny was done only by the President personally. And seventeen cases were opened against him. But who cares, he had contained sinisterism.

And this was a time of social upheaval and change from divine willed Islamic precepts to forced will law as from the mouth of the uncouth. The media became unthinkably vicious, and no one cared that they were not speaking truth and the gory falsehood was repeated to date and as and when convenient, making false base that children were killed in the Lal Masjid. And no one talked of the fake woman's guise of Burqa in which the despicable clergy Abdul Aziz tried to sneak smuggle him out after abandoning his men. His truth was empty of content and he was a fake Maulana. He was going to escape but he was caught. He had been challenging from behind the walls of the Lal Masjid, where he had stored guns and weapons and self-immolating human bomber jackets. And even in April 2013 TV anchors like Mohammad Osama Ghazi and Shahzeb Khanzada poured out venom of hatred against General Pervez Musharraf, with total disregard to General Pervez Musharraf's cognitions for the country to serve his countrymen. Ace journalists like Hamid Mir writes in his column on 25 April 2013 in Jang Newspaper:

Agar Woh Bhag Gaya Toe Pata Chalay Ga Kih Khas Aadmi Kay Liyay Koee Qanoon Naheen: If he ran away, then it will be known that for a particular man there is no law.

In this expression the Urdu used is of hate and disdain and seduction. Hamid Mir used his verminous language. The despicable word 'Gaya' is used for a lowly positioned - an inferior being and Hamid Mir has shown distasteful writing. These lines are not at par with the status and credentials of a C-in-C and a President. But hate makes one blind, be he a journalist or Maulana Khadim Husain Rizvi spitting and spurting venom against army and the judiciary. And here, hate and imbalance of mind brings out that language for a *Mohsin* – the benefactor of the country and for respectable institutions which is not the characteristic of a Muslim.

And the superior courts have nicked their reputation and let lose their hate and vengeance campaign to harm Pervez Musharraf. There is apostasy in the air, the world of reason has to acquit them of their diatribe of implementing trimmed Islam. How thankless the national character is, it is coloured in the edifice of these miscreants, forcing the will of the reasoned to bow to untruth! These are the samples of the Talibanized era after the 2013 general election in which the Taliban are force thrusting the victory of the Islamist parties, like PMLN, PTI, JUI, Jmaat-e Islami. These parties were hoisted up by the Taliban to freely campaign their election campaign, but no secular parties, like PPP, NAP, MQM. They could not hold meetings, since bomb blasts were made in their meetings with several dead. The country wearing the cloak of democracy was practicing anarchy.

This was all because the *Adl* or justice was missing in the creed of the faith of the Taliban and of the Taliban like. But Adl had the top next place after Tauheed in the fundamentals of the creed of Muslims, the followers of the Asna Ashr Imams - the Shias. Adl was property of God to be owned and the Shias had it in their *Usool-e Deen* – the fundamentals of faith. And it did not suit the Taliban brand faith, who had to defend the ideology of their ruling forerunners.

And what cause was driving the centre-right and the right-wing political parties towards harsh politics of revenge against General Pervez Musharraf was the fear, weakness and their vulnerability to lose to him in one-to-one bashing. In May 11, 2013 election, which led them to grab power through the Taliban menace, who would not let the secularist parties hold open public meetings and only PMLN and PTI, they allowed to freely convene meetings and blare their propaganda, and others if held meetings, there was bomb blast, due to ineptness in understanding the religion they followed.

The *Adl* or justice is hub of the nature's free turning wheel for bringing peace and the knowing of God rule in the society to which the long-term ruling General Ziaul Haque who hopped on the driving seat of the State's carriage had no far-sightedness to see and entice the society to embrace justice without reservation. He manipulated them do injustice. The religious precept claimers of Islam, today are viciously defending the honour of the Prophet SAWW, to which the loved Prophet does not need their shield of fake support. His strength of divine character is deterrent to the barrage of the uncouth mind and invitation to the conscious mind to defend his sagacity and his Marfatul Nafs, the recognising of his innate characteristics. Yes, the Prophet SAWW wants his grave be pilgrimage to and Durood and Fateha offered which they decline, though they loudly roar of love for him SAWW. And the Prophet SAWW wants that for the pilgrim to keep him tied to his Habib Allah, in whose praise God the Gracious is not tired of praise.

But one thing is certain, the Providence did not equip the Generals with the intricacies of the jocular humour, and they could not overrule their inept tendency not to be dictatorial and falling in injustice. And they were not given insight to see into the spread plan of Nature and the Generals were not an entity charged with a *Qaed's* duty. Duty of Rahbar – a leader. They were locked to command and not necessitated to speak heart-warming, accent oriented, crisp, invigorating, eloquent, decorative, doctrinarian language with elocution in the vernacular of Urdu. And the Generals could master all the intricate tactics of warfare, but not the temperamental secrets of invigorating men and master the syntax and the grammatical structure of the beautiful language to give invigorating talks and arouse piquancy, intoxicating the nation with eloquence coated of justice.

The General who hanged the Life Filled in the quiet hours of the morning, fell to his ignominious death for crudeness in the middle of nowhere and kept burning and consumed by fire. But his performance aside; when looked at the performance of the larger number of the

Generals and men at arm; it was surprising to see 93000 men surrender and then brought home from captivity by the wizardly Life Filled – not a General, but the wizardly master of eloquence was being caged to be slung from the cross bar and they did not raise not even a finger in protest and see with their open eyes the thread of life of their mentor and *Mohsin* - the benefactor, cut crudely by a bean of a bent shoulder General. It was fair to say, it was ingratitude and debacle to mar the good name and the rectitude of the army generals. The army is an institute that must protect righteousness and it must decorate humanity with ethics and morality, and they have their vault of purity of character filled Shuhuda, laying down their lives for just cause but they did not open their book of laurels on this occasion of the demise of a kind soul of the nation and kept it shut.

And the armies of the nations were never a weak force of submission, but a strong head of applaud and veneration, for never to bow to aggression, and what a beautiful history it would have been if the 93000 men had shed their blood and stood their ground and fallen in their blood. What a splendour it would have been in their defeat turned victory. But truly all that was needed was to win the hearts of the people of the East Wing and if it had seen that day, it would have been true leadership of General Ameer Abdullah Khan Niazi.

None the less the army with the bulk of its Generals as they fashioned themselves, with their near right righteousness and their large degree of righteousness illuminating their path into active certainties, and they as much a match to the dexterous flights of the prestigious killers, were an indispensable species, pioneers of freedom and unity. They were needed with their ability in centralism to hunt down the killers throughout their set hidings in the wilderness of the country, to search them out and haul them up from out of their maze of the hide outs and let them encounter for once the social laws in vogue in the realm of justice, they were so unconcerned with.

But whereas the Nawab of Ralah of whose realm of statehood, we will introduce shortly was thinking of disbanding the army in consequence of his personal evaluation of its utility in God rule and greater moral ascendancy and for reason of a greater universal application for the world at large than the suffering of the loss of a certain number of talented citizens killed one after the other in the

Nawabdom as the listed targets by the terrorists of the Sipah-e Sahaba, and others misguided calling them ace of religion, the army was retained. The Nawab's thinking of the army not to retain carried its main reason that the army fought war not by the approved method of God - that was using 'sword' where human quality of courage and valour emerged, but instead they used devices and tried these devices outdo the devices of the combatting force and this brought carnage, and their use required taming inside in them secondary qualities of cunningness and cleverness that aroused curtailment of the qualities like of courage, bravery and consummation of spiritedness to relevancy to God justice and the device was contagion to bring cowardliness, the thing the Nawab abhorred.

And the General who had hanged the Life Filled had amply demonstrated that he excelled in these abasing virtues and was infested with these. And for that it was little surprise; when he was still planning the authorship of his ten years retention in the saddle of power, someone triggered a spark in the sky and it became a ball of fire and brought him down hurling on to the ground with his paraphernalia and all his plans went up in smoke. In this act, the Commission of Inquiry thought 'the mishap was an act of God', a retribution. But it was not so. God said in the Holy Book Quran, Aayet 9:70:

"...It was not God who wrongs them, but they wrong their own souls."

God least wanted any one to suffer any pain. The pleasure of God was to see only orderliness. But it was certain God did not like excess in words or in deeds done against any of His creation by any of His creation, even in as small act as weighing and measuring and not doing fair deal even as tiny as the bite of the morsel of an ant. It was retributed with punishment. The Wali of God Hazrat Ali Ibne Abi Talib AS. has summarized God's law and declared:

"It was going to be the cardinal principle of my rule that
any one taking any one's belonging, even equal to the portion
of the right as tiny as the morsel of an ant, it will be retrieved
from him and returned to the rightful owner."

-: . :-

I

POMP AND SHOW OF
SEVENTEEN-JUDGES-BENCH

VIII

A writer has his right to assemble facts and pick pragmatic choice words to narrate to make it public property but has no right to distort fact or let distortion slip in even unintentionally during narration. He is only entitled to highlight facts through appropriate words. But we see the words used by the authority of the majestic bench of the seventeen judges in Pakistan that was the shot tower to fire the ball of trumpeted morality, uses the salvo of the words of immoderation that hover back at the hooting conjunct conceptualizing with their entails. The order from the seventeen judges benches further injured the reputation of the judiciary already injured and in ruinous state from its previous disrepute of judicial murder of the country's ace Prime Minister, politician and outstanding individual Z.A. Bhutto. The judiciary can go on offering apologies and begging forgiveness and paying homage to the victimised soul, by visiting this Shaheed's grave but they cannot exenorate them of the guilt that is smearing them and they cannot bring back life.

The appointment of seventeen judges to give judgement on the NRO – National Reconciliation Ordinance that they gave on 16 December 2009, to say the least, was murky. The appointment of such a large bench was betraying the secret that they wanted their package of justice served as public entertainment and it endorsed as perfect word for the might of the sheer weight of a large bench whatever its merit in following the Islamic principles. Slippage verging on to lapses and deviation in the verdict of the judgement passed were betraying intention camouflaged under the sheer weight of the authority of the bench. The scheme in the formation of a large-number of benches of

17-member judges was, it will cushion out the guilt and the blame, which, however was bound to erupt through the judgement that they were determined to pass, despite that the conscious and the professional ethics were dictating otherwise.

Look at the Judgement, the seventeen judges cast on the NRO validity, they say:

"The code of Allah demands absolute equality of right between all people without any discrimination or favouritism between man and man and between man and woman on any count."

Then referring to Quran, the judgement vis `a vis the immunity-claim, by the President for his holding the office of the President, says:

"This verse of Quran clearly establishes equality of all men and women on the basis of common parentage and as such discounts all claims of superiority or discrimination for any person or group of persons. There is no rational or logical ground for such claims and therefore it is unreal and unnatural to demand discrimination between man and man or between man and woman on any account."

The learned judges of the 17 judges' bench in the National Reconciliation Ordinance (NRO) validity case hearing say, all men are equal, but the Holy Quran says in numerous places all men are not equal. The Aayet 2.253 starts with message:

"All these messengers whom I have sent, among them, some have been given superior status over some, in them some are such with whom God conversed and raised others stations in different ways..."

It is obvious, the Munafiq is not equal to Momin, the Jahil is not equal to Aalim. The devoid of good deed – the Fasiq-o Fajir is not equal to the Muttaqi, and the Ummah is not equal to the Anmbia. And such discreditable statement is unbecoming of a judgement. Further in Aayet 103, 1, 2, 3 God says:

By the declining day.
Man is in loss.
Except such who believe and do righteous deeds and between them do the exhorting for truth and the exhorting for patience.

What this Sura emphasizes is that the majority of men have placed them at a loss, except a minority that have faith and did good deed, prompted each other to take to righteousness, and observed patience and not did tyranny and violation and treaty of unjust manner etc.

The souls of all the judges must be in torment for running into assumptions and passing slighting remarks. This in the judgement is showing a prejudicial mind, a judge in the panel writing the judgement refers to immunity as one of the reasons for corruption. He says:

"The anti-corruption and penal laws have remained ineffective due to their inherent defect in adequately meeting the fast-multitudinous growth of corruption and bribery. Corruption in high places has remained unearthed leading to a popular belief that immunity is attached to them. To combat corruption the whole process and procedure will have to be made effective and institutionalised."

The assumption to say that immunity is giving rise to corruption in high places is professorship to say corruption is in one top high place, without quoting specific incident or the corrupt. This generalised statement is not expected from learned judges especially when they are forming a panel of 17 judges. And then their judgement says:

"Besides all human beings are servants (ibid) of Allah and therefore equal. They are created by Allah and all are his servants alone. As such they are all equal and enjoy equal rights in all areas of life. In His service and obedience, all humans are equal and stand on the same level without any discrimination, all as one race and one people before Him, no one claiming any special privileges and honours."

All the above paragraphs in repetition of one point is without elaboration of any specific case. The judgement of the seventeen men bench says all men are equal, but the Quran says all men are not equal. And such fallacies in judgement make the judgement of no consequence.

God has given enough intellect and insight to the thinking man, especially with the expertise behind his façade of years of conditioning into justice to investigate the pros and cons of the matter with dedication to fairness and in this fiasco of the formation of a bench of 17 judges, only one judge was enough to give judgement in totality and the umpteen number of judges were a futility to consider a one-point petition that its matter pertained to.

And what a beautiful thought behind NRO was stringed through three words of National Reconciliation Ordinance. The phrase coined was to bring in a national spirit of give and take to enter in activity to turn the wheel of progress faster, but it was jammed by the self-glorifying team of the 17 judges in the name of justice and accountability. These 17 judges behind the bench have done harm to the nation of Pakistan that for a long time its effect of their slashing the spirit of the philosophical insight into the matters of reconciliation will be felt. Only they should have endorsed it and put conditionalities to make it more profitable for the nation.

Internally their administrative approach is that the Chief Justice of the Supreme Court allows the Chief Justice of Punjab, Khwaja Mohammad Sharif to avail palm-greasing, worse than the NRO provision. This chief justice Khwaja Mohammad Sharif announces and acknowledges, 'I feel subdued by the favours of Shahbaz Sharif.' Such chief justice has no right to represent the judiciary of Pakistan, who's conscious is quashed under the load of favours. Hazrat Ali the Maula, declared by the Prophet SAWW was placed as fourth Caliph under the philosophising edict that: 'power of Imamat and the Nabuat must not be placed in one place –i.e., in the Hashemi House.' And these regimes of unholy practices are possible where above adaptations are possible. Hazrat Ali as Caliph of the Umma says:

'If a judge is sitting in the chair of justice and accepts a favour, he is Kafir - infidel, and if he accepts a bribe, he is Mushrik (worse than a Kafir).'

Then the judges are Qazi, not executive authority. The admonishing stick of the contempt of court raised to quell a justified questioning is contrary to the principle of moralistic dispensation. Science of correct ruling will quell every squabble. The moralist in the judge must be standing high unable to be weighed down by the slathers of money or by the threats against him to not give correct judgement - that is going to be adverse for on the trial and is going to be an example as a reforming dose. The judge as moralist must exercise his moral, the Khassa (chief property) of justice.

But where is moral gone to, the records are filled of judgements where the terrorist is set free from the court despite his admittance that he committed murder, he did bomb blast and killing. And the excuse given is that not sufficient proof against the accused was submitted to the court. There was no witness coming forth (case of Sipah Sahaba Haq Nawaz Malik). This is a pathetic scenario. The criminal must have been punished for his admitting the crime, the crime had occurred, there should have been clear verdict of guilty and consequential punishment given by the judge, despite paucity of witness.

The Qazi was cautioned by the Ameerul Momineen Hazrat Ali AS., to having treated him (the appellant) with courtesy higher than the defendant. So, the Hakim or the Commander who is executive can admonish the Qazi, but the Hakim cannot be admonished but only criticised. And the judiciary trying to play the role of the executive through their orders to cut or fix prices, open a case, or lodge cases, or send letters or make appointments bypassing seniority and issuing orders to dismiss a government servant who is not showing obedience to the judiciary is *Bidat* – innovation not allowed. It is exceeding jurisdiction of the judiciary which is not falling within the purview of the Islamic culture and within the domain of the judges. In Nahjul Balagha Hazrat Ali says (maxim 441): "Whoever views himself with respect, views his desires with disdain."

The judges are the most focussed centrally placed serving members of the government. In the society and in the chair of the judge they must force them to remain most perfect. They cannot be left to be wavering in judgement and if they do, they have to be corrected; the intellectual guidance to them must be provided from the highest source in Islam – like by the Aayetullah in Najaf or Qum. And they should know Fiqah; Hanafi, Hunbali and other as well as the root of the Fiqah(s) - Fiqah-e Jafaria as well as the legislation. And if a judge knows only one kind of law of jurisprudence; he is half judge and should cease to function as judge. The judge is that absolute power who is above party politics, above Maslaki edicts, personal likes and dislikes; he is only servant of justice, a servant of God.

Giving birth to a non-existent issue in the appeal submitted for hearing is out of moralistic jurisdiction beyond the judge's authority from moralistic point of view and it points to his bias if he does so, increasing his jurisdiction tending to be punitive. It encourages dissidents and is against the defendant, and the judge must remain neutral. He must not raise a wand or flash a bite to lure towards his conceived judgement. The judges were given to judge the validity of the NRO and they opened a case of suspected corruption against the President of the country. And in this case an element of arrogance of the *Qaziul Qazat* - the Chief Justice emerged, where he says: 'The seeker of the immunity i.e., the President should come to his court and he will grant, what he thought appropriate.'

Whereas the Islamic way will be, there is no immunity applicable to anyone, only the faithful will prevail, but the Fiqah of the majority group of the Muslims – the Sunnat wal Jamaat gives immunity to the general Sahaba from any criticism of them or alluding any fallacy with them and the definition of the Sahaba given is very liberal – anyone who has seen the countenance of the Prophet SAWW is a Sahabi and immunity to this unknown quantity of Sahaba is highly controversial. This aside, the tradition in Islam has been set by Hazrat Ali Karam Allah Wajahoo, when he appeared in the court of the Qazi as appellant. So, it was not without precedence that the Hakim appears before the Qazi. But the exception was, he was not summoned - and a president can appear in a Qazi's curt, but the Qazi must be clean of blemishes and be faultless. But the Qaziul Qazat Iftekhar Mohammad Chaudhari who wanted the President of Pakistan to appear before him was not without blame of corruption[12]. And from moral point of view his authority was slighted by his own act and the president must be cautious to go to his court. Then the court cannot set aside the law and be dictatorial ignoring the constitutional provision of amnesty given to the president by the astute law of the country and ask the president to

---

[12] Iftekhar Mohammad Chaudhari is alleged to be exceeding his authority as CJ, in using his position to provide advantage to his son Arsalan. The CJ's conduct is of politicising the judiciary. He takes loan from the House Building Finance Corporation and uses it inappropriately. His court releases all the terrorists and he became directly responsible for the murder of the Shia Muslims by them. Then the country's Parliament and Senate sided, not allowing reference against him filed by Senator Faisal Raza Abedi to be heard. And his restoration movement by the lawyers installing him back as CJ was thus an act and implication of disastrous nature. He also exonerated Nawaz Sharif in the case of plane carrying General Musharraf, and he disallowing it to land in Karachi, and his exoneration of Lal Masjid agnostic Maulana Abdul Aziz, was damaging to public interest and contrary to justice, since he was responsible in killing, bullying and rampage and carried weapons in the Lal Masjid.

go to the judge to seek it from him when it is already made valid by the law of the country. All such fluid orders betray confidence in the CJ and the justice system.

The matter is further complicated if the Chief Justice is fastidious and arrogant. The full court bench of the 17 judges has earned the name of Imperialist Bench - termed by Lawyer Naeem Bokhari, and the Chief Justice Iftikhar Mohammad Chaudhari has earned the name of Firaun – Pharaoh termed by Lawyer Ali Ahmad Kurd, and the panel has earned the name of 'biased judiciary' – termed by Human Rights Worker, Asma Jehangir. And with that entire paraphernalia of the court ostentation on display, the public has found the judiciary under Iftikhar Mohammad Chaudhari politicised, radicalised and biased, and scantily equipped with the functional virtue in the field of moral standing. And the personal performance of Iftikhar Mohammad Chaudhary at the Association of the Bar of the city of New York in November 2008 was rated as disappointing and embarrassing to the lawyer's community of Pakistan, though he was granted the honorary membership of the association.

Thus, in finding a specific matching word to describe the talents of the Chief Justice Iftikhar Mohammad Chaudhary, it was no pleasure in mentioning that President Musharraf when he was in the presidential chair of Pakistan called him a 'Third Class Man', that coming from a president, whose merit was, he was not accused of misuse of power, this remark makes the Chief Justice a cause of concern for the country. But politics is a multi-dimensional beast and if in the hand of men fighting for power, they will use it, believing they are right and if wrong will be forgiven for using it.

The panel of the seventeen judges was accused to have surpassed the appellant's prayer and have gone in clauses of constitution uncalled for, and included these in their order with their likes and dislikes, ordering the government to send a letter to the Swiss Court for the trial of President A.A. Zardari. The government was further instructed by them; they must carry out their orders, whereas the constitution of the country and the international immunity laws forbade sending such a letter. The insistence of the court was for accommodating their politically motivated justice. And the prime minister had to resign. This was due to arm twisting taken too far. A country caught in by such irresponsible marginal judiciary is bound to see instability.

That was a show of sneer the judges made in their effort to enslave law to interpret their longing wish. It was not like of the judiciary but like a heavy roller flattening with spikes all order of the state and spreading chaos. The judiciary must be guided by *Adl*, which carries the functional precipitous order creating balance and equilibrium in a system. The Adl or justice was in the fundamental of faith of the adherents of the Fiqah-e Jafaria and the judiciary must make a knot of it for its conduct in unimpaired justice. This Usool-e Deen – the fundamentals of faith were given to the Muslims by the God-appointed Imam, Imam Jafar Sadiq AS. whose appellation is Sadiq – true speaking and he should be the idol of the judiciary of Pakistan. But unfortunately, this Adl – generating the finer existence of virtues was not included in the fundamentals of the faith of the Fiqah Hanafia, which the Pakistan judiciary take into account to act under the Fiqah-e Jafaria.

The Usool-e Deen or the fundamentals of the faith given by the Fiqah-e Hanafia for twelve hundred years has ruled the Sunni school of thought. But it has produced dismal result. The paucity of Adl, if it will appear should be no surprise as the fundamentals of the faith did not carry this Wasf of Adl – the quality of God as prime feature in the fundamentals of faith Fiqah-e Hanafia.

And how not the views of the Sunni fellow men will change with the extreme views thrust by the later day Imams like of Ahmad Raza Khan Brailwi whose edict Ahkam-e Shariat (edicts of jurisprudence) p. 138 (14 Nizamia Kutub Ghar) says:

Shia Murtid Say Bhi Zyada Khabees Haai. Shion Ki Majlis Mein Jana, Siyah Kaprday Pahenna, Marsia Sunna, Nyaz Khana, Haram Haai Aur Oosmein Shirkat Moojib-e Lanat Haai.

'The Shia is more wicked than the apostate. To go in the meeting of the Shias, wear black dress, listen to Marsia, eating offering is Haram (unlawful) and partaking in it is cause for curse.'

In fact, Fiqah deviated from the divine dictum has let lose disruption and terrorism, it is filling in even the respectable institutions such as judiciary, army, political party units, mosques, Madrassah, and in the government offices. And a drastic turn away from the Usool-e Deen giving mis interpretive meaning to Adl – the justice of God is creating Fiqah incompatible with absolute reality and the life pattern is in clash with the reality. The Ummat has made the issue of the Khatm-e Nabuat such a matter of life and death, as if this is the last string holding the ship of their Eeman (the faith) and all acts of virtuousness are on hold and without it the mast will go down to the bottom and the keel of the ship will be up on the top. The point is the Khatm-e Nabuat is final and no claimant of Nabuat left any immediate effect, so why waste energy on it and why be upset.

The logical approach without committing sin should be to be large hearted and let the non-believers in the Khatm-e Nabuat finality, prove the non-validity of the Khatm-e Nabooat. The Muslims can allow the argument to be presented. And the must be allowed to let them live. They will spend their life and will have no evidence to present. Rather than excommunicating them, the rationale is wait and enjoy the failure of the claimant of prophethood. Let there be claims of prophethood, let them come with arguments and evidences, they will fail and see disappointment as has happened in history.

The Usool-e Deen and appropriating Fiqah is needed to address problems, and visions righted by following the principles of the Aehlebaait-e Athar of the House of the Prophet SAWW. In this errand, either the Usool-e Deen Jafaria may be followed wholly or essential Usool – the principles extracted and adopted by the brother Sunni Muslims, done by a panel formed of the Shia and the Sunni Ulema(s).

The members of the judiciary are mostly the followers of the Fiqah-e Hanafia, they are delimiting them by being satirical in the NRO judgement sited by them. It is only half constructive and basically sophism. This is due to the Adal element not functional with its majesty to harness the mind of the judge. In this situation an Usool-e Deen alluding that every happening is the act of God is allowing men of judiciary not applying mind with its hundred percent capacity towards carving out Adl. There is an example, they take fifty years to decide whether the house belonged to the owner or to the occupier. Through this time marked ineptitude caused by mind not sharpened by the Adl in the faith fundamental, a fearful incompetency arose of 50 years of delay in the judgement. This allowed the occupier to occupy and the owner to be deprived of his rights for fifty years and the inference was, it was the consent of God to be so. After fifty years the judgement came in favour of the owner that the house is his. This was a case of a house on street fifty-one in the Nursery Bazaar PECHS, Karachi.

The glorious Qazi courts of the past days in the days of Hazrat Ali had no contempt of court rulings to shield them but only their dignity and virtue assailed all contemptuous notions. The antecedents and the conduct of the judge kept contempt at bay from them for their exemplary behaviour. They commanded respect because of their spotless character, who will give judgment after one hearing from the plaintiff and the defender and the case will be decided. The judiciary today in Malir Session Court is giving date after date and delaying passing the verdict of judgment. The judiciary is allowing time after time to the appellant at the cost of the defender. The paraphernalia of the trails of the orderlies, court attendant, and the tool of the contempt of court, lawyer's support and false decorum to give them importance are the likes they are surrounded with, and these are delaying justice served.

-:. :-

I

THE JASHN-E BAHARAN

IX

Jashn-e Baharan was one wilful name given to the events of celebrations, designed and cut to fill the poetic days of celebration to present light moments of fleeting charm and entertainment. It was culmination of the celebration of gaiety and thanksgiving. The two words Jashn-e Baharan were the twin, mind pleasing words from the vocabulary store of the spoken languages in the land of the seasons and songs to pamper the spirit. The name attracted and invigorated all to participate in the proceedings of the celebrations. And this twin word in meaning and sound conveyed fully what the linguist wanted.

The Jashn-e Baharan was speaking of a long custom voluntarily created by the folks. They celebrated the coming of the spring, which pampered spirit and vitalised one to be cheery. The spring charmed the man with the songs of the singing birds floating in the air and man wore on smile and was thrilled. The season's yellow flowers enlivened the atmosphere with their fragrance, and the fresh breeze made man recite poetry and he burst with jovialities ensued from him. And the season was tonic for the repressed and downcast. The spring made the needy of smile and agility, rejuvenated, celebratory and filled with cheeriness.

It is said Nizamuddin Aulia did not smile for twenty days. The devotees were worried seeing the Wali has gone quiet and they were beating their heads. The devotees loved Nizamuddin Aulia for his austerity from undesirable, for his keeping fast and his spiritual intensity that what he said became true. Then one day in Basant some women passed from there, wearing yellow *Oardhni* – the stoles of yellow colour. Ameer Khusroo was his one devotee who dearly loved Nizamuddin Aulia, he took one of the stoles from the Basant dressed woman and covered his head with it and started to do a *Dhamal* – jumping rhythmically in the manner of the mendicant. This made Nizamuddin Aulia smile and there was great joy and celebration for it that he, Nizamuddin has spread smile. And this tradition they continued later each Basant since then. And the mirth of the Jashn-e Baharan flows on the waves of joy.

My eight-year-old granddaughter Batool Ali from Visconsent Maquin USA has worded the joy of spring in her poem for me. Many thanks to her and deep thanks to her parents. We present her poem here:

The Sweet Smell of Spring

Spring is my favourite season of all,
I love it more than winter and fall,
I see tulips and daffodils,
and I have picnics on bright green hills,

Spring is when baby animals are born,
and farmers grow crops of corn,
I see baby duckling and a fawn,
and sunrise is so beautiful at dawn

April showers bring wet rain
May brings flowers and watermelon and grain.
Bright yellow sun like honey dew,
and skies are a nice shade of bright blue,
Seedlings are planted in the ground,
and birds make lovely singing sounds,

Spring brings moments of heat,
and the air smells so sweet,
Spring is a wonderful treat!

Batool Ali

The Jashn-e Baharan was one name of a twin words collection, resplendent with its eventful days, rendering people feel cheery and satisfied and assured of plenty. It was celebrated once a year and the participants sensed the spiritedness of the environs, as soon as they brought the name 'Jashn-e Baharan' on their lips. The rising inflection uttered in the words gave the sound that carried the sense of pleasure. It unshackled the spirit to express egalitarianism and goodwill. The participants came to this pearl of the cities Lahore having a history as royal as the dynasties of them for celebrations from far and near for the abounding fun and joy and embracing its spirit there. They came to its precincts to enjoy the food varieties served by the festive stalls and restaurants in the food street and these were the substances and the evidences of the spirit of the Jashn-e Baharan.

The masterly simple chefs with their smiles and unassumed importance displayed a variety of food dishes in the hot vessels placed on plates in the food street. There was Hareesa - the crushed meat cooked with saffron and *Urad ki Dal* with *Tardka* of *Ghee* - deep spoon sizzling hot butter poured on the dish, with it every grain of the Dal soaked in ghee, and the *Seekh Kabab(*s*)* with choice varieties of bread - *Qulcha, Girda, Taftan, Roagahni, Sheermal* and *Nan, Puri, Paratha* whatever the fancy chose. Then there was *Helwa*, and Bhoona and Qorma and the chefs each of sweet tongue, bent on to please the distinguished customers. They served pleasant food and service of excellence. And did all to enhance the celebration of the Jashn-e Baharan.

Then there was the folk's game, the *Kabaddi* match – and the other was Dangal. The kabaddi player from one team came out from his half of the field, challenging the opposite team players. The players of the team tried to catch him, not let him return to his half of the field and the player on the attack tried to touch one of the opposite team players calling *Kabaddi Kabaddi* all the time without breaking his breath, and if he touched and returned to his half of the field, he was winner. He had knocked out one opponent player whom he had touched, and it meant one point for his team. and if he did not touch some player in that event, he was taken as out. And if he touched someone, then his return to his half was blocked by the opposite players, all of whom shifted and moved all the time to surround the opponent, taking positions to stop him returning. The game created lots of excitement and in this game each player from each team repeated the call of Kabaddi Kabaddi, challenging the opposite team members.

The *Dangal* was a wrestling competition in the *Akharda* - the pit of soft earth. The atmosphere was serious, each contesting party weighing each other and trying to outsmart each other. There were blue, green, pink *Pagrdi*(s) - the turbans and silken *Lachay*(s) – the robes that the wrestlers came wearing them, showing their status and value, and announcements of their names like *Sojha Pahelwan Chakia Wala, Pattha Jabir Pahelwan Baddari Wala were* made by the announcer, when they came towards the Akharda. And every wrestler's name was taken with his teacher wrestler's name. There was prestige at stake and the clan name standing for one-upmanship, associated with wrestling. They displayed their skill, ferocity and their extreme fitness, trying to overthrow the challenger in the pit. And this was a show that agitated the blood to run speedily in the body, with shock and tampering pleasure.

And the Jashn-e Baharan had it all. The horse trainers presented *Asal Nasl* horses - the thoroughbreds. And farmers showed their husbandry, presenting all furbished beautified pretty look cows and bulls, all pinned up, smartening themselves to show their value to the referee, who saw their legs were sturdy, skin was shining, and the milk bag full and loaded to be awarded top award. And all this was the paraphernalia and the decorative asset of the Jashn-e Baharan. The people had suddenly so much to enjoy from these celebrations. Smiles took over glumness on the faces and clouds of dismay disappeared and fun and frolicking ruled, and excesses and fuming angers never showed up and there were songs and pleasantness everywhere.

The spirit of the Jashn-e Baharan was one honeysuckle that was never to end its fragrance and its flourish. It was stroked with the melodies of the *Qauwali(s)* – the songs composed for eulogising the admired – the cream of humanity known. The spiritual baskets of nature God sent to the ordinary for their reform and polishing their presentation of themselves in the world. This was the cultural might of the Land of Seasons and Songs. Its singers intoxicated the audience with the lure and the appeal of their lyricism. The Qauwal(s) presented meaning infested, beautifully worded lyrics, lifting and enlightening the soul.

And elsewhere in parallel with Qauwali, in the hinterland of the Land of Seasons and Songs, there was *Kajri*. The Geet that was simple and rhythmic. The unique expressive and impromptu vocal poetry presented by the vision-overtaken, meritorious unschooled poets. They were spirited performers and entertainers. They were presenting everyday experiences of the common man in sentimental verses, coined, then and there and describing the conversation of gods, praising gods who praised God in responding to a rival Kajri reciter's challenge and he responding in Kajri Geet – the song directed at him.

These were the forces, lifting sadness and creating cause for differentiating between happiness and sadness. And prompting man to live longer and be thankful to God for life. They made environ alive, celebrative and the spirit touched by moving pleasantness in the system and no remorse. The singers with power indefinable with prideful lyricism and correct vocal expression in the dialectal delivery, mostly Poorbi, spoke and sang in the Land of Seasons and Songs, and presented the verses. This was creative art in poetry, not seen in any foreign land in its equivalence – the extempore performance of Kajri. The sample words of Kajri in the Bhao (in the weight) of Kajri in the Sawan Ka Mast Mahina (in the lustful lustrous month of spring) are:

> Gawan Mun Bhawan Na Bhaway
> Laya Nay Nawa Nay Mun Doe
> Aai Bha Wana Na Nan Doe
> Ee Na Nawa Nan Doe

The performers of the Qauwali imagined them standing before God, singing the composition of poetic verses, bringing in originality, uniqueness and the fervour of Wajd – the ecstasy. And the performers' personal subtleties were backed by their Khanwada – their family traditions dedicated to the art of singing. Their correct expressions in the linguistics, their enhancing poeticism and the charm of their magnificent personalities, kept the listeners spellbound - captivated by their presentation. And each and every moment of their company was enjoyment. Their performing grandiose with the might of the artistry and their captive attractiveness conveyed enough to attract even the sages, the angles would like to join if permitted by God. And they were revealing beauty, verse by verse, and lifting the soul to enter in the domains of pleasantness.

And then there was the wonder world of musk and honey, the lady's vocal art, the dew pure souls with charms abound, singing the spring songs of 'Malhar' – the mode song of rain, and they sang songs invigorating all, reminding them that the Season of the *Baharan* – the intoxicating spring was there in full swing. They tied their swings to the greener than green trees, and their long swing showed impassioned cheeriness. They sang songs of praise eulogizing the season and the Creator of all creation, to have created this season. And they told the ignorant to stop for a while and ponder on the dimensions of life.

بہار کو ممتاز خزاں کرتا ہے
اَللّٰہ فرق عُنصرکا عُنصر سے کرتا ہے
خزاں اپنا سبق بہار اپنا سہرا لے
خوشگوار دنیا خدائے تعلا نقش کرتا ہے

سیّد اطہار حسین

Bahar Ko Mumtaz Khezan Karta Haai
Allah Farq Unsar Ka Unsar Say Karta Haai
Khazan Apna Sabaq Bahar Apna Sehra Liyay
Khushgawar Dunya Khuda-ay Tala Naqsh Karta Haai

The autumn makes stand out spring
God makes difference of element with element
The autumn taking its lesson, spring taking its garland
God the High makes the pleasant world imprinted

-: . :-

1

THE POET AND THE NATURE

X

The poet's rationale was touched and his poeticism aroused by the literalist in him associated with his compositional fervency due to the spring, the cause, the poet becoming intoxicated by the allures of the spring season spreading its manifest all round him that evolved the finest couplets stroked by the zest of his capacity of Ishq – the frenzy for the world to hear and enter in ecstasy. Then as the side benefit his literariness added to the literature the verses of extreme delight and subtlety – the masterpieces carrying deep thought. And poeticism from him was that rare gem that holistic professionalism, rigour of deliriously said entail of love of feverish communication that would put back soul in the dead.

Describing of the invigorations of spring, poet Meer Taqi Meer in his style, dictum, genre and the subtle - original in the art of poetry, says in his couplet:

کچھ موج ہوا پیچاں اے میر نظر آئی
شاید کی بہار آئی زنجیر نظر آئی

Kuch Mauj Hawa Pechan Aay Meer Nazar Aa-ee
Shaayed Ki Bahar Aa-ee Zanjeer Nazar Aa-ee

O Meer, some twisting and turning is seen in the air.
Perhaps the spring is here; and I see the shackles.

Now poet Meer Taqi Meer has excelled in describing the charm and the effect of the spring season in this couplet. He says, zest has sprung up in the air and it is so, since the spring season has arrived, and now

103

because of its effect on me, I will become high spirited and infected by its charm and will lose my senses, and they will chain me and lock me up with shackles in my feet since I would have gone in uncontrollable zest.

Poet Meer Mohammad Taqi, nom de plume Meer, year of birth 1723, obituary year 1810 AD, came from Agra from an aristocratic family. He came to Delhi and became of Delhi. But when year after year, ravages by Ahmad Shah Abdali and others starting from 1747, and even continuing from prior to that and its continuity became unbearable, as these ravages brought ruin[13] to Delhi and all this bore effect on Meer Taqi Meer such that in 1783 he said farewell to Delhi and moved to Lucknow.

Lucknow was the bastion of poets, Meer Taqi Meer went to a Mushaera, a meeting where poets recited their verses in exuberance of their being. There, the people saw a new face and questioned each other about him as to who he was, as if the stranger was an intruder in the gathering. At that moment Meer Taqi Meer said on spot an off the cuff stream of verses of poetry which are literary treasure. These are remembered for the sentiments the verses conveyed. Meer Taqi Meer received tumultuous applaud and Nawab Asafud Daula immediately ordered a stipend of 300 Rupees a month for the poet. This made the life of Meer Taqi Meer pleasant in Lucknow.

We remind of Ghalib, in his time that came later received a mere Rs 60 a month from the British Raj, who so poorly treated him and then this little payment would be against his property taken over by the British. So, the British did not take care of the poets and it was because their intellectualism failed to penetrate the Urdu barrier.

The poet Meer Taqi had said a long ode at the entrance of the door of the Mushaera when he was looked at upon with misgivings that was carrying disdain in it and they questioned where he was from. Only three quatrains are quoted here, complete poem can be read in the *Kulliyat-e Meer* or in the research work of Professor Ralph Russell,

---

[13] The carnage of Delhi by Nadir Shah in 1739 was most devastating, which was in retaliation to the killing of his soldiers by unscrupulous noblemen in Delhi, despite indemnity given to his troops after he had defeated Mughal Emperor Mohammad Shah, subduing Delhi in the year 1738-1739.

British Baba-e Urdu, died 2008 at the age of ninety, whose death was a great loss to the Urdu language, and why such people die:

Dilli Mein Aaj Bheek Bhi Milti Naheen Oonhein
Thha Kal Talak Dimagh Jinhein Taj –o-Takht Ka
Kya Bood Bash Poochho Ho, Poorab Kay Sakino
Hum Ko Ghareeb Jan Kay Hans Hans Pukar Kay.

Dilli Jo Aek Shahr Thha Aalam Mein Intekhab
Raehtay Thhay Muntakhib He Jahan Rosegar Kay
Oosko Falak Nein Loot Kay Weeran Kar Diya
Hum Raehnay Walay Haain Oosi Oojrday Dayar Kay.

Pardhtay Phirein Gay Galyoan Mein In Rekhtoan Ko Meer
Muddat Rahein Gee Yaad Yeh Baatein Hamariyaan
Bul Bul Ka Shoar Suun Kay Na Mujh Say Raha Gaya
Maain Bay-Dimagh Baagh Say Bahar Chala Gaya.

In Dilli today they do not get even alms
Till yesterday who thought of nothing except of crown and throne
What do you ask of (my) whereabouts, O dwellers of the east?
Thinking me helpless and poor, so laughing loudly.

Dilli that was the city of choice of world
Where there only the select of profession lived
That was robbed and turned into ruins by the sky
I am dweller of that much uprooted world.

I will go around reciting in the lanes these narrations in Rekhta
O Meer
For long these talks of me will be remembered.
On hearing the chattering of Nightingale, I couldn't contain myself
Me of no brain, walked out of the garden.

Meer Taqi Meer earned great love and respect for his tender and short versed poetry which spilled pathos, little merriment and humour. The pathos sprang from him, because when he moved to Lucknow his son, daughter and wife died and also there was an ingrained effect on him of a failed love, but the poet had a big heart that came from the thankfulness to God. But generally, the culminating effect that the poet possessed was restlessness in his spirit because of events in his life. The early failed love which was inflationary to his tenderness was due to an indiscreet beloved not responding to his love in measures of his expectations, and it turned him into a tender-hearted poet. Meer Taqi Meer had such a unique style of saying poetry of short verses, in a meter with deep meaning that he was called *Khuda-e Sukhan* – god of poetry in Rekhta - the Hindui language, which he nurtured, marrying it with the idioms of the Persian language.

But besides Meer Taqi Meer establishing his place in the world of literature as an immortal poet, the immortal poetry of the great poet Asad Ullah Khan Ghalib is a hallmark of the *Adab* (etiquette) - the literature is ever thankful to. But poet Ghalib acknowledges the greatness of Meer Taqi Meer in the verses of his couplet:

Rekhta Kay Tumheen Ustad Naheen Ho Ghalib
Keahtay Haain Aglay Zamany Mein Koee Meer Bhi Thha
You are not the only Master of the mixed language (Urdu) Ghalib
It is said there was a Meer in the gone by days

When Poet Ghalib embarks on describing the merriments the spring brings, the spirit of the poet touches the all-time high literalism, and he acquaints the reader with the nature and the flavour of the spring season through his literariness and the similitude he creates takes the reader to the state of reality. Poet Ghalib has produced extremely mirthful literature in Urdu and the Farsi language which is the heritage of the Land of Seasons and Songs and the reader is charmed as well as wonderstruck by the poet's literary genius. In his one couplet he describes the birds, which are welcoming the spring season, or the spring's effect on the birds as the spring spreads its wing over them. The poet describes these and speaks:

Aamad Bahar Ki Haai Jo Bulbul Haai Naghma Sunj
Urti Si Ek Khabar Haai Zabani Tayuoor Ki

106

The arrival of the spring is on its way that the nightingale is
loading the air with songs
The rumour is spread in the air through the tongue of the
birds in their sprucing and singing.

Nature presented such lushness in spring and such were the allures of
this season that the shackles Meer Taqi Meer saw, all saw, only the
effects and the invigorations that worked on them was different. The
lush green scene in the nature, and the scent of the spring swayed
another genius - poet Rabindra Nath Tagore. With mirth, he describes
of it. And he did that miracle in poetry, lured by the spring and its
charm that it earned him world fame and the Nobel Prize. And
Rabindra Nath Tagore was great.

But before we proceed further, we begin with the praise of God,
versed by Sant Rabindra Nath Tagore. Here is the Hamd – the God-
praise. The words from Geetanjali, transferred in the Urdu poetry form
by the poet Sayed Zaheer Abbas. Dr Awan Chishti writing a prelude on
it says:

"In Geetanjali there is Vedanti and unitary existence thinking also
present." The reader will find its evidences in the following Musaddas
of Tagore:

Aai Khudawand-e Jahan Fatirul Aflak-e Azeem
Aashiyan Mein Bhi Haai Too Arsa-ay Aflak Mein Bhi
Too ki Haai Husn-e Sarapa Teri Ulfat Hi Faqat
Kaar Farma Haai Azal Say Khas-o Khashaq Mein Bhi
Rung Say Saut Say Khushboo Say Yahan Zahir Haai
Too He Auwal Meri Dunya Ka Too Hi Aakhir Haai

Phool Nazrana Yeh Mera Teray Qabil Toe Naheen
Per Too Chahay Toe Yeh Husn Mein Yakta Ho Ja-ay

Rabindra Nath Tagore
(Translated by Sayed Zaheer Abbas)

So great are these poets that if they existed before the times of Moses
and Jesus. AS s may be God would not send so many timed Sharia- law

codes. The words of poem of Rabindra Nath Tagore even after translation are a spiritual reality and the thought and humility of Rabindra Nath Tagore are wonder filled. Now I would not want tens of Mullas running the premises of the Masjid with haphazard sermons, but one Rabindra Nath Tagore singing out another Geetanjali.

Translation:

O God of the universe creator of the great skies
You are in the nest as well as in the span of the skies
You that art the whole beauty, Your love alone
Is in invigoration from beginning in weed and straw also
From colour, from sound, from smell, it is evident here
You are the first of my world, You are the last

The flower for presentation is not worthy of Your status
But if You wished so it may become in beauty unique

Rabindra Nath Tagore was born in 1861 in the province of Bengal. The poet died in the year 1941. He came from a Brahmin family and earned great fame and was known as *Sunt* - the Saint. In his life time, he established his name as writer, thinker and reformist. He was a poet, thinker, writer, composer, a playwright and Gyani – acquiring spiritual knowledge, all at the same time. Rabindra Nath Tagore has greatly enriched the Bengali literature by his writing. He wrote *Geetanjali* – the offering of the songs, in the Bengali Bhasha which was a great work, and it brought him fame. He next sat down to write its translation in the English language and when the Irish poet William Butler Yeats saw that, he was thrilled with it. He wrote a preface to it and Rabindra Nath Tagore won the Nobel Prize for his Geetanjali in 1913.

The great poet wrote to Indra Devi Chaudharani from London and spoke. "I don't know English and yet how I could write this English" and he said:

"It was *Chait* (Bahar, Sawan or spring) when I sat down to write. The mango trees had started showing *Boar* – the flowering on them, and there was sweetness in the air. And in this season each fibre of my body was pulsating with vigour, vibrating and singing. And I said, I must take advantage of it and write, and I wrote."

Rabindra Nath Tagore was referring to the limitations of his extents in the English language and yet the effect of the spring season did not allow him cordoned off and it carried him to the heights of fame. The season invigorated his faculties to write and express, and he simply let loose his capability to produce masterpiece. He started the translation of Geetanjali in the English language in spring in Bengal, of which he completed most part there. The remaining he completed in England and won immediate recognition as writer and the Nobel Prize laureate in literature.

The poet had written in his letter to Indra Devi; he did not know English language - he was that humble! Rabindra Nath Tagore has translated several of his poems with the same ease, comfort and simplicity in the English language as he wrote these in his Bhasha, the Bengali language. The sweetness of his writing is the hallmark of his greatness. Among his short stories in prose, he has written 'Kabuliwallah'. It is a narrative full of affection and oozes out love and is interpretive of a father's love for his distant small daughter. It describes the tenderness of human nature and it touches hearts.

Rabindra Nath Tagore for his laureate and fame was invited as royal guest of the Shah of Persia, Raza Shah Pahlavi in 1932 and then by the King of Iraq and he was given Royal welcome by these Kings, who had blood of nobility in them. There was another poet who was a contemporary of Rabindra Nath Tagore, poet Allama Sheikh Mohammad Iqbal who obtained a doctorate in Philosophy from Munich, and while Rabindra Nath Tagore won international fame, Allama Iqbal still could not take his fame beyond the borders of the Northern Punjab though he was literary - most figure of his time. But his cluster of poetry confined only to the defence and the glorifying of Islam and not addressing the humanity at large - not discussing the nature and life. The highlighting of the Islamic grandeur is no innovation, but repetition of the stereo type, but describing nature is. And in spite of his rating, he is accredited to be the thinker of the state of Pakistan, but he does not claim so and himself denies of it. Allama Iqbal himself writes in his letter of 4th March 1934 to E. Thompson as quoted by Poet Faiz Ahmad Faiz that we quote here:

"I have just received review of my book. You call me protagonist of the scheme called 'Pakistan'. Now Pakistan is not my scheme. The one that I suggested in my address is the creation of a Muslim province – i.e., a province having an overwhelming population of Muslims in the North West of India. This province will be according to my scheme, a part of the proposed Indian Federation."

Allama Iqbal despite all these honours accredited to him was not recognised at the level of Rabindra Nath Tagore in India and he seems to have resented it for being ignored at all fronts in comparison to Rabindra Nath Tagore and especially for not to have been considered, for the Nobel Prize.

This was apparent when he did not congratulate Rabindra Nath Tagore at his laureateship nor wrote a letter of thanks to Rabindra Nath Tagore when he called at his house in Lahore at Mayo Road. Allama Iqbal however had an excuse for the latter; he was not in Lahore at the time when Tagore called at his house. And he could not have welcomed him, he was away, out of the town.

Quaed-e Azam Mohammad Ali Jinnah paid tribute to Rabindra Nath Tagore at his demise in 1941 in these words: 'I am certainly grieved to hear the sad news of the death of one of the greatest of India's poets, philosophers and Social Workers...'

Rabindra Nath Tagore obtained his knowledge from the *Upanishads,* the teachings which based precepts on negations to materialism. The poet worked hard in his life. He sat in communion with God each day from three in the morning and remained in meditation for two hours. He was known as Guru Dev, and his father Dev Vindra Nath Tagore was known as Mahan Rishi. He would often be day-long in the state of meditation - that is in the *Bhagti* or *Maraqbah* – losing his self to uplift his soul.

Dev Vindra Nath Tagore was comfortably placed in life. He was even called wealthy. He had built an *Ashram* in the south of Bengal as a refuge: a delightful place of scenic beauty for consolidating prayer through meditation and there was an orchard of trees - a grove to enhance tranquillity, it was a perfect setting for peace and quiet. Rabindra Nath Tagore's flight of thought took off from there through his Maraqbah or meditation. And what this setting produced was serenity. The Indian Congressman, Maulana Abul Kalam Azad describing the charm of Rabindra Nath Tagore's personality writes about him, expressing his thoughts in the Urdu language, and the picture the Maulana draws of the poet was of a prince made of gold heart, of which the translation is as under:

"In 1936 December, I saw him for the first time. It was a frail body he carried, but full of sparkling of the earlier youth. His long bright hair was shining like the lines of silver streaks falling on his shoulders. He of a graceful face with cheeks filled with colour and of a texture of the pomegranate and was bringing out magnanimity that with composure and peace engulfing him. He had put on a gold colour *Chogha* – a cloak going down to his ankle, and a pair of brown colour slippers were his *Zeenat-e-pa* - the decorative having the honour of being associated with his feet."

I as writer feel so proud to have translated this narrative so truly in the words of Maulana that his soul, blessed be it, must be pleased and my adorned poet's soul equally pleased. Maulana Abul Kalam Azad was a N*erm Dil* – soft hearted Muslim. He was against Muslims making a separate state of Pakistan. He was true leader and the visionary. The Muslims had to excel them and not get engulfed. But Quad-e Azam, Mohammad Ali Jinnah when his keeping united with India effort was frustrated, he made Pakistan and in his last dying days, this great leader saw circuitousness at play. He was nearly abandoned by the ambitious political leaders, establishing their constituency but the masses were the true litmus of love for the Quaed-e Azam in Pakistan. And they continue to pay galore homages to their Quaed-e Azam.

Rabindra Nath Tagore so loved books and reading that he said:

"The worm wonders why the man not eats the book up."

Tagore was so much in union with reason and demonstrating it preserving virtue, approved by the Wali of God Hazrat Ali AS. that heavenly reward for him beyond doubt is seeking him and as due deposits it in mirth in his lap. The Wali of God Hazrat Ali AS. says:

"He who is engrossed in literary or philosophical problem, enjoys a constant pleasure."

And how not it will be true, it is saying of Ali the Wali 'who is gate of the city of knowledge'. It is saying of the Prophet of God, Hazrat Mohammad Mustafa SAWW. About his love for God, Rabindra Nath Tagore's says:

"I am a singer whose employment is with God, singing for God in the presence of God." And what newness in thought Rabindra Nath Tagore produces.

Hazrat Ali AS. about his gnosis of God says:

"I am at that pinnacle of faith, whereof it cannot increase further, even if all the veils between God and man are cast aside."

And my God! what simplistic introduction of the achievement of the height of the man's zenith - the door of the city of knowledge identifies to the man.

Josh Malihabadi

Josh Malihabadi 1898 – 1982, was accepted to be the most vigorous poet and an impactful literalist of the modern day. He invented the word *Tagoriat*. He meant by it, philosophy, friendliness and the humanity of Rabindra Nath Tagore. Rabindra Nath Tagore was pride of India - the Nobel laureate of literature for his Geetanjali and Josh Malihabadi for a short spell was under the tutorial spell of this genius and god of literariness.

Josh Malihabadi transferred Tagore's thoughts and work from the Bengali Language into the Urdu Language. When Sirojini Na-edo recited Josh Malihabadi's poem *'Tuloo-e Sehar'* – the breaking of the dawn to Tagore in Lucknow, Tagore called Josh, *Sehar Gah* – the dictum of dawn. Rabindra Nath Tagore invited young Josh to his residence Shanti Nakteen for him to further enrich his experience. Josh went there and stayed with the great poet for six months and it was enough for the young poet to learn of the Tagoriat.

Josh Malihabadi was titled *Sha-e-ray Inqelab* – poet of revolution. His following couplet illustrates his mode of poetry with revolutionary expression against the British Raj:

Parcham-e Tameer-e Nau Jab Charkh Pe Lahraega
Asr-e Pareena Ka Aewan-o Kalas Tharraega

When the flag[14] of the new foundation will flutter on the sky
The decades old palace and dome will shake with fear

Josh Malihabadi started a magazine called 'Kaleem' and wrote for the freedom of India. He was awarded Padma Bhushan medal in 1954 by India. However, despite that he migrated to Pakistan in 1958 to serve Urdu. Pandit Jawahar Lal Nehru insisted on him that he stay in India, but he came to Pakistan. In Pakistan he was not received as well as he expected for the views and the belief, he held of being Punjatani, and he ever regretted coming to Pakistan, of which he says in the following verses of quatrain:

Kis Ko Aati Haai Maseeha-ee Kisay Aawaz Doon
Boal Aai Khoon-khwar Tanha-ee, Kisay Aawaz Doon
Chup Rahoon Toe Her Nafs Dasta Haai Naagin Ki Tareh
Aah Bharnay Mein Haai Ruswa-ee Kisay Aawaz Doon

Who knows the Jesus like healing who I call?
O devastating loneliness, speak who I call?
If I remain quiet, every breath sting like the bites of snake
In sighing pronouncedly, there is disrepute who I call.

There is so much disappointment and remorse evident from this quatrain that it speaks of the discrimination already in 1958 just after eleven years of the existence of Pakistan against the Shias. That is evident from the monologue of the verses of Josh Sahib who was very unhappy in Pakistan and felt terribly neglected in the new hostile world antagonist to the Aehlebaaiti faith Muslim and he had allowed him to enter in to serve the Urdu there.

The poet's literalism indulges in describing man and the woman entity. He describes how nature arranges the beauties of the genders:

Mard Ko Tohfay Mein Dee Shamsheer-o- Tadbeeray Hayat
Aur Aurat Ko Chiragh-o Bar Bat-o- Qand-o-Nabat

---

[14] Pakistan and Bharat were not in existence but the will and common desire of independentce with their flags was there and the poet calls it flag of new construction that suits to India and Pakistan both.

Mard Kay Aaza Ko Bakhsha Sang-o-Ahan Ka Jalal
Aur Aurat Ko Subah Ka Lauh-o Shabnam Ka Jamal

Gave man in gift sword and deliberative power for finding way
   of life
And to woman lamp and violin and sweetness and greenness

To Man bestowed limbs of the majesty of rock and iron
And to woman glittering of morning shine and grace of the dew

Poet Josh Malihabadi sees life's compatibility with nature in the physique of the mountain girl. In the following couplets he describes life with similes and metaphor, drawing the words by observing the nature.

Oh, Banat-e Koh Ki Kard-yal Jawani Al- Aman
Puttha-roan Ka Doodh Pi Pi Kar Hoo-ee Haain Jo Jawan

God's refuge! Oh, the intensity of the youthfulness of those
   lasses of the mountains
Those that have attained their youth drinking the milk of the
   rocks

The poet says another couplet drawing attention what the nature holds in its folds in beauties:

Aa Rahi Haai Baagh Mein Malin Woh Ithdlati Hoo-ee
Muskuranay Mein Laboan Say Phool Barsati Hoo-ee

There comes the woman gardener walking coquettishly in
   the garden
In smile, shedding flowers from her lips on her way

A poet has no inhibition in not lavishing praises for the scenic beauty of nature basically for his profession of filling expanded ideas in small number of words and is using his literariness and intellectualism to excel in thought generation and convey to his reader and listener, what

114

embodiment of brilliances of etymological string he has created through his poetic articulation.

The thinker in Sunt Rabindra Nath Tagore says in his monthly magazine Sadhna - a periodical on ethics: "Except for a mere bit, man is under obedience to the writing of God and the written law of Nature, but by his self, he is completely at liberty."

This philosophic exemplary outpour leads into the reality of life and it is extreme in Irfan – the gnosis said by the poet.

This elucidation by Rabindra Nath Tagore in his magazine was consistent with what Imam Jafar Sadiq AS. said in answer to a question about Jabr-o-Aekhtiar - how bound and how independent man was. The elucidation by the Imam that how far the determined-fixed ruled the man's freedom was in practical demonstration given by him through most basic and elementary explanation for understanding the gist and the meaning of the subject without misgivings.

The Imam asked the man who raised the question to lift his one foot and then he asked him to lift the other foot simultaneously. The man could not lift his both feet simultaneously and the answer was; the man was only that much free; he could do some things and could not do some things.

Poet Sheikh Imam Bukhsh Nasekh said of this with such elucidation:

Chala Adum Say Maain Jubrun Toe Lipti Taqdeer
Bala Mein Pardnay Ko Kuchh Aekhtiyar Leta Chala

When started from eternity under compulsion, the destiny
    wrapped itself round me
To land myself in trouble I took some independency with me.

It is possible to have a very great discussion on this couplet that this book will not allow, for it is beyond its purview, decree and scope.

Rabindra Nath Tagore says: "One who runs from wife and son and the responsibilities of life, was running away from God."

Now I have no inhibition in saying Rabindra Nath Tagore is the true interpreter of the Hindu religion. The philosophy he is presenting is no different than what the Islamic teaching is. And we stop here.

This remark was obliquely directed at Prince Gautama Siddhartha and Prince Mahavir, they are ethical law-givers to millions of souls on earth. Rabindra Nath Tagore is deriding their decision to abandon their family, notwithstanding for the cause of the search of truth. The abandonment of the family to find the solution to misery and pain which has been for centuries inflicting man, was no excuse to shun the first duty, though for the search of truth and God. The misery haunting men, making a nest in their homes was the doing of the man himself. The duty of the incumbent was to the nearest concerned and first was devotion and attention to the family. For Rabindra Nath Tagore running away from one's first responsibility to shoulder the neighbour's responsibility and carry his burden was no recipe to eliminate misery in life. The solution was to craft, blend and produce the needed ointment for the either necessity in parallel.

Also, Rabindra Nath Tagore publicly upbraided Mohandas Karam Chand Gandhi, when he eluded the 1934 earth quake in Bihar to the retribution directed by God for well to do and wealthy not looking after the poor and lowly.

But this was an all-time conviction of man that collective punishment was awarded to a people for the failing of the leading men of the society and those at the helm of the ship. So, the allegation by Mahatma Gandhi was not farfetched and Rabindra Nath Tagore's upbraiding of Mahatma Gandhi was not quite tallying with God revelation. Society with no spirit of charity from the affluent will be cause of collective punishment from God. The allegation by the Mahatma was the regulatory law of Nature, the all-time belief of man was that a collective punishment was given by God for the failings of the top men and the affluent of the society not making charity and sharing the discomfort of the deprived.

The silent voice of the Mahatma would say: 'No human action is without having a consequential effect on the near neighbours and the far neighbours.' And the Mahatma's proclamation was an extrapolation of the Aayet 16:112 of the Holy Quran and his reprimand was based on the Quranic precept in the distribution of wealth, where man's disobedience and thanklessness to God were not condoned. Providence had entrusted Mahatma Gandhi with certain responsibilities as leader of people and at each stage of his life he has discharged that duty with a saintly touch. The world is thankful to him for reviving the concept of *Ahinsa*. And as a gesture of thanks to him, his birthday on 2nd of October is commemorated as International Ahinsa Day - the nonviolence day. For his achievements he was given the title of Mahatma. And it is said the first person who brought this word on his lips for Mohan Das Karam Chand Gandhi to decorate his name with, was Rabindra Nath Tagore.

Mohan Das Karamchand Gandhi is a name taken with love and reverence for the lesson of *Ahinsa*[15] - the nonviolence he gave and showed that it was a force to achieve success. The extremist Taliban, the Salafi and the Wahabi terrorists are today all over Pakistan. They are doing immense harm to the fibre of the nation, by killing the Shias. If they do not act as Muslim and act as mercenary to kill Shia on the instigation of Wahabi countries they must turn to Mahatma Gandhi to follow his nonviolence of Ahinsa, where an Ahinsa practicing Hindu is nearer to God than a murderer of peaceful people.

Out of this insight into the brilliancy of Mahatma Gandhi and Rabindra Nath Tagore, if there was any inference to be drawn, it was that chastity was not the exclusivity of any stock of people, it was distributed all over the world in proportion to their sum of the origin. Chastity was not of any colour and property of any religion it preserved itself for any people to inherit it, it was every body's property and asset who advanced towards it. Mohan Das Karam Chand Gandhi practiced attaining chastity. He kept more fasts than he ate and his teaching was never to speak a lie and he even vexed some people for his teaching to forgive the tormentor. And he was mastering these qualities, he did not go in Ruku and Sijdah, but was declared *Mahatma* as well as *Bapu* – the great soul and father of nation.

The golden principles of any religion were formed of three desirable things: Chastity, Love and Justice and Mahatma Gandhi personified these virtues. He was assassinated for insisting on justice when he insisted; 'the share of Pakistan be delivered to Pakistan.'

---

[15] Ahinsa existed as a metaphysical force between 6th century BCE to the 1st century CE, Upnishads revealed over this period as prose and in verses, as Vedas had bearings on it, but its truth was revived by Mahatama Gandhi and shown by him, how to use it as a force.

The excellences of Mahatma Gandhi's mind were seen in the traces of his speeches even as far back as February 4, 1916 when he went to the podium and gave a piece of advice to his countrymen. This was the occasion of the opening ceremony of the Banaras Hindu University, where he says:

"It is not enough that our ears are feasted that our eyes are feasted, but it is necessary that our hearts have got to be touched and our hands and feet have got to be moved... If we are to retain hold upon the simplicity of Indian character, our hands and feet should move in unison with our hearts."

Mahatma Gandhi's contemporary and his equal in fame and stature in greatness was the other father of nation, Mohammad Ali Jinnah with his honorifics of; *Baba-e Qaum,* Quaed-e Azam. It was a pleasant coincidence that either of them took their origin from Gujrat. The trait of Jinnah and Gandhi was the same and their professional qualifications were the same and either were remembered in history as father of nation. The only difference between Gandhi and Jinnah was, Gandhi was a Brahman of the Bhagti tradition and Jinnah was a Khoja Shia Asna Ashari. And Gandhi was freelancer, he extracted wisdom from where he got and had respect for all. Jinnah was a believer in the infallibility of the Twelve Imam(s) of the Aehlebaait, but either of them were sons of soil and either controlled the destiny of millions of humans.

Quaed-e Azam was guided by the theology of the Shia edict, prominent in it was *Adl* – the justice and the problem in it for all the Muslims to follow was; whether fatalism - Jabr or Qaza - the fate controls everything, or is it free will - the Aekhtiyar or Marzi or Khood Mukhtari that prevails and led men? Al Quran says, Sura Raad, Ayet 13:11: "Verily, Allah will not change the condition of a people as long as they do not change their state themselves." This emphasised on Aekhtiyar and made Jinnah take the course he did and carved a country for the beguiled people of the Muslim of India. He created a secure country for the Muslims, because he believed in free will and he was of the class of Asna Asheri; here was no limit to the applicability of free will until you found thing unreachable falling in its place of unreachability due to you.

Quaed-e Azam did not live long for further spectaculars to occur in his life, to present to his nation he had formed. And there was deviation and the country became a cradle of not thinking and not feeling and pseudointellectuals. He would have made it a bastion of God fearing, religious and spirited Muslim State, but unfortunately contrary to his vision, the country became home of extremism. And this was cause of hate of the righteous Shias and element of despotism.

And in this the influence and the meddling of the external power centres claiming to be champions of Islam were the chief exploitative forces for deviating the country from the path of truism and the chief of them was Saudi Arabia. Saudi Arabia and the Gulf Wahabi States had money and they controlled all facets of extremism in Pakistan by pumping in large sums of money to build their factional Islam to strengthen their kingdoms. They exploited the ignorant regional Muslims, turning them to heterogeneity and be extremists, and not let the Shia faith prosper in these regions to the east of Iran, which might be an asset to Iran, since the growth of Shiaism was a danger to their kingdoms. And they were the deciding factors for the pathetic state of the whole region. There was daily murder and bomb blast. Not only that they exploited *Johla* – the ignorant, and sent them to enter in Syria[16] to destabilise the regime there which followed a closer Fiqah conforming to the Shia Fiqah.

And this *Fitna* or mischief was created to break the bond of Syria with Iran. This was a larger scale plot involving America, Israel, Saudi Arabia and UAE. But why Britain must enter in this war against Syria is not clear. The Army Chief of Britain, General Sir David Richard said: "Britain must go to war, ground targets would have to be hit". He also says, "I see myself as a moral soldier," ref. Daily Telegraph, July 18, 2013. But what morality it is to help those people who dig out long buried dead for 1200 years from the grave - Sahabi Hajr bin Adi RA was exhumed and insult to his body was given by the Daesh. Then they bombed and destroyed Shia shrines. The Islamic morality and motto are:

'Our hate is for God and our love is for God'

---

[16] The Pakistan Taliban claim in July 2013 that they have sent hundreds of their fighter to fight against the Syrian Government of Bashar Hafez al-Assad, by joining the Syrian rebels.

In this, love for arousing piety for the love of God and hate and disdain for unscrupulous and tyrant are conclusive and the last word in ethics and is ultimate. The impasse in the progress of the formation of a balanced Islamic State of Pakistan came, when the slogan started in Pakistan; *Pakistan ka Matlab Kya, Lah-e Laha Illal Lah* – (what is the meaning of Pakistan, there is no god but God). This was a new slogan in Pakistan, floated in late 1950s by the desperate Mulla out to sit on the pony of power - take over the country and defeat the intelligentsia whom they could not defeat otherwise. Hysteria was raised to save Islam and that Islam was in danger and they thrust the idea that the country was founded to save the faith of Islam, which it was not true. Islam was never in danger it was the malicious faith of the follower which put it in danger. They took laxities in life in forbidden.

Truly the country was founded to safeguard the economic interest of the Muslims and the Muslim culture. Islam was not an issue, there was no danger to it, only danger to the weak faith Muslims. The genuine longing to excel in Islamic culture were hailed and respected by the Hindus from whom the Hindus learnt patience and took intellectual council. But for economic obstacle and for the build-up of the Muslim character a safe haven had to be built to preserve the Muslim culture and Pakistan came in existence. The people had resisted the onslaught of the Hindu culture for long and retained Islamic values. But it had received some dents through the free hand of the Hindu culture which was trying to mould it. And Hindu culture was fascinating; it had a character of a Bail, the creeper that covered up the tall tree with it its leaves for its unchecked growth.

Therefore Quad-e Azam Mohammad Ali Jinnah accepted in a hurry as he said, 'a moth-eaten Pakistan'. He accepted a land mass as was on the plate and achievable. Under the British, the people were already leading a Muslim life as they wanted, perhaps with less friction between the factions of sectarian divides and it was a credit to the British. So, the purpose of Pakistan was not the necessity to raise fortification for Islam in the country. The borders of Pakistan were not to safeguard Islam, it was to save Muslims from economic debacle that was coming to them after freedom.

There was only one fear haunting the thinking Muslims that was of the Tatas and the Birla - the giants of the economic hubs in the undivided India, ruling the economic infrastructure that they will rule over the Muslims in the economic field, and the Muslims were going to be a second and a third-class citizen. But the Hindu majority always felt subdued by the might of the Muslims in the intellectual and the linguistic field that was active and working. However, it was feared, the Hindu culture will camouflage the Muslim culture, once their majority was in power, but the practice of the religion was never in danger. In fact, the Hindus admitted the best thing in Islam was the congregational prayer of Namaz, and they took inspiration from it.

So, the slogan of 'Pakistan Ka Matlab Kya, Lah-e Laha Illallah' was deceiving and gave rise to a cult that turned the country into a nation of bigoted (narrow-minded), prejudicial, self-deceiving, where clergy emerged to propel their conceived untruth to corrupt truth and strengthen clan ideas and regional interests of racist nature. It was also fed with the 'fuel' of sinisterism of the extremism of the Punjabi class to rule the country, even if needed revolting against Islamic benevolences with an eye on the campaign to crush the Shia faith as far as possible, as this sect checked falsehood.

In this movement of the creation of Pakistan, a great shift in thinking and its evolvement at the juncture, when the entire world values were going to be challenged and modified and a power centre evolved by this creation, one view of great consequence was of the congress politician Maulana Abul Kalam Azad, who vehemently opposed the partition of India. And his remarks and views are a hundred percent total truth prediction what is happening in Pakistan today. The history lovers must read the speeches of the Maulana, especially that in the Calcutta mosque.

Once Pakistan was made, the orthodox Muslims changed their views to new-trend - oriented class of Muslims. They changed from the fundamentalist to an opinion biased class. They changed the getup of Pakistan and moulded its destiny by giving vein to thinking of an Islam confronting with the Islam of the Aehlebaait of the Prophet Mohammad SAWW. They aired an Islam which was in contradiction to the *Hadiths-e Saqlaain*[17]. It was an Islam which was also contrary to

---

[17] This Hadiths said: 'I am leaving behind between you, two weighty things: One Quran and the other my *Itrat* – my progenies. For as long as you will hold on to the two, you will

the one known by the Quaed-e Azam and his perception will go against it and it brought the worst form of militancy in Pakistan. And I have this to say:

عشقِ گریا غافل و کُند نہ ہو جائے
روانے اَ شکِ فغاں کہیں کم نہ ہو جائے
فقط عرفان کو حاصل ہے دائمی قدرت
تعریفاتِ خُوگری کو روکیے نفس ہوَس گیر نہ ہو جائے
س ید اطہار حسین

Ishq-e Girya Ghafil-o Kund Na Ho Ja-ay
Rawani-ay Ashk-e Fughan Kaheen Kum Na Ho Ja-ay
Faqat Irfan Ko Hasil Haai Da-emi Qudrat
Tareefat Khoogari Ko Rokiyay Nafs Hawas Geer Na Ho Ja-ay

Crying for love may not become, inattentive and blunt
The flow of tears of grief may not become less
Only gnosis (God knowledge) possesses permanent power
Stop praise of self-style lest the self becomes owner of lust

Unfortunately, also, the countrymen of the leader who kept humility in the forefront: the Bapu of India, Mohan Das Karam Chand Gandhi's people also developed in their country a tight fist staunch religious lookout abandoning the liberal culture, such that it created buffets of intolerance and harassment to the minority religions, and even the domination of their liberal minded film industry could not hold them back on their traditional course. And they started talking of 'return home' - the Shuddhi of the converted to Islam, to return to Hinduism. They believed their country was liberated to restore the dignity of the Indian nationhood and they worked to restore their national dignity through the force of conversion to their old vedic faith.

The situation exists in India where though the scripture says only to revere the cow as mother of civilisation, but she was given the

---

not be lost.' It was in contradiction to this prophetic edict that Hazrat Umar ibn al Khattab had said, 'Quran is enough for us' and that trend and practice continued in spirit and letter with the Muslims in general from then on to the later times.

status of sacred mother and killing and eating beef became blasphemous. This is so in 21 states out of 29 states in India. And their radical religious groups and the BJP of the Indian Prime Minister Narendra Modi are campaigning to have a ban on cow slaughter. It has become Hindu rallying point as is the issue of the Khatm-e Nabuat for all Muslims in Pakistan as a fashion.

Only in their money earning film industry the Hindus and the Muslims work together as one body and help keep a check on the extremism. They forget their religious differences, and on the whole the countrymen did not let loose the vile culture of repression and murder as in the country of the Quaed-e Azam, on the pretext 'save Islam'. The Islam of their derivation was a meaning they coined, to hide the meaning and gist of Islam that it not be the way of the people.

The thinking was corrupted and the country turned into a religious idiocy where a murderer was hailed as *Ghazi* – conqueror. The nation of the confused Muslims had all the apparent signs of the Muslim features, but it was little prepared to meet the harkening of God in Aayet 29:1 that the Muslims will be tested. And the Muslims in Pakistan were not ready and submissive to the twin authority mentioned in the *Hadiths-e Saqlaain* – the *Itrati* and the *Quran*. Murder of the Muslim Shias was common after announcing a hit list by the terrorists who called them Muslims and the will of the judiciary and the administration was missing to protect the Shias and was at variance to snub the terrorists.

Quaed-e Azam Mohammad Ali Jinnah, so disapproved discriminatory treatment based on religion that his one remark about Mahatma Gandhi was: "I have nothing to do with this pseudo-religious approach that Gandhi is advocating." Quaed-e Azam meant Mahatma Gandhi was putting in more than one half of his talent and force for the Hinduism in the Indian politics. This remark had emerged from Quaed-e Azam while Mahatma Gandhi was speaking to Durga Das in London.

The state of Pakistan, Quaed-e Azam founded was a settled necessity in his eyes to save the Muslims from exploitation, but they started exploitation of themselves. It was to be the home of the moderates, where love and respect was to be found abundant for all, but it featured contrary to that. Time and again Quaed-e Azam expressed that motto through his speech and showed by his action to be moderate. Jaganathan Azad was an Urdu speaking Hindu poet living and working in Lahore for a literary newspaper. His family had already left for India after partition and he was staying back. On August 9, 1947, Quaed-e Azam sent a message to him through one of his friends at Radio Lahore, asking him that he wanted him (Azad) to write Pakistan National Anthem.

Poet Jaganathan Azad died in 2004, but before that he reminded of his service that he wrote the National Anthem. He informed the song was sent to the Quaed-e Aazam Mohammad Ali Jinnah, who approved it in few hours. It was sung for the first time by the Radio Pakistan Karachi and remained the National Anthem of Pakistan for one and a half year, which afterwards was replaced by the national anthem written by poet Hafiz Jalandhari. Through his national anthem, he became a legendry name in Pakistan. The words of the Azad's song of the national anthem were:

Aai Sir Zameen-e Pak
Zarray Teray Haain Aaj Sitaroan Say Tanbank
Raushan Haai Kaehkashan Say Kaheen Aaj Teri Khak
Aai Sir Zameen-e Pak

O land that is pure (free of foulness)
Today your fragments are brighter than the stars
Today your dust is brighter than the Milky Way
O land that is pure (free of foulness)

Quaed-e Azam's philosophy of work and logic was that religion should not be sitting at the apex of state policies and only ethics, morality and humanism be the show piece of the character of the nation and this is the necessity in face of so much faith difference among the Muslim fundamentalists. The discordance in the faith of the believers is visible in hate and murder all over Pakistan and yet the religion is the prime concern. There is at present a peace talk on with the Taliban, proposed by the Taliban and accepted by PMLN government of Nawaz Sharif. But they have not even honoured their word to lie low for at least the period of the talk and have murdered thirteen police commandos and injured 58 of them on 13 February 2014. And because politics is self-centred in Pakistan, the political parties seek power only to rule. The PMLN is continuing to present sacrifice of the innocent citizens to rule the country. And the murderers using strongarm tactics, force the politician through murder to yield to their brand of Islam, although they are not more than 5% of the total moderate faith followers of the country, but their terror weapon is strong to make definitions of logic, reason and justice altered.

The ethics says that even if the state is carrying 99.9% majority faith of one class, even then that class cannot be given sanction to gobble up and destroy the 0.1% faith minority that represent a different entity than them. It has right to exist along with the majority faith, whether democracy or no democracy, and the state must not yield to the ibn Tamayya doctrine of annihilating the differing. There was total institutional revolt and militancy in ibn Tamayya doctrine, which is followed by the Wahhabism.

Rabindra Nath Tagore came from a different culture because of his bred of mind. He possessed knowledge much richer than the conventional learned in politics. Among the Muslim Learned who valued him are Abdur Rahman Bijnori, Josh Malihabadi and Quaed-e Azam Mohammad Ali Jinnah. He followed Vedic religion, and the vedic wizards claim the Quran is the gist of the Vedas. Rabindra Nath Tagore recognised people of meritocracy and his philosophy was simple, extend love to the hard working, whether poor or rich. And he though a Brahman, seemed to have no problem of touch ability to non-Hindus. He had a debate with Albert Einstein on metaphysics in 1930. Albert Einstein became Nobel Prize laureate in photo electric effect and Sunt Rabindra Nath in glorious literature. The Sunt had a scientific and perceiving mind and his adequacies were ruled by his logical mind. In one of the songs in Geetanjali, he says:

"Leave this recitation of the prescribed and obdurate submission to the fixed determined - the idol worshipping and leave the counting of the beads - the incantation made in their praises. O you! In the temple, in one lone corner after barricading everyone out; whose worship are you doing? Open your eyes and see that God is not in front of you. God is there, where man is overturning, pushing and dislodging hard rock, and where there are road workers, breaking the stone to bed them on the road. He is with them."

And salute to him. This saint-poet has said very powerful and long rhyming verses in his Geetanjali. He says in one of the poems:

> *Tumhari Kiran Pattay Pattay Par*
> *Bhar Deti Haai Pran*
> *Tumhara Prakash Punch Kay Ghar Mein*
> *Jaga Deta Haai Gan*
> *Baray Pyar Say Geoti Tumhari*
> *Tun Par Meray Aakar Utri*
> *Hirdaai Sahla Rahi Uski*
> *Vimal Hatheli Aan*

> Your rays are on each and every leaf
> And fill the souls
> Your universe is in the house of the bird
> It awakens singing
> With extreme love, the glow of Your Self
> Has come to descend on my body
> Its (glow) is stroking my heart
> With purity having come into (my) palm

The poet then like a teacher, in the wisdom of the prophets of their days says:

> *Kaun Kahta Haai Sub Chord Ja-ega*
> *Maut Jub Thamay Gee Hath Tera*

> *Jeevan Mein Jo Toonay Liya Haai*
> *Oosay Marrund Mein Laychalna Hoga*

> *Iss Bharay Bhandaar Mein Aakar*
> *Khaali Hi Chaldega Aakhir*

> *Lenay Ko Jo Kuch Bhi Haai Tera*
> *Bhali Tarah Say Lo Tub Tum Ja*

Koorda Kurkat Ka Yeh Boajha
Jo Toonay Dunya Mein Batora

Butch Jaega, Janay Ki Bela
Sub Kashr Kar Ja-o Gin Gin

Aa-ay Haain Iss Dharti Per
Suj Dhuj Lay Shrungaar Saja Kar

Raja Kay Vesh Mein Chalo Ray!
Hunstay Marteyoo Paar Kay Oos Utsau Mein.

Who says all, thy will leave behind?
When the demise of death will catch thy hand

Whatever thou have collected in life
Thou will have to take along in death

After coming in this topped up glamorous fair of the
     world
Will thou leave empty handed at last

Whatever, is thine for your taking
Take in a goodly way and then go there

The burden of that trash
Thy collected in this world

Will be left behind at the time of departing
Give all that away in its count

(We) have arrived on this earth
All pinned up with the trappings of decorations

(O you lost) Go in the guise of a King laughing
Over to the place where one reaches after death.

-:. .:-

127

I

THE BLESSINGS OF THE SEASONS

XI

The transition from summer to winter in the Land of Seasons and Songs was interceded by one intermediary season, the autumn; that was the co-link between the two seasons. It cushioned the transition between the two extreme seasons. When this season ran the soil was rejuvenated and the nutrients were returned to the soil and it was readied for use in the spring. It was time when the leaves fell from the trees and rustled on the ground, and the simplicity took over the nature. Petals dropped from the sockets of the flowers and flowers seized to bloom and the nature was like the sheep shorn of its fluffiness. She made barren of her woolly looks and her cuddliness stripped off her and transformed to unassuming looks and left to the cares of the Mother Nature, and she stood on her slim feet to start and rebuild her fleecy admirableness again.

Or was it like the tall ship, with its forays of sales, devoid of wind on the high sea and the rigs hauled down and it wobbling on the waves, waiting for the wind to come to let her set sails, when it will dip its bows and splash water, tearing the waves and prodding and surging forward once again.

Or was it like the bride in the Land of Seasons and Songs, resplendent in her *Solah Singhar* –with her sixteen embellishments, symbolic of the vanity she represented, which just she shed off and was standing in her simplified grace, casting her looks into the oceans of times and looking into the futures with bemused expectations.

Or was it like the huge armada of ships of combat readiness, anchored to fish and try feed its compliment.

None of the imagery in words however intricate could explain the effect of this season on the man's nature and the lesson the nature was set to give to its brood. This was the nature's way to say that what once paraded had wound up its drubbing and the changes were in offing and it was the nature's inevitable in her management in ruling the world. The repeating phenomenon year after year were lessons to prepare man for the change he was to experience. He was prepared by the nature to say good bye to one that was, and welcome the one that was to come. Such were the designs of Nature to give sustenance to life.

The autumn was dispelled by the season of sternness - the season of severities which held off all moderations, and the shivering and shuddering became order of the day for the people. There was howling wind and biting cold that gripped the people, and people started to equip themselves by furbishing them to stand to face the season's battering.

The instinct of the birds exceeded that of the men. The birds had started their farsighted preparations at the very first glimpse of the season and furbished their nests with additional cosiness by laying additional twigs and bits to their already well-knit crocheting. They gave it further subsistence to ward off the extremes of the cold and barricaded themselves against the onslaught of the piercing thrust of the cold.

The rodents and insect eaters and amphibians, those denied love hid them in their burrows to sleep the winter off. The tree climbers went in their pits and holes in the trees, sealing off themselves against the harshness of the winter and the heftier of them sat the winter out in their natural habitat, conserving their energy. And there were preparations all round to face the cold in the manner and the way what suited them.

Those possessing least, made the least of the preparation. They took out their old cotton quilts and spread them in the mild winter sun to give a bathe of sun rays to become warm and free of staleness. And that was the best in the preparation the poor did. But the affluent purchased fancy pure silk, satin or chintz for their new quilt tops and a matching mercerised cotton length for the underneath bottom and ordered the tailor to stitch these with frills attached and the affluent had it filled with fluffy new cotton by the *Dhunya* - the cotton shredder.

The Dhunya came with a dumbbell and bow of taught cord of guts of lamb or of the goat and he hung the bow from a peg that he hammered in the wall. He started shredding the new cotton, striking the chord with the dumbbell that produced crests and troughs of nodes and shredded the new cotton in a big fluffy heap, guiding the bow and pushing the vibrating cord in the cotton heap. The cotton shredded by the cord, produced the rhythmic singsong note of Trrung, Trrung, Trrung and fluffy pile was piled by the Dhunya in a big heap.

He filled the quilt with the shredded cotton, pushing it into the far corners of the quilt and levelled the quilt, readying it to be of comfortable thickness all- over and using his slim stick made the quilt even and cosy. And a kingly length and breadth emerged. Then all it needed now was its threading. And unless the Dhunya was required to do the threading of the quilt, he was paid off and bid farewell. The ladies in the house did the threading in a patterned design, and produced a new attractive quilt, otherwise the local Darzi - the tailor was called and his expertise in threading produced the finest quilt desired.

When the quilt was ready, filled with the freshly shredded heap of fluffy cotton, the result was warmth and comfort and smell of new cotton of the quilt. And there was no denying the fact that this was one single item that man so desired and which so contributed to his comfort that he loved lying covered with it. When the wind was howling and it was freezing cold and the sun was shying away, only presenting a mild glow, the quilt compensated for the missing warmth. And it was a definite source of warmth. Man, then so hid him, wrapping the quilt round him and spending his hours of peace covered in its cosiness that he felt sheltered from all harm.

Those with what least was their possession, and those with their places a degree higher than the outright dispossessed and those with crown of a king on their heads and those with the bred of mind excelling in intelligent manipulation of thoughts and those devising theory of everything and presenting premise and axioms, none could say they were not equal in quest, whining to be covered by the quilt readied and filled with equal amount of fluffy cotton of even thickness, threaded to pattern to keep its shape and warmth, when the cold came to attack them. This was the equality lesson in the trimming of the behaviour of the privileged and the dispossessed alike, all drawing comfort alike from the cosiness of the quilt and protecting them from the severity of the winter. And this was a lesson to all in the basics of joy man derived as his share from the season's equal treatment to all with no discrimination made against any. This was the nature's covenant as its basic pledge to all.

The winter season with all its severities of cold and shiver, was also liberal, it brought streams and streams of joys to the people of the Land of Seasons and Songs. It brought plentiful varieties of gifts of eatables abundantly available to all. The exclusive in these was *Gurd* – the dried molasses. It was the season's most outstanding gift. The Gurd was one fistful lump of the overly cooked and evaporated sugar cane juice, obtained by heating it on the field *Choolhas* – the open make-shift stoves made in the fields. Deep cauldrons filled with sugarcane juice were placed on the Choolhas, and the juice was boiled to its set point and condensed and a long arm scoop was used to scoop out the concentrate on a jute mat. It was shaped and solidified into the fistful lump of sweet Gurd.

Gurd was the standard commercial product, made with the least of the gadgetry and sacks and sacks of Gurd were brought to the *Mundi* and heaps and heaps of it were sold. The beneficences of the Gurd were as varied as to increase the heights of the children, make food palatable and provide energy to the marketers and activity in the market. Mandis with brisk merchants selling the Gurd sprang up on fixed days in the *Qasbah* – the big villages. There the sweet smell of Gurd spread out from the Gurd stalls in the Mundi hung in the air and it enhanced the Mundi. The Gurd was within easy reach of all, and its aromatic smell so filled the market and created so much of cheeriness in the Mundi that the Mandis thrived on it, and it so conveyed the feeling of abundance of eatery that all felt assured that they lived in the land of plenty.

The Peshawari Gurd was one variety of the many kinds. The vendor sold it as the chief item on his push cart and said, it was *'Sardi Ka Dushamn'*- the enemy of the cold. This Gurd was in small Dala (piece) with excelling looks in its golden colour. The Peshawari Gurd carried broken almond and groundnut mixed in it, which peeped out from it and its gold colour invited attention. The vendor made a small pile of it on his push cart - the *Thdela* and it competed with the Helwae's delicious sweet.

131

The Risawal was the season's other outstanding gift. It was a delicacy made on the field Choolha – the open stove. Small quantity of rice and a large quantity of sugar cane juice was cooked for long hours in a large pot. The rice blended with the juice concentrate and a delightful product Risawal was obtained. And there was nothing sweeter than Risawal. Coconut pieces and almond flakes were added to the Risawal and the simplest in the novelties of the season was obtained. Sometimes a drop of Kewrda was added to it and it was a cherished dish of the traditionalist taken with milk or with thick top cream of the milk obtained on slow cooking on low heat. The Indian buffalo milk when simmered on slow heat produced an excelling thick layered cream which added maximum taste to the Risawal.

Hola was another pleasure of the season. It was late winter gift, when the tender chickpeas in their shells were ready to be plucked and the Hola trees with branches laden with Hola buds were pulled out with their roots. And heaps and heaps of these Hola trees were placed on the fire from the shrubs and dry twigs in the open field. The buds sputtered and were roasted to a brown roast. The smoke of the fire made the Hola smoke-flavoured, and these had a unique taste. It was eaten with the blend of chilli, salt and garlic, the mixture ground on the kitchen stone slab – the *Sill*, and it didn't fail to please all.

The Hola tree's tender leaves were also a delicacy for their piquancy and were nibbled with the ground chilly - garlic - salt Chutney. The Nature had packed energy in these tender tiny leaves and their acidic sharpness and piquant taste were a novelty and the favourite of the ladies.

Roasted Hola and the Risawal were recognised inexpensive delicacies, meritorious to be sent to affectionate neighbours and friends in generous quantities as gift or present. This tradition of sending presents from one to the other were the gestures of warmth and friendliness of the people, and these etiquettes spoke of courteous life and of good humour the people had for each other in the Land of Seasons and Songs. And the Nature was kind to the people in the Land of Seasons and Songs, there was *Bajra* or the millet, liberally used in the winter. This was the cheapest of the farmer's food grain. It was poor man's wheat at half the price of the wheat. The Bajra bread made from Bajra flour was crushed with Gurd in plentiful quantity of Ghee and a fine *Maleeda* emerged from this mix. It *was* an excelling home produce in sweet. It was the simplest of the wonder foods in the farmer's house, which boasted of taste and nourishment packed in one, and it was a product of fashion, presentable to honoured guests and it pleased the eye, satiated the appetite and guaranteed instant energy by breaking down into energy particles.

To add further to the pleasantries of the season was the most outstanding present to the strong toothed the sugar cane itself, called the *Ganna*. The tender juicy *Ganna*, fresh from the Bigha(s) and Bigha(s) of spread sugar cane fields was stripped of its hard-outer skin using the sheer power of the teeth and a *Ganderi* – a bite of the sugar-cane pulp was snapped away and the strong teeth wrested the juice from it and its dry pulp was thrown out. The young and the old, both equally enjoyed it, chewing the Ganna. And the winter changing its mood from harsh winter to pink winter all through its run of the four months, kept the faces rosy and provided a series of persistent edibles to the people. For this the people were thankful for what they were and where they were, in the Land of Seasons and Songs.

The soil, the climate and the mineral rich water of the river produced the varieties of roots and flowers and of these, one was Gajar – the carrot. And Gajar Ka Helwa was made in the houses in the winter. It filled the body with energy and if it was black Gajar, it had enhanced taste and softness. The black Gajar Helwa was beyond tastiness ever normally one came across. Then there were a variety of Helwa(s) produced from gram lentil soaked and ground and then roasted in Ghee or from flour of Moong lentil, or from granulated wheat flour – the suji (semolina), or from egg yolks and flour - the Anday *Ka Helwa*. It was semi hard and when it was put in the mouth, it instantly released a burst of flavour and fused its fragrance all round in the mouth.

And there were plenty of varieties of pleasing standard Helwa sweets made in the houses. The ladies showed their artistry by giving the Helwa, varied texture of softness and hardness. There was soft Helwa saturated with Ghee and the hard diamond shaped Helwa cut out from the hot prepared Helwa cast on the tray. It was crisp, fragrant and tasty. And the Helwa was preserving itself for a long time and these spoke of the ladies' art in cookery. The dry solid Helwa was given geometrical shape by slicing the freshly cooked Helwa spread out on a tray when it was just about to solidify and the necessary constituent of all was the adequate amount of sugar, fragrance and select nuts put in, and it was to yield taste.

But the most talked of Helwa was the *Gajar Ka Helwa* – Helwa of carrots. For its taste and looks, its flavour and texture and for its health benefactions, it is the most outstanding Helwa. The black carrot when it was fresh, the Helwa excelled in taste. The black carrot was diced and simmered in buffalo milk. The buffalo milk was higher in density and carried rich fatty cream which could be seen floating in the milk. Saffron and sugar were added to the Helwa and when the Helwa was ready, no grain of carrot was left standing in the Helwa, it was blended in the constituents and turned into a placatory semi solid Helwa, soft in texture, and of fragrance which travelled far and in taste such as to be remembered for long. *Chandi Ka Waraq* – air-thin silver foil was delicately placed on the Helwa making it look distinguished. And almond and pistachio flakes were liberally sprinkled on the Helwa.

Then there was the unerring *Turri* so lovingly served in winter. The dried fruits were soaked in water and it were ground and roasted in Ghee and turned into a pleasant soup. The Turri was beat all the delicacies in nourishment. It is a soup with infinite in taste, for warmth and strength. For increasing haemoglobin, it is an invaluable asset. A hot bowl of Turri is most suited when the diagnosis was insipidness, which had hit the weak due to deranging exhaustion and weakness. A bowlful of this vitalizing delicacy if given to the person will make him strong and it is consistent in its ready cure. The Turri is most suited to be taken when the winter season sets in.

The constituents of Turri were almond, pistachio, sultana, *Chiraunji, Chohara* - the dried dates, coconut and *Char Maghz* – the four seeds of gourd, watermelon, muskmelon and pumpkin. The standard practice was; the dried fruits were soaked in water then ground on the *sill* – the household hard-stone slab, and the fruit paste so prepared was roasted in sufficient ghee with one or two pods of cardamom and an appropriate quantity of water was added and the Turri soup emerged in silver colour; something inviting in looks and full of taste and there was no one who could say they had tasted anything finer than the soup of Turri.

And what a world we have and how blessed we are, never would we like to change our planet with another. On this planet we have the best of everything. The summers and the winters and each of a different characteristic, each accrediting ruggedness but of opposite nature and each distancing them from each other and sitting on the opposite end of the diagonal of the elliptical orbit. They were creator of their foundational seasonal phenomenon for their positions that was guaranteed by the diurnal spin and the annual rotation of the mother Earth.

The arrangement of the solar system held the seasons in their embedding, and the summer and winter occupied a foray of a wider chord in the span of time of one circle round the sun, and each of these spreading their benevolences for a longer period with differing spectaculars and fervour. These seasons patterned life in the moulds of their distinctive colour and people's response to them was, either they were panting or they were shivering by the pledge of their extremism.

In winter, *Angethdi* – the earthen bowl holding live charcoals was slipped under the *Moonj Ki Palung* - bed made from rush twines and the warmth reached to the bed occupier, sleeping or awake. And outside in the village-shed, *Keekard* twigs and wood chops and logs were burnt in the corner of the shed; where the elders drew their *Moandha* – the stool made from reed sticks – the *Sirkonda*. And *Palung*(s) of Moonj were pulled close to the fire and *Huqqa* - the Hubble bubble was passed from one to the other for drawing their puffs. The Huqqa had padded flexible tube, moistened with water and its bubbling sound arising from its brass vase, giving fascinating sound in the dim of the light. The water in the brass was catching air that came passing through the tobacco placed in the *Chilam* - the necked bowl on which embers were placed, which burnt the tobacco and the tobacco laden puffs of the Huqqa spread the smell of the *Khameera* - the sweetened tobacco in the spaces around.

Khameera was made from raw tobacco, knitted in molasses and a rich smell travelled from the Huqqa all round when it was puffed. Its smell was so sweet that even the novice was drawn to take a puff or two from the Huqqa. The tobacco of the Huqqa was prepared by mixing *Raab* - the molasses with raw tobacco and fragrant spices in proportionate quantity were added to it and the mixture was pounded using bare feet. The mixture yielded into a bitter sweet tobacco. It was a unique perfumed tobacco. This tobacco, half bitter half sweet, suited the occasional smoker. The tobacco shops that prepared *Khameera* smelt so sweet that people deliberately whisked past the shop where the perfume hung in the air and they inhaled the air laden with tobacco perfume.

The Huqqa in the dim light of the wood fire, in the village-shed in winter nights had a mysterious effect. The village elderlies were bound to each other through it. And Huqqa was their chief attraction to assemble in one place under the shed to talk and exchange views and pass news. The Huqqa was puffed and a pause was taken in the talks to afford them to think and review. In this time the listeners waited to listen to the reply and the elderly puffing the Huqqa took his time to reply. And the Huqqa was the tool to bind the folks to one another and was their asset and simple luxury.

The fun that the winter provided was described by Poet Nazeer Akbarabadi – from Akbarabad, present day Agra. Poet Nazeer Akbarabadi died in the year 1830 at the age of ninety-five and live full life thanks to God. Nazeer Akbarabadi – Sayed Wali Mohammad has written long poems. The poet's one *Qita* – continuous verses of poetry on one topic the winter is quoted here:

Jub Mah Aaghan Ka Dhalta Ho;   *Tub Dekh Baharein Jarday Ki*
Hans Hans Poush Sanbhalta Ho;   *Tub Dekh Baharein Jarday Ki*
Din Jaldi Jaldi Chalta Ho;   *Tub Dekh Baharein Jarday Ki*
Aur Pala, Barf Pighalta Ho;   *Tub Dekh Baharein Jarday Ki*
Chilla Khum Thoank Uchhalta Ho;   *Tub Dekh Baharein Jarday Ki*

When the month of Aaghan[18] was sliding away;
Then see the fun, the winter brings
When the month of Poush was smilingly edging in;

---

[18] Aaghan is the 8th month of the Hindi calendar and corresponds with October-November in time. It is followed by the month of Poush.

136

Then see the fun, the winter brings
When the days were running away fast;
Then see the fun, the winter brings
And the hoarfrost was melting away;
Then see the fun, the winter brings
Shrieking, slapping on the thigh, jumping;
Then see the fun, the winter brings

The poet has used the word *Khum Thoank*. It is customary that a wrestler when he is challenging his opposite number, slaps the thigh, as soon as he enters in the earth pit. It is called *Khum Thoankna*. By that he has thrown challenge to his opponent who responds by slapping his thigh to show he has accepted the challenge. The poet has used the word to say that slapping the thigh in the severe cold is involuntarily challenging the cold.

The falling snow stimulates the poets more in the West, than the budding flowers in their sockets that were swinging in the breeze of the spring and were venturing tickle the feeling of the poets in the Land of the Seasons and Songs. Poet James Thomson beautifully describes how it was when it snowed. He lived where snow fell and so he describes it. Poet James Thomas writes:

Through the hushed air the whitening shower descends,
At first thin – wavering; till at last the flakes
Fall broad and wide and fast, dimming the day
With a continual flow, the cherished fields
Put on their winter robe of purest white.

But the poet in the Land of Seasons and Songs smells of the sweet scent of the earth and the evening and the morning spells of spring and he writes about the flowers and the breeze. The poet conditioned by the melodiousness of spring in the environs of the Land of Seasons and Songs bursts out with lyric speaking of flower and bud and fragrance and the morning serenity in the Phulwari — the flower bedecked garden and he yields:

137

غنچہ ہے سحر ہے قرار ہے تازہ دمی ہے
مہک ہے خوشبو ہے، امتیازِ و خوشنمائی ہے
پھیلی ہوئی ہے تازگی فضا میں یوں او دا ئم
جس طرح کائنات میں بر قرار تیری خدائی ہے

خلقتِ خدا کو خدائی کی ادا نظر آئی ہے
درس وتدریس سے اسمیں وفا بھر آئی ہے
خوشگواری کا اب سبق دیتا ہے خلقت کو
کیسی ارتقا کیسی حسنِ وضع اسمیں آئی ہے

تقّد س عجز ہے سجدہ ہے بار شفقت ہے
مومن پنہائی میں پیمبر ہے، بار بردار بارِ امامت ہے
کیا خوب نظامِ قدرت وجود دیا رب نے
نہ انتہا ہے نہ ابتدا ہے ثبت ہی ثبت ہے

سید اطھار حسین

Ghuncha Haai Sahar Haai Qarar Haai Taza Dami Haai
Mahek Haai Khushboo Haai, Imtiyaz-o Khushnuma-ee Haai
Phaaili Hoee Haai Tazgee Feza Mein Yuun O Daem
Jis Tarah Kaenat Mein Barqarar Teri Khuda-ee Haai

Khilqat-e Khuda Ko Khuda-ee Ki Ada Nazar Aa-ee Haai
Dars-o Tadrees Say Oosmein Wafa Bhar Aa-ee Haai
Khushgawari Ka Ub Sabaq Deta Haai Khilqat Ko
Kaaisi Irteqa Kaaisi Husn-e Waza Oosmein Aa-ee Haai

Taqaddus Ijz Haai Sajda Haai Bar-e Shafqat Haai
Momin Pinha-ee Mein Payamber Haai, Bar Bardar Bar-e
Imamat Haai

Kya Khoob Nizam-e Qudrat Wajood Diya Rub Nay
Na Inteha Haai Na Ibteda Haai, Sabt Hi Sabt Haai

There is sprout, the dawn, the stability, there is freshness
There is scent, sweet smell, there is distinctiveness and prettiness
Spread in the air is freshness so O Permanent
Like in the universe is Your stability of Godliness

To the creation the blandishment of the Godliness of God is in sight
With teachings and lessons, faithfulness has filled in him
Now he gives lessons in good mannerism to the creation
What an evolution, what beauty in mannerism has come in him

The sanctity is humility, prostration, weight of affection
Momin in solitude is messenger, load carrier of the burden of
    Imamat
What a beautiful management of the providence gave existence
    the Provider
Neither there is endlessness, nor beginning, only writing and
    writing

The ferocity of the heat burnt and scorched skin in the summers and people hid their heads under the shades of the cools of the trees. The hot scorching wind, called *Loo* blew outside, and the look of places was a deserted emptiness. Lobes of hot flame arose from the bare stone-roads of no tarmac. The fierce sun sent flame, burning the road and no one dared put their feet on them. It was only when the heat subsided in the evenings and people found the cool was returning that they came out. Water was sprinkled on the ground and sweet smell arose from the soil and life that was stilled due to the blistering heat of the high noon, returned to normal and briskness of life returned.

People wore thin cotton Kurtas - loose sleeve shirts of *Malmal* - the muslin and came out in these dresses. And took them around; some went to stalls for *Thanda-ee* – the cooling drinks of herbs, and some went to shops to buy *Lassi* – the whizzed yogurt with sugar and crushed ice. While others went to buy drink from liquor shop which had pungency and odour. They were free of bounds to negations and submitted their comprehensive alertness to pseudo alertness, entering in that state putting out their step from the door step of the shop. They trotted along exuded but with lesser alertness of mind. The drink's benefactions had worked on them dragging them from the professed sober to professed drunk in intoxicated state. It arrested their discerning mind and pushed them into dither, to a definite emptiness of mind, which they did not know of. These were the kinds of drinks that pounded on the drinking and subjugated minds and dwarfed man's mindedness to mindlessness and they went willingly to the shops to be in that state. The drinks' smell stuffed the air and the vicinities with their pungencies and punches.

But there were other drinks also, with exceptional virtue in them, they improved sanity there in was instilled purity in the drinker. These were simple and filled with fragrance. They vitalised body and were of demureness and of qualities of goodness in their character. These were the *Sharbat* (the sorbets), ready to nourish life vein and strengthen heart and embolden mind. These sweet in taste and pleasant in fragrance drinks, pleased all. Their classification was of large variety in the Land of Seasons and Songs, so much so that some were made even from tamarind with its acidity and its punch intact. Its virtue was counted to help sharpen mind and soothe disposition as it helped blood circulation. Others of its kind were prepared from ground almond and milk and still others from fruit nectars. And still others prepared from the seeds of swelled *Balanga* in water, with measured quantity of lemon juice and sugar. But all these taxed the pocket.

And that which cost nothing and came bowing with submission to please the soul and strengthen the mind's moorings was the evening gush of breeze, lush with fragrance of flowers and drenched in the scent of the soil, laden with these. It was bent on providing bliss and benefaction to the recipient. It invigorated the soul and strengthened the body. The breezes, fresh in their virtue in trail swept all through the evenings, rejuvenating the mind and typifying the grace of the summer evenings of the Land of Seasons and Songs.

Money was not in abundance with the people of the Land of Seasons and Songs, and their needs were small and simple. They tilted land and reared buffalos and bullocks. And they produced little grain to self-suffice their needs and never enough to earn luxury. And all told they suffered shortage of commodity and the shortage of money that was the handicap staring in the faces of the peoples. But despite the shortage of money, one or two glasses of Thanda-ee or Lassi, at *Duanni* or two Anas - English Tuppence a glass were not an impossible proposition - beyond the means of the people if they desired to buy a glass or two of these drinks. The ingenuity of the hard-working Lassi and the Thunda-ee shopkeeper made it possible for them to buy, since the shopkeeper kept the price low. They used muscle power, rather than the cleverly designed machine to whizz these drinks. And ensured not to tax the pocket of the aspirants, desirous of the drink and served these to the customers at the Lassi shop with the choice of sweet Lassi or a salty Lassi, of quality and in volume that suited their pockets.

The people in the houses also prepared a variety of drinks. They knew of many kinds including of Thunda-ee. Thunda-ee needed great care in its preparation. It was fruit of labour, friction and attrition of kernels of musk melon, watermelon, pumpkin, gourd seeds along with some poppy seeds and *Kahoo* seeds. Kahoo sharpened the mind and so did the flower buds of rose and rose-petals, which were added to the Thunda-ee along with a small quantity of aniseed for its cooling characteristics. All this was pounded and ground to fineness and the very best in drink was obtained. Thunda-ee was served in the cool of the afternoons in the subsiding heat of the summer day. It demanded lots of labour and minute details observed in its preparation, but it excited an all-round flurry. And the pleasure it was to yield could be seen in the twinkle of the eyes of the awaiting recipients - the children when it was served. They had waited patiently to sip the incredible taste laden drink for long and now it was presented to them.

Among other nourishers that recouped energy in the summers were the *Kulfi* – the cone of the luscious ice cream. It was made from milk, sugar and ground dried fruits. The mixture was filled in a steel cone and frozen to become Kulfi. And there were so many varieties of it. One of the varieties of Kulfi, greenish in colour, brought intoxication and jovialness in its eater. This was *Bhang Kulfi*.

The customer after eating this Kulfi entered in a state of joviality which lasted for as long as the *Bhang* or the hemp - some called Ali Booti, worked to relax the mind by diluting the problem to make the self-happy. There are two ways in it, sluggishness or over occupation – enhanced activity. It is not clear which way the Bhang worked. But it brought a soothing state. It made alertness deadened and the deciphering of the understandable ordinaries impossible. Bhang was an herb and it gives the Kulfi green colour and fills hilariousness in the eater, sending him to exhilarated laughs. Men chuckled and mused with each other and even the trivial non-significant things appeared amusing to laugh at and these tickled them. The eaters of this Kulfi could be detected from a distance by even the most aloof observer.

But contrary to the men laughing and acting carefree after taking the Bhang Kulfi, there were men in the Land of Seasons and Songs who opted for the opposite what the Bhang did. They took *Afewn,* the opium. It took them on tours to the land where they felt deep holiness, virtuousness was engulfing them, and they thought it extremely meritorious to be gone into that state of mind. It hit them with deliriousness and an obsessed contentment took control of them, and they felt every bit contended with what they were and, in the state, they were.

The pitying pitied them for the state they were in and called them *Apheonchi,* and to those who smoked opium with chopped betel leaves mixed with lime, for their state to enter piqued in drowsiness – that was their appearance, they were called *Madakchi.* These were rather hilarious names given to the habitual opium takers, because the words describing them suited to their desiccated physique of their body and the condition they had entered in, of their spongy mind and skin and bone thinness of body. And it spoke of the nature and the content of the people of the Land of Seasons and Songs, who didn't want to be hurtful to others for their personality but not deny the fun and the pleasure out of the mimic and the arbitrating judgements on them. The condition the *Apheon-chi* and the *Madakchi* had allowed them to enter in; was suggestive without ambiguity that either of them was not suited to produce work of any credibility, but just a living soul incapable of harm to others.

The Kulfi man brought a variety of Kulfi(s) in a *Matka* - a large pitcher placed on a pushcart of three wheels to the customer centre. He had wrapped the pitcher with a red cloth and kept it moist; it helped the Kulfis in the Matka stay frozen for longer period. The customers swarmed the Kulfi man as soon as he arrived, and he swirled his hand in the pitcher when an order for a particular Kulfi came and when he brought out his hand, he had held the right size and the right flavour Kulfi, what the customer had ordered. There were many kinds of the Kulfis in the pitcher with ice chunks, covering the Kulfis, but he rarely peeped in the Matka to see and locate the Kulfi he had to pick what the customer had asked for, such was his expertise in locating and picking. There was never a chance that he was going to feed his customer a Bhang Kulfi, if he had asked for the pistachio one, and either of these were present in the pitcher in plentiful numbers and each green in looks.

The search and locate expertise of the Kulfi Man was perfect and he picked and lifted only the particular type of the green Kulfi from his pitcher the customer wanted, even if it was dark and late in the evenings his expertise worked. And he handed out the Kulfi on a piece of banana leave with an equal measure of concern of sanctimoniousness for everyone. He squeezed out the Kulfi and jump deposited it on the piece of the leaf with an adjudged accuracy to let it settle as of automation in the centre of the leaf.

The little Kulfi man was *Pawitr* that is to say he was clean of impurity and purity filled from the time of his birth. He was of a cast that carried a distinction of trust worthy purity about him for everyone to take Kulfi off his hand. And he had to push and half spin the Kulfi to land on the piece of the banana leaf and save his fingers touching the foul surface of the banana leaf that was now held by the unknown of the cast. He had to save himself from being contaminated by not allowing his fingers brush touch the banana leaf piece that was in contact with the assumed foul man. And the Kulfi man was not concerned how sophisticated the eye brows the customer had and how he looked, his concern was to keep aloof of him and his treatment was universal. And this was in effort to satisfy all classes of his customers, some of whom were even of a higher cast than him, and were critical and observant that the Kulfi Man maintained the required ethical standard in cast class distinction and he remained uncontaminated.

The Kulfi men worked hard for preparing the Kulfis. These Kulfi men kept hygiene and taste of the Kulfis in the forefront. There was never a chance of one getting a maligned stomach after eating their Kulfi and everyone who ate their Kulfi praised the taste of the Kulfi. The customer never had to run to the fields to relief him of stomach pressure built up with bad Kulfi(s), which was a consequence to be feared from the modern-day caterers. The Matka Kulfi men never allowed such mishaps. They were not the mass-producing caterers whose standards slipped now and then and a poor lingering taste sat on the tongue, and men had to run to the fields. The Matka Kulfi men were clear of this blemish.

The major ingredient of the Kulfi was milk and the minor was Kewrda water. The Kewrdawater was produced from Kewrda flower whose essence was transferred in the water. Kewrda was a corn shaped flower and the nature's straight gift to the people of the Land of Seasons and Songs. The Kewrda flower was reputed for fragrance and the Kewrdawater was a dilution of the concentrated essence from the Kewrda flower. The Pansari sold Kewrda water and only a few drops of this wonder in food and *Sharbat* were enough to make it fragrant and pleasing. The fragrance of Kewrda valorised anything it was sprinkled with and it supplemented the recipient food with its virtues and the Kulfi man used it for the benefit of his customers.

The plant of Kewrda was remontant (blooming more than once in a season) and its long leaves grew into rich thickets, but the tree bore only a few flowers, blossoming along among the leaves covered by them and spreading fragrance all round, making the air laden with scent. The Kewrda fragrance filled all the places and when the sensorial came in contact with it, tension was taken away and pseudo sadness was replaced with cheerfulness. The snakes loved the Kewrda fragrance and they made home under the thicket drawing close near to the stem and laid eggs there and brought out their young creep.

Adding only two drops of Kewrda essence, in ten thousand drops of water was enough to make the Kewrdawater. It was bottled, and its fragrance remained intact for a very long time and the Pansari sold it. And like the rosewater, it was used for sprinkling on faces, on the *Khash Ki Tatti* – the thatched screen of the fragrant grass, to give cool fragrant vapour and sprinkled in the assemblies when the scholastic speakers were presenting *Kathas*, the narrations - revealing the mythology of the past gods. Like rosewater it was sprinkled on the *Matamee* – the mourners beating their chest with hand or when using chain hung with knife blades in the processions of the Muharram, and when blood flew from cuts. It was immediately sprayed and It healed the wound.

The fragrance concealed in the leaves of the Kewrda plant was absorbed by the cachou when it was spread on the leaf by the Paan eater. The moist cachou absorbed the Kewrda fragrance from the leaf and the fragrance enriched cachou filled the breath of the Paan eater with the Kewrda fragrance. The Paan had the age-old custom and its significance. The *Paan Beerda* when lifted when taking a vow, it symbolised pledge to fulfilling a vow and support from the eater to the donor. It meant the eater is going to honour the pledge he made.

The Nature was kind to the people of the Land of Seasons and Songs. Its land was filled with the botanic wonders of unique kinds. Like the Kewrda tree, there was the *Bela* flower bush tree, its flowers carried sweet mild smell, and its white colour reminded of purity. Then there was the *Chambeli* flower with its unique fragrance of utmost in fragrance the nature provided. And man was blessed, there was the yellow bell shaped *Champa* flower, it was so sweet smelling that the snakes became its captive and were entranced by its fragrance and they made their homes in the vicinity of the Champa trees, hiding them in its crevices and climbing to its branches to wallow themselves up in Champa fragrance.

And there was the *Joohi* flower - the night blooming little Chambeli - the Jasmine with its climbing habit, and Nature was kind in the gift of fragrance with its varieties to the peoples of the Land of Seasons and Songs. They only had to sow a seed in grit and soil, and it responded with a parent plant that grew. The Nature attended the seeds from its germination till its tree was strong, lavishing it with the abundance of air, light, heat and moisture to quicken it blossom. Leaves and branches shot out and flower buds raised their heads and daily fresh bunches of flowers laired them on the plant and sprouts sprang out, and tender branches shot out and Nature was incessant and thoughtful and worked round the clock for the people of the Land of Seasons and Songs.

-: . :-

1

THE TRAVELS OF THE PEOPLES

X II

The cold spells in the Land of Seasons and Songs were of extreme severity and putting step out in this weather for a journey was an endearing task. It was suggestive of no pleasure that could be drawn from taking a journey in these conditions of harrying severities. It was to provide no exhilaration to anyone who finally embarked on a journey and took to the errand of going through the perils of journey.

But despite this handicap of the weather severity and the time related shortfall in the facility of travel which clung with the people of the Land of Seasons and Songs with their fluctuating fortune that pulsed with the benignity of their rulers, whose ambitions to rule, ruled their deteriorated benign performances which paced the provisioning of the facilities of travel meagre and wanting, and the people had to travel in these prevailing conditions.

The level of apparels to the people the facility the governance could provide was of extreme scantiness, bordering to negating the requirement of adequacies in the sufficiency of clothing to hold back cold and the wind piercing through to molest and attack the body. And the degrees of insufficiency corroborated with the vulnerabilities of human limitations to tolerance, exceeded all limits. But in spite of these limitations and shortcomings, a vast population of the people from the countryside to countryside made massive counts of movements and made travels in these conditions in their unassuming lives.

People travelled in observance of the rituals and rites of their set beliefs on the calls of religion they followed. Then they travelled to make their normal and urgent family visits to their near and dear ones and to answer to the call of their duties and to discharge their obligations and responsibilities that befell on their shoulders. And the severities of the weather and the vagaries of the climatic abruptness of changes could not stop the activity of these people of this vast Land of God.

The greater number of the people travelled on foot, only some travelled on bullock carts and some comfortably placed in life on bicycles, and some on horseback and others in sedan chairs or the palanquin lifted on the shoulders of the *Kahar(s)* - palanquin bearers. Occasionally people went to avail the service of the *Aekka* - the horse and cart on which they sat and made journey far faster than what they could do on foot or on bullock cart. Of course, to avail the facility of the Aekka, they had to go to the *Aekkewan* – the horse and cart driver and settle a fare to hop on the horse and cart to start their journey. But by far the largest number of the people travelled without anything to ride on. They travelled walking on their bare feet with no shoes on them, showing they had no requirement of any reliance on the need of a pair of shoes.

This was because they had God gifted tough souls of the feet and could travel barefoot on rough and rocky terrain and flat muddy land with equal ease, notwithstanding the vagaries of the weather standing in the way. And they travelled bare feet, more bound by the style of their living and their tradition than they gave any thought to express the pain it might cause to the flesh constituting the sole they possessed. These tough people showed a pre-formed habit and a heightened ostentation not to change their contentedness to live as they lived in the circumstances of their creation, not allowing their overbearing in contentedness and their practice of detached seclusion enter adventurism to probe into any professionalism and generate money to spend what they had to spend on buying a pair of shoes. And that was why they did not own a pair of shoes for walking with, and also did not want to know of them, and never thought of a pair of shoes as primary an object of any primal importance and continued with their style of living as they ever did - disowning a pair of shoes.

Some among them, even if they did possess money for buying a pair of shoes, showed a whole lot of affinity to travelling bare feet and did not want to spend money on a pair of shoes, and they felt just as comfortable without a pair of shoes as those with it, and were amply demonstrative of it by showing an all-out reliance for walking bare foot, making good use of their God given tough soles of their feet, walking on hard stony grounds and on soft mud tracks with equal ease, and never showed, they were missing the luxury of a pair of shoes which were a paraphernalia ready to strip them of their ruggedness.

And so, even when they did have a pair of shoes, they walked as of preference bare foot and hung the shoes for display as a token of their high possession from the end of their *Lathdi* – the staff of solid bamboo, of close knots, which they kept oiled with great care and carried along with them for self-protection on journeys to territories foreign to them. Their Lathdi pivoted on their shoulder with its major part extending behind them and the shoes hung, slipped one over the other at the end of the Lathdi from the last knot of the Lathdi.

The shoes were taken off from the feet and hung from the Lathdi for saving the soles of the shoes from getting worn out, and instead the soles of the feet were used, because they knew the soles of their feet were not a thing to wear out, but the soles of the shoes were. And thanks to the Merciful God, Who made the soles of their feet so tough and endearing that it allowed them take liberty with their soles of the feet, which saved the wearing away of the soles of their shoes.

But with all that on, giving circumstantial evidence of the era and the prideful custom and the cultural norms governing the reason for the walking men travelling bare feet, there was one other good reason for walking bare feet and hanging the pair of the shoes from the Lathdi. The commodities were short and hard to get at, and the shoe maker (the Mochi) making the shoes was not easily got to. Only one heard of a person who lived somewhere out at a distance in the hutments that he made a pair of shoes, and that he was an artisan - a Dustkaar and made cheap pair of shoes from raw hides of the grazing and chewing animals, like deer, nylghaus, antelopes or *Sanburs* - the horse size deer with his golden hair cropping. These species were hunted to get their hide. The shoemaker made a hard-wearing pair of shoes from these Sanbur class hides. The wearer only had to go and hunt, skin the species, eat its meat or give away to one who ate, or leave it to the beasts. He took the hide to the craftsman – the shoemaker - Mochi to get his pair of shoes made.

The shoemaker examined the hide brought to him and used the tanbark of some tree like the *Sheesham* tree, oak or hemlock and tanned the hide. After the hide was so cured and treated, he stretched it to remove its shrinkages and hammered it to a doughty compactness. The craftsman then started to cut the soles of the shoes and its uppers. The soles he made from the thick, compacted part of the hide and the uppers from the thin soft part of the hide, keeping the utility requirement of the tough and the soft part of the skin in mind. And the all-eager shoe wearer wanting the shoe made with all perfections, sat watching the craftsman - breathing down his neck and watching his every move with his open eyes that he puts the best of his skill to make a lasting pair of shoes for him. He sat all through by the shoemaking, watching the shoemaker closely.

The shoemaker cut each piece of the leather to measurement, using his best cobbler or Mochi skill and sewed them up, readying the shoes. But there was no guarantee from him that the shoes were going to be kinder to the feet, and that they will not bite the skin of the feet, though he advised to use plenty of mustard oil to keep the shoes soft and no matter how much mustard oil the wearer put to soak the leather to keep it leathery as the shoe maker had advised, it still most rudely bit his feet and scraped off a chip of the skin from the top of the toe and at the back of the heal. And this was one other reason the shoes were hung from the end of the Lathdi to allow the bitten skin get healed and as the economics to save the sole of shoes was in sight, invariably the traveller had to hang his shoes from his Lathdi when he was out on a long journey on foot.

The compulsion then to hang the shoes from the end of the Lathdi were of three kinds; one when the wearer had to hang it to let his bitten feet be healed, the other one when he wanted to save the sole of the shoes from getting worn away and the other when he used his precautionary instinct and took the shoes off to hang them from the Lathdi to save his feet from being bitten. These were fairly understandable reasons. But the reason to hang the shoes from the end of the Lathdi to make known that the prideful individual hanging the pair of the shoes from the Lathdi owned a pair of shoes, betrayed the era of the heightened deprival and the era of simplicities, and this ostentation was of significance showing love of materialism, showing conservation of their precious possession. This impressive display was made by the most backward but the most simplistic of the people.

These simplistic people came from the forlorn hill tops, where the cultural ingress of the enlightened twentieth century had not touched its borders and where time stood still and the awareness had not been awakened in the primitive tribes of the docile *Muss-har* - the race mostly found in the hills, only some of them on the plains doing *Kahar* duties - lifting sedan chairs of the gentries, or there were other slave like race, the breed of *Chamar* living in the plains doing skinning of dead animals, or like the tough *Paasi* doing on order killing of the rival for someone. They did the slaying of the enemy of the paying with dagger, cutting the enemy's throat for small payment. These they did in the dark of nights in the *Khet Khalyan* – in the barns and associated threshing field, where they found the innocent enemy sleeping.

The trait of displaying the pair of the shoes hanging at the end of the Lathdi was to do with their cultural bind and their primitiveness tied to their class. This was by their own design and their discretion as they were bound to depict it in the practice of protectionism, where in all events they had to put a bold front hiding their deprivations and displaying their exclusive possession - the pair of the shoes they owned, and this was the show of the heightened ego. Showing innocuously, with heightened pride and that was the prime reason out of the major reasons when they hung the pair of the shoes at the end of the glistening well-oiled Lathdi.

That was why those hermits for their intellect and alertness as their hallmark and their uprightness as their elbow-rest, with their superior meditative power backing their thrust to look into the world spread before them, with their coiled hair forming a knurl over their head, feared those shoes and snubbed the temptation they aroused to put them on and make a display of their possession. They also feared their invasion on their freedom of movement for their deliverances of the bitten feet. But more so, the major reason for their not using the shoes was; the hermit was averse to killing the Sanbur for hide for the shoes and that's why he did not wear the shoes. Instead, he wore simple *Khar`aoon* – the wood slipper wear with its front carrying a mushroom stud that he positioned between his toe and the second finger and gripped the stud by the two fingers.

The hermit with that Khar'aoon stud caught between his toe and the second finger, travelled with them lifting these clear of the ground as if laced to his feet, as he strode walk on the rocky ground, in and around the vicinity of his hermitage on the rock filled hill. These were the cluttering sound makers on the hill tracts. And it was the custom of the beasts that when they heard the cluttering sound of the Hermit's Khar'aoon nearing them, they cleared his way. The hermit walked in these simplistic of the foot wear, near and far from his hermitage with an elegance that was a part of the style of the hermits of his class, ready to peep into the future and bring out prophecies, and prophesy for the morrow.

The prophecies were the gift of his perceiving power he had achieved expertise in it through the means of yoga of meditation, through his controlled breathing, and the stillness in the posture of abyssal silence he entered in, supported by dietary and the control of self in the practice of abstinence, harnessing his mind and attuning the self to achieve purity. And for achieving to these degrees of manifestation, the hermits falling in this distinct class of attainment, placed their huts where even the sound of the barking of the dogs could not reach to their ears to disturb their concentration.

These hermits were after the purification of their inner self, rather than any longing and preference for worldly possessions, and they were hermits not seeking help from any external god, epitomised appearing as portraits in picture forms, presenting gods as God, but after the Wasf – the qualities or the virtues of God for self-support and they relied rather on the power of their soul for the realization of truth than god in a wooden structure or a figure carved from stone of a beautiful human. They searched deep into the inner recesses of their soul and formed their destinies by their own makings. The vehicle taking them there was their ruggedness and it did all to make them stand on their feet in vigour, for identifying them with God and the God's ways.

The only limit was their meditative input and the pouring in of purity and concernment of detachment from vile, and putting labour in the perseverance to bringing out the power of mind to capture vision and enter into the realm of Godliness. And there was no limit to the extent to which they could get to and obtain closeness with the Ultimate Reality – God of the universe. And when their input was unlimited, they said they had united with God. But what was the definition of God the hermit attuned his self to? Only the hermit knew, for these were hermits who demonstrated disposition of complete faith in them and were a world within their selves and could see of the realities not in the sight of others.

These were some of the variants of the cultural wonders to be seen in the Land of Seasons and Songs by an absorbent eye that was never tired of seeing wonders scattered round. These repeated them with frequency and interval in the span of space that complimented to the country's absorbability to spectaculars and creating numina (deities) and classes of human so mystically endowed with power and ability to be coasting with God.

These hermits carried an aura of holiness around them, revealing of their distinctiveness. And these gifted hermits had reached to the climaxes of aggrandizing charms and held these numinous tendencies apparent and concealed and were adored for it, and they were around the corner, but still not to be frequented and reached to by the ordinary and they were not to become too easily got to. But the hermits were a class of their own and the pride of the very cultural might of the Land of Seasons and Songs. And it was something to do with the seasons of the four climates, distinct and auspicial that propelled men and hermits to attain their mystifying grandeurs. And to find these hermits one had to search them and travel to solitary places.

سفر ادیان کا تحفہ
ملا اب مدینہ، کربلا و مکہ
محبت دم بھرے اینجا واونجا
کرو خالص ذہن ہر جاہ کربلا و مکہ

ہوں مسلم ایک اخوّت میں خدایا
کریں زیارت و طوائف برملا
خدا سیدھا سا ہے معبود انکا
بُلاے کربلا، نجف، مدینہ، مگہ جو اسکا
سیّد اطہار حسین

Safar Adyan Ka Tohfa
Mila Ab Madinah, Karbala Wa Makkah
Mohabat Dum Bharay Eenja Wa Oonja
Karo Khali Zehen, Her Jaah Karbala wa Makkah

Hoan Muslim Aek Akhwat Mein Khudaya
Karein Ziyarat Wa Tawaef Barmala
Khuda Seedha Sa Haai Mabood Oonka
Bola-ay Karbala, Najaf, Madinah, Makkah Jo Ooska

Journey is present to the religions of the word
Now got Madinah, Karbala and Makkah
Love spreads warmth here and there
Make your mind sublime every place Karbala and Makkah

The Muslim may become one in brotherhood O' God
May Do pilgrimage and circumambulation openly
Their God is simple deity poised
Calls him to Karbala, Najaf, Madinah, Makkah who is His

-: . :-

1

THE STORY TELLERS

XIII

In the season when the evenings were serene, and weather permitted, the *Palung(s)* (the carry cots) were spread out for sleeping under the glitter of the night sky. There, under the spell of the night sky glittering, the storytellers turned them in the fervour of imaginative mood, and their furtive minds carved out fantastic stories from their fertile story webbing minds. They were intelligent and prankish men like the Hafiz Sahib, and the only essential characteristic about them was their common inheritance to be a jovial personality and they brought out innovative stories full of gimmicks, fantasies and galore ventures' excessiveness.

Hafiz Sahib whose credentials no one had ever bothered to ascertain to test of his being in the class of the *Hafezeen* – those who recited Quran from memory, everyone had accepted him Hafiz as he presented him to them for his witty and a ready to answer mind. He had probably acquired the title of Hafiz from his father and he thought it was a *Mansabí* or a hereditary designation - the family-owned-title. Because for all his apparent habits he revealed, his aptitude had little to do with the memorisation of the Holy Quran in his mind. He was cut only to be an excellent storyteller. But he had other amusing habits. His plucky walk and his conversing in a manner that invariably attracted other's attention towards him was his asset.

Hafiz, who was formally called Hafiz Sahib, came from another town. He was sent by his employer to the farfetched place, who wanted to get rid of him and had sent him to the hilly isolated terrain. He had come to the top of the mountain that God forsaken rocky mountain place, the locals called it 'Thargatwa' for its rugged terrain on an eight-hour climb from the plain below; negotiated by riding in a

154

palanquin which the Muss-hers lifted on their shoulders to climb to the mountain. Hafiz's employer had assigned him an intermediate class of duty there. He was sent there to collect samples of herbs and he said, "What the healthy animals did not eat was herb," and he collected and dispatched these in abundance to his employer from there and on each assignment, he received money. So, it was for his wit that he lived.

Hafiz lived, where the locals lived. He had coined a two-word phrase for them *'Yan-heen Kay'* - you locals - or you belonging to this place. And sometimes he called them – *'Jhan-een Kay'* and he meant you silly - he meant you belong to a class who has haziness in mind and all that. But he would not openly express so and he would muffle the sound and only those who shared his secret and his coded spoken words, knew what he meant, and had difficulty controlling their laughter. He would use the word ten times during his short sentences he spoke with the locals, pretending that to be his *Takiya Kalam* - the expletive and a way that was an associate of him that was not rid able by him, which he pretended, which the locals having a slight disadvantage in the linguistic ways thought odd, but remained cheery with him. And he would also use the word *'Yan-neen Kay'*, that was the commonly understood expletive and that meant 'you mean that'. So, he will fill his talk with, *'Yan-heen Kay'*, *'Jhan-een Kay'*, *'Yan-neen Kay'*.

And he would give a farfetched meaning he supposedly understood of an obvious explanation that was given to him by the locals and use *Yan-neen Kay*, to give them stimulatory assurance that he understood their problem what they were saying if he noticed any lingering doubts developing in their minds about his intention, then immediately he would use *Yan-heen Kay* or *Jhan-een Kay* in the trailing of his sentence drawing attention of the local to otherwise meanings. And with his *Yan-neen kay* he gave a divergent explanation of what the local was saying that he supposedly understood. On which the local corrected him for once again for him to have wrongly understood his problem, and there was always some muddle in the talk.

The word *Yan-heen Kay*, you locals, Hafiz used had a subtle behind it. At the turn of the 19th century the British Colonial Administration was trying to systematically classify and record the population pattern and traits of different people. The local converts to Islam were found in this exercise to retain their Hindu names and customs. Of these the Muslim weavers were slightly more backward, and for retaining their traits and customs they were given the derogatory connotation of *Jolaha* – the ignorant class, and that became their appellation. And soon in these times, with time on, the Jolaha started calling them *Ansari(s)* to gain an equal status within the fraternity of the Islamic communities and to be at par with the Ansaar(s) – the helpers in Madina who had extended invitation to the Prophet SAWW, then received and hosted the Prophet of Islam Hazrat Mohammad Mustafa SAWW in Madina and helped settle the newcomer Muslims from Macca. So, their help was of vital importance and they were called Ansaar.

But despite adapting the name of Ansari the tinkling of the past ways of their living was still dominating the nature of these converts now purified, and they were still following their community trade of weaving, using hand looms set in a pit, dug in the ground in a room of their house. This was menial work, and monotonous in nature and was in no way a task that sharpened wit and aroused any charm and geniality in them. And the Benares Gazetteer of 1909 said, "The Jolaha have always taken a prominent part in religious quarrels."

Hafiz moved by their aberrations and blurring even in marginal matters, and they being hostage as they were to their customs in their Jolaha precincts which was acting as their precursor in all their behaviours, had specially coined the word *Yan-heen Kay* – you locals for them, which somehow befitted their activity. But Hafiz used this phrase Yan-heen Kay for the suspicious Hindu also who felt disturbed with him, whom he found baffled and confounded when he used this gibe.

The other subtle diminishing the status of the Jolaha and others amounting to a subtract of credits from being assimilated as brainy and benevolent people pushing Hafiz locate their name by the pick of the word Yan-heen Kay – you locals, was that the general people, who were there in these backward areas of the country had contributed to the flourish of no art and to the advancement of no culture and they simply lived their lives, which was observed as a negative point and not a cognizable credit of any kind by Hafiz.

There was no genealogy to speak of among them of persons like Mohammad Ali Jinnah creating a country, or like Mohan Das Karam

Chand Gandhi reviving Ahinsa, or like Mao Tse Tung launching his long march for great leap forward, putting China on its feet, or like Imam Roohullah Khomeini, demolishing imperialism in Iran and revolutionising the world, or like of Prince Shah Karin Agha Khan of philanthropic disposition, patron of fine architecture, awarding prizes in architectural excellences and serving to enhance people's facilities in health or like Agha Hasan Abedi building mighty BCCI and giving to the third world monetary help, including funding to the Carter Centre and other Carter charities.

These locals simply lived and despite progress of time in front of them unreeling daily happenings, they were unconcerned with it, keeping their door of knowledge shut. And they continued going to the fields to meet their call of nature and used cow-dung to burn to cook their food and reflected abyssal ignorance about anything not indigenous and remained contended with their standstill or reverse progress. And Hafiz for these questioning traits with them and with no incurring zest shown by them to philanthropic tendencies, or excellences coming out of them to harness culture and beautify civilisation or generate money to enrich the world in thoughts and means, called them *Yan-heen Kay*.

Hafiz one day was sitting when a local walked in to him. He was Hindi local. He had eaten something, and his stomach had gone bad for that. He went to the *Hakeem* – a sort of inferring and intuitive doctor. The Hakeem had come to practice there in this detached mountain place called Naugardh primeval in its looks, on top of the mountain. The local went to him to get treatment, for the Hakeem (s) had a lot of self-faith in them and were very good at solving stomach problems. The local went to him for his unsettled stomach cured and the Hakeem gave him something and he started passing mucus.

The local had never found him in that state. He thought his intestines were being cut and made to be purged and thrown out of him. When he went to the field for relieving him, he saw only mucus there, and that had become very frequent and intense, he had to go sit squatting for long and pass lots of mucus and he was very angry with the Hakeem. He thought the Hakeem purposely had resigned him to die like that and soon there would be nothing left of his intestine. He was bemoaning like that and came to the Hafiz Sahib to complain to him about the Hakeem, whom the local thought was from one of the kith and kin of Hafiz and had given him medicine to die. The local made gruelling faces and expressed pain and fears and repentances for going to the Hakeem at all. And he said his mistake was, he ever went to the Hakeem.

Hafiz listened to him among his lots of butting in of *Yan-heen Kay* and sometimes *Jhan-een Kay* and also *Yan-neen Kay* and was bemused to hear of his story and his fear of his intestine. Hafiz dismissed him finally after listening to him at length and said to him, "Listen Yan-heen Kay, the Mars is in the sixth house of the Zodiac and it is casting its harassing influence on you and is sending you to the fields for purging mucus."

He said, "Take red-brick-coloured thread and wrap it round you to simulate you are a Martian and the Mars will think that you are a Martian and that will be the secret to befriend with the planet and your mucus will stop."

It was then when the local was talking to Hafiz and Hafiz was briefing the local that he thought of a story and declared to the young team of the story listeners that tonight he was going to tell a new story.

Hafiz had invented a new story then and there, while he was listening to the misery of the local about his suffering from mucus purge that how his intestines were being cut and thrown out. The story came from the shoot of his imagination. The episode of the local made Hafiz invent the story of *Hakeem Sana-ay*[19]. The young team of the story listeners on that good news from Hafiz that they are to hear a new story that night wound up early and spread their Palung(s) close to Hafiz's Palung to listen to the new story Hafiz was going to tell. The night was still and quiet, and silence prevailed on the plain of that mountain-top and the stars were shining, and these seemed all so close all round to the story listeners at the height of the mountain, as if they were going to listen to the story. There these general conditions

---

[19] The real Hakeem Sanai was a Persian poet of Afghanistan in the times of Mehmood Ghaznavi. His tomb is in Ghazni near Kabul in Afghanistan. But the witty nature of Hafiz had invented the name 'Hakeem Sana-ay', which alluded to the the herb Sana and its qualities.

prevailed in the atmosphere, enough to boost trigger Hafiz's mind and Hafiz had a mind seethed with humour and he started the story:

"Sometimes back a very able Hakeem lived in a kingdom. He had a very nice *Matab* – the clinic, with a patient examination place and a prescription dispensing workplace. The Hakeem sat in this Matab and examined the patients. And medicine was dispensed by the Attar – the dispenser against the prescription written by the Hakim. One wall of the Matab had a wooden frame with chest of drawers, which carried herbal medicines and the Attar had an apprentice (Shagird) to bring to him medicine from the herb stock, placed in the drawers and elsewhere and the *Attar* sat there and prepared and bound the medicine pack and dispensed these to the patients.

The Hakeem was very famous for curing all kinds of ailments. He had a son whom he wanted to teach everything of the good practice of the *Hikmat* – wisdom of practicing in the herbal medicine, but the son whiled away his time and did not learn anything about Hikmat while his father lived, who one day died.

Now the responsibility of running the Matab suddenly fell on the shoulders of the son to serve his town's men, but he did not go near to the Matab since he did not know anything about Hikmat. Luckily for him, his father the great Hakeem had married him to an able wife, who when she saw there was no way out of the misery taking hold of them due to poverty surrounding them and the people of the town expected the Matab to be opened and the son of the Hakeem serve them in the fashion his father was serving them, she pepped him up and said, "you can do it if you keep your wits about you."

She asked him, "Over all these years that you were with your father, do you remember anything of the names of the herbs that your father served to the patients?"

He said he does not remember of anything except of the *Sana* – the cassia senn. He said, "I saw Sana was given as laxative."

Now sana – the dried pods of the cassia plant were a mild laxative, but the great Hakeem his father used it in numerous ways, which were related with the classical knowledge of the Hikmat. He used it, to purge fear and worries and he also used it for bringing out repressed ideas and unpleasant experiences of the patients into conscious awareness after overhauling the patient and ridding them of the

159

patient like condition and he also used it to unravel philosophic deep sitting thoughts in the patients, revitalising their existing traces of genealogical philosophic links in them and achieving to enhancing their character to revering status. And he also used the Sana for purging hardened faeces in constipated conditions and evacuating the stubborn knotty faeces of the patients that had been resting inside hidden, disturbing plausibility of normal health. In such instances of the hardened cases, he used a fair amount of the Sana on them. But the specialty of the Sana was that if it was used purely for purging, and if used in excessive measures, it induced very excessive purging.

The wise wife of the young Hakeem was very pleased to hear from her young Hakeem husband of 'Sana' that he knew of, and she said, "That would do, now you go and start the Matab," and she said to him, "You open the Matab and sit there in the manner of your father and give the dose of the Sana to your patients."

The young son of the great Hakeem put on the big white turban of his father on his head and went and opened the Matab in the manner of his father and the wise wife put his name on a nameplate, which read: 'Hakeem Sana-ay.'

The people when they saw the young carefree - a disaster of a son, at last is taking to his father's way, they were very pleased. They became convinced of the hereditary transfer of qualities and said all this was a family trait and they were excited at the prospect of the new Hakeem sitting there in the Matab, waiting to serve and he in all appearance ready and fit to serve them. But still they watched his Matab from a distance till he had proved his worthiness for assuming the office of the Hikmat.

After some time, a *Dhobi* - a washerman came to the young Hakeem. He was in trouble since his donkey was lost and he had to carry the load of the washing on his back from the riverbank to his house each day after the wash, which the donkey carried. And now that the donkey had disappeared, he could not carry as much load as the donkey did and he was lagging in washing and had to listen to the abuses and threatening talks and listen to all the 'Daant' - rebuke of his customers each day. Some of them even threatened to beat him up for not washing their clothes on time. And the washer man was in deep trouble since the donkey was lost.

The washer man pleaded to the young Hakeem to bring cure to his problem as quickly as possible and set him to find his donkey. The young Hakeem said, 'there was no problem, you will find your donkey' and he gave him a full load of a heavy dose of Sana to put him to find his donkey quickly.

The Sana immediately started its work to make the washer man run to the fields into the bushes all day and night and in one of these runs while he was purging himself, he encountered the donkey. Some bits of the purging flew and fell on the ears of the donkey, who was hiding in the bushes there. The donkey curled his ears in disgust and flapped them to rid of the purge and the Dhobi knew who flapped the ears and he jumped from his place in the bush holding his Dhoti — waist piece and caught the donkey by his ear.

The washer man was very angry with the donkey that he put him to so much trouble of purging before he let him catch him. He brought the donkey home. But by this time, he was exhausted due to purging and he lay him on the cot outside. His fellow *Dhobis* saw his condition like that and they decided to take him to the young Hakeem to inform him of the recovery of the donkey and to ask him that the job was done and his purging was not needed now and he stop it. They lifted the cot on their shoulders and carried to the young Hakeem. The young Hakeem when he saw the washerman is being brought to him sprawled on a Palang, thought this was it, my end has come, the washerman due to purging has let go life and the Dhobies are bringing the dead Dhobi to put life in him. He saw trouble coming closer and closer, and he at once as fast as he could started reciting:

Jallay Jalal Too, Saahebay Kamal Too, Aa-ee Bala Ko Taal Too. Jallay Jalal Too, Saahebay Kamal Too, Aa-ee Bala Ko Taal Too.

'You of glory and greatness, You owner of perfection; the trouble that is coming now push it away!'

This was the repeated call given to God to quickly come to aid and rescue the reciting from the coming disaster. The young Hakeem recited the imploration in desperation as fast as he could, repeating it faster and faster to be quickly effective

The Hakim quickly repeated the vird faster and faster to God to quickly come to help and rescue him from the coming disaster. Because the young Hakeem thought the Dhobi due to excessive purging had let go of life, and the Dhobis were bringing his dead body to him to blow life in him. He recited the imploration in desperation as fast as he could, repeating it faster and faster to be quickly effective.

These extreme implorations were made in extreme distress by someone caught in unexpected deep trouble. And the intensity of the imploration and its vigour of repetition spoke of the seriousness of the problem. And the recitation mode was direct to God, for Him to come and save the neck of the pleading, already fast landing in trouble and the troubled beseeched to dissipate his trouble. This invariably amused God, and this recipe provided a fair guarantee that the trouble will evaporate. And luckily it happened just in that like manner for the young Hakeem. The Dhobis were bringing the Dhobi to him sprawled on the cot because of his lots of purging that he had done, he was left with very little life in him to walk to the Matab of the Hakeem on his feet, but the Dhobi was still alive and breathing.

When the young Hakeem Sana-ay came to know of the case that the donkey was found, and the Dhobi was alive, he thanked God for that but soon he was asked by the team of the Dhobis to stop his purging.

This, the young Hakeem did not know anything about, as to what to do and what not to do, to stop his purging. He ran to his wife and said to her, "Begum I was saying, don't push me into it, now this is it, the end of me. As soon as the Dhobi dies, the other Dhobis will kill me. I have seen them washing, how they smash and wring: *"Woh Hamein Patakh Patakh Kay Mar Deingay"* – 'they will smash and smash me against the ground and kill me.'

And the young Hakeem was bewailing, "Now there is no chance of my remaining alive and now there are only moments left of my life and you are going to be to be a widow in this world."

The young Hakeem was doing 'Baain' – heart rending talk like that and said, "I wish I had not listened to you and had not sat in the Matab and started that Hikmat."

The wise wife of the young Hakeem listened to the wailing and the Baain – lamentation of her young Hakeem husband and realised the matter was serious but she kept her wits about her and she said to her young Hakeem husband, "Calm yourself down, and control yourself while I think of something" and she went round in the house, looking for something to work to nullify the caustic effect in the stomach of the fallen Dhobi and arrest the emotional breakdown of her young Hakeem husband and she found a lump of *Gurd* – a piece of dried molasses in the house. She picked it up and gave it to her young Hakeem husband and said, "Go and give this Gurd to the Dhobi immediately, he needs some strength to hold on to life and then we shall think of something afterwards."

The young Hakeem rushed with the Gurd to the Dhobi and gave it to him to eat it immediately. And as soon as the Dhobi took the Gurd, its constituents immediately started working. The bitter and corrosive effect of the Sana started dying down, and the Dhobi soon recovered his strength. He was rid of his purging and turned fit and well.

All the Dhobis profusely thanked the young Hakeem for being so great a Hakeem and solving their problem. And all the Dhobis praised and admired the young Hakeem. The patient Dhobi now cured so thanked the young Hakeem and promised to him to wash his clothes free all his life, with *Kalaf* and *Abrak* – the starch and with shine of mica applied on them and so promising all that to the young Hakeem, all the Dhobis left for their homes.

The news of the young Hakeem's mastery in Hikmat spread all round like wild fire. And he became a full-fledged famous Hakeem instantly afterwards, and there were two wonder medicines the Hakeem used; the 'Gurd' and the 'Sana' through which he conquered all the ills and solved all the problems of the people. And people started coming to him one after the other with problems.

One day a tailor came to the Hakeem. He had lost his needle and he had to sew lots of clothes of his customers given to him for sewing for Eid, and Eid was near and his needle had got lost and the tailor was worried to death that if he did not sew the clothes and returned them to the customers before the Eid, he is going to be in trouble, he will have nowhere to hide his face. He said people will beat him up and chase him out of the village. Hakeem Sana-ay said, "I understand your problem" and assured him he will find his needle and gave him a hefty amount of Sana for curing his ill and removing his misfortune quickly.

The tailor had a frail body and after a few hefty purges from the Sana spread his already weak and frail body on the bed. He was weak and thin and with the purging there was nothing left in him and he was

163

inching nearer to death and lay himself on the bed. His relatives thought his worries had taken him to this end and he will be no more with them and they gathered around him in this hour of peril to be with him at the last moments of his life.

The weak tailor was lying on the bed and his eyes were up looking towards the ceiling, then suddenly he saw the needle stuck in the spider's web above his head in the ceiling. The needle had flown up and got stuck there when the tailor was giving a good shake to a dress he had finished sewing. The weak tailor hardly able to mumble a word raised his first finger up towards the needle, and his relatives who had all gathered there, started wailing, thinking he was pointing towards the High God to inform others that his time was up and he was about to meet Him and he was saying good bye to them and to this transitory world. But the tailor meant to point to the needle stuck up above his head.

The tailor was very annoyed that his relatives cried so hard for nothing and not listened to him and not followed the direction of his finger and in anger raised his shaking finger again towards the needle and mumbled the name of the needle in this weak condition, which no one understood, and people started wailing louder, thinking he is now informing of his hurried departure. The tailor was now furious and shaking with anger raised his finger up and this time there was greater wailing. There was great consoling to each other and everyone thought he was hurrying his departure from the world, but the tailor was very, very angry and contemptuous at the wit of his relatives, and he pushed his finger higher up and this time at that very moment someone saw in the direction of the finger and saw the needle stuck in the web and they understood why the tailor was raising the finger up each time and the wailing of relatives that he is nearly gone was for no cause. And so, went the story and there were always plots added to it.

The needle was taken down and given to the tailor, and they rushed to the Hakeem to inform him that the tailor has got the needle, now he needs to be put to stop purging. The Hakeem hurried to send the doze of Gurd with them and the purging of the tailor stopped with it and everyone was so thankful to the Hakeem. The tailor pledged he will sew all the clothes for the Hakeem for life, free of charge.

The story webbing mind of Hafiz knew no bounds in producing new scenes and plots, drawing them out of his mind. The weather spurred him, and the keenness of his story listeners made him keep adding fantasies to the stories. Hafiz said:

"The fame of Hakeem Sana-ay's miraculous cure reached to the King and the King was in trouble. He was facing a threat from his enemy King who had massed a big army at the kingdom's doorstep. The enemy king said, "Boundary or no boundary, he was going to march and take the capital." And he was getting ready to attack the kingdom and the King was very worried indeed. The King sent for the Hakeem to come to his help and turn the tables on his enemy and solve his problem.

The wise wife of the Hakeem when she heard of the call from the King, said to her young Hakeem husband:

"The Dhobis did not kill you but be sure the king will certainly kill you, if you fail to win the battle for him, so do as I say." She said, "You enter in the King's fort like a big big Hakeem. This is battle of wit, and you have to first win the support of the courtiers to win the battle, and defeat the King's enemy."

The wise wife of the Hakeem took charge of the whole situation and sent a message to the King to send two bullock carts to carry the books of the Hakeem and she asked the King that all the courtiers should be assembled in the courtyard outside the palace to receive the Hakeem when he enters the palace gates.

The King sent two bullock carts pulled by pair of strong oxen each, and these were big carts and she had not many books. The wife of the Hakeem therefore put many bricks on the deck of the bullock carts and covered them with *Ghas Phoos* – weed, dry grass and straw and she put the few books the Hakeem had on top of the Ghas Phoos to make the bulk of the books look big. And she gave the young Hakeem a hundred-arm's length long white *Safa* – the turban, and told the young Hakeem to start winding on his head when he starts entering the gates of the fort. Also, the wise wife told her young Hakeem husband:

"As you enter in the King's fort start winding the Safa on your head and let its length trail, so that it is dragging itself on the floor and you keep yourself busy winding the turban, as you enter the fort."

This she said was to tell the courtiers how big and wise a head you had, full of wisdom, like the overflowing trail of the Safa, And the wise wife said to her young Hakeem husband:

"The Kings go by the words of the courtiers, so do not forget to impress the courtiers that you have as wise a head as the huge white turban you were wearing." And so briefed, the wise wife sent her young Hakeem husband to the King's palace.

All the courtiers had assembled outside in the palace courtyard of the fort before the Hakeem arrived. They received the Hakeem whom they knew, his intellect and two wonder medicines solved big problems. This was exactly as the wise wife of the Hakeem wanted. The courtiers when they saw the Hakeem enter the court yard of the palace with two cartloads of books with Hakeem winding the Safa and its trail trailing, bowed their heads and were convinced that the Hakeem held great knowledge and all the likely opposition from anyone of them doubting in the ability of the Hakeem to solve a military problem disappeared. And as for the King, he was all ears to listen to Hakeem Sana-ay's diagnosis for the problem his kingdom was facing.

The Hakeem after hearing something of the problem immediately made the successful diagnosis and ordered to gather all the Sana and all the Gurd there was in the kingdom. He also ordered that all the fat *Koonjrdas* – the vegetable and green leaves vendors in the kingdom, all of them with fat bellies and huge bottoms be gathered on the high ground, where the enemy was masquerading. And all the Koonjrdas – green grossers have their buttocks facing in the direction of the enemy line. He said they were to be utilised in the battle. And he announced one Tola of the Sana to be given to each fighting soldier and two Tolas of it to be given to each of those fat Koonjrdas.

The news of the preparations by the King reached to the enemy King through his informers and spies, and the spies, least to say they were bewildered. They wondered what the King was up to. They knew for sure he was up to some tricks laying trap for them, gathering Sana and Gurd. The enemy King found out that there was one Hakeem Sana-ay who was doing it all and he will give Sana to the King's army and the Gurd was a diversionary tactic and so was the gathering of the hefty Koonjrdas. And they were sure the Sana was to pep up the army so on that information they gathered steam to defeat the king completely.

They therefore, also started gathering all the Sana that there was in their kingdom and they did not give importance to Gurd. And since they had found it was one Tola that the Hakeem Sana-ay had prescribed for the King's army, they decided to give two Tolas to each of their troops and before the King gave it to his army they quickly served it to their army to be one up and they all lied flat in the battle field with their mess and the King's army recovered sooner for they took only one Tola of Sana and also there was Gurd behind it and they charged after taking Gurd on the wearied soldiers of the enemy King and ran over them.

Their victory was made further easy by the hefty Koonjrdas. Before the army charging on the enemy, the hefty Koonjrdas whose stomachs were so very strong that it took the Sana and only responded to the Sana in measures that they created only foul nauseating gas and started farting. They were immediately ordered to swing their bottoms from their positions towards the front line of the enemy and direct the gases towards them, which when it reached diffusing its stink to the enemy, they thought the King had invented some poisonous gas and was directing this foul gas at them and they were all frightened to death and gave up.

The battle was won without much ado and the enemy was routed without much resistance offered by the enemy King. Most of the enemy soldiers were captured half faint and pretty exhausted and the enemy was completely run over and defeated.

Hafiz seemed to be greatly against the expansionist armies fighting for territorial expansion. Such battles were in greed, not for exporting a superior ideology and Hafiz always gave some account of debacle in such fights and in this took aid of ridiculous statements by creating extraordinary plots in the battle.

Hafiz under the glitter of the stars in the sky and the trail of the shooting stars[20] across the sky and the listener's expectancies to hear fantasies; on the flat top of the Thargatwa Mountain, produced each

---

[20] Shooting star is a flaming stellar projectile of a speck of cosmic dust, heated with friction into flame and glow.

night new fantastic story. One day he would tell the story of a mighty demon and the next day of a sweet, humble Prince and the next day another new story to the listeners. And the listeners always wanted to hear from him of his praise worthy extolment of meek and weak and denouncement of extrication of devils.

One night the young listeners were all ears to Hafiz, when he told the story of a 'Demon and the Princess'. The Demon was the big fierce *Dev* living in his magic fort in his hideout and he had an eye on the beautiful Princess of the kingdom. The Demon abducted the dainty Princess from the King's palace. The Princess was only strolling in the garden when this happened. He abducted her to his hideout and turned *Tiles* - a connivance of trick on her and confined her to a bed in his hideout – the magic fort.

The Tilism was that when the Dev exchanged the *Sirhanay Ki Patti* with the *Paitanay Ki Patti* – the head side wood with the feet side wood of the Princess's bed, the Princess became unconscious and when he put the sides in their original positions the Princess became alive. The Dev made the Princess sleep when he left his fort and made her awake when he returned by exchanging the sides. The demon after his day long excursions would come in the evenings and after making the princess awake, will ask her to marry him. But each time the brave Princess refused, and she continued to deny marrying him, till at last her Prince in love with her, searching her in every nook and cranny, found her.

The Prince had to cross many, many hurdles of fiery rivers, fierce jungles, deserts, after these he came across a fierce lake in which water globules were rising from its centre, and these were travelling towards the shore of the lake and were red blobs of blood from the mouth of the Princess, each blob coming to the shore to the feet of the Prince and turning into a jewel. The Prince when he smelled the jewels, they were giving the smell of the Princess. And the Prince knew that the Princess was at the bottom of the lake.

So, the Prince swam hard towards the centre of the lake against the waves of the water, but the waves were forcing him back, dispelling him stay away, but he swam against the forcing waves and he had to use so much force that blood came out of his mouth but he did not stop and continued fighting with the force stopping him to get to the centre. The two drops of blood from him and that of the Princess each

168

advanced and combined, floating to the shore and together turned into bigger jewels than before – so said Hafiz!

After a great fight against the dispelling force at last the Prince reached to the centre of the lake and entered the whirl pool. There was a gate below and the Prince had to heave and push the gate to open and enter in the magic fort wherein the Princess was kept captive in one room by the Dev. The Prince searched in the fort looking for the Princess and at last found the Princess. She was on a bed and drops of blood one after the other fell from her mouth, which, were swept by the lake and they turned into jewels at the shore of the lake. The Prince had found the Princess, but just then the Prince heard a great rumbling sound getting nearer to him and he hid him below the bed. A huge Dev entered in the room of the Princess and the Prince saw the Dev is sniffing and his prying eyes are searching something.

The Prince saw the Dev exchange the head side wood of the Princess' bed with the feet side wood. This made the Princess wake up and he said to the Princess, he smelled of human smell and said; *Bun Manus, Bun Manus* – there is human, there is human here. But the Princess was surprised and she said she was the only human that there was in this place.

For the Dev(s), the human beings were inferior creatures and the Devs were of the superior kinds of race, and all the Devs called the human beings '*Manus*'.

Hafiz said, the *Parayana* - discourses of the past on religion, revealed the first King of the Land of Seasons and Songs was Manu Svayambhu – the self-born. When god Brahma decided to create Manu, he had him born of him - as his own being. Manu was a hermaphrodite, he had both male and female reproductive organs as some flowers have, and he bore two sons and three daughters from him, from whom a series of Manus a kind of human race of the kind of Adam like features were born and Manu had started their origin. Hafiz said, the superiority notion of the Devs over human was in keeping with their claim that because they were made from smoke, some of their kinds from fire they were superior to human made from soil. Also, that they had a larger variety of races among them than human and each race of them competed for domination of power on earth and the women class of the human were their weakness.

When the Dev came in the room and made the Princess awake to enquire her if she will marry him. the Prince saw his method and when the Dev was gone, he made the Princess awake as the Dev had done. The Princess became a blossom of joy to see the Prince and the Prince knew no bounds of joy to have the Princess alive and safe. The Prince said to the Princess, next time when the Dev comes to ask you for marriage, ask him where he keeps his *Jaan* – the soul. The Prince said he will destroy it once he knew where it was, and they will be free. And he then put the Princess in the state she was in for Dev to find the Princess in that state he had left. The Dev when he came again repeated the words, Bun Manus Bun Manus, after he awakened the princess by exchanging the head side with the foot side and the Princess replied, it is me the human. Then the Princess asked the Dev. "I want to know where your life resides."

Now this was an intimate question asked by the Princess and the Dev thought the princess was turning her attention towards him. The Dev thought she was inclined to give consent of marriage to him and the Dev told the Princess that his soul resided in the parrot. There was a parrot sitting high up in the vault of the wall. The parrot was concealing him with his wings.

The demons kept their lives safely stowed away with great care in contrivances not to be suspected of carrying their lives in them. And this demon had kept his soul in a parrot that sat high in the niche of the wall. So, with that secret known now it was easy, when the Demon was gone, the Prince made the Princess to awaken herself and he reached to get the fake parrot in which the life of the Demon resided and he had to use all his force to push his arm to reach to it, because a barrier of unseen force resisted him and stopped his hand reach to the parrot.

The Demon was on visit to a far-off place, but immediately he came to know that his soul was in trouble and he rushed back hurling him to reach to the parrot, but the Prince's hand had already reached to the neck of the parrot and he had started to strangle the parrot, squeezing life out of the Demon. The Demon slumped at the door of the Princess' room and as he fell the fort started crumbling. The Demon had fallen at the last minute and the Prince's life just saved from the iron hands of the Demon reaching to the throat of the Prince. But the Prince had wrenched the parrot's neck and the demon was dead.

The fort disappeared and everything suddenly turned real. The Prince and the Princess found they were standing in the middle of a desert, and there were only jewels left there. They took a collection of big and small jewels and started walking through the desert in the direction of the palace and at last reached back to the palace where the Princess lived. The King was full of joy that the princess was liberated by the Prince. Everyone celebrated and acknowledged Prince's bravery and the King married the Princess to the Prince and they lived happily ever after.

Hafiz one night told the story of a sweet Prince who was victim of his rival brothers. Hafiz said a very sweet Prince lived in a kingdom with his five Prince Brothers. The sweet Prince was the youngest among them and he was more loved by the King for his good nature than the other five brothers. The five brothers were jealous of the sweet Prince and thought he was the cause of the King not loving them so much as him. So, they poorly treated him and had no opportunity not to abuse him. The Prince was treated harshly and deprived of good things and forced to wear tattered clothes by the brothers who made him look a lowly person in the palace.

The good-natured sweet Prince suffered all this infliction. Then one day there was a Soyember in another Kingdom. This was an event in which the Princess of the kingdom was to sit in the Soyember and all the Princes were to assemble from different kingdoms to try to win the hand of the Princess through competition between them. The custom was, in these Soyembers a damsel, whose match was sought, either herself selected her husband from the eligible men gathered or the Princes gathered, solved a riddle in the assembly of the competition arena and won her as spouse.

In this Soyember there was going to be a contest, and the princess was to be married to the winner. It was a haughty beautiful Princess and it was a tough Soyember. Many Princes had come to contest in the open Soyember in the kingdom and so were the five brothers who had come there, but had forbidden the sweet Prince from going to that Soyember.

The sweet Prince was left behind, so he went to the hills as he was dismembered as a prince. There he heard the moan of someone coming from a cavity in the mountain side. It was a poor demon imprisoned in the cavity shut by a huge boulder of rock. The poor demon was bound by the magic spell and was made powerless by his rival powerful demon. And the poor helpless demon could do nothing to get out, till the sweet Prince passed from there. The Prince heard the voice of the demon appealing for help from behind the boulder. The demon pleaded to get him freed. The Prince took pity on him and brought a big log of wood and made a fulcrum of it and toppled the heavy stone with a heave and the demon was free.

The demon was very grateful to the Prince for freeing him. In gratitude he plucked out seven of his hairs from his head and gave them to the sweet Prince and said to the Prince, "I will appear in front of you on seven occasions, when one hair of these seven hairs you will hold facing to the sun. Then whatever wish you will make, I promise, I will make them come true."

The Prince thanked the Demon and took the seven hairs to the palace and on the first day of the seven-day Soyember, the Prince remembered of the demon's gift and showed one hair to the sun. The Demon immediately appeared in front of him. The Prince said to him, he wants to go to the Soyember. The good demon provided the sweet Prince a princely dress, horse to ride on, which was decorated with a *Kulghi* - the plume on his forehead and a matching saddle was on the horse and the horse took him to the Soyember flying. And on each of the seven days, he showed a hair to the sun, and on each occasion a different dress of a different colour, with a flying horse with saddle of the colour of the Prince's dress appeared in front of the Prince.

The horse was always wearing a *Kulghi* – the plume on his head, and took the Prince to the Soyember where the haughty beautiful princess was, who was waiting for beautiful and gallant prospective fiancé to appear in the contest to match her. She had agreed to hold a Soyember only to prove that there was no bride-groom to match her in beauty and charm, but this prince was to outdo her.

The five Prince Brothers who had arrived at the Soyember; hoped one of them will win the hand of the haughty beautiful princess and they wanted to show to the King father that they were more talented than the sweet Prince whom he so dearly loved more than all of them. But every day at the contest in the Soyember, a young Prince wearing a veil on his face excelled all the Princes by flying his horse high in the Soyember and pass showing him to the Princess. For when all the contestants had failed to take their horses high up by spurring the horses to jump, the sweet Prince's horse took off and made a very high jump in the air coming in level with the *Jharooka* – the narrow opening in the wall where the Princess was sitting. The prince could not be recognised, and certainly not by his brothers, whom they thought they had left him behind and the Prince every time reached face to face with the Princess of the Soyember and struck her with small soft ball as was to be done in the Soyember. The condition to win the Princess was to hit the Princess with ball in the middle of her chest right in the centre.

The Prince each time came in level with the haughty beautiful Princess sitting in the window an opening in the high straight wall, there each time the haughty Princess was hit with the ball and as the Princess's condition was that she will marry only that Prince who could make his horse jump that high and hit her in the middle of the chest in the Jharooka, full ten feet high in the high wall, the condition was met. But the next condition that the cotton ball bouncing back after hitting her in the middle of the chest, the Prince should catch and present that to her as evidence, was not met.

The sweet Prince hit the princess with the ball each time as desired by the Princess, and it hit her in the middle of the chest between buds and bounced back at different angles and came into the hands of the Prince. The Princess had announced the ball will carry her scent when it hits her at the right place and she had announced if caught on its bounce back by the Prince hitting her and he presented the ball to her, she will marry that Prince but the princess was being frustrated.

No Prince could do that save the sweet Prince who had now done it six times on six consecutive days running, as was the condition and the sweet Prince had disappeared after hitting the Princess at the right place. And the Princess kept waiting for the ball to be presented to her, but the sweet Prince made a mystery of him; he disappeared each time leaving no trace of him for fear of his Prince Brothers discovering him, and the beautiful haughty princess was beaten and very infatuated and she desperately wanted to catch him.

So, on the last day of the seven day contest the beautiful haughty Princess sat in the Jharooka with a *Chakkoo* – a small knife, by her side with aim to throw it at the invading Prince to let knife pierce in the calf and if he gets away on this last and the final day, he will be caught for that knife wound. And she threw the *Chakkoo* at the Prince as soon as he had hit her on the chest on the seventh day and the Chakkoo went straight aiming at the calf of the Prince but pierced in the ankle of the sweet Prince and the gash of the wound became the Princes' mark for him to be caught the following day in the kingdom, as he limped in walking.

The following day the foot soldiers went out to comb the kingdom to catch the man with a wound in the ankle and found the sweet Prince limping and hiding among the poor and tatty in the kingdom. He was carrying the wound from the Princess' knife and was limping and was easily caught. And he was such a good-looking tattered clothes sweet Prince and sneaking one glance of the Prince by the beautiful haughty Princess, the Soyember was declared concluded and successful and the proof of the ball with scent to be presented to the Princess was not asked for and the two were happily married together.

Hafiz's teacher in story telling was the nature's academia. It gifted to him vast imagination and flourished him to pluck ideas on the spur of the moment from the air and produce fantasy filled fantastic stories, which he carved out from the fantasies of his imagination, producing one story after another, but in it he did gauge the mood of the listeners. The stories formed a vivid picture of another world unknown. And the vividness was so real that to all his story listeners, for the world he created and described existed and they were spell bound with excitement and his story telling was inexhaustible.

The rise and fall of his voice and the dressing of the ordinary words with an angle of twist and his formidable expression, and every now and then opening new phases in the story, kept the listeners spell bound. And sometimes the story never ended, and sleep overtook the listeners. The story was then completed the following day. And there was no end to the stories that Hafiz could fabricate for the listeners.

The female storytellers for their class and sophistication they carried had more of fantasy filled stories instilled in their minds than men could ever boast of. The female storytellers drew truth and untruth instilled in their minds one after the other from the archives of their memory, and for their nature they could tell more intricate stories than their male counter parts could do. They went even further in excelling men by their acute feminine-touch in the inventiveness of the stories. The vernacular presented was a produce of them. These original and first time told, producing unmatched words, making the class of story, unique of words decorative to the story of the feminine class, and their uninhibited feminine-phraseologies, deploying expressive words and their vast vocabulary at their disposal with their modulation of voice and their instinctive feminine concepts, gave such a flavour to the stories that these rivalled all classes of stories that could be told.

Some stories had to be repeated, again and again by them on the vehement insistence of the listeners, young and old alike. All young and old listened with equal fervency and made *Farma-ish* – the request with cherishing, to be narrated to hear it again. These stories had such fascinating names, as 'Gul Bakaoly', 'Subz Kabooter', 'Chandan Haar' and the likes. These kept the listeners spell bound, their pulses rising and falling at each curvaceous turns of the fantasy being webbed in the stories. It raised great curiosity in the boys and girls to explore the unknown world of the fantasies and brave them with the adventures they heard, encountered by the heroes of the story. They believed these actually existed and the stories were seen to have a great moral building influence on them.

The invigoration of the weather with gentle breeze and the smell of the soil, its perfumery smell, were the patting for the story tellers, who were feeding ideas to the listeners and spurring their imagination to later produce all classes of stories. The categories of the stories, lavish in humour, adventure, fantasy, love, faithfulness and betrayal by the cruel hearted, were not designed to drive points in the severities of ethics or propounding discipline of religion; they only aroused healthy curiosity and ethos and there was the lasting decency that was cast in the central character - the hero or the heroin of the story.

But the storytellers could not have produced the stories and entered in the fantasies they transcended and myth and mania they built, unless the listeners were supportive, listening and giving their consent through their exclamations of 'Au', 'Oh'. 'Ji' on the stories being constructed and narrated and these acknowledgements during the story telling supported by nodding and humming, were telling the story teller that they were listening. It bucked up the story teller to comb his mind to revel and produce further intricacies in the story.

And it was certain; no environment was more conducive to produce stories of fantasies than that in the Land of Seasons and Songs where the sky was lit with stars, and filled with its numerosity and the breeze serenaded producing freshness, coolness and calm with prevailing universal quietness. It was a different world conducive to the variety of functions indicative of God qualities, plausible and comprehensible. It supported the fluxing of the mind to produce tender ideas, and such was peace around in these conditions that it invigorated fantasy in the thinking unlimited, and mirth stood by in its lingering consistency.

-: . :-

1

THE VILLAGE WEDDING

XIV

The village weddings in the Land of Seasons and Songs were a very special occasion and of these the summer weddings were unique. Everyone in the village concerned himself with the wedding and had taken upon him something to do by him. It was a case of *Abdullah Diwanay*[21] - Abdullah gone crazy, a proverb for showing frenzy in other's affairs.

There was no end to the festivities in the village wedding. The bride groom's wedding party carrying *Laddoos* – sweetmeat balls, it brought from the *Helwaee* - the sweetmeat seller, and *Peendees*[22] made in the house by the ladies from dried fruits, Ghee, sugar and *Sooji* – semolina (granulated wheat flour), mixed and bound in balls, to be carried with them as Shagun – as good omen of wedding, all redied, with the Sooji and dried fruits roasted in Ghee and added with sugar and bound as balls with both palms. In addition to the sweetmeat, *Toakra(s)* – basket full of fresh fruits, and dried fruits in red cloth-cotton bags, white sugar and *Chohara* – the dried dates in several red cloth bags were taken for distribution at the end of the *Nikah* - the marriage solemnization. Along with these tokens for good gesture: bride's dresses of silk and of Satan decorated with laces, - a minimum of 14 pairs of these dresses, packed in a steel trunk with boxes of bride's jewellery, perfumeries and cosmetic taken as Bari for the pride. All those fineries and with *Doolha* as the centre piece of the wedding,

---

[21] The proverb was: *Begani Shadi Mein Abdullah Diwanay* - in others' wedding, the outsider not concerned with it goes mad, running around amuck to managing it.

[22] This hand bound sweet ball was so special that it was always made on the occasions of weddings and births in the houses for good omens and cheeriness.

the party left for the bride's village. It travelled on four Aekka(s) from Rala to the railway station Bharwari to travel down the three stations away to the Rasoolabad station and from there to start on foot to Kurrah Sadat the bride's village.

The train was pulled by the hissing locomotive run by the coal fuel. The coal was burnt and It raised steam that pushed the pistons and turned the wheels and the train carrying the wedding party, with engine belching out dense carbon soot, hissing and whistling and filling the nostrils with carbon black soot of engine exhaust ran rhythmically, wheels beating the rails, producing a rhythmic sound, not unpleasant colouring the journey stopped when the station came. But till then there was more filling of the nostrils with coal soot for people in the front bogies, next to the locomotive. The train took the wedding party, treating the passengers like this to the Rasoolabad Railway Station of the bride. There every one of the wedding party got down from the train and started the journey for the bride's village on foot taking the Pug Dandi – the walkway Kachcha path through the sowed crop. The load of the wedding Bari – the bride groom side present of sweets and Chohara- dried dates for distribution were lifted by one person.

The wedding party walked on the winding walkways through the fields, with their load of the wedding presents and all the villages falling on the way to the bride's village were hailed as the donors of the bride by the jubilant *Baraatees* (wedding participants from Doolha), and chuckles were raised, and there was no end to zest shown by the bridegroom's party. Each one of them feeling on top of the world for going to bring a bride to their village from another village. Each one feeling they were winners and victors.

So, with fun and frolic at its highest and jokes cracked all the way the bridegroom's party with their Doolha walking somewhere behind, reached to the sighting distance of the bride's village and halted outside the village. The bridegroom was taken to the reed hutment, with its reed walls and reed roof pitched on a level field and the Doolha was given a towel and soap to wash and freshen him, removing the soot of the train and then he was given a brocade *Choordi Dar*

Pyjama – the slim leg pyjama and brocade *Achkan*[23] – the knee-deep long coat with open overlapping front halves with cotton buttons sewed on it and he was dressed up. Soft muslin, pink *Safa* - the turban was ceremoniously wound on the head of the Doolha and he was given to wear *Naagri* brocade shoes. These had to have their toes tapered and a piece of leather at the toes end curled to symbolize a Shah's footwear.

The design of the shoes was important, it was to notify that these were the shoes of the *Nau Shah* - the New King. These were laced with *Kla Battoo* – with gold and silver threads. These Naagri bridegroom - shoes were slipped into the Doolha's feet. And *Sehra* – the groom's strings of garland - the flowers in strings were tied round the *Safa* dropping down from the forehead of the Doolha over his face down to his length and he was now a Shah and was given a handkerchief to place it on his mouth to cover the lips and the tip of the nose and he had to manage breathing as best as he could and maintain that posture of the Doolha and he had to display his four days old *Henna* done pink hands while holding the handkerchief.

Four days back the *Rasm-e Maanyoun* - the ceremony of glistening the bridegroom was held at his village house. His face, arms and feet were rubbed with *Uptan* – an application prepared by grinding turmeric with mustard seeds – Sursoan Kay Beej on the *Sill* - the kitchen stone slab and it was mixed with gram flour and *Badam Ki Khali* – the oilcake of almond to nourish his body. A few drops of milk were added to it and it was Uptan. The *Na-ee* - the barber came daily to rub it on the Doolha. This was going to arouse newness in furtherance in the Doolha and make him shine with the rubbing of the Uptan.

The Uptan was rubbed on the Doolha's body for many days. And then afterwards his soles of the feet and the palms of the hands were given application of Mehndi - the henna. A blob of Mehndi was formed into a circle on each of the palms or a geometrical pattern of triangle or star was made by the sisters. The Mehndi left a deep maroon mark on

---

[23] Sometimes in some villages the Doolha was dressed in *Angarkha* which had flared front halves, the right half over-lapping the left half to which cotton strips were attached to tie them to each other.

the surface of the skin. The palms as well as the soles of the feet were so decorated, for which a generous reward of *Neig* - hard cash was paid to the sisters by the parents of the bridegroom and a generous payment of reward was considered auspicious on this occasion in the house. This Neig was distributed by the sisters among themselves and to far or near sisters and there were many cousin sisters of the bridegroom - all from the relatives, they were given their shares.

The Neig was the sisters' right and the parents paid that with cheeriness and immediately the sisters put the Doolha under the protection of the *Kungan* - a small bright red ball of cotton, decorated with gold laces and a tiny length of a shiny lace strings hanging as a bunch of extra flurries from the little Kungan. It was tied on the Doolha's wrist to symbolise the emergence of the Doolha out of the shy young man, knocking around unnoticed in the village. The Kungan advertised his Doolha status when he moved around or sat around among his friends. And the Doolha or the *Nau Shah* was the central figure on all the occasions till his marriage solemnization was over. And he was of immediate attention with his newness in conscious gathering. He was given milk sips by the sisters and *Peendi* - the hand bound sweet balls of dried fruits with semolina roasted in Ghee to eat, of which each bound ball was tenderly bound by pressing a small quantity of loose Peendi in the palm of the hand.

Each day till the Baraat left for the Bride's village for Nikah, the *Dholak* - the small drum was played in the house and the Dholak sound meant to accompany the marriage songs, arousing the frenzy of wedding. These songs were the cultural heritage of the folks of India. The names of each relatives of the Doolha were taken in the *Dholki* song with some misnomer added on the spot by the ladies while singing for fun. And different songs were sung each day in the house, and each day saw prolonging of the *Dholki.* The song session continued till the day of the Baraat, when the bridegroom and the Baraat left for the Bride's village.

There in the bride's village the protocol was that a representative came to meet the Baraat, to invite them to enter the village and the wedding party flanked the Doolha's horse on each side and formed the ensemble of the jubilant Baraat. The lookout of the bride's party informed of the Baraat's progress of march to the bride's house and the reception party assembled at the reception line. And the Baraat arrived with the band of the instrumentalists lined in front of the ensemble in their coloured tunic, marching on the wedding tunes with drum beating and trumpets blaring, and the *Taasha*, the cymbals of brass plates beating each other in clash and there was jingling from the little Taasha and the shrilling noise of the clarinet at the highest[24]. The Doolha was on the horse's back and his long length *Sehra* – the strings of flower were hanging in front of his face, curtain-covering him from head down and the remaining length was resting folded in front of the Doolha on the horse's saddle and the *Shahbala* was sitting at his back, with Doolha displaying an adapted shyness as briefed by his wards.

The *Shahbala* was no other than the little five-year-old nephew, or any one of relation, dressed as a mini Naushah. He was Doolha's assistant to give support to him and he adroitly caught hold of the Doolha's Achkan at his back on the horse. The Baraat in that formation of family traditions inched forward on the journey and arrived at the Bride's house entrance of open space in its sweet time. The wards of the Doolha were propitiating all the time by throwing coins over the Doolha's head for God's mercy and favour, ranging round the Doolha's horse. And at the reception line the bride's elders were standing at the bride's house, the propitiating elder emptied the last of the reserves of the coins in the bag, throwing over, above and across the Doolha and after that final propitiating, the Doolha dismounted from the horse and the coins were all the way swept clean of the ground by the poor, menial workers and other charity collectors.

Everyone who mattered from the bride's side was present, forming the reception line and some hurrying to join in, and every zest and courtesy was shown and honours accorded to the Baraat individuals. And the Baraat was received with all the courtesies on display by the donors.

The bride's wards had left nothing lacking in preparations to make their house look bridal. Long before the Baraat was due, they had treated the house to make it look bridal to do its face lifting. The walls

---

[24] In the Molvi houses this ostentation of music band brought by groom's party was not allowed. But it was an innocent indulgence and it brightened the occasion.

and pillars of the house were given new looks by fresh cladding with the best clay from the soft soil brought from the pond's side. And the entire house was hand lapped with clay mixed with the chaff of the straw. This was so done at the bridegroom's house as well. And a sweet smell came from the walls and the floors of the house. And everything was presented freshness and he to swear of its newness. The outer face of the house was given a coat of lime wash and the best of preparations were made for giving away every body's love in the house - the frail and elusive little girl now turned into *Doolhan* - the bride.

The bride was aggrandised with the *Sola Singhar(s)* – the sixteen embellishments (done to an Indian bride). Her palms and feet were maroon coloured with Mehndi to make them look pretty and made giving the Mehndi fragrance. *Missi* – the red lead, darkening powder was rubbed on her gum to make gum look dark and the teeth whiter. The lips were made to look delicate by applying a film of paint of *Roghan* – a delicate oil, then *Afshan* – the sparkling tinsel specs were sprinkled on it to make them shine and look attractive. The bride's shyness was enhanced, and the submissiveness of the smile made attentive.

The corners of her eyes were filled with *Kajal* – the lamp-black to give them a look of the *Chashm-e Aahoo* - deer like eyes, and her hair was combed back and plated with *Choti* – the *Paranda* – turned into plating. Her nails were given a coat of magnificent shine of her choice and she was perfumed with the *Itr-e Sohag* – the nectar of unique fragrance. And her attractiveness arrested in her for the husband on the first night of the marriage as contracted out through this civicism being efficacious with *Sohag* for wifehood and readiness into the plausible life of happiness. Now she was a declared, certified and turned into a Doolhan. And the final seal of the Doolhan - the *Nuth*, the large gold ring was slipped into the lobe of her dainty nose and she was declared bride, and Cleopatra could fill all her hair with gold dust but could not bring the allure of this bride of the Land of Seasons and Songs.

The *Gao Takias* - the elbow rest pillows with velvet covers were placed on the white *Jajam* – a large one-piece white cotton sheets spread on the floor over thick cotton Durries covering the length and breadth of the veranda and its front platform where the Baraati (s) were to sit and a couple of special Gao Takias were placed for the Doolha where he was to sit. And he was given a silent vivacious welcome when he came extending appropriate attention to him. But first the Baraatees were seated and all the guests of the bridal side were seated on the Jajam, and then the Doolha was brought in the company of the courting friends to sit at the centre seat with his long Sehra fully covering him, and he was only to throw back the long end of his Sehra and unveil his Naushah's bright face after the solemnisation of the marriage by the *Maulana*(s) — the revered religious heads.[25]

The Sehra had to be long, as long as possible, only for the sake of etiquette it had to be kept a little shorter than the length of the Doolha. The picture of the Doolha was drawn by Poet Ghalib. This poet has said many Sehra(s). He says in one of his *Sehra(s)* — the praise of the Doolha's trimness in Sehra. The poet says:

Yeh Bhi Ek Bey Adabi Thi Keh Qaba Say Bardh Ja-ay Sehra
Raeh Gaya Aan Kay Damun Kay Barabar Sehra

This also was showing of a disrespect that the Sehra exceeded
the length of the Qaba - the long coat.
The Sehra (in shortness) came down only up to the skirt of
the garment.

Poet Ghalib says that it was the prevalent custom to make Doolha graceful by decorating him with a long Sehra, and wards longed for a very long Sehra hanging from his forehead down to the length of the tallness of the Doolha, but the Sehra all the same got down to the level only to below the knee to observe the comfort of the Doolha.

The Baraat was seated and glasses of *Sharbat* were served to the Baraati guests, then *Paan* wrapped in *Chandi Ka Waraq* — silver leaf, were placed in the *Khasdan(s)*, small silver tray with cover of silver

---

[25] There are two Maulanas in the Shia Muslim marriages; as in the Nikah of the Prophet SAWW with Bibi Khadija one from the bride's side and one from the bridegroom's side.

dome, and higher brand cigarettes of 555 from England were served and ash trays placed round for ash flicking and cigarette butts stubbing. And it was seen to that everything was in its place to make the guests feel honoured. The prominent members of the Baraatees and elders of the Doolha were already garlanded at the reception line and when all courtesies due to them had been observed, the proceeding on hold for the solemnisation of the marriage was put on the move for the binding *Seegha* – the formulaic words of contract of marriage to be initiated and gone through. The advocate for the bride was led inside the house to the chamber of the bride to seek her consent for the marriage to take place.

When the clergy returned with the bride's consent the two clergy advocates - Maulana(s), started the exchange words of the solemnisation of *Ankahtu*. The Bride's Maulana said, 'I have given' and the Bridegroom's Maulana said, 'I have accepted the wedlock', with each speaking on behalf of their respective clients getting married and bride's Maulana announced the value of the dower sum agreed to between the wards of the Bride and the Bridegroom that to be given by the Doolha to the Doolhan.

The wedding *Seegha*(s) in the Hindu custom were *Shabd(s)* – the words spoken by the *Pundit*. *Agni* - the fire was witness of the proceedings and the solemnisation was completed with Doolha and Doolhan taking seven rounds of the Agni. At each circumambulation, prayer was made for the prosperity and a long-lasting companionship. The proceeding there were kept elemental and more fundamentally endowed, which have been long drawn and designed to cover as many shades and aspects of life as possible through rituals.

After the Nikah solemnization was completed by the Maulanas, the wedding dinner was served to the Doolha, Baraatees and to the guests. The food quality was ensured to be equivalent to the occasion; tasty, pleasant, appetising and of choice. At least two Saalun – curries, two breads – Nan and Sheermal, Raeta, lavish Pulao and Zarda were served, and elsewhere in the Hindu wedding, Puris, Kachuaris, Bhajis, yoghurt, *Achaar* or pickles and Tar-Halwa as sweet dish were served. This was the climax of the wedding and the Baraatees were bidden farewell who left with the bride and she was sent with tears flowing from the eyes of her near and dear ones.

The wedding party with Doolha and Doolhan returned to their village and the Doolha's wards started the wedding feast celebration of the Valima – a feast from the Doolha next day. Villages after villages were invited in the Valima – this was wedding dinner in jubilation of the happy wedlock. Large heartedness was shown on this occasion by the Doolha wards, who invited a very large number of guests to the Valima and a furore of activity was programmed in the Valima. The kith and Kin of the Doolha ran round, helping in laying the food and looking after the guests from the villages. Villages in turn by name were called to come and sit at the Dastarkhwan – cloth spread on ground on which food varieties were placed.

All the big landowners in the villages - the *Mukhyas, Chaudharis, Talluqedars,* village chiefs were present. Then the villagers were provided entertainment after the Valima dinner. It was the culminating point of the wedding celebrations. One entertainment was *Nautanki* which staged plays for the villagers and the other was a dance and songs session. The entertaining team of the *Tawaef* presented dance and songs and the jokers or the *Bhand(s)* made hilarious jokes.

The Tawaef presented catchy songs with gentle dance on the floor spreadover with carpets. They were brought from the town and were a necessary component of suburban joy of the villagers' society. The higher status of the House of the Doolha vouched the deployment of the Tawaef that they be given floor to present their show. The entertaining ladies were called *Tawaef* and never called with the bad name of *Rundi*, the word was distasteful. And though they were an exclusive class, a tragopan, the brilliantly coloured pheasants in human form, but they were feared to be mixed with. Some of them were called *Kanjri(s)* and chuckles were raised and a swirl of the eyes of the villagers appeared at the mention of their names. They were an elite class but an alien to the village society – a sporadic outcome of the larger society but emerging as a class of a sophisticated entertainer and a class by themselves.

The classic Tawaef(s) showed a disciplined courtesy and mannerism and retained their dignity and knew the grades of respect to be given to the classes of men and presented top entertainment to bring credit to those who brought them to their doors for offering entertainment of an enjoyable evening that invariably ensued from them. These ladies waived their wastes and swung their bottoms and swirled themselves and sang illusive songs, and their co-male partners provided security to them escorting them, also acting and forming as their musician troupe and instrumentalist team, on whose instrumental tunes, these entertainers sparkled and put their charm and performance to allure the audience.

The *Sarangi Sazinda* – the fiddle player helped them with the shimmering throb of the sound of the Sarangi, inciting them to excel in their performance of the *Mujra* – the dance and sweeten their songs. And the *Tablachi*, the drummer thrilled them perform, resonating their limbs of the supple body, bringing out their flexure and feminist charm, and the ladies played their part and fantasised imagination of the village gentry, and each lady's performance was alternated with the performance of the *Bhands* – the *jokers* equipped with a variety of tricks in the fun of tickling men and making them laugh. They produced humorous talks and made gestures and performed acrobatic and presented fun wearing funny clothes and facial make ups and the lady singers during their performance took intervals to powder their nose.

The ladies' *Mujra* was for the males only gathering. There were no provisions for the participation of the ladies in *Pardah*. It was another matter if they peeped through the slits of the bamboo screen hanging on the windows or peeped through the cracks of the doors or obtained certain glimpses from somewhere that suited them from where there was surety they will not be seen from outside.

The Kanjri(s) sang inexact songs cognate with their styles. And the Tawaef(s) sang masterly songs copying the voices of the goddesses of the film industry, Ishwarya Roy, Rekha or Meena Kumari, and presented alluring songs from the pick of the compositions of the renowned poets. Their pronunciation of words most correct and crisp, and the style of delivery of poetry set to make standards and please the soul of the litterateurs, and they were a necessary component of the society and themselves an elite class. They gave colour to culture and if it was Greece, they were Aphrodite – the goddess of love.

The proof of their being elite was provided by the British when in Lucknow the British ruined their class, along with other elites of the society under allegation that they took part in the rebellion against them. The Tawaef's jewelleries and properties were seized under allegation of their openly aiding the rebellion of 1857 - 58. And of them the Rundi(s) were the lesser talented in the art of sophisticated entertainment. They allowed their easy virtue follow the path of the forbidden profession, and they only hardly found a place of respectability under the elite name of Tawaef – the society girls, and a Rundy would hide her behind the Tawaef class.

In the wake of the Tawaef's presentations a new elite class emerged out of the seam of their artistry to serve literature and Wijdaniyat – the ecstasy. This class sang elusive poetic songs and they were professional sangfroid and sanguine, nourishing aesthetics and leading men enter in *Wijdaniyat*, the state of love for God. And they were as respectful as the Queen of England gracing the throne of England. They carried the names of Abeda, add to it Parveen, Munni Begum, Noor Jehan and the outstanding of them – the Queen of Bollywood Lata Mangeshkar, Aasha Bhoshley and the princess of them Nazia Hasan, and the competing alluring Ishwarya Roy, who set up tempo of the nations. And the ladies came out of the Pardah and sat along with men to listen to their invigorating *Ghazals* – the poetic love songs and the Sufi culture was not left in the woods, it was dusted and polished through songs sung by them, and fantasy was fetched to match the purity of mind. They held the audience captivated and mesmerised and they cooed themselves with accurate phonetics serving literature. Of them the melodious Munni Begum sings such deep-meaning lyric as:

Qudrat Nein kya Mazaq kiya Aadmi kay sath
Jeena Khushi kay sath Na Marna Khushi kay sath
Maain soachta hoon yeh bhi Faraybay Khuloos haai
Hans kar jo Baat Karta haai koa-ee kisi kay sath

What joke the providence has made of man?
Neither living with happiness nor dying with happiness
I think this is also deceit of sincerity
When someone talks with someone laughingly.

The performance of the Kanjris so appealed the academicians, that they opened academies to teach their knack to their academy students. Their graduate students attained excelling mastery in this art, and not only that they crossed all binds set by the Kanjris; they exhibited their navels and more. And the Kanjris were aghast and marvelled at their readiness to display their navels and flesh beyond that the one half of their rose buds.

Emperor Jalal Uddin Mohammad Akbar, Shahenshah-e Aalam, Zill-e Elahi, Maha Bali, Akbar-e Azam for the limitations set by the Kanjris on exposed performances, observing moderations in what they displayed of the finenesses of their persons while putting their acts as entertainment to the audience, did not like to call them *Kanjris* or *Kachris* - meaning the discarded little rubbish! He called them *Kanjish* and the Emperor listened to their songs.

Alexander Pope says of the chasteness in AD 1735 in his 'To a Lady', (Epistles to Several Persons):

Virtue she finds too painful an endeavour
Content to dwell in decencies forever

Alexander Pope's analysis of the people's behaviour is; it is too difficult to attain virtue and people live as their senses dictate. And the senses such dictated that a whole industry of entertainment was erected following the sensuality and easy virtue in big cities of India.

India was a model country for using music as prayer and as source of entertainment. The varietal openness of the culture was little seen so varied and so immensely enjoyed without expanded elaborative stages by the overall complex of people as there. The grading of the chiefs of the villages and their stalwartness revolved round one fact, that how much land was owned by them and what dowry they gave to their daughters when they married them, and whether if they excelled in these traditions, they were admired as traditionalist generous, and that if the Mujra was facilitated to be seen and enjoyed by the folks at their wedding galore.

The princes in the Land of Seasons and Songs were weighed in emerald, and ruby and diamonds on their birthdays. The standard of the dowry from the ordinary chiefs was; 4 hefty milk giving water buffalos, 6 cows, 25 goats, 25 *Murabba(s)* - 625 acres of farming land, two female servants, one male servant, 100 quilts, ten to twenty kilograms of gold and lots of utensils.

And an untold amount was spent on the marriage and the justification for the entertainment was sought from the Quran, saying the entertainment was a part of the marriage of their offspring and the sanction for it on the weddings, extruded was from the command of Aayet 7.33. Its liberal interpretation provided them what sanction they wanted to meet the dictates of the customs of the society. The words of the Aayet 7.33 were:

"Say, my Lord forbade only indecencies such of them as are apparent and such as are within, and sin and wrongful oppression, and that ye associate any one with Allah for which no warrant hath been revealed, and ye tell concerning Allah that which ye know not."

The interpretation taken was; 'indecencies' and association of externalities with God was forbidden and it sufficed their notion of assumed warranty extended to them by God of the Universe that no harm ensued from their indulgences into the entertainments, they had organised.

-:. :-

1

THE NAUTANKI

XV

The Nautanki was an indigenous creation, a play enacted on a stage, with mixed enactments of dialogue, action, dance and display of facial makeup and dress changes in running times. It mostly presented characters of legendry famous Indian heroes, covering their field of activity. The Nautanki performers opened their entertainment boxes personifying the celebrated to the village audience and they attended it mind and soul and it was a big social event. The summer weddings included the Nautanki in their programmes for the villagers. It created a flurry in the people and it was staged by small drama companies. The local boys of a team of only a few produced a variety of programme and they presented these plays under the open sky which ran all night till the morning. The Nautanki was a great entertainment for the villagers. They sat glued to it all night.

The jokers cracked jokes and mimicked. The actors made dialogues and sang. They leapt out from behind the side screens on the stage and one and the same actor changed his costume and appeared with different make up to do a different role. And there were sprinkles of solo dances in between the acts. A slender boy from among the Nautanki men was dressed and given look of a girl and he did what the best of the female dancers did. People so much enjoyed the Nautanki.

The stage or the *Marsah* was made by joining the *Takht*(s) – planks fixed on four legs and a continuous wide stage was obtained. The Takht was the most essential piece of the Nautanki component. The device had to rumble when the actors jumped on it and groan when an actor threw someone on it and it had to be silent, making no contribution of noise of its own when the sound of the *Ghungroo* – the small bells tied in bunches on the ankles of the dancer's feet struck the

Takht on its plank to tinkle in rhythm with the sequence of the feet stamping it in the dance. The Ghungroo had to respond to the tempo of the dance in perfect harmony as was wanted of it and at each of the *Thumkas;* the bursts of the stamping by the dancer, the stage had to comply with its rigidness to stand vigorously silent for the sound of the jingles of the softness of the Thumkas to be listened to by the audience.

A sheet of canvas was spread on the Takhts, end to end and the traditional stage was formed. It was flood lit with gas lantern light. The main curtains on the Marsah were hung at the front and at the back of the stage using bamboo poles, and narrow curtains were hung on the sides of the stage. Within these backgrounds the Nautanki was staged and the audience sat all night and watched, and the actors entertained them.

Moonj Ki Palung – the carry cots of rush strings, were spread for seating prominent audience in the Nautanki show. The more numerous general audiences sat on the durries spread on the floor. Others sat anywhere they could find a place to sit on. And such was the spirit on these occasions that those sharing the limited space on the Palung(s), some six to eight peoples squeezed themselves in the space available for not more than four people, and never complained to the other that he had occupied more space than his share.

The villagers came with their bundles of *Beerdees*. These *Makhrooti smokes* - tapered tobacco rolls, from the leaves of the Dhak were the *Desi* smokes - the native cigarettes. They were filled with tobacco at one end that was lit to burn tobacco and the tapered end was used to puff the Beerdeeirdi. And these were the cheapest of the smokes and unique in their class. Clusters of *Dhak* shrub grew everywhere on their own in the spacious land, of the Land of Seasons and Songs and these were used for making Beerdees, and lots and lots of Beerdees were made and puffed. And if anyone made the best use of tobacco, it was the Beerdee maker, he made harmless-proof puffs, putting in it measured tobacco to do no harm, only kill urge. The Beerdees glowed in the dark of the night all over the Nautanki ground, its smoke floated in the air. It seemed, as if lots of glow-worms were burning their fractious candle power to light up the darkness of the night. The audience as such were a welcome crowed burning the Beerdee.

191

The cigarettes imported were not brought to the Nautanki ground as the simple villagers had no means to buy them, they entered the market about 1944, and this product from the West had to wait for the affluent times to come, and these to edge out the Beerdeeirdi(s). There were two well-known kinds of cigarette brands then in the market; the Players and the State Express 555, both came from England and were sold by the chemists in the towns and were bought by the affluent – customers of means and stature. But the Beerdees were sold in abundance with guarantee and certainty of their virtue. The other cause was medicinal analysis that the cigarettes did not help digestion whereas the Beerdees did.

The Beerdees had another value in facility and possessed a definite edge over the cigarettes. These extinguished by themselves and everyone could throw the butts of the Beedrees safely on the floor anywhere, these extinguished quickly and became the natural habitat of the earth, whereas the cigarettes did not extinguish and required stubbing, and were a litter. And then the village *Pansari* – the small grocery shopkeeper kept only bundles of Beerdees. Only sometimes when the smoker asked the Pansari for the expensive Beerdee made from the *Aabnoos* tree leaves – black wood tree, he said he didn't have that.

The Nautanki was an ensemble of boys only group. It was an all-boys' show. Only six to eight of them formed the Nautanki team. They carried the Nautanki paraphernalia on their shoulders from one place to another where Nautanki was called to stage its show and the entertainment they provided to the spectators was spectacular. They out stripped their small size in every department of performance and their small size was their strength for many reasons, and one was they had no controversy. Their act was Mubah – carrying permissibility and everyone enjoyed every bit of the Nautanki.

The drummer's fingers tapped the drum diaphragm in the middle portion of the diaphragm and it was for soft heavy sound and the edge of the drum was struck with fingers for a crisp twanging sound and the base sound was created with the mound of the palm, hitting the centre of the drum with it and each event was characterised with a hard and a soft note of the sound rising with its assigned note to depict of the event. Then there was a signature tune, a different sound announced at the start and the end of different events. And there was so much to enjoy in the varieties of the tunes.

The actors articulated their voice; bringing out masterly sound when assertive to stress a point and used whisper with gentleness when the sound required was to be soft and melodious, and they did what their act demanded. And the *Maskhara(s)* – the jokers, cut hilarious jokes. Then the actors came from behind to give a vivid scenario of the daring of a dacoit and the funny dresses of the *Bhands*- the comic actors, spoke of the light moments. The presentation of the *Thumries* by the dancers, were accompanied by the whistles from the audience and sound of horns from them. The noise and shrill sound were created in accolade to acknowledge the surpassing standard of the dancers. These performing talents were out from nowhere and were self-created. All these performances presented professionalism, making all sit at the edge of their seats, alert and all engrossed not to miss a moment of the Nautanki.

The popular drama staged was the 'Sultana Dakoo'- the robber baron Sultana. The dacoit moved with his team of fierce men challenging the police authority and the commissioners. He went to rob the plump rich, who were stacking wealth and not letting it be circulated among the people. Sultana Dakoo was both admired and dreaded, and he behaved sovereign. His band of dacoits were ready to die for him and do anything daring he ordered them to do and they were a dedicated force.

Sultana Dakoo robbed the stingy-rich who did not give in charity to the poor, and he said he put wealth on its feet. His fortress was in the foothills of Himalaya overlooking the barren planes of Najibabad and because there was nothing to loot there he came down to Delhi. He and his gang arrived on horses' back with a big whip and never made a secret of it, as to who the next stingy-rich was, he was going to rob by raiding. The police arrived at the scene before him, but the police always found, they were duped and fooled. They could not catch the Dakoo.

The Dakoo by his natural superiority in wit, spoke English in his Git Bit like English, and forced the police to fall in and stand to attention. The police wore half pants and a *Khaki* wool strip called *Patti* wrapped round their calves from knees down to the ankles and they did not know English. They were in *Khaki Safa* or turban of cotton, which was folded in strip, some fifteen arm's lengths long, and it was wound on a *Koolha* - a turban former. In this outfit of the uniform, they stood to take orders. In their Khaki Safa, they had a pink *Jhabba* – a pink cotton twine that was clipped on to the right side of the Safa. This presented a perfect obedient police sepoy in uniform and he was all attentive to act at the Git Bit[26] in which orders from the Dakoo were passed to him.

This police dress was of the better times, when obedience was of prime importance than getting to know the trick of an ingenious robber, who appeared in his Git Bit like a perfect commissioner. The Git Bit was manipulation of a few words of English spoken in the accent and command of the Gora Sahib. The police stood erect, head high and pulled their chests out at the command of the Dakoo. And the Dakoo wore English Sahib's Birje - pant with flare at the hip and tight at the ankle, and a Khaki cork hat with brim and he shouted the Git Bit. And the whole contingent of the police men did not understand a bit what Git Bit was spoken, save to smartly pull their chests out at these commands.

In these times of serenity, there when theft, and the other murder the whole town stood still in remorse and was stunted. And the citizens did not know of dishonouring of a woman. This crime did not exist. This was a crime against the dignity of man. His manliness did not allow any excess on the weak woman. Even genuine love was illegitimate, only if there was mutual honourable family consent for establishing a relationship was allowed. And police had more moralistic duty to perform than dealing in violent crimes. One's fate was accepted as his lot and forced means to change one's own condition through robbing and slaying was unknown.

In these peaceful days actions of deliverances were done and there was Nautanki. Half of the secret of the success of the Nautanki was the dress - the costumes they wore on the stage. It made a man into a Dakoo and a boy look like a girl. All that the Dakoo needed was a moustache, and a girl that she needed was a fourteen-inch-long human hairweave, rouge, lipstick and powder, which changed the

---

[26] A native not familiar with the English language or a talk in vernacular that was beyond him, not understandable by him, called it Git Bit.

faces to look as they wanted and the dainty boy was changed into a girl. And the other secret was the versatility of the actors. The Dakoo spoke *Git Bit*. The Git Bit of the Dakoo confused the policemen who had come to catch the Dakoo. The policemen thought the big *Gora Sahib* – the English Sahib had arrived and it was he who was talking to them in that Git Bit.

The Git Bit was the language of the *Gora Sahibs* and also of the *Desi Sahibs* who spoke that in the fury of the command, when they were issuing orders as the urgent messages in the emergencies, and the police constables thought one of the Sahibs was standing in front of them, but it was Sultana Dakoo, issuing emergency commands and they paid every bit of police attention to what they could interpret from the fury of the command as was being flung at them, and they saw to it that they stood erect, chest out and did not move from their place where they were stood erect and ordered so by the decoit.

The great Dakoos were great managers. They did little shooting and produced maximum intended result of robbing without shooting, and the Sultana Dakoo was its enlightened pioneer in robbing. He treated the police with the kill of a great manager. He stood the police at attention while his robber team were at work robbing the stingy-rich in the house, whom the police came to protect. His team of Dakoos entered in the house and the robbers told the stingy-rich they were Dakoos and had come to rob him. The stingy-rich became so panicky that he immediately wetted his pant and the servant was sent running to bring for him another pant, but he was shouted at to bring out the hoard his master had stacked in the house and lay that before them on the floor.

All the stingy-rich were baddies. They did not give in charity and did not help others and used the hoard to collect compound interest by giving money on interest. The stingy-rich was not willing to hand in keys to bring out his hoard. But when a whip cracked in the air, he hurried to ask the servant to bring out the hoard. The Dakoos then asked the servant to bring a rope and the silly servant quickly brought the rope and the Dakoos bound them to the pillars and put gag round their mouths and went out leaving them bound in the house. The police stood at attention as commanded by Sultana Dakoo and waited for further orders.

Sultana Dakoo commanded in crisp Edwardian Urdu in which the Gora Sahibs spoke to the police; *'Sipahi Platoon Munh Udhar Karay Ga'* - the constables will turn their faces to the other side, and then he shouted the command, 'About Turn'and the police about turned smartly and the Dakoos sat on the horse with the loot and left the scene.

Sultana Dakoo is considered as a folk hero. He robbed the stingy-rich, who did not give in alms and charity to the poor and hoarded money. He robbed and gave the bulk of what he robbed to the poor and he was credited to be doing equitable distribution of wealth in the society but the British rather than give him an O.B.E., hanged him from the gallows, in 1940. Sultana Dakoo died but till today has his name engraved in the memory annals, as a worker to bring in equality in the economic order.

The famous Laila-Majnoon story was another highly emotional and heart-rending drama of the Nautanki plays. The way the Laila ran looking for the Majnoon in the desert storm in the desert was a display of pure innocent love of beloved to the loved. It was another favourite of the villagers with its legendry powerful characters - the Qais and Laila which the Nautanki presented. Qais Bin Mulawwah was lover and Laila his beloved. Qais was from the desert and Laila from the urban town. The love story of Laila and Majnoon was enacted showing the equal intensity of love Laila held for Majnoon, and the vice versa what Majnoon held for Laila.

The young Qais who had turned *Majnoon* that is gone crazy in the love of Laila roamed in the desert. The cost of the love of Majnoon for Laila was always peril for the Majnoon. The drama was; The Laila of the Nautanki sat high above in a gallery, seven feet high and the Majnoon sang song from below, spreading his arms, and when the song was over, Laila made a jump from those seven feet heights above, down towards the Majnoon.

But Laila had a tilt and she went face down on the ground and the Majnoon could not catch her and she fell badly tipped on to one side just short of the Majnoon, behind a thin curtain between them. And the Majnoon then spread his arms out and started to wail and sang another wailing song.

The Laila had to be a boy who was light weight and had some feminism about him. Such a boy's face was made pretty with lipstick and powder and the Majnoon was a rugged desert man with wild grown beard sand blasted and looking insane with hair frayed and clothes torn.

-:. .:-

Part II

Man and the Excellences

II

THE NAWABS AND THE KINGS

I

The Nawabs of Awadh- the Shah of the country of the land of Awadh were kings. And among them the last Nawab of grandeur, Nawab Wajid Ali Shah, God bless his soul was a great benefactor of the people of his Nawabdom. His highness was of a perfect Shah, and disposition of poet, musician, dramatist, spiritualist, literalist and his belief to making life and history of great attraction of excellences. A voluminous book is needed to present his life sketch and that would be only scantily covering it. This Nawab carried a great pioneering spirit for the cause of the cultural excellence of Lucknow, its heightening and its enrichment in his reign 1847 – 1856, born 1822, died 1887. The compact of Kushta with its medicinal miracles to embolden manhood was a source of vigour for him and had a prominent place in the life of this Nawab.

The Kushta with its specifics of its ingenious chemistry was a mystery for many but an assuring pack of legitimacy to a limited few, and seen all altogether in its historical perspectives, it raised great hope in all for generating robustness of manhood. The Kushta by the dint of its constituent components and its process of preparation was expensive and it was suspiciously looked at upon as something unmanageable due to the lack of circumventing knowledge that was gaping in its use, but it commanded intervening respect due to its virtue. The Kushta literally was juggernauting of the metallic product it was; burnt, pulverised and refined for turning it into a priceless energy booster. It was a product that had intense power and had its grades and potencies and was one preparation in the art of alchemy that suited the pocket of the rich.

The well-equipped in the art of Kushta making will tell, there were many varieties of these, but the Kushta from sapphire, ruby, topaz,

201

gold and silver had special place in the list of its varieties and these were the pushers of energy that elevated and placed one at a higher level of energy platform for man's functional abilities in the department of reproduction. And the precious Kushta metals for summoning forth the ingenuities of the Nawabs, were pulverised, refined, and fragrance permeated and it turned into a palatable energy booster.

The comprehensive human qualities in elation and exaltations of man if they were graded in the grades of achievements, the last Nawab of Awadh with his individualistic form, stood at the attainment of a very high standard of spiritual standing. He brought out the chewed residual of the *Paan*, made from the betel leaf with its elemental dressings, enriched with Kushta and spat it in the spittoon in preparation for the second and the third submissions of the prayer of the day to bring him near to God. The spittoon stood in the area adjacent to the *Wazoo Gah* - the place to purify one through ablutions and it was adjacent to the *Hammam* - the place for cleansing one and taking bath. It was placed at its place of location by the attending *Mehtar* and the residual of the Paan spitted in the spittoon rested in the spittoon. It was giving powerful fragrance, which was noticed by the *Mehtar* who went there for his duty near to the placement of the spittoon.

The attendant Mehtar, who was also familiarly known by other names as given to him by the people as they thought fit for the lowly placed in the society, was considered otherwise differently by the Nawab because of his such an important assignment of duty he was responsible for. He was entrusted with the ridding of the pots and pans carrying human excretory waste, letting the houses remain habitable and denuded of foul smell, keeping hygiene tapped securely in its place and letting it fly its flag of cleanliness triumphantly in the society. The men in this profession of vital importance were given the name of distinction in the Nawabdom by the Nawab; they were called by the likeable name of *Mehtar* which meant - the noble master.

It was in the culture of the Nawabdom to call these assignees 'Mehtar' rather than *Jamadar, Bhungi, Choorda* or *Dome*, that were also some of the varied names given to them, which were also very prevalent in the circles of the Nawabdom. But persons more articulate in choosing the name for the functionaries in the class of cleansing pots and pans, besides that also if they will be doing the sweeping service that was so indispensable to all, called them by the name of Mehtar and the Nawab approved of it. And the Nawab's preferences went for the selection of the word Mehtar for calling the functionary by that name, rather than by the name of Jamadar, Bhungi, Choorda or Dome.

One reason assigned for not preferring the words Jamadar and its other associate names that could be thought of contributory to the non-preference by the Nawab and that appeared plausible was: in the vernacular which was spoken in the Nawabdom, the words starting with 'J' were not representative of so many sweet and affectionate words in the language as those starting with 'M'. Besides the word Mehtar was thought of by the culturally motivated, and by the Nawab himself by virtue of its meaning, subtly more morale boosting in nature than any other word for the lowliest of trait doing the service defined in the duties of the Mehtar. And this sealed the evident reason for the preference of the word Mehtar by the Nawab and the greater number of the people of the Nawabdom followed suit to the Nawab's preference and to the backing given to it by the culturally motivated and they took to calling him by the name of Mehtar more in preference than by any other name.

And as for the words Bhungi or Jamadar or Choodra or Dome, all these were turned down and discarded as an outright reject by His Excellency the Nawab and by all the culturally motivated, dedicated to enhancing the culture. Because each of these words were neither that sweet sounding in phonetics, nor conveying that elated a meaning that imagination in the higher realm of taste and acumen for cultural motivation sought for generating the elective list of the vocabulary of linguistic distinction to meriting their selection.

The Mehtar so defined, went to the Hammam as was the assign of his duty and he came across powerful fragrance adjacent to him, emanating from the fragments of the chewed residual of the Paan of the Nawab. The chew was residing in the spittoon that had been dutifully stood there at its place by him for the use of the Nawab. He had a go at it. He took out the bit of the residual and ate it up! This was sufficient to make his wife - the *Mehtarani* lodge a complaint against the Mehtar of cruelty on her.

The case was lodged in the female quarters of the Nawab's Harem that her Mehtar was very docile, dormant and manageable before, but since he has taken the residual of the Nawab's Paan, his requirements have changed and he has become ferocious and she was finding him unmanageable. This lodging of the complaint by the Mehtarani spoke of the power that was stored in the Kushta which it ensconced in the Paan, carrying the constituent components of the Kushta as a whole.

And this incident betrayed the secret of the formula of Kushta making for all to know of it and to benefit from its alchemy carried behind it by the alchemist that he had evolved and designed to meet the specifics of the requirements of the Nawab, by shaping the Kushta surface out of the ingenuities of his alchemy to equip the Nawab to visit his one hundred and twenty and some said three hundred and sixty legal mistresses – the legal secondary wives along with his two *Mankooha* – married wives - the crown triumvirates of the Nawab in binding relations with him on permanent basis to bear heirs. And all others being categories of legal secondary wives, whose lawful status in terms of the contractual marriage by the *Nikah-e Mowaqqat* - the wedlock of time bound contract under Aayet 4:24 of the Holy Book Al Quran was not of permanency, but legal that the Nawab enjoyed[27], and they a such were justified as of legal status. The Aayet 4:24 had given sanction to Nikah-e Mowaqqat without any later abrogation. The Aayet said:

*"And the women with husbands but those who came in your custody
(off the infidels from the battles are not unlawful), this is the written
law of God that on you (is binding) and besides these women
(other women) are lawful to you if not for fortification but for purity
and astuteness, in exchange give them their statutory gifts you
mutually agreed to, of course with those women you have made
Mutah give them that stipulated Mehr – the dower."*

---

[27] The British misunderstood this legality and exploited it as his weakness of nature, calling it debauchery and brought down his rule on this pretext. They annexed Awadh as it was a rich yielding land.

Then there was the Aayet 4:3 to say on the subject:

> *"And if you fear that you cannot act equitably towards*
> *the orphans, then marry such women as seem good to you,*
> *two and three and four; but if you fear you will not do justice*
> *(between them), then only one or whatever your right hand*
> *possesses (slave girls – Kaneezen)."*

These verses of Quran amply allowed the Nawab not to have to hide his requirement, interpreted as sensuality in which he took liberty in deriving ecstasies from women, to what the varying for political reasons called abasement, or his ways in transgression, which was farfetched for his class in obedience of God and with the insights into the God's laws and by the application thereof he aggrandized him with, and liberalized it on his self was all in consultation with the edicts of Quran. And it was the purity of mind that dominated and tamed the unruliness residing in the nature of man, not the repression of legitimacy by squashing a lawful, by brandishing it as unlawful - as if not permitted by God that was done by the 2nd Caliph of Islam who had transgressed. In truth he was so obsessed for its clamping that he spoke pridefully of making three Halals, Haram for the Ummah, which was unthinkable in these days of developed higher and deeper understanding by the Muslims.

The legal status awarded to these fair bevies – the pleasure sources, under the verse of the Quran was not negotiable near the concomitant fundamental belief of the Nawab and he did not allow its privatisation rights and its provisions turned into deprivations by any soloist!

Khalifa-e Rashid II Hazrat Umar bin Al-Khattab during his reign of Khilafat had stopped *Muta-an-Nisa* – the timed marriage with women. The Nawab ignored that daring adventure of the caliph and had its improvisation availed and made it accessible to all in the domain of his kingdom in all its totalities. And in pursuance of this provision from God; among predecessor Kings, albeit in the land of crescent, with their absolute rule in the past eras, His Majesty's equal, like Khalifa Al Mamun, reigned 813 to 833 A.D. had legalised it in his domain that was spreading over Arabia.

And hosts of these God's creation of fairing praise and beauty were visited by the Nawab in one day, followed by the night, and no one complained from among them of being neglected by the God fearing Nawab! And this was the gift of Kushta. He was short of time to visit them in the compact of a day supported by the night, and still had more energy instilled in him, left stacked in reserve to spend on them than their frequency of demand arose, and the energy was bubbling in him and it was in waiting for spending. And the good Nawab was benevolent and justice was appropriated by the God fearing and God loving Nawab on all of them.

Out of them, those who bore no children remained *Begum* and those who did bear children, became *Mahal* and were honoured and given higher respect and allocated higher allowances. The girls, when they were heralded in, and entered in the Palace, they were known *Khwaseen* – 'special people. And when the Nawab liked any one of them, she became initially a *Pari* – a fairy, and was accorded the title of Pari – a creation of legendry charm and excelling attraction and beauty. And the good Nawab did not look at any one of them fairing beauties unless they entered in the solemnisation of the relationship of the temporary marriage through mutual joint preference and consent. Whereafter they stayed under the term of the marriage for as long as they continued to be wedded to him under the *Muta* - the temporary marriage, till the expiry time of the term came.

The historians have used the word Mistress for these legalized fair sexes offering their exuberance and charm to the Nawab though they were eligible fully legalised serving ladies in contract marriage. Their status was of *Kaneez* – a servant with no sense of shame or implication of sin touching their status in purity, and they were not mistresses in the sense as used in the lands of Europe where the Nawab's contemporary - the predecessor-Kings prompted, egged and engaged fair ladies in other's matrimonies as their mistresses.

Emperor Bonaparte, Napoleon I, Conqueror of Europe entered in a shattered and gobbled up Poland in 1880. He was adored and admired and welcomed by the populace. His ambition was to see a united Europe under French control. The populace in Poland saw in him a liberator of their nation from Russia, Prussia and Austria. He was to reunite Poland, as it was a united country before. The Emperor's eyes fell on the beautiful Countess Maria Wilensky. Her status was of a married woman. Despite this status, the emperor advanced with his neophyte manner to possess her.

Now if it were Emperor Jahangir of the Land of Seasons and Songs, he would send a nobleman in chase of the nobleman who owned the beauty - Mehrun Nisa as his wife, whose beauty had pinched his heart since the time when he was just a Prince. And now when Emperor, he was to have her freed from the bondage as a married woman to another person and legalise his union with her. Therefore, the nobleman Qutb Uddin Koka was sent to nobleman Sher Afghan, who was owning Mehrun Nisa as wife. Qutb Uddin Koka was to lay down terms to him to free his spouse for her to be installed as Empress with the title of Noor Jahan for her beauty, and if the negotiations failed, the nobleman was amply equipped by the Emperor through the paraphernalia of force to put down the nobleman at his refusal before he suffered dishonour?

But here in Poland Countess Maria Wilensky was egged by the patriots of Poland to submit herself to the Emperor and the husband looked the other way. She was coaxed to consider it her patriotic duty to court the Emperor, while she was still in the count's matrimony.

Maria Walewski was led to the Emperor and she was on national duty. And Maria Wilensky says the emperor was like a hungry lion and accompanied the Emperor for three years, where the Emperor went to different lands and when she conceived and borne a son to Napoleon, Napoleon learnt of his manliness and then to meet the need of a legal heir of his throne after him, he off loaded Maria Walewski and divorced his barren Empress Josephine and married the Austrian Princess Empress Marie Louise. This he had to do because the sword of Church hung on the heads of men with the axiom; 'one man one wife'. And these ungodly things were happening because the Kings and Men were not allowed to avail the benefits of the sanction of more than one wife to them as allowed by God and as the nature of man demanded it, as was the nature – the Sarisht of the man's past.

There was a Hadiths to say: "One Namaz of a married person is bigger than seventy Namazein of the unmarried." The implied meaning is: woman is a means of nearness to God. So, the Church has deprived men of attaining what is permitted by God.

Maria Walewski was off loaded, and in this Napoleon should have followed the course Emperor Jahangir took and would have had all round sympathy with him but as it was that was the highest of the follies Napoleon made to abandon Maria Walewski. He lost Poland as his hinterland to make retreat as he lost sympathy of the people. His other reason for losing their sympathy was for his treatment of Pope Pius VII who snubbed the Emperor's relation with Maria Walewski and he lost 2/3 rd. of the support of the Poles, who were a diehard Catholic nation.

زندگی کا اثاثہ محبّت و مروّت ہے
جس نے پایا قنوت و سکون رحمت ہے
ساری عبادت کا خلاصہ پاکیزگئے ذہن
عورت حلال نہ ہو تو زحمت ہے

عورت اللہ سے قُرب کا ذریعہ ہے
ایک سے زیادہ شادی اسلام کا فلسفہ ہے
شادی شدہ کی ایک نماز بقولِ نبی سِتّر نماز
غیر شادی شدہ کا اللہ سے ستّر نماز کا فاصلہ ہے

بارے، غیر مسلم سمجھے فلسفہ حائل
میخ نہ نکالے فلسفہ میں مرحبہ ہو قائل
ساری کا فنا ت کا کھیل انتہائے ضبط و صدق
پارسائی اللہ کے قرب کا وجدان و خاصان اے اہل

پس کہ لازم ہے مرد کر لے شادی
ایک لازم ہے گر ہو دو کامیا بی
کسکو آداب سکھائے اب انسان
کر دیا خالق نے کام آسان آدمی گرفتار مرضِ بد نامی

سید اطہار حسین

Zindagi Ka Asasa Mohabbat-o Murauwat Haai
Jisnay Paaya Qunoot-o Sukoon Rahmat Haai
Saari Aebadat Ka Khulasa Pakeezgiyay Zehn
Aurat Halal Na Ho Toe Zahmat Haai

Aurat Allah Say Qurb Ka Zariya Haai
Aek Say Zyada Shadi Islam Ka Falsafah Haai

Shadi Shudah Ki Aek Namaz Ba Qaul Nabi Sattar Namaz
Ghaair Shadi Shudah Ka Allah Say Sattar Namaz Ka Fasla Haai

Baaray, Ghaair Muslim Samjhay Falsafah Hael
Mekh Na Nikalay Falsafay Mein Marhabah Ho Qael
Saari Kaenaat Ka Khel Inteha-ay Zabt-o Sidq
Paarsa-ee Allah Kay Qurb Ka Wijdan-o Khasan Aai Ahl

Per Kih Lazim Haai Mard Kar Lay Shadi
Aek Lazim Haai Gar Hoe Doe Kamyabi
Kisko Adaab Sikhaay Ub Insaan
Kar Diya Khaliq Nay Kam Aasan Aadmi Giraftar Marz-e
    Budnami

Translation

The possession of life is love and kindness
One who got piety and calm that is blessing
All the worship has its gist, the purity of mind
If the woman is not Halal (lawful) she is trouble

Woman is link to the nearness with God
More than one marriage is philosophy of Islam
One Namaz of the married, word of the Holy Prophet is
    seventy Namaz
The unmarried has seventy Namaz distance from God

Why not the non-Muslim must understand the philosophy
    interceding
Not be objecting to this philosophy Bravo be convinced
The game of entire world is extreme tolerance and
    truthfulness
Chastity is intuition of nearness to God and particularity O
    deserving

But its compulsory that man does marriage
One is compulsory if two it is success

209

To whom man will teach manners now
The Creator made the matter easy, the man captive
of defamation

Napoleon Bonaparte was forced out of his imperial palaces and exiled to the rocks of Elba off the coast of Tuscany in 1814, but then it was only Maria Walewski from Poland, who showed her loyalty to him. She arrived in the Island with their son Alexander and her jewels and offered the jewels to the Emperor. The Emperor gracefully declined to take any of that but felt consoled he had a friend and as for Marie Louise the Empress of Emperor Napoleon, she acted not like a high-class gentry to meet her obligations she owned to the Emperor and never bothered herself about him. She fled from Paris and comfortably lodged her in Vienna. She lived with her toddler prince son with an attendant and in full bloom.

Emperor Napoleon Bonaparte had kidney problem from his early age and died at the age of 51 in 1821 of kidney failure in the Island of St Helena due to lack of medical care in his second exile, after his defeat at Waterloo. The Emperor in the Island had cause for complaint that the British Governor of the Island did not call him Emperor, but called only General Bonaparte. This was a penny-pinching attitude a large-hearted governor would not show. When Napoleon Bonaparte was first exiled to Elba, he carried the title of the Emperor of Elba and ruled over its 110,000 people. But here in St Helena, he complained he was not treated even as a royal, but while there, the opportunity came his way to write his famous biography.

Napoleon Bonaparte was called great, not without reason. When after conquering Milan, his forces entered in the city, his forces were in tatters. Napoleon himself was wearing uniform that had patches on it and his army was extremely poor and in a destitute state. There was a need of looting and robbing the city, but Napoleon ordered his generals that anyone found looting, grabbing or snatching, he be shot. He said he does not want to be remembered as robber in history.

"A man should feel ashamed of robbing another man. The brave and intelligent only think of other's benefaction." – Emil Ludwig's biography of Napoleon.

Back to the Land of Seasons and Songs; the fateful events occurring to shape the history were that Mirza Ghayas Beg from Yazd Iran, was from a Shia family. He came to Agra, to old Akbar Abad with his wife Asmat Beg, sons and a beautiful child daughter Mehrun Nisa to the court of Emperor Akbar. The Emperor awarded Mirza Ghayas Beg the title of *Aetmadul Daula* - reliable of a ward/ circle. About this time Sher Afghan Ali Quli Khan, from the court of Shah Ismail II of Iran, came to Multan, some 400 miles away from Delhi. He joined the army of Khan Khana there and fought well in the Sind campaign and was raised to the noblemen status at the court of the Moghuls. He was favourably looked at upon by Emperor Jalauddin Mohammad Akbar - the Shahenshah, and was married to Mehrun Nisa in 1594.

The beauty of Mehrun Nisa was renowned and when Prince Saleem became Emperor in 1605, although he had eighteen of beautiful women for courting him as spouses and of them as prominent a spouse, as the daughter of Raja Uday Singh - Princess Maan Bai, but he was carrying the scar of the loss of the beautiful Anaar Kali. The delicate Anar kali – the all love of the all-heart, Prince Saleem. He could not be united to her, although the Prince was the precious most precursor and starter of the dynasty from whom Moghul emperors were to ensue, but was not allowed to be united with her and she was cast alive in between two walls to die there suffocated by Emperor Akbar, because her mother was a commoner or was, she a concubine of the emperor. Prince Saleem was now Emperor Nooruddin Jahangir and there was nothing to stop him having his way and obtaining Mehrun Nisa.

He obliged Sher Afghan by allocating him lands in Bengal and then appointed Qutb Uddin Koka as governor of Bengal, and sent him there to negotiate with Sher Afghan to free Mehrun Nisa from his matrimony. But Sher Afghan considered it a matter of honour and found it offensive what the governor demanded, and he was a better fighter and killed the governor and then fled with his wife from his stronghold but was hunted by the troops of the governor and in the fight with the governor's army was killed at their hands. He was killed at the end of the year 1606. And the generals of the Emperor's army proved they were robots rather than of live minds. However, they were cause to produce an Empress for India that was exemplary and an example in behaviourism.

Mehrun Nisa was brought to Delhi after the battle where Sher Afghan was killed, but her loyalty to Sher Afghan would not allow her that the Emperor take hold of her hand and make her his wife. For five years she resisted and carried the grief of Sher Afghan and then she had to ultimately give consent for her marriage to the Emperor in 1611. She was thirty-one then, but still a belle - the most beautiful Mehrun Nisa of all the most beautiful women known of the time. She was first given the title of *Noor Mahal* – light of the palace, then in five years, title of *Noor Jahan* – light of the world. And she sat behind the *Chilman* – the translucent hanging screen, and put her hand on the shoulder of the Emperor and guided him in *Jahangiri Adl* – the renowned justice of Jahangir.

The delicate Anaar Kali, because she was a commoner was disallowed to be married to the Prince by Emperor Akbar the Great, though she was love of the all-heart Prince Saleem. And although the Prince was born after much prayer and beseeching to God through the intercession of the Pir-o Murshid – the spiritual leader, Sufi Hazrat Sheikh Saleem Chishti and the prince was the jewel of the eyes of Akbar and mother Joda Baee the Rajput princess, yet such were royalty norms.

Emperor Akbar after years of no heir born to him travelled to the city of Fateh Pur Sikri with his Rajput Queen - Rajkumari Jodha Baee of Jaipur to the doors of the saint Sufi Hazrat Sheikh Saleem Chishti and requested him to pray for him for the boon of a son to be born to the Queen. So, prince Saleem was born after much longing and prayer and his every wish must be met, but not when it comes to blood degeneration. The wish of the prince in matters falling below the dignity of the Royalty could not be entertained by the lofty Emperor.

As for Hazrat Saleem Chisti's boon granting the Emperor a son, it was perfectly with in his purview. The authority to give a son was the scope of the Walis. Angel Gibrael came to Bibi Maryam and said I have come to give you a son and Hazrat Eesa AS. was born. The other boon granted was by Imam Husain AS. to pastor Bahira. He was only five years old in 6 AH - 626 A.D., he was in the company of his Grandfather the Messenger of Allah, Hazrat Mohammad Mustafa SAWW that a Padri – clergyman from Bab Al Saghir Damascas came to Madina. He went to the door of the Messenger of God and saluted the Prophet and said, 'You are the last Messenger of God and you can read the Lauh-e Mahfooz, please check if I have any sons scribed on the Lauh – the plate,'

The Prophet checked and said, 'the Lauh is blank for you.' The pastor wanted sons and was leaving sad and dis-hearted. But he knew that a thing can be written on the Lauh-e Mahfooz and once it is written cannot be erased, but if a thing not written can be written and so he looked appealingly at Imam Husain AS. searching in him if he would make the Ata – the endowment, and he cast a supplicant's appeal in front of him.

The totality is, an Imam is always an Imam, whether these are the days of his infancy, or the days of youth, or grown to maturity or when he entered the stated pithy of Imam hood. Imam Husain AS. said, 'I give you a son.' The Prophet SAWW said, oh but by fate he has no son and Imam Husain said, 'I give him two sons' the Prophet interrupted again and the young Imam said, 'I give him three sons' and the Prophet interrupted him reminding him of Bahira and his fate, and it happened seven times and the Imam each time gave the Rahib a son. The Prophet then said to the pastor now seven sons are mentioned on the Lauh-e Mahfooz, and the priest had seven sons born to him.[28]

Each singularity of event under the cosmos is carrying an entailing information. This whole cheerful narrative of the generosity of Imam Husain AS. was revelation, introducing the jurisdiction of every one of the Punjatan, wherein each had their authority and power independent of the other and each were benign to degrees, levels and extents as to decide by their immediate disposition to meet the Hajat – the requirement of the beseeching the benefit he was seeking.

---

[28] This narration has been heard continuously from many sources. The Rahib came from Helab. This miracle is mentioned in Karamat-o-Mojzat Ameerul Momeneen AS., by Hujjatul Islam Andurzgo, also in Majmooa-ay Mojzat Bahraat by Seqatul Islam Waez Khurasani. After the Imam granted him seven sons the Rahib requested the Imam to come and visit him. The Imam accepted it and the Imam's head after he was martyred in Karbala was taken by the army of Yazid to the monastery for a break of journey where this Rahib was. He saw a light emanating from the head and he requested the troop to give him the head for the night and took the head, washed it and placed it on the pedestal and light emanated from the head and it was the fulfilment of promise of Imam Husain AS. that he will to come to the clergy Bahira that he his head was there.

Sufi Hazrat Sheikh Saleem Chishti's authority was a Wali, though never even comparable with the authority of the Imams of the Aehlebaait, yet he was an Arif — one having insight knowledge and would consider it an honour if an Imam of the Aehlebaait called him his servant, he carried the authority to bless the Emperor with a son. Hazrat Sheikh Saleem Chishti in return only asked the Emperor to put the son's name on his name - Saleem. The danger was Emperor Akbar could equally have named his son after the Rajput Hindu names, which would have been a burden on the Wali.

When Prince Saleem was born after seven years of restless waiting and now the sustainability of the dynasty of Emperor Jalal Uddin Mohammad Akbar was assured, the Emperor was filled with thankfulness, hope and glee. It was a very major event in the history of the Moghul dynasty and in the Empire history of India. In this empire was nearly the entire Land of the Seasons and Songs. Emperor Jalal Uddin Mohammad Akbar had to match the Moghul majesty with the momentous event and he ordered to open the seals of the vaults of the treasuries.

Three Crore Rupees, 100,000 Bighah[29] of land and three hundred villages were given away in thanksgiving on the birth of the Prince. The Prince then was weighed on his birthdays in Pearls four times, in Turquoises the fifth time and in Rubies the sixth time over his numbers of years as he grew. The Prince was the dynasty saviour and the gift of God and all the worldly cares and comforts were provided to him and nothing was spared that he wanted that was not provided. But Heaven high strict control was kept on him in observance to the norms of Royalty and he was not allowed to marry below his station.

The Prince was given in the care of the Sufi Sheikh Saleem Chishti whose gift he was, and was left in Fatehpur Sikri for his coaching. And tenderness in the heart and respect for justice was so deeply entrenched by the Sheikh in him that he found in the weigh balance of justice even his beloved Noor Jahan guilty of an inordinate shot of arrow from her that had killed the lowly rural. Noor Jahan was ordered to be put to sword by Jahangir to serve justice that was life for life and

---

[29] One Bighah = 1936 sq yards. One Canal = 605 sq yards. One Acre = 4840 sq yds. (66 feet x 660 feet), One Marla = 30.25 sq yards

tooth for tooth, but Jahangir tremblingly prayed to God to save her life.

And if it were not for the reparation – the *Deet*, his beloved and talented Noor Jahan[30] would have been put to sword. The Jahangiri period was renowned for justice, which God loved. Serving justice and enforcing injunctions of God is the greatest service the God's servant can do on earth and that Jehangir did. Jahangir to his credit has written his autobiography, *Tuzk Jahangir* – the grandeur of Jahangir, showing his literary capability besides his unmatched leaning to the cause of the merit of justice, and his rule was of aristocracy and meritocracy – not democracy, not monarchy of absolute power.

Contrary to the Kings under bond – not allowed to do what they could not do against Sharia in the Land of Seasons and Songs, exception was in the Muslim Ruler of Europe, Ali Pasha of Albania. He exceeded effrontery about whom Poet Lord Byron 1788 to 1824 says, 'He was a fine portly person with 200 women and as many boys[31]' and he says, 'Many of the lass he saw, very pretty creatures they were.' In Europe there was aversion to polygamy but this latitude was perfection as seen in Islam. Here in Europe the Church clamped the liberty of men and kings to access to acquire more than one wife, and it deflated into the sin of sexual relationship between men and men and to a level as something fashionable and permitted in the Greek society[32] for strong bond between men. And Greece was the hub of the pride of the culture of Europe.

And what dysfunctionality of righteousness and the trampling of the man's right it was! Among the Kings, bound, frayed, ostracized and disallowed availing God's sanction of more than one wife was King Edward V111 son of King George V; disallowed a hypothetical operating

---

[30] The arrow she threw from the bow to prey a wild deer hit a Kissan - a peasant. He died and the Jahangiri justice came in force and the innocent of intentional killing Noor Jahan was sentenced to death, but for provision of Deed, it saved her life.

[31] This indulgence with the male gender of the Pasha was not allowed in Islam but of the ladies in the class as Kaneez or servants in service had no restrictions or inhibitions and it was permitted.

[32] Islam disallowed homosexuality and dealt the offence with severe punishment because of its pre-knowledge of its hazardous disease of syphilis it harboured to detriment health.

of two wives and reaping the advantage of the logic of God's sanction in marriage and saving his throne. The King had to abdicate the throne to marry Mrs Wallis Warfield Simpson. He had to sacrifice his throne to put at ease the parliament and the Archbishop whose concern was saving the purity of the blood of the Royalty which was going to be transformed from pounds weight to ounces if the King of England was to marry a two-time divorcee. In all this the charm and the captivation of Mrs Simpson overwhelming the King was the straw that broke the camel's back. For the relief of the king, the Archbishop and the Parliament were unable to find the solution available from God they worshipped. Its conveyance though was revealed through His last Messenger, but that was negated to the detriment of the society. And the innate saying sprang; 'Mrs Simpson pinched the King of England', was allowed to prevail.

And as to the breakdown of the restrictive law, raising challenges to the Church's jurisprudence; Louis XV of France's behaviour was an open protest against the Church; he housed a bevy of young girls near the Palace of Versailles where he serviced them, excelling his great-grandfather Louis XIV in this demeanour of match game. Louis XV created the rank of official mistresses and put them to occupy recognized positions in his court. The bevy of young girls regularly serviced by the gallant Louis XV were equivalent to the *Laundis* – the slave girls which were allowed in the Shariat of Islam but not in the Shariat drawn by the Church, still the King indulged him unrestrained by any Shariat of the Church and freely exploited what the bevy had to offer. All this was a repercussion to the clamp on the sanction given by God of availing more than one wife, and there is no Church big enough on earth to throw a challenge to God, Who stationed His premise and laws.

Of the Kings in Europe, only the King-in-Waiting of England, His Highness Prince Charles Philip Arthur George, Prince of Wales, Earl of Chester, Duke of Cornwall, Duke of Rothesay, Earl of Garrick, Lord of the Isles and Baron Renfrew, Prince and Great Steward of Scotland deserved sympathy! He had excuses against the beguiling done to the Kings of Europe by the Church and for the reasons:

When Diana and Charles were married consonant with the 1689 Bill of Rights and the 1701 Act of Settlement of Parliament, Diana held a permissible spark of the infancy of love for an imagery James Hewitt, and Charles had a full flung, flaming - impermissible love for real Camilla Parker Bowles and she was out with her sparking determination to saddle herself on the pony representing the gem of the ruling cliché of the reign of the Duchess of Cornwall and enter the Royal House of Windsor with its peace supporting her.

And it was easy, since Princess Diana was nagging and complaining and since she threw vases at the Prince, and was strong spirited and considered the Prince old hat and of behindhand. But the Prince was that who considered even Descartes, Voltaire Leibniz, Locke and Rousseau old hats with their enlightenment into grooming culture through reason, 100 years old. And his enlightenment and entelechy in boosting the survival of mother earth, was his concern and advocation for building houses such that where birds such as swallows and swifts could make their nests for their comfort, and his saying was, "It is immoral not to consider those other species that share this planet with us." All this prove he is more innocent and of gold heart than the circumstantial evidences submitted their records.

And Camilla Parker Bowles though not in degrees as beautiful, was caressing and of kind words and she conducted as appropriate. And Diana though justified and of pretty looks, but a dear which leapt out of bounds. And liberalism in the guise of materialism was victorious, only the price paid was the cash of spiritualism! There was divorce and then vague liberalism to marriage.

The universal demand of prevailing normality on the Royalties were stringent and their binds were of onerous. The status of Royalty demanded its heraldry must not shake hands with pretentions, and beauties carved and dissuasion to un-exemplariness established. It was in all practicalities possible that Charles could have had two wives as the law of God permitted, and for this; the doctrines ruling the west, needed changed for fullness of life taking hold of man, and forced destiny disallowed to take its course and Diana thereby could not be divorced and she would reconcile to the hard reality in vogue in the society of two wives.

The world looks for ready precedence, it continues to look towards the houses of culture - the Royal Houses for standards evolved traditions, and fashions created, and idealism generated, and the duty as such of the Royalty was to present idealistic precedence, and not addendums of commonplace. They ought to create exemplariness in them to harness minds and mould them to enlightenments and the most formidable source to draw these from, with ethical and humanly views, is the House of the Aehlebaait, the house of the Prophet Mohammad Mustafa SAWW. And look at them, they marry more than one wife, continue with politics of reason, prayer of intensity of continuous uplift of self, giving charity by way of demonstration and in secrecy and lay down lives when needed to stand in defence of righteousness.

But virtue has many forms and Diana divorced or not, she was princess of the hearts and there was no one like of her to come to them with straight sanction of the parliament and the consent of the Bishop. And her innocent eyes told when she came to them, she had not seen ignominies that debauched world and her beauty were without match. It permeated to the inside of her and spread to the outside of her to cover her. She received ovations at her Cinderella wedding, and when she left this world, she was declared Cinderella of Nature. Her last journey through the kingly streets of London was breath taking; nearly the entire world halted for two minutes and prayed for her for forgiveness.

Where then there was left any burden of sin if she carried one on her shoulders, of neglect and permissiveness. There was a fair guarantee that that was gone. She had not shed human blood, she had not told lies, but the balance sheet was she was treading the soil of Africa to salvage the victims of Aids. The tragedy is she was not given time to redress her with *Tobah* – the penance, and her end came. The rare shyness with the acute smile was gone and she was not preserved. They better preserved instead the smile that was not so known that of Mona Liza.

Talking of the binds of the Church, in all these Kings beguiled and weighed down by Church doctrine, only the brilliant 16th century King Henry V111 was exempt. He was strict on morality and the assumption was that he sought to marry more than one wife as permitted by the Holy Quran, where the Providence permitted Kings and Men what suited them best. But because the will of the Church prevailed, his six Queens suffered the fate of: Divorced, Beheaded, Died, Divorced, Beheaded, Survived.

Of these the second Queen Anne Boleyn was executed in 1536 on the accusation of infidelity and the French poet Lancelot de Carless wrote a 1,000-line poem about her promiscuity. But unfortunate as it was, it was again related with the Church's one-dimensional freedom of one wife to men and of not allowing bigamy or polygamy i.e., allowing them having more than one wife. The Queen Anne was driven to take five lovers to produce a son for Henry. She was afraid of the first Queen, Catherine of Argon was divorced for not producing a male heir and there was intermittent impotence of the King in her way, and the King craved for a male heir and the Queen was desperate to produce one. And this led to the unholiness created by extraneous.

The men following the Church doctrine, could never break its sophism of 'one man one wife' imposed on them, although the law of the Gospel allowed the contrary and the earliest Church permitted it to own more than one wife. And the rule was simple; God allowed men to take more than one woman as wives in contractual marriage, but inhibited polyandry and made women to have only one master as there was only one master of a soul. The women were allowed to have only one husband and that God issuing the approvals and injunctions was the same God Whose message was of the same substance in Gospel, as in Torah, as in Quran and in ancient Vedas[33].

But despite such ease from God the order was disorderliness, there was a goddess of love Aphrodite, she sprang from the oysters and gave birth to Eros, the god of passion. And Casanova the famous took to his profession of morale evil and he tasted undeclared marriages. He would start dinner with twelve oysters and then he was ready for the bevies. And there in the Land of Seasons and Songs the order was, the goddess of love Sarasvati sprang as the daughter of Durga and she occupied her seat on the water flower lotus and initiated the music of Sitar – the three stringed guitars and sang morning song *Bhairwi,* the first thing as her prelude and observed chastity as consort of Brahma. So, the populace followed the order of Sarasvati and Brahma.

---

[33] Only we see in the Mahabharat Druvadi has five Pandu brothers as husbands, but the pretension offered was Lord Vishnu said to her, each morning she will be virgin after bath.

Jalal-Uddin Mohammad Akbar Emperor of India reigned from 1556 to 1605 AD, and never was such majesty on display as shown in practice by Akbar. He imprinted the annals of times with sovereign decisions using his great intellect, and though he was not so educated, but bless Khan Khana the teacher and ward of Akbar, he had sufficiently equipped him with the basic of learning and emperor Akbar's capability to analyse situations in correct perspective left nothing wanting. *In his rule Shia and Sunni went to one mosque and Franks and Jews to one Church and observed their own form of prayer.* And followers of Hinduism paid no Jizya and their damsels were married and brought to the Royal house and carried equal family right.

This Shia tenet of justice — what God does is justice was the character of Emperor Akbar. Shah Tahmasp I of Persia had obliged Emperor Akbar's father Himayoun regain Delhi's Kingdom in 1555, Emperor Akbar had Shia proximity in his character. More so, his Shia character was due to the influence of his Shia General, Wazir and *Ataleeq* – prime minister and tutor, Bairam Khan Khan Khana who had shielded Akbar to ascend to the throne of Delhi. Akbar's Harem consisted of three hundred legal wives and when the number of his wives in his harem reached to the figure just to three hundred and one, he took a strict decision.

The constant rejection of the status of his married bevies was declared not legal under the Islamic jurisprudence in vogue in the court as issued by his Sunni Qazi. It made him rethink of its validity, the Sunni Qazi disallowed *Mutah* - the period contractual marriage and that facility in the scripture of Quran existed. The Emperor therefore turned down the Qazi verdict and solved the problem simply; he dismissed the Sunni Qazi and appointed a Shia Qazi whose interpretations into the contractual marriage was as allowed in the Quran. It allowed him declare all of them legal, with their various status they were enjoying and the Emperor said, 'morality under the shield of simplicity was God's and man's proviso.'

Emperor Akbar's reign was the grandest period of Mughal rule. And the lowest in power and prestige was of Mohammad Shah's 1738 – 1739, of the Mughal's house. Nadir Shah like Ameer Temur Lung had appeared suddenly on the horizon of power for his brilliant insightfulness as conqueror. He tore apart bondages of poverty and class distinction and emerged as a ruler of historic importance. Nadir Shah rose from the background of a shepherd's family and became Emperor of Delhi by snatching throne from the Moghul Emperor Mohammad Shah. Mohammad Shah was a dynastic king with kingliness running in his House for five generations. And for that clique of distinction a *Vazir* – minister of the court of Mughal Emperor Mohammad Shah, directed a concealed insult at Nadir Shah and asked sarcastically, "What was your *Shajra-e Nasab* – the family tree?"

Now Nadir Shah was an ordinary son of a shepherd and he had risen to be king and could not have claimed five generations of kingship behind him, so he replied, "I am *Ibn Shamsheer, Ibn Shamsheer, Ibn Shamsheer, Ibn Shamsheer, Ibn Shamsheer* – I am son of sword for five generations. And that scared the life out of the minister and he was dumb quiet.

The Afghans invaded Persia in 1719 and deposed the Safavid Shah in 1722 and Afghan ruler Mehmud Ghilzai 1699-1725 murdered a large number of Safavid Princes. In one stroke he had massacred all the leading citizens in Isfahan when they were called as invitee to a feast arranged for them. The Afghan tyranny and the ruthlessness created the necessity and emergence of a Nadir Shah a rescuer and leader and the Providence picked up from the ordinary of them and gave rise to him to be ruler.

In 1727, Nadir Shah offered his services to the heir of the Safavids dynasty, Tahmasp II, 1704 -1740, and he staged the re-conquering of Persia and drove the Afghan out of Khurasan and then conquered Herat, Qandhar, Kabul and Punjab and how often the world sees the cause appropriating itself. That was evident in the shape of Nadir Shah - the *Makafat-e Amal* or the suffering for the misdeed or the Karma was paid back as return of doings to Mehmud Ghilzai, he was brutally killed by his own people and these events were convincingly the *Shahadat* - the established proof of the existence of God.

Nadir Shah Afshar 1698-1747 AD, ruled as Shah of Iran from 1736 to 1747. He has been described as Napoleon of Asia and the like of Alexander the great of Greece for his military genius. He raised a standing army of 375,000 men laced with modern equipment. He built a Navy that conquered Oman, and drove the Ottomans, Russians and the Afghans out from Persia and became so powerful that he removed the Safavids from the throne of Persia who had ruled for 200 years and became Shah of Iran in 1736 and founded Afsharid dynasty. He was assassinated in 1747 by the Qizilbashi conspirators in Khurasan. When he became isolated due to his use of absolute and indiscriminate power. Nadir Shah Afshar's successes were phenomenal and he is credited for restoring Iranian power.

When Nadir Shah went for Ziarat to the Rauza of Hazrat Ali – Maula, lord of all soul declared by Allah and Rasul, an honour that will never come to any human again. At the mausoleum of this Maula, Nadir Shah saw a huge crowd of blind and lame sprawling there outside in the courtyard. He enquired from his noblemen who these people are. He was told they are the needy praying at the shrine, some for the restoration of eyes, some for limbs and some praying for other needs. Nadir Shah had such an unshakable faith in Maula Ali that he knew that they were not praying hard enough with sincere devotion and for that their prayer has not been realised. He ordered that he is going inside the shrine to do Ziarat and when he has come out of the shrine if still, he finds a blind with no eyes and lame not healed and needy standing unanswered with his need unfulfilled, he will have them put to sword, their heads will be severed from their necks.

Nadir Shah went inside the mausoleum, he kissed the Zaree – the silver lattice of the tomb of his Maula and paid his respects and when he came out, in this time the blind and lame had prayed so hard that the lame got healthy limbs and the blind their eye sights, and those sticking around for collection of alms and charity who had no need to pray ran away from there. These needy at the shrine were comfortable, receiving alms and charities and food that was fed to them and they did not need to pray deep down from their hearts, but Nadir Shah's sword forced them to do that.

Besides his military genius, Nadir Shah had other qualities. He stopped open *Tabarra* – damnation, the curse sent by the populace of Iran on the first three caliphs. They considered them not deserving the rank and the post of the Caliphate and were of disservice to the faithful. The Tabarra was sent on them after the prayers in the mosques during the Safavids reign. Nadir Shah for uniting all various factions of Islam stopped that.

Some men who were instilling revolt against his reign were weeded out by Nadir Shah and kept under observation, but they fled from Persia and Afghanistan and took shelter under Mohammad Shah in Delhi. Nadir Shah asked for their repatriation to him, but Mohammad Shah in Delhi so disdained the idea of surrendering them that he neither sent a reply to his letter nor disowned these men. This annoyed Nadir Shah. He first conquered Qandhar in 1738 and then seized Ghazni, Kabul and Peshawar and then advanced through Punjab and captured Lahore, and then turned to India and marched towards Delhi. The Moghul army was defeated in February 1739 at Karnal and Emperor Mohammad Shah was captured. Nadir Shah entered in Delhi in triumph with Mohammad Shah.

Next day word was spread that Nadir Shah has been assassinated. The Moghul noblemen taken over by this rumour revolted against the conqueror and killed many of Nadir Shah's soldiers. This infuriated Nadir Shah and he ordered his soldiers of general massacre. The resisting noblemen in Delhi and all behind the plot, in one day 20,000 men were killed. Mohammad Shah slumped to his knees and begged for mercy.

He had to hand over the keys of the treasury and he lost all the Royal treasures and with that the Peacock Throne that was taken by Nadir Shah to Persia to be part of the treasures of the Persian Empire. Nadir Shah stayed in Delhi for six months and thereafter returned to Iran, leaving one of his generals, Ahmad Shah Abdali behind as governor of Punjab, who had risen in Nadir Shah's army from his personal attendant to the rank of general of the Abdali contingent and was with him in the India campaign. The plunder seized by Nadir Shah from India was so huge that he stopped taxation in Iran for three years and prices fell there and there was general prosperity in Iran.

Mughal dynasty was weakened and a new power centre rose in Lucknow. The dynasty of the Nawabs 1722 – 1856 was established in Lucknow by the Nishapur Shahs whose first ruler was Nawab Burhanul Mulk Sadaat Khan 1722 – 1739. The Nawabs of Awadh were the legend for the sophistications they introduced in their distinguished courts and in the back-sitting tertiary territories under their rule to make life full of refined mannerism. And people hesitated to take their names until a mention of regard and respect was made for them.

Of them the last Nawab, Nawab Wajid Ali Shah was extreme in benignity in the acts of benevolence and commanded great respect for him in the hearts of his people for maintaining very dignified ways about him, and for giving rise to a culture to its people of fine etiquettes and practice of hospitality.

In all his known life the Nawab kept his self-bound to the spells of noble acts. This had earned him a distinction for carrying acknowledged accomplishment in spirituality in him. This was the view of the accomplished with their standing in the realm of spirituality who were of high distinctions, and they lent to bow a respect to this spirituality elated Nawab for his standing in benevolence and his purity of mind. The incident of the case of the barber in his service spoke of the degree of the purity held mind in sanctimony and in elations he held for which he was given such acknowledgements.

The case was that the Nawab's barber was bit of a buck – a Ban-Kay – a self-pepped. He tried to be fresh with the Nawab and spoke a bit discordantly, bereft of the regards due for the Saidanis - the pious ladies taking descent from the progenies of the House of the Prophet of God SAWW, who deserved reverence for their purity. And this incident spoke of the extent to which this Nawab Wajid Ali Sha's mind held the *Saidanis* in reverence. The barber spoke thus: "*Huzoor* - sire, I got married again. Now I have married a *Saidani*."

The Saidanis were ladies of Hashemi descent and the word Saidani was singular and was restricted to defining the feminine offspring – the descendants from Hazrat Ali AS. and from Bibi Fatimah Zehra SUA and men asking for their hands had to be equivalent of their status and of a worthy descent. And the barber was disruptive of the respect he ought to have shown to the ladies of that calibre – the Saidanis. Now being Nawab's barber meant he was a man of position and of reach and he won this distinction of getting married to a Saidani who was some poor destitute Saidani.

The Nawab who immediately saw the degradation of the status of the Saidani, due to this casualty incurred by the barber was furious, and said to the menace:

"You married a Saidani and didn't your eyes go burst – *Teri Aakhein Naheen Phoot Gaein.*"

And the barber had it, his eyes went burst, he became blind. The horror effect of the barber - his transgression on a poor Saidani was too much for the Nawab. And a shocked Nawab spoke words which homed in. The barber knew of the spirituality of the Nawab. We are not clear whether he recovered his sight, but understand this barber must have recovered his sight after his seeking pardon.

The *Bankay* (singular, Banka) of Lucknow were a class who had adopted attitude of carrying no problems, they dressed in the dress of thin *Malmal* or muslin white *Kurta* – the loose flowing white shirt with stiffening starch applied to its sleeves by the Dhobi and the sleeves pressed in a fashion to show crinkle as to present many, many wavy folds of tidiness. They wore it, be it cutting cold to establish their oneness in toughness. And for impressing the style of manliness that supposedly they will carry, they kept a moustache with its tips raised upwards and they had a full head of long hair to present the style to look impressive. The shoes they wore had a pointing toe with a furl and curl of prominence and they walked *Mastana* – swaying their body. And they projected their personality they wanted to air about them that they stood by their promise whatever the consequence and conveyed the cult that they may be trusted even for a proxy commitment, come what may.

The Bankay had taken to the principle by evolving their style in interpretation of Aayet 2.177, which was a complete definition of a reliable praying Muslim which was their point of adaptation to fashion their living, whereby they felt bound to put their face towards Kaaba to say Namaz and doing charity and searching in it to be haughty. So, when they made promise they were equal to their words, standing firm in hardships and difficulties and had claim to be abstemious – the *Parhezgar* with their virtues of rugged face and rugged manners.

The Nawab with his humilities overriding his sanctity and his insights dominating smoothness into sanctitude and grace dominating man's share of prejudices, with his postulates revealing all his virtues of sanctimoniousness above all fallacies, accorded a very high degree of respect to the ladies of virtue and to the ladies of pious descent and to those falling in the class who liked to follow suit to the dictates of virtue in life. The Nawab gave a whole-hearted support in preserving the status of this silent class in virtue, and in this venue as response, the ladies maintained and preserved the dignity of their finer class, which was the status awarded to them by God. These ladies in the Nawabdom commanded deep respect and were of reverence and they were shielded from the eyes of the males who were disallowed by the defined set laws of the Book of God to cast eye on them.

An enclosure of two Purdah walls made from two sheets of cotton was formed and held on all the four sides of these ladies by the *Mahram* – men before whom the law in Pardah allowed them to appear in their chasteness without veil. And they were led out between the two walls to board a waiting transport when coming out from their house and they were all the time kept in Pardah. And the Mahram, as defined in depth were those on whom the ladies could cast their eyes at, due to being in kinship, if that kinship permitted for them to come out unveiled before them by the *Shariat* – the divine law.

The ladies nevertheless and in spite of these restrictive bindings and stringent etiquettes had to play a very great dominating role in the conduct of the affairs of their male members in moulding events that concerned them, which without their participation could be perturbing to them and to the society. However, they showed judiciousness and did not let their presence become participative of the male company, keeping themselves behind curtain and staying within the four walls of their houses, but fully exercising their authority. And their participating had become a matter of very great necessity for its weight it carried, and it had become a high influence-bearing tow line in the formation and the patterning of the society.

And perchance in a Sayed's matrimony if a Saidani came, who was dark skinned, like in the case of Sayed Riyazul Hasan's Mankooha Saidani, he would show extra love and devotion for her, standing beside her bed with glass of water and medicine because she was prone to be sick and on that always way behind in getting ready when going out to visit relatives and in taking part in family functions. The Sayed will show additional devotedness and wait cheerfully for her, till she was ready. And even if all signs appeared of being late to meet the schedule of the function, she still, despite it could spell, 'first she has to comb her hair, then powder her face, then take out a dress and open the box of jewellery for wearing in the ear, i.e. wear the ear-ring

226

one suited to the occasion,' and she will tell a long list of things needed to be done, but the typical Sayed, in Sayed Riyazul Hasan would cheerfully wait and on no account show any vexation, but only a greater display of love for her because she was comfortable with herself and was a dark skin Saidani, with charm not dull.

The Nawabs of Awadh were Shia Muslims and there was nothing amiss in justice in their rule and there was an excellent tradition of impartiality in their realm. The Shias and the Sunnis were treated equally in the dignified rule of the Nawabs of Awadh. The Chief Secretary – the *Munshi-ul Sultan* was Sunni. The Chief Minister – *Vazir* - the *Munsirim-ud Daula* was Sunni and the arrangement for the Majalis and of the *Imam Barda* – the mansion of the Imam(s) allocated for function commemorating the anniversaries of the martyrdom of Imam Husain AS. and the celebratory functions of the birthdays of the progenies of the Prophet of God SAWW were in the hands of Sunni. The Majalis of Moharram were held with regularity and the pathos to devotedness of mourning, and the arrangements of its running were done by the Sunni. The *Amanat-ud Daula,* or the Paymaster - the *Bakhshi* paying salaries and allowances was a Sunni. And no one cared who was Sunni, who was Shia in the rule of these Nawabs.

The citizens had little time to put labels on each other as to which faith they belonged to what was their religious trend was not concern of any one nor shown any reservation for it, this was out of etiquette. The boon of it all was, the inter religious and race relation was in harmony in the Land of Seasons and Songs, which was never seen at its best, as in the times of these Shia Nawabs of Awadh. Many prominent Hindu noblemen built their own Imam Bardas with *Shah Nasheens* – the royal pedestal on which Alam – the standard of Hazrat Abbas AS., Tazias and replicas of the shrines of the Holy Imams were placed. The Nawabs participated in the festivals of Dewali and Holi and the populace had very little left they would not participate in each other's celebrations, in happiness and in sadness.

The common trait and the national pastime of the folks of the Nawabdom was of training and keeping the *Kabooter*(s), the pigeons, *Bateir*(s), the partridges, *Toata*(s), the parakeets, the ring-necked parrots. These were kept as pets and greatly cared to and the Toatas were taught to speak. Partridge and quail were led to fight. These fights were organised and Kabooters were trained with such expertise that when the trainer whistled or made a coded sound, they immediately turned back from the flight to their trainers and there were pigeon keepers everywhere. And it was considered kind and livening to keep Kabooters. A fistful of sum was spent on purchasing fancy and high flight Kabooters which made fast turns and tacking in the flight. They rolled in the air in their flight and these were called the *Uran Kabooters*.

The *Patti Kabooters* carried a thin band of feather f colour round their necks and the *Laqa*(s) had long neck, white feather and large sharp eyes and graceful appearance. These were kept in the houses and these livened the surroundings. They hopped in small hops and made fluttering small flights and sat from one place to another in the houses. And then there were the *Shirazi*(s), they had alternating bluish and brownish feather and the other was the *Jungali*. He was gruffy and parent of all of them and the Jungali was sold by the *Chirdimar* – the bird trapper for two Paisas a Kaboter and the Shirazi(s) were kept and trained by professional breeders i.e., *Kabooter Baaz*. These nuggets of the breeds fetched to the breeder from the *Ba Zauq* – of taste hobbyist, from sixty Rupees to ten thousand Rupees a pair of Kabooter.

Some people kept the tribes of the pigeons in a *Khaun* – a cavity made in the ground. A belly shape pit was made for housing pigeons in the court yards of the houses. The Khaun had *Kabook*(s) or small square slots, suited in depth and cut all round in the wall of the belly. The circular mouth of the belly was entrance and exit for the pigeons. A *Chabootra* or square raised platform was made near the wall of the house and the Khaun was located at the centre of the platform and the pigeons descended in the Khaun belly and went to their home slots in the warmth below and each pair needed two slots, one for male and one for female. The characteristic of the pigeons was they did not change their mates and their offspring took to them.

The opening for the entrance in the Khaun was made of a comfortable size circle. This was covered in the nights by a *Jhau-wa* – a heavy basket, made from the lentil *Kanrd* – stalks, of the plant *Arhar* - the *Toor*. The Jhau-wa kept the cats away. They were always lurking round to get the pigeons. The Jhauwa was bigger than the *Tokra* but all these were made from the *Kanrd* sticks and the Jhauwa because it was big and weighty kept the cats from pushing it to the side, away from the entrance.

The *Tokra* was a close knit, sturdy large basket and its match the *Tokri* was light and small. The word Tokra, in keeping with the grammar of the language spoken in the Land of Seasons and Songs suggested of its masculinity. Its name was in keeping with the nature's desire of masculinity donated by its rising 'aa' sound to it, and the nature likewise allocated dominance of strength put together through its Kardein (stalks) in its share, and it was of a strong weave, made from slim but sturdy brown twigs for its generic class from the Kanṛdein of Arhar – the populist lentil plant. And for its masculinity, it withstood to take strong knocking about and went through rough handling.

The Tokra and the Jhauwa for their weight and bigness, and their sound ending with 'aa' conveyed of their masculinity and a confidence encircled them, reposed in their being for the user of their sturdiness. And out of them, mostly the Jhauwa was placed on the mouth of the Khaun, for it tended to be bigger. It was also sparingly knitted with heavier Kardein, and by its nature allowed air and light to pass through its slits or spacing into the belly of the Khauon below, but no other extraneous thing to pass through it. The pigeons did not feel estranged, cooped up and suffocated for the grace of the Jhauwa with its weight apprehending its displacement, watching the entrance and parrying the cat and shut the entrance securely.

At one edge of the Khaun in our house in Rala, sat snug a five feet high stand with its platform for the birds to land, perch on it. And grain and water were placed on the floor in earthen bowls for these birds to peck, drink and wet their wings in water. They pecked grain and drank water and bathed their feather with great display of joy, cooing and trudging the place with their short walks with smartness.

The Khaun and each of the pigeonhole were white washed with lime-water, and the floor of the belly was given a regular cleaning to keep vermin away and keep the pigeons healthy. This pigeon house was in my grandfather's house of Sayed Nazim Husain – an extremely considerate and a manly man in Mauza Ralah, Tahseel Sirathu. Some thirty pigeons lived in that Khaun and they were living in that pigeon house from since when, I do not know. I saw them fluttering out in the mornings from the Khaun, when the large heavy Tokra - the Jhauwa was removed by my 12-year-old uncle Sayed Anwar Husain and the entrance door was opened for the pigeons to start their day's errand. Grain and water mostly the birds filled themselves with was from wherever they went flying to peck.

The hens laid eggs in their slots and brought out their broods and the pigeons were sometimes less and some times more in numbers and they formed a good part of the topic of conversation between my young uncles. Anwar Husain and Ashoor Husain. My grandfather God bless him, so loved the pigeons that he always found time to play with them. He would put a grain of *Bajra* – the millet or some such grain in between his lips and the pigeons would come walking jerking their heads gracefully, with raised necks and intentional display of pleasure and gently peck the grain from the lips holding it. It was evident from their style, nature and grace of walk they presented that they were parading in pride to display of their worth.

The passion for pigeon seeing them flying and going high and seeing them do aerobatics had kept the last Nawab of Awadh so bound to them that in his last days in this world in the days of his exile to Matiaburj, this gracious Nawab bought a pair of pigeons for Rs 25,000. A team of pigeon keepers was employed by him for training and keeping them healthy for making high flights and show their acrobat. At the time of the Nawab's death, some twenty-four thousand pigeons were living, bred and managed by a team of pigeon keepers for the Nawab in Matiaburj.

It was said of the pigeons that they were of Sayed race among the birds. They showed extreme reverence to the House of God - the Kaaba. Thousands of pigeons lived near *Haram* in the precincts of Kaaba, but they never will cross the Kaaba - flying over the Holy Kaaba not cutting the rectangular column space above the Kaaba. These Sayed birds showed their respect for Kaaba, and wondered when they saw woman were struck repeatedly by the *Mutauwa(s)* – the clergies appointed by the Kingdom of Saudi Arabia for kissing the impression on the stone of the foot of Hazrat Ibrahim AS. at the Moqam -e Ibrahim. The ladies came to kiss the stone on which the Holy Prophet had stood, when he was building the Kaaba with his Prophet son Hazrat Ismail AS. The impression of the foot was glass encased, but they were hit for kissing it, since in the neo-Wahabi faith it was Bidat - schism to kiss the *Shires* – the signs of Allah.

Simultaneously there in Kaaba the turbaned clergy, Mulla Makki was giving sermon in Urdu - giving lessons in the exegeses of Quran. He held his group class after Maghrib, the evening prayer. On September 29, 2003 he was elaborating Aayet 34:14 to his pupils who were huddling in a semi-circle in front of him in the open courtyard near Kaaba. Makki was saying:

"About Hazrat Suleiman AS. they say, he kept standing after his death, with nothing happening to his face or to his clothes. The confirmation of this happening is found in the books of the Jews, but they cannot be relied upon, since they changed their Book Torah. Other ones are the Shias whose books describe[34] this, but they cannot be relied upon since they distort facts and in their *Fiqah* or jurisprudence it is all right to make lies and they are *Kazib* – the liars. The Jews and the Shias do *Ghulu* – make true of untrue in their books and cannot be relied upon for the statement they make about Hazrat Suleiman AS."

He was freely preaching dissent, accusing Shias of lying in the courtyard of Kaaba in disregard to any reverence Muslims show to each other in the Haram. And those men sitting encircling Makki were listening to his diatribe and he was preaching spite and discord in Kaaba for 200,000 Muslims from Kuwait, Pakistan, Iraq, Indonesia, Malaysia and England, excluding the 400,000 from Iran, who had to hear him. He was allowed such platform to burst his spites, but he was not the only one preaching hate and dissent; there were others, with their groups, who came out with such preaching that Hazrat Ali was never born in Kaaba and they were Kazib who say so.

Such preaching is bound to change the thinking of the attendee students, instilling in them attitudes and precepts of hate and discord and ignore history and not knowing of God will, and power. These sermons springing from the precincts of Kaaba from the *Ulema-ay Soo* – scholars of negativity are against the ethics of Islam. But the Saudi

---

[34] Aayet 34: 14 says Nabi Hazrat Suleman AS. died but kept standing supported by stick and no one told Jinnat of his dying till termite eating his staff made it hollow and it broke and the Corpse fell then the Jin knew.

Kingdom seems to endorse it and they have allowed many horrors to happen.

The Nawabs of Awadh were pillars of culture and decency. They were prides of Nawabs, known for their excellence, and heaven high finesses. Their affection for the masses, suaveness, refined culture, rising epitomes, articulations and their created fashions were their hallmark of their cognition in state of affairs. The *Matbakh* - the kitchen and the kitchenettes equipped for cooking and fashioning the food for the last Nawab of Awadh, was a laboratory of rare known functions, charged for excelling in food quality of taste and aroma, with artistry and imagination applied to the utmost in the presentation of the food.

This was a laboratory that had attained mastery in innovation, in originating delicacies and producing standards in food, and it continued to sweep its own record of excellences in the art of cookery and decorative presentation. It equipped itself with talents and skills of great chefs, not to fail in the functions it was charged with. It was there where elegance was bred, and style evolved for the cultural grandeur in the fashioning of the food of nourishing looks and of taste with creativity in the cooking of the food, concealing taste in their bosom, which was to be discovered with the pleasantest of surprise on the first crush of the bite. Matching utensils for cooking were shaped and created and crockery and vessels for serving were of the legendry exceptional qualities, kept immaculately shining for serving food and laying varieties of dishes for dazzling the eyes and meet the expectations of the invitees.

Great ingenuities of the chefs were on test at all the times and they had to keep endeavouring to be at the set mark of fine taste and sublime ways of the Nawab, and the chefs did not fail in their assignment and met the stringencies of the demands set by the Nawab and produced unique dishes that amazed many - the elated courtiers and aristocrats who had the honour of sitting at the table with the Nawab and they did not fail to express their praise and wonder for the flavour, looks and the quality of the food. The Nawab did not sit to dine alone without having these guests of taste and men of merit and they were from among the noblemen who carried unique talents as courtiers of the Nawab.

The great chefs of His Excellency the Nawab prepared simulated rice of which each grain was carved from soaked and peeled almonds, cut to resemble the rice kernel. These great chefs prepared *Murgh Musallam* - the cockerel was roasted with its stomach filled with special stuffing of roasted dry fruit of Chiraunji, Sultana, Khaskhas – the poppy-seed-paste, Ja-efal (nutmeg) and Jawattari, fried and ground onion and delicately proportioned dry coriander with measured black pepper. Sweet aroma emanated from the roast, loading the environment with its enticing smell and the Murgh Musallam itself in looks when out was a roast of pink tinge, carrying a glaze of the golden shine and armoured with the marvel of immutable perfection.

The definition of the cockerel was that the bird was bred, grown, and blown to full maturity with feather shining to present a healthy look to the critical eye examining the cockerel. This energy laden cockerel was done Zabah – made Halal, skinned and its stomach filled with preparation of finely ground mixture of choice dried fruits and the chest sewed, and the whole Murgh was put in the envelope of heat of glowing charcoal emerging from healthy logs in a special pit of a thought-out pattern made from clay. The oven was ingenuously made from clay in which smokeless flame was diverted from the wood to the roasting section and rich flavour of the ingredients seeped in, in the limbs and the ligaments of the Murgh.

The Murgh of the Murgh Musallam possessed energy equivalent to forty Murghs. This was done through high powered breeding and rich feeding to the Murghs in hygienic clean environment of the barn, where, out of a group of forty Murghs, one Murgh was cut in the name of God for the rest thirty-nine to feast on its meat. Then the next Murgh was cut the next day and given to the remaining thirty-eight and the process continued till the last cockerel was left and that last had the strength of forty Murghs and that became the adornment to take the shape of Murgh Musallam, decorating the dining table of the Nawab. The Murgh Musallam was based to give a pleasant sweet, alluring aroma emanating from the sweet ingredients placed in the Murgh cavity.

It was in this state of its exuberant purity and delicacy, tinged in a gold colour look, with its emanating luxurious aroma from the spice's combination melted in its chest that the Murgh Musallam was brought to the table of the Nawab in its freshness. The look of the Murgh Musallam was an exacting reddish golden colour to overwhelm the guests and heighten their appetite among other delicacies present. And all the guests seated only waited for the Nawab to take the first morsel from it before they lent themselves wholly to do justice with the Murgh Musallam placed in a large dish. It was the way of the Nawab that he did not dine without guests and the guests were that asset of God who brought fortune to where they went and when left carried away any misfortune if it was there. And it was God rule as He SWT liked this exuberance of invitation.

It was something to be said of the chefs that they were never tired of producing ingenuously thought of new dishes of surprise for presenting these to the Nawab, whose one approving nod, further spurred the chefs to producing further imaginative dishes of outstanding taste and quality. It was the style approved of the *Darogha Matbakh*, the Superintendent of the Food Development Processing and Presentation Department that whereas the resemblance of the food grain served was to be one of a familiar grain farmed off the harvesting field, the taste it produced was to be different. Whereof an element of surprise was sought on the faces of the sophisticated sitting at the dining table, which was monitored for its appearance to emerge on the faces of the surprised diners, which showed it in full expressiveness as the abrupt flash in their eyes, when they found their estimated expectation of the likely taste they imagined to encounter, was way laid behind the reality of the excellence they were experiencing in encountering and enjoying the taste.

And the diners became an unknowing victim of the design of the Darogha Matbakh as they were flashing the expression of surprise for his record. It was registered at once by the attendants serving the invitees. And it was a score point of excellence of the dishes the Matbakh had produced and it was noted and registered for devising future excellences and earning praises.

There were six kitchens of the Royal household and the dishes of exclusivity and variety were prepared there in each, matching to the standards set by the Royal Matbakh, and the Nawab had the benefit of enjoying the best of the dishes from all of them, sent to him by the relatives. Also surpassing this practice; if someone from among the noblemen and relatives wanted to send to the Nawab a *Tora* – a full tray of food dishes: the standard of the Royal Tora was, one hundred and one trays – round brass trays tinned to shine or a solid silver metal trays polished to shine, or a silver plated brass trays, or *Sheesham* wooden trays of rectangular shape, each covered with a silver polished dome-cover, all full of food and each being carried by a line of men and women one behind the other, and the trays placed on their heads.

The trays carried food for one person, and a dome covered the trays, all again covered with a white cloth and an over-cover of an ornate covering of silk or satin and the trays carrying the main courses of standard defines and types from among those produced by the Royal Matbakh. The food was accompanied with a variety of sweet dishes, with *Achar* tray - the pickles as support item to enhance the taste of the main courses.

To name a few of the food varieties of the Tora sent to the Nawab; the following varieties as standardised by the Royal Matbakh were the cogent kinds: In the rice dish class: Pulao, Mutanjan, Biryani, Kushkha, Saada or plain rice. In breads class: Sheermal, Taaftan, Paratha, Chapati, Phulka, Roti, Raughani, Parat-dar-Parat Hawaee Chapatis – the thin chapatis of several layers separated by the film of Ghee. In meat dishes: Qorma, Bhuna Goasht, Pasandah, Doe-Piaza, Kofta, Shorbay Dar Gosht, Qeema, Qatla, Kabab; of which, there were several approved varieties. In the sweet dishes: Sheer Barunj, Shaahi Tukrday, Muuzafar, Feerni, Safaida as well as Murabba(s). Then there were; Achar(s) and Chutni varieties to support the main courses. And these formed a trail of one hundred and one trays of the *Khwan* – the pack of the eatables of the Tora.

The price of one Royal Tora was Rs 500 in these times, which in the periods of some Nawabs was accepted in cash in preference to the ostentation of the actual Royal Tora sent to the Nawab.

Nawab Salaar Jang Haider Beg Khan was a relative of Nawab Shuja-ud-Daula 1753 – 1775. During the reign of this Nawab, Nawab Salaar Jang paid a salary of Rs 1200 a month to his chef. This was the highest salary paid in any court in the Land of Season and Songs to a chef. The chef made gorgeous Pulao for the *Dastar Khwan* of the nobleman. The Pulao would be so rich and mighty that no ordinary person could take more than a few gulps and easily digest it. But Nawab Salar Jang ate heartily that Pulao, with sips of cold water.

The chefs were very much the pride of possession of the noblemen. They were tenderly treated and envied at by other noblemen for someone owning a wonderful chef. And the chefs had a delicate nature, and were not to be annoyed otherwise the quality of the food was affected as the noblemen found out. The chefs were very much valued for their ingenuity and what speciality in food they created and what the chefs could do with meals to feast. And it was accepted the chefs possessed some philosophic tendencies.

In the reign of Nawab Asifud Daula 1775 – 1797, one chef came to the Nawab; he was asked what he made. He said he cooked lentils. He was asked what wages he took; he said five hundred rupees. In these times the clerk in the office took less than twenty rupees a month. The Nawab agreed to employ him, but the chef said he will take the job on two conditions. He was asked what they were. He said the first of them was; when the lentil is desired to be eaten, he must be informed of it two days earlier and the second was, when the lentil was readied and laid on the Dastarkhwan, the Nawab must eat it straight away in two minutes.

The Nawab agreed to the terms of the chef and the chef was sent to the kitchen. After two months the Nawab remembered of the chef and sent order two days ahead to the chef to prepare lentil two days later. The chef prepared the lentil in two days' time and informed the Nawab the lentil was ready. The Nawab was busy, discussing some important political matter with some foreign visitors. He asked the chef to lay the lentil on the Dastar Khwan; he will be coming after one minute. The chef laid the lentil on the Dastar Khwan and waited for one minute and then he went to the Nawab and reminded him of the lentil. The Nawab was still busy. The chef waited a minute longer and went again and reminded him of the lentil, and after a third time reminder when the Nawab still did not come to the Dastar Khwan, the chef picked up the lentil and emptied the bowl on the roots of a dead tree, its stem had dried up long, and he left the palace.

The Nawab when he came to the Dastar Khwan, found neither the lentil nor the chef. The Nawab asked where the chef was, he was told he picked up the lentil, ditched it on the roots of the dead tree and left.

The Nawab asked to look for the chef, but the chef was not found. Later it was reported that the dried-up tree on whose roots the chef had poured the lentil, its stem became green and it was reliving and blossoming.

نوابی کیا تھی شانِ وحدانیت
علی کی تیغ زہرہ کی عبادتِ وحدانیت
زرق برق جلوه حسنِ کردار نمائی
اثر ایسا تھا دنیا پہ آجَ تک بھولی نہ انسانیت
سیّد اطہار حسین

Nawabi Kya Thhi Shan-e Wahdaniat
Ali Ki Tegh Zehra Ki Aebadat-e Wahdaniat
Zarq Barq Jalwah Husn-e Kirdar Numa-ee
Asar Aaisa Thha Dunya PehAaj Tak Bhooli Na Insaniat

What was Nawabdom glamorousness of Oneness
Sword of Ali (AS.) worship of Zehra of Oneness
Glamour and light manifestation beauty of character display
The effect was so on the world till today the humanity did not
    forget

-: . :-

II

KUSHTA AND THE MA AL LAHAM

II

The word Kushta literally means a poisonous substance, but it is not. It is a metal or mineral burnt or roasted to make it eatable. The metals or minerals so treated become calx. They have gone through a change of state and become a pack of energy and an ultimate source for reliance on to farm off energy off them. They have their grades and efficacy and are substances known by the meaning infested word of Kushta(s) and serve the depleted of energy. Whereas the *Ma Al Laham* – the liquid extract from the meat, is the Kushta's organic partner. It is meat juice in liquid form, and Kushta(s) and Ma-al Laham(s) have a twofold function; they prevent ailments taking over human, build fortification against the ailment's attack on the vulnerable and then in the department of capability of reproductivity the show their Jauhar – quintessence and supply energy.

Of the Kushtas; one type of them coming from natural metamorphism (change of form) are called *Salajeet*. It is nature's special gift; nature supplies this mineral ready to farm energy off it. It is in solid state, also in semi solid state and it is known for its potency to supply energy. It is found in rocks and boulders of the mountains and the collectors of the Salajeet, scrounge it from these rocks which have been piled one above the other by nature and form the pretty face of the mountain sides.

Salajeet was found at all levels of heights in the steeliness of the mountains, especially where the baboons lived. The baboons were the indicators that the Salajeet existed in those mountains, and whether it was Ghazni or Turkham, the more the baboons, the better the chance for the errand man to find the Salajeet, which in its raw form was a

238

bubbly, light metallic, steely product of pleasant smell and it was a rare substance.

The Salajeet man sold the Salajeet at one thousand times the price of the easily found ferrous metal – the iron, and the *Pansari* – the shopkeeper of spices and raw herbs kept these in small quantities along with other herbal medicines and raw herbs, such as grass, roots of flourishing herbs, dry fruits and seeds and rare plants' flowers and he was always proud to show his possession of the Salajeet collection to the prospective buyer, if he noticed the customer was knowing the worth of the substance. He said he had purchased that from the well-tried Salajeet man of integrity and said he had to do a fair amount of haggling with him to obtain that precious genuine piece of Salajeet, he was holding in his hand.

All the Salajeet collectors will tell the baboons were the real hurdle in the collection of the Salajeet from the steepy mountains. The baboons whose muzzles resembled in blackness to the colour of the Salajeet, had done a lot of licking of this energy charged rock foam, and the baboons had gained their sturdiness out of the determined licking of this product emerging from the rock fissures. The baboons considered they were the real claimants of the Salajeet at the source of the rocks and did not like any one tampering with their environment and taking chunks of solid or the fluidal Salajeet, off their mountains. And when the opportunity crept their way, they most forcefully swung and crashed their dangling tail on the face of the Salajeet collector and that was done at the most inopportune moment when the Salajeet collector was busy screwing out Salajeet from difficult corners in the mountain rocks.

This was certain to produce its ill effect. The Salajeet collector eventually fainted, dropping down over on the rock and the baboons fearing the consequences that the harmed and others will launch an attack on them fled from the site in panic. And in all that happened there, the Salajeet man had the severest of the blow on his face, and the dangling long tails of the baboons, all the time frightened him. But the value of the real Salajeet was such that the advantages accruing from its collection, it yielding hard sovereign silver coins, far outweighed the ill effects of the crashing tail of the baboons on their faces, and the Salajeet men remained undeterred and went scrounging the Salajeet from the mountains to keep the Pansari(s) well supplied and the resurging patrons in the Nawabdoms were kept well dispensed with its packs.

The raw Salajeet was moderated, before sold. It went through a long process of treatment before it was ideally suited for the consumer. The Salajeet was washed, refined and tampered with milk. It was beaten and appropriated with medicals of choice by the specialist of the Salajeet to enhance it for yielding defined strengths in grades and qualities. It then became the ultimate price laden yield and was sold in small packs as Salajeet. It needed a monitored consuming, since before the consumer had to see the adverse effects shooting off its use, he needed expending the energy it transferred into the user. If the input of the energy bound in the Salajeet grain taken in, was not balanced with the output of the energy that required expending after the Salajeet was administered, the imbalance created hurt the body. The Salajeet was for the purposes of emboldening life in the department of sensuality, making the user vigorous, losing his peacetime, until he released the energy.

Beyond the excellences of the naturally obtained Salajeet, transferring their benefits in human body, at par with it, there were the manmade Kushtas. And of these, when the natural pearl was turned into the *Kushta Murwareed*, a formidable booster of energy emerged. This Kushta was renowned for its potent strength - for its ready energy it possessed in its inherent chemistry to embolden those seeking renewal of life in them. Its deployment did that, and vigour appeared bustling in the user, over filling him and if he stayed put, he landed him in jeopardy.

All these potent energy transferors were in most demand in the months of winter. Kushta Murwareed was the product produced from the pearls of lustre brought out from the deep waters of the sea by the divers in the sea. They had to be perseverant, armed with the skill of holding breath and enduring the pressure of water under the depths of the layers of water over them as they descended down in the depths of water to search out pearls and they were at war with themselves to find pearls from the sea rocks in their descents, even when it was a manageable sea depth, where they took themselves to inspect, select and bring out mature, shut sea-shells from the depths of water. The shell's pearl was taken out from the shell, then boiled in the thorny leaves of *Chauka* - the 'Sasbania Aculeate' for an excelling lustre and for improved hardness. The pearl was now declared ready as a piece of valuable find for ornaments and for medicinal use.

The docile sea rocks, rising like walls from the depth of the sea, kept the shells lodged in their crevices, where the pearls were mothered inside the shells. Others of them were hanging at different layers and water mothering the pearls at correct temperature, and the layers of sea water weighing down on them and rubbing the shell, formed an adequate force on the shells to make them resilient for the culturing of the pearls.

The sea environment boosted the pearl, forming an unyielding gloss on the inside surface of the shell giving a lustre filled surrounding for the initial pearl inside the shell, and a scraped hard solid surface on the outside of the shell for the protection of the pearl. And the tiny fancy of the pearl as dust that nature had lodged in the shell for the initiation of the pearl was safeguarded, and it developed those inherent qualities in shaping its richness such that it turned the realism of the tiny pearl in the shell into a lustrous and sumptuous growth that was the nature's design and its generosity to form the pearl of lustre. And praise be to God!

Kushta Murwareed was prepared from the natural pearls, breeding in the sea or cultured in the man-made sea like environment. The Jauhar or the essence of the almond was transferred to a handful of pearls through heating. The quantity of the pearls so treated was put to attrition in a *Kharal* or the mortar, pulverising the pearls with a pestle. Simultaneously sprinkling Kewrda water on it and doing a lot of attrition with Kewrda water for twelve days. The cost of attrition was kept low by deploying unskilled labour and the progress was monitored over 10 to 12 days of its attrition. The pearls turned into particles and then into smooth powder. It was then that the pulverisation was declared complete, though never perfect to the satisfaction of the critical user. He always thought that it needed more attrition to make a finer powder. And there was only a finely measured quantity that could be taken at one time and never more, even by the most formidable and experienced in its consumption.

A bachelor past the prime of his youth, but still young at heart was restless to enter wedlock with a lass - someone from out of the ordinary, and this desire had so far kept him bachelor, he was that critical in choosing a spouse that none passed his critical fixed standard. His standard was that the house he entered in, where he was to choose the bride be immaculate. If he observed, there were minor shrinkages on the bed covers, and if it was so that was enough to arouse repulsion in him to reject the prospect of marriage there, and the most outstanding in the society turned him down for his small frame of body and cheeks not that rosy, though he was princely in the mannerism.

He heard of Kushta Murwareed what it did. God bless his soul, he tried to come out of the state of his bachelorhood through the help of this wonder gift of the nature by utilising its assets to make him look rosiest on his next matching day falling shortly with a higher class in the society. Lots of people from the would-be bride's side were coming on this occasion to approve or reject his hand of offer made on his behalf by his near and dear ones to the bride's wards and the bride was of an outstanding family and of extreme charm.

On such previous occasions the team of the authority-holders of saying yes or no, on three occasions had rejected the gallant proposal made for him, on his behalf. The good intentional proposals as a norm were made after match-making, keeping the long-lasting generative interest of the contenders in mind with an eye on their fair looks and after ascertaining of the compatibility of the families going to unite with each other. And this point was always foremost in the minds of the families and was the fundamental rule in match- making. But in the case of this princely bachelor proposals were always made beyond the matching points between the suitors. All attention was paid to concentrating on the looks and the personality of the bride and that she is coming from a family of the highest strata in the society and as soon as these virtues were located the proposal was made.

On this occasion like before, the proposal was made on his extreme conglomeration of whimpering to and pestering of the relatives. And the spouse marked by him was the most outstanding in the circle of the society, who were known to the family. In this he had been successful in shaking off the relatives' dormancy and the proposal was made. Cheered up to see that the consensual obligation was progressing, the friends, well-wishers and sympathisers came forward and all extended their good wishes, effusing cheeriness for him and there was all the general backing from his special chef as well, who always stood by him. And this was the occasion when the proposal had to succeed and not meet its fate of the likes of the past. All the previous ones which had fallen flat, and success had brushed past him were for the cause that pointed to making an over match and falling in a surpassing proposal category but still it was made and the result was never triumphant, and he was never to admit that it was his over ambitiousness.

And on this occasion to ensure that success was not neophyte and slipping away, he equipped him with the weapon of Kushta Murwareed, whose secret in vigils he had discovered, and he pinned all his hopes on the wonders of the Kushta. He decided, laced with the record of its sure heavenward successes that the best chance of winning the hand of the fair lady was, if he took a fair amount of Kushta and made his cheeks roseate, which he did. And that was with the most sanctimonious intentions to pep up him and fill his small frame with energy and present an emboldened look to the crucial decision makers of his fate. But the Kushta's natural trend in infusing energy worked fast; his condition deteriorated fast due to the diabolical heat energy released in his body from the exceeding quantity of the Kushta, he had taken.

The Kushta became vigorously functional in his not too robust a frame of body and by the time the evening arrived, when he was to dress up, drawing from among his branded expensive shirts' collection, with matching *Neelam* and sapphire cufflinks and princely *Sambhar's hide* shoes or one from among a string of expensive shoes he had, of *Goh* skin - skin of the desert creeping and occasionally fast running creature not so frequently seen unless one went to look for them in the desert, and from the shoes of crocodile skin or from calf leather shoes and other fancy shoes; he was all scarlet head to toe, and anyone could see he was burning the fluidity of his life at a very fast rate.

An emergency was declared, and he was rushed to the safe guarders of life and ailing reversers to health - the doctors in the hospital. They finding his condition was precarious detained him in the hospital and kept him under observation and the unlucky contender could not take part in the *Bur Dekhauwa* - presenting one's face and mannerism for the match making. And he could not captivate hearts and win approval from the assessors giving passport to marriage. And our destined to remain a bachelor was deprived of the fair occasion of hitching an Audrey Hepburn and dragging her inside the margin of approval. And the prospect of becoming bridegroom was snubbed. The doctors sent him home the next day after resuscitating life in him to full.

The Kushtas therefore, so pounded one with energy that it was a problem to contain it, as the innocent enthusiast had provided evidence of proof. The energy imparted by the Kushta had to be expended suitably in a time bound period. The Kushtas as such were a boon as well as a banality. It could be a dangerous pack of energy capsule if unauthorizedly used. But those dexterous in its use went on unmistakably searching for the Kushtas and they successfully negotiated with their inner inundated of energy, whereof it succumbed to take them to higher realms of life. The demand and the number of those seeking the Kushtas increased as the winter season took hold and its use propelled men exuding energy, and bouncing around at will.

Of these energy pack immutable benefactors meeting social needs, *Ma al Laham* was another kind – a certain well tried and stable propeller of energy, competing the Kushta. It was a medicinal food and its preparation and making needed exceeding care and also it had a durability of not long freshness. And had a hush-hushed status. It was for filling energy in the deserving of special class, made for very special individuals, those highly placed in the stations of life, the Maharajas and prosperous Seths. Ma al Laham had a gentler taste and a pleasanter disposition. It was meant for the metaphorically indispensables whose longevity was wanted to be determinedly extended, and who were thought deficient in vitality the meat provided, as they were prohibited to take meat or had themselves voluntarily built around them a fence inhibiting them to take meat in its recognisable form, even if the meat was cooked and dressed.

The Ma al Laham was extract of meat and it was stronger than the meat. It did wonders to the deficient of meat. The diagnosis was that the incumbent had fallen deficient in iron and he had become slower in cognition and was lethargic in handling tasks. Such deficient in iron and for want of that, deficient in red blood cells, were diagnosed for treatment with the Ma al Laham and they were really those who were under the bondage of the gripping spatial extended society and had to do what the society norm demanded of them - become aversive to taking meat in any solid recognisable form. But they needed revival of their form and vigour that was purportedly not sticking with them by any means and they needed leaning on the ingenious manipulator who could provide them with quick gullible form of drink that pulled them out of their deprecating condition. Candidly speaking, they were brought to life from the condition dead on to their feet. The Ma al Laham pulled them out of their condition and took them to their former state of agility when they were positively diagnosed beaten down by the deprivation of red cells and they must take it.

The product was prepared from select *Laham* – the meat taken from a collection of a vast number of defined Halal birds, live-stock, excluding cows and buffalos – only birds and animals of nature's free and palatable species. The profitable selection from among the birds were cocks, partridges, wild ducks and Jungali Kabooter – wild pigeons, and in animals, goats, deer, ram (sturdy male sheep) and their kinds with all the essence of life they carried. The meat was appropriately weighed down with an adequate quantity of *Kheera* - cucumber and *Kakrdi* - long thin cucumber, and four kinds of famous kernels from the watermelon family. The combination was distil-processed in a *Karam Beekh* – a distil, the equipment of brass retort, tinned on the inside of the device.

The ingredients were placed in the hold of the Karam Beekh to extract juice through distillation. The droplets of the extract travelled through the neck of the retort and condensed in the receiver. The form of the ingredients had changed to a new pleasant liquid and all the benefits of the Laham were retained in the collected liquid. This was preserved and presented to the valued deficient of iron with the label of the Ma al Laham. It was a high value costly product, falling only in the means of affordability of affluent rich, only suited to the spending dictates of such affluently rich as Maharajas, fabulous Mahajans, the business magnets, and those who fell in the ranks of His Highnesses and high in the society. It was kinder to the user. The taste, smell and the quality of the Ma Al Laham were of pleasantness and its excess use was not a source of any anxiety. It did all to increase tolerance to absorb stress and was the ultimate choice for life sustenance and cell regeneration function.

Ma al Laham otherwise when extracted under high pressure from a device called *Bhubka*, wherein entry of air was not allowed, with its lid sealed with clay – *Chikni Mitti*, all round the lid, it was rated as the richest Ma al Laham, higher in quality than that obtained from the *Karam Beekh*. The outside microbes in the Bhubka were not allowed to make contact with the constituent components in the hold of the Bhubka during the puritanical change of their form to pure droplets of liquid. The condensed droplets were captured in bottles and classed as higher-class Ma al Laham and were labelled as 'Ma al Laham Oola' – the high rated nectar.

These energy-propellants transported one, to the higher realms in the specifics of life. And in their bottled state they were an all-season energy transfer product and were considered unique what the ingenious Hakeem[35] had produced. The effort and the expenditure spent in obtaining this splendid liquid was every bit well worth. The relief it brought to the patient was phenomenal. The glow it transferred to the consumer on his face, sat on his cheeks turning him roseate. And although it was well suited for all seasons, it was a product that went on increased demand and use in the winters.

Besides these manmade ingenuities strengthening man's ability in all departments of cognizance in combating disease, nature had provided all kinds of aids to the peoples of the Land of Seasons and Songs to strengthen their physique, and reign in slides into depletion of their health. These came through the medicinal features of special trees. These trees were the botanic wonders of nature in the shape of Neem trees, Peeple trees and Burgad trees providing cure to illnesses. Among these trees, the Burgad tree was very medicinal; it had mind and will to demise illnesses. Every fibre of the tree contributed to health and extended life in the man. It was a full-time dispensary of Nature which remained open day and night and served the people.

---

[35] The word Hakeem stood for the solution finder – a man of intellect, filled with literary commitment and experience in diagnosis from inspection and by pulse reading – observing regularities and the irregularities of the heartbeat.

The Burgad tree or the Banyan tree gave man what specific it had - that was the long life and wisdom. It strengthened health and helped the helpless. Its cool shade provided shelter to the tired and its sweet fruit satiated hungry and exhausted, making them strong. Its leaves, bark and the milk that oozed out from its trunk at the slightest of incision anywhere on its vibrant body were medicine, and every bit of the tree was medicine and cure, eradicating disease. The Burgad tree was such a beneficial tree that the earlier people called it *Maha Varist* – the great teacher of great authority.

The Burgad tree with its deep-down spread roots, and its long knitted and wavy beard and its formidable dynamism, gave shelter to the needy and restored his health and vigour by fanning air full of health. The tree rid harassing ailments and it not only cured the illnesses of the common cold but cured illnesses down to the terrifying cancer, it was one functionary in the vast world of vegetation which filled the lap of the mother bereaved of a child with a healthy child in her lap.

The Ayurveda – the science of the sages' way of life, claims that to let the nature bless a mother with child, she should get tender sprouting leaves of the Burgad tree, then an equal number of betel nuts and an equal amount of rose chest nuts and grind and mix them. Then if it administered to the devoid of child in measures of only one tablespoon-full of the mixture taken for thirty days with milk, it was enough for a baby to land in the lap of that mother.

The Burgad tree stood in great honour in the kingdom of vegetation. Lord Buddha sat under the Burgad tree and attained divine wisdom and the Burgad tree became renowned for wisdom. Prince Gautam Siddhartha sat in the company of hermits and tried by the conventional ways to achieve union with God. He exposed his body to self-torture, bearing discomfort and observing asceticism for six years, practicing austerity for revelations to dawn on him and way to *Nirvana* – salvation open to him, but the fulfilment in the measures of satisfaction to his self, did not come to him.

He then went to sit under a Burgad tree and engrossed him in meditation. The environment of calm serenity under the tree, provided by the Burgad tree, led Lord Buddha to attain enlightenment on the forty ninth day and he found his meditation revealing mysteries and the floral gifts descending from heavens. Lord Buddha established link between him and Wisdom, and it became the binding knot into the entity of the High God's Oneness. The faithful clustered round him and the great religion of the Buddhism sprang to formation and the Burgad tree since then has been known as the tree of wisdom, and the tree vouched to help and protect the philosophy of meditation.

The Burgad tree vouched, if anyone wanted to be wise and he striving to establish link from the worldly surrounding to the heavenly surrounding, he should go to sit under the shade of the Burgad tree and surrender his self to meditation. It will turn him head to toe in the personification of knowledge and God- favour with power and principles to attain higher life will flow to him. That was the phenomenon what Lord Buddha demonstrated. But for the lesser souls the comfort was; the meditation leading to revelations by sitting under the Burgad tree was not a compulsive dictate of any real necessity after the meditative input of Prophet Hazrat Mohammad Mustafa SAWW who attained revelation in the environment of Cave Hira, where God entrusted and empowered him establish edifice of faith to show the man the way to salvation and its attainment in life, while he lived controlling his desire, keeping within the functional environments of his created surroundings.

The Burgad tree for its immenseness, a thousand of years of life had its first recorded origin from the middle of the Mesozoic era 100 million years back. It formidably gripped the mother earth with assuring grip and showed majesty. Some Burgad trees in the villages of the Land of Seasons and Songs were so colossal that a whole village with their beasts and burden could sprawl under the shade of the tree and still its space unfilled.

And sowing a Burgad tree was to open an account for thousands of years of blessings accruing in the name of the person sowing it, because of the help extended by the tree to the people that formed charity by the deed of the sowing. The charity ensuing by the service rendered by the tree is recorded in the name of the person sowing the tree, and the charity in the name of the sowing becomes so enormous in numeric that it becomes immeasurable and it keeps increasing, multiplied countless times and the bliss overflows, and takes the planter's soul ascending in the endless journey to ascendancy - to the heights of elation, not imaginable by the extension of any imagination. And as extrapolator optimist we say:

The reward for sowing any tree is just as much as sowing a Burgad tree, be it a Neem tree, a People tree or a tree planted that was only giving shade, below which tired could sit to take rest. Or it could be a tree, only to fan purified air or one that bore fruit or one that flowered, spreading fragrance and cheerfulness, or one whose utility was fulsomeness or medicinal to stand by the needy to rid him of his ailment. The joy of planting a tree Charles Dudley Warner 1829-1900, expresses: "To own a bit of ground - four thousand miles deep, to scratch it with a hoe, to plant seeds and watch the renewal of life – this is the commonest of delight of the race, the most satisfactory thing a man can do."

Even with two negativities in his bag, Hazrat Ans Bin Malik diminishing his status of a Sahabi, denying remembering the event of Ghadeer-e Khum and not submitting his allegiance to the rightful Caliph Hazrat Ali AS., when stated a heavy weight Hadith was reckoned with reverence. Hazrat Ans Bin Malik states the Prophet SAWW said:

"Anyone who plants a tree or did agriculture, then when human or birds or animals ate something from that tree, or they were benefited from the fruits of his agriculture then that would be counted as his Sadqa - alms-giving, and it will be an act of Sawab, – the unburdening of the penances from him and bringing him to elation."

Hazrat Ans Bin Malik even after conveying this totally motivating Hadith, does a disservice by denying of what happened at the Ghadeer Khum, after he had heard the Moazzan's call of Hayya Ala Khairil Amal - a totally new article of faith in the Azaan he had heard, then he was asked by the Prophet SAWW to call back the gone far Hajjis. Still, he did not remember the event of Ghadeer. And the rules in ethics are very strict for the Muslim, the Sahaba are not masses, they are truthful entity. Prophet Hazrat Eesa AS., was Messiah and harbinger of civilisation in the west and east. He was conveyor of love and rectitude; he gave further insight into the continued blessings and rewards flowing to a fortunate from the good acts he did. Hazrat Eesa AS. was passing through a graveyard that he saw a dead was being penalised there. The dead was being inflicted with torments. Hazrat Eesa AS. hurried to pass from that place quickly. He AS. passed from that same place after one year, this time that dead was being lavished with ease and was receiving blessings. The Prophet paused and praised God and asked the reason for it and God spoke:

"O Eesa Ibne Maryam, this man has left behind a son who after one year has grown and says Bismillah ir-Rahmanir-Raheem - I begin in the name of God Who is Kind and Merciful. This boy when he becomes of age is going to be extremely virtuous and he will help people, feed orphans and will show the people righteous path. I have therefore forgiven the sins of this man who is his father."

Now, what deep effectual lessons in thinking, God created to stress the importance of learning. He uses His revered Prophet to convey God strategy. What God said to Hazrat Eesa AS. was that; good acts left behind by a dead were a source of recurring reward for him after he departed from this corporeal world where he had sowed the seed of good act. And when it flowered, it was his harvest for the hereafter.

But the true treasure of man and the secret into the cure of the sick and the guidance to the lost, way gone in vacillation in the inverses of goodness: to lift their souls and illuminate their path to success and satisfaction and thereby haul them from their submergence in degradation to attain sublimity was the word of revelation of the Holy Quran, with its immediate beneficences: the Aayat 3: 132,133,134 which say:

"And obey God and the Messenger so that mercy may reach to you. And run for the forgiveness of your Lord and to the paradise as wide as heavens and the earth provided for the God fearing, who spend in the way of God in the ease of plenty and in hardship both and control anger and forgive others. God loves the good doers."

The word of Prophet Abraham AS. in the Sura 26, Aayat: 80, 81, 82, 83, 84, and 85, 86 of the Holy Quran was another deliverance to open the heart and put inducement in the heart and accommodate compassion in the self for even the adversary. These Aayat elevated heart to include in the prayer good for the enemy, seeking his forgiveness. The verses of the Sura says:

80. And when I fall ill, that's Him, Who heals me.
81. And He, Who makes me die and will raise me again.

82. And He, from Whom, I have ardent hope (He) will
forgive me my sin on the Day of Judgement.
83. Lord! Give me knowledge and wisdom and
unite me with the righteous.
84. And in the generations to come, keep me remembered
with good mention.
85. And make me also from the inheritors of the garden of comfort.
86. And forgive my father, for he is from among the erring.

And another way to salvation was the Hadith of the Prophet of all kindness, Hazrat Mohammad Mustafa SAWW:

'One who recites daily 4 Aayat of Sura Baqarah and then the Aayetul Kursi and then three Aayat of the last Suras of Quran, he will face no suffering or will come across any untoward incident occurring to him or hear of any unpleasantness.'

These Aayat and Ahadith are the open way to salvation to all, be they Munafeqeen, the hypocrites or wholly angel like, characterised to the vigour of goodness to enter in the realm of mercy through the dint of reciting these Surah. It will salvage them all, such is rule of law of God in reward and justice, applicable universally.

All these incentives infused in man are to conquer the evil and attain bliss. So, the world is concluded to carry two forces, the force of Godly virtue and that of the evil forces under the control of Shaitan. These leave their effect temporary and permanent. And the individual is a motion bound spec, looking for salvation and shelter and has duty to know what is right and what is wrong. And his intention if harnessed by goodness, generosity, civility and kindness, determines his status in the realm of goodness and the personification of good forces, the Nabi, Imam, Aehlebaait and God Himself help him.

And all the Godly forces will respond if they are approached to, but the bad forces will act against whenever they had their way and that's why there are formulas given by the good forces to overcome the evil forces, and man is free to determine his course.

-: . :-

II

THE GENIUSES OF THE NAWABS

III

Nawab Amjad Ali Shah 1801 – 1847, ruled for five years 1842 to 1847. He was father of the last Nawab of Awadh, Wajid Ali Shah who reigned for five years from 1847 to 1856, died 1887. From among the Nawabs of Awadh, Nawab Amjad Ali Shah was so well educated that he became a *Molvi* - one devoted to Godly occupation. His concern was making the populace like himself - abstemious and God fearing, with a lookout of religious bondage. He was not running the Nawabdom with the majestic touch of Kings, but with business in mind to establishing the writ of the Sayeds. He replaced the Sunni law that was operative through the Mufti since the time of the Mughals and appointed a Shia Mujtahid – the eminent Ghufran Maab AayetUllah Sayed Dildar Ali to implement Shia Jurisprudence. And he did no politics, only statesmanship. More Sayeds held departments in his time than at any other time before.

This Nawab created a department of *Mohakma-ey Marif-e Sharia* - Department for Acquainting with the Rules of Religious Laws. Its Head was *Mujtahidul Asr* - the highest Shia scholar and authority in the Islamic jurisprudence of the day. And the jurisdiction of the Mujtahidul Asr was enormous. The Nawab also created a department of *Mohakma-ey Sadrul Shariyat*. This department carried the central authority for introducing Shariat Law and practice of religion, e.g., *Namaz* – the set prayer, *Munajat* – supplications, *Ahkamat* – compulsory in obedience. But in spite of his Molvi mind and its trait, he also did laudable things decorating his capital Lucknow.

Nawab Amjad Ali Shah did so much to introduce Shia philosophy, which is emulation of the highest clergy – the Marja – the decision-making leader in religious edict to evolve piety and abstemiousness as a necessity like the daily bread. But in his Nawab's role, he was not negligent of the entertainment requirements of the generalities of the public and of Nawab kinds. He took into account the vast weakness of the inconsolable and the phlegmatic to meet their need through the edicts of religion and those groaning and calmly complaining of deprivation. He created a department of *Mohakma-ey Arabab-e Nishat* – The Department of Opulent of Means to Happiness. It was managed by a cluster of bewitching fair ladies who organised its activities. He built bridge on River Gomti and mettled road from Lucknow to Kanpur.

The Nawab also established an exclusive school of 'Shia Theology' and named it *Madarsa-e Sultania* - Royal College. All the students there were paid a stipend at various levels. It was brought in existence since there was no Shia School till that time. The students till then for learning religious practice were sent to the only Sunni established schools, but after the establishment of this college, they were diverted there.

The Madrasa-e Sultania had ten boarding rooms. The curriculum and the intended set up were such that its management necessarily was given in the hands of the Mujtahidul Asr, Sultanul Ulema Sarkar Aayet Ullah Maulana Sayed Mohammad Husain Naqvi. The British when they annexed Awadh in 1856 saw it right in their wisdom to close the college. This unfortunate move was to cater their requirement of stronger foothold in India, driven by the conduct of expansionism. One would immediately think if the British had not closed the college, it might have been a seminary at par with those in Qum and Najaf. They closed this college, and did great disservice to the Shia Faith and to the Muslims, only they allowed a similar college to be established where English was taught. It was established at Aligarh in 1875 as Mohammedans Anglo Oriental College, which became Aligarh Muslim University in 1920.

The title of Sultanul Ulema was given to Ayetullah Sayed Mohammad Husain Naqvi by Nawab Amjad Ali Shah in 1742. This Ayetullah was first ever in the Land of Seasons and Songs who had completed his research as Mujtahid and qualified to be Ayetullah after studies at the religious centre of Najaf-e Ashraf in Iraq. The previous first Mujtahid to return to India after studies in Karbala was Sayed Dildar Ali 1752 – 1820. He campaigned against Sufism in Awadh and sheltered the Shia faith and did other Shia faith connected services. These were so fundamental that after these Ulema, the learned in Lucknow never gave up their *Khidmat-e Ilmi* – initiative to strengthen modes of learning. They barricaded disapproved and created morale aptitude through the virtue of their self. And provided authentic religious interpretive services to the faithful of Islam in general and to the Shia faith followers in particular. A string of Ulema to their credit take their descent from them; thanks to the pioneering work of the Nawabs of Awadh. This rise of the blue-blooded Ulema was possible because of the triumphant emergence of the Nawabs.

This service of the Nawab Amjad Ali to retain exclusivity of the religion through learnedness and diverse manifestations was pioneering a general trend of Shia religiosity. For all his services Nawab Amjad Ali rendered, he was buried in Imam Barda Sibtain he had built in Lucknow. In Muharram people light candle at his grave and offer *Sura-e Fateha* to the soul of this pioneering Nawab.

The Nawabs of Awadh were from Nishapur Iran, and here in the Land of Seasons and Songs were classed as Rulers of Nishapur Dynasty. The last Nawab, Nawab Wajid Ali Shah ruled from 1847 – 1856, died 1887, he was a poet, playwright, a humane and a great patron of arts. He showed an equal religious bend of mind per se of his father.

When the Nawab went out it was a procession. There were two lancers who carried two silver boxes ahead. They received complaints from the subjects, which were dropped in the boxes. The Nawab had the key of the boxes and when he reached back to his palace, he opened the boxes himself and issued instructions to redress grievances and he wrote the instructions in his own handwriting. But the East India Company made the sovereign rule of the Nawabdom difficult.

From the year 1773, and in next thirty years, Awadh surrendered half of its territories to the East India company. And not only that the East India Company imposed a British run army whose salaries and perks the Nawabdom had to meet and the company made repeated demands of loans and Awadh the garden of granary and queen province of India was made impoverished by the incessant cash demand of the British, due to which this kingdom ended in 1856. The British seceded it of which they had long decided to take this action. And if they had not done that the world would have had a centre of excellence in behavioural science of good manners, love, respect and example of purity ordained life. And it was all because of the military victory of the British in Plassey in 1757 and their infatuation of 'Rule Britannia, Britannia Rules the World' and there was fair and foul means all dedicated to rule.

ہمارا سلام نواب امجد شاہ کی دوربینی کو
مہکتا اودھ چھوڑا انصاف کی ترجمانی کو
نواب امجد شاہ کی شان گوہر یکتا کی ہے
کو رعناؤ ی کی ی دف ن یتم رہی ڑھد ا ے کک ھ س ین امام م لی
سیّد اطہار حسین

Hamara Salam Nawab Amjad Sah Ki Doorbeeni Ko
Mahekta Awadh Chorda Insaf Ki Tarjumani Ko
Nawab Amjad Shah Ki Shan Gauharay Yakta Ki Haai
Mili Imam Husain Kay Barday Ki Mitti Dafn Honay Ko

Our salute to the far sightedness of Nawab Amjad Shah
The pearl shines not melt to the vagary of the times
Nawab Amjad Shah's dignity is of the pearl of uniqueness
Got the earth for burial of the Barda (court) of Imam Husain (AS.)

-: . :-

II

THE ECCENTRICITIES
AND THE NAWABS

IV

The Nawabs of Awadh were great patrons of culture, acts of courtesy, solace to grief stricken, hospitality to guests were the enjoinments. Culture was dusted, fragranced and raised to the towering heights in their period, and Lucknow the capital of the Nawabdom since 1784 was the breeding ground of courtesy and by 1847 it was at its pinnacle. Nawab Wajid Ali Shah after dinner was taken to the *Pandan Wali to* give rise to the culture of blazonry. This lady made Paan. She was a lady of gorgeous fashions. She wore decorative apparels laced with embroideries of high value and displayed her art of Paan-making by dressing the Paan. The betel leaves were layered with a blazonry in applying the Kaththa and Choona, showing sophistication and excessiveness in mannerism, and the *Gilory* – the Paan of the cone shape was made, tucking its ends in, and wrapping the Glory with *Chandi ka Waraq* - the thin most silver leaf, nearly of no thickness. *Chandi ka Waraq* was made from square nuggets of silver, which were placed between tough leather folds and beaten with mallet till the nuggets (several folds of leather with their nuggets placed one above the other) expanded to papery thinness to become thinnest metal leaves. It was wrapped round the Paan for presentation. The Paan thus wrapped had become shiny and of tempting looks. And it will be seen that a small amount of silver was eaten with the paan. This culture of decorating the Paan by wrapping it in Chandi Ka Waraq, was also evident in covering sweet delicacies of Helwa with *Chandi ka Waraq*.

The Pandan Wali placed the Gilory on the silver plate of the silver *Khasdan* – the glory dish – the betel-leaf dressed with lime and catechu, carrying a small quantity of betel nuts was turned into a cone and edges tugged in, called Glory. The Khasdan was an elegant piece of silver dish artefact to hold Paan with a decorative dome cover carrying chequered punches on its silver dome. The domes were also plain with an elegant protrusion for lifting the dome to uncover the plate on which the Paan Glories were placed. After bowing and presenting *Aadab,* the courtesies to the Nawab, she presented the Paan to the Nawab lifting the cover of the Khasdan and then ceremoniously she ate the Paan herself. The Nawab did not eat the Paan, but simply watched the Pandan Wali make the Paan and present it to him with her style and courtesies and her artistry put on display.

The Pandan Wali was paid one guinea by the Nawab for presenting the Paan, and for her protocol of unpredictable in the artistry of the use of flattering court language to please the Nawab. She was further given a *Pandan Kharch* - the Paan gadgetry maintenance allowance for the upkeep of the Pandan decorum from the treasury and this was to give a new dimension in the growth of culture and the flourishing of the art in the Nawabdom. The artistry in the use of words, coining new feminine phrases in excellence or in adiaphora came from the innovative mind, fertile and visionary, flowing from the neuron cells of the unpolluted chemistry of the mind of the Pandan Wali and she was paid to maintain her state of mind in tune to produce gorgeous proverbs. 'The best manner was for man to stop at his limits and not to exceed his status.' Saying of Hazrat Ali AS.

The Nawabs what they represented were Kings, but the style of the Nawabs in stateliness had a show of aloofness from the kingliness. They had replaced kingliness with an acute display of uniqueness of their character in academicism. And then it was swathed with the dauntless love for the progenies of the Prophet of God Hazrat Mohammad Mustafa SAWW. In this display, there were their sophistications at work in bringing to light the divine of the progenies of the Prophet SAWW through their literary and reformative works. These Nawabs did not wear crowns of the Kings, but an adornment showing learnedness – which was Safa with a plume and a modest diamond or some ruby crest. But alas the Nawabs were soon found without a state and without portfolios and in fact in times mostly penniless, with only their names remaining alive and interesting.

Some of these names and their phonetics pleased the ears and they jingled of the era of the Nawabs. These were names like, Nawab Chhakkan, Nawab Achchhoo, Nawab Ghasita, and Nawab Sun Dus. All these words were unassuming but of pasty sweetness and sat fixed on the lips, and though they were conveying only faint specific meanings but were linchpins of the vocabulary of the vernacular spoken in the Land of Seasons and Songs in giving a trail of the eccentricity of the Naw-wabi is carrying a whole lot of history with them and defining the character and the complacent nature of the named, and the sound of these calibrated paradox generated love and commanded restraint respect to be shown to them, for their penitent fortune of losing their kingdoms.

The Nawab Sun Dus was under age, so the transfer of wealth to him was withheld by the British colonial power, and when he became of age and heir to the estate of his ancestor Nawabs, he received all the accumulated dues, since he had become of age 18 on the first of January 1910. Immediately he was paid all the money, and as soon he got it, he became lavish, prodigal and reckless, started spending burning the wick at both the ends, throwing his money - burning ten-rupee notes as cigarette and gave most of it in service to be served to easy virtue class. He was rich on first January 1910 and was a beggar on 31st December 1910 and he was named 'Nawab Sun Dus' – the Nawab of Year Ten. Then there was the Nawab Chhakkan after fast spending all his wealth, he took the keys of his empty vaults and hanged these with the *Izarbund* – the chord of his trouser and walked with the bunch of the keys hanging from the end of his *Izarbund* and the keys made the jingling sound of *Chhun Chhun* and he got the name of 'Nawab Chhakkan'.

And the renaming was not limited in the Land of Seasons and Song, it spread up to Britain; Sir Arthur Stanley Eddington was an astrophysicist, when the astronomers spotted that certain numbers had an apparent coincidence in cosmology. Sir Arthur Eddington set out to show that this coincidence could lead to an ultimate theory of the universe. When one of the researchers proved that the dimensionless number was closer to 1/137, Sir Arthur fiddled crude fudge, and added one to his cosmology of 1/136 and the Punch magazine renamed him as 'Sir Arthur Adding One'. This stance detracted the physicist community from Sir Arthur. He was Knighted in 1930, Born in 1882, died 1944 - a known British Astronomer and Physicist. He was professor of astronomy at the Cambridge University and he investigated into the internal constitution and the luminosity of the stars.

كبھی ہلکا نہ ہو بوجھ نرم خوئی کا
ادب کے ذوق کا تسلیم وفا کے موتی کا
سبق پیغمبری اور امامت کا یہ ملا ہم کو
اخوت پاس ایمان کی پونجی دمساز قضیہ عقل جوئی کا
سید اطہار حسین

Kabhi Halka Na Ho Boajh Narm Khoee Ka
Adab Ky Zauq Ka Tasleem-e Wafa kay Moti Ka
Sabaq Paaighambari Aur Imamat ka Yeh Mila Humko
Akhwat Paas Eeman Ki Poonji Dumsaz Qizya Aql Joee ka

Never lightened be load of kind heartedness
Of relish of literature, of greeting of the pearl of faithfulness
The lesson from the Prophethood and the Imamat reached to us
Brotherhood near, capital of faith friend, object search of wisdom

-:.:-

II

POETIC EXCELLENCES

V

The poets of the courts of the Kings, Nawabs and the Maharajas in the Land of Seasons and Songs received a comfortable stipend as remuneration to meet their need as poets serving literature with unimpeded zeal and the poets performed their functions as committed to them. They had to keep to a very high standard in the art of literary commitment, delivery packages of praiseworthy poems, work in Qasida Go-ee, in lavishing praises on the Royal through poetry, enhancing comprehension in depths of matters of subjects. The court poets were like the goose clacking and running towards the master as soon as he appeared. There was no harm in using flattery and sophistries, this had explosive effect on the rulers and it pampered the literature. And the turnover of these had to be regular, a timely thing in releasing lineament and predicament. Then the poetic contribution had to be innovative making excessiveness in the linguistic expression, extravagant for exacerbating all limits in exaggeration in relating to the King's eulogies. They had to say couplets in the court to convey of the King's elations in the style:

"The thin crescent on the sky is not the crescent of the new moon. It is the image of your eyebrow appearing in the mirror of the sky, O King."

I had to say the following couplet carrying the above meaning, short of recalling the poet's verse. There was a beautiful couplet said by a poet that unfortunately has slipped my mind. Since it is such exaggeration that one will seldom come across - a logico-mathematical knowledge, where the poet applies pleasant flattery, then imagination of height to place his eulogising object at sky rocketing height, using mathematical bit in determining the reality of the image opposite in the mirror of the sky. The couplet in its originally having slipped my mind I have to manufacture as under:

هلا لِ نو توایک پر تو ہے شاہ کے ابرو کا
آسماں ہے شیشہ نُماں عکس لئے ابرو کا
سید اطہار حسین

Hilal-e Nau Toe Aek Pertau Haai Shah Kay Abroo Ka
Aasman Shisha Numaan Aks Liyay Abroo Ka

The new moon is image of the brow of the king
The sky is like mirror taking the image of the brow of the king

In the vein of exaggeration: in one of the sessions, a Nawab was drawing puffs from the long tube of the Huqqa - the Hubble bubble. The tobacco was burning in the Huqqa's Chilam – the tobacco container, in which there was a metal plate which separated the tobacco from the embers that was brimming the Chilam and the tobacco sizzled and gave smoke that entered in the water vessel of the Huqqa where it was filtered, and the puffing tube for inhaling the smoke carried a nozzle to draw the smoke. The Nawab drew on it and it made the sound Gurd Gurd, Gurd Gurd. This *Gurd Gurd, Gurd Gurd* made time slow down, and a hush of peace seemed to appear and the atmosphere was one of ease and comfort, of pondering and leisure, ready to favour exploring mystiques and enter in literalistic domains. One of the litterateurs there was fired by the melody of the sound of the Huqqa and he floated a *Misrah Tarah* – a line for completion of a verse, a hemistich before the thinking gathering there to say a verse in the same meter. The Misrah Tarah had a subtle, encountering the activity of the Nawab. It was floated to be matched with. It was:

Bejan Bolta Haai Maseeha Kay Hathh Mein
The lifeless speaks in the hand of the Christ

Now look at the flourishing mind of the poet, how he marries the reality of the Prophet Hazrat Eesa AS., whose deployment of hand

261

makes the lifeless turn alive and speak. And here the lifeless Huqqa in the hand of the king speaks with its Gurd Gurd.

How subtly this verse is created that carries duel meaning; one obvious meaning, the Hubble bubble is producing sound in the hand of the illustrious Nawab, the other the metaphor of Masiha used as a statement that the Prophet Masiha has the Qudrat – the providence to make the lifeless speak, which is the miracle of Hazrat Eesa AS.

Poet Nisha Ibn Insha – a humourist poet 1927-1978 was there at this moment and he immediately produced the matching verse of the subject matter:

Huqqa Jo Haai Huzoor-e Moalla Kay Hathh Mein
Goya Keh Kaehkashan Haai Surrayya Kay Hathh Mein

The Hubble Bubble that is in the hand of the high honoured
As if the Milky Way is in the hand of Surrayya - seven stars in
    the sky

The poet may have been fired by the imagination of the spiral
    of the pipe of the Huqqa and he compared it with the
Kaehkashan – the Milky Way to elate the high honoured Nawab,
    in whose company the poet was sitting.

The poets had to touch the height of exaggeration in the eulogies of their patron Kings, and say exclusive words of flattering excellences. In eulogising the King in praise of the auspiciousness of the reign 1837 – 1857 of Emperor Bahadar Shah Zafar the poet exacerbates realities in words for the Emperor:

Dey Agar Zaagh-o-Zaghan, Baaiza, Toe Paaida Ho Huma

If the crows and kites lay eggs, then Huma gets born of these

Poet Nawab Mirza Khan, with nom de plume 'Dagh' said this poetry in eulogy of Emperor Bahadur Shah Zafar in Delhi. He said this poetry to highlight the imagined heightened rule of the Emperor who ruled for twenty years over a limited empire confined to Delhi from 1837 to

1857 then he was arrested by a captain of the British cavalry and exiled to Rangoon. Now think of the fall of fortune, from the eggs of crows and kites only crows and kites could come out, but the poet says Huma will come out O' king! Your rule is of such beneficence. The greatest beauty of the poetry is exaggeration, but this is height of exaggeration to say from crows and kites Huma will come out.

The bird Huma was that rare legendry bird that was not seen, and could not be sworn that it existed, but it existed in fantasies and in the poetic language. It was said of it that if it cast its shadow fall on someone then that someone at once became a king and the poet says your reign O king has brought that change in what lands that you rule that the eggs of the crows and kites of that place will produce Huma. This was the height of exaggeration but the poets were called upon to exhibit that imprudence. Hazrat Dagh had said this poetry of exaggeration of highest order in elation of Emperor Bahadur Shah Zafar in whose court he served, the litterateurs valued measuring exaggeration in the weigh balance of imprudence and lavished praise for it.

The exile of the Emperor Bahadur Shah Zafar by the British to Rangoon was unfortunate. The Emperor was 82 years of age and a thorough deep rooted and wise poet and he sums up helplessness speared by tyranny and said the following historic couplet, and the poetry is indebted to him to have narrated history that worldly power has no continuity. The British also lost all the power and returned to their island country. The Emperor poet says:

Ketna Haai Bud Naseeb Zafar Dafn Kay Liyay
Doe Gaz Zameen Bhi Mill Na Saki Kuuay Yar Mein

How unfortunate is Zafar for the burial
Even two yards of land did not get in the environ of friends

The poets had to show extreme reverence and a heightened awe for their patron Kings. A poet in the Deccan (South) when he came to know that Nizam of Hyderabad Mir Osman Ali Khan was going to pass by a certain spot and was walking on foot, he quickly worked on his skill and pulled out a *Ruba-ee* - a quatrain. He put it on display card in a position so that the Nizam could see it and give him some reward for it. Only three verses were completed, when before the fourth verse of the quatrain comes out of him, the Nizam appeared there. The Nizam happened to look at the quatrain and saw only three lines there. He asked the courtier accompanying him what happened to the fourth line of the verse. The poet who was standing there, said:

Roab-e Sultan Ko Dekh Kay Misrah Phisal Gaya

Seeing the awe of the King the line slipped

The Nizam was himself a poet of Persian and Urdu languages, he repeated the line of the poet '*Roab-e Sultan Ko Dekh Kay Misrah Phisal Gaya*' which was a verse in its own right and carried the weight of appeasement and flattery. The Nizam though detested flattery, but ordered the poet be awarded Rupees one hundred as bursary, and a monthly stipend of Rupees fifty be fixed for him. In these days the salary of an average clerk in offices were just under Rs 30.00 a month.

Hazrat Dagh, 1831 – 1905 was described as the greatest poet of Delhi. One of his disciples was Poet, Pandit Roy Narayen Arman. For having been a pupil of Dagh, he said he was *Ghamanda* – a nose upturned, that is to say he feels bombastic. Now there is a word *Ghamand* – it is vanity i.e., entering in a state of proudness in the Urdu language but there is no word '*Ghamanda*'. And from the sound of it, it was supposed to carry the masculinity bit of Ghamand – state of being proud. And this poet was so proud in his pursuit of being a pupil of Hazrat Dagh that he said he was 'Ghamanda'– which word he introduced in the language to say of the higher form of Ghamand – one having very, very high pride. And he exaggerated things in the style of his mentor Hazrat Dagh. He has said a poem whose title was 'Ghamanda', one couplet taken from it reads:

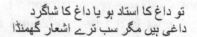

تو داغ کا استاد ہو یا داغ کا شاگرد
داغی ہیں مگر سب ترے اشعار گھمنڈا

Tu Dagh ka Ustad Ho Ya Dagh Ka Shagird
Daaghi Haain Magar Sub Teray Ashaar Ghamanda

You be a pupil of Dagh or teacher of Dagh
O Ghamanda! – nose upturned; all your poetry is
    blemished - spotty

Here we divulge a little bit in the specifics of the Urdu language and wade into it, to assimilate some of its beauties. The spot may be sometimes a beauty and sometimes a blur, and a defect, but here the poet generally means they are defective. The word *Daaghi* – carrying *dagh* or smudge, spot of defect, although it is an ordinary word, but has been beautifully used by the poet, giving it double, triple meaning, and one of it was having a link with the name and the person of his mentor; Poet Dagh. And the poet in this poetry subtly reminds himself of his humbleness through addressing his self as Ghamanda that he is proud he is pupil of Dagh. This elaboration has been given as it would be made in an Urdu class.

Pandit Roy Narayen Arman Ghamanda has said that poetry and his mentor has said the following couplet that is an oft repeated couplet by the Urdu speaking class, a satirist's concoction, used to summarize a situation of conclusive end, in the Land of Seasons and Songs:

Hazrate Dagh Jahan Baaithd Ga-aiy Baaithd Ga-aiy
Saainkrdoan Jootay Parday Uthd Na Sakay Late Ga-aiy

The honourable Dagh sat where he sat by will.
Hundreds of shoes beating received, did not get up sprawled there

Now this poetry appears humorous and simple, but there is so much thought behind these verses. These verses of poetry are impervious to softness and speak of stubbornness of one adamantly pursuing his course, and it is completely a novel verse. Despite religiosity in the pursuance of determination showing stubbornness, the verse says, if he was pushed and kicked and tried to be dislodged, he will not be rising to stand, but lie down; his resilience was of that order that he will not give up that what he has held but will go to pieces for it.

The founding of the poetic literature in versifying an idea in the Urdu language is incomparable. The imagination of the poet transcends all limits in classics when he expresses fantasies and systematic thoughts, the matches and contrasts and vigour in educative poetry and the outlines of the prototypes in his mind all when beautifully written is masterpiece. Its vigour could be excruciatingly penetrating. In touching the limits of exaggeration, one poet turns his attention to the lowly thing, to the shoe and exploits its lowly status, and spurs imagination to entertain thought; and says it was studded with the bright rays of sun. As it is, it is a normality that the sun's rays will fall on the shoes, but look how the poet is manipulating word and showing it how an exaggerator can exacerbate the punch of exaggeration in bringing the lowest thing to high elation. The Poet says:

Paposh peh lagaee kirun aaftab kee
Jo baat kee Khuda ki Qasam laa Jawab kee

(Exaggerating an event, the exaggerator said):

Studded the ray of light of sun on the shoe
By God! Whatever talk he made, he made something incomparable.

The poetic thought and its intenseness of expression could be as penetrating as to tunnel through the barrier of impracticality, and enter conventionality and transcend the borders drawn by the rules of the language. And it is the command of expression and the vigour of thought that drive the language yield and say what was hidden to the ordinary but was obvious to the poet, and he conveys it in the lures of poetry. And it is the prose writer's talent that when he becomes excited and his imaginative pronouncements are filled with fantastic ideas, his prose turns to poetry:

Sir Walter Raleigh after a life of adventure and glory became a prisoner in the Tower of London and was executed on 29th October 1618. That was discreditably filled act, immensely shocking to all, especially more so when it was learnt it was to appease the Spanish Empire and its King, Phillip III 1578 – 1621. He was King of Spain, Portugal and Algarve. His Empire then was at its heights. The Spanish sent a stern note of displeasure at the deaths of their nationals, killed by Sir Walter's field team in their pursuit of the hunting of gold. There also against him was allegation of his conspiring against King James I of England in the country. He was accused to have opposed James I going to be installed as King.

Sir Walter however, on the King's approval later, went to find gold mine in Guiana by deploying his expertise and talent. He met some Spanish settlers resisting him there, they were killed in the duel by his expedition members, and although in the duel that erupted, killed among his men was his son also, but the British appeasing to the King of Spain cost the nation Sir Walter's life and he was executed and there were justifications forwarded that his execution was because of his earlier court sentence. Sir Walter writes about his death, and he turns prose into poetry:

"O eloquent, just and mighty Death! Whom none could advise, thou hast persuaded; what none hath dared thou hast done; and whom all the world had flattered, thou only hast cast out of the world and despised: thou hast drawn together all the far-stretched greatness, all the pride, cruelty and ambition of man, and covered it all over with these two narrow words, 'Hic jacet'." – "here lies."

Sir Walter Raleigh, explorer, poet and historian was born in 1552 in Devon. He had risen to the heights of immutable of the country in several fields. During the reign of Queen Elizabeth, I, he was granted many monopolies and favours by the Queen, including the governorship of Jersey in America. He composed History of the world and many treatises. His account of the voyage, 'Discovery of Guiana' contributed to the legendry story of the City of Gold - El Dorado.

Sir Walter Raleigh's chivalry was quoted world over; he threw his mantle - the robe which represented a considerable part of his estate, on the ground for Queen Elizabeth to walk dry shod over a puddle. Also, he scribbled verses of poetry with diamond on a pane of glass for the Queen to win her favours. Such was Sir Walter Raleigh; he featured in the 2002 BBC poll as one of 100 greatest Britons.

Talking about originality in thought process in poetry, and putting exacerbating thought in the minimum of words, in this art poet Mir Taqi Mir was a wonder. The poet is known to excel in economising words and saying very much in very short lines that will reverberate in meaning for readers to draw what meaning was valid with reasoning to be drawn from the depths of the words and enjoy as much as they wanted out of the couplet. No poet in any language could say poetry of the like of Poet Meer Taqi Meer, unless it was Meer Taqi himself and the language was Urdu. Showing of his wittiness and his goodness of character, this poet speaks of the corporeal love in the clamp of a few words of charm. The poet says:

Sakht Kaafir Thha Jis Nay Pahlay Meer
Mazhab-e Ishq Aekhtiyar Kiya

He must be a proofed unbeliever (the hardy heathen), O Meer,
Who first adapted the religion of love (fell in deep love - did Ishq).

The poets were pitiless with the power of their expression, and poetry was their truth weapon and its grammar were making one close his eyes and go in trance. They talked of *Bulbul* – the song bird of love, and of roses, and tried to measure the thinness of the thin waist of the excelling imaginary beauty by the measure of their poetic metres and lures, using flight of thought, carving out the finest picture of the Mashooq – the beloved. Poet Meer Taqi Meer equipped with all these in abundance says through it:

Nazuki Ooskay Lub Ki Kya Kahi-yay
Pankhardi aek Gulab Ki si Haai

What to talk of the delicateness of her lips
It is like a petal of rose.

This couplet however also speaks of the culture and the entire ways of the East, where the thinness of the lips is liked in preference to the fullness of the lips, that is liked in the West and it is more an object to be looked at and pleasure drawn from it rather than indulging in any exploration of its curve and texture, as done in the West and this was again in line with the silent love practice of the East to contain oneself and make no display of practical appreciation.

Poet John Keats born October 31, 1795 in London, died February, 1821 in Italy. Expressing of the trend in the West, says of it:

'Give me women, wine and snuff until I cry out "hold enough"'

Poet Keats has a high place in the list of the poets. He died young, and in consideration of the laurels of his literariness, if he makes a wish for pleasure that may be excused. He went to Italy in the last days of his life when his health was failing, with a definite termination of life in sight. He went for a change of air and restoration of health, but cruel death snatched him away from the world of literature. His treats of three poems are considered the finest in the English language.

And speaking of the *Sokhen Parwari* – the oeuvre of poeticism, when seen at its extreme heights, it was the fragrance of the poetry of poet Ghalib in Delhi that brought intoxication to souls. When this poet embarks on literary exploitation - turning language into a piece of literature, he stretches imagination into extended extensions. The poet describing the intensities of the casting of the frolic attractiveness of the eye from behind the shades of the bows of the eyebrows says of it:

Abroo Say Kya Haai Iss Nigah-e Naaz Ko Paywund
Haai Teer-e Moqarrar, Magar Iski Haai Kaman Aur

What connection that delicate glance has with the eyebrow
It is still piercing arrow, only its bow is different (the eyebrow of
the hard-hearted ripper.)

And it was in the nature of poet Ghalib to say a thing to make one's imagination toil to derive meanings off his verses. Then to have reached to some concerted decision on the conveyance made by Ghalib that was meant to be the gist was not unanimous. Poet Ghalib says:

Sabd-e Gul Kay Talay Bund Karay Haai Gulcheen
Mizda Aai Murgh Ke Gulzar Mein Saee-yad Naheen

The flower gatherer shuts (as flower) in the bottom of flower
basket.

The good news for you O Fowl is that the bird trapper is not in the orchard.

The poet is addressing the fowl that is so pretty in his colour of feather that it looks like flower. The poet says, O Murgh – O worthy fowl - you are filled with deliciousness, and you are always preyed at for your desirable meat. The meaning drawn from the verse is that O cockerel, if you are caught by the florist due to his habit of his gathering flower, thinking you to be a flower, there will shut you in his basket at least you will be in contact with the flowers and the good news for you is that you will be caught by the florist and not the bird catcher who is not present in the garden.

The poet is perhaps saying your similarity in likeness to the flower is so near to it that along with the flower, the flower picker may lay his hand on your neck and catch you and shut you in the basket as his habit, and the good news for you is that the bird trapper is away, and chances are you will be caught by the florist, if not, you will be meat of delicacy on some one's table.

Among other things, poverty has been attacked by Mirza Ghalib in his poeticism. With affluence kissing the feet of the opulent, farmers making unprecedented production of fruits and producing grains to feed them, *Helwaees* – the confectioners making *Samosas* to fill them, caterers laying tables dressing with delicacies to feast them, the people so indulged them in the *Aftaar*, the extras of the subsidiaries helping the revival of the taste in the mouth at the breaking of the fasts at the sunsets that there was hardly a reason they should not keep fast. There was too great a temptation of these mouth-watering varieties for keeping the fast and it was even holding the non-fasting from staying away of non-fasting even though they faced some physical discomfort. Poet Ghalib says this in his style.

Jis Pas Roza Khoal Kay Khanay Ko Kuch Na Ho
Roza Agar Na Kha-ay To Naachar Kya Karay

One who has nothing to eat after breaking his fast?
If he does not eat the fast; what shall the helpless man do?

270

In another place in his poetry, the humour of poet Ghalib expertly highlights poverty and at the same time ridicules the mega-rich ways, the poet says.

Roza Mera E-man Haai Ghalib Laykin
Khaskhana Wa Barf-aab Kahan Say Laoon

Ghalib! Fasting is the hub of my faith, but,
Where from I bring the *Khus* screen (to stay in), then water, cool as
    ice - at the breaking of the fast.

Khus is a grass, its sticks are tied to form a thick screen using its tender twigs, when water is sprinkled on the screen it effuses fragrance and gives out cool vapours in the living place. And the rich spend their time there in the heat of the day. An attendant ensures it was kept wet and it was the way of the living of the rich, and Ghalib says where from he shall get that facility for the fasting.

Poet Asadullah Khan Ghalib felt satisfied even when not keeping fast. Maybe he relied on the extrapolations in the meanings of the words in the saying of his Maula Hazrat Ali AS. extruding necessary comfort what needed from the trait of skipping the fast. The Wali of God had said:

"If you suffice yourself with the minimum of provisions for sustenance then God will be *Raazi.*"

Poet Ghalib says of Meer Taqi Meer:

Ghalib Apna Yeh Aqeeda Haai Ba-qaulay Nasikh
Aap Bay Bhara Haai Jo Moatqide Meer Naheen

Ghalib my conviction in the words of Nasikh-pupil of Meer is:
    He is unfilled (not learned) who is not convinced of Meer

The faith of Mirza Asadullah Khan Ghalib in Hazrat Ali AS.'s Wilayet – divineness was so deep that not a Momin will easily reach to that pinnacle of faith. He so despised the enemies of Hazrat Ali that he said O God, if nothing I did in life to please You, make my body fuel of fire in

271

the hell so that I may burn the heart of the enemy of Hazrat Ali AS. This is the extreme in devotion a Momin can bring out to be weighed in the weigh balance of love for the Holy Ali. And what magnanimity cannot be talked of Ghalib whose Irfan is so complete. It is said, this quatrain in its meaning and gist was his last poetry, before he died. May God bless his soul and place him in the Jannatul Firdaus, near to his Maula. The quatrain reads:

گر زندگی میں کچھ نہ ترے کام آسکا
ممکن ہے بعد مرگ ہی کچھ کام آ سکوں
ایندھن بنا دے مجھکو جہنّم کا اے خدا
تا کہ دشمنان علی کے کلیجے جلا سکوں

Gar Zindagi Mein Kuchh Na Teray Kaam Aa Saka
Mumkin Haai Baad Murg Hi Kuchh Kaam Aa Sakoon
Eeindhun Bana Day Mujhko Jahannam Ka Aai Khuda
Ta Kay Dushmanay Ali Kay Kalejay Jala Sakoon

If in life I could not be of much use to You
It is possible, after death I may be of some use to You
Make me fuel of the Hell O God!
That I may burn the hearts of the enemies of Ali AS.

This quatrain shows extreme devotion and gnosis, Ghalib carries.

There are two subtleties in the last couplet of the quatrain. One is: The poet asks, he be transformed into another existence – the fire, as opposed to be burnt physically as the enemies of Hazrat Ali AS. will be burnt, and the other conveyance in the last verse is that the enemies of Hazrat Ali AS. will be burnt in hell. And the genius of poet Ghalib is not easily recognised unless one comes across his multi meaning verses.

The Shahs of Awadh whose hearts throbbed with love for Imam Husain AS. and for the progenies of the Prophet of God Hazrat Mohammad Mustafa SAWW, have said some very fine elegies. The last Nawab who's *Takhallus* - nom de plume was Shah and his distinguished name was Nawab Wajid Ali Shah, in his own hand writing has written Holy Quran and has said odes and some touching elegies on the sufferings and the martyrdom of Imam Husain AS. A couplet from his verses describing the majesty of Imam Husain AS. to which utter aversion is shown by the faithless in Islam, reveals the Nawab's *Moaddat* – the deep love for the Shah-e Karbala – King of Karbala, Imam Husain AS. The poet says:

Ha-ay Madaam Bosa - Gahay Mustafa Jo Ho
Aaisa Gala Ho Shimr Ki Shamsheer Kay Liay

How very sad, for always: that which was spot of kiss
of Hazrat Mustafa SAWW
Such throat becomes the virtual object of the dagger
of Shimr-e La-een[36]

Vis-`a- vis Nawab Wajid Ali Shah's lament, the historian Sir W. Muir comments on the response of Imam Husain AS.:

"that Husayn having yielded himself to a treasonable[37], though impotent design upon the throne, was committing an offence that endangered society and demanded swift suppression."

This is such a pathetic comment coming from the throat, not heart and the cultural depth of linguistics. A history writer should not give his comment about rightness or otherwise of an event, unless he was in knowledge of the ethical matter of the subject. Sir W. Muir could not fix the meaning of allegiance in his mind, which was forced on Imam Husain AS. by Yazid. Giving Allegiance or not doing allegiance was the right of a free people. Yazid on the throne of Khilafat was leading a debauched life as a ruler and thrusting his ways on the Ummah. He said no angel came no Wahi came and thereby wa deforming Islam, against which Imam Husain AS. had to rise as his duty entrusted to him for his hereditary status of Imam. If Imam Husain AS.

---

[36] This word Laeen refers to the pushed away from the favour of kindness of God. The etiquette of a Muslim is to point out the degradation of the abysmal status of the murderers of Imam Husain AS. and his companions, sons and brothers, and attachment of word Lanat with their names is in consistency with God value.

[37] Astaghfirullah! The historian does not know the significance of Masoom, he brings him to downfall of using treason for Imam Husain AS. The Aimma and Anbiya (Prophets) were incapable of sin, colossal or minor. The downfall of Umayyad and theirn regime liquidated but the peace and stand of Imam Husain AS. is on the rise.

had not risen against the impiety of Yazid, the Imam would have failed in his divine duty and that was impossible for him and more serious than his neck separated by the henchmen of Yazid. And shirking his duty was not in the aegis of the Imam designated by Allah. The Imam's martyrdom brought awakening in Islam and separated falsehood from the truth. In this stand of protecting God values it was not only the Imam, there was his brother – the great Abbas AS., the children, friends and companions and they created such precept and example in the world of upholding righteousness that it is for ever a beacon of light of truth and forbiddance that the poor of means Momin gets the jewels of handful which quantifies him as the richest being filled with Eeman.

-: . :-

II

THE LAND OF AWADH

V

The land of Awadh was full of *Momineen* of conformity to the preaching of the divine Twelve Imams. Such Momineen were high in *Asmat-o-Paairavi-yey Foghan* – chastity and practicing grieving, building human character by wailing and resorting to sorrow and simplicity, living in the style of Nabi Yahya AS., who though was a *Masoom* - infallible, but bewept vehemently for forgiveness from the High God.

And this was the surest and the most effective prescription for cleansing the heart, shedding sins, and curing the ailments of the soul, and the land of Awadh was distinguished in its practice. Its men recited the Holy names of the High God, and of the fourteen Masoomeen of the House of the Prophet of God Hazrat Mohammad Mustafa SAWW. It kept them inspired to stay away from falsehood. And historians will fail in their writing and presentations unless they, introduced the character and the model of living of the fourteen infallibles the Momeneen of Awadh followed. And these Momeneen referred to, were Shia Muslims and no land boasted to produce the like of them.

One poet of the Aehlebaait surpassing in contentment and thanks giving lived in Lucknow. He and his family lived a destitute life, facing hardship. One affluent of the society, devotee of the Aehlebaait went to him to be of help to him. He had brought an amount of money for the Momin, but the Momin poet would not take any of it. The affluent then thought of a way. He brought a sum of money and said to the Momin, I have brought this money, and it is an Amanat- an entrustment, please keep it with you till I come, whenever I would. And he hoped the Momin might use it for himself. The Momin said if it is an Amanat, do not give it in my hand, just put it there. The affluent put it there and did not go to the poet Momin for a long time. Once when he went there, the Momin said to him Bhaee (brother) where have you been, I am now old and weak and cannot die peacefully unless I have returned your Amanat, which is lying there as was kept by you. Please take it so that I die peacefully. This was the Hasab-o Martaba – nobility and designation of the Momin which was so in all the fields of life, and this was due to the emulating of the qualities of the Aehlebaait and devotedness to the Aehlebaait.

The Ulema of the Shia faith with their sobriety in the virtues of *Fughan* – the crying, followed the precept of their Maula Hazrat Ali AS. who cried vehemently in front of God and the Ulema entered in that Halo of their Maula. Maulana Sarkar Sayed Dildar Ali and his venerated illustrious son Sultanul Ulema Aayetullah Al Uzma Sayed Mohammad Husain Naqvi were the gems of the Land of the Seasons and Songs and they issued directions into the *Shia* faith precepts in Lucknow and it was accepted without argument and vacillation, every one putting faith in their directives. The people felt secure and guided by the authority of learnedness, purity of character and heart in peace of these Ulema, with their practice of righteousness. Moved by the living of the Momeneen of Awadh I have the following quatrain to say:

مومن نے نفس کی طہارت سے نہ فاصلہ رکّھا
نفس کی پاکیزگی کی ڈھال عمل کا اصلحہ رکّھا
اللّٰہ ہر معصیت کے رخنہ سے مضطرب ہوتا ہے
عشق اللّٰہ کے داعی نے اہل بیت و رسول سے واسطہ رکّھا
سیّد اطہار حسین

Momin Nay Nafs Ki Taharat Say Na Fasla Rakhkha
Nafs Ki Pakeezgi Ki Dhal Amal Ka Aslaha Rakhkha
Allah Her Maasiyat Kay Rakhna Say Muztarib Hota Haai
Ishq Allah Kay Daee Nay Aehlebaait-o Rasool Say Wasta
Rakhkha

Momin did not keep distance with the purity of the soul
The soul's purity the shield of deed kept its weapon
God at the innovation of every sin becomes disturbed
One beckoning love of God kept link with the progenies and
Messenger

The *Ilm* – or the learning of an Ayetullah must be heaven high and it is imperative on him to promote and do revival of learning in the Umma – the nation of Islam. The Ayetullah with his sea of knowledge and high in *Amliyat* – action bound was the kingpin of the religion of Islam. Ordinarily a PhD was specialised in one field of knowledge, but the Ayetullah was of knowledge in up to ten to fifteen fields of learning and there was no limit to the maximum. These scholars were born after thousands of men were born and they stood like rock of virtue in the perseverance of faith. And the Marja (the leader) is the proofed, rolling in the flux of knowledge, and his illumination in erudition is through his prayer, devotion and submission to God, which is spread over his 51 Rakats of Namaz over the day followed by the night prayers in his life, and there is no limit to the stretch of the mind's faculty achieved through purity and abstemiousness.

Along with his fifteen to twenty PhDs in the fields of various Ilmiat – the learnings of dedication and integrity and the knowledge of the *Marja-e Taqleed* – the resort for conformity will be associated with faith practice and the purity full life; controlling the modern onslaught of extraneous attacks, blunting these by his inner self strength. He is independent economically through the Khums he receives. Thanks to the system given to the Shia jurisprudence by Imam Mehdi AFS, the Marja has political and spiritual independence. Man is born with need and if need is pacified, purity has no bar left not to rise to zenith. And there is no individual in the world who has a guaranteed freedom from extraneous influence in public office as the Marja-e Taqleed of the Twelvers Shia. He has millions of men in his *Aeqteda* (following) for his one virtue: piety, which brings in retentive knowledge. Knowledge and purity are tied together in higher self, and the individual is in constant bliss, free of economic burden, and thanks to the system the Imams of the House of the Aehlebaait have created. God approves of it for the system continues shedding bliss as an automated phenomenon and man and the system of God are beneficiaries.

King Mohammad Ali Shah 1837 - 1842 in Lucknow in 1839, built the Jaama Masjid of Hussainabad. When it was completed, he asked the Sultanul Ulema Ayetullah Sayed Mohammad Naqvi *Rizwan Moab* – Keeper of Heaven - of Dignity, to lead the prayer in the mosque. The King had very good relations with the Sultanul Ulema, but he refused to lead the prayer or himself offer prayer there. The reason came to be known was; a portion of the mosque was encroaching upon a private property. The King was horrified of the consequence; he immediately moved to obtain the ownership rights for the piece of the land encroached upon with agreement with the owner and after the settlement of the payment and the legal transfer of the land to the King was made, the Ayetullah consented to the King's request and went to lead the prayer in the mosque.

Shah Wali Ullah Mohaddis Dehlawi was a Sunni faith adherent Aalim. He explains; the Khalifate representing the Holy Prophet SAWW is of two aspects: one, external that maintains peace and political stability and the other internal caliphate given to those who work for the strength of the religion. In this vein of foundation, the work of Imam Husain AS. was severed by Yazid, by putting allegiance demand on him AS. Then Shah Wali Ulla wrote translation of Quran in the Persian language which was the common language of the time, years 1730s. He wrote with important marginal notes, about a hundred Sunni extremists assembled outside Fatehpuri mosque of Delhi and encircled him with intention to harm him. He had a small band of followers and a rod. Raising the slogan of Allah Ho Akbar, he turned upon them and forcing his way came out of the mosque safe.

Shah Wali Ullah's teaching are replete with Jihad on the pattern of Ahmad ibn Tamiyyah of Syria, whose follower was Ibn Mohammad ibn Wahab and thence rose the Wahabism. Shah Waliullah criticised, learned and the Sufias of his time. When Shah Waliullah roughened the Shia precepts, Maulana Sayed Sarkar Dildar Ali wrote three books as treatise in defence of the Shia faith - elaborating Islam from the view point of the Shias of Ali – the friends of Ali, which were record and an initialisation in such service in the Land of Seasons and Songs.

Shah Waliullah Mohaddis Dehlavi was born in Muzaffargardh in 1703, died 1762. He was a reformer, philosopher and theologist and it hurt him that the Muslims were divided into factions. But he himself had to follow a faction. He was from Hanafi Sunni school of thought and he looked at the solutions of Islamic state from the Sunni point of view of defence of the traditional belief of the superiority of the first three caliphs of Islam over others. But even before Pakistan People's Party introduced the slogan of 'Roti, Kaprda Aur Makan', Shah Wali

Ullah had dealt with this subject of social need and viewed it in the light that not 'whole nation' should have the same uniform standard of clothing, food and house facility, but everybody should have right to ownership at the level of the facility according to his abilities. And this is meritocracy – not equality of right, as is supposed to be in democracy. Democracy is restrictive of the merit system as it is pluralistic; the vote right of equality is equal. The system of government created in democracy has failed. If there is meritocracy practiced there is no need of foreign policy. The elected representative is not out of the merited in democracy and of quality but product of push in the race of contest through money, coercion and force on the voters and there is no sufficiency of appreciation for this system of government.

Democracy in Islam is not as practiced in the united states where no state has a right to interfere in another's domestic affairs. But in Islam the laws of governance are universal and the resources are shared all over by the country. But the federated states practice meritocracy of preference to monistic rule. if monistic is a better form of government and the pluralistic form of government is a failed system of government, then there should be as many regions to govern as possible for pockets of welfare states as run in the United States, but the desired form by Islam is as they are manageable, with the uniformity of the distribution of wealth and it has freedom to practice religion of variety, but not abusive to one another.

The geographically bounded resource centres of the provinces of a country have the first right over these resources, as this will be the law of the meritocracy – Auwal Khuwaish Baadhoo Derwaish – first must treat one's relatives then others. But many fallacies are emerging from the individual and the personal concepts of the leaders of political parties in Pakistan, where they want to do away with the feudal system to flatten this concept in Islam of gradation and in it merit evolve, status accorded by piety and virtue and the effort put in. In Iran they are successfully running the Wilayet-e Faqih system of government, which is based on meritocracy.

Shah Waliullah Mohaddis Dehlavi was exceptional, otherwise literature from the Maslak of the Sunni school of thought, was in one way or the other lopsided – not preferring meritocracy. Only the finest Ulema and Mujtahid were from the Shia secure religious unity, printing and publishing literature and removing the darkness from the world. And the Shia Kings and Shia affluent, were never negligent of not supporting the deserving. The first King of Awadh Ghazi Uddin Haider 1814 - 1827 left a very large bequest for supporting the deserving, from which income allocation was dispersed to the Mujtahid of each of the cities of Najaf and Karbala. After the British annexation of Awadh the responsibility of the distribution of money was taken over by the British and in 1900 they decided to increase the number of recipients of the bequest to ten Mujtahid in Najaf and Karbala and attempted to use it to influence the Mujtahid politically, but they underestimated the spirituality of these Mujtahids and met with God snub and failure.

Lucknow was the pride centre of the land of Awadh and the culture and the etiquette of Lucknow were Islamic political laws. The courtesies offered by one to the other under the prodigious Nawabs of Awadh were the glorious traces of the distinguished house of the Aehlebaait trimmed to show the prosperity of the Nawabs of Awadh. It was seen to that the glass of water when offered to the thirsty, was placed on a tray and covered with a decorative cover and served with the utmost courtesy. And the style of this culture of Awadh bore such distinctive influence on the people that its permanency has stayed till today on the lips of the people of the Land of Seasons and Songs, in such phraseologies as 'Pahley Aap'- 'first you Sir'. And these phraseologies continue to be part of the living memory of the people in the Land of Seasons and Songs, reminding them of the Lukhnawi Andaz – the manner of Lucknow – a continuity in the bestowal of generosity and hospitality of Imam Hasan AS, who would run a running Dastar Khwan for the hungry and destitute.

The etiquettes went outside of the palaces; to the limits beyond the capital city of the Nawabs of Awadh to hinterlands and to the world of other capitals spread to vast territories and the etiquettes exceeded and the excessiveness of the etiquettes verged on to foppishness and it was summed up in one-word Lukhnawi – belonging to Lucknow. The mannerism of it was called the Lukhnawi Andaz – the characteristic style of Lucknow and for all its exuberance and the show of ostentation of mannerism in presenting formalities it carried, it was also excessively loved and excessively ridiculed.

A Lukhnawi was once travelling in a bus. The bus stopped at one stop on the road and a hawker came with some farm fresh tender *Kakdri*. The Kakrdi(s) were long thin cucumbers. Their skin was softer and tenderer than the thick cucumber. These were lovingly called as cukes, but better known as Kakrdi. The Lukhnawi bought a few Kakrdis from the hawker to quench his thirst and freshen him. He inspected each Kakrdi and then peeled the skin and made delicate thin slices of the Kakrdis and in this way proceeded to eat the Kakrdi. Now there was hardly any skin on the tender Kakrdi(s) to peel off, and then making fine slices of already thin Kakrdis was an indulgence in excessiveness for preparing to eat the Kakrdi, and then he was making such a show of small morsels he was taking by biting small pieces from the thin slices of the Kakrdi, repeatedly going through the act.

A Sardar Sahib was watching the indulgence of the Lukhnawi for a long time, prolonging his eating, dwelling on the inspection of the Kakrdis and having the Kakrdis bared of its green skin. It was already an excessive etiquette to peel the Kakrdi and to throw away the perfectly eatable tender skin of the Kakrdi and then to make thin the slices of the already thin Kakrdis and eating it with such pomp as to delicately lift and eat the evenly sliced Kakrdi sections with intrinsic attention. This whole act continued in front of his eyes. He couldn't take it. The Sardar Sahib was fed up of the Lukhnawi Andaz and to show his disgust, he called the man selling the Kakrdi and bought some Kakrdis from him and making a show of it, he grabbed a Kakrdi and demonstratively smelled, it and then broke it with a snap and took a full harsh bite at it. This made some sputter come out and the man sitting next to him started sneezing.

Sardar Sahib looked at the man and spoke. "Bhai Sahib, I am eating Kakrdi and you are sneezing?"

On this the man said. "You see I am catching cold from the sputter of your Kakrdi". He said, "We don't eat Kakrdi the way you are eating."

Sardar Sahib said. "Oh yes, and how do you eat Kakrdi?"

The man replied, "You see that person there, we eat Kakrdi that way."

Sardar Sahib on that revelation asked him. "And where do you come from?"

The man filled his chest with pride and bulging it said, "I am a Lukhnawi."

This made the whole riddle become clear to Sardar Sahib and he knew now the reason for this excessiveness. Sardar Sahib came from a region where these etiquettes were foppish, ridiculous and vain.

And they considered the Lukhnawi(s), so exacerbating the etiquettes passing reasonability that while introducing their Lukhnawi colleague to someone formally making judgement in categorising talents, said, 'Sahib Inkay Pudinay Kay Baaghat Thhay' - Sahib they had gardens of mint trees. This was pun and fudge with hidden sarcasm to say, 'Sahib they are the people who exaggerate ordinary patch to garden make it look a marvelling fancy.' He meant to say they came from where they called their residence - Ghareeb Khana a poor man's house but meant it was Daulat Khana – the residence of well to do. if they are hungry, they will say they are full stomach, if they lived in hutment, they will say in God's provided shelter. Now these are qualities to show self-elation and thankfulness for the Lukhnawis but for the colleague from Punjab where the Sardar Sahib came from were blaring fits of anecdote of deliberate self-classification.

The Pudina, i.e., the mint plant was grown only in small patches. It was used only for digestive purposes and for problems associated with flatulence, and used in small quantities, therefore it was not so widely grown, only in patches, but to ridicule the Lukhnawi colleague, his colleague from the region where Sardar Sahib came from, would find an innate word for the Lukhnawi for his excessive etiquettes and say of the patches of the Pudina fields - they were Baaghat - big gardens, deliberately indulging in excessiveness to ridicule the Lukhnawi colleague. And the Lukhnawi felt so pinched at that, and considered it a barbarian cultural invasion.

And when the Lukhnawis thought of their correct rhythmical stress on words in producing deliveries of the vernacular in vogue, with correct accent, letting out correct pronunciations and infusing rules of grammar in its delivery, producing Saut-e Hasna – pretty agreeable phonetics to listen to, pleasing to the ears and that they were helping the language in elocution hoist the distinctive flag of fluttering flourishes, making the language methodologically effusive;

they thought their new locals, they were rubbing shoulder with were unthankful to their linguistic services.

The Lucknawis considered the unceremonious jibes flung at them was their derating by their new associates and that was ingenuine and the Lukhnawis called them invasive, idolum and affixing false mental picture of interpretive and refined Lukhnawis. And the sarcasm used in introducing them, trespassing the judicial authority of probity and fairness. And the Lukhnawis promoting awareness and revival of the Islamic Ummah and propagating renascent Islamic ideas among the cadres, especially among the religious scholars to respond to the masses need all a trivial knot, to call their patches of the mint field a garden of the mint.

And the Lukhnawis delirious temperament considered the appealing lights sitting behind the news desk as newsreaders, with their nonprofessional inserting and stuffing unnecessary of inept words in the texts, stretching it, and for that racing with it as news items on the news desks and making news construed of countless worthless words construed from non-legitimate pieces of information in the short pack of time and conveying little from it, presenting degraded jarring vernacular of less than middle class performance – a product of outcome of their backing. And repeating a break during the news announcement were illogical link - not sticking to the professionalism to deliver what was to be delivered with ease, and composure. And the field reporters forcing the listener to listen to their news guff stuffing – with little of material reporting, and more repeating and filling the text with unwanted and considering them doing exaction of service to culture, most suited to the composure of the audience.

And those accent filled newscasters in their media channels on news desk never pronouncing Ghaain better than Gaain and Qaf(s) not better than Kaff(s) and Khe(s) not better than Khhe(s), not adhering to the crisp pronunciation, and in speaking applying their sweet willed butts and composure and ease, and not attempting deliver sentences with stress and accentuation to produce sound with cadence, and their ripple less voice hammering the diaphragms of the ears, not doing justice to the vernacular, and violating the rules of the pretty language Urdu, as if Urdu was an orphan. This lethargy and definite willed determination to produce the language tinged with the local flavour, the Lukhnawis found was not acceptable. And the Lukhnawis hastened them to heraldry, to let not slips and detours turn into belligerency.

The horrific irrationality, the defection from the service of literality, serving their commercial interest was most done by the prominent news channels, harassing the public, and clobbering at the government to mould their mind and go by their way of thinking, enraging and exacerbating extremism. It is so, since they are having no accountability to answer to and they are not devoting them to do their duty as part of pride, as demanded of professionalism in producing excelling standard. They are more concerned running commercial advertisement and imposing their notional religiosity on others all for money filling their till.

And their obnoxiously, annoying and tasteless signature tune is so bad as to be called self-deception - message without target, suited only to the taste of the insensitive, away from the Islamic discipline. The signature tune should be a marshal tune of some orchestral masterpiece, but it is one rudimentary tune of ripping music to rip composure and not sooth the ears. These channels are destroyers of culture, repeating inferiorly worded advertisements to fill the TV transmission time, violating ethical rules. This is all because of the lack of sincerity, also their non-dedication to professionalism and lack of exercise to handle diligent challenging work, unable to follow the practicing religious scholars who equip listeners to unearth beauty.

The columns in the renowned newspapers of the country were never produced writings-of-value in comfortable readable size of font. Then the columnist content is parochialism with blatant smearing of the targeted, mostly angling to protect and air extremism. All hypotheses of cure to extremism were discussed in the papers and on the TV, but it was superfluous discussion, making murky waters with it of muddiness. In all this tragedy, the preferred faith is of clear prominence and Adl the justice is led to the parking bay. Adl is the sheet anchor of the ship of life and it is not touched, since it has not been introduced in the faith fundamental of the majority of the Muslim believers. And Adl or justice in the fundamentals of the faith is next to *Tauheed* – the Oneness of God and brings immunity from error. Adl was cure to block the ills of impairments. It was a devised compact of faith with continuation into Quranic adherences, fully barring fallacy to emerge. But the four great factions of the Fiqah did not have Adl in the fundamentals of the faith. It was missing there and there was possibility of the numericity of errors. It was necessary to rendering service to the masses and keeping them attuned with God qualities.

And the dearth of the cultural excellence and absenteeism of talent, was due to lack of sobriety. There were no Anis and no Dabeer born in the region called Pakistan, no Ghalib, neither Mir Taqi Mir. If Iqbal was there, he was producing literature on military glory of past:

> *Bahray Zulmat Mein Daurda Diyay Ghorday Hum Nay*
> *In the fearsome seas of challenge, we ran our horses.*

Iqbal in evolutionary stage all the time was an unsettled soul. So much controversy resides in the clasp of Iqbal that he is all inconsistency – sometimes great, sometimes ready to be unsound. If Iqbal was identifying him of Ali and Fatima, but ultimately not bowing at their door and was following a different Fiqah. The literary beauty without practicality was mistaken reasoning. The cohesion to didactic and awurd - the coming of the revelatory thoughts from the majesty of nature came through the ingress of the sublimity flowing from the House of the Aehlebaait. Iqbal was going through phases of change starting with his *Shikwa* and *Jawab-e Shikwa*[38], in his poeticism a general revival effort of arousing the passion of Umma, through the reminder of the past and invitation to enter the past glories and derive inspiration. He was endeavouring to invigorate and resuscitate Ummah to saddle on the ibex of power, but never to help roll back the general deficiency in the faith fundamentals, or himself showing such depth in purity as of Meer Anis, who says:

> *Door Baitha Ghubar-e Meer Oos Say*
> *Ishq Bin, Yeh Adab Naheen Aata*

---

[38] This is a set of two epic poetries in Musaddas (six lines stanza). In his earliest poetry, he narrates of patriotism. Later his poetry addresses the Nation of Islam. His early poem Shikwa in 1911 received severe criticism and he was conferred the misname of Kafir. Two years later he wrote Jawab-e Shikwa - reply to the grievance, to remove the stigma of Kafir from his name.

The dust of Meer sat away from him
If no love of God, this culture does not spring up

Meer Anis has chosen the tiny word 'Ghubar', ordinarily meaning dust, but here the meaning is ostentation, backwardness and it huddles in all aspects of worthlessness in a being. The word is extremely unassuming but so meaningful in the context used by the poet. It is carrying the central intended meaning of ego away from him. It is astonishing what command Meer Anis has on the selection of words and in the power of expression he will display.

Lucknow had its own distinctive version of Urdu and its own unique style of people. One Lukhnawi in the days of his youth, when the young hopefuls dreamt that fantasies will be coming, and kissing their cheek on their own accord, dreamt that his dream-fairy will land in his lap. The fair ladies of fairing beauties driving cars around, in these days were few and far. The Lukhnawi however was dreaming that one of them will hit him square by her car, and it will open the way to the mine of the wealth of love and beauty and he says in his Lukhnawi Urdu:

Tamanna Haai Ki Kissi Haseena Ki Car Kay Neechey Aa Jaoon Aur Ba-ain Hanth Ki Chan-guliya Mein Choat Lagay, Aur Khoon Bhal – Bhal, Bahay.

'My longing is that I be run over by car of some extreme beauty and my little finger of the left hand gets hurt and blood from it flows Bhal, Bhal – gushing out unchecked.'

Look at the innocent desire of being run over by car and only the little finger of the left hand be hurt. The young Lukhnawi expected that after the car hit and he run over by the beautiful dainty fairy of his dream, he will have aroused sympathy in her heart and this assailant will throw a smiling glance at him and there after the gates of heavenly comfort will open for him.

This wish was in keeping with the burning silent love shown by the young, devoted to the profession of loving, in the Land of Seasons and Songs and their passivity was ready to take all knocks of rejection inflicted by the beauty and rudeness flung at them and yet they standing erect with virtuousness of love intact for the dainty beauty. This show of timid chivalry and taking knock on the knuckles was the standard in the show of true love in the Land of Seasons and Songs. Whereas the appetizing power associated with the sensory cognition in love in the West was a business deal, and each party had to meet their commitments for the pleasure of the other.

The poets of the Land of Seasons and Songs, explaining this virtue associated with the love-kind permitted in the land have written many professing *Ghazalyat* – poems of form dealing with the subject of love, conveying subtleties of the reflexes profuse with the intensity of progress towards rejection, but poet continuously lurking towards progress and prosperity. One poet of the East addressed the Western lover where the sun was not so much out to burn the skin, shrink it and toughen it, to take the knocks of love, mildly taunts at him for the organizational demise in love super fluency. The poet says in the voice of the famous lyrist Mehdi Hassan's challenging verses with tasty flavour of uniqueness of love-kind which prevails in the East, as opposed to the surface skimming love in the West[39]:

Jo Chahetay Ho So Kaehtay Ho
Chup Raehnay Ki Lazzat Kya Jano
Yeh Raz-e Mohabbat Haai Pyaray
Tum Raaz-e Mohabbat Kya Jano

What you want, you say
What will you know of the bliss of keeping quite?
This is secret of love, my dear
What will you know of the secret of love?

The Lukhnawi who wished to be run over by a Haseena's car was for humour than carrying any longing to meet a real dainty beauty taking only the farfetched expense of damaging his little finger; it showed the kind of humour that went around in the society and these were the

---

[39] This paragraph was written some twenty-five years back and since then the realities have changed in the west. The love is not on display there anymore on the streets and the lanes. It is bottled up and shown in Islam dominated behavioural order.

spices of life. This takes us to the early days of the Bollywood film makers when the cult of oblique love ruled the principles of film making which they shot for the screen.

In the films in those days of 1944 - 45, great stars like Surraiya, Madhubala, Nimmi, Nargis, Noor Jehan, Dileep Kumar, Raj Kapoor, Deva Nand, Santosh Kumar, Rahman and others, in league and individually, appeared on the screen and outdid one another in the cult of love. And the beauty inf the names were that these heroes had to have Hindu mythological names to sound attractive and sweet on tongue, like Raj Kapoor, Deva Nand, Dileep Kumar. The Muslim names with bare names of Sifaat – the qualities of Allah did not fit in the film industry. E.g., imagine a name like Allah Ditta or Tanweerul Haque Musaddaq as film heroes. This is so mouthful that in love portrayals, these were biting the ears. The tongue will yield that miraculous exposition that its exhibition will close the film industry and it will either collapse or travel in the direction where were elements more on Islamic philosophy than of the entertainment. The Muslim names could not display of the corporeal love with that zest and the sophistry as needed of them by the film industry, so they turned to the names of neutral appeal of Sanskrit oriented names.

But now in these modern days of activation and stringencies of group performing, action filled stage performances, the pseudonym has moved in the direction of real Muslim names with mostly Khan suffixes and affixations with the exception of Bachchan for distinction. And the great fun in the display of sincere *Majnoonana* (vehement) love has been lost somewhere. Now the Screen Ace Actor Amitabh Bachchans drags the Extra Actor, pulling and punching him in the face and on the ears and kicking him with a flying kick in the bar and in show of very hard kicking the old cult of love has been thrown out of the window, and soft melodious whispering confession of the invasion of love taking over the actors and the actresses on the screen is put to ruins.

And of them the least interested in love scenes are the Khans, who are truly from the land of *Naswar* – the sniffing thing. Sultan Alauddin Khilji 1298 A.D. had four classes of Noblemen or Ameers: Khan, Malik, Ameer and Sipahsalar and the top were Khan and they continue to maintain their Haakmiat – the governing role, which has little space for love. That is why these Khans give love look of murky look – diversionary in attribute to goodness. And it is true, it is least expected of true Khans to display tender love with their ancestors' history of making mountains of the skulls. But still of the Foursome born to display talent in the Bollywood, viz; Aamir Khan, Salman Khan, Shah Rukh Khan and Saiph Ali Khan, to be fair at least the first two did not let their front apron of shirt be contaminated with love, the other two were a bit relaxed and the third and fourth were well submerged in it. And the hardest hit for screen performing love, completely averse to it was Amitabh Bachchan. He had no inkling of it, only showed his majesty of fist and bang with his shoes. But their manifestations are shining like glazing honey with perfect Urdu and they serve entertainment and literature alike. And Bachchan is capable of even pouring the song waves into the ears and delivering Sanskrit vernacular. And the least love portraying of them -Salman Khan has shown his family prevalence, he adroitly sticks to his ancestors' profession of conquering territories, based on that he conquers infatuated hearts brimming with love for his muscular toughness, when he displays to them his toughened muscles.

In those days (in 1940s), the Bollywood film makers would film the story of Laila Majnoon. This was an adventure in which deep love of Qais for Laila had turned him into a *Majnoon* – someone gone crazy. Qais was a victim of love for lovely Laila. He loved Laila more than his life. But this was an arduous love since Laila was daughter of the Head of the rival Arab clan and the exhibit of love from Qais ibn Mulawwah could not be tolerated by the rivalry hit parents of Laila. But they were beaten by the reciprocity of Laila to Qais. And the intensity of the Majnoon's love was the ultimate in the measures of the *Majazi* love - the corporeal love that had broken all bonds and record.

This love had emerged from the depths of the silent Arabian *Sahara,* the desert and the world cherished the Laila Majnoon love. The screen based its cinematography on the versions of this love for a very long time, till they learnt other tricks and till then it was the guiding and dominating fundamental love story in webbing the plots of the scenes of stories in love in the days of the theatres on the modest size cinema screens of the Land of Seasons and Songs.

In the early days of the Bollywood cinematography, the screen story was cut to support to be screened in black and white. There the dejected hero would sing song on the screen, with lyricism drenched in remorse and filled with agony:

Chal Jahan Gham Kay Maray Na Hoon
Jhooti Aasha Kay Taray Na Hoon

Take yourself to where there were no one hit by tragedy
Where there were no stars of false hopes.

Now in these verses, while the first line was tolerably acceptable Urdu, but its match the second line was disaster. A concoction of nonsense versed and dragged in and filled as a line to make the meter of the poetry be complete but breaking all rules of conveyance of sense filled thought. Everyone knew there was no such thing as the 'stars of false hope' - there wasn't such a thing. But the screen requirement made the song emerge from it and no one cared about the linguistics so long as the tune was catchy. And Bollywood took off from these pedestals and gone on to its flights of richness of success. From that level of no rules observed in grammar, it rose to its today's zenith. Today it is second only to the biggest industry in the world of entertainment.

And thanks to its new-found sense of perfectionism, now it cannot allow any more mis conceptual expressive poetry of the like of the film of the yester years. Then they studded purely Hindi words in purely Urdu couplets to get the metre right, but now they have such professionals in every field of cinematography that it is pure professionalism at its best and it is staggering. They have been progressing by leaps and bounds and now manage to entice and produce actresses like Aishwarya Roy who plays the role of the famous society girl - *Tawaef* Umaru Jan Ada of Lucknow and she will sing song of deep-seated meanings on the screen lush with Urdu terminology. In one of her songs in a film describing her plight of being neglected by a nobleman, an important someone in the society, played by Abhishek Bachchan, her husband, she presents high class pleasing poetic lines in her song:

Tumhaari Mehfil Mein Aa Ga-ay Haain
Toe Kyon Na Hum Yeh Bhi Kaam Kar Lein
Salaam Karnay Ki Aarzoo Haai Idhar Jo Dekho Salaam Kar Lein
Yeh Dil Hai Jo Aaa Gaya Haai Tum Per,
Wagarna Such Yeh Haai Banda Parwar
Jissay Bhi Hum Dekh Lein Palat Kar, Oosi Ko Apna Ghulam Kar Lein

This is perfect poetry in the genre of Ruba-ee. And pleasing too. And here is the translation.

I have come to your gathering then why not should I do this work?
I have longing to salute you - if you look this side, I greet you
This is the heart that has flung itself on you - otherwise truth is O'
Bunda Parwar - promoter of us ordinary – (its meaning also conveys the sense: you of high caring or you the non-caring)
Whoever I look at by turning back, I make him my slave.

And their industry (The Bollywood Film) has come a long way; they will deal now in philosophy, politics, education, economics and in multidimensional subjects and have left the Laila Majnoon love story way behind. That was their springboard and that served the purpose. But still Laila Majnoon was a powerful drama of pure love flexibilities in the freedom of human faculties and it was presented in a dignified way with purified versions in love in the Land of Seasons and Songs.

Many poets and litterateurs have described the plight of Majnoon. Poet Nizam Ganjavi was born in Azerbaijan in 1140 AD, he describes in his lyric, the peak height of love that Majnoon had entered in. Then his logicality of love allowed no flexibility and he charged to places wherever his self will find Laila. The poet Nizam Ganjvi says for Majnoon:

Choon Bar Dar-e Khaimah Ee Rasheeda
Mastana Sarod Ber Rasheeda
Laila Gufti Wa Sang Khoori
Dar Khoordan Sang Raqs Karda

When (he) arrived at the tent (of Laaila's wards)
Lost of awareness of his existence, he drew the
verses of songs off him

291

He was speaking 'Laaila' and was receiving hits of stone
While rained with stones, was dancing.

Poet Ghalib describes of Laila and Majnoon in his subtle as under: The interpreters have opened a whole chain of office to describe the meaning of the couplet said by poet Ghalib. Each interpreter is deriving a different meaning out of it, reflective of the mood and the angle with which he looks at the couplet and interprets according to his fancy what he likes. And each cannot be disputed for their authenticity. The poet says:

Qiyamat Haai Kay Suun Laila Ka Dasht-e Qaais Mein Aana
Taajub Say Woh Boala Yeoun Bhi Hoata Haai Zamanay Mein

It is eternally impossible said he, after hearing that Laila came to the desert of Qaais

With surprise of strangeness he spoke, does it happen like that also in the world (that Laila meets not Qaais)?

Interpreters say, Laila did not meet Majnoon because of the etiquette of Pardah, although she went there lost in love of him, only thinking of him, searching for the Majnoon, yet she refrained from meeting Majnoon. And if the analysts' views were taken into account there were many possibilities in the approach to the meanings that can be written. In explaining of the couplet here, since it will take too much space and there will be considerable deviation, the writer will restrain him from being drawn in its explanations. But elsewhere, including in the *Adab* or the literary portion of the Jang newspaper London, the *Tabserah Nigar* – critic and commentator, Partau Rohila has sufficiently covered it with explanatory literature as analyst and has done it beautifully.

Majnoon was so lost in love of Laila that one day while he was going all lost thinking of Laila that he crossed a man who had just settled for prayer in the open on the ground. He had just entered in the *Niyat* of the prayer that Majnoon appeared there. The man had taken all due precaution that no one should cross him during his prayer. He was a *Darzi* – a tailor, so he had driven in the soil his steel measuring yard in front of him and had taken all due care with driving the *Satar* – the inhibiting curtain in front of him in the ground so that nothing should come in between the curtain and him in his direct contact with God, and he had started the prayer after that elaborate preparation, and the Majnoon despite that crossed passed in between the Satar and the man.

The man was furious, he broke his Niyat and immediately caught Majnoon and slapped him on his cheek and said didn't you see I was praying? You crossed from in front of me in between the Satar and me. The Majnoon after that slap on his cheek said, 'I am sorry Sir, I did not see you.' And then the man was more furious and slapped Majnoon's cheeks harder and said how is it that you didn't see me when I was standing clear for prayer? And then on that his supposed to be disqualification Majnoon spoke thus:

"Sir, I was so lost in the love of a beautiful woman of the world that I couldn't see you, but you tell me, how you saw me passing in front of you, when you were standing before such a Magnificent Beloved One of Majesty and Beauty."

Majnoon had presented logic and awakening of conscious and the Darzi, the ego of the trail of prayers he did which helped no one except him. But the haunting logic and acuteness presented by the Majnoon straightened many Namazis in their presenting themselves in the submission of love to God. Darzi improved in the standards of faithfulness to devotion to God and Majnoon proved he was right the distinction of love, even be Majazi is Godly. Love bound two people, and Majnoon was faithful to his beloved and was thinking about her even on his way, but the Darzi was not faithful to his Beloved for Whom he had stood to pay his submission. He was not thinking about Him, but thinking of no trespasses should be made between the Satar and him and he even jumped at the Majnoon to beat him up as soon as that happened and violated the fundamental of any faith of being patient, it was his showing of no connectivity with God which thanks to Majnoon, he corrected.

Nawab Wajid Ali Shah was a great patron of art and culture; he took extreme pleasure from the plays of the ladies in *Rekhti*. (To pronounce the word Rekhti, the 'khe' sound is brought out with lips spread opened, and sound brought out from top of throat). The Urdu phonetic 'khe' is difficult to pronounce in the English language for its phonetic, which has its deficiency. The Rekhti were poems in the language of the ladies of the elite class and Nawab Wajid Ali Shah brought out a ballet known as *Rahas* in Rekhta where women showed love to the elated and glorious Lord Krishna.

The language of Rekhti was in idioms, peculiar to the conversation of the women. Wajid Ali Shah himself acted in the drama as male actor and he had chosen for him to play the pastoral life of Lord Krishna. The *Gopi's* or the milk girls had a burning love for Lord Krishna, and very powerful expressions were possible using the language of Rekhti. The ladies' role of the Gopi(s) was played by the *Parees* - the beautiful ladies in the Nawab's Harem of which there was no shortage and the Nawab played the role of Lord Krishna for his exclusive majesty that suited his station and elegance.

The Nawab had a script prepared under the title '*Indersabha*' or celestial court, by one of his court poets. This was a drama of *Hindu Rahis* where Krishn Chand puts himself to dance with the Gopi(s). It was very popular drama with the audience. In general, everyone was invited to it, when it was staged on special days in the seasons of rejoicing. However, this practice died down when the Nawab's rule ended in Lucknow. This spirited conversational programme, extending the scope of the language for stage drama of Rekhti died down, and the British were the cause for it.

To cater to the taste of the select class of the society and to bring in humour when the committers' fate was cause to bringing in their abasement for, they not wading in rationality and not strengthening hagiology (literature dealing with the lives and legends of the saints), the poetry of ridicule or *Harsiya* – condemning the enemies of the Aehlebaait was given birth to. It was customised and enacted behind curtain. This was contrasted to *Marsia* – the elegy, which highlighted the tyrannies of Yazid's army in Karbala and simultaneously glorified the bravery of the oppressed Imam and his companions' and children's and brother's, protecting through it, righteousness. The Marsiya composition was for lyricism delivered from the *Menmber* – the stepped high chair on which the speaker went to sit on the second or the third step to address the audience. But the Harsiya was recited without such formality.

After the *Soze-o-Salam* - the dirge and salutary recitation that was recited by a recognised team of at least three members, consisting of a *Marsia Go* – the main grief reciter of highly specialised adeptness and his two *Bazoo(s)* – the arms who intoned the verses of the lyric to be in step with the Marsia Go. Thereafter the Marsia reciter took the Menmber. The Majlis was addressed by Marsia presentation. There was no *Khitabat* – address by a clergy. This was more of the literary genius distinguishing in paying homage to the Imam and his family and friends than the episode to be narrated in detail. A particular aspect of the tragedy was elaborated in the language of erudition and literary excellence was tied to the analytic virtue of some hero of Karbala.

The etiquette in the Soze-o-Salam was that in its submission there was to be no *Gitkiri* – train of lyrical sound, undulation with falls and rises successively in the voice. A persistency of disincline in the undulation of the delivery was presented in the Soze. But in Salam it appears permissible if appealingly done. Only one dip and one rise at one pitch was permitted in Soze, but ripples were allowed, and it had to show either sadness or pride depending on the verse type said. And the main address of the Majlis started after the Soze-o-Salam ended. The Majlis concluded after the narration of the Marsiya verses if it was entirely a Marsiya Majlis, otherwise the Zakir went to take the Menmber and he addressed the Majlis. These were the Muharram Majalis proceedings.

The substance of Harsiya was different to that of the Marsia, which was a combination of drama through poetry and ridicule lavished at the characters who had forgotten the station and the status of the Prophet SAWW and brought hurt, tyranny and death to the dearest of the progenies of the Prophet Mohammad Mustafa SAWW in Karbala and in times earlier to it and later to it to the Imams and the progenies of the Prophet SAWW. And Harsiya was for these men who had forgot decency and became frigid i.e., turned to ignoramus ilk. But because the description and the enactments in it were likely to hurt some, who were disposed to condone these acts of excessiveness, it was open only to explicit audience, and if an alien joined in, he must have been prepared to hear deficient lavishes of praise to their idols.

For this reason, these activities were held behind the curtain in privacy, away from the eyes of those not wishing to be exposed to it and unlikely to enjoy it.

But in exclusion to Harsiya, and to Marsia and to all flowery poetry there was another genre in ploy behind the curtain where all participated jointly to have fun. It was called *Hazel* – the unapproved poetry. The poets played with words, describing the scenes of – the loo, the defecated impurity parting. The excelling poet in this art of poetry was poet Chirkeen of Lucknow. The Hazel was presented in the *Mushaeras,* which were poets' vocal presentations in the assemblies of poets and audience, where this genre was expressed in appropriation to match an occasion. This poetry never failed to stir bursts of laughter.

In the days, when the facility of toilet - loo in London were all well provided in a well organised way, these were large public lavatories, it cost then one penny to use these, and that was for unlimited period to occupy the seat. These times were that good. There was one such large underground lavatory in Leicester Square. One English Poet paid a penny for the loo door to open for him but he was rewarded with very little benefit from it after sitting on the commode. He therefore wrote on the wall in the loo:

> Oh, how I feel broken hearted
> Paid a penny and only farted.

The poet in this poetic thought brought a flash of subdued laugh to the reader, but it failed to touch depth in meaning and subtlety in expression. It dispersed only one item of information in isolation and that ascribed to the specific grief shown by the poet on parting with his penny in that unprofitable manner. Only incidentally it threw some light on the monetary weight of the penny coin, which then, in 1956 - 57 was still a stern monetary denomination of reckoning. Even the ha-penny then carried weight and was duly receipted. But even with all that said in its defence, the couplet lacked power of carrying allegory in it; it was plain and flat.

But poet Chirkeen in Lucknow credited him by saying such in depth verses in Hazel poetry that it raised astonishment and expectations as to what could not be said using this genre. The poet says:

Urda-ay Urdti Naheen Sitki Bardi Paadoan Say
Urda-ay Deta Haai Chirkeen Pahaar Phuski Say

The tiny pebble is not flying with big farting
Chirkeen is blowing away mountain with his small farting

This was a difficult poetry of a different genre in characteristics. And what really, this poet Chirkeen in Lucknow was saying in his style was that he was that competent that, what little things others could not do with big efforts, he did big things with little effort.

Poet Chirkeen is said to have had said beautiful poems in *Ghazalyat* of love filled poems in his early days. His *Bayaaz* – the copy book was stolen and the content was published as their own. Poet Chirkeen was unaware of it. He went to Hyderabad Deccan and in a Mushaera recited the verses of one of his Ghazals and he was booed at on that, as people thought he had stolen the Ghazal from the published book of someone else's. Chirkeen was very annoyed and he vowed to say verses only such that no one was to steal and call his own and he then adopted the genre of Hazel.

Many charms filled Lucknow, and the most was from its rich poetic tradition and its poets. Lucknow was full of poets and it hummed with *Mushaera* - the assemblage of the poets, where they recited the verses said by them and received accolades from the audience.

Many prominent poets and scholars had moved from Delhi to Lucknow. The Nawabs of Awadh were forthwith in offering their patronage to them for their poetic abilities. The Nawabs themselves said poetry and it was a great time for the Urdu literature. Thoughts and lore floated across the land far and deep, with *Misrah Tarah* – line set for completion of verse, and it was matched by the responding poets to the same depth of literary excellence as they were challenged to match the hemistich, and the excellences were matched with excellences. And there was a definite linguistic rivalry between Lucknow and Delhi – the 'Centres of Urdu'. The Lukhnawi poets and literalists sent the following half line - hemistich to the Delhi poets for their royalist literariness to match the line of the verse and complete the couplet if they could.

Natawan Hoon Kafan Bhi Ho Halka

I am frail the shroud for burial should also be light.

The Delhi centre replied with the matching line that was equally demanding and delicate in nature as the original demand in the hemistich. The Delhi poets reply was:

Daldo Saya Apnay Aanchal Ka

Put the shadow of your stole (on my corpse).

Delhi and Lucknow had emerged as great centres of the Urdu language. Though the first Urdu newspaper Jam-i-Jahan was founded in Calcutta by Harihar Dutta in 1822, but Urdu basically was nourished by the mind of the Muslims and Calcutta was a pillar not the building. Another centre or the anchor sheet of the Urdu language was Hyderabad, but it did the renowned services of research, translation and the founding works to cater for expanding the word contents of the Urdu language. And this centre also patronised Islamic art and culture. This was under the patronage of the Asaf Jahi Kings, especially under their vigorous King the seventh Nizamul Mulk, Mir Osman Ali Khan Asaf Jah V11, Nizam of Hyderabad.

The learned Nizam and his ethos of civility was such that with his high title of 'His Exalted Highness', he folded his arms and sat on his legs folded listening to the Moharram Majlis addressed by the *Zakir* - the speaker, who narrated the tragedy of Karbala in the *Aashoor Khana* – the *Khilwat Hall* where the Majlis in the month of Muharram was held for mourning the martyrdom of Imam Husain AS. And this culture was of the elite from the south to the north of the rulers and the ruled.

The British loved this culture, but they could not take all at once the twin of the culture and the unchecked Nawab Wajid Ali Shah ruling the Nawabdom of Awadh. He was given the misnomer by the British of debauch. The Nawab was declared feisty and immoral, and by dint of that they occupied Awadh in 1856. And it was the superiority of weaponry, regimentation and intrigue that won the day for the British. They moved the troops of the British East India Company towards the capital of Awadh on the pretext of debauchery by the Nawab and laid siege to the capital - the one excelling in charm and grandeur all the Paris and the Petersburg for its stucco architecture, and distinguished for its name for having been founded by Lord Rama. This deity the Lord educative of moral selected the place for its founding for his brother Lakshmana, the devout god of fidelity, and for the Rishis and Munsee to be their praying field.

Lucknow boded of moderation in interracial relations, it bred harmony between various races, it promoted tolerance and civility. The poets there, produced poems which helped rule of Amr -o Nahi – the desirable and forbidden - Fatwa -the edict. But all that was rudely interrupted and the advance of the culture was halted. That entire ploy of the negativity was possible due to the defeat of Nawab Shuja ud Daula at Buxar at the hands of the East India Company in 1764. After this defeat the Nawabdom was not allowed to communicate with other states and the spirit of the nation, and of the people to defend and fight was demolished. Whereafter the Nawabdom never took off militarily or politically except for the cultural and the architectural excellences. And the East India Company never stopped meddling in the affairs of the state. The greatest sufferers of the havoc brought by the East India Company were the Shias and this was a universal setback to the subcontinent of India and then of course to the emotionality of the world.

British East India Company obtained its foothold in the Land of Seasons and Songs in 1698. The Company started the career as travelling salesman, locally called *Boxwallah*, a pejorative term used locally, since they carried a box with their samples when they travelled upcountry. Fortunately, they were allowed to hire three villages at the mouth of the Ganges in the principality of Calcutta (Kalkatta) including Calcutta in 1698. Following that foothold given to the company, a grant in 1717 given by Moghul Emperor Farrukh Siyar to buy thirty-eight villages for a three thousand a year revenue payment and permission of trade granted for trading with the inland mass of the country from their base, thy had a fortified home. Thereafter it was easy for the company to increase its presence and influence and they left behind the company's one hundred and fifty years of political and military dormancy and started interloping in local affairs till Hindustan felt it. But they never stopped, till they reaped a sound victory against Nawab Sirajud Daula of Bengal at Plessey in 1757 where they captured and executed him. The British for all this could rule for only under two hundred years.

This entire ploy of skilled politics was possible but there was intrigue and conspiracy. Lord Clive enticed Mir Jafar the *Bukshi* or the commander-in-chief of Nawab Sirajud Daula to a deal of handing him over the Nawabdom of Bengal, Bihar and Oridisa, if he held back the artillery and his mounted army from battling and abandoned the Nawab.

Mir Jafar did that and stood his army at stand still watching the fall of the Nawab, what horror it was! The Nawab pounded the British with Guns, but rain came pouring in and it wetted the gun powder where after the British charged and captured and executed the Nawab. Mir Jafar was made Nawab - the first Nawab of Bengal of the Najafi dynasty, but soon he realised his folly to have betrayed the Nawab and in two years he stood against the British and entered into a pact with the Dutch, but the Dutch were overpowered by the British and Mir Jafar had to abdicate in favour of his son-in-law Mir Qassim. The reason of Mir Jaffar's betrayal of Nawab Sirajud Daula was not perfidy but he thought he was humiliated by not giving him the chief ministership, and instead of him given to a Hindu courtier and unfortunately this betrayal changed the fate of India.

Nawab Sirajud Daula took reign of Nawab of Awadh after his grandfather Nawab Ali Wardy Khan died. He elevated the Hindu Kasturi, Mohanlal to be his Diwan-e Aali - Prime Minister. This post was a higher post than Mir Jaffar's Army Chief and he so resented it that he decided to somehow remove the Nawab and become Nawab himself. This was done in Pakistan by General Ayyub Khan to President Sikandar Mirza.

As commander-in chief, Mir Mohammad Jafar Ali Khan with his ambitions was a suited person for control and leadership and was powerful enough with entire army under his command. The British as such found in him a target to prey at and conspire against the Nawabdom. And where Nawab Sirajul Daula showed one deficient trend, he did not follow the established pursuit, 'Auwwal Khuwaish Baadahoo Darwesh', it had its toll. He should have done Silah Rahmi – kindness towards one's relations and given the prime ministership to the kith and kin rather than to one not Nishapuri and history of India would have been different.

The British did not have to face the power of unity in India and they carried the day. They were well entrenched in Bengal and Ordisa and now ready for future expansion and ultimately held entire India and though later an alliance between Shuja ud Daula, Mir Qassim of Bengal and Shah Alam II of Delhi was forged to dislodge the British, but that was too late and the British under Clive could not be stopped in their expansion of power. And they started using their successes after domination over India to enter in plantocracy. They ran tea, coffee and indigo industries. And the British managers could count on the local police and magistrates to keep their workers in line. And India's raw material was carried to England and machine-made British goods were imported to India.

The Poet of the East, Allama Mohammad Iqbal summed up the ways they should not have used and what they aught have used - the fairways of the conquerors. He points out this in the subtle of his couplet.

Ya Aql Ki Roobahi Ya Ishq-e Yadullahi
Ya Heelay-e Afrangi Ya Hamla-e Turkana

Either the foxiness of wit, or love of Ali (hand of God Hazrat Ali)
Either pretence of the English, or frontal attack of the Turks.

The poet has a right to shed disparaging insult and taunt at the British, but nations in power game have used all means at their disposal to win a war. The Yazidi forces stopped water from reaching to Imam Husain AS's camp for three days to wear out his army. Imam Husain's children in Karbala cried with thirst. Then when the Prophet SAWW was raising a siege on Khyber, it was not conquered even with the change of commander after commander. The Prophet then at last used his superpower Hazrat Ali to conquer the Khyber. So, the objective of all in the war was to conquer the battle. And depending on their ethical and spiritual attainment of height used foul means and of God quality used the combatant prepared to meet all eventualities.

History speaks of Ameer Muawiya raising the copies of Quran on the tips of the spears in the battle of Siffeen and he won the day, from whom perhaps the British learnt deception and borrowed the idea in war strategies for winning their war. Ameer Muawiya Bin Abu Sufyan was made Governor of Syria by Khalifa-e Rashid II Hazrat Umar Ibn al Khattab after the death of Muawiya's brother Yazid ibn Abu Sufyan in 639 A.D. And the trace to the origin of the evil in the world is fathomable. Muawiya's fate was in ruin, with Hazrat Ali in power. His precision in righteousness would not allow him sit as governor and so Muawiya deployed all means to hold on to his power.

So, the history is full of intrigues in the theatre of war. And the fairest warrior cannot be given guarantee of victory, war is a frontage of truth and untruth and only courage and conviction win the war.

The manipulability of the weak faith by Muawiya in Hazrat Ali's army by raising the Quran and in deceit of making appeal for peace, immediately created a group of *Khwarij* in the army of Hazrat Ali AS. They demanded of Hazrat Ali to call back Malik Ashtar, the general reaching out to defeat Muawiya. That saved the day for Muawiya, and his cunningness became the outstanding subterfuge in history.

There were many junctures in the world where evil prevails and demolishes goodness. Muawiya had at last established his dynasty through wrangle, using *Fitnah* and subverting peace. He next established the tradition of *Tabarra* – slandering Hazrat Ali AS. For 80 years the Umayyad engaged them in sending Tabarra from the *Menmber* – the pious pulpit of the Prophet SAWW on Hazrat Ali and Muawiya bribed and hatched conspiracies and pulled down the fifth Caliph of Islam, Imam Hasan AS. Imam Hasan was embodiment of peace and decency and Muawiya poisoned him. The world learnt treachery and illegitimacies from these covert evils and the British in Bengal were deep in it. Only fair set of rules was pursued from day one to the last in war by Hazrat Ali AS. and the world is obligated to follow him.

Four scores of years earlier Mirza Ghalib lamenting the misfortunes of his countrymen had said what Allama Iqbal said later:

Gulshan Mein Bandobust Ba Rang-e Digar Haai Aaj
Qumri Ka Tauq Halqa-e Bairoon-e Dar Haai Aaj

The arrangement in the garden (in India) is of a different nature today
The collar of the pretty dove (India) is the circle in foreign place today

Poet Ghalib made that comment, seeing the political scene in India. The British had closed the Madrassas and the Pathshallas and had hindered the *Fiqhi* postulates and training of Islamic mind and were the stumbling block to the education as they opposed the Islamic concepts in the management of Shara-ee norms in all the fields of life. Their training method and schooling they introduced was segregation, and they prepared talents limited to a certain level and imparted, only pockets of management skills to educationists suited to the secondary positions to train students for them to run the administration of India.

Mir Anis, like of Mirza Ghalib was the literary preen and his equivalent in Lucknow, earlier he had said verses in the same vein as Ghalib did in Delhi. Mir Anis felt he had lost the entire flurry that was Lucknow once the British occupied it. He summed up the annexation of Awadh in his *Ruba-e* - the quatrain, thus:

Afsoas Zamanay ka Ajab Taur Hooa
Kewn Charkhe Kohan Yeh Kya Naya Daur Hooa
Gardish Kab Tak Nikal Chalo Jald Anis
Ab Yan Ki Zameen Aur Falak Aur Hooa

Sad! The world has taken to strange ways
Why, O rugged old sky how come this new era emerged
For how long this suffering! Leave and be out soon Anis
Now the sky and earth of this place have become different

Mir Anis was associated with literature from his birth 1802, till his death in 1874. He saw the reigns of the Nawabs of Awadh, Saadat Ali Khan, Ghazi Uddin Haider, Abul Mansoor, Mohammad Ali Shah, Amjad Ali Shah and Wajid Ali Shah. Mirza Ghalib was born in 1797, died 1869. Ghalib saw reign of two emperors Akbar Shah Saani and Bahadar Shah Zafar and the period of either poets had seen great spell of the poetic *Kalam* – the poetic works due to the patronising of the literature by the indigenous sovereigns.

-:.:-

II

THE LAST HURRAH

VI

The last Hurrah was given to the Nawab of Awadh by Maharaja Kashi Naresh of Banaras State. The Maharaja requested the Nawab to honour his state with his gracious visit, when the Nawab was on way to Matiaburj, on his journey of exile.

Kashi Naresh Maharajas were of outstanding princely standing in the comity of the Princes for their titles of Kashi Naresh. They held exalted seat in the Chamber of the Princes. And to their subjects as Maharaja Kashi Naresh, they were virtual gods for their last names terminating in *Narayen* - uniform with God. And the title of Kashi Naresh was for holding the seat of rule at the holiest of the sites – Kashi, known from the ancient times as sacred as Shiva. His Highness King Kashyap in the years before 1200 BC in the gone past eras had laid the foundation of the city of Kashi. He had put the seed of Hindu mysticism there for asserting peace and for germination and flourish of the Hindu mystique. The River Ganges was the river of salvation and did its *Aabyaari* – the watering, flowing through its precincts, outside the doorsteps of the temples and the river watered the plains of Kashi flourish and yield food crop. The Pundits sat in the inner temples continuously doing *Jap* – recitation, deleting the count of the Master Time - the destiny, leading to the Dooms Day – the Qiyamat that was inevitable, but praying for greater number of eras to appear for prayers to continue, till it came.

Maharaja Kashi Naresh(es) were deities and benefactors of the Hindu religion, with largesse of heart for coexistence with other religions. They had profound respect for the Sayeds. The Maharajas enjoyed great love and respect from their subjects. When the Maharajas appeared to present their glimpses to their subjects riding in an open Rolls Royce Bentley for *Hawa Khori* – to freshen up in the evening cool air - going from the *Qila* – the fort, to the *Rani Bagh* the state garden or on the country drive to be of oneness as the God's nature, or to attend a state function, there was an announcement by the drumming of two drums – the ceremony called *Naubat* – the beating of the drums to alert the subjects that the Maharaja was being taken out of the palace.

And at each outing even if it were a jaunt or a trip to the tennis court, all these innocent indulgences were monitored by the subjects, and rows and rows of the loyal subjects when the Maharaja passed them, bowed to deep bows and raised the slogan of the greeting of *Har, Har Mahadev* - let the high piety flourish. And the greeting travelled in waves after waves from the standing to halt men, to greet the Maharaja and the Maharaja exuberant and thankful to God for assigning him elation, raised his clasped hands to salute and greet back his subjects.

The city of Banaras was a district town of the Nawab of Awadh. And Mansa Ram was in the service of the Nazim or the Mayor of the city of Banaras, Mir Rustam Ali who stayed as Nazim of Nawab of Awadh till 1738. During his service with Mir Rustam Ali Khan, Mansa Ram had become wealthy and Rustam Ali Khan had made him Zamindar of Kaswar. In 1739 Nawab of Awadh Saadat Ali Khan for 12 Lacs of Rupees appointed Mansa Ram successor to the Nazim Mir Rustam Ali. Mansa Ram very soon died in 1740 and his son Balwant Singh ably administered the Banaras region and in 1739 the Nawab granted him the title of *Rifaat Wa Awal-i-Martabat Raja Sri* Balwant Singh Bhadur and granted him to retain the revenues of Jaunpur, Ghazipur and the Chunar districts.

Raja Balwant Singh built a fort in Ramangar in 1754. His coronation to wear the crown of Raja was done by his father Mansa Ram while he lived. The British Empire after 1918 further elevated the Rajas of Banaras to the order of the Maharajas with their patches of recognized territories starting from near the outer limits of the Nawabdom of Awadh, and they had a viable state run efficiently by efficient administrators and there was nothing amiss. They were already from the Gautam Brahman Clan as the notary Hindus and God was kind to them.

Raja Balwant Singh had chosen to build the fort on the other side of Kashi, on the bank of the River Ganges. It was a predominantly Muslim countryside, and he had to fall back on the Hindu strength. They started to recite the Sanskrit Ashlokes and read Ramayan loud lyrically in his capital and the Maharaja built the Mansa Devi ambassadorial intervening temple for the Praja – the subject to interface with deity and next he evolved the staging of Ramlila – the theatrical enactments explaining of Lord Rama's life and of his ordeals. Raja Balwant Singh did this pioneering work to strengthen Hindu belief and enforce Hinduism and he resurrected lost Hindu glory.

The festival of the Ramlila was held every year by the Banaras State in Ramnagar. The ruling Raja was present at every *Khund* – sections of the episode of Ramlila. He would go to the sites of the theatre, riding the elephant and the Ramlila moved from site to site and Lord Rama's history was enacted from the beginning of his birth in Ayudhaya to end in Ayudhaya travelling through the Bun- the forest and going to Lanka and back to Ayudhaya. And the state flourished; Ramayan was read aloud and farmland cultivated with three crops and art was encouraged to prosper and trade flourished and there was plenty in the State.

The last of the Maharajas of Banaras was, Maharaja Vibhuti Narayen Singh died on 25th December 2000 at the age of 73. He was adopted as son of the last Maharaja Aditya Narayen Singh, who wanted a son as heir to the state. The Maharani was blessed with one; she conceived a son, but the quack said she was carrying a girl child in her womb and there was no need of girl child and the child was aborted and thereafter the Maharani never conceived a son. Or for that matter any child at all, and Vibhuti Narayen was the young sapling from the Maharani's family, he was adopted by the ruling Maharaja as heir apparent in 1934 when he was six years old.

In 1939 when Aditya Narayen died, Vibhuti Narayen Singh became Maharaja under the regency of the British Raj. And he was under scrutiny by the assessing to how he did as ruler of the state. He successfully saw through the traditions of the state continue in all their immediacy. And Maharaja Vibhuti Narayen did not fail to show the Maharaja majesties as desired of him. This Maharaja not only proved worthy of the Maharaja bearings, he emerged as a distinguished scholar of Sanskrit, Purana and Vedas and he was a renown literary person and became Chancellor of the Banaras Hindu University.

When Maharaja Vibhuti Narayen Singh was young *Kunwar* or Prince, his name was Chandra Bhal Singh, he was sent to Jaipur for education and because he was still a minor, the state Managerial responsibility was transferred to Sayed Zamin Ali Zaidi for his capabilities. Sayed Zamin Ali came from Kajgaon, with its literal meaning 'a not following straight path village' or bent or defective or a crooked place of a village. And although there was no evidence to suggest of that about the village, but the village was still known by that name. And it was said of Kajgaon - a suburb of Jaunpur:

'If you took the name of Kajgaon first thing in the morning you would not get breakfast, and if you met a man from Kajgaon first thing in the morning you would not get meal all day, if you travelled to go to Kajgaon you will be lost in the way.'

This berating of the Kajgaon Wallas was enjoyed by the diehard Sunnis and the Meer (one up) Shias alike. There was one more reason for their berating and that was; the people of Kajgaon were extremely stingy in spending money. Sayed Zamin Ali ruled Banaras State as Chief of the State for over three years when the Maharaja was undergoing education and he showed his mantle in stringency. He drew a meagre salary from the state treasury, travelled in the run out classic of the time – a four doors car, though of chrome hinges and the doors handle still shining, but prominently showing its status of old model. Zamin Ali was a tall handsome man, extremely fair skin with pinkness on the cheeks. He was a known stingy and thrifty in spending state funds. I once went to his residence with my maternal uncle whose wife was in relation cousin of Zamin Ali. It was a large D shaped state-owned bungalow, but no guards and no servants visible, he was President of the state, but lived simply, even the collectors lived a pompous life.

Zamin Ali's stinginess was very renowned. He had a pair of trousers of corduroy made to measure from England. He sat somewhere and when got up; his trouser got immediately nicked on one side of the hips. He therefore sent his trouser to a tailor to mend it. The tailor for symmetry puts a patch on each side of the hips. This was Zamin Ali's best pair of trousers. He therefore wore that trouser and went to the annual sports events of the Banaras state, and because he had a bumpy buttock, the patches stood out and perhaps looked good. When the state functionaries saw him wearing a trouser with a 'D' patch on either side of the hips, they thought it was a high fashion and many of them had their trousers patched up like that, with 'D' on each hip.

The distinction of Kajgaon was that the Sayeds lived in that village and the word of the Maharaja for them was that if a Sayed from Kajgaon were to be appointed to a post; they were to be appointed in the State without asking them many questions up to the posts of *Tahsildars* – the Revenue Officers. And for any one from Kajgaon for qualifying for such posts, they had to be a Sayed and this was Maharaja Prabhu Narayen's word or *Farman*.

Till to the time that Maharaja Vibhuti Narayen was of age, ready to shoulder his responsibility, Sayed Zamin Ali acted as the ruler of the state till 1943 and when the Maharaja had completed his education, Sayed Zamin Ali's caretaking ended and the Maharaja started his functions but still he had to heavily lean on Sayed Zamin Ali in the running of the State.

Molvi Sayed Irtiza Husain of Meerut was Head of the Urdu and the Persian Department at the Meston High School Ramnagar, and the Maharaja's birthday was due, he was invited to school ground covered with tent and carpets for the celebration of his birthday at this prestigious school, later it turned into a University. He accepted the invitation and came to the event. Presents of one Guinee by each of the teachers in brocade pouch were offered to the Maharaja. Molvi Irtiza Husain wrote the *Isteqbalia Nazm* – the poem of greeting. The verses of the poetry that I can remember were:

Huzoor-e Pur Noor Dam Iqbalahoo
Hamari Mehfil Mein Aa Rahay Haain.

Chiragh Maddhim Vibhut Naraen Ka Noor Raushan
Jidhar say Aa Rahay Haain Ya Ja Rahay Haain

His illustrious honourable, full of light, may his good
fortune remain always at heights
Is coming in our auspicious assembly

The lamp's glow is low of Prabhu Naraen's light bright
From which ever direction he comes or is going

The Nam de guerre – pen name of Molvi Sayed Irtiza Husain was Natiq. He was a learned, educationalist also virtuous and his speciality was that he addressed Majlis, detached from conventionality. It inclined to be faith refreshing and informative in nature and fulfilling the elegy requirement to the utmost. In his Majlis-e Husain, he by bringing in untapped topics, showed all through his superior knowledge in history of events. When describing of Janab Fizza - the maid servant of Janab Fatimah Zehra SUA, he described of her high virtue, which was due to the direct reaction of the influence of the honoured Bibi Fatima Zehra SUA. He elaborated Janab Fizza's subtler and loftier status and addressed such Majalis in 1944 when Zakirs were not so conversant and fluent to speak on such topics as speaking on the life pattern, *Zuhd* - the abstinence, and the competencies of Bibi Fizza RA's understanding of Quran.

The State of Banaras was rich with forests, the Providence had lavished the state with hills and mountains, standing on the earth to remind the majesty of the mother Earth. The mountains were lush and dense, boasting of their forests of bushes and Chiraunji trees and Tardee trees with a vast variety of beasts and graziers, birds and fowls, these were fed by the forest and lots of game were in offing for the Maharaja Prabhu Narayen and it was a vast hunting ground. He ruled for over 42 years and went on the hunting spree of tiger, cheetah and lion, shooting from *Machan* – a raised platform, well-hidden behind the foliage, sometimes on trees, and the *Hakawa*, the team with their drums cordoned the beasts and drove them towards the Machan of the Maharaja aimed at them and ensured to kill the tiger in one shot, otherwise these powerful beasts attacked and if escaped and began killing human. And the Maharaja had lions' and tigers' skins with skull hung on the walls of his palace museum, the skins still shiny and fresh and vying with their colours shining.

The burly lions roared in the State's chain of the Vindhya Hills and the grizzly bears roamed freely in the valleys and feasted on the *Chiraunji*, the small cobnuts, whose fruits grew in bunch and the tall lush Chiraunji trees, would be laden with them. The burly bears were only interested in the sweet-sour pulp of the cobnut and these ate them and showed no disposition to crunching the small hard nuts of the Chiraunji which they left in their dung and the women with not much means of livelihood collected these from the forest and washed them and took out kernel as a commercial product and took the kernel to sell to the town's people. And these were wholesome, since no foulness had touched them.

Maharajah Prabhu Narayen Singh died aged 75 in 1931. The State of Banaras flourished in his time and the Maharaja ate only the first Puri, turned out from the freshly filled wok with Ghee – each Puri had to be fried in each fresh scoop of fresh Cow Ghee and the Rani mother personally inspected the Puris for their genuineness and the Hakeem of outstanding expertise stood to advise him on health matters.

My maternal grandfather Molvi Hakeem Sayed Mazhar Hasan, with his spirituality backing him and his Sayed purity elating him, and his expertise in the Science of *Tib* – the Unani way of Medicine explicating him, and the bona fide education from Lucknow Tibbiya College decorating him was courtier and Hakeem of the Maharaja, and the Molvi Hakeem accompanied the Maharaja even on such adventures as *Shikar* – the hunting of the tiger, and the Maharaja would send him gift of trays of valuable wares, with gold guineas and his appreciation and this nobleman would have a variety of game birds and meat of eatable noble animals at dinners in the seasons of game.

The Molvi trait was linked with Hikmat. Hikmat was wisdom and Molvi Hakeem Sayed Mazhar Hasan was a Courtier, Librarian, Hakeem and Writer of the History of Banaras State. His History of Banaras State was in four volumes printed by the press in the fort of the Maharaja Banaras. He also wrote several books and treatises on Unani medicine, known as Tib and its Urdu was more Persian dominated than the present-day vernacular of Urdu. He would frame sentences '*Wastay Iskay Karnay kay*' instead of '*Yeh Karnay kay liyay*'- i.e., for doing this. His books were donated by his son to the Aljauwadia Arabic College Banaras, founded by Maulana Zafrul Hasan Sahib.

Molvi Hakeem Sayed Mazhar Hasan was a distinguished nobleman, he was also Imam Juma of the Friday-prayers at the Talia Nala Mosque in Banaras. And the Namaz-e Juma was the supporting pillar of a state and for the Imamat of the Juma prayer a conversant and knowledgeable prayer leader with knowledge of current affairs of the word, laced with Taqwa – the piety, was needed. One who could give first of the two sermons in the Juma prayer on Taqwa -piety, and the second on current affairs, such Imam would lead the prayer as Imam. Molvi Hakeem Mazhar Hasan lived in Ramnagar and will go to Talia Nala on the other side of the river by crossing the River Ganges in a *Chappu Kishti* – the manually rowed boat on Fridays and there were no Qasr Namaz for that distance and sometimes he went by his Tanga with his *Saees,* the groom.

Molvi Hakeem Sayed Mazhar Hasan died in 1942, born 1880. His son, Hakeem Alhaj Sayed Mohammad Jafer, God bless his soul was also Hakeem, Librarian of Banaras State, and in Hospital Management as physician of Tib at the State's Central Hospital in Ramnagar, he also ran his Matab in Ramnagar. Below is picture of Molvi Hakeem Mazhar Hasan.

Allama Sheikh Ali Hazin was teacher of Shah Abbas Sani II, the Safavid King of Iran. Abbas Sani II deputed one trustworthy youth, named Nader as attendant to him. One day the Sheikh asked him to bring a glass of water, Nader brought the water in a clumsy way and the water spilled on the Allama's cloak. The sheikh called him poor of manner and admonished him to be more careful in future. Nader Quli Beg was of imperialistic bent of mind by nature and he took offence from it, and time progressed and he went to far heights, and conquered Herat and Qandhar in Afghanistan and then took over as the Shah of Persia.

He introduced him as Nadir Shah. He was not a forgiving kind and so the Sheikh left Isfahan and came to Banaras in the Land of Seasons and Songs. Raja Balwant Naraen Singh, Raja of Banaras came to know of the credentials of Sheikh Ali Hazin and of his learnedness. The Raja went to him (sometime after 1754) and personally requested him to coach his son Chait Singh and Balvant Singh donated a large piece of land in Banaras to the Sheikh. Sheikh Ali Hazin was a poet and is compared to Allama Shibli in the Persian poetry. He has written 266 books.

Sheikh Ali Hazin built a mosque with no roof - a one room structure and one veranda on the land donated by Balvant Singh and started the *Dars* – giving lessons in apotheosis. The Maharaja provided the boundary wall and a large gate and the place was used as graveyard also of the Muslims, known as Fatimaan Qabrastan. Later Jauwadia Arabic College (Jamiul Uloom Jadidia) was founded by Maulana Mohammad Sajjad Al-Husaini son of Jawadul Ulema, Aayetullah Sayed Ali Jawad Al- Husaini in 1928 on the land donated by Raja Balwant Singh. And its Sawab must be reaching to Raja Balwant Singh.

Banaras State was a *Rajwarah* – a Princely state. A fair number of Jinn, Bhoot, and Ghost lived there. The Jinns a creation from smokeless scorching fire had their codes and philosophy of life and the Bhoots were not a creation but the lost souls – an outcome of their doing in the life, but they were having existence. The Bhoots did not like the day light, but the Jinns appeared all the times with changed appearances and the Ghosts in their attires paraded the places of their burials. Of them the Bhoots were the desperate lost spirits, of failures in their duties and obligations, when living as human. But they had a chance to avail of the respite of the cyclic rebirth into another life, if their intention was to do good in that birth when they will have connection of soul with the body. And their rebirth must not fail them for Mukti – seize from rebirth as was believed by the Hindu Mut, as for the religion of Islam it believed in only one birth. The logic stands verified, since the concerned believer in Islam had discharged his duty observing his full obligations in his life, which was requirement of Mukti.

If one wanted to meet these spirits, the jinn and Bhoots, he had to go to the Mharaja's state, where they lived in Maharaja's disused buildings. Some of them were out occupying distant sprawling houses of the Maharaja that were only occasionally used by him, but these houses were kept spick and span. And the Jinns and the Bhoots proved they had eye for exclusive places. They occupied vacant houses and the more spacious the better, and would never share its premises with an intruder. And never one of them would trample the right of the other.

The Maharaja knew of their dwelling and granted these spirits rights of freedom and considered them subjects of his state since they had opted to live in his territories. And of them, the Jinns were reciprocating and helpful and the Ghosts serene and quiet and the Bhoots tolerant if they were not disturbed and encroached upon by anyone trying to takeover overwhelming them in their spaces.

When their Royal Highnesses, the Kashi Naresh Mharajas came out in their regalia of a Kashi Naresh Maharaja attires, with their entourage following, flanked by escorts and displaying the flags of the House of the Narayens in their finery, and the Maharaja riding the prestigious elephant on the occasions of the Ramlila(s) – the folk theatres. It was a rare occasion. The Maharaja rode the royal elephant of tallness and massiveness and of majesty, with the elephant's designation. The elephant had to be dominating one, surpassing every other elephant of the state. The exuberance of its massiveness and its spectaculars was to present it carrying the kingly *Houdah* – the Maharaja's *Sangha Shan* - the moving throne on the back of the elephant as the unique artefact. And there was a sense of majesty conveyed through it.

The Houdah or the haudaj on the elephant was turned into a court, decorated with the Narayen Mharajas' insignias, with glittering umbrella shaped canopy covering the Maharaja and the attendant at its rear in compartment on the Houdah, at attention with a deluxe whisk with its handle of gold, jade and amber, sweeping laterally with gentle motion. The attendant, airing its sweep over the Maharaja, and the *Mahaawat* – the mahout or the *Feelban* planting him on the head of the elephant with his prick-steel held in his hand for passing commands to guide the exactions of the elephant's trunk, now raising, now coiling it and its body stencilled and painted in curving traces. And the Mahaawat wearing a wound pink turban and he glittering in the glitter of his tunic, and the Maharaja's kingship glittering for being

314

Kashi Singusth Maharaja and the gold trappings of the elephant hanging down - across its width from atop its massive tallness. Brandishing glamour, dropping down to touch the ground, but not so, only to suit to the dazzling grandeur of their Royal Highnesses' elations of the Kashi Naresh Mharajas.

Just then the principled Jinns, the moderate Ghosts and the unpredictable Bhoots joined the procession in display of their loyalty and their presence, forming rows to parade at the back of the procession. In this formation the gins will be the first-row major category specimen and in this set up, the grace and honour travelled ahead of the Royalty of the Maharajas of the Throne of Kashi. And the subjects stood by to hail Hur Hur Mahadev (pleasant blessing every moment O great king) with their palms of hands joined and raised in salute. And the wish of Hur Hur travelled with the procession rising from the lines of men.

Kashi in its exclusivity not far from the Maharaja's capital perched on the other side of the holy river. And the holy river touched all the fringes of Kashi banks of the Maharaja's capital. And on both the banks of the holy river, the sun worshippers offered the stream of water to the sun, pouring it out of their brass pots to the rising sun, first time showing its face bringing to the world bright morning.

Of the three invisibles realism falling in to join the procession, the jinns were the earliest creation. They were made of smokeless flame of fire and they had emotions and religion and gave account of their deeds on the day of the resurrection - the day of judgement. The characteristic virtue of their soul was, the good ones of them submitted allegiance to and acknowledged the authority of the Twelve Imams of the House of the Prophet Mohammad SAWW. The Quran said of the jinns and men in Surah 15: 26 - 27.

> *"We created man from dried cracking with sound clay,*
> *mouldable into shape."*
> *"And the Jinn we have created in foretime from*
> *smokeless intense fire."*

And because the fire professed fieriness and was refined, the Jinns were fiery and refined. They had emotions and lived a long life, as long as one thousand years and more and travelled a thousand times faster than man and they spoke in voices resembling men and could touch and react with kinder feelings and they could possess men and sometimes they were also possessed by men stronger than them in will power and power was where piety and forbearance was stronger.

And there were bad Jinns and good Jinns and the good Jinns were always a race of extreme respectability, the obedient creation of God. They envied man's capability and befriended with them, if they found a soul compatible with their good nature, they would befriend with that human. One of these jinns had chosen to befriend my maternal grandfather Molvi Hakeem Sayed Mazhar Hasan Hasni and brought present to the Hakeem, and the Jinn was offered every Thursday or on special occasions, delicacies in the empty large downstairs portion of the house, placed in the Taaq – the niche.

The incident leading to the friendship between Molvi Hakeem Sayed Mazhar Hasan and the Jinn was that Molvi Hakeem Sayed Mazhar Hasan had just joined the service of the Maharaja. He was given a room to stay in, in the fort. At night after a busy day when he came to his room, he found a stranger was sleeping in his bed. The Hakeem did not find it polite to wake him up, and he slept on the floor. The next day the same person was again sleeping in his bed and the Hakeem again did not like to awaken the sleeping stranger and for his perseverance to tolerance and distinction into patience made the stranger Hakeem's friend – the stranger turned out to be a Jinn.

The Jinn stood by Hakeem Sayed Mazhar Hasan and was of numerous services to him. Later the Maharaja gave him a big house in Ramnagar near the fort. On occasions when special dishes were prepared in the house for *Nazar* – the offers to the progenies of the Prophet SAWW, the Hakeem ordered a special plate full of delicacies be placed in one of the niches of the wall in the downstairs veranda of the house, which remained empty, not dwelled and hence not lighted and looked forsaken. Presumably the food was taken away by the Jinn or what happened to it was not clear, but I saw it staying there for a day or two.

The Maharaja Kashi Naresh requested the Nawab of Awadh to grace him with the honour of his visit to his state and the Nawab accepted that. Afterall the Maharaja was the Nawab's creation in

Royalty. The Nawab in these times when there was distress must have weighed the invitation of the Maharaja as a great solace. He re-routed his journey adding several scores of miles of travelling to the capital of the Kashi Naresh for a day stay. His Excellency the Maharaja felt singularly honoured and spread red carpet over the mile-long road to his fort in reception of the Nawab of the House of the Shahs of Awadh. He also erected *Gulab ki Tatti* – pick roses Knitted string fence. The rose fences on the road stood at intervals all along the road down to his capital.

The Gulab ki Tatti were placed along the road to subdue effluvium if anywhere coming to the way of the Nawab and for fear that the Nawab might not catch a sight which might be cumbersome to the eyes of the Nawab, and for the fear that he should not see a thing such that it simulated an untidy presentation and was burdensome to the eyes of the Nawab.

These were the impeccable, implicit display of hospitality accorded to the honoured Nawab by the Maharaja Kashi Naresh. He was the honoured Royal guest of the Maharaja of the House of the Narayens. Such meticulous elaborate planning for the reception, thought of for a royalty by a royalty, spoke of the sophistications of the Royalties of the Land of Seasons and Songs, who were of a class and distinction who understood the fineness that were required to be presented to the supreme and sublime rulers of the land.

-: . :-

II

THE MATIABURJ

VIII

Matiaburj in the south of Bengal was the place where to Nawab Wajid Ali Shah was exiled by the British. This abandonment of scanty houses became a living city, for its fate bringing Nawab there. The siege of Lucknow and the demolishing of the state of Awadh was started, it put in operation and the Nawab was made without his state and rule and dislodged from his city. Minute by minute news of the *Ferangi,* the White – now, they are approaching to the *Chowk* – the meeting point of four roads, now they are approaching the Gate – the entrance to the inner city, came to the Nawab and they came and annexed Awadh. And people till to the last minute remained busy bucking the fight of the *Teetars* – the partridges, reared and trained to fight out to death, and each one of the partridges having a famous warrior's name.

Nawab Wajid Ali Shah was sitting when the British Commander entered his palace. All the servants and the courtiers had run away, leaving him on his own. They had hidden themselves. The Nawab was without any attendant. The British Commander asked the Nawab, "Everyone else fled and got away, why didn't you?" The Nawab replied, "There was no one to slip the slippers in my feet.

The Commander was chivalrous; his root was in Englishness which had floating sense of the gotten general perfection. And for their distinctive admiration to a Royalty and the snobbishness that propelled the English and affixed their courtesies to suit to the measurements of the recipient's stature that set their style of governance and established their standards, the commander found, there was Nawab in front of a mere Commander, and the Commander in respect of the majesty of the Nawab, overwhelmed by his cool composure and his grandeur shedding its effusiveness, picked up the slippers of the

318

Nawab and slipped them in the feet of the Nawab and after that he symbolically arrested the magnanimous Nawab and the fate of the Nawabdom concluded.

Nawab Wajid Ali Shah had many talents. One touching Thumri he expresses in the Poorbi verses when he was being lifted in the Palki -the palanquin for once to people to taste the words of Thumri. The piercing intensity, this Thumri carries can only be felt by the knowing of the language. The tender hearts might roll out drops of tears, which will show their humanitarianism grown to full blossom.

The Nawab exactly said the following drenched in remorse song at the departure from his ancestral home:

بابُل مورا، نیہر چُھو ٹو ہی جاۓ
بابُل مورا، نیہر چُھو ٹو ہی جاۓ

چار کہار مل موری ڈولیا سجاویں
مورا اپنا بیگا نہ چُھو ٹو جاۓ، بابل مورا۔۔۔

انگنا تو پربت بھیو اور ڈیہری بھئی بدیش
جاۓ بابل گھر آپنومیں چلی پیا کے دیش، بابل مورا۔۔۔

Translation

Father my home (the moon) is getting separated
Father my home (the moon) is getting separated

Four palanquin-bearers get together decorate my basket
My own hard hearted is getting separated

Father my home (the moon) is getting separated
Father my home (the moon) is getting separated

The courtyard became mountain and the doorstep became foreign land
Go father home your I (am she) going to lover's land

Father my home (the moon) is getting separated
Father my home (the moon) is getting separated

319

Debauchery was harmful and offensive to the society, and Lord Dalhousie on accusation of debauchery supposedly by the Nawab, had commissioned the Resident of Awadh, Major General Suleiman 1849 to 1856, to determine whether or not the kingdom of Awadh should be annexed. The Major General reported:

"He (the King) has never been a cruel or badly disposed man, but his mind naturally weak has entirely given way, and he is now as helpless as an infant."

This was a coded message to say, the annexation was a total possibility on two counts, debauchery and incapacity of mind to rule. And Lord Dalhousie's commission in the authority of Major General Suleiman was a guise to deceive serenity and the Major General reported all wrong. The king was rated the best of the litterateurs among the kings of Awadh and there was no plausible reason to annexe the Nawabdom, save the dictates into the immorality of expansion and greed of grab of land.

The King's moral standing and his scholarliness in his own time and in later times were so clearly elucidated in the words of Kanwar Durga Prashad Mehr. He writes in his Bostan-e Avadh.

"No King like him ever rose up from the soil of Hindustan with such erudition in scholarship and arts. And in his manners no ruler raised the banner of kingship on Indian territories with matching genius and intellectual attainments."

This is the glowing tribute to the outstanding ruler of Awadh (India) of Durga Prashad Mehr in his Bostan-e Avadh whom the British so brutally berated for the mere treachery to grab his land on the strength of the might of guns and the shame of immorality.

Then there is Mr Jones in the court of the Proprietors of the East India Company, on 24 September 1856 he says in his speech, reference: 'History of Indian Mutiny'.

"The King has been charged with being guilty of vices and debauchery; but he was told on good authority, that few people were more moral than the King of Oude in that respect."

Then, Sir W.H. Sleiman, in 'Journey through the Kingdom of Oude' says:

"There never was on the throne, I believe a man more inoffensive at heart than he (King Wajid Ali Shah) is."

But despite these tributes paid to Nawab Wajid Ali Shah, he was banished to Matiaburj on charges of moral ineptitude and his kingdom annexed and justice is firm Islamic fundamental principle, not a social need as in other religions of the world, where for accomplishing their pursuit they may sacrifice it, and the virtue keeping beating its chest.

Luckily, much to the relief of the British, in one-year time after the annexure of Awadh, there was a revolt against the British starting from Meerut and then spread to Delhi, and it expanded to Lucknow in the next year 1857-1858 of the annexation, and that provided an excuse to the British to continue with the annexation, since much of the Awadh had joined in the rebellion, and the British hold on Awadh was sealed. The greatest harm that came off it was the demolishing of the society and its flourishing culture of Lucknow.

The Nawab was exiled to Matiaburj and resigned on a pension of twelve Lacs, Rupees 1200,000 a year and the income from his Nawabdom of two Crore seventy Lacs 270,00000 a year was swallowed up by the trading Company Bahadur East India Company. And the Crown in England as the final act in the consolidation of the British power, ordered to shift the seat of rule from Calcutta to the capital Delhi in 1911.

The East India Company governors were appointees, representing the British Crown, during their nearly a century (1858 – 1947) of British rule. They set up the same system of rule as of the able administrator Sher Shah Suri during his brief period of rule of five years of full monarchy from 1540 -1545. This monarch died in 1545 during the siege of Kalinjarport in an accident of gunpowder explosion and then soon the Suri dynasty fell to the Mughal King Homayoun, who was earlier defeated by Sher Shah Suri, but he re-conquered Delhi. The Mughal dynasty had endowed the British a well organised governmental system, including the provincial rule they had introduced.

The British in Delhi finding the governmental system already running smoothly went to add some paraphernalia to it to aid their rule. They constructed country wide railway system, made canals, opened courts, renewed and organised postal services, established universities and colleges and gave codes of practice to civil and military services and established order. And the British also eliminated the Thugs as did Sher Shah Suri.

The Thugs expertly threw a loop round the neck of a wayfarer and strangled him and robbed him of his possession on roads and on the highways. They were well organised to even rob the whole company of men of their possessions. They did not miss the wayfarers and small caravans and followed them and bought and sold them between their groups in their sectors and zones of the wayfarer's journey, till one band from them finally succeeded in throwing the cloth loop with coin in it round the neck of the wayfarer and their expertise ensured that the coin sat at the centre of the wind pipe precisely, so that they could easily strangle their marked victim.

The disciplined rule of the British had no place for their professionalism to strangle and wrench practiced in their domain of rule and they were eliminated and they also eliminated the Sati in which the women sat on the pyre to terminate their lives by burning themselves in grief of their dead husbands.

Nawab Wajid Ali Shah, till to the last of his existence in this world of remonstration and deceit continued with his effort to build a world as stipulated by the Prophet of Islam. And in spite of sufferings the Nawab was going through, he maintained the decorum of the king he was, and this style was nowhere to be seen in the rulers of the lands. He had styled a way of giving charity to the poor, where long strips of gold in bunches were cut by the female appointees in the service of the Nawab. They stood on the balconies and from that height cut the gold strips, so that when the pieces of gold strips fell below twisting and turning, they created a sparkling effect that pleased the eyes of the Nawab and it was charity and social service. The descending pieces when they reached below were rushed at and picked, swept clean by the needy poor.

This was the level of charity given by the Nawab when he was deprived of his kingdom and confined to the city of Matiaburj in the south east of the Land of Seasons and Songs and he had but only a fraction of his wealth left with him and the rest was gone. But the charity and the alms- giving was not stopped at whatever level it could be dispensed with to the poor.

A second Lucknow had emerged in Matiaburj. The Majalis of Moharram, the Imam Baargah and its *Zeenat* – the adornment of the Sheh-Nasheen – the high seat with standards of Twelve Aimma, i.e., Punja of the name of each Imam and Hazrat Abbas AS. stood in graceful drapery and replicas of their shrines were stood, honoured and illuminated. The poets and the shopkeepers, all assembled there in the fashion of the grandeurs of Lucknow. And the dancers with their art and the singers with the melodies of their voices, bevies, and street charmers free to perform their expertise, all sprang up there to show their glitter.

Dr. Aslam Farrukhi of Karachi University said *Dadra* and the *Thumri* style of music, originated from the genius of Nawab Wajid Ali Shah and bees of men came to gather where the Nawab was and visitors from Europe came to see the city that was created there where the Nawab was in Matiaburj. Of the Nawab's descendants, one trace was in the great grandson, Prince Anjum Quadir – Chairman of the King of Oudh's Trust and President of All India Shia Conference; he was still residing in Matiaburj and commemorating the memory of this genius of the Nawab.

The Nawab before he was exiled to Matiaburj offered to the British that he will cover the road from Lucknow to Matiaburj with silver coin if he was not exiled and if they left him alone to stay in his capital in Lucknow, but that was not to be.

The Prince of Wales Albert Edward ascended the throne of England in 1901 as King Edward VII of England and Emperor of India, after Queen Victoria's demise. He came to visit Lucknow in 1876 as Prince of Wales. Lucknow was once glittering as the vibrant city of India, basking in the culture of its creation, now it was overpowered and subjugated, and the free spirit of its people shackled, owing all to the disparaging disunity and self-injury at the battle of Plessey in 1757.

The Prince presented colours in Lucknow to the First Battalion and then went to see the Nawab of Awadh in Matiaburj to pay his courtesies to the Nawab. The Nawab said to the Prince of Wales. "My son you have come at a time when I do not have much in my possession." The Nawab then gave a walking stick to the Prince, studded with gems. The Prince thanked the Nawab and brought the walking stick to England where the diamonds studded to it were found to be so rare that they were not ordinarily assessable. The gracious Nawab died in the year 1887 and an era ended and gone, never to come again.

And what the British did wrong was to arrest and depose the Nawab. It was easy to conquer a territory but not a culture, and it is rare to build a culture and impossible to impose a culture.

The British to help facilitate their takeover of Awadh, had put for propagation many defaming odd stories about the Nawab of Awadh, against the person of Abul Mansoor Sikandar Jah Padishah-e Adil Qaisar-e Zaman Sultan-e Alam Meerza Muhammad Nawab Wajid Ali Shah but the spirituality of the Nawab was adamant to narrate the events otherwise:

The Earl of Mayo 1869 -1872 was residing in Calcutta as Viceroy of India in his Government House. He decided to pay a courtesy call to the Nawab and went to Matiaburj to pay his respects to the Nawab. The Nawab reciprocated the gesture and went to see the Viceroy in his Government House. The Viceroy received the Nawab with full honours and with all due courtesies. He was sitting and making conversation with the Nawab and then something came upon him - the instinct of, "Rule Britannia, Britannia, rules the waves (world)" overtook him. Entering in the mode of fascism, the Viceroy picked himself up and went to sit on the Presidential Chair in his Government House at a place higher than the Nawab. This was a deliberate wounding to belittle the Nawab. Wajid Ali Shah was quite hurt. He stood up and without saying a word left the Government House.

When the Nawab reached Matiaburj about forty miles from the Government House, someone asked the Nawab. "Your Excellency you left the Government House without bidding farewell to the host – the Viceroy." The Nawab replied. "Who would I have bidden farewell to; I saw only a corpse in that presidential chair and not a living person."

It was not long after that what Nawab spoke that the Viceroy was killed by a convict in the Andaman Island. The Viceroy went there to make a tour of the Island and the convict killed him. And they knew it was the Nawab's word, which had brought the end of the Earl of Mayo. But this was hushed up.

An early Portrait of Nawab Wajid Ali Shah

From the collection of Guru Pandit Ramlal of Bhopal

And whether it was a policy of the British parliament that the East India Company went on the errand of architecting a superiority cult in its men was not clear, since prior to 1798 the company men, every bit followed the local ways and wore local dresses and even ate Paan and then when Governor General Richard Wellesley took over Bengal 1798 – 1805, the men were ordered to show aloofness from the locals and establish their sovereign right over the populace.

-:.:-

II

FAITH AND POLITICS OF
M.A. JINNAH RA

VIII

No one can describe the genius of the Qaed-e Azam Mohammad Ali Jinnah more accurately than Stanley Wolpert. He writes in his book 'Jinnah of Pakistan':

"Few individuals significantly alter the course of the history and few still modify the map of the world, hardly anyone can be credited with creating a nation state, Mohammad Ali Jinnah did all three."

The greatest homage that can be paid to the Qaed-e Azam is that he gathered all the Muslims on one platform under the banner of his leadership and there was no Sunni and no Shia, no Kafir among them, they were all one mold of Eman in duties and responsibilities with higher considerations to create a country where there was to be Wahdaniat and security for all. Today Muslims of Pakistan are adrift, establishing there formed Fiqah and recluse believes about the divine property holding Aehlebaait and they are declining holding on to the Hadeeth-e Saqlain, in which the Prophet SAWW said: 'I am leaving behind two heavy things, one the Quran and the other Itrati – my fragrance – the Aehlebaait, as long as you will stick on to them both you will not be lost (go astray).' And since after the Qaed-e Azam none of the leaders have worked on this idea of uniting the Muslims. Today the nation believed in the right of the majority, but the Surah 103 of Quran Wal Asr says, only those are at advantage who preach of peace and show patience:

Wal Asr; Innal Insana Lafee Khusr; Ilal Lazeena Aamanu Wa Amilus Saali Haate Wa Tawa Saw Bill Haqqi Wa Tawa Saw Bis Sabr.

326

Verily man is in loss, except such as have faith and do righteous deeds and join together in the mutual teaching of truth and of patience and constancy.

What Stanley Walpert did not mention was the fourth direction that the Quade-Azam turned the attention of the Momeneen of the new nation to be for each other of righteousness:

In his speech on the occasion of the first Constituent Assembly on 11ᵗʰ August 1947, Quaed-e Azam said: "You are free, free to go to your temples; you are free to go to your mosques and to any other places of worship in this state of Pakistan. You may belong to any religion or cast or creed that has nothing to do with the business of the state." This extract in conformity forming the words of the Quaed-e Azam was from the God's revelation in Quran, from the Aayet of Aayatul Kursi that said; 'La Aekra ha Fiddin'- there is no compulsion in religion.

And then Quaed-e Azam said there, "... you will find in the course of time, Hindus will cease to be Hindus and Muslims would cease to be Muslims not in the religious sense, but in political sense."

This was all a vision taken from the leaf of the great Aayet 103 - the pattern of the rule for the country as envisaged by the Prophet SAWW, but instead there appeared dictator General Ziaul Haque thrusting him in self-aggrandisement who worked against this philosophy of bringing Muslims on one platform and damaged the unity of Islam by such slogans as, *Apna Aqeeda Chhordo Naheen aur Doosray ka Aqeeda Chherdo Naheen* – don't leave your faith and do not prod into other's faith.

He secretively worked to segregate the Muslim from contacting each other and removing their differences. If the principles of faith are not discussed in an atmosphere of cordiality, the truth cannot be reached at and religion cannot be served. And Ziaul Haque was distinctly anti-Shia and winked to the Talibanized Sunni delegation to take action against the Shias whereby their houses were burnt in the northern territories, and their properties ransacked, and they killed. The description of this event is given in the book by Asghar Khan, "We shall never Learn from History". And Ziaul Haque created Gumrah-e Deen, the misled of faith.

گمراہ دیں ہیں اس طرح آزادی سے پھریں
مقتل میں جس طرح سے منافق وہاں پھریں
صد پند سود مند نہ لقمانِ حکیم کے
رازق کا رزق کھا پی منکر مومن کے سے پھریں

سیّد اطہار حسین

Gumrah Deen Haain Isqadar Aazadi Say Phirein
Maqtal Mein Jiss Tareh Say Munafiq Wahan Phirein
Sud Pind Sood Mund Na Luqman Hakeem Kay
Raziq Ka Rizq Kha Pee, Munkir Momin Kay Say Phirein

Wayward in religion so freely roam
In the slaughter field like the disbeliever roam there
One hundred counsels of Luqman the wise is not fruitful
Eating and drinking provisions of the Provider the deniers
   roam like believers

On the unity of Shias and Sunnis, Imam Khomeini, the Marja al –Taqlid says: "Those who show discord are neither Sunni nor Shias; they are agents of superpower and work for them." On another occasion he says: Muslims are brothers and will not be segregated by the pseudo-propaganda sponsored by corrupt elements." And contrary to that dictator Ziaul Haque said Apna Aqeeda Chhordo Naheen Doosray ka Chherdo Naheen- he insisted on segregation, and extending the premises of Stanley Walpert – no revolutionary leader possessed the piety and piousness of mind as did Imam Roohullah Mustafavi Moosavi Khumeini. And Quaid-e Azam Mohammad Ali Jinnah was most true to Islam and summed up as guideline the gist of the Aayet Wal Asr... for the nation.

Quaed-e Azam Mohammad Ali Jinnah RA was born on 25th December 1876 in Karachi, died on 11 September 1948 in Karachi. He went to the Sindh Madrassah Karachi, studied at the Bombay University and at the Lincoln's Inn London where he was admitted in 1893 and was Barrister-at-Law in 1896. Mohammad Ali Jinnah became the most successful lawyer in Bombay. He joined Indian National Congress in 1906, but left the congress in 1913 and served as leader of

All-India Muslim League from 1913 on, and there were two words now, 'Leagy and the Congressy'. All the Muslims big or small were Leagy and the natural segregation had taken place. But still there were many Muslims in the congress party who believed in, the roots should not be cut.

Quaed-e Azam was adored by the Muslims and he was so upright that the Muslims could shed their blood for him. There was no Muslim born in the subcontinent of India with such authority as Mohammad Ali Jinnah. He was of the Shia Asna Ashari *Aqeeda* Muslim. The Nikah or the marriage solemnization of Mohammad Ali Jinnah was performed by a Shia Aalim, Sheikh Abul Qasim Shariat. Quaed-e Azam Mohammad Ali Jinnah's family belonged to Ismaili Agha Khani Khoja, but Qaed-e Azam was converted to Shia Asana Ashari from the Ismaili Agha Khani sect in London by Maharaja Mohammad Ali Mohammad Khan Muhib, father of Raja Mohammad Ahmad Khan of Mahmudabad.

Quaed-e Azam was an active member of the Khoja Shia Asana Ashari Jamat in Bombay, his wife died in Bombay and she was buried in the Khoja Asana Ashari graveyard. Mohtarma Fatimah Jinnah when she went on an official tour to Bhakkar Mianwali to tour and meet the people she did Matam-e Husain in the Imam Baargah Mahajereen Bhakkar and identified herself to be Shia. But what is Shiaism? It is love of the Mutahhar – the progenies of the Prophet SAWW, those who have God gift to purify others.

Ata Ullah Shah Bukhari Ameer Majlis-e Ahrar[40] said he was against Jinnah because he is a Rafzi – to Shias they called Rafzi (a word coined for those who did not accept the first three caliphs as the true caliph), and no Shia could think of joining Majlis-e Ahrar, but one Maulana Mazhar Ali Azhar carrying a Shia like name was an active member of Majlis-e Ahrar. This person said Quaed-e Azam was Kafir-e Azam. And they pretended that the Shias say Quaed-e Azam was Kafir-e Azam. And none of the Sunni Ulemas, including Maulana Husain Ahmad

---

[40] From lower middle class, they sponsored Satyagardh movement – 'holding on to truth' concept introduced by Mahatma Gandhi, that Quaed-e Azam opposed. The Ahrars were former members of All India Khilafat Committee. They were pro-congress, anti Ahmadi and addressed Quad-e Azam as Kafiir-e Azam. The party collapsed after Pakistan came into being.

Madni, Head of the Darul Uloom Deoband, India, Allama Hameed Uddin Mashraqi of Khaksar Tahreek, Ameer of Majlis-e Ahrar Attaullah Shah Bukhari and founder of the Jamat-e Islami Maulana Abul Ala Maudoodi were happy with the leadership of the Quaed-e Azam, because he was a Shia Muslim.

When Quaed-e Azam Mohammad Ali Jinnah died in the governor House in Karachi Maulana Anisul Hasnain Rizvi of Sadat Amroha was called. An official vehicle went to bring him to the Governor House and under his supervision the washing of the body of the Quaed was done according to Shia precepts and the Maulana said the Namaz-e Janaza, later the state Namaz was said by Allama Shabbir Ali Usmani at the site of the burial. At the time of the burial the Talqeen as given in Shia practice was recited by Mohammad Husain Baltistani.

When the funeral procession of the Quaed-e Azam started from the Governor House for burial, all around there were Alams of Maula Abul Fazlil Abbas and the coffin was moving under cover of Alam - the standard of Hazrat Abbas AS. and on the Pharaira - the banners was written Ya Husain AS. Ya Abbas AS. Then a big Majlis-e Aza was held at the Governor House and large banners of publicity were written[2] to say; Majlis-e Aza-e Husain AS. for the beneficence of the soul of Jinnah Qaed-e Azam RA.

Quaed-e Azam Mohammad Ali Jinnah was strongly entrenched in the Shia Asana Ashari faith but he had a thorough knowledge of the Fiqah-e Hanafi – the Hanafi School of Jurisprudence of the Sunni Sect, which showed up in his historic address on 17 March 1911 to the Imperial Legislative Council in Calcutta on Muslim Endowment Bill – Waqful- Aulad.

The Islamists (extreme view holders) led by Majlis-e Ahrar had a policy of sectarian divide. They could not bear the leadership of Islam snatched from them that was enshrined in the Asna Asheri faith Quaed-e Azam followed and they called him Kafir and he was an impeccable character, upright and of integrity. Unfortunately, his work and sayings have been deliberately hidden or even belied upon and distorted and his true sayings have been limited to be shown only within the precincts of the academic centres. Because his quotes and slogan are too directional and of critical accolades that point at the glory of the Aehlebaait – the infallible members of the house of the

Prophet SAWW. The Islamists want domination over Shia faith and this means chaos in Pakistan. The Shias are the moderators of extremism, only they do not compromise with untruth, but the Islamists have crossed all borders of prejudice and have not assimilated the philosophy of Islam.

In 1946 when Quad-e Azam went to England with Viceroy Lord Wavell, Congress Party leader Jawahar Lal Nehru and League stalwart Liaquat Ali Khan, together with other notaries accompanying him in this journey, King George VI, King of Great Britain and of British Dominions and Emperor of India invited them at dinner on the night of Ashoor-e Moharram. Quaed-e Azam after seeing that schedule on board the ship said he will not attend this dinner and before the ship reached London the schedule had been changed. The British did not want escalation of discontent and knew now of the reason, the Karbala and its importance.

Mahatma Gandhi used to come to the Quaed-e Azam to meet him at his house in Bombay. On the 20th of Ramzan, Mohammad Ali Jinnah RA told the journalists tomorrow on the 21st of Ramzan, he will not meet Gandhi Jee. The Journalists asked the reason he said tomorrow is 21st of Ramzan. The journalists expressed their lack of knowledge about the significance of the date; Quaed-e Azam said, you have no knowledge that it is the day of the martyrdom of Imamul Muttaqeen Hazrat Ali ibn Abi Talib AS.

Mohan Das Karam Chand Gandhi, Mahatma and Bapu of entire India, offered Mohammad Ali Jinnah the leadership of the undivided India. This was largeness of heart of Mahatma Gandhi. But the feeling of pain for the Muslims in the heart of Jinnah was in equal match and Mohammad Ali Jinnah did not accept the whole India Presidentship. And these were great decisions Quaed-e Azam made for the Muslims and created Pakistan. The Hindu Dharm in undivided India was not the problem it was the majority Hindu Dharm ruling over the Muslims with their hold on the economics in India and Quaed-e Azam wanted Islam carry the mainstay hoisting the sail of Unity, Faith and Discipline the Quranic injunctions and launch the boat of Pakistan in the waters of Irfan – gnosis and flight of thought. And the secularists had a field day advancing their theory that Quaed-e Azam was one of them and the Islamists rebuked Quaed-e Azam that he was not one of them. In fact, till today the lower middle-class Muslim disowns Quaed-e Azam. What tragedy befell on the Islamists not to see beyond their nose hampered by their prejudice?

Not understanding logic of positivism, not grasping linguistic eloquence but raising objection is the trait of the *Maslaki Aalim(s)* – the abundant of learned, dedicated to their particular schools of thought from defunct religious seminaries. Of these, doctor of medicine Dr Israr Ahmad writes in the Daily Jang London of January 23, 2007: "The sentence of Quaed-e Aazam (Mohammad Ali Jinnah) in his speech of 11th August 1947 that:

"Anqareeb Pakistan Mein Na Muslim, Muslim Rahay Ga Na Ghair Muslim Ghair Muslim Rahay Ga."

Soon in Pakistan, neither a Muslim will be (identified) a Muslim, nor a non-Muslim, a non-Muslim.

"Kaash Woh Yeh Alfaz Na Kehtay." Wish he had not said these words.

And he adds, "My opinion about this sentence of the Quaed-e Aazam is that the secularists forward it as a supporting argument in their favour."

Unfortunately, what was a beautiful guide line from the Great Leader, advising to build a peaceful, idealistic state where the Muslims, Hindus, Sikhs, Parsis, Christians and Jews will enter in a state of brotherliness and develop respect for each other, though each retaining their religion was looked at as predominant in influence over the Muslims by the weak faith extremists.

However, the slogan of Hindu-Muslim Bha-ee Bha-ee, was cheerily taken by the Muslims and the Hindus alike in the pacifying days before partition. It spoke of reciprocal feeling of the undivided India. But the Maslaki Aalim raises objection to it and Dr Israr Ahmad sees fissures in the Great Leader's noble thought taken off from *La Aekraha Fid Deen'* - there is no *Jabr* – no arm twisting in the religion.

In fact, this Maslaki Aalim, Dr Israr Ahmad had a greater agenda, he said about Imam Husain AS. that he was not a martyr, in the presence of Dr Kalb-e Sadiq on the 9th of Moharram- 2006 on the PTV. He said, "He was a slain person."

Dr Israr Ahmad claimed to believe in the Prophet of Islam Hazrat Mohammad Mustafa SAWW, but did not believe in his words that Husain will be martyred in Karbala. 'The Prophet SAWW wept when Imam Husain AS. was given in his arms as new born baby and said he will be martyred in Karbala; I have just been informed by Angel Gibraeil.' So, the Ministry of Religion In Pakistan must not let disturbance and misgivings occur on this account and keep faith on the track as shown by the Prophet SAWW. The incompetent become easily disgusted, they got a country and now want all minorities to change their faith to their way. In the beginning Quaed-e Azam did not want a separate country for the Muslims and was all along striving for a united India with Hindu Muslim Unity. The British had decided to give independence to India, but the Congress rejected Hindu Muslim balance of power in the central government and as President of the All-India Muslim League Qaed-e Azam had little choice left but to blunt a Hindu raj syndrome once the British left, since the Congress insisted the British leave India and the discretion of the extent of the level of rule to the Muslims will be decided by the Majority Hindu.

A British Cabinet Mission of three members was formed by the Prime Minister of Great Britain, Clement Attlee to evolve and form a constitutional body in India, which arrived on 23 March 1946 in India and it had to ultimately propose of the partition because of the disagreements. Quaed-e Azam Mohammad Ali Jinnah was President of All India Muslim League from 1916 after joining it in 1913, at the same time he was a member of the Indian National Congress till 1920. And he resigned from it when Indian National Congress launched a non – cooperation movement to boycott the British rule and take hold of power.

And God was kind to send a leader for the Muslims in the shape of Mohammad Ali Jinnah. His every move was calculated cladded with constitutional expertise. There was no match to him. Jaswant Singh, the ex-foreign minister of India, after five years of his research released his book 'Jinnah, Partition and Independence' on 18 August 2009. He writes:

"Mohammad Ali Jinnah was the most outstanding figure among the contemporary political leaders of India." Jaswant Singh was a high-ranking party member of the right-wing Hindu Bhartiya Janta Party, the BJP and he found Quaed-e Aazam a bigger leader than Wallabh Bhai Patel, Jawaharlal Nehru and even Mahatma Gandhi. For praising Mohammad Ali Jinnah, Jaswant Singh was expelled from the BJP by its leadership, but he basked in the glory of speaking and presenting truth and he served his religion better than any of the leaders in the higher echelons of the BJP with their agenda of revitalising the Hinduism. But what has hit the ill-informed Pakistani rising from the ranks of Wahbism is to take away the sole effort and achievement of Quad-e Azam and open it to share by Allama Iqbal, who says in his letter of March 4, 1934 to E. Thompson as quoted by Poet Faiz Ahmad.

"I have just received review of my book. You call me protagonist of the scheme called 'Pakistan'. Now Pakistan is not my scheme. The one that I suggested in my address is the creation of a Muslim province – i.e., a province having an overwhelming population of Muslims in the North West of India. This province will be according to my scheme, a part of the proposed Indian Federation."

Quaed-e Azam was a patient of Tuberculosis and it is sheer human determination that he stood to face so much hard work and achieve the mission in the short span of his life of 72 years from 25 December 1876 to 11 September 1948. His last message to the nation was on 14th August 1948:

"The foundations of your state have been laid and it is now for you to build and build as quickly and as well as you can."

And his wish was; a particular religiosity will not be the destiny of the country, and made the dominating fundamental in the nation's life, but equality for all to be bred and observance of moralistic values practiced.

In January 1948 a minor communal riot erupted in Karachi. The Editor of the Karachi daily, Sindh Observer, Mr K. Punniah wrote some provocative editorial castigating the government. The administration wanted to take action against the editor, the matter was brought to light to the Governor General, and it was stopped. Then the officials prepared a draught ordinance for the Governor General to promulgate to detain anyone for some time without trial. Quaed-e Azam tore up the draft, saying all his life he has opposed 'black law'. This was the unique leadership of Quad-e Azam and salute to him.

Quaed-e Azam was a modernist. He changed his religion to Shia faith that was guided by the infallible Imams, So, Quaed-e Azam abandoned his attachment with his old faith. Thus, Quaed-e Azam's jurisprudence spread not only up to presenting a country to the Muslim nation but also, enlivening the mind of the Muslim nation to use its faculties and mark the truest branch of the religion and take it up. When Lord Louis Mountbatten was appointed Viceroy of India in February 1947, he quickly became friend of Pandit Jawahar Lal Nehru, but Quaed-e Azam disliked him. Though Mountbatten had charm, wit, personality but he had a stigma of homosexuality attached with his name and had scruples with his wife. And for Quade Azam these departments of life created the essence of ethics, whose demand were as strict as to stay away from one polluted.

Quaed-e Azam's personal charm was stately and stood out everywhere and his charismatic personality accepted all sorts of dresses and these were becoming on him. He has worn Agha Khani velvety tunic with wound Safa, brimmed hat and suit, Sherwani and pointed black lamb wool high wall Topi – given the name of Jinnah Cap and stylishly used monocle with a front pocket chain watch in his Sherwani dress. And he was also fond of Havana Cigar. In billiard he would thoroughly judge to a 100% pocketing the billiard ball. The acumen he used in politics was in precision to his pocketing the billiard ball. And what a man he was. A modernist and a hard upright politician were sitting in him.

The beauties in Quaed-e Azam were seen and obvious to all just as light from the sun is not hidden in all weather, his immortality was not hidden. It was known from his life his name will live and what a tribute it will be, if a grand place is created and his statue is erected in Karachi. Quaed-e Azam was a stern man and this was due to his integrity in his profession and in his life. He presented the specimen of a man where there was no bending, no appeasing since he had firm character. During his early practice as barrister, he always impressed the client with his uprightness and the client went to him to take their cases. In one case a well-known businessman Haji Abdul Karim was summoned to the court on some serious charges. He went to Mohammad Ali Jinnah and asked him how much fees he will charge. Jinnah replied Rs 500.00 per day. The Hajji was a frugal person. He asked for how long the case will last; I have in all five thousand rupees; you take this amount in return for your entire service in this case.

Jinnah said he will not accept that and his fee is rupees five hundred per day. Either you pay me this fee or you can find another advocate. Abdul Karim accepted his condition and Jinnah won the case in three days. His fees worked out Rs 1500.00 which he took from him. He was offering him Rs 5000, which he declined. Now there is quite a lot of tidiness of mind evident from this incident. Quad-e Azam believed in Halal Risq – legitimate earning of each day.

During the early days of Jinnah's practice Mrs Sarojini Naidu Feb. 1879 – March 1949. Political activist, poet, first woman president of Indian congress, called nightingale of India met him. She sensed the tall character of Jinnah hidden in his apparent sternness. She writes about Jinnah:

"I have not seen such contradiction between anyone's apparent characteristic and his real character. He is high of stature but extremely lean and thin and in appearance looking so weak. His manners are of affluent, but his physical delicacy is a deceiving curtain before it, behind which is hidden unusual power in intellect and strength of character. He is dry and irritable and keeps himself to himself and usually does not meet people with open arms. His manner is usually dictatorial. But those people who know him, know well that behind his pomp, haughtiness and arrogance, there is hidden a very attractive personality." Taken from the book 'Jinnah Namah', by Khalid Siraj.

When his illness became worse Quaed-e Azam went to Quetta and then to Ziarat for recovery but the climate did not suit him there and he returned to Karachi and what a contrast in ungentlemanly behaviour and the shirking of the responsibility. The response from the nation to this precious gift to Pakistan was of aloofness – the men at the helm of the government, sent a Dakota, Douglas DC-3 plane to bring him back, but not even a third degree official went to receive him at the Mauripur Royal Pakistan Air Base and worst of all, only a Red Cross tin roof ambulance was sent to carry him from the base to the

Governor House. Today when the countrymen will read it, they will be hurt by the behaviour of their predecessors, to their great Quaed.

The vehicle gave way, it broke down for two hours on the road and Miss Fatimah Jinnah sat in the ambulance on the bench and the driver and the ADC stood outside and the heat of the day and in it the sick Quaed-e Azam suffering the failures of the officials. After two hours his English military secretary arrived with another ambulance and it was announced the Quaed-e Azam died that same day. The evidence points at the wilful negligence of the Prime Minister, who did some politics. Even in those days there were cars put on road by makers that did eighty miles an hour on reasonable roads and ice cream plants were sold for installation deep down inside in the isolation of country with conveyor belts for turning out packed and wrapped ice cream bars and there was no dearth of means but only that of will. And the least the nation can do in atonement is form a commission to write the history of Pakistan to pay honest tribute to Quaed-e Azam and his uprightness be taught in the schools.

The tussle between the Prime Minister and the Head of the State, the Governor General or the President is repetitious in Pakistan. It is because, the Muslim nature is not suited to democracy. It is conditioned to receive directions from absolute and flawless authority. It needs to be ruled by a King, a pious and wise, a Faqih. And there is a King available for Pakistan!

When returning after performing the first and the last Hajj, the gracious Prophet SAWW was ordered by God on the way to Madina to immediately declare Hazrat Ali AS. his successor. The place was Ghadeer-e Khum. The Prophet asked Bilal to make call of Azaan and sent Ans Bin Malik to call back the men gone ahead and those trailing, and the Prophet asked for the Kajawa(s) laid for him to make a Menmber to speak and the Prophet SAWW gave a long sermon and said *Mun Kunto Maula Fa Haza Aliyun Maula* – whose so ever I am Master this Ali is his Master and he put a pink turban on his head and if the Prophet SAWW is our Master Ali is our Master. And a king for Pakistan maybe chosen from the worthiest trails of the descendants of Hazrat Ali. And what a bliss it will be to have a Sayed lead the nation as King. The Adl or justice will be the highest priority after the *Tauheed* – the acceptance of the Oneness of God. The practice of justice will determine the rule of law and order in the society. And this kingdom will have soon extended from Pakistan to Arabia and the Salah in the Kaaba will be led by the Aalim acceptable to all the Muslims.

I was invited to a Sunni wedding in 1968 in the DHS. There were many prejudiced Sunnis in the gathering. Outside in the poorly lit light a Sunni spoke to me not knowing that I was Shia, 'Jinnah was a Rafzi'; it had been eighteen years since the Qaed-e Azam had died and his Mazar had a few haphazard growths of trees around. The Sunni said, 'we shall put one or two *Mujawirs* – attendants at the Mazar and the Qauwals will go there on Thursdays to the Mazar with their Dholak – small drums hung from the neck and sing Qauwalis and there are trees and bushes growing and the boys and girls will go behind those bushes in the dark to make use of the place and in this way, we shall bury the name of Jinnah.' And this Sunni was every bit expressing the feelings of the Madrassah he came from, who disliked Qaed-e Azam because he was a Shia, not caring what he did for them. They openly used mouth to give rise to unchecked expression in vulgarism.

Field Marshal Mohammad Ayyub Khan after he took over the country gave an address in the Royal Albert Hall in London and said, 'the Qaed was a sick man.' And when Ayyub settled down in the saddle of power, he opened international tender and gave first award in architectural excellence to the Turkish Architect and affectionately built the Mausoleum of the Quaed-e Azam on a raised plinth of marble. And where as it was true the Quaed was in a sick man's body; but he was 'High' and 'Determined' and was 'Badshah'- a King!

In the deep hinterland in India, there was a village Kurra Sadat near Fatehpur Haswa that was my Nanehal, where there was only uneven mud road to go to on the *Baail Gardi* - the oxen driven carriage, no postal service, no Aekka to ride on. One cold morning in 1948, the news of lament spread in the village:

Pakistan Ka Badshah Toa Mar Gava

The King of Pakistan that is so, has died.

There was a hush in the village. Then one villager said, 'He was not their King,' then the other said, *Woh Wahan Ka Badshah He Thha* – he was King of that place all right.

And that summed up the true status of the Quaed-e Aazam (king of Pakistan). That was so, due to the genius in the sick man's body whom not only his nation but all other nations admired. And the Shia Khoja community to which the Quaed-e Aazam belonged to were to be thanked for bringing up such talent. The silent massive work they do for the cause of the service to humanity is exemplary and admirable. And their discipline in time keeping in the general Muslim events, in the Majalis the Muslims must learn from it.

Pakistan resolution was passed in Lahore in 1940, after that it was only a matter of time that Pakistan was to come in existence. A poet in 1942 said in Bhadohi the following verses in love of the Quaed-e Aazam.

Musalmanoan Ki Halki Phulki Si Kishti
Jinnnah Ki Badoulat Khuda Kay Saharay
Chali Ja Rahee Hai Kinaray Kinaray

The Muslim's feather light boat
Because of Jinnah and helped by God
is keeping its course and going on by the bank of the river.

The Ottoman Empire was defeated by the European powers, wiping out the Muslim Khilafat that was running for the last six hundred years, 1299 – 1922, it was spanning over three continents at the height of its power in the $16^{th} - 17^{th}$ century, controlling most of South-eastern Europe, West Asia and North Africa. This was unprecedented power. The Europeans joined together to break it and occupy Ottoman territories and under the treaty of Serves in August 1920, Britain and France liquidated the defeated Turkish Empire. Then they proceeded to create new Arab protectorates in Arab territories.

At the British Parliamentary Committee of the British House of Commons Mohammad Ali Jinnah said: "...The Khalifa is the only rightful custodian of the Holy Places according to our view and nobody else has a right. The holy places should not be severed from the Ottoman Empire under the Sultan." Look at the courage and far sight of Quaed-e Azam!

Together with his statement before the Parliamentary Committee Barrister Jinnah also submitted a memorandum to the British Prime

Minister elaborating the viewpoint of the Indian Muslims on the Ottoman Caliphate and the future of Turkey. Already through the Balfour Declaration in 1917 the British government had pledged to the Jews to plant a Jewish State in Palestine. Quaed-e Azam was very hurt with what was happening with the great Muslim Empire, it being dismembered. On returning to Bombay on 17 November, 1919 he said to the Daily Bombay Chronicle, which he headed as Chairman of the Board of Directors, "the British were so persistent in striking a blow at the integrity of the Ottoman Empire".

And he was thrilled when Kamal Ataturk hurled back the Christian aggressors of Europe from Turkey, trying to bring its population under their slavery. When Kamal Ataturk died in 1938, Quaed-e Azam said:

"Kamal Ataturk was the greatest Musalman in the modern Islamic World. The remarkable way in which he rescued and built up his people has no parallel in history...in him not only the Musalmans but the whole world has lost one of the greatest men that ever lived."

Raja Sahib of Mahmudabad had spent 30,00000 thirty lacs of rupees to make the All-India Muslim League session in Lucknow successful in 1937. That session pumped life in the All-India Muslim League (AIML), after that it picked up election seats. It was a large amount Raja Sahib had spent for the success of the AIML and truly he had spent most of his wealth on the making of Pakistan and he wanted an Islamic State with Sunnah and Shariah. But Quaed-e Azam wanted a Muslim Liberal Democratic State and Quaed-e Azam was against a theocratic state, since there were over 70 sects in Islam and each claimed its interpretation of Islam of truth. Later in 1970 Raja Sahib wrote Quaed-e Azam was right. But he had left India due to ideological strain on this subject and started residing in Iraq.

When Quaed-e Azam went to Quetta for the change of climate, for recouping of health, he was not getting better. In this condition he remembered of Raja Sahib Mehmudabad and called him from Iraq to Quetta. He was the only reliable friend with him in whom he could confide. And Quad-e Azam said of controversies he faced from high in administration. Raja Sahib Mehmudabad listened with very grieved heart. Raja Sahib of Mahmudabad in his last days was a penniless prince. He was offered repeatedly certain levels of posts in the reigns of President Iskandar Mirza, and in the periods of two consecutive

Generals, General Mohammad Ayyub Khan and General Agha Khan. Though these were high posts but not commensurate with his roll he had played in the achievement of Pakistan and the stature he carried and he replied, "He has sacrificed only his wealth not his nobility."

Raja Sahib Mehmudabad died on October 14, 1973 in London and according to his will he was buried in Mehshad, the city of the 8th Imam of the Aehlebaait, Imam Raza AS. This city was the holy city of Iran due to the presence of Imam Raza AS's. tomb there. It was when Emperor Raza Shah Pehlevi ruled that I visited the Rauza. Emperor Raza Shah will go yearly to sweep the ground of the Rauza till 1978 when in January 1979 the empire was abolished.

I went to the Imam's presence in 1973 in my Hillman Avenger car driving through Europe to Iran and I first visited Holy Qum, because Imam Raza AS. said so that his pilgrims first go to the pilgrimage of Massoma Qum. From Qum I drove through Iran to Khurasan and presented myself at the Rauza. I am so thankful to the Imam for his so many welcome gestures to me, these appeared on their own accord. The Rauza was not built yet as it is transformed to its majesty now. Outside the entrance door in the courtyard was a fountain. An Irani was just concluding his Ziarat recital from a pamphlet in his hand. He extended his hand and gave the few pages book to me. And armed with the recital of salutes to the Imam I entered the door of the Rauza after kissing it. And there inside I was the only pilgrim. The Rauza dome and walls were filled with Tikone – triangular cut mirrors embeded in the wall surface. And I circummambulated the Rauza and saw a King resting in the tomb with a very large crown on his head. And it was kindness of Imam Raza AS. to show me one of his states of his existence and grace. Ever since I have been several times to the Rauza of this Imam of eloquence. And each time I feel I have been gifted with a present from him. Alla Humma Sallay Ala Mohammdewn Wa Aal-e Mohammad. Before Emperor Raza Shah Pahlavi was uprooted, he started majestic construction of the Rauza, completed subsequently.

Quaed-e Azam executed his Will on 30th May 1939 in Bombay. By this Will he bequeathed his house with land situated at Mount Pleasant Road in Malabar Hill Bombay, his shares, securities and bank account to his sister Fatimah Jinnah. And he made a bequest in favour of his other sisters, brother, Anjum Islam School Bombay, University of Bombay, Arabic College Delhi. His entire residual Estate including corpus was divided in three parts and one part each was given to Aligarh University, Islamia College Peshawar and Sind Madressah Karachi.

He directed his executors to set apart Rs 200,000/-, which then brought Rs 1000/- per month in return, to be paid every month to his daughter during her life time. After her death corpus of Rs 200,000/- was to be divided equally between her children.

According to records available with the Estate of Quaed-e Azam, the Will was executed and all payments to the beneficiaries of the Will were paid, except the bequest in favour of the Aligarh university, which was ordered by the High Court of Sindh to be retained in Pakistan and held in Trust constituted under orders of the Sindh High Court for payment of income earned thereon as scholarships to poor, needy and deserving students on merit. The Quaed-e Azam Aligarh Education Trust continues to function up-to-date and has granted more than 5000 scholarships to students for graduate, post graduate studies in Pakistan as Jinnah Scholarship.

کر دیا خالق نے کرم خاص مسلمانوں پر
کر دیا درِ خداوندی وا مسلمانوں پر
رہنما محمد علی جناح کو بنایا بہ خاص اِذن
ایسی جوشیلی فزا نہ آئی پھر مسلمانوں پر
سیّد اطہار حسین

Kar Diya Khaliq Nay Karam Khas Musalmanoan Per
Kar Diya Daray Khudawandi Waa Musalmanoan Per
Rahnuma Mohammad Ali Jinnah Ko Banaya Bah Khas Izn
Aaisi Josheeli Faza Na Aaee Phir Musalmanoan Per

The Creator embarked on doing particular kindness on the Muslims
Opened the door of Godliness on the Muslims
By special edict made leader Mohammad Ali Jinaah
Such exciting environment again not came to the Muslims

-: . :-

Part III

Fate and the Man

III

Bachchu the Horse
and Cart Driver

I

Fate is an event quantified by time that is ever in motion and man's effort and God sanction is pre-written, but freshened addition is added on the beckoning of man to pre-written event slate. The story of Bachchu *Aekkewan, the* horse and cart driver narrates is, there in his share of beneficence and kindness, the events created out of his command to his horse modify the Loah-e Mahfooz (the Preserved Tablet) and add to it new generous bestowals to his fortune, not by his call for it but by the generosity of nature.

The story of Bachchu *Aekkewan,* horse and cart driver starts from his rudimentary village in the Land of Seasons and Songs that was where two rivers met, where Bachchu *Aekkewan* lived in his village, whose lanes were track paths of mud tracks and they squeezed, wavy and of bends. And the recognition to the village was given for the cluster of a few mud houses and two red-brick houses that had sprung up for pride. All sitting and occupying their claimed spaces with their preferred orientations in their preferred cardinal directions what suited to their fancy, and all of sizes and outline as suited to the means of their owners occupying them. The paths were not paved, and the roads not built — not yet in the detached villages such as where the horse and cart driver Bachchu lived, whose full name was Bachchu Yarwah.

The village had two wells, one *Imam Barda* and one site of a holy grave untested for its powers, one mosque and one Karbala where the dead were also buried. These stood near the village and served the villagers. And these were the prides of the village and the houses had their roofs at modest height and occupied length and breadth what was manageable in means.

Bachchu was known and recognized as Bachchu Aekkewan, or more generally, simply as Bachchu without the qualifying affix of the Aekkewan and he was a horse and cart driver whose track of life record dominated by the monastic clash inviting incidents and his insistent ways were of such charm and extent in follies inundating his life and occurring on their own and happening so often tampering and disturbing serenity that it attracted the attention of many for their profound vigour they frequented them with all through his profession in his life. And this gave a sample of the Indian ology for study led through his spoken apt and his persistent ways for which he was rudely chastised and buffeted by others. But his form of his expressions continued to open a floodgate of distinctions for him, all rushing his way and he by dint of these became an object of proven distinction. And the phenomenon associated with it became the basis for him to be picked as the subject of this story.

Bachchu lived in a mud house which consisted of a small room with its mud roof carrying a veranda with a *Chhappar* on it. The Chhappar was a thatched shed for providing him general comfort. The Chhappar served for his living and cooking when there came occasion for it. It stood on two pillars of stout stems that were trunks of two *Babul* trees – the Akacia trees, which were hacked and each of them cut to give the Chhappar a graceful height and a kind slope and these kept the front of the veranda open. And the back of the Chhappar was supported by the mud wall. So, this much formed the house. The Chhappar was thatched with long grass brought from the pond side where it grew in abundance. The grass was dried loosely bound and stacked on the Chhappar and strapped to the ribs of the Chhappar.

The room looked into the Chhappar shed, and the Chhappar looked at the village passage-way which past the Chhappar front, squeezing itself between the Chhappar and the village well that was opposite the Chhappar veranda. The passage-way in this arbitration squeezed itself sufficiently. Allowing the room of the house left with ten arm's length of depth each, for Bachchu to feel comfortable in them.

All the villagers went to and fro through that suddenly squeezed passage-way which immediately opened up at the end of the Chhappar, once it cleared the Chhappar and the plinth of the well, and it merged into the open space of the disarray of the remaining few mud houses of the village on its one side and the ploughed fields for crops on the other side and after a short distance, it became a broad passage and joined the wide mud road which took the villagers to the town.

The house Bachchu lived in was left to him by his parents, both of who had passed away when he was still young and growing, and there was only his aunt left to look after him. The small room with its earthen walls and its earthen roof, stacked with fine grain earth brought from the pond-side was knitted with the chaff of the straw and clay and chunks of it stacked on the wood ribs laid across the roof logs, and it formed the flat roof of the room and the room together with the Chhappar formed the house. And it stood as symbol of security for Bachchu, providing him all the luxury Bachchu wanted, exempting him of any curiosity of a brick house of fractious part per million uranium and thorium in them, creating their environment of discomfort. And the luxury of a mud house in the hot summers was different with its coolness and peace, which the red brick house dwellers did not know of, and they missed it.

The small room had a solid wood door of Sheesham wood that was the gem of the house. It fixed itself in the solid thick wall and the room boasted of a high sitting slit-window, large enough to allow light and air to enter in the room and watchful to bar the hot sun rays and the gashes of wind and cold in the winter enter in the room. And the basic requirement of light to enter in the room and the room keeping its coolness intact in summers and warmth in winters was assured through the thoughtful high sitting slit-window, and that was all that was needed to wither the weather off by the contended parents of Bachchu when they had built the house, which was now the proud heritage of Bachchu, which entirely sufficed him to meet the house need.

The space in the room safely took, in its corner everything that was of immediate concern to Bachchu in the horse and cart accessories and gadgets, stowing the harness and the bridle of the horse. And for the storage of its meat and fodder and grass bundles, ample space was available on the floor, even it affording some squeezing space for Bachchu to lie down and stretch himself if he so wanted.

Bachchu led his *Aekka* - the horse and cart out of the village passing through the muddy road for a short distance and then led his

Aekka to the wide Kachcha (unmetalled) road and once he was on the wide Kachcha road, the horse ran on it and the road took care of Bachchu and the horse and cart and took them to the town.

There were no cross roads, no overtaking from behind and no tarmac or compacted broken-stone roads all along, till his horse and cart hit the metalled Grand Trunk Road built by Sher Shah Suri, on which the Aekka rode and then got down off it, landing with a thud on the continuing soft Kachcha road, and only for the abrupt interval that Bachchu's horse and cart was on the Grand Trunk Road, from the time the wheels of his two wheeled horse and cart hit it and rode on its concreted surface and started to grind it that there arose a familiar metallic sound of the wheels embracing the road, and the sound of the embracing of the two produced by the rubbing of each other, was the familiar sound which Bachchu's ears waited for to detect through it the condition of the soundness of the metal ring cladding his horse and cart wheels. And it was always pleasing for Bachchu to know that the metal rings sounded so far so good on the two wheels.

This was the pleasure sound; Bachchu was always alert to hear and enjoy listening to it. The sound was akin to the joy of the cannoneer's perceiving ears, finding his cannon ball landing at the middle of the most sought-after target. And Bachchu dwelled with the likened feeling of achievement of the Commander of the General's artillery, sitting in his field command centre and hearing the news that the cannoneer had scored the hit at the target. And Bachchu for a few lurching rounds of the wheels of his horse and cart, flamboyant with the assurances extended to him by the fanciful grinding sound he heard to say, all was well with the rings of the wheels of the horse and cart, rumbled his horse and cart with joy pervading in him that all was well.

The soil in the part of the country where Bachchu lived was fertile, and its fertility was due mainly to the generosity of Nature that looked at it kindly. The fertility of the soil was further supplemented by irrigating. The soil was irrigated with the sweet water drawn from the well by the sturdy bullocks, which pulled the *Jhore* - that was the *Moat*, the leather cask, full of water. It was called *Pur* when the bullocks rushed and ran with the heavy Jhore laden with water, and all ought to know that the *Pur* was the name for the state when the leather cask - the *moat* or the *Jhore* was full of water and was being pulled and hauled to the top of the well by the heaving run of the bullocks, and when it was heaved out of the well the etymological authority of the Pur ended and Pani Dena - *Sincha-ee* – the act of irrigation started.

And that one precious piece of leather container - the cask that brought water out, was of such vital importance that it and its performing acts were given so many loving names by the people of the region and the region echoed with such loving names with their sweet sounds gifted by the vernacular spoken in the region of this God blessed land.

The land where Bachchu lived, typified by the charm and the custom given to it by its people, reciprocated by giving them in kind a dialectal characteristic of the flavour of uniqueness, typifying their uniqueness with its sweetness and heightening their charm for the stresses they placed in between the sentences shooting out from them, with the exorbitance in syllabifying which they thrust in the conversations. The *Pur* helped them produce good harvest after the fields were quenched of thirst by the sweet water that the *Jhore* lifted from the well. The water laden Jhore was pulled clear of the mouth of the well by the barely clad industrialist farmer, and the *Amrat* – the nectar of life the water was let flow in the receptor basin and it channelled itself running to the fields, rushing to reach to the far ends of the fields through the furrows, made by thoughtful branches in style by the watchful farmer for the yield of the crop, and the saplings grew lush and became sturdy.

And the farmer was thankful to the two rivers Ganga and Jamna spreading their sequel and commitment there, after their union with each other. The two rivers through their joint pool of the wealth of water in their swells and swoops blessed the land with a deep down moist of the soil, fertilising the soil for the yield of crop. And the soil yielding a rich harvest with the two rivers' joint fertilisation, helping the farmer in his endeavour, and he was thankful to God and to the commitment for him.

In this sequel it was again something to do with the union of the two rivers, merging in one in this part of the country and flowing together unionising them, satiating the land with water that there was plenty of grass. Lots of grass grew there in this sweet land for free taking by the *Ghasyaras* – the grass croppers. They bundled the grass and sold to the horse and cart drivers so very cheap, which kept the fares cheap and the wealth of the country circulating.

The horse and cart driver Bachchu mostly bought these bundles in generous quantities, more than enough for the need of his horse. It was only when there was not a good earning that day that the bundles, he bought were just that little less as the earning was. The horse that needed full stomach of grass each day did not like it and considered it pinching her assured feed. And it was on such days that there was a big problem waiting for Bachchu, because the horse was not of a disposition to forgive Bachchu for that folly of short supply in grass.

The horse was of the female class - a mare. She was tall and well-built and needed lots of grass for munching. You couldn't tell the difference between her and the next horse of her size standing beside her, unless you peeped with a searching look and noticed a gendered something of a horse was absent in her, and a gendered something else of a horse present in her. It was only then that the difference was evident. And her spontaneous release of energy vis-à-vis her build was equal to two three horses, smaller her size and weight. And because her requirement of the grass in accordance with her weight and size was on the high side, she resorted to her way of resentment for her lack of feed by making violent kicks to the foot board with her heels, jolting the cart and the passengers on it and announcing her unwillingness to pull the load of the passengers and not moving forward when the grass was served short to her.

The mare kicked the footboard, treating Bachchu in equal measures in reciprocity which was, 'you get as good as I got', and it was a tit for tat from her, and it was only when she had her fill of snappy kicks to the footboard and after Bachchu's lots of spurring and showering of shame on her that she budged, and that grudgingly and with difficulty took to the road. The horse that was to say the mare, otherwise was a cooperative sort, and she cared for the pitiable Bachchu for the hard work he did as much as she did herself, and both knew that together they did lots of hard work for their living. But the horse never liked to see money earned in the day's wage not spent evenly and she always liked to see Bachchu not spending her share of the earnings on things other than food and fodder required to be purchased for her.

And it was in her nature that despite her generous feeling of sympathy towards Bachchu, she sometimes resorted to kicking the footboard just for the hack of it. And whenever she felt the repetitious, monotonous phenomenon of Bachchu forcing the iron bit in her mouth, blinkers against her eyes, noseband round her muzzle and slipping crupper under her tail and tying the girth round her belly, strapping her with harness, backing her up and forcing the shafts of the cart to hitch her to it, making her look not a reliable trustworthy creature, but a dispute making beast. Whereas she was a horse with a pedigree and not a mixed breed and her pedigree vouched she was of attributes. And she deserved treatment as something important.

But Bachchu like professional would back the mare with affection, doing 'Choh, Choh' to hitch her gently to the shafts of the cart, and she knew it was an unavoidable necessity, and she knew she was stuck with it for life. She could not relax a bit, no matter how weary her legs were, she had to stand fixed at a spot, she was halted at. She was halted on the roadside in a queue, waiting, waiting for how long God knows for the passengers to appear. And the flies screwed their head fins and tongue in her eye corners and ears. And though Bachchu showed all considerations to her, affectionately patting her on the flat of her neck now and then and keeping her in good humour, but her being tied up to remain standing exhausted her.

And she felt just then it was better to run on the road than standing that was turning her legs stony, there then her coat was rippled with air and the flies were fanned off when she ran on the road and she felt important being on assignment. And to stand in the queue with flies drilling in her eye-sockets and pushing their antennae in her muzzle, and some squatting on her face and entering their claws into her ears, taxing her patience and turning her into easy rage was the outcome. So much that even with all her inexhaustible strength of patience and the build of her horse of not an easily demisable patience, their atrociousness was beyond her not to force drive her to exasperations and put her to vent her feeling of desperation through wily repeated, violent swinging of her head, violating the rules set by the law enforcers of horse's behaviour to be standing still in queue on the road side.

She was required to keep her head and neck straight and stay in the queue by the law enforcers that was police. She had to be standing in line with the front horse and cart and keeping her body, from muzzle to tail as straight as an arrow, not to pull to the sides and remain still. And it was a bit too much even with all her steeliness she carried and the formidable strength that anyone could see she possessed but she failed not to break the rule and let her desperation raged into temper and let off steam by giving bangs on to the footboard with her heels that were the loudest on these occasions, meant to make the announcement with all the force of disapproval in her. And if ever any one thought there was no logic, this was it – the exasperation had won over the patience.

All the horse and cart drivers took a day off and were on that day off the road and so did Bachchu. He had fixed Sundays as his day off and this meant that for that day the repetitious up and down parading, on the stirringly dismal, all too familiar, the only road of the town was stopped, as also was stopped any excursion with special passengers for destinations beyond the outer limits of the town, and also stopped the jumpy starts and stops at the call of the passengers, sovereign in their manners in the issue of their commands: putting Bachchu to stop now, go now, and that so relieved Bachchu and his horse that it was to Bachchu like a richly endowed one month's vacation of a gentleman of means in the West, in the jolliness of the Riviera.

On these Sundays, Bachchu took his mare for wash and bath to the river. And it had to be in the earliest hours of the mornings before the sunrays came out from behind the horizon. He had to keep to the superstition that haunted the horse and cart drivers that the horse must not be seen taking bath at the riverbank after the sun was out. He took his mare to the riverbank just then when the cool morning wind serenaded the river side, and mist laden air did its duty to tone up everything with freshness, when the vaporous fumes rose from the river surface, and serene quietness prevailed everywhere, and the sun with its streaks of rays was below the horizon. The sun waited to inundate the spaces with its full glare of rays with their brilliances, still hiding behind the line of horizon. And a mystic prevalence was prevailing around the riverbank environments in depths. Just then Bachchu took the horse to the river bank to administer the wash and bath that had become due to her after a full seven days lapse.

The mare so much enjoyed the wash and the scouring on her coat that she gave several approvals of neighing and whinnying, and Bachchu willingly took the compliment, and Bachchu was always glad that the horse found her true colour of the coat, dark mahogany revealing to full extent after the wash. And the mare herself marvelled at the spotless shine of her coat and the roundness of her hooves, which prominently stood out after the rubbing and scouring. Bachchu himself on these Sundays entered in the river and took long and short dips and let the water with all the copper and gold and sulphur and all the Brahman purity it brought riverfull from the high mountains rub him and with its gentle flow wash off the dirt deposits and grime that had stuck on to him for full last seven days, in spite of his daily treatment he gave to him on the well's plinth, splashing him with water.

The bath enhanced the sanctity of life. The nature appeared so kind on Bachchu, bestowing on him favours countless. The Flautist was all the time playing His flute, only the fortunate had the ability to absorb the melody. The Bountiful had opened the doors of charity, only the recipient had to present his *Kashkole* and fill it with the abundance of the generosities from the Decorous. And Bachchu as much as he could, assimilated of it in his being. He washed and rinsed his clothes and scrubbed and cleansed him and made him pretty look as much as others thought of him. And the cheerfulness that nestled in him through it lasted for the whole one week till to the next Sunday. And life was never unkind to Bachchu and he could never think of even making the slightest of complaint to arouse the faintest of doubt in any one's mind that he did not have most what he wanted.

But, to have all the desirable in life was exceedingly difficult and not possible to achieve and there were demands associated with desires that at times had to be curbed and Bachchu had to put a hold on cooking a meal for himself. The cooking of meal exceeded the means of a horse and cart driver and negated preservation of self and Bachchu had to submit to the dictates of his meagre earnings to save the firewood and not cook.

The firewood was expensive, the woodcutter, the *Lakarhara* brought the wood from the wood forest by chopping off dry branches and tying them round a centre log from his wood, making a huge cone – the *Qunda* or if smaller one the *Dhann*, either he carried on his shoulders with its centre log resting on each shoulder and it was a huge collection of burning wood for cooking. He brought it to the doors of the houses and for all this he asked was six Anas from the buyers, but that was expensive for Bachchu and it took lots of wood to cook. And Bachchu had to bury the desire of it, if it ever raised its head, he took what bread and onion, bread and salt or bread and mango offered in food.

Bachchu collected mangoes from the mound of the pond, there were clusters of mango trees there. The mangoes fell from the trees and they were there for anyone to collect them, lying there ripe and sweet. They also fell from the trees and lay by the road side of the cross-country Grand Trunk Road, built by that ornate King Sher Shah Suri. He fired the imagination of the British, who took over India to rule like him. The mango trees planted by Sher Shah Suri were every one's property and these decorated the road and were a showpiece of the thoughtful planning of Sher Shah, known and remembered for his reformative skill and for his trend setting mind in the pain taking welfare of his people. He was remembered for the style of his rule.

The trees stood on each side of the road in solemn ovation to Sher Shah Suri, Emperor from 1540 to 1545 AD. They spread their branches and had assumed giant tallness to lent coolness and calm to anyone taking shelter beneath them, providing therapy to the resting with clean pleasant air they blew. And dropped ripe mangoes and Jamun from each tree of its kind on the ground, which begged notice of the passers-by to be picked up and eaten. Bachchu found ground sprinkled with ripe mangoes early in the mornings, and he only needed selecting and picked up the best of them, as much as he wanted and had no problem for his meal.

Bachchu also relied on *Bhuna Chana* - parched gram and *Murmuray* – parched corn and *Laee* – parched rice kernel. The *Bhunjuwa* roasted and parched the grams; corns and rice kernel in the graded heat of the heated sand, which he heated in his *Bhard* – the fire-place. This was his furnace, the contrivance for parching grains. He parched the grains in several large belly graded of heat, largemouth pitchers mounted on the *Bhard,* the kiln he had engineered. The flame diverted to its pockets and he sold the parched grains fresh and hot and so much of it and for so little a price and they were marvellous. And the Bhunjuwa was a wonderful man. And Bachchu could buy as much as he wanted at a cost next to nothing. He sat cross-legged on the floor of his veranda and ate these with onion, chilli and salt and these were wonderful substitute for meal.

Bachchu also relied on *Settu.* It was the cheapest of the foods, purchased from any of the two tiny shops open for all hours in his village. He first knocked at the door of the house and called the shop owner, adding to the name of the shopkeeper with the title of *Mian* or *Lala* whatever the shop keeper's caste and class demanded the prefix. If Bachchu wanted, he could buy Settu for two or three handfuls of any grain kind; gram, corn, barley, wheat, maize or whatever in exchange, if he did not want to part with his coins or if he did not have any of it. He could get what he wanted on barter from his two village-shops. *Settu* was prepared from parched barley flour. The Settu Bachchu bought was salted and chilli added to it. He also bought plain Settu. He knit it in water and it turned into one full blown food and Bachchu had the choice in Settu of sweet Settu and salty Settu. He made sweet Settu by adding *Khand*, the raw brown sugar in the plain Settu and he had lots of choices of quick food.

Roti or bread was sold at the kitchen restaurant of the town. The *Bawarchi* - the cook sold the Roti fresh and hot direct from the griddle and the cost was next to nothing. The Roti was the mainstay of Bachchu's food with *Mattha* – the sour milk. The Mattha excelled all the accompaniments of bread, it was sumptuous and pleasant, the pleasantest of the foods.

Most of the houses made Ghee in the village and so much Mattha was produced collectively in the village that they would rather give a bowl or two to their neighbours than ditch it as waste. Milk rich in cream, from the buffalos and cows was simmered and increased in gravity and it was coagulated to become yoghurt, then churned in plentiful quantity of cold water in a *Matka* - a large pitcher. The *Chachh* or the aerated cream, the butter - the raw Ghee floated on the surface of the water. It was scooped off, and plenty of Chachh or Mattha with its sweet smell and mild sourness was left in the Matka as a by-product - a unique health-giving product of excellence.

The custom was that no one bought or sold Mattha, it was always given free, and Bachchu had bowls of Mattha coming from the houses. Mattha contained fair rich traces of butter and Bachchu soaked his bread in the Mattha and swirled his lump of salt in it and it made an excellent meal. When he wanted sweet Mattha he added *Khand* to it and Bachchu had the choice of sweet Mattha and the salty Mattha. Mattha was the lifeblood of Bachchu. It was excelling for plain drinking and it filled the depleted hibernating with energy and did lots of good to its consumer. And Bachchu helped himself with a copious quantity of Mattha. It kept his form and health envious and free of worries and filled him with energy, ready to take the strain of day-long run round with his horse and cart.

Khand was brown sugar. All the Parchoon shops kept sack-full quantities of it. It was sold dirt cheap, and it was in plentyful quantity around. Even the tiniest shops sold brown sugar. The refined white sugar was expensive, it was four times the price of the brown sugar and the brown sugar made Bachchu's Mattha just as sweet. The Khand or the brown sugar had molasses and mineral traces and the sugar goodness was intact in it, and it had a cooling effect on the nerves and was good for the lining of the stomach. Bachchu could tell that Khand on health score was better than the expensive grainy white sugar. The commercial monopoly holders after Bachchu's find, found the virtues of Khand that it helped the briskness of life, and they made it five times dearer. The trend setters and the lovers of naturalness started not only adding Khand to their coffee drinks, but to the cake tops and the cake masters began sprinkling it on their dough and the cookies.

Bachchu, occasionally breaking away from the monotony of taking parched grain and putting aside the unassailable requirement of fire-wood consumption, once in a while became lavish, especially in the winter times and also when fancy took over the restrictiveness and desire overpowering his denounces; he made tea for himself and boiled rice and took rice with tea with the sense of gratitude and felt as if all the privileges were standing humbly in his presence, appeasing and rolling out their foray of taste and nourishment and Bachchu felt he had exceeded the means in the attainable to him. Rice and tea were a strange combination of food for some, but for Bachchu it was at once a sweet, a food and a relaxant.

Right from the time the good parents of Bachchu left this world of remonstrance and penitence, for another world whose coordinates could not be determined, and dimensions ascertained and the believer's share of comforts gauged with any competitiveness, and as to where Bachchu's parents had gone, no scientific physical evidence could explain and shed light on, and no epistemology could make any revelation, save words of Holy books which gauge humanitarian attitude and their vogue of reverences they allocate to God appointees. Bachchu's parents with either of the two standings were in comfort and solace that their son in this world is accustomed to give exploitation and rivalry was in the cares of his aunt and she was his warden. But only after a short time as it seemed when he was still to enter into the firmness of youth, as was the inevitable end of everything good that bowed out from the arena of its performing stage, the aunt of Bachchu bowed out, and said goodbye to this world of astute discords, one offering no assuages to pain and only discomfort and she left Bachchu on his own to face all the harshness of the world.

So Bachchu was left to his own choices in this world of competition and rancorous ways to formulate his own rules and pounce at adversaries to force out rewards off the chest of the world which had it in her holds. And Bachchu could learn no more lessons from his aunt in handling the affairs in deriving earnestness out of pandemonium and safeguard him as best as she taught him, and she had left him. Bachchu could not enjoy her company for long. And Bachchu's Aunt was the last of his parents and when she was gone, Bachchu felt all that he could call his own had perished.

Bachchu's Aunt was a lady of wise worldly ways and of a generous disposition. She had left for Bachchu a horse and cart - the Aekka to open the way for him to establish his recognition, and revamp the family name to extolling and distinction in the God's vast world of distinct attributes, and here he did exactly that, through deploying the horse and cart on excursions bound by a day's ploy, around and about places, which started from the town centre where he led his horse and cart to, three and a quarter mile away from his village to conquer odds. And through his maintaining dignity, Bachchu met all the challenges that faced him and earned honours and rewards, interposed by admonishes and apologies from the people of consequence and he had glorified the authority of a straight man, thanks to his Aunt.

The Aunt of Bachchu easily stood in a class that was with flourishes of distinction and out of the ordinary, and the degree of her extraordinariness was in the significance of the time she was born in. She was born on a Thursday in the early hours of the day when the powerful planet Jupiter had returned to take its position in the Zodiac, twelve years three months and thirteen days after her set round, in the sky, and the planet was casting the greatest of the benevolent influence on all, and good fortune and opulence was cast in ampleness in the destined portions of the Aunt of Bachchu as the mark of her luck. This reflective reality was not known to the in-laws of the Aunt of Bachchu that opportunity and good fortune was one of her baggage and that was following her around. And it was their greatest drawback that they did not know of the celestial forces tracing her footsteps to help her. They only looked at the short-term quick haul in reward and adjudged the Aunt of Bachchu by the gold and dowry she had brought with her to their house, which she had brought precious little and that in a very insignificant quantity from her parents. And from day one it was not any exhilaration to them that the obviously short worldly goods were her baggage and she had not brought with her emerald and gold.

Bachchu's Aunt was married to a distant village, two scores of miles away among different people unknown to the parents of the Aunt of Bachchu, eight years before Bachchu was born. She was immediately put to a lowly esteem by the in-laws with lots of taunting and maltreatment administered to her, since she had not brought the desirable quantity of dowry with her. And she was every now and then sent to bring the deficient quantity of gold and dowry from her people to them.

And the last time she was pestered, and she went to her parents to bring the gold and the deficient dowry from them, her parents had left this world of trial and tribulations and the house in which they lived had succumbed to a flat heap of mud for not being able to bear the battering of the wind and rain and take stand against harshness. The Aunt of Bachchu had no gold and dowry to return with to the in-laws and did not return to them this time and lived permanently away from them.

She went to live with her sister; the mother of Bachchu and took charge of Bachchu. And this was due to her skill and the extraordinary talent in perceiving the affairs and thereof from her a certain intelligent manipulative talent and special capability in handling the affairs of the horse and cart running under varied situations, emerged in Bachchu.

-: . :-

III

Gorays the English Whites

II

The Aunt of Bachchu, besides her good fortune and comparative worldly ease that possessed her for one to enjoy her company, had all along herself possessed, skilful manoeuvring into the power of perceiving and it's registering into retention a sharp mind for interpretations and general exploitation, and she knew how to lookafter herself. She went out level with these related assets, brimming to full, stored in her brain for its deployment in handling the situations of extraneous discords for extracting excelling results and looked for a job where the *Gorays* – the Whites lived, and she successfully downsized the Elite Englishman in his garrison to agree to employ her and secured the job she had found suited to her talents with her terms.

The Gorays - the Whites were an outstanding brand of men. They had a religion and a natural gift of art and science which they exhibited with the deployment of primacy of reign and the exercise of brain. Their home island eased its shores into the surrounding seas with hundreds of estuaries, from the north to the south of their island country, with its shires and boroughs, with Devon's undulating hills, and the Welsh towns of long legendry names, with village brass band, and Midland marshes and Scottish heights. And they had birds, Robins, Herons, Owls, Doves, and Larks, and wild flowers; the primrose, daffodils, thyme, dog violets, and fine flavour English asparagus, trees and shrubs which wore distinct summer and winter garbs.

And the Gorays had Shakespeare, Dickens, Keats, Byron and Kipling and Newton, born in their midst, and what a beautiful country they had. And the country stood on the firm foundations of the pillars of literariness and it was a learning centre and of military fashioned traditions and accommodative to various religious thoughts and tolerant to vice and virtue. And the people from north to south carried a uniform tradition in food recipe, entertaining them with Yorkshire pudding, roast beef, gravy of stock and roast potatoes; Irish stew, Scotch broth and apples, rhubarb and custard dessert, and did not miss truffle and exported their oysters and made potato their staple diet. They preserved their Royalty and drove themselves to empire building and nationalism was their representative inadequacy, but they were not of Caligula or Nero the notorious emperors and nothing of height with them in apathy was bothersome to others. And for obduracy they said:

'Seeds of potato-berries should be sown in adapted places by the explorers of new countries.'

Captain Young was Commander of the Doon from the Ghurkha war in 1815 till to the uprising of 1857 in Meerut, Delhi and Northern India (the British called it mutiny). Capt. Young was an Irishman, and he liked Irish stew, which had a small quantity of special potatoes in its recipe. He received a fresh crop of potatoes from Ireland and sowed them in the foothills of Himalaya in Garhwali and grew the potatoes there in 1820s. Till then potato was not a known vegetable in the Land of Seasons and Songs. He encouraged the farmers to sow potatoes and soon it became a popular veggie there, used in so many dishes. Captain Young had really to thank Sir Walter Raleigh for his introducing the potatoes in Ireland and thence for his intense liking of the potatoes. Sir Walter Raleigh had introduced potatoes and tobacco in Ireland in about 1580.

The Island of the Gorays was remarkable. It was an upright angel, standing all by itself on its feet, unlinked to any culture, it produced a culture and a language that leapt out to be language of the world, though the island was isolated, but self-sufficient, it was of a topography of pleasantest features, and of sufficient length and breadth to give its people a language that worked in all situations, written and spoken then it had a King and discipline. And the island ruled and weaned success, allowing failure to interrupt its onward march to glories only rarely.

And its people in the discharge of their duty stood by their posts, and so dedicated that the Titanic while going to sink, the postmen prepared their strategies to save the registered mails disallowing their thoughts wager to save their lives. And the people so loyal to their Monarchs that they ruled in their name the world over, and their army pushed the astringent as collective community as ordered by their Iron Lady to assert action as far out as to the far-off Falkland Islands.

Queen Victoria was born on 24th May 1819 in the auspicious hours of the epoch of British ascendancy, and its significance was, she survived two attempts on her life and proceeded to become the most charismatic Queen of England – a warm hearted and lively Queen. In her time industrial expansion took off, and empire became of such dimension on which sun never set. But it was said of Queen Victoria "Chamrdi Ja-ay Toe Ja-ay Damrdi Na Ja-ay." (The skin may be taken away but not the quarter penny). She is most talked of Queen of all the sovereigns of the British Empire. The British Empire reached to its zenith during her period of rule and became the foremost global power. She was Queen of England and Empress of India and she was called grandmother of Europe for her 9 children, 41 grandchildren and 87 great grandchildren, most of whom she married in the royalties in Europe.

The Queen engaged a cook, Abdul Karim from the Land of Seasons and Songs. It was tried that he is taught English, but he failed to learn any of it in spite of efforts. The brain of the Queen so worked that she never failed to make the most out of the least she made in her investment, and she reversed the process of teaching and learning. She gave Abdul Karim the title of *Munshi* – someone able to write dictations and with ability, and she put him to teach her Urdu. It was doubtful that he showed any flare of teaching anything, least of it the Urdu, and he achieved no excelling result on this score either, but the Empress of India on her own efforts taught herself most of the essentials of Urdu and her competence rose to such a level that she filled her diary with notes in Urdu. And awareness arose in England about Urdu and an unseen good happened to England. It created outstanding men of knowledge in the Urdu language in Britain.

Dr Gilchrist translated Shakespeare in Urdu and composed Urdu dictionary. He was Head of the Department of Hindustani Language at Fort William College Calcutta, which was centre of learning of oriental studies from the date of its founding on the 10th July 1800. Dr Gilchrist served the Urdu language raising it to the status of advanced language from the *Lashkari* or the trooper's language used in the market place as the conversational media between the peoples to the courts as the common language. He added vocabulary to its *Rekhta* - the mixture of words. In the initial stages of the language, Urdu was, but a collection of borrowed words from Turkish, Persian, Arabic and the local Prakrit with verbs taken from the Hindi. Dr Gilchrist's work unfortunately ended when Governor General, Lord Dalhousie with a change in the policy of the British India Government closed the college in 1854.

But the effort by the British to promote Urdu was more political, than love for the language foreign to their Island. Persian was the court language for centuries in India in the courts surrounding the strongholds in India, which was reflective of Indian Shahi influence and to reduce its influence it was necessary for the British to build Urdu.

Lord Macaulay 1800-1859 was member of the Governing Council of East India Company from 1834 to 1838. He advocated in his speech in Calcutta on February 1835 to replace Indian nation's languages with the English language as the medium of education. The Governor General of India William Bentinck approved the proposal on 7th March 1835 and it became the corner stone of British-India educational policy and remains largely so till today.

About the trace of linguistic standing of India, in a pathetic note Lord Macaulay says:

'A single shelf of a good European library is worth the whole nation's literature of India and Arabia ...'

And he says:

'What the Greek and the Latin were to the contemporaries of Thomas More, 1478 – 1535 and Roger Ascham, 1515-68. our tongue is to the people of India.'

It was said of Macaulay's knowledge and personality in as early as 1826; it was 'Overflowing with words and not poor in thought, liberal in opinion but not radical. He seems a correct as well as a full man. He showed minute knowledge of subjects not introduced by him.'

And considering what heterogeneous people were making up Indian subcontinent, it was perhaps a good thing if a common language spoken by all was the media of education. But the English language and the method of teaching was so trimmed that in the process, intellectual slaves were created in aid of British rule.

Dr Gilchrist returned from India to England and continued to serve the Urdu language. He opened Urdu Teaching School in England. He has written some seventy books and papers to bring English and Urdu close to each other. His service to the Urdu language was devotion to a cause that effect nations and this sworn devotion was again shown in the person of Professor Ralph Russell of London University died 14th September 2008. His phenomenal service to the Urdu language has earned him the title of British Baba-ay Urdu – the British Father of Urdu. For thirty years this soul served as professor and head of the Urdu Department of London University. He was decorated with Sitara-e-Imtiaz by Pakistan for his services of promotion of Urdu.

The title of the Baba-*ay Urdu* – Father of Urdu, in service to the Urdu-e Moalla – elated Urdu, was given to Molvi Abdul Haque, b.1870 d.1961. For fifty years this dedicated man held the post of Secretary and then the post of President of *Pak-o-Hind Anjuman Taraqqi-e Urdu* – 'Pakistan and India Society for the Advancement of Urdu'. And Molvi Abdul Haque was a revered celebrity, and he says:

"The amount of work Dr John Borthwick Gilchrist has done for Urdu is just as much as Delhi has done the serving of Urdu to make it rise to its heights."

The title of Baba-ay Urdu given to Molvi Abdul Haque raising him to the celebrity status would have been an uncontroversial achievement of him, but for one shortcoming: Although for forty years Molvi Abdul Haque remained secretary of the Anjuman, serving the Urdu language yet his statement comparing the services rendered by Dr Gilchrist to the Urdu language at par or even higher to the services of Delhi, has to be taken with a pinch of salt. Molvi Abdul Haque did a disservice to himself because of his feeble logic he has put, he says:

"So many *Ahadiths* – the traditions of the Prophet SAWW have been described in reverence of the *Aehlebaait* – the progenies of the Prophet SAWW - said to have been said by the Prophet SAWW that they cannot be true."

Molvi Abdul Haque did not understand the height of the Aehlebaait also he made little of the fact that prominent Prophets declared successor to them from among their families; Prophet Moses AS. made his brother Aaron his successor, Prophet Ibrahim AS. made his son Hazrat Ismail AS. his successor and Hazrat Ishq AS., and likewise Prophet Hazrat Mohammad Mustafa SAWW made his brother Imam Ali AS. his successor and these successions were with divine consent. That's why the Prophet SAWW had repeatedly to say words in praise of the Aehlebaait for holding divine succession and divine appointment of the Imamat. And Molvi Abdul Haque must register that the Prophet SAWW does not say a thing unless it is from God, having His consent.

It pleases to write, that the English are of tender heart, especially to children. And whether it is a characteristic that the religion has infused in them, or it is the race characteristic that emerges in the races, is without doubt true of them and they are doubly covered with it. They would be horrified to know there have been Arab races which have buried their children. To the greater creditability of the English; in a charity appeal by the BBC 'children in need' TV show on November 19, 2010 in seven-hour telethon, by the end of the show at 0200 GMT, the celebrities had contributed £18, 098,199. The organisers hoped it will be more than £39 million once all donations were in, and God must be pleased over the performance of Englishmen of England. There was no remuneration matching this performance, which the celebrity gave as their call of passion of love, demanding no recognition. God says in Aayet 2:271:

If you give charity in open (making it known and publicised) this mode is acceptably good and if you give charity in secrecy (without publicity) this act is much better and it (charity/alms) atones for many of your sins and God is well aware of your sins.

The village of Pinner was some ten miles away from the centre of London. In the 18th century it was bound by 4000 acres or 33 Hides of land. The village ran two horse buses of which each seated eight people inside, one on each side of the coachman and the strong horses of the bus ran with that number of passengers jog-trotting. Then there were two-wheel horse and carts in the village which carried meat to the retail butcher, and some of them collected scraps calling 'Rug and Bones, Rug and Bones'. The village had a manor house, a tavern and an Ale Houses and the villagers reared cattle, and the farmers cultivated land in a set pattern till 1601, cultivating on a three-year cultivation rule. For the first year they sowed wheat, oats, barley or peas, for the second-year crops of beans, oats or summer corns and for the third year the fields were left uncultivated to regenerate by the decay of the fallow.

The cows were fed on the undergrowth, which they digested and produced milk and milk was plentiful. The fallen wood, furze or bracken was free fire-wood for the villagers. The pigs were fed on acorn which was easily available and meat was plentiful, and there were about four million pigs all over in the island and only fifteen million people. And the villagers paid one penny a year per pig to the lord owning a wood, and for it they sent their swine to run in the woods and the pigs were left there and they fed them from the wood fruits, roots, grass, earthworms, rodents and snakes.

The Parish Church of Pinner of high Episcopal authority ensured religious practice in the village and the villagers adhered to it. The villagers assembled at the Parish Church and sang hymns and read Gospels. The women dressed with the head covers of bonnets and hats and men wore hats and bowlers. And time travelled as if on a tricycle. The people were of simple nature, endearing and of contentment, of mannerism and sweetness. My colleague, Philosopher Alan Johnston of Pinner Philosophy Group, who has a tendency to be Sofi like – quiet, mannered and wise says:

'Heath Robinson was living close to Pinner, and it was tribute to him that the Pinner Council has decided to honour him, and open 'Heath Robinson Museum' in the national heritage house of Emma Lady Hamilton in Pinner.'

Heath Robinson's name is adjectival producing complicated mechanical devices, gadgetries and contraptions. He had brainwaves and the name 'Heath Robinson' was a maxim for making effectual or ineffectual functioning gadgetries, each admired, and people's appreciation is unbound for individualistic ideas in this angelic island.

The adjectival *Gorays* or the English White was a pseudo name that came off their association with the Land of Seasons and Songs due to their white skin. They had an affiliation to the culture and the languages of India, particularly the Urdu language, and had a soft corner for the variety full India. And the Aunt of Bachchu missed no opportunity to exploit this situation and went from her village to exercise her skill on the Gorays, right there in their very garrison.

And her wide vigilant eyes fully opened and observant in this world of inflictions and sufferings, construed favourable result of securing a permanent employment for her, without bargaining the surrender of her independent mind. She had no difficulty in finding the long-term remunerative job of 'Fowl Keeper' in the house of the garrison commander - the Elite Englishman, who exercised command and control of the garrison. And in it was the full nod of consent of the Elite Englishman's Begum – the benign English Lady of the house.

And though her job was only a fraction of a degree higher in distinction above the charwoman, but in assumption she made it to carry an unprecedented importance in the house of the Elite Englishman. And the aunt of Bachchu ensured that the job yielded the greatest of the benefits the world was holding in its covert chest and it yielded to her.

یہ گورے فکر انسانی میں مثالی ہیں
نمایاں خوب خوبی میں جمالی ہیں
محبت آتی ہے انکو، راہ اخلاق عقلی
شستہ کلامی کی مہارت علم کے شیدائی ہیں
سیّد اطہار حسین

Yeh Goray Fikr Insani Mein Misali Haain
Numayan Khoob Khoobi Mein Jamali Haain
Mohabbat Aati Haai Inko Raah Aekhlaq Aqli
Shustah Kalami Ki Maharat Ilm Kay Shaidaee Haain

These whites in concern for humanity are model
Well distinguished in goodness love inspired
They know love, way of ethics of wisdom
Habit of civil talk and lover of knowledge

-: . :-

III

THE ELITE ENGLISHMAN

III

The horse that pulled Bachchu's *Aekka,* was given to Bachchu by his Aunt. The horse belonged to the Elite Englishman who used it as a double in his carriage. The Elite Englishman sold the horse because she behaved erratic and had become unreliable. She tried to bite someone when she willed and kicked as if she was not a pedigree horse of the thoroughbred class, but a less-bred, third degree hinny, and for her erratic behaviour, the Elite Englishman sold her cheap as punishment to her, and Bachchu's Aunt who had an eye for a good deal, quickly grabbed the opportunity and took the mare in her possession by her noseband at the throw away price of just under her two months' salary.

The Elite Englishman had employed the Aunt of Bachchu for keeping his cocks and hens in trim shape of which he was very fond. These were the prime days of the *Gorays* in the Land of Seasons and Songs, their loading the Indian mind with elaborations and ostentations gave them magical power to rule that knew no bonds. The Tommie paraded the streets in the towns and on the platforms of the railway stations in crisp military uniform with boots of metal toes and metalled heels, and bent down and kissed sitting woman on the platform without any inhibition and with audacity and they thumped the ground in pairs and the regimental detachments had Scottish Bagpipe ready to serenade outside the dining halls of the regiments and posh dinners were served to the commissioned officers in celebration of one or the other event and mercurial vitality of some officer after boozing was on genuine display. The booze made them drop on the floor and peddle their feet as if they were peddling bicycle.

The aunt of Bachchu went to the house of the Elite Englishman and of his Benign English lady in the local garrison to do the slice of the

368

duty of looking after the cocks and hens of the Elite Englishman. The Elite Englishman adored the free parading cocks and hens, he was particularly interested in the cocks whose, varied colours fascinated him captivating his temporal imagination of these creatures features, in particular the shining feathers of the wings and their graceful swaying rose comb, and the best of all, was the bowing stiff shiny hackles, and their glossy shining plumes of rainbow colours, the admixtures of golden-red, orange-yellow and dark-brown and such varieties of colours as nature bestowed them were all very fascinating to the Elite Englishman. And what fascinated most to him was their short step march, and their crowing over, giving the *Baang* (the dawn crowing, announcing the arrival of the morning), all these things pleased the Elite Englishman and he looked at them as object of fascination and gratitude for being in the world and gave each of them individual affectionate names.

The flock of these cocks and hens were kept in an enclosure especially prepared for them, and appropriate arrangements were made by the Elite Englishman for their comfortable living that these cocks and hens had to have. An adequate low roofed quarter of refuge – the *Darbah* or the hen's house was built in a guarded enclosure for them to huddle in and rush out of it as they would require when they wanted to, and adequate safe environment was created for them to live in and prosper there in seclusion of fear, and the area was made out- of- bounds for cats and dogs and anything to do likely remotely resembling to be enemies of the cocks and hens.

These domestic creatures were a spectacle of alluring beauty for the Elite Englishman and were left free to run around in the yard, they were in. Only once in a while they were paraded before the Elite Englishman when the Elite Englishman thought it was time to see colours. And those of them that did not show off colours or spiritedness were summarily whisked away from the parade and never seen again. They never appeared again in the squad of the flock. When the evenings arrived for these creatures – that was the dark of any shade, say a cloud passing overhead, they hurried and bunched together closely and hurled them in the Darbah, closing any gap between them and huddled themselves together in tightening security, and any wayward creeper encroaching in, in their four walled refuge, no matter what the intention of the wayward creeper was, it was jointly attacked at by the fist-tightened force. And frogmarched and destroyed. And this was done most adroitly as the punitive measure, as they rightly thought the place was very much theirs - the place of their retirement and no encroachment could be permitted.

This was admirable, and thanks to this practice they lived, and with that lived the job of the aunt of Bachchu, whose status though only at par with the charwoman, but had shot up and risen much higher above the classification of her job in the house of the Elite Englishman for her contrivances on the cocks and the hens and her knowledge how to keep the Elite Englishman's adsorption to bright colours of the cocks and the hens actively spurred and alive. That was by her keeping their feathers as shiny and bright coloured as possible. For this she on the quiet and with discretion as her tool, fed the cocks and the hens with fine cut pieces of tender meat which they readily digested, and looked healthy and bright.

In face of the evidential circumstances that presented themselves of the showing of the odd flare for colour infatuation of cocks and hens that the Elite Englishman showed, if ever an Englishman was to have had an acknowledged eccentric tendency, then this was one case where the saying fitted well and good. Because to keep some one employed for cocks and hens to keep their feather shining, was exactly the case where the blemish fitted just and right of eccentricity. But the eccentricity in the case of the Elite Englishman was a trait not easily understood that whether it was a rogue, or an asset contributed by his individualism, and it was not clear as to how it modified the exacerbation of the Elite Englishman's disconcert to worldliness that was a weakness inherited by most; but it rendering disaffection in Englishman for it and there were questions to be raised about it.

The only thing evidential that could be located positively and seemed to emerge with plausible evidence about the Elite Englishman's approaches towards life, were the rise of a group of narrow sharp peaks of inordinate virtues that the Elite Englishman possessed, and these were the throw away habit what he showed in parting with his worldly possessions on the one scale of virtue, and on the other scale, the corporeal managerial tendency he possessed. It showed itself peaking, in the one track following of his unforgiving mind not to forgive any one showing lack of adherence to punctuality in time keeping.

And due mainly to the assertiveness of this later flourish of the Elite Englishman that although the Aunt of Bachchu enjoyed a unique status for her keeping the cocks and the hens in the trim of shape and their shining colours mesmerising, she had to make a relentless additional definite effort to keep her status at par at which she enjoyed it, and keep her popularity floating there and that was by arriving at the garrison to her duty place on the express of time at the dot, just when the sun was preparing to launch its first streaks of rays over the dome of the sky, but having its face still hidden and not out in any prominence and still slightly below the horizon, though all determined to immediately pop out its forehead.

The Aunt of Bachchu never allowed the sun peep out to be noticed by a discerning eye, even if when he enjoyed all the freedom of visionary power, expressive and inherent, and in however hurried ascendancies his hallo was to lead sun rise from across the line of horizon to emerge to light the day in laudable brilliance. The Aunt of Bachchu was there before any such occurrence occurred, and she never allowed any shilly-shallying or dithering steps to force her submit to the requirement of any appeasing to any one for any late arrivals, and she every time arrived at the garrison very much on time, on dot to start her duty.

The regiments inculcated in them principles in their daily routine, what the top brass instilled in them, and it was in the regiment of the Elite Englishman that everything that was to be done was to be done on the dot. With no leeway to anyone to show any laxity. The Elite Englishman who was more regimentals than the regiment in inception, and had never relaxed himself a bit over the years, nor allowed those under his worthy command to relax a bit, had him and the rest of the regiment always on tiptoe. Well! Except, when his innocent indulgence crept on him allowing him loosening of his self, by taken over by the command of his inbred faculties of allowing itself overwhelmed by the mesmerism of the colours of the cocks and the hens to let it sit across on the inroads of his reasoning, whose doors then got shut, holding him back then exercise judgements of legitimacies. It was then, only on these occasions when the regimental coordinates of discipline

371

were cast aside, when he showed some inordinate creeping indulgence to watch colours of the hackle. Otherwise, it was out of question that anyone under his command or he himself takes any exacerbation latitude in laxities of any nature suggesting freedom of non-regimental nature.

And he could not imagine for one moment, the Aunt of Bachchu could be allowed to be a variant and be late and not start her cock and hen vigilance on time, which true to her sense of command of duty that abounded her inside out; she never failed herself in her punctuality of timekeeping, and was always there on time. She always arrived on the duty at the fixed time. For which she had to first walk briskly and then take the first horse and cart going on the Kachcha road – she could catch one the earliest, going to the Railway Station to meet the first early train passengers to be lifted. And from there she reached to the garrison on the other side of the station, walking fast like the fast wind to where the Elite Englishman and his Benign English Lady the important two were making history in implementing the time keeping. And she always reached there at the garrison bang on time, meeting all the rigours set in the regimental timekeeping, and reached there without any detour in punctuality.

For the reasons of her punctuality in timekeeping and the considerations bordering and including the magnanimous generosity of the Elite Englishman and the benevolent nature of his Benign the English lady, the Aunt of Bachchu could buy the horse for almost free. And with a definite plan in her mind to steer Bachchu lift him in rankings in life, she bought a two wheeled vehicle - the *Aekka* she found standing idle at an owner's premises. He was glad to get rid of the Aekka and clear his space and she bought it at cheap price, doing the favour to the owner and transferred the rights of the horse and the cart to Bachchu for his owner ship, and that's how Bachchu got the name of Bachchu Aekkewan.

Besides the distinction of being called 'Aekkewan', there were some other good reasons for Bachchu's badge of distinction and his recognizance around, and these were varied, including his slim frame of body, drawing other's attention to its flexure and glistening, then his wheat coloured complexion and the build of a bird's nest of hair on his head which was a human showpiece of wooliness, which kept his head covered with dust and fly spits and which only got a chance on Sundays to get straightened and washed at the river side. Otherwise on other days its wooliness only received some soaking from one bucket of water on him in the morning baths and water having difficulty penetrating to the roots of the headful of hair, did a simulated exercise of going through the hair roots.

And of course the other distinctive feature that stood out for the recognisance of him in the peculiarity domain was the tell-tale story of the spread over of a large mouth, he used liberally to bring out choice words for communication with his horse, with their sprawling meanings, which flung their discord wrapping in most of the times others, due to the gestural insinuations of some undesired imaginative folly that supposedly he saw floating in them, and the folly, falling covered comprehensively by the expanse of the meanings of the words shot out from him. Which was to say the least, when a person firmly established that it was directed at him or her, it not only was disturbingly unsettling for him or her, but it sent him or her into a state of stunning shock and become, uneasy discomfiture, which destroyed their total composure for the day they had started with earlier to tackle the day.

And to top it all, there was the sign of the permanent invading smile, sitting on his face, mischievously threatening his victim's composure, although he had nothing to do with it. But that confounded matter, coupled with the words he spoke, that was defining visible follies detectable in his unintentional target, and the two of these created a very unsettled environment all around there, creating perfect misgivings about his intention in uttering those words to what soever places his horse and cart duty took him to.

-: . :-

III

THE FAR-OFF SCHOOL

IV

Bachch represented to his Aunt, all she could call her own. He was the first and the last thing in the world for her. She was his guardian and the only aunt in the world. She did everything to raise Bachchu into a hardworking and a straight man. But in what she could not make provision for was to send Bachchu to school even if she fought tooth and nail to overcome all the invisible subduing forces working to inhibit the lowly stationed like her, to send her ward to school, even if she became a hurricane to undo and sweep aside all the threatening jam, locks and inhibitions that gnawed at her to keep her bound by the parameters that restricted the aspirations of the lowly stationed like of hers to rise a notch higher in the social order raising their faces towards knowledge and learning. The social set up was such that even if it was a Buddha's tallness coming to rescue her, she was unable to tear apart the customs that weighed down on her and on the equals of her class to unshackle the bondages of the classes of the society. She could not have undone the fixed norms of the society at large and generated means to educate Bachchu beyond read and write rudimentary words at the maximum.

The tradition was that no family of the stature and the standing of the Aunt of Bachchu were appropriated to possess and enjoy status other than that had befallen in their lap, and the lowly in the station of life were not to reap the benefit of the fruit of education by sending their boys or girls to school. And there were factors ruling it and the most was the scarceness of money and their class could not come up to send their boys to school in the days that the aunt of Bachchu lived. The society had its claws stronger than the will of the weak. And the Aunt of Bachchu had largely to be contended with the fate and the

374

dictates of the society and submit to the harshness of the silent law that made inequality rule all along an all-around operating fundamental, and the law of the ruling dominating the class was sovereign, not allowing Bachchu class of boys to be sent to school.

In any case even if the Aunt of Bachchu stood up against all the invisible odds, subjugating all the striding hurdles suppressing and trampling the linchpin that conducted the manner and the behaviour of suppressing by the higher class and stuck her neck out and made herself tall with undeterred efforts to send Bachchu to school, there was no school that ran in her village or the next village or one, in the near vicinity of her village, and this meant that the boy had to be sent on a long walk to school, two and a fair portion of the next mile on foot, when taking a shorter route through the fields. But the Aunt of Bachchu was adamant and she took Bachchu to the school.

The school had one teacher and a deputy teacher, and it possessed all the features of a school, but was bare of facilities. The obvious need of a school, tables and benches were not there. The class room was a long room with battered windows in the outer wall, and hot and cold gusts of dusty wind came into the room, and dust and gusts came all day. The floor of the room was in level and the walls were worn and the roof of the room carried heavy logs and the environment of the class room was showing paucity of care taking. The pathway to the school was the foot-track with pebbles placed on either side of the path to mark the path and these features created a semblance of school and gave authority to it to impart teaching.

The school in the days of its monopolizing popularity, teaching no more than necessary in moral building, and raising students to attain proficiency level in linguistic expression and excellence in the art of reading and writing in the vernacular of Urdu and Farsi, added with competency in learning to solve arithmetical problems, determined the future of standing of the qualified in the society. And science was not taught to the boys; it could bring in heretic tendency in them. Afterall science claimed man took origin from carbon particle. The school in those days of its exclusive prominence in teaching had two rooms filled with boys.

But since schools of institutionalised enterprises known as the missionary schools, like the Trinity Schools, Madrassahs and

Pathshallas had sprung up with their competitive ferocity, concentrating on early segregation of mind of the boy through religious lessons bending them to strict discipline for adherence to the fundamentals, they carved from the religion they advocated, the school was in difficulty: its attendees had fallen in number and it was limited to only one class room. And the other room of the school had become adjunct, due to its disuse. And only room with its frontage remained functional in the use of the teacher and was recognized as wholly the complete school. The single classroom was called the school, with its assembly of a total number of thirty-seven boys who together formed varied age group, covering ages from early seven to late fifteen.

The room or the school had one distinctive possession though; it was the prestigious eight-day clock in mahogany frame. It was hung on the wall under the vigil of the teacher. For other things besides the clock, there were two arm chairs, one table, one stool and a corner cupboard. The stool was used by the teacher to take down the eight-day clock and hang it back after winding it to full on the eighth day of the week. The clock gave the teacher the authority to muster the assembly of the students on the dot at eight o'clock in the mornings and authority to discharge the class at four o'clock in the evenings as the clock struck four, and the clock was a very valued possession of the school. And as for the students, it was a consolatory prize for them to understand from its ticking arm that the time of their strenuous occupation of keeping themselves glued to the book was bit by bit coming to the end for the day, as they glanced at the clock once in a while, nearing to the end of the school.

The only thing that could be said about the teacher and the least said the better was that; if ever he was kind to anything and to anybody then it was that eight-day clock which he put on his lap on the eighth day without fail with delicate care and wound it till the spring gave the sound 'pong'. He wound it as taut as it could go and filled life in the clock to its brim, and he did not forget to carry out this on the appointed day, since the clock allowed the teacher to command the words, 'shut your books, and go home,' when the hammer struck the gong at four. Only on Fridays the class was wound up early at three o'clock and the boys were bee lined to proceed to the grass field, adjacent to the school on to its side to play 'Korda Chhupa-ee' for one hour in the cool when the sun had gone many degrees down in the sky.

The boys sat on the grass in a large circle and a lash was made from a *Gamchha* – the shoulder scarf of a boy and the teacher who was referee in the game, gave the lash arbitrarily to a boy, and the game started. The boy crouched upon the lash hiding it as best as he could and ran around the circle behind the sitting boys and softly dropped the lash behind some boy, who in his opinion was slack and was not likely to discover the lash dropped behind him. Then if he had completed his round of the circle and the boy did not discover the lash was lying behind him, he by the rule of the Korda Chhupa-ee won the right to pick up the lash and start lashing at the boy for not discovering it.

The boy with the lash running round the sitting boys had to spot a really slack boy to drop the lash behind him, using his best estimate that the boy was really slack and he will not detect the soft lash when placed behind him. But if it was to go wrong and the boy discovered that the lash was laid behind him, he grabbed it and if he had fulfilled the condition that he did not look behind and only his probing hands found it, then he immediately pulled it from behind him and ran with it after the boy who had dropped it behind him and if he caught him, he was free to start lashing at him with it and do so till the boy managed to escape and threw him in the place that was vacated by the boy now lashing him.

This part of the game aroused intense excitement. It brought out lots of bucking up for and against the boys. Sympathisers, prompting one or the other of the two and the most of it was against the boy who had made the erroneous judgement of not selecting a glum boy but an ace of a boy who discovered the lash and was now lashing him. The boy being lashed had lost the sympathy of the other boys because he had given away in the trick of softly dropping the lash and it was easily discovered. And he ran hard, not knowing where to, to escape the lashing that were now mostly landing on his head.

But if the boy who had dropped the lash had completed the round of the circle and the targeted boy was really slack and did not discover that the lash was dropped behind him, then if the referee who was always the teacher sitting on chair placed on the grass, thought that the lash was within the reach of the probing hands of the sitting boy and it had not been discovered for inaptitude, at once signalled the OK sign and the lash was picked up by the circling boy and he began whacking the boy still sitting glum.

On this unexpected treatment meted out to the boy, he jumped in air like a spring toy and ran sprinting for life to get out of the reach of the whacking, and the boy with lash chased him till he threw it down in disgust for not being able to catch the escaping boy and he then rushed to quickly occupy the place vacated by the running boy. And the boy finding the chase was over, returned and picked up the lash thrown on the ground and he started a new round of the game.

The fear of getting whacked in the game brought out the sprinting ability in the boys, it enabled them escape from the whacking or the chase for it to do whacking, in either case they were put to hard exercise, and it took away vanity and aroused discipline. No one could violate the rules of the game. And in this game each one was for himself and everyone was allowed to run and chase and whack and every student loosened himself, either whacking or being whacked and there was a great fun in the game.

The teacher took immense pleasure from the whacking, dodging and chasing and he had a good laugh. The teacher thought, the *Korda Chhupa-ee* game created comradeship and spiritedness in the boys and it vouched for arousing sportsmanship and a whole lot of better understanding between them and wiped off mugginess. He was of the opinion that it inculcated power of point-concentration and increased the power of listening in the boys and it bred attentiveness and discipline in them as the game demanded of them to be every bit attentive and be listening to the sound of the drop of the soft lash that was of soft cotton scarf.

The scarf for the lash was borrowed from a boy in the class, whoever carried a large scarf on his shoulder. It was twisted and folded into a lash. And it was in the nature of the lash of the scarf that it made little sound on the grassy ground when it was dropped behind a boy, and the boys required deploying their full hearing faculty they were born with, directed to detecting and listening to the softest sound of the drop of the lash behind them.

The teacher had organised the Korda Chhupa-ee game for the boys because he had no provision for spending on game material or employing a game keeper as there was nothing in his game fund to spend on the games. It was in the book that once in a while the game kitty will be filled by the *Sarkar* – the administrators running the finances of the state, but it remained lean and empty as ever. And the teacher not knowing, no other way of providing cost free game to the boys was always well satisfied with his ingenuity in thinking and producing in the physical training domain what he had arranged, infusing many appropriations in the boys highly suited as a replacement in the absence of any spending cash in the game's coffer.

The teacher taught all the subjects that the students of the class needed to learn. And the least that could be said about the school was that there was more thrashing done in the school than there was teaching, whereas the latter was thought to be the primary function as expected of the schools. But the teacher had put it in the second place, next to thrashing. And there was little *Khushkhati* – the printing of letters done by the boys on their *Takhti* - the wood slab, and more done to correcting the tips of the pens made from the wild growing reeds, collected by the boys from the pond's side.

Of the reed's types, one reed type was *Sarkanda* and the other was *Click*. The Sarkanda pen had pulp all along the inside of the stem in its belly. When it was dipped in the ink, the pulp absorbed the ink, running it longer when writing and kept the pen tip moist for a long time and the Click had no pulp, it had a hollow bore with discs inside at its knots, all along its length and it could not absorb and retain the ink, but the tip of the Click pen was stiff, only the tip required lifting the ink from the inkpot more often. It however gave an assured feeling to the student that the tip was not going to fail in a while as the tip of the Sarkanda pen did.

The pens had to be made correct to the defined specifications as laid down by the teacher for their tips to be of such and such width, and of such and such thickness for a flexible travel to and fro on the surface of the wood slab and the pens had to have a prick in the tip of the pen with such and such pricking force to achieve correct split in it for side movements on the writing slab, and the tip had to be given a slanting cut on it of such and such inclination to let it adopt and invest itself to obtain correct form of the word by sticking to the dimensional features of the letter under print along its curves, and take to flatness in the straight portion and to curving in the curved portion of the letters to give correct shape and form of the words being printed on the wood slab.

And these specified preciseness in the shaving and the trimming of the reed and care in its selection, finally formed the pen and its tip, and these were such specifications formulated by the teacher of binding do's for carving the pen out of the reed that the teacher had little confidence in others for achieving these rigorous standards in making the pens, and he took this errand upon himself each time a boy had a worn-out pen. And it was more frequent than not.

And the teacher would rather forego his lunch of parched gram and parched rice, sometimes these mixed together, and he will be shaving the worn-out pen and correcting it in his lunch break, rather than let the broken pen be left waiting without its due re-shaving that was needed after the lunch break immediately soon, and the progress of the class could not be compromised. And in any event the teacher saw to it that he did not stretch his lunch, and took his lunch in as little a time as possible. Only he dwelled on the dried slice of the mango *Achar* – the hot pickle, and he took a pot of water afterwards and sometimes a carrot as afters, but never during all these performances he took off his turban from his head, and kept decorum of his person.

The standard of the fluidity of the ink was another define set by the teacher alongside with the depth of its black colour quality that was considered by him a strong factor in achieving pretty letter printing the boys had to develop through handwriting. And the boys and their wards did all to meet the standard. As school orders had great priority for the parents.

The black ink came from the lamp-black of the kerosene lanterns and as also from the mustered oil Diya – lamp with wick in it burnt to collect the soot. The better ink was obtained from the mustard oil lamp-black. It was deposited on the inside of a small dish placed over the flame of the Diya - the small dish holding oil and wick and burning the cotton wick. The dish was placed in the *Taaq* - the niche in the wall and the soot rose from the burning wick and it deposited on the dish. The black soot and water were mixed to make ink. A small amount of gum was added to it to correct its fluidity so that it did not run on the slab or form blobs on it.

The boys went to the *Babul* trees in woody areas and collected gum from the trunks of the trees. They screwed out the gum blobs from the tree trunks and from its branches. And the standard in the fluidity of the black ink was maintained. And for the blue ink the boys had to go to the *Baniya* - the grocer to buy the blue tablet to make the blue ink.

All this home exercise was to meet the requirement set by the teacher and the rigour of the teacher was, he could allow a boy deposit a blob from his running nose on the writing wood slab and blur the words printed on it, but hack it, he could murder the boy for having a word misprinted and misrepresented for its correct height and thickness and flatness at its turns and bends and it not assuming its correct form. And everybody held his breath as the teacher came and inspected it. And the draught-stricken room, hit by cold lurking in with fresh gusts entering from the open windows, had the boys in difficulty holding their running nose.

The progress of the class was under continuous scrutiny and the survey of the teacher, and the surveillance of his masterly eyes adjudged the writings whether correct or otherwise as the words were printed by the boys on the wood slab, and the printing progress was monitored by him on the wood slab with an eagle eye, and there was no getting away from it not correctly printed and not achieving the standard, and he could kill a boy for not doing the writing correctly, than letting the boy go on tracing words from his pen unbecoming of the art of letter printing and spoiling the reputation of the school.

And in appropriation to his determined ways alongside with these rigours of standards, the teacher had set his mind at the rigours of discipline. He had evolved, entirely his own sweet hours created ideas of teaching and of maintenance of discipline. And all told, the teacher had set himself to be a strict disciplinarian that was every bit evident from his all white *Safa* – the turban on his head and his white flowing two-piece robe, the Kurta and the loose cotton pyjama he wore. His deputy was even stricter, whenever he took over, he wore likewise turban but instead of pyjama a one-piece cloth, the Dhoti. And both the teachers believed that the fundamental of discipline stemmed from thrashing and that was the best way to keep the boys straight and behaviourally fine and above mark. And they saw to it that it was carried out rigorously and steadfastly, without letting laxity come in the way of the appropriateness of a particular punishment that suited one, who in their opinion deserved that treatment and they administered that punishment at once.

The teacher had devised a means of pressing the boy's finger by sandwiching it in between two sturdy pencils of fair thickness for lesser offences, say a boy was forgetting his lesson. And he continued prolonging of pressing the finger till the boy went crimson and blue or in the case of a feebler one, loosened his muscle and sufficiently wetted the floor. And he resorted to the use of stick for slightly higher offences; say a boy was leaning his back on to the wall, making the wall behind him a back-rest cushion. Or say a boy was making use of the wall as a tree to climb on; when a rodent, like a mouse ran towards him and he was forced to do so.

This happened on the occasions when a mouse popped out of an unexpected hole, which was not there the previous day and the mouse in its frenzy to enter in its lost hole, tried to socialize with the boys sitting on the jute mat spread over the length of the room and touched past one of the boys on its swift frenzied run aiming at the hole where he wanted to enter in. But finding the hole covered by the mat sat at on by a boy, the mouse turned swiftly back towards his previous point of emergence to make his disappearance final there. On seeing the mouse whizzing round in his trip to and fro on his swift feet, there was a great commotion in the class, and all order disappeared. And the teacher who did not know; what the excitement and screams were about, immediately spotted the boy screaming most and had his devised punishment out from his rules book and administered on him at once to quell the commotion and it subsided to full that had ripped the class temporarily.

But the teachers despite their firm conviction in the virtues of thrashing which they did, to bring out the best in the boys in Wazadari – in formalism and elegance, also deeply believed in *Shusta Kalami* - the mannered way of speaking and they taught that with great stress of intensifying intensity, identifying its virtues to the boys. And the only most status reducing *Kalama* – the sentence of bursting intensity to rid the boys of propensity to preposterousness who had brought discredit to themselves by uttering some unbecoming word for some unfortunate reason which came on their lips, not expected of them; the teacher would say:

Na Soorat Na Shakal Choohay Kay Bill Mein Say Nikal

Neither pretty face nor having pretty looks found a hole o
f a mouse and came out.

رشد حاضر نظر آتی ہے وہاں
جہاں اقدار سماج و راسخی وہاں
کس طرح دفن درزمیں نہ ہو غبار
جہاں ذوق استقامت داری وہاں
سیّد اطہار حسین

Rushd Hazir Nazar Aati Haai Wahan
Jahan Aeqdar-e Samaj Wa Rasekhi Wahan
Kis Tareh Dafn Dar Zameen Na Ho Ghubar
Jahan Zauq-e Isteqamat Dari Wahan

Rectitude is present is seen there
Where there are values of society and treading of
righteousness there
How is it the ill will not be buried in earth
Where there is desire of standing straight there

Bachchu saw all this going on, on the first day of the school he was brought to by his aunt to satiate her piquant idea guided by her better judgement thrust on Bachchu, and instigating him join the school, now was genuinely so scared with all that formality he saw that he never returned to the place to sit there the next day.

Bachchu thus from the early years of his boyhood had no schooling given by a school under the command of teachers of virtue and had grown unschooled. And he had to pick his wisdom from the multifarious open University of Nature for learning all the expertise in the use of the vocabulary of the vernacular he spoke. And he mastered

383

the art of expressing from the floating slang of the vast reservoir of words formed of the traditional, artfully spiced, plucky and cosmic words spoken by the sweet tongued folks of the region, he lived in. The usage of which on all occasions and in all conversations was in practice in every nook and corner of that part of the country where Bachchu lived and people were soaked with them and their flavour.

And the slang so added spice to life that Bachchu could swear it was totally indispensable for him. And that this way of conversation that he knew of and was expert at, was spread as far out as he travelled on his horse and cart to places that were way off his routine journey and beyond his daily one day's runs.

-: . :-

III

THE MARE

V

Bachchu used the security of the room in his house for keeping the belongings of the horse; the bridle, harness, and things like curry-comb, food and fodder, grass bundles and stock of gram and pitcher to soak gram. The bridle he hung on the stout peg in the wall pushed in and filled with clay. He kept the harness on the slab and the floor space was taken up by the grass bundles, food and fodder of the horse. These occupied most of the floor space in the room and Bachchu slept under the thatched *Chappar*. His horse occupied the place below the tree on the other side of the passageway, and the horse was always in sight of Bachchu. And the narrow passageway in front of the house was always busy with the villagers going to and fro to places they required to go. The villagers saw the veranda when they were coming and going by it.

There was an understanding between Bachchu and the mare that she would neigh every now and then at intervals from her lodging, where she was tied to the pegs by the trunk of the tree to inform Bachchu of her presence there, and Bachchu would reply back in a voice of 'Ho' to inform her that he was aware that she was there well fastened to the pegs. Because once in a while the horse would break loose, uprooting the pegs and run dragging the pegs along with the rope hanging from her neck and rush to the grassy land and pasture. This was because on such days she was hungry when Bachchu had not enough in copper, nickel and silver coins to buy sufficient grass and fodder for the horse. Otherwise, there were days when he had enough of these coins earned and he saved some coppers for the rainy days.

The mare whose requirement of grass was never less, conceded nothing to Bachchu in not buying anything less in grass than she was used to. And indifferent with what hit Bachchu, when the grass was not there, she uprooted the pegs and ran in *Dulki* – the trot and sometimes raced *Surpat* – galloping for the pasture where she found fine short grass ready to be gorged to make up for the loss of the grass, she missed not provided by Bachchu. And the mare not being of the compromising type to let her suffer with hunger and discomfort did that more often than not. And she sometimes did it and ran to the grassy land simply to gorge her in the pasture, in spite of her fair share of grass that was provided to her by Bachchu.

It was on these occasions that Bachchu was most worried that the horse might run in somebody's ploughed and furrowed field or enter in somebody's lush green crop field and ruin them trampling with her hooves, leaving the pasture behind for even softer *Chaara* - the tenderer food of shoots of barley or maize or corn etc, which were ready to lure her. He would quickly run after the horse to catch her as soon as he discovered she was gone. And the horse, seeing Bachchu coming near to her would jerk her head and trot away to another spot getting away from Bachchu. This exacerbated Bachchu's worry and he would shout to whoever passed nearby where the horse was: '*Pakardh Liha Ohka, Pakardh Liha Ohka*', '*Pakardh Liha Ohka*'- catch her, catch her, catch her. And he meant to say to him, catch hold of the horse by the dangling rope from her neck.

This sentence stirred quite a problem. A lady sitting there in the bushes under the compulsion of her need at the call of nature, became very panicky. The lady was observing her routine call of the day and she had taken due care to obscure herself in the thicket and she thought she was safe, when suddenly, she heard the call of 'catch her, catch her', and the call was growing near and near. She sprang up from her position she was sitting in on the feet crouching on the ground position and she sprang up and took to her heels; because she could not think of anything else other than Bachchu was enticing someone to catch her. She managed to whisk herself away from the scene and ran with her body and soul and only rested herself after she had reached to her people and was safe among them.

Bachchu however had not any inkling of the lady running across the field that she was scared and had not in the least any idea that the scariness of the lady was because of his call of 'catch her, catch her,' and he most diligently concerned himself with the mare that was on the loose, calling out 'catch her, catch her', putting all his vocal and lung's power calling out to passer-by there, and pointing with his fingers towards the mare which was also the direction of the lady running, and he also running towards her to catch the mare and calling out catch her, catch her, quiet unconcerned with the state of the lady who was panting and exhausted. And at the end of her run when the lady had just made it to reach to her people in safety, she was all not sure what happened and why, she was being caught and she was scary and white face.

Bachchu had such a pang of fear about his mare running into somebody's cultivated field that at nights he dreamt of the mare entering somebody's field. And while sleeping in his slumber loudly would shout 'Catch her, Catch her.' And only Bachchu was capable of such an extraordinary display of human vulnerability to assumed fear of damage caused to someone's property through his investiture on something on which he did not have any control that could bring out producing full blown loud sound while he was under full submission of the demand of sleep and it was an acknowledged fact that no one else known there among the villagers could produce the sound of yelling like of 'catch her, catch her' that Bachchu produced while asleep. And it was only Bachchu's domain who could do it. But genuine science vouch it could happen with men of extreme symbiosis of caution. And it was Bachchu's conscious that made him produce full throated loud sound while under full submission of the demand of sound sleep with deep slumber.

This, yelling of Bachchu in the middle of the night caused quite an unusual situation in the neighbourhood; the ladies were sheepish of coming out of their houses in the nights in case there was a beckoning for them to be caught by someone. And these village womenfolk had to go to the fields to meet their call of nature in the company of the Saheli(s) – the girlfriends and sometimes alone in odd hours, which these village folks were used to doing, and these bursts of loud calls of, 'catch her, catch her' had made them very panicky that they will be caught by someone lurking around there. And many of them thought Bachchu was outright a nuisance and some were ready to swear he was of poor conduct, yelling out 'catch her, catch her,' when they were minding their business and keeping themselves to themselves and least expecting trouble in the nights, by his 'catch her, catch her', making them vulnerable to be caught and mauled by someone.

And to say the least, these bursts of the yells 'catch her, catch her', when most unexpected in the nights, had made the ladies all extremely edgy and had created an outright uncertainty about their safety while on the call of nature. And the yelling was a blow to their freedom of movement and a cause of harassment to them. Besides that, it had cast a fatal doubt in the minds of the ladies about the health of Bachchu's mind. And they felt a need to be cautious during his presence around, when he was seen near about, and was visible to them in their close vicinity.

And the ladies as a precautionary measure, in spite of a sane look of appearance on Bachchu's face Bachchu presented to the ladies, they did avoid his closeness to them. And the ladies never had no-reason not to pass rude remarks and gaudy taunts at him when they found him prancing around and hustling himself disconcertedly there about, near by the proximities of the ladies where they were, and it was then, when Bachchu heard hideous cutting remarks about his state of mind from the ladies that he said, 'was it not for the committed men chasing their galloping horse and they were teased by the unthinking'. But Bachchu overlooked the hurling of cynicism on him and considered the ladies act a socialising. And he had no malice against the charming ladies.

Bachchu except for such snubs as the ladies lavished at him that he had to take and not utter a word contrary to the feelings the ladies spelled, otherwise, had a peaceful life in his village. There was God given everything. The wide free flowing river was there, the village well with the sweetest of water was there, and there was the gift of the whole wide world around and about him to enjoy life and feel the mirth of God's boon to man as his personal fiefdom, loaded with privileges, and the nature's approbation never stilling itself not to be obliging man and ensuring to see that man was comfortable, enjoying; sun, air, rain, the boon of plenty of the never-ending grace and gift of God. And Bachchu thanked God for it and ignored the remarks of the ladies. And to Bachchu the joy of being able to thank, was joy by itself that washed the ladies' remark and Bachchu felt there was nothing that was good in life that he had to have and that he missed. But what he missed in definite count of assuring negation was a wife.

His youth was turning into full blown manhood and it was ready to pass from that region of the perfect model state God had positioned for man to be in the prime of things in newness and he was moving forward to step into an unknown realm of life where a progressive ageing was to ride on him like a fiend with its piercing claws, taking hold of him and driving him at a faster pace towards the subduing of life to one of still flatness, and the void of not possessing a wife had started haunting him and it was pricking and discomforting.

He was not able to get a wife, because of the wretched passengers, Bachchu thought; they did not come forward to be picked up in abundance to be carried to where they ought to be taken to on his Aekka. Bachchu blamed the passengers and called them 'wretched' because they were so miserably short in numbers to be carried to places, to their destinations they were to be taken to in frequency of trips for a fair collection of a fair day's earning. And the shortfall in their numbers and the trips to places was so meagre at times that he did not earn enough, even to keep him and his horse going and keep afloat to be meeting the bare needs of life, and Bachchu thought what when he got a wife, how will she be cared for.

Then there was another worry that raised its head haunting Bachchu's reasoning, and that was, if he did bring a wife, how he will cope ridding himself of the free flow mouthfuls he spurted out at the most ill-conceived moments, which hit one person or the other, though he had no intuitive knowledge of it happening, and which happened through his saying that what he had to say, to smother his horse with the vocabulary of the most roughened slang that emerged of him all on their own, lush with slighting remarks and full of decorative *Aekkewani* terminologies of dualistic expressions that few could claim to be innovative of, what if they had a mind-set ever so fully rich in the linguistic department. It was only the expert realm of Bachchu's genius, thanks to the erratic behaviour of the mare that he of automation came out with such fanciful punchy slang at the spur of the moment, appropriate in suitability to match to the uncertain temperament of the mare that no expert of linguistics with all his/her determined individualistic expertise in any appropriateness was able to match it with and produce the like of it.

Bachchu's retort to the horse with proprietary infestations of punch and charm, with expanse in the meaning of absorption, excelled all articulation in the linguistic approaches and it appropriately cut across the horse's deliberations, subduing the horse's aggravation in right measures to drag settle her on to the course of the display of normalcy. And with it in the ultimate the horse behaved. And thanks to the repetitions of Bachchu's buoyant diminutive commands, over the period of time, she had listened these shoot outs from him that she had become attuned to them in hearing, registering and yielding to obey them and she had become a registry, and would turn her ears to be directional to absorb what they were to hear in wordiness springing out of Bachchu and his joviality.

And Bachchu, invigorated by such conditions that suited the delivery of the colloquialism with full abashing of the mare, used his loud mouth ranting, concerned him with no other vernacular of kinds than his Aekkewani slang and produced unique self-created words he was expert at, producing them freely and without inhibition when the mare misbehaved and when their liberal use was called for by the occasion. But sad as it was these were ready to ruffle one person or the other, though unintended who unfortunately happened to fit in, in the span of the meaning carried by the expression that could never be alluded as a subjugation of them or any misjudgement of Bachchu in extruding those words out of him. And however, misconstrued they were, they were never an intentional injury and the molesting means of disguised infirmity of someone even distantly removed from its intended meanings and their spans. And Bachchu's mind was plodded with fear that his vocabulary might sprinkle propensity extruding as infuriating insult by the wife, which was not meant for her.

This habit of Bachchu of addressing the mare with meaning infested, self-created words in a twisted vernacular of cutting slang, allusive in nature that he readily heaved out of him, had thoroughly penetrated into his simple conversational style and it was not under any checks and bounds of him as to when they came out of him and where they came out of him. To quote an example for illustration to the non-conversant with his spoken apt of the wealth of the store of the slang he had kept amassed in his mind's archive that revealed themselves with no articulation applied; he was bound to say to his horse if she showed any waywardness at the time of the moving off to take on to the road, as the horse was in the habit to walk slanting on to one side or there were occasions when not moving at all and twisting her body and giving jolts trying to be awkward, so Bachchu would say:

Arrat Haai, Burrat Haai, Aeinthuth Haai, Goeinthuth Haai,
Hill kay Naheen Deyt, Phus Maarat Haai.

She twists. She stiffens. She hardens herself; she pulls her muscles. She doesn't budge to move. She lets off wind off her.

If spoken in plain vernacular, interpretive of his retorts understandable to the ordinary not conversant with the slang of the region, especially with Bachchu's twists decorating it further, these words were the charming monopoly of disdain thrown at the sickening hardened carrying lots of waviness in expression, expressing and interpreting the moment-by-moment muscular distortions and contractions of the mare for which art in expressiveness was evolved, substantiating her action through word harmony. But such were the etiquettes of Bacchus's decorative slang that though the behaviour of the mare demanded that a full slang maximally released at her oddment be released, but he deliberately did not induct in words of higher degradation, such as '*Sasuri*' – a referral to the demoting of the status of mother-in-laws, so much spoken in that part of the world where Bachchu came from.

Sasusri was used for clear degradation of the addressee intended demolished, alluding and implying her connectivity with the mother-in-law. And if Bachchu had used it, it would have been for personifying the mare as the mother-in-law. This mode of speaking was frequently adopted in each such situation of disapproval, and the word was repeatedly used and it was so common an expletive used in this part of the country where Bachchu lived that it was inserted in every fifth word in the conversation, and it was used as profoundly as the word not quotable, used in frequency and repetition in the West.

And if the word Sasuri had been used by Bachchu, it was most likely quite appropriate for the class of the performance the mare was putting forward to him on these occasions. But this was beyond Bachchu to take aid of such impolite implicative and use them in his sentences, no matter how stubborn the mare was and how pressing the requirement was to get her moving and he only used the degrading words in the class of *Phus Maarat Haai* - lets off wind off her.

Now normally the simple phrase *Pus Marat Haai*, carried the meaning of: releases wind off her, and this was to mean that she was suffering from some kind of indigestion and she lets off puffs of wind voluntarily or involuntarily from her vent. But any alluding made, in the use of this word to convey the meaning in that context, if any one thought so, Bachchu made and appropriated, was making a gross mistake and a mismatch to his imagination and to his dispositional skill. In his intended use of the phrase he made, this was bordering on to the terms of philosophic intonations, and it was an outright excess on him in alluding that he meant to convey that meaning of *Phus*, as the ears heard, and the person making so blatant an accusation on Bachchu was using total indiscretion in insinuating that that inappropriateness in words were deployed by Bachchu which was impossible at his expertise level of the usage of words.

The obvious meaning alluded to his intentional conveying of thought was far removed from what Bachchu said. He was using it for its other meaning! What he meant by the use of the word *'Phus'*, was not the puffs of wind coming out with miasmic tendency from the vent of the mare, but only that she was short of energy and she was not showing enough courage and was not up to what she was supposed to be doing - putting in excelling performance in the display of good behaviour to run on the road just when she was required to do so, with passengers seated on the cart and no misgiving left to be catered.

But it was certain that this word 'Phus' if heard by someone with Urdu and Hindi language speaking and interpreting ability, and with a clear disposition to extricate meaning from it, and the person took a plunge into the intricacies of the word, going into the meanings hidden behind it, though the word was of seemingly simplistic phonetic, but if the person was to detect with a given certainty that it was directed at him or her, then there was nothing to speak of; there was bound to be trouble. And under all circumstances to say the least; if it was a lady of strict disciplinary coordinates, controlling her environmental concerns and carrying representative potentials of certain rigid mannerism, then there was nothing to speak of it, there was going to be a very big problem, right at the spot.

But to Bachchu, the word 'Phus' and those that accompanied it in the conveyance of the meaning what he wanted to convey to the mare, which he derived from the vast vocabulary of the hidden collection, residing in the dictionary of the spoken slang in the air that thrived in the environs he lived in, meant to carry no harmful meaning to anyone, who so they were and whatever their performing behaviour was.

These were only the natural means of stimulation, meant to be effective on the mare and were the masterly words of punch, intense in their power of coaxing and were the pick of the slang, used as whip to harness the mare and make her move. And without their liberal use Bachchu found the mare simply did not budge and it was not at all unusual for Bachchu to use these spurring words for the mare in frequency as repetitious as was the shifty behaviour of the mare, and the shifty behaviour of the mare was more frequent than easily ignored by Bachchu and he was dragged in and prompted rather unknowingly to be using these free flow expressions in situations he was caught in, most frequently.

And Bachchu had not the foggiest of the idea that these words were not spiritedly taken in by some who were foreign to the rich slang and were not sporty, not ready to enjoy the exhibits of the contradictive vastness in the meanings of the words and their linguistic intricacies, and were ignorant of the richness of the slang and sadly ill equipped to absorb the conveyances in the expression he was so competent at.

And Bachchu not knowing these blossoming difficulties of foreign to the slang which they sadly showed, used these artfully carved, fit for the occasion, sweetened with the sound of musical therapy, meaning carrying dexterous words, and used them at will and anywhere, and anytime all round where ever he went with his horse and cart, in the deployment of his horse and cart work.

And for those who had an apt to hear these slang, there were two places Bachchu was to be found with his Aekka – the horse and cart, one was the railway station where he spent one half of the day to pick up passengers from the trains when these arrived at the station and the other place was where he was for the rest of the time - the Aekka Stand in the town.

Bachchu's Aekka service was good. The spokes of his Aekka wheels were large and the Aekka had high seats, and the passengers enjoyed a high seat Aekka ride. They were always pleased with Bachchu's Aekka service except on occasions when the mare's mood was shoddy and they wished they were not sitting on the high seat Aekka. Because then she jolted the Aekka and the whole Aekka shook and there was no guarantee for how long the mare was to continue to jolt the Aekka and as to when she was going to revert to her working mood and take to the road, because on these occasions she preferred to aim at and kick the footboard.

However, in spite of this abomination displayed by the horse that disturbed and discontinued the composure of the passengers, of whom some even panicked to starting preparations to disembark, still many generic deliberately chose to sit on Bachchu's Aekka to listen to his routine commands that he issued repetitiously in earnest to his horse that they noted the contents of the comments he passed concomitantly on the performance of the mare all along the way, appropriated to her performing behaviour, were so generously entertaining with freedom of speech filled that men with alluring austere to be unsmiling, sought and sat stubbornly on his Aekka to steal a smile. And all the passengers never did have a dull moment while taking a ride on the Bachchu's Aekka.

-: . :-

III

THE RAILWAY STATION

VI

Bachchu for his calculating, dexterous and innovative use of the slang had earned a place of high popularity among the visitors and the travellers frequenting the use of the Railway Station among whom he was known, and was looked for by them for travel with him. And of the two places that Bachchu stood his Aekka to offer transport service and was bound to be found at one or the other of them; one was the Railway Station and the other the Town Aekka Stand. But of these two places, Bachchu's Aekka was always found at the Railway Station when the train arrival time was due. The Railway Station Aekka ground otherwise remained empty of the Aekka(s), when there was no train arrival time.

The Railway Station was the nerve centre of the town and it was a busy place. When the train times came, people rushed to the railway station from all the directions, and the station was filled with people all in their tidy, washed and clean dresses, seemly suited for the occasion of travel and to outdoor works. And though the Railway Station had the simplest stone building and only a bare minimum in structure, it spoke of its importance. It served as the vigorous artery to the outlining villages, and it spirited its function from only two rooms stone blocks structure. One room was the station master's room and the other the rest room, adjacent to each other. The rest room was for the first-class passengers, who were invariably the *Gorays* - the Whites and the rest room boasted of having all the facilities for them.

The Gorays needed a large arm frog chair in the rest room with a large mirror and a toilet with a small mirror, which it had, and the station boasted of its stallion importance. It stirred activity all round in the town, and it stood attendant at the country-wide rail track system passing, edging the town. And the station as it stood there, it was at the select place, in the middle of the town on its one flank along its length. The station had threefold long platforms, which were a guide if anyone wanted to know of its status. Three numbers of long passenger trains including fast express trains halted there at once, and the trains were the communicative arm of the British India and the station's centrality compelled all the mail trains and all the express trains; all to halt there.

The Railway Station burst into the flurry of activity (as seen in years 1944 - 45). It was a rumpus when the train arrived at the station. A great hustle and bustle took over the station. The shrieks of the hawkers, the fretting of the passengers, the hurried movements of men; all sprang up at once at that one instant. The hot tea sellers with their steamy hot *Purwa Cha-ay* call, filled the Purwa — the baked clay mug to capacity and moved swiftly around with their tea vessel, and the Purwa made a hundred frequencies singing sound as the tea was soaking in the virgin mould, singing of the uniqueness of the Purwa tea and the Purwa guaranteeing of the savour of the Purwa transferred to the tea and vouched of the Purwa's newness. The tea in the Purwa was filled to its brimming fullness, which was the speciality of the Purwa-tea-hawker at the Railway Station, and people rushed to him and warmed themselves with the Purwa tea, and people said the Purwa tea was the best of the teas.

The *Purwa*(s) were clay mugs without a handle on them. The potter cast these from the finest clay brought from the pond's basin and its sides. The mould of the Purwa was baked in the kiln, till each grain of the clay of the Purwa moulded and fused with one another and its structural purity gave the authority to the hawker to make the call of '*Purwa Cha-ay*' at   the high pitch sing song note, alternating with '*Garam Cha-ay*' - Hot Tea in sonorous syllables in a modulated pitch, especially cut and reserved for use at the railway station. This call aroused instant flurry to go running to get the Purwa tea from the hawker and people were thankful to him in the winter misty morning to be served with hot tea. Even the most dormant, sitting at the far end of the train compartments, got up on their feet at the call of the hawker and rushed to him and he obliged them with the steaming hot tea from his portable tea vessel, which carried red glowing charcoal, also burning log pieces in the lower pocket of the vessel to keep the tea sizzling hot.

The passengers were also attracted by the hawker selling *Anday Garam* – hot eggs, whose peculiar voice added a new note in the air. The Anday of those days were a rare thing. These came from the birds freely running in the open fields in the villages, all bred there to lay hard shell eggs and as tasty as the pretty looks of the chicks that came out from them. And the station with its specialities was truly special with its name **Bharwari**. It served a whole region famous for its guavas, *Qalmi Aam* - the grafted mangoes and Jamuns - the rennet.

The customers who knew of it cupped their ears to listen to the chant of '*Tazay Amrood*' - fresh guavas, and rushed to buy them at the first call of the hawker. The hawker called only once at intervals and remained busy weighing them to the customers. These were sweet and juicy guavas of soft texture and of such flavour that no region in the Land of Seasons and Songs produced the like of them. Their enormity of size, softness of flesh, sweetness and yellow colour was their uniqueness.

Then there was *Chinya Badam Wala,* the hawker sold roast groundnut or *Moong Phali,* calling out *Moong Phali Taka Pao* – groundnuts two Paisas a quarter kilo (it was two farthings a quarter kilo of groundnuts). The passengers hurried to buy the groundnut and some called him to come to their compartment window. The groundnut was fresh and crisp and the hawker paraded briskly all over the platform selling it from an open tray for all to see the quality of the groundnuts. It had crisp fulsome groundnuts with no staleness and no pony nuts hidden in their chests. The hawker sold six trays a day when the trains arrived and earned five Rupees - one Pound Sterling a month from it and he was twice as happy as the yellow turbaned *Chaukidar* of the police force.

The Chaukidar was police Ahelkar - a field worker at the lowest rung in the police hierarchy. He was paid three Rupees a month and he was assigned to take rounds of the villages under his charge at nights when everyone else was asleep. He called '*Jaagtay Raho*' - remain alert (awake) and made thieves run away with his rounds. They could not do *Naqab Zani* – making a hole in the wall of the house to enter in. And his call kept crime at bay. He reported to the *Thana* – the police station, each month or once in a fortnight or after one week when his turn of the call for reporting to the police station came. And the once-a-week reporting earned him one-rupee additional salary. The Chaukidar(s) were the police eyes and ears and they came to speak to the *Munshi* or the *Moharrir* – a constable who was picked up for his competence in Urdu writing and reading, to write the happenings in each *Aelaqa* or sector of which the Chaukidar spoke of their status.

The Moharrir or the writer scribed the statement of the Chaukidar; how many babies were born, who died in the village, what men moved in and what men went out from the area and who they were. The Chaukidar had to tell especially of the movements of the men with criminal records, called the '*History Sheeters*'. And all the Chaukidar(s) returning to the Thana one after the other stated of the occurrences in their Aelaqa – the sector and it was recorded in the register.

The three Rupees a month that the Chaukidar was paid sufficed him to meet his simple needs. The monetary strength of the Rupee was formidable, it was minted in sterling silver and the Chaukidar prided on himself for his position, though he was only a part-time *Ahelkar*, yet his work was important in the running of the administration. He established the authority of the police in his area. The Police Constable was one step higher to the Chaukidar in the hierarchy of the police, he took thirteen Rupees a month and he was full time Ahelkar of the police, and he was responsible for order in his circle of the villages. He had a number of villages under his charge, but went there only when he was assigned as police official on duty and these were meticulous thought forming rules to run a government efficiently.

The labourer took four Anas a day. The Raj and Mistry - the builder and artisan, eight Anas a day and the Rupee fetched a load full of grains and grocery. And *Damrdi* – the copper coin one eighth of a *Paisa*, and *Dukrda* – the copper coin one fourth of a paisa or pica, equalled in monetary value to the farthing, which had started fading out, but the *Dhhela* and *Taka* – the half pica and two picas copper coins were still weighty coins. In three hundred Rupees the villagers built comfortable mud house from clean, live and fragrant clay soil, brought from the pond's bed by the labour. Gold was sold at twenty Rupees a *Tola*: equal to eleven grams by weight, and silver could be purchased at the rate of two Tolas for one Rupee. The government survey of the year 1875 said the per capita income then was 2 Pound sterling per year in the Land of Seasons and Songs and peoples were contended, peaceful and purity full. They died early and lived a cheerful life walking and taking part in activities when they died and were assured of finding two yards of land free of cost for burial.

When the trains arrived at the station, the passengers from the train rushed to buy the eateries. They were in a frantic hurry and everything they bought was without need to deeply examining what they bought. They had a cheery confidence that whatever they bought at the station was assuredly good and they were never disappointed. Their only worry was to hurry back to their seats lest the train moves off and left them behind, since the trains stopped for only three minutes at the stations. It had a long, long journey ahead, and they rushed back to their compartments, manoeuvring and zigzagging through the crowed at the platform as soon as they had ceased the goodly thing they wanted. They hurried to get to their compartments before the guard waived his green flag and whistled for the train to move off. And stations after stations, there were regional specialities. There was Jang-Shahi kay *Laddoo, Mathura Kay Peyrday, Multan Ka Helwa, Banaras Ki Rewrdi,* Jung Shahi Kay Moti Choor Kay Laddoo all famous and tasty specialities sold by the hawkers at their respective stations.

All these events; the hawkers making their shrieking calls in their high pitched modulated tone, fashioned to reach to the far end of the train to the buyers and they rushing to him, and the hustling and humming noise of the people, the hurried time bound boarding and getting off from the train by the passengers, some loading their luggage in the train and some unloading these out of the train, the whistle of the Guard and his waving of the green flag, signalling the locomotive driver to move the train, the activation signal bells in the station master's room and their clanging metallic ball noise, the waving and the farewell bidding by the escorts to the travelling relative or friend wishing them safe journey, created a unique scene at the railway station and this was the Railway Station of Bharwari.

The spectre of the activity lasted for as long as the train stopped and then started to move off and after that the hustle and bustle died down, leaving the platform a solitary place, bereft of people. This spontaneous eruption of activity at the railway station was incredulous for its intensity and it was only to be found at the railway stations of the Land of Seasons and Songs and it repeated itself many times in the day, when the trains arrived and left. It brought abrupt cheeriness at the railway stations and abrupt calm of dullness. It was a display of the nature of its people and their customs. And though these railway stations could not compete in grandeur with the showpieces in structure and intensity of traffic of the railway stations like of the Grand Central Terminal of New York or the London's St. Pancras or the Paris' Gare d'Orsay - now a museum, but the railway stations of the Land of Seasons and Songs were unique in their display of social life and there was no event to match it which integrated people as one, thanks to the Railway Stations.

The Railway Station of Bharwari transferred all the liveliness it generated to the town, and the town was thankful for it. And though the town had its own flurry and significance and spoke of its history it had hidden behind its existence from its past, disguising it in its present, it still was a sleepy town. Though it was there in its trace in the times of the Imperial Mauryas 322-185 BC when Chandra Gupta Morya established an organised administration, also in the times of Guptas 320-455 AD, who lifted the Land of Seasons and Songs from the ancient past and transferred it to the medieval present, also it was there when it was passed on to the Rajpoot Maharajas of the decaying past with their times they shared between them in rule, with patches of glowing and fair glowing periods from 6th century to 1027, and then also, it was there when the Maharajas handed it over to the Ghaznavid.

And Ghaznavid 997 AD, handed it to the Ghauris 1191 – 1240 AD, and them to the Aibaks and them to the Bulbans and them to Khiljis and them to Thugluqs 1320 - 1413 AD, and them to the Sayyeds 1414 – 1450 and them to Lodhis 1451-1526 AD, who passed it on to the short lived dynasties of the painstaking and impressionist ruler Sher Shah Suri, until the town was transferred with its destiny into the hands of the Majestic Moghuls, from whom it ultimately landed into the lap of the *Gorays* - the British Whites and in their times the virtual state of the Nawab of Ralah sprang up, with the English elites still the masters, playing the tunes of Scottish Bagpipes in the times of Bachchu Aekkewan, who plied his Aekka in the town and helped the town with his endeavours and inputs and his unexpurgated talk with his horse.

کیسی دریا دلی تھی تسکین و امن کی
باغ باغ آدمی تھا گو کمزوری تھی پیسہ کی
نہ کوئی ہاتھ پھیلاتا تھا مانگنے کو
نہ غیرت اجازت دیتی تھی ہاتھ پھیلانے کی

سیّد اطہار حسین

Kaaisi Darya Dili Thhi Taskeen-o Aman Ki
Baagh Baagh Aadmi Thha Go Kamzoari Thhi Paaisay Ki
Na Koee Haath Phaailata Thha Mangnay Ko
Na Ghaairat Aejazat Deti Thhi Haath Phaailanay Ko

What a generosity was of satisfaction and of peacefulness
Man was filled with happiness though there was weakness of
    money
Neither any one was spreading hand to beg
Nor self-esteem gave permission to spread hand to beg

-:. .:-

III

THE NAWAB OF RALAH

VII

The Nawab of Ralah symbolised in the book is an ideal ruler of Godly principles. His was a virtual state in the Land of Seasons and Songs, where peace and serenity ruled the mind and the genetic of the people, and where goodness in the state warded off all calamities of all forms, and the minds of the people ruled the places and their purity chastised and tempered the national character to exhibit divine virtues. Murder was unknown and theft if done was to feed the belly and not to rob to deprive the other of his possession. And meritocracy operated. And God was pleased with the His Highness the Nawab. And Nawab was a descendant of the Sayeds and a servant of the Aehlebaait of the Prophet of God Hazrat Mohmmad Mustafa SAWW. And the name of the Nawab was His Highness Bannay Sayed Athar Husain Naqvi Nawab of Ralah. And his motto was submission to Aayet 5:8:

'O faithful to please God be prepared to give witness for the pleasure of God and the enmity of any tribe may not involve you that you start doing injustice, you do justice this very is very near to forbearance and fear God because what you do God certainly knows that.'

In the Nawabdom of the Nawab, crime was non-existent, terrorists did not exist, and peace prevailed and people were God fearing and no judge existed who did not serve justice and left an offender unpunished and no politician existed who did politics to get rich. Politician did politics to serve and no one appeased one preaching but not himself acting. It was a theocratic state and there were no factions of Islamic sects and there was only one sect of Islam, where respect to the venerated of religions was supreme. In this state its

Nawab of Ralah His Highness Nawab Bannay Sayed Athar Husain Naqvi

towns were filled with peace and contentment, and its people showed fine spiritual characteristics, and kindness was visible at each corner and at each bend in the life of the Nawabdom and the people all good and loving to each other. Its chief town was Bharwari with its quiet importance and the capital Ralah was straddling the suburbs and the vicinities like a rider on a beautiful horse. Such was the idealistic state of the Nawab of Ralah.

The town of Bharwari with its significance and its ancient history in the apparel it donned and the suburbia status it enjoyed, with its faint trace of its passing glories of the eras of the past, was a high perched town of merit and ascendancies. It was a *Mundi* where granaries were bought and sold. But people struggling for survival, which was evidencing its existence of no more than a collection of a few unimposing brick houses and only the aggrandising adequacies of the road side pockets of sellers of eateries and green grocers selling berries, water melons, carrots and vegetables in their *Jhabis* - the scuttles made of the *Kardein* - the stems of lentil plant *Arhar*, and some made from the bamboo strips. The town though had a post office and a kitchen restaurant with two *Takhts* – the flat wooden bed-stead for seating men for eating their meals. The restaurant for its roof was covered by thatched shade of long grass. These were stacked on cross beams which were placed on the support logs of sturdy wood.

403

The customers placed their plates of food on the Takht – broad bench to eat. The criterion of the measure of the bigness of a town in the Land of Seasons and Songs was that how many *Helwaee(s)* it had, which also showed the economic strength of the people and such towns were loved for spreading fumes of good and pleasant smell of frying in the Ghee, and sweet smell of the sweets. Bharwari had one Helwaee, and his shop was lavish with sweets and it liberally spread the smell of the Ghee Puris fried and customers swarmed at the shop. And there were granary merchants with their varieties of heaps of grain, and also shoe shops and *Bania* shops selling spices, grains and Settu and *Misry* – dough from sugar. And there was the *Mahajan's* big shop where cloth for shirts and *Bundees* was sold in the measure of yards.

The Mahajan(s) were recognised for their successes in business of buying and selling merchandise and for that reason all the Mahajans were objects of respect. The villagers going to their shops, sat there in an orderly manner to get the cloth cut in yards. All the cloth for *Dhoti*, *Lungee*, *Bundi* and *Kurta* was sold at the Mahajan's shop. The *Latthda* - the fine long cloth and the *Markeen* - the coarse long cloth, came from the cotton mills in Lancashire, rolled on cardboard, smelling of newness, and these were sold at the controlled price and the villagers had to sit patiently and not spread out over the spaces of the shop till the cloth was cut and given to them by the Mahajan's shop attendants.

These assets of the town, in its dreary quietness but harmless cosy environment and unassuming posture gave recognition to the town of its importance. Though it had only one straight road passing through its length from the middle of the town and scattered single-story buildings of red bricks standing on to one side of the road and a few houses pot-marking, up from the flat land they occupied that looked at the town, gave it the status nearing to the defines of a town.

The town however was generous and fed the needs of many of its associate villages that stood in homage to it, stretched around at distances where from brisk walking men came on foot, on bullock carts and on donkeys, with their granaries from their fields and barns, hurling them into the town and did their selling and buying. But everyone who came to the town had to hurry and finish the business before the darkness censured the town. Since only the kerosene oil lamps with the exception of one or two gas lanterns in the shops lit the street and the town length, and illuminated the face of the town.

The surging power of electricity had not reached to the town yet, to brighten the face of the town with the flick of a switch and help the town eschew the darkness spread there. The roadside oil lamp-posts were non-existent as they stood in the towns of similar stature to decorate the town and light its face, by putting their spirited flickering glow to illuminate the road for men coming to the town to feel cheery. The light cheered, and the darkness dulled the spirit. This town was bereft of the road side lamp-posts, though others of its status had one, of which they had fancy varieties, even though they could not boast of owning a railway station on the loop of prestigious railway track of the Land of Seasons and Songs.

But the good thing about the town was; it had broken-stones compacted road without tar or bitumen on it. The horse and cart drivers found the bitumen was a pain after it melted in the heat of the blaring sun. It stuck to the rims of the wheels and hindered it to turn and the horse and cart drivers preferred broken-stone roads without bitumen. The wheels turned freely on them. And although the horse-shoes wore out faster on them, hooves getting knocks and getting chipped off on the bare stones, but the horse and cart men knew they couldn't have the best of both worlds at the same time and they had to be contended with one that came their way. But they agreed, there were differences among them on the merits of the roads. However, all preferred the bituminous road in winters when the bitumen hardened giving a fine smooth road and the compacted broken-stones roads in summers when the bitumen that melted was not there.

But there was one thing the horse and cart drivers never disagreed on, and it carried their consensus opinion that the soft Kachcha roads leading to the villages were the worst for the wheels when rain poured. They were then at these times plain horror - a lumpish thud, worse than the heated up sticky bituminous tar covered road in the town. And to Bachchu and to every one of the horses and cart drivers' fraternity they were a harrying horror and each of them suffered in equal measures.

Bachchu had to be up early in the mornings when the stars still glowed in their dim glows, faintly twinkling but decorating the canopy of the jade sky and the approaching morning and the streaks of the rays of the sun were in recess, hidden behind the line of the horizon, and the remnant of the stars were studding the sky. Bachchu had to be up just then. He had cut the demand of the sleep to a minimum and it stood him in good stead. His health and physique were all the better for it, good and at prime for work and his mind suspended itself in the state of alertness, ready to guide him in the adversities when his horse was going to be stuck on the road, trying to be awkward.

And it was only Bachchu's domain of sturdiness in physique and health radiance that in spite of his sleep punctuated by yells shooting off him of 'Catch her, Catch her', involuntarily making exclamation from the deep gorges of the throat of his mouth while asleep, cajoling the passers-by to catch the mare which he never stopped not seeing in his dreams, and she not stopping running away to the fields, and the yelling by all measures that should have had their tolls on him bringing in degradation in the assimilation of energy when he slept, needing seeking quiet serenity to recoup energy, instead it taxing energy and he physically interrupted in the sleep by individuals invading his sleep by shaking and poking him and he rudely woken up by the most affected for his yelling and kicked, still despite these handicaps he was up early before the dawn came and always felt a vigour when he was up, and his anatomy was all primed and charged, forcing him to dash to the field to do what the call of nature demanded of him to do.

The birds sat on the branches of the trees, twittered and chirped. The crickets poked their heads out from mud, shrilled and peeped. The frogs flashed their eyes from the grass, croaked and squawked. The fire flies let off flashes of light brightening spaces around with their fractions of candle-power in their tails; all provoking Bachchu's attention. But Bachchu had little to do with these invigorations at work to oblige him be thankful to nature, incessantly imploring his attention and trying their best to motivate him think of God's purpose of creation and of the nature's wonders around him, reminding him of God's justice controlling their existence. But they mattered little to Bachchu.

Bachchu's mind was set to happening nothing other than what he ought to be doing. He could only think of the survival of his self and of his horse and considered the frivolities of nature excessively scouring his brain to come out of the preoccupation of his mind and he was not ready to take anything else which was contrary to his planning and purpose. These, attractions, God made, begging his attention to divert his brain towards them was of no substance. He had little time to pay attention to other introversions and had time only to pay attention to the intentionality of his mind's preoccupation that thought only of his scholastic methods of the *Aekkewani* – the horse and cart driving.

The disconcertion associated with the non-worship of God - not spending one moment of thought into the purpose of creation was a dividend of purposelessness in life, said the Great Teachers. It always put one in a tearing rush, always having him fighting with problems. But Bachchu said there were more important demands than worship and spending his morning prime time in it. And his worship was excelling when in his routines he excelled in the exclusivity of the horse and cart professionalism. And Bachchu rushed to attend to the needs of the horse rather than to the methodised worship. The think cap worn to discover God's purpose of creation, Bachchu said will be worn later, when opulence visits him and gives him profoundness and strengthens his didactic and Bachchu said:

شب چو عقد نماز بر بندم
چہ خورد بہ امداد فرزندم

Shab Cho Aqde Namaaz Bar Bandam
Che Khurad Ba Imdaad Farzandam

When I want to pray at night

I always think about what I shall feed my child tomorrow morning

This was so as Bachchu did not know of the secrets of a God related life consideration and here is what I have to say through my Ruba-ee – the quatrain:

مشک و عنبر سے جڑی قسمت ہے
خدمت خلق گر فرض و غائیت ہے
کیسی سادہ ہے زندگی خود کی
جب محبّت حصولِ عبادت ہے

407

روح داد بخش گر عمل والی ہے
روئداد نہ کھولے قدرت دم بدم حامی ہے
ناز قدرت کرے اس پر ایسے اطہار
جیسے والدِ پسرِ باادب پہ واری ہے

سیّد اطہار حسین

Mushk -o Anbar Say Jurdi Qismat Haai
Khidmat-e Khalq Gar Farz-o Ghayet Haai
Kaaisi S adah Haai Zindagee Khud Ki
Jub Mohabbat Husool-e Aebadat Haai

Rooh Daad Bukhsh Gar Amal Wali Haai
Ru-aydad Na Kholay Qudrat Dum Badum Hami Haai
Naaz Qudrat Karay Oos Peh Aaisay Athar
Jaaisay Walid Pisar-e Ba Adab Peh Wari Haai
Joined with Mushk and Anber is fate
Service to humanity if is duty and objective
How very simple is one's life
When love is the gist of the worship

Soul the just if active is doing duty
Providence not opens to analyse doings, it is at each step his helper
The providence so prides at him Athar
Like the father is sacrificial on his obedient son

But Bachchu's dictate of mind was so cut that it remained preoccupied with the entanglements of occupations demanding his immediate attention and he remained occupied with concerns for the mare and was completely dedicated to her wellbeing. He returned after he was free from the call of nature to rush to the mare to give her a quick *Kharaira* – the brushing with the curry-comb, on her neck, shoulder, back, belly and croup, and the horse's chief asset the legs. He rubbed her to remove the sweat deposits on her coat and massaged her to open her pores and warmed her up, and this was the preliminary in preparing her for work ahead of her over the day.

He stroked her fore-lock and folded her legs, lifting each to inspect the condition of the iron-shoes, nailed in the hooves and this was very much liked by the mare. She obtained a momentary relaxation with her feet lifted and her knees folded and her hoofs taken in hand for inspection of their soundness, and Bachchu did not disappoint her. He then brought new grass to her and gave her soaked gram, mixed with bran and wheat husk in the manger and let her eat that in her own good time.

Bachchu then tidied the horse's lodging, this was one thing he was not neglectful of, lifting the horse's overnight dropping. His mare's lodging was in the open, in full view of the village folks. All the villagers passed from there and no one would like to see the bed littered and untidy. The tiny flies bred fast in the dropping if left lying and Bachchu always carried it to the dung heap of the village to let it dry there. It became dried cake and was used in the kiln by the *Kumhar* – the potter. The potter burnt it in the kiln and potted jars, pots and clay toys which was sold by him so very cheap because of the free kiln fuel.

-: . :-

III

THE BLESSED TILAK MAN

VIII

The well in the village of Bachchu belonged to all the village folk. They were thankful for this vital necessity catering the need of all of the villagers. Its sweet water was a blessing. It was given to them as present by the Blessed Tilak Man - the merchant with a *Tilak* - one finger mark of yellow paste of Sandalwood drawn vertical on his forehead. He was seen with this symbol he drew for good luck on his forehead after his morning prayer. The Blessed Tilak Man nursed a *Choanti* - a lock of hair, he had grown at the back of his head that distinguished him further. He took due care of it and it shined, gracefully curled. He had built the well for the villagers, after divining and prospecting for sweet water and the well was dug out where the prospector's pointed the earth that sweet water was lying under. The well was dug and a square platform was built around the well rendered with stone slabs, which was called *Chabootra*. And though the Blessed Tilak Man was gone, and no one knew where he went, but he was remembered for his great present he had given to the village. It was generous good work. And it was his magnanimous good-hearted intention that the earth had sprung out sweet water from the well.

All that was known of the Blessed Tilak Man, was that he came to the village once a while on his large spokes Aekka driven by his *Saees* – the groom. The Saees always stood behind him. And when his Aekka came in the village, there was a great excitement, the villagers gathered to honour him for his visit. He wore a sea-gull white *Bundi* and a sea-gull white *Dhoti*, and nothing more was known of him. But the man with the Tilak Mark on his forehead had earned a place of reverence in the hearts of the villagers, and each villager remembered

410

him with affection and blessed his soul each time they used the sweet water of the well and the well was the dearest of the possession of the villagers.

After tiding up the horse bedding, Bachchu went to the well and drew a pail of water from the well and threw it on him, the water was warm. The sheath of water enveloped him with its silk touch, and it was therapeutic and a rush of pleasure surged through him. The entire smother that had stuck on Bachchu all through his passenger carrying run-rounds; the salty sweat drying up on his body, the incessant obstinate flies leaving behind their dirty feet marks and their mess on his feet, arms, calves and then the attacks of dust of indeterminate whirlwind freely roving all through the town that covered him with the layers of dust, all were washed off, and he was clean and fresh, now ready to be cutting through the dust and muck met in the day.

Bachchu was at once thankful to the kind Nature to provide warm water in the mornings when it was chilly and cool water during the day from the well when it was hot and Bachchu thanked the Blessed Tilak Man for building the well. After taking the bath, Bachchu entertained him with one pot-full of the mineral rich water of the well with a piece of Gurd which his Aunt in her days when she lived in this world kept in the *Matki* - the small pitcher that she had left for Bachchu and Bachchu always replenished it, since after she was gone. If there was some *Misry* – the solidified sugar in the cloth pouch, a relic again his aunt had left for him, he would take a piece from it in preference, and replenish the pouch with Misry as often as he could.

The Misry was expensive; Bachchu bought it from the *Perchoon* shop in the town. The tiny shops in his village did not keep Misry, it was something special and only the Bania sold the dough of the Misry in the town. It had moist softness and had pleasing taste. The Bania said it was made from sugar cane juice concentrate, with a drop of sweet oil, some arrowroot and liberal Kewra essence, and the concentrate was bedded to solidify, which turned into the dough of Misry and it was laudable. Bachchu chewed a piece of the Misry and sensed it coat his mouth with sweetness and he absorbed it, letting its taste dissolve in his mouth and let its lingering trace last long round his mouth. And the sweet mineral water of the well provided further nourishment and there was nothing amiss not to start the day. And Bachchu started his day with thankfulness for the rich shedding of favours the Nature made from its lap to fill the poor's need.

Bachchu always closely inspected the harness to see if it needed any mending, before harnessing the horse. The tugs and the bands took strain all day and needed inspection. When in the town, he will take the horse and the cart to the *Mochi* – the cobbler if any mending was needed. The cobbler was his friend and he knew how to mend them. He was a versatile man and he also shaved and trimmed the hooves of the horses, and nailed the iron shoes on the hooves and the horse and cart men did not have to pay a large sum to him for his services.

Bachchu patted the mare with affection before leaving for the town. He guided the iron bit in her muzzle and the sensitive moment for the horse was over, then he pulled the bridle, backing her to the cart affectionately and hitched her to it and with that done; both Bachchu and the mare were ready to begin the day for what it had in store for them. Bachchu only made the familiar sound of the 'Keqhue Keqhue' that the mare knew what it meant and where to go, and she started to take the determined steps with an air of assumed importance that was akin to all the journeys she took cheerfully in the mornings for the town. And it was in the horses' nature to show some jolliness to run when they were put to run after a lapse and rest, if they had nothing to hold in complaint in their bellies and the mare did exactly that.

Bachchu did not come across any passenger to be picked all the way to the town. It was all an empty field of land, only crops and rows of Mango and Jamun trees stood on the one side of the muddy road on which the Aekka ran and he only heard the sound of the lurching of the Aekka as it ran in the stillness around him and heard it rebound from the Jamun and the Mango trees' trunks reaching to his ears like piece of music repeated rhythmically. And he thought of one pleasure then in this state of mind that he so longed for in the mornings; it was the crisp Purees and Bhaji of the Helwaee at his shop.

The Helwaee freshly turned out the Purees from the cauldron and the Bhaji he made in another cauldron and sold these hot and savoury. He did something to the Purees and the Bhaji that the cluster of customers swarmed at his shop and the hum and the buzz of the customers and the aroma of the frying Puree travelled far reaching to Bachchu on his way to the town. The flavour of the frying Purees in Ghee entered his nostrils heightening desire for it to entertain himself and Bachchu drove the horse straight to the Helwaee's shop and jumped out of the cart. And he did not forget to pat the mare which was to wait by the shop from where he and the horse could see each other.

Bachchu hopped in the Helwaee's shop and there when his turn came, received his crisp Puris and fluid Bhaji from the Helwaee on the Banana leaf and his fingers twitched to deal with the ravishing thing at once. It was a compliment to the Helwaee for his recipe that such taste of the Purees he produced. The Helwaee served the Puris and the Bhaji on a fresh, clean piece of banana leave piece and Bachchu did not leave a tiny trace of the Purees or the Bhajee on the Banana leave and had every bit of it divulged and transferred to the recesses of his stomach where they should be gone to invigorate the functionary veins of his vast enervated complexes of the frame of his body that needed these to nourish and energize them in whatever quantity, the means of a horse and cart driver would afford them.

It was only when the passengers were a lush crop to be carried all day to their destinations on the to and fro trips that Bachchu could spare a few copper coins for buying crisp and delicious *Jalaibi*(s) from the Helwaee. The Helwaee squeezed the Jalaibi mix dribbling from its pouch and made a spiral in the heated Ghee in the cauldron. It fried the Jalaibi to a measured brownness, then he dipped it in the sugar syrup and it turned into the delicious Jalaibi. The Jalaibis were so delicious that Bachchu could swear he did not want the guilt and gold, but the Jalaibis. And he attributed it to the earnings from the blessed passengers.

When the Jalaibi was weighed and handed over to Bachchu by the purist Helwaee on the dough of the banana leaf, hot and sweet, smelling of the cow ghee, out from the cauldron, soaked and dripping the sugar syrup, a something at the correct temperature, of golden colour and exuberant in sweetness, he thanked his two wheeled horse and cart for the very best attainable in life. And Bachchu with satisfaction spread across his face, with its glow radiating off him was more than assured, what a good thing life was, and what not it had in store to delight man.

The mare on these occasions was inquisitive. She glanced at him once in a while from where she was standing to see what Bachchu was having at the Helwaee's shop, and when she saw Bachchu was enjoying Jalaibis, she immediately began to think of the earnings, whether it was spent equitably on her and whether her share had reached to her in grass and feed in appropriate measure. And if she felt she had been in any way deprived of her share in the split of the earnings, she immediately flung two kicks to the footboard when Bachchu arrived.

Bachchu was all too familiar with the drama that unfolded when he treated him with Jalaibi. Because no matter how secretly he negotiated the fares with the passengers, it was thanks to her days, when the mare was with the Elite Englishman where she had feasted herself so well, and so much of fine meadow grass she had gorged that it had done lots of good to her. It had sharpened her wits into the extraordinary in seeing and hearing sound clear and it had equipped her with a build of a strong body and dexterity in her head. Her eyes and ears had become sharp and flawless, as perfect as the fresh shiny blade of grass with its symmetry that nature had taken care in producing it with cognition, and it perceived the lightest sway of the breeze, that made it dance, so did respond the mare's ears that could pick the faintest of the sound of the fare negotiated and its fixation and her eyes by the scrutiny of the number of the passengers riding the cart, whose bars were on her shoulders, commanded the neuron in her body connected to brain to signal the calculation of the total income in fare that was coming. And now she wanted something better than grass – Moti Choor Kay Laddoo to add worthiness to the feed deviated from the normal.

The mare in seeing could penetrate her deep gaze on the objects with a searching look, and in listening grasp up to the last words of the secretive most talk going behind her, way out of the range of the normally endowed, and her build of the body reflected in the bangs she could give to the footboard with the lightening loud thuds and thumps to draw attention of Bachchu. Her impartiality arousing resentment in inequality of distribution of the earning was stronger than her affiliation with Bachchu and unless this was removed through some unique formula, producing replacement, something like Gurd or Laddoo, she was not going to stop banging.

The mare had a glistening on her coat. Her muscle and brain had turned incredibly agile and piercing in functioning. Her mind was extremely accurate. And she could catch within the purview of vision and that of audibility, anything with perfect precision and never miss a thing even when the occurrence was way off at location out of her sight. On seeing the number of passengers, and after scrutinising their bearings and screening their vulnerability to Bachchu's dexterity, and monitoring and listening to the negotiated fares, she could tell with absolute accuracy, how much Bachchu was going to collect at the end of the journey and her share of feed was calculated by her.

And she immediately visualised she deserved finer things than grass. The mare behaved even if Gurd was served to her, otherwise, there was bound to be trouble and her kicking away of the footboard was exactly in proportion to the amount she imagined she was mistreated and plundered. But this sensory cognition of the mare of uneven distribution of the share was a fig of her imagination. It was ridiculous to think that Bachchu could make distribution not applying fairness. However to pacifying a misled beast who was his partner and for his name's acquittal from anyone's figment of imagination having notions that Bachchu was rarefying him in his unchanging fairness, and that the prorating of the distribution of the shares he had made was inaccurate, and that the mare was deprived of any portion of her due share of which there was no possibility, still for precaution, Bachchu stroked the mare on her forelock and said, 'Hoar, Hoar - calm down, calm down, let go of your anger. There is a good filly; I will make it up for you.'

Bachchu thereafter, immediately dug his hand in his pocket in the recess of his Bundi and pulled out from the reserve silver coins he kept for emergencies - those coming as epidemic - as eye infection, or virus with fever or such enemies of health which made a horse and cart driver a dump for a few uncertain days. And Bachchu would like a responsible realist set at solving the problem created by the mare and proceeded to buy what the mare liked to be entertained with.

The money Bachchu kept in the recess pocket was mostly needed besides illnesses, also to cushion his days of some eventual layoff periods of non-income, and for fines. The fines were paid as penalties by the horse and cart drivers for offences, as determined by the law enforcers. All the horse and cart drivers kept a reserve with them and so did Bachchu. He would draw from the untouchable reserve to buy a lump of Gurd for the mare, bought by him that same moment. Then he filled split-gram with husk mix as feed for the munch of the mare he carried in her nose-bag over her muzzle behind her ears and the Gurd he fed her from his hand which pleased the mare, but not entirely unless she was also given repeated pat on her neck and a stroking on her forelock to make up for the excess, she imagined was made against her.

The ability to draw money from the purpose-marked reserve, spoke of the status of the horse and cart drivers vis-à-vis those carrying scuttles slung on their shoulders on pole ends going round as pedlars, selling fresh vegetables they brought direct from the farmer's harvested fields to the customer's doors, or those selling 'Gurd Ki Putti' – the flat sheets made from the Gurd-syrup with sprinkles of roast peanuts, or those peddlers and sellers selling Rewrdi – the sugar concentrate knitted with Kewra essence and arrowroot, covered with sesame in blobs.

The Rewrdi hawker sold the Rewrdi with heightened pride, announcing of its crispiness, guaranteeing of its shooting out bursts of fragrance of Kewra shoot in the mouth at each crunch, and the Gajak hawker what he sold was the crusty rosette biscuits. He made these mouth filling delicacies from the white sugar or from the brown sugar concentrate after knitting it with a copious quantity of crushed sesame. These were the typical of the populist nibbles, and the hawkers sold considerable quantities of it, but still the horse and cart driver outdid them in the class distinction and in money earning.

The horse and cart drivers carried more reserve with them than any of the hawkers and they were again high on the rung of social ladder in comparison to the loaders in the *Mundi*, who carried sacks of wheat, rice or lentils and other grains on their back, in and out of the granary shops to deliver the sack to the customers' houses or did *Begaar* (labour hired for carriage of a load for one off job). The amount of reserve held by each of these hard-working men was the indicator of their social status in relation to one another.

The sturdiness of monetary standing of one over the other, each one of them understood of each other. And all these treats that Bachchu gave to the mare from his reserve were out of the gracious generosity and a bold gesture shown by Bachchu to please the mare rather than her due that she ever deserved. And that spoke of the good temper Bachchu kept with the mare and this he did so that there was no foot-dragging by her when she was called upon to get moving after the passengers had seated on the cart. She had to begin moving then at once as soon as the passengers were settled, and when she was ordered to move.

Bachchu charged the fares from the passengers not more than the passengers willingly paid for the journey, and Bachchu showed flexibility in his fare charging. He had fixed different rates of fares for different passengers. He would charge the highest of the fare from those who were out on a spree, travelling for enjoyment, and would charge a low fare from those who were going out on their daily run of work and the lowest fare from those travelling on a stricken journey, the journey forced on them for reasons beyond their control that could not be seen into, and the journey was not out of their free will that they were travelling. The nature of the journey that the passenger embarked on was adjudged by the trained eyes of Bachchu, and the trained eyes of Bachchu had attained absolute accuracy in gauging the true status of each passenger's journey purpose. And Bachchu placed each passenger in the appropriate fare bracket and charged only accurate fare commensurate with the passenger's journey type.

But there were occasions when the trained eyes of Bachchu faltered and then there was a fair haggling, verging on to a row that erupted in the course of the fixation of the fare. And this haggling and wrangle was all picked up by a seasoned passenger who knew every bit of the details of the fares in vogue and remembered in absolute terms what only twelve moons back he had paid and what he paid before that. And he felt free to do a fair bit of molesting and even clobbering of Bachchu as the fare demanded in his eyes was every bit exceeding that in vogue and was in his un-faltered knowledge active and safe within his memory system. On such occasions Bachchu having been struck by the falters of his judgement and confounded by the unflinching superior memory of the passenger had to go back to his first principles of fare charging, and rescued himself from the debacle by accepting what fare the passenger offered to him.

The Nawab of Ralah, who was ruler of this part of the country, approved this system of fare charging in his country, which was a payment of fare by the passengers, according to the pleasure they drew from the trip. The Nawab was inclined to think that the horse and cart drivers were the best judge to determine the extent a passenger was out enjoying his journey, and they were allowed to fix the fares and also make adjustments in cases when it had to be done on the vehemence of a passenger if he had his own views about the fare. And whether if these distempering argumentative settlements hampering the passenger readied the passenger to do the clobbering of the horse and cart drivers, the Aekkewans had to yield. But the Nawab had strict laws in the Nawabdom to avoid such situations of doubts and featherweight arguments arising between horse and cart drivers and the passengers were to entail no retaliation. If argument arose out of the vehemence of the passengers: the horse and cart drivers were to give in, in these situations.

And the Nawab was immensely appreciative of the horse and cart drivers and of men driving the oxen drawn bullock carts - the *Baail-Garees* for carrying granary, blocks of stones, bricks, lime and such heavy loads and goods requiring muscle power for lifting and transporting these. And the Nawab had a special praise for the genteel drivers caring the Baail-Gardi carriage – the oxen pulled carriage drivers, deploying their care in carrying the children to schools in their oxen pulled carriages, with roof and seats and the safety door, with pedestal to enter in the carriage and leave the carriage.

The Baail-Gardi carriage drivers took tender-age school children, mainly little girls to school. The service of the oxen pulled carriage drivers; taking the children to school and bringing them safely back to their homes was considered meritorious service in the Nawabdom and they were allocated a place of distinction in the Nawabdom for their genteel ways of tugging in the children to their seats and opening the door and daintily helping them out of the carriage and bringing them to their respective houses. They wore pink turban of distinction on their heads by which they were readily recognized in the Nawabdom and they were given appreciative look by all, wherever they passed from, driving their oxen carriage.

Also, the Nawab was very appreciative of the men carrying materials on their heads – the *Beggar*(s) – the handy men picked from the Mundi to carry loads and bundles on small tips and the Nawab was particularly appreciative of the *Kahar*(s), the men lifting the *Dolee*(s) – the sedan chairs on their shoulders and also large palanquins carrying *Begemat* – the genteel ladies in Par-dah on social visits, to their neighbours' houses.

The Kahar(s) helped keep the dignity maintained of the nobility in the Nawabdom. They were totally indispensable to the gentry when a visit across the town of a social nature was intended and the place was far for their dignified self to walk on foot and expose their finenesses to be traversing without availing a ride to mount on or be carried in it. And it was not a comforting sight for all to look at such dignitaries to be without a ride, since all became concerned; worrying with speculates, if any mishap had hit that the unfortunate dignified elite that he was walking on foot without availing a ride.

The Nawab was grateful to all these hard-working men for the carriage of men and goods and he considered them all greatly contributing to running the brisk social and the commercial aggrandise of the Nawabdom. Which thanks to their contribution was on the flourish and the Nawabdom was enjoying peace and prosperity that was a source of contentment to its people and to His Excellency the Nawab. People were thankful to the Nawabdom and cheerful with a show of unity and discipline, and there was order all round in the Nawabdom and it glittered with their peaceful citizenry and the orderly living and their rectitude towards each other.

The Nawab was a man of letters and a man of straight virtue and of outstanding qualities and pious habits. He deliberated for the advancement of the culture of open heartedness in matters in his Nawabdom and honour for the name Mohammad, Ali, Fatimah, Hasan, and Husain; this was part of justice and had set a system of justice in the Nawabdom, where justice was served immediate. The Nawab believed justice delayed was no justice. And the Nawab had order prevailing in his Nawabdom. There was neither killing nor shame, nor begging by the easy money collectors, nor encroachers on the roadsides with their goods illegally occupying space meant for walking and men loitering on the road crossings. Nor there were imposters and swindlers, promising chunk of profits to investors and taking hold of their savings and divorcing them of what they invested by robbing them. Nor there was cluttering of the roads by the push carts with sale goods and only flimsy articles on these, littering these roads and fleecing the customers by selling nonstandard merchandise on soaring prices. Nor there were unscrupulous shop owners occupying greater portion of the pavements meant, placing their goods there meant for walking men. And there was no profiteering and no snatch and grab in the Nawabdom.

There were some individuals though in the Nawabdom, in loose flowing habit they donned for the radiance of their simplicity, with beard on their faces - the embodiments in appearance and in reality, of good nature, who did rounds of dwelled areas, passing through lanes and streets in the Nawabdom, carrying Kashkole - the begging bowl slung from their shoulders. They made chants for alms in the Nawabdom. The Nawabdom treated them not as an unwelcome extravaganza, but a source of spreading discipline likened to God virtue. They sold no merchandise and were aloof of mutilating values and were genial and legitimate good doers. They were appreciatively looked at upon by the Nawab and the people of the Nawabdom for reminding the people of virtuous deeds and for having inhibitory influence upon the people to keep away from the fallaciousness. And what they did was to bring serenity and calm in the Nawabdom, and they were recognized as *Faqeers*.

The Nawabdom considered it very much in order for the Faqeers to raise their chants and they asking for alms in the name of God. Their chants reminded all, of the existence of God and the Nawabdom of the Nawab was a monotheistic state believing in one God, and the chants of the Faqeers were thought of by the Nawabdom to induce the spirit of alms giving which was an order from God which helped destitute and those deserving help. The alms met the wants of the needy and made the people large hearted. And the Faqeers were considered a vehicle through which the inducement to goodness was homed in, in the people.

Contrary to the Faqeers who were welcome, there were also beggars alongside them in the Nawabdom, plying on the roads and lanes who tried to trick others, making the people believe of them destitute, whereas they were not, and were professionals using beggary to scoop money from the pockets of the people. They faked a wound on their body and a female carried a baby in the arms which they drugged to make him look sick and invalid. This was to gain other's sympathies, and they were rogues and impostors. But they thrived on the sympathies of the kind hearted and were mostly successful in collecting large amounts of charity at the exhibition of their fake miseries and arm bandaged as if wounded that duped people into believing that their miseries they spoke of, and the wounds they showed were genuine. And overtaken by the tender feelings, the donors hurried to bestow alms and charity to them, and when these fake Faqeers got exposed, they earned extreme general despise and lost all sympathies of the people.

As opposed to the fake Faqeers, the genuine Faqeers in the Nawabdom with the display of their authority they generated through their variant soothing and disciplining chants that came out of their composure and their graceful behaviour, coalesced people to affinity to God values that brought serenity and blessings for them. With their *Faqeeri* virtue filled with abstemiousness towards the worldliness, with their adherence to the names of the Punjatan, reminded the people of the virtuous pious of Islam and they were welcome to collect alms freely in the Nawabdom. They were the benefactors of the society and were qualified in the eyes of the Nawabdom to beg through their exhilarating chants, and they were symbolic of the reminder of the duty that befell on the shoulders of the rich to look after the poor. And the greater the Nawabdom approved Faqeers there were, the greater was the discredit note tugged at the back of the rich that they were not fulfilling their responsibility of looking after the need of the poor and the destitute and the Faqeers reminded the prosperous to remove the stigma sticking to their names.

The Nawabdom approved Faqeers did not go out on their calls to use their unique, monosyllable, rhythmic rising and falling centripetal voice in the deafening swamp of the all note screams and bickering going on all round in the day, dwarfing the sane voice. They went on their calls in the cool of the evenings when darkness had spread and there was quietness and when sound travelled faster and reached to the deeper depths to the funnels of the man's cupping ears. And in response to their call God loving men hurried to give them what they could, in bread, flour and coins. And the Faqeers gave them more than what they received from them through their prayers and blessings from the depths of their hearts, in words of sooth, coming out of their good nature, which was a force and it subdued the donors to be humbler than the humility.

And the donors knew they had boarded the carriage of blessings and were thankful to the Faqeers for coming to their doors and carrying away their load of remorse and sin and their abhorring conceit. And were thankful that the Fakeers generated for them conditions for receiving virtuous environments and comfortable homes in the Heaven. There magnanimous abodes, for the immense kindness of God became their entitlement for their small kindness they showed in the world. The donors were rendered resplendent services in the paradise, cushioned with gladdened contentment and elation, and it was a reality, not a wishful thinking, as it was the firm promise of guarantee issued by God to those who associated their lives with charity.

It was on this note of the promise from God that the masterpiece of the dissimulative skill of one of the Town's Nazim[41] from the *Baldiati*

---

[41] The institution of the local system of governance was revived by General Pervez Musharraf in his tenure of Presidency. This system of governance was blocked by the lower cadre politicians.

Nizam –i.e., local administration, took form of applied reform. The Nazims had emerged, picked up through the elective process to administer areas of their recognizance, and the Town Nazim's inception turned to precision of action, and he raised a simulated team of Faqeers to go around to dismiss problematic beliefs by making chants and arousing spirit of understanding and compromise, among opinion clashing zealots.

Some of these zealots killed select class of people and threatened the lives of the surviving of them for not subjugating to the whims of their beliefs they believed in, which they wanted imposed on them. And because it was not coming to be; they turned to greater violence and started intense killings. Killing the select categorised, who were marked by them in desperation that surrounded them and killed in disregard to what happened to the grief-stricken women who were widowed and the children who were orphaned, and the mothers who were deprived of their dear sons, and the sisters of their brothers, and the sons of their fathers.

The zealots who killed, continued with their horrendous act of the sin of killing since the imposition of their whims did not work on their targeted select class of people who were the followers of the five holies, and the fear was that it was not going to work forever. And it was certain their mission to impose their belief on them was to be a failure because of the discernable feeble concept they put across to them to be followed. And because it was not to be, the killings all the while exacerbated. It also exacerbated the already inbred intolerance between the killers and the killed, otherwise fundamentally a people of one brotherly nation, but the killers did not recognise and did not celebrate the ethnicity they offered.

The intolerance grew stronger day in and day out and became like a massive trunk of over nourished tree with deep down roots spread out far and wide with its indiscreet tentacles. It shredded the fabric of the society, all of which was a consequence due to the devotional zeal of their loyalty syndrome to their heroes of the early days of Islam to the point of worship. The sanctum of perfection, who evinced stout sound traits and battle rich record, they placed in the background and placed the secondary virtue ahead, and this was organizational failure of mind and heart. And this had created a great moral decadence and an all-round failure. And the higher the devotion to their first placed heroes, the greater the growth of intolerance between them and the greater the killings of the varying with them.

And the intolerance brewed itself to such extreme that they went out chalking the walls and road side spaces with slogans, 'Shia Kafir'. Whereas need was that they reviewed and reformed themselves, but instead of burying the hatchet, they headed for the sowing of the harvest of abiding enmity with the discriminated Shia. And no alchemy helped. They were blowing their limbs through bombings, and in the process earning, eternal diminution in their standing and status near God.

And spurning all reasons leading to sanity and shutting their hearts to show religious concurrences, unabatedly continued with their decorous act in their eyes; the killing, hurling bombs, spraying bullets and ashamedly blowing to pieces the praying in the mosques with bomb jackets on their bellies and throwing projectiles from distances, and staging open terror, fearing none. They were challenging sanity, and shaming man. And their missionary zeal for killing did not stop. The news of the killing reached to across the seas into the lands beyond, and it put people in awe, since the law could not lay hand on these adamant resourceful killers who had backing of the powers from the Arab land of the new kingdoms and killed misinterpreting the Aayet 9.123 of the Holy Quran:

> "O ye, who believe, fight those of the unbelievers
> who are near to you and let them find harshness in you,
> and know that God is with the duty bound."

They therefore murdered and threw the bodies in the river Tigris and seventy dead were nothing to them. Only if they killed 32 to 36 Shia Muslims, they earned the title of Ameer and that was the modest aim of the killers. The killing made them enter in *Tareeqat* – mystic way of life and reach to near the *Haqeeqat* and exempted them of *Namaz* and *Roza* and allowed them to go straight to the *Jannat*. And there were prodding from the Wahabi powers, who wanted them remain adamant on killing, and not adhering to democratic norms and it led them to tear more human bodies apart, and attack revered shrines of the pious high God appointed Imams, spraying bullets on the praying in the mosques.

The lack of wisdom, driving the killers to do the killing is summed up in the proverb of Hazrat Solomon AS. quoted from the Holy Bible:

> *Wisdom cries out in the street*
> *In the squares she raises her voice.*
> *At the busiest corner she cries out;*
> *At the entrance of the city gates she speaks:*
> *How long, O simple ones, will you love being simple?*
> *How long will scoffers delight in their scoffing and fools*
> *hate knowledge?*
> *Because I have called and you refused, have stretched out*
> *my hand and no one heeded,*
> *I also will laugh at your calamity;*
> *When panic strikes you like a storm,*
> *Then they will call upon me but I will not answer;*
> *Because they hated knowledge and did not choose*
> *the fear of the Lord.*

The bible with subtlety warns, wisdom is calling to respond to it and not to ignore knowledge and God says if you refuse My warning and not heed, I also will laugh at your calamity.

This problem was also discussed in the Aayet 6.151 of the Holy Quran:

"And don't go even near abased desires, whether they are reachable openly or in the secret, and do not kill any living of soul whose killing God has made unlawful except in lieu of any right"

And despite that the killers followed Quran, they ignored its warning. There was the clearest word in Quran against killing, but they continued with the killing, till their deprivations in attaining their objectives became a source of desperation to them and they went on the spree of killing more formidably than ever before, using grenades and machine guns on religious processions in the Land of Seasons and Songs for a spectacular greater killing, demolishing human finenesses and there was no one to stop them.

425

The police was busy shining their shoulder brass, the army was busy marching on the tunes of victory, the judiciary was busy framing masterpieces of excruciating verbosity, leaving room for evasiveness; the press was looking over their shoulders not taking up pen to show honest diligence and stand straight not lopsided and go to shield the hapless victims, and the media was selective in presenting realities and becoming evasive to arrow at the culprits and even took to glamorising the killers. And whereas all were servants of the Unitary God and the upper echelons, but all were showing insincerity, and lack of astuteness. With the learned and the cleric among them turning opinionated, there were none left to serve God, and the target killing went on unabated all along in the years 2002 to 2013 from Khyber to Karachi.

The Jamat-e Islami instead of weeding was watering and strengthening the growth of weed and thorn of intolerance and was endorsing extremism. In a big gathering on the 4th of October 2004 in Naushehra, Ameer-e Jamaat Qazi Husain Ahmad 1987 - 2008 says, "... *Hum Inteha Pasandi Kay Khelaf Naheen Haain.*" - We are not against extremism. He served as crutch for extremism. He had his Thunder Scout, Shabab-e Milli and Jamiat-e Tulba; all weapons laced and standing behind the extremism to back it up and they continued with the disruption as if that was an order in Islam. On the performance of Qazi Husain Ahmad, a poet has said:

حوالہ

ہو موسم گل اور بت حور سرشت
بھر بھر کے مجھے جام پلا ے سرکشت
پھر چاہے کسی کو بھی مری بات نہ بھاے
میں کتّا سے بدتر ہوں جو لوں نام بہشت

Ho Mausam Guul Aur Buut Hoor Sarisht
Bhar Bhar Kay Mujhay Jaam Pilaay Sarkisht
Phir Chahay Kissi Ko Bhi Meri Baat Na Bha-ay
Maain Kutta Say Budtar Hoon Jo Loon Naam Bahisht

It is the season of spring, idol and wine
Filled and filled pegs gives me the turned bad

426

Then be it if no one likes my talk
I am worse than dog if I take name of paradise

Whereas the poet, philosopher, astrologist and algebraist and holder of knowledge of Quran, Umar Khayyam 1048 – 1122 AD of Nishapure pleaded for moderation in his Tabah – the style of his liberal nature:

Mun Must Wa Too Deevana
Ma Ra Keh Bard Khana
Sau bar Tora Guftam
Kum Khoor Doe She Paaimana

I am out and you madly out
I have to go to the house (you in no condition to help)
I told you a hundred times
Drink little only two or three goblets

Despite that their next Chief of Jamaat-e Islami Munawar Hasan calls the extremist terrorist TTP Ameer Mehsud killed in the drone attack, a martyr, though he was responsible for killing 50,000 citizens, and Munawar Hasan calls the army soldiers killed fighting against him *Halak* – killed - meeting death. And so perfect was brain washing that a graduate engineer of Jamaat Islami goes to the terrorists to help and gets killed with them in Miramshah in North Waziristan on 29 November 2013 in the drone attack.

The extremism had penetrated even into the body of the judiciary. In the time of Chief Justices Iftekhar Mohammad Chaudhary, there were 346 Shias killed between October 2011 and August 2012 and no terrorist murderer was executed by the court of Chief Justice Iftekhar Chaudhari, but he released such terrorist of Lashkar-e Jhangvi as Ishaque Malik who openly boasted of killing 12 Shias. And despite Lashkar-e Jhangvi are declared a terrorist organisation, police are deployed by the Punjab Chief Minister Shahbaz Sharif at the residence of Malik Ishaque for his protection.

And the judiciary under Iftekhar Mohammad Chaudhary refuses to hear several thousand Shiite prisoners languishing in jail in Pakistan for 13 years. Ishaq Kazmi has not been heard by the courts and neither has Iftekhar Mohammad Chaudhari heard him over five years. This unprecedented practice of discreet persecution of the Shias is going unpunished in this corporeal world but will not to be so in the world of the hereafter, where each judge responsible for it will face his retribution.

The news in 'Jang' London, January 22, 2008 reads: "Extremely dangerous prisoners escape from the Quetta ATF Cell. Usman Saifullah and Shafiqur Rahman were involved in 32 sectarian crimes (killing of Shias). After the escape of the prisoners, the security has been further increased on Imam Bargahs and other important places."

The Jang London news further said. "According to the sources, one person came to meet the prisoners the previous day and after putting *stamps* on their wrists, he took the prisoners with him."

The Sipah-e Sahaba was founded in 1980. Their faith forbids celebrating the birth of the Prophet SAWW, but the secretary general of the Frontier Region of the Sipah-e Sahaba in 2007 went to lead the procession of the Eid Miladun Nabi in Parachinar – a majority Shia country and raised the slogan of *Husainiat Murdabad, Yazidiat Zindabad*. A bullet came and he was hit by it and the Army of the Islamic Republic of Pakistan sprang into action and sent a helicopter to lift him to the hospital. This diversion of resource to save an extremist vouched the survival of extremism. The forces of sanity are far from saving Pakistan from ideological derailment, rather are aiding it quicken its pace. The hypocrisy was the curse of the country but it can never be diluted, such entrenched position it has organised for itself.

The doctrine of peace and law abidance is being shattered and the Chief of the Tahreek-e Insaf, Imran Khan pleads for negotiations with the terrorists, and says he is in touch with the Taliban and the result of this contact was they bomb blast on the 10th of Moharram, killing mourners who were taking out procession in Karachi on the 28th of December 2009. Forty-seven Azadar were killed and over 70 injured and within five minutes of the bombing, the miscreants started setting shopping complex on fire, burning down 360 shops and creating over 15 billion rupees of destruction of the merchandise, and in its wake produced joblessness and public disturbance.

The hypocrites, press, media, the hidden hands started blaming the police and the administration for the fire and the merchandise losses and shielded the Tahreek Taliban Pakistan who on each occasion claimed the responsibility of the bombing. The anchors in the TV talk shows always diverted the talk away from the Lashkaray Jhangvi, Jaish Mohammad, Jundulla and such like, since either they were afraid of them or are working in tandem with them.

They advocate the cause of the terrorists and demand the resignation of President Zardari since he initiated military action for the first time against terrorism of the Taliban in the Northern Territory of Pakistan in Swat, and he is considered to be Shia faith and there is open and muted hate for him in all quarters. The trend was openly displayed by the Secretary General of the Pakistan Muslim League Q. Mr Mushahid Husain Sayed on 27 December 2009 in the TV talk show he tells Imran Khan, 'Have your Sherwani ready for takeover in 2010' and a hype was created that A.A. Zardari will fall in December and Imran Khan, shedding a charming feminist shy was loving that remark. And Imran Khan surprises the nation of Islam: he pleads to negotiate with those about whom Aayet 2:8 says:

And from mankind are some who say: We believe in Allah and the last day, when they believe not.

If they believed in Allah, the awe and the fear of Allah will make them pious and keep them from killing. At present they are cutting the throats and playing football with the heads they cut of the soldier, and the soldier they ascertain in their captivity was Shia.

And despondencies hung in the air, houses emptied of their occupants and they moved to other lands where they should not be gone to, and people held their breath and prayer places were emptied and people were forced to practice *Taqayya*[42] – doing

---

[42] Taqayya had various forms, but the intention is preservation of truth and the self. Taqayya, all said was the highest form of faith. It was preserver of soul and system, whereby the soul flourished. The highest in Taqayya was displayed by the Prophet SAWW and Hazrat Ali AS. when the Prophet asked the Wali to sleep in his bed to look like him to save his (Prophet's) life in the night of the migration, when the enemy stood outside the house with sword drawn all night to slay the Prophet in the morning. They continuously monitored and found the Prophet sleeping, but it was Ali, the look like of the Prophet SAWW!

prevarication, hiding their beliefs and parrying inquiry about their faith's identity.

And fear took away self-assuredness and escapism replaced concerted stand against mayhem and wails spread sorrows over regions and tears shed, but no solution and no accession to bring the terrorists to chastisement to force break and enter the nexus of their dens of fallacies and tear it down through the force of logic and love or might took hold. And no slash stick was taken in hand to bury the fallaciousness. It was left only to the Imam Mehdi A.F.S. – the Imam of the age to come and address the menace and demolish the awning giving cover to the miscreants.

In this torment of killing and mayhem, there were vast regions in the land of Seasons and Songs that emerged to make morality further directionless. They marred their names by giving refuge to the killers and protecting and can-watering the plant of extremism. They allowed their four walled revered places, God's prayer houses like Lal Masjid, turn into tailing grounds, teaching to raise pupils with distortions in their minds to bomb their bodies for blowing others. And Baitullah Mehsud and the Swat Taliban Chief Fazlullah stood behind the Lal Masjid with their Taliban menace and the show of hate for the Shias.

When a group of army infantry was taken hostage by the Taliban, their extremism picked out 18 Shias from out of the troop captured and slew them by cutting their throats and released others and they said they were out to establish Shariat-e Islam, but this was prejudice topping barbarism. This was dastardliness of heart and outright obduracy against God's loved servants, an agenda to installing Wahabi faith. It was Sipah-e Sahaba, Lashkar-e Tayba and Lashkar-e Jhangvi's agenda and each were on the road to precipitate their scheme with the help of the secret hand. This secret hand hoped to use these demonstrators of hate as a reserve force in the future war with their trumpeted enemy - India, and at what price, corrupting the nation, it was a perilous act for the dim glim of the battle success.

Poet Khalilullah Khalili was born in Kabul in 1907, died in 1987. His quatrain is printed (thanks to the Octagon Press, London). The quatrain wails:

Yak Qatra-e Khoon Ke Bar Zameen Mi Uftad
Az Khatam-e Aasman Nageen Mee Uftad
Hushdar! Ke Az Aah Yateem-e Mazloom
Bas Kungra Kuz Arsh-e Bareen Mee Uftad

A drop of blood that falls on earth
From the ring of sky, the jewel falls.
Beware! From the sigh of the orphaned oppressed
The highest height from the high sky falls.

And I know the pain of Pakistan the misguided have brought to it and say the following:

نفس برباد ہوا قاتل کا کرکے قتل انسان
عذاب چھا گیا گردوں تک بعد قتل انسان
کس قدر ظلم سپاہ صحابہ اور لشکر جھنگوی نے کیا
دم بخود فرشتہ، دین پامال، رو دیا انسان

سیّد اطہار حسین

Nafs Barbad Hua Qatil Ka Kar Kay Qatl Insan
Azab Chha Gaya Gardoon Tak Baad Qatl Insan
Kis Qadar Zulm Sipah-e Sahaba Aur Lashka-e Jhangwi Nay Kiya
Dum Bakhood Firishta, Deen Pamal, Ro Diya Insan

Soul was destroyed of the assassin after the assassination
    of human
Retribution stretched up to the sky after the assassination
    of human
What great tyranny Sipah Sahaba and Lashkar-e Jhangvi did
The angel is stunt, the religion trampled, the human crying

A country which always ran on some kind of aid and grants, if a threefold amount of aid in Kerry-Lugar Bill shape is passed by the Senate of the USA with conditionality to destroy terrorism and extremism and protect nuclear assets from these terrifying men. It was wisdom and leadership of USA. But it was demonstrated against, by the Jamat-e Islami activists in Karachi on 2nd September 2009 and

431

prominent TV Anchors condemned the bill and poured propaganda into the ears of the innocent listeners in their programmes, describing it as sell out of the country. This was not selling out freedom but reason; they saw extremism was going to be obliterated, which is their prayer-wheel, and they barricaded from airing it, and the army saw their freedom into governance trimmed and cut to size and their accountability brought in vogue, so they also opposed it. And what tragedy what shame the country of Pakistan has not gone through. An investigation must be made against the conspiracy.

The specialists, the educated class and corporations were thrilled over the passing of the Kerry Lugar Bill. They saw in the bill, access to the EU and US market opening for them. The stock exchange in the country was on the boom and investment in the country from the outside world began to trickle in but the gloom cast by the media engulfed the country and any voice raised against the USA was a welcome note for the terrorist, whose ultimate aim was to grab power, and that was possible if Pakistan was weak to bridle it as their pony to saddle on and charge with their deficiencies sitting on its back as imposters with their blunt spear of heresy to poke in the people.

In the wake of all this the burst of Asif Ali Zardari on 27th of December 2009 in Naudero that he will 'pull the eyes out of their socket' was the sober up speech - a warning and thwarting of speculations, all round in the air. Sarcasm in the air due to the media, and the rude poetry of 'Sanbhal Jao December Aa Gaya Haai' was given so much publicity that it appeared as if an earthquake is about to come with its tremor to demolish the capital and the army adventurists were investing in political activity, though it was not their domain (see the politics of the day in the Zem TV and Pak Politics programmes of these times).

In the name of literature and behind the façade of politics, sarcasm and bitterness was made asset to destabilize a forward looking political party. This poetry was abominable and an open license to attack on decency.

The armed forces of the country as of their duty must only use reason rather than they lace their boots to march on their capital and knock at the door of the presidential palace as was the rumour in those days. And the judiciary should be reminded; they should shorten their robe to save them tripping over.

The worsening events struck the chords of the heart of the Nazim and he rose to dust off despondency. He placed his Faqeers in position, armed with their chants to do the weaning away of the killers, from doing killing and remind the intellectuals of the Punjatan's inculcated purity in people through their conduct. And through the pouring of reason, alluring, soothing and appealing chants which the Faqeers raised, it penetrated through the killer's hardened ear bones, eroding their fallacies that the killer's dedication to killing abated, and the chants untangled the Anchors from the tightening net of the heresy that had entrapped them and had webbed around them a mesh of puzzlement.

The Faqeers scrapped off the thick deposit of heresy and the foul notions that had surrounded the killers otherwise of erstwhile sanguineness which was overpowered and stunted and their reasonableness of mind deactivated, disallowing them court with sane behaviour. And thanks to the Faqeers, who did their chanting fearing none but only the failure of their mission, they cleared the fallacy about the attainment of abode in Paradise by reminding the misled killers, the interceding power of the Punjatan and of the God's command in His Book of Guidance – the Holy Quran, verse 28.83:

"Abode of the hereafter We assign unto those who intend
no high handedness or mischief on earth and the end betterment
is for those abstaining (from evil)."

The Faqeers of the Nazim devoted as they were, with their hearts pure and free, putting in their *Iffat* – the abstemiousness and the odorous beggar hood to remove fallaciousness to wean success out of the despondency that had spread all round in the Nawabdom. They succeeded, the success had at last come their way, on their call of:

Nazr-e Maula, Niyaz-e Husain

Jo Dey Uska Bhi Bhala, Jo Na Dey Uska Bhi Bhala

Your offer to Maula, your present to Husain

who gives blessings for him, who does not give blessings for him
    also

Also, they made the calls of:

Allah Kay Naam Ka, Punjatan Kay Naam Ka Sadqa, Khaairat

In the name of Allah, in the name of the holy five alms, charity

Then the Faqeers gave the blessing: God may reward for your charity, God
may make your intentions right, God may fulfil your legitimate wishes.

And the act of the Nazim, disguising the good intention behind the
drive for the revivalism of the sanctity of religion and making the
beggar hood of the Faqeers an antidote to extremism, in the manner
of the 'Bahloolian' treatment of moulded presentation to eradicate
social disease was derived from the great philosophy of Taqa-eya - the
dissimulation or hiding of the actuality. Defending the virtue against
the attack of ignominy and ignorance and attaining the desirable by
routing out the illness from the heart of the misled for the sake of
goodness.

    And the word Taqa-eya - hiding actuality for the sake of removing
danger and threat to save life, came from the collection of the words
bound in the Arabic thesaurus that was there all the while for the
seeing, till the Nazim saw it and he precipitated the philosophy behind
it into acquisition of healthy society, using the resource of the Faqeers
and their silent lessons they gave in measures appropriate to even keel
the rocking ship of civilization, hit by fallaciousness and he was
successful. He abridged the dispersion into cohesive affection. And the
Nazim's act pleased God, the Prophet of God, and the catchwords of
the Faqeers gemmed with the names of the Punjatan – Mohammad
SAWW, Ali, Fatimah, Hasan and Husain AS. with their style in the
formulation of the begging chants, reminded all revitalise their faith
under the Aayet 7.96 of the Holy Quran.

"And if the people of the township had believed and kept from evil, then we should have opened for them blessings from the sky and from the earth...."

-: . :-

III

THE LADY WITH UMBRELLA

IX

There were times in the life of the Nawabdom of Nawab of Ralah in the Land of Seasons and Songs, when its very existence was in danger due to the external power's meddling and meritocracy in danger and threat to unity and dictation in the affairs of the Nawabdom. They were ready to scuttle its freedom. They had sinister intentions about the Nawabdom and tried to stop it breathe and tried terminate its existence. But they could not damage even the jib of its one of its dinghies, thanks to the Faqeers of the Nawabdom, who lavished it with their *Doa*(s) — the prayers to God, and the existence of the Nawabdom continued and its throne remained assuredly stable with its feet firmly grounded on the firm ground of its hierarchy of the purest of pure fourteen; Nabi, Fatimah, and the twelve Aimma and the Nawabdom continued to flourish with its strides in scholasticism.

The exclusivity of God's kindness on the Nawabdom was because the Faqeers took the names of the chosen ones of God; Mohammad, Ali, Fatimah, Hasan and Husain — the benefactors of humanity. The righteous remember them and the pious emulate them. People in their prayers through them warded off danger to the Nawabdom and it remained stable, and people kindred and contented, of orderliness and thanksgiving. And people spoke with one voice, affectionately of one another and were in loving bond with each other and all praise for the Nawab to have infused such spirit. The people were thankful to the Nawab and the Nawabdom and prided themselves for the morale and the material achievements they were enjoying. The state was earthly utopia they were living in. People wore pleasant expression and bore pleasing manners and it was the custom in the Nawabdom that no one went out from their houses until they had dressed them

436

respectfully in pleasing manner, attiring them tidily and covering their heads and shoulders, and bringing out cheerfulness and gleam and livening their surroundings.

And everyone there, in the Nawabdom looked picturesque and spick and span and no one scruffy and untidy. And it was to be said, everyone believed in the saying that 'no one sees what you eat, but everyone sees what you wear.' And they dressed well. A good formal dress had the highest place in their eyes and they worked for a respectful society, and coarse eating and fine dressing was the accepted norm of the people and the established way of living in the Nawabdom. And people were thin and slim and graceful, with no belly protruding. They ate frugally but ate tasteful and fresh food, and only that much was put on the Choolah – the stove that was consumable for that hour of the day - dispensing with the need of cluttering the Nemat Khana – the holder of novel things.

The chief dresses of the Nawabdom were the closed collar Sherwanis, either of long length or of short length, but loose carrying flare, letting body breath and they wore turban or high walled boat-caps – the Jinnah Cap, then round cylindrical caps - the Fez with tassel, the Gandhi or Nehru cap, then turban wound in fluffed comfort. Then they put long shawls on the shoulder- the stoles in the Shastri manner, with embroidered border, giving a Shastri look. And the outstanding dress among them as the pace setter was the Shastri dress. And the Shastris were the principled ideologists with their three thousand years old grounding in the Land of Seasons and Songs. Their shawls and the flowing white loose *Kurta* of knee length, decorating their Aryan tallness, with pure white *Malmal* – muslin cloth *Dhoti* wrapped round their waist, down to their ankles was their distinction. The Dhoti covered the legs, and the end of the cloth was brought up and tugged at the back of the waist girdle of the Dhoti to provide ease of manoeuvring. And their frisk movement in their brown leather slippers strapped to the feet, spoke of the grace of the dress, and they negotiated the corridors of learning, marginalizing all fashions dare challenge their style.

The Shastris were standards in education and principles, in selection and wearing of the dress and they were such an asset to the Land of Seasons and Songs. They were not only admired for their

Shastri dress but also for their knowledge of the *Shastras* - the treatises of the religious laws of Vedic origin. The Hinduism was derived of it, and mannerism, learnedness and abilities of the individuals originated from the Vedic Shastras.

The Shastris ancestors were semi migratory people who herded cattle and their society was the master race who spread out from Caucasia. They divided their society into three main groups: priests, warriors and herdsman and as far back as perhaps the fourth to the third millennium BC in the *Koah Qaf* – the Caucasus Mountains and the east of the Volga River they lived, whose one branch went to Iran and the Indian branch mostly came from Iran and for that they were called Aryans. Their one branch came direct from Caucasus. And together they evolved precursory Sanskrit and God inspired Rishis and Munis subscribed to the Shruti (heard and transmitted by the sages) and Smriti (remembered by the ordinary human beings) scriptures and formed the sacred *Sharia* – the Vedas.

They divided the society by the Vedic law into four classes of casts. At first the division was non-rigid, and people could cross over from one cast to the other. Then centuries later it became as rigid and sharp in division as two opposite banks of a river and the law of non-reversibility had come in operation and one individual of a group only belonged to that group. Of them the first was *Brahman*, equated with the Brahma, who was life giving, and Brahmans were the source and the root of everything, and jurisprudence was for them to interpret and they were Kings and knowledge holders of the Vedas. After them came the *Kashtris*, the holders of sword to wage war as warriors, then the *Waish*, to act as traders and farmers, and last, the *Sudras* - the serving menial class, and of them the lowest were the scavengers. So, the followers of the Vedas had created four distinct rigid castes; they had to live with, with its boons and handicaps, and the society had rigidly shaped itself and life's existence moved smoothly.

Whereas elsewhere in recognition of their purity and chastity that commanded their exclusivity to divine ties that is in Islam, one exemplary caste carrying distinctiveness were the Sayeds. But all else of their kinds down the ladder carried the same attribute of worshipping of one God and all of them were brethren, forming one *Ummah*, the nation. But there were infidels forming groups who could not be controlled and had their rigid interpretations contradictory to reason casting dispersion in God authority.

In the Nawabdom of Ralah, there were classes of men, besides wearing the predominantly worn dresses in the Nawabdom, they were wearing trilbies and fashion tailored suits to be contemporary. They also slipped on bush shirts and slapped on head brimmed cork hats and appeared in breeches and dared the sun with its ferocity touch them in the sun-drenched days. And so equipped, they went out sheering their way in the Nawabdom to places of their assigns.

To substantiate and compliment the fanciful donning by the males of the Nawabdom, there were matching veils of the modest ladies and the excessive veils of the extra modest select class high echelon dress conscious ladies, making the end of their Saris covering their heads as *Ghoonghat* - a drooping to conceal their captivating face and with it cover and conceal the nature and beauty of the hair to halt the prancing eyes' glaring reach to their headful of alluring asset. And they in this prominence guided their personality around. And there was fast colour *Lehenga* – the loose pleated skirt with small fancy *Kurti* and then the fitted *Choalee* – the body blouse worn by the hard working pleasant of manner and of good mood ladies in their working outfit.

Then there were the fashion wears of the *Sharara*(s) - the loose long flared skirts and with it the matching *Kurtee*(s) - the mini shirts with *Reshmi Dupatta(s)* – the silken stoles, plain or with lace of golden laces on the edges. Also, there were slim trousers with crinkle, baggy on the hips, called *Choordi-dar Pyjamas*, and then there were the rustling sound of the silk *Gharara*(s) - the embroidered large flared trousers with end and middle, decorated with ornamental *Gota(s)* – the laces of gold colour or of silver colour stitched to the Gharara, with matching short Kurtee(s), cut to fit the contour of the body to make the donning look taller than their tallness. Then there was the *Malmal Chuniri* – the crinkled stole of multi-colour muslin further enhancing the grace of the wearer or in its place there was Dupatta, the stole without crinkle to cover the shoulders and head to enhance modesty. All these dresses enhanced gracefulness and spoke of the wearers design consciousness.

Then in the style of the hairdo, there was tight plaited Choti – the end of hair hanging as single plait and sometimes in two plaits, and sometimes plaits folded or hair simply coiled and a silk bow or a rosette was tugged on at its centre, or a fresh rose flower string wrapped round the *Joorda* - the crest. These were the fashions that delighted even the mundane. And these were the distinctive pride dresses of the Nawabdom, and there was to be no intermixing in the dresses that a male was to look like a female or a female aggregated herself in looks to look like a male. These graceful dresses were all the approved dresses in the Nawabdom and were looked at upon with admiration and all wore these.

There were some ladies though, who prided them for their short hairstyles and walked in certain tunics and dresses cut and fashioned from the fabrics of stunning design, not easily seen in the Nawabdom, with an umbrella held in their hand. It served them as a proactive tool against the eventualities as those showing up when they had to put their step out in the climbing sun's heat intensity, and it was unbearably hot. They used it then against the sun's merciless blazing, which was ready to scorch their worthy to defend pretty face and their much cared for hair, and the suns onerous was all too set and ready to burn their skin and bleach dry their hair and dull their bright face that had to be protected. Also, they used it to serve them on the occasions of the not seen in rain, when it poured and its wetness drench stained and softened the starch of their clothes making it sticky, not suited to their grace.

Conversant with its use they also utilized it to parry someone who in their judgement unmistakably came closer to their being, and he seemed to be heaving in nearer to their proximity swayed by the stagger of his feet. Additionally, the umbrella carrying ladies also utilized their umbrellas sometimes outright in the extreme as an aggressive tool for hitting, poking and parrying someone whose evident mannerism was questionable and who in their faint judgement was asking for it, allowing the lady's pomp and brightness sway him, taking hold of his better judgement and he was closing the distance between him and them more than was desirous.

The umbrella carrying ladies with their advocacies, advocated for correct attitude in Pardah. These ladies in the observance of the norms of Pardah were very much unlike the ladies of dominating veils, or the ladies in Burqah, covering from head to toe with eyes opened in a slit or covered with thin seeable cloth or net, or ladies with long

Chadar, a sheet covering them, only allowing a slit remaining open for their eyes. They were not like them. Also, they were unlike the ladies showing the fashioned excessive *Hijabs* – keeping their face and body features open to establish the charm of their personality, but head in religiosity need fully covered. And they trying dodging God, but He was only mused. The Umbrella carrying ladies observed no Purdah like these ladies. But these were ladies who powered the infusion of their puritanical thoughts in the society. And were never disallowing a major happiness not touch them. They believed life was for living and the Hijab was symbolic and their vigour with norm was essential.

Poet Jigar Muradabadi 1890 – 1960 was a top poet in Ghazel Goee. He said romantic poetry. He writes about the necessity of Hijab:

> *Zindagi Thhi Hijab kay Dum Tak*
> *Barahmiyay Hijab Nein Mara*

The life was peaceful until Hijab was operative
The exceeding of Hijab Killed (the peace)

The umbrella carrying ladies did only the essential in the Hijab as commanded by the Book of God, in the Holy Quran in Aayat 24.31. The Aayet said:

"And say to the believing woman they keep their eyes low and guard their private parts of their body and they should not reveal their self-beautifying to others, save that which reveals it naturally, and they should put their stoles on their breasts and display their beautifying of self to no one except to their husbands, fathers, husbands' father, sons, husbands' sons, brothers, or brothers' sons, or sisters' sons, or their women, or slaves whom their right hand possesses, or male servants free of physical needs, or small children who have no sense of the shame of sex; and that they should not strike their feet in order to draw attention to their hidden ornaments. And O ye believers! Turn you all to God that ye may attain bliss."

The umbrella carrying ladies drew inspiration in Pardah from the foregoing Aayet and equipped them with the essence of its teaching and did not show their embellishments and facial decorations to unidentified and kept their eyes low. And if anyone of them had her nose upturned to add further beauty to it or one who had her face done up through the precisions of the surgeon's surgery, they covered it as commanded in the Aayet of Pardah and did not show it. Otherwise, they showed their eyes, lips, nose and face, no matter how beautiful God had made them. And they did not put a cover on their nose, and also did not put a stiff black cloth hanging in front of their face as some ladies did from the Arab lands with a pair of holes cut out in the black cloth for eyes to see and they looked freak. This was beyond the umbrella carrying ladies. They only covered their hair to present orderliness and ensured that they did not present a dehumanised face.

The umbrella carrying ladies said, anyone who did excessive Pardah; it was the same as people over ate and over drank and they said excess in Pardah was a bother, and no one called upon them to submit to it. There was no creedal fence raised for it. But they equally despised any one baring open their femininity and not honouring them with the respectability given to them by God. God had accorded them a female status, be it the queen of the film 'Queen', appearing in premier and winning Oscar 2007. She was priding herself on her dress and making finicky emotional gestural motions, saying about her dress:

"It was all made for me so I didn't have to have any under wear. It fitted me like two angel's hands. I cried when I put it on, it is a work of art."

The Sun news reporter writes: "(she) giggled cupping her boobs to illustrate the point."

The umbrella carrying ladies detested this obnoxious liberalism and considered it least befitting to a lady, even if she was picked to personify as Queen of England in the film. The Umbrella carrying ladies laid stress on precepts of good acts drawn from the precedents presented by the progenies of Prophet Mohammad Mustafa SAWW and said:

"Ostentation of Hijab of fashion or the show of Pardah for creating distinctions for the self, hindered harmonising relations between races."

And they said in their eloquence:

"It was not entirely the responsibility of the ladies to keep the chastity of men intact and unmolested by their charm. Investment in the maintenance of Pardah and its unabated pursuance and its spirit had not to be singularly the ladies' responsive effort to keep men in chastity, men also had to keep their eyes low and not race them, and they ought not to load their selves with what derided men."

Aayet 4:34 said: These men (the Kamaoo/bread earners) were the maintainers of women:

Arrijal Qwamoon Alan Nissa

But at the same time if the woman had their own earnings, they had their rights on it. By Aayet 4:32, if they earned *Taqwa* – the abstinence, it was theirs, if they earned *Neki* – piousness that was theirs and if they earned wages and wealth it was theirs, only they had to take permission of the husband to go out to earn.

But the Deobandi Scholar, Mujibur Rahman of Deoband Darul Ulooom says, 'it was Haram for the woman to go to work'. And these Ulema from Deoband believe theirs is the sect for whom the Prophet SAWW has prophesied that they are the only one destined to enter in the paradise. And if they had choice, they will send all the rest to hell.

But that controversy aside, the women were made weak by design in their structure by the Creator and were not meant for hardwork of onerous, like running marathon and doing wrestling. They were cut for light sports, wearing respectable rigs - not spectacular shorts or a wear such as not hiding their feminine parts associated with them and they were not permitted to share premises where there was a single man and she by herself alone. This precludes the post of a secretary that would not be suitable for a Muslim woman.

It was about the beginning of the fifth century BC, when even the concept of God was not very clear in parts of the world that sage Lao Tzu said the classic words of wisdom in China in the ancient book Tao Te Ching. It has since then been continuously read. This sage stresses on a straight approach for harmony and order in the society. His philosophic discourse says:

Give up sainthood, renounce wisdom,
And it will be a hundred times better for everyone.
Give up kindness; renounce morality
And people will become filial and kindly.
Give up ingenuity and renounce profit,
And thieves and robbers will disappear.

And to be in step with the sage the Nawab of Ralah added:

Give up abuse of Pardah
Abundance of goodwill and respectability will follow

The umbrella carrying ladies were of intelligent manipulative class and showed piquancy and adapted to the Taoist wisdom. They showed valour and exhibited an unmistakable articulated capability to meet the demands of each and every situation through the implementation of the utility of the umbrella, in hitting, parrying and providing grace to their person. And these ladies in their profession of aggressive handling of the umbrella were not discouraged in the Nawabdom by the Nawab of Ralah. They enjoyed a status of respect and high standing, and there was a prospective fear shown of them by others and even the naivest never thought of making even the most rudimentary violation of any unapproved behaviour enacted around them.

The ladies in any case were very quick to detect any violations and treated them in the manner that was most appropriate and disposed of the cases then and there, right on the spot by using the umbrella as a poking, hard hitting and a thrashing tool.

It was one of those days when destiny springs to crystallize eventualities into realities, rising from the rock bottom recesses where it resides, and it was the day when it was touching the other tip of the scale of the spectrum of springing eventualities, bowing to lend a kiss to the apparent looming adversity in whose succession things tend to go wrong in the life of a horse and cart driver, and it was one of those days from the pools of the fateful days destined to appear in the life of Bachchu Aekkewan when his mare was feeling she was cheated; not fairly treated. She refused to budge when the full load of the passengers was seated on the Aekka – the horse and cart, whose reign Bachchu held in his hand.

Bachchu first prompted the mare with his *Keqhue Keqhue* sound from his mouth which originated from his tongue pressing the uvula and lower Qanoon lip open and the mouth resonating allowing sound out to make her move, but there was no response. He then used the pepping up tool, and compared her to Hitler, pepping her to make the prideful move the way Hitler moved, and drew the parallel between her and the haughty Hitler, saying:

Nikaal Ghordya, Nikaal Qadam Jaisay Hitler Nikalat Raha, Chal Ub

Step out horsey, take out step like Hitler used to put step out, go now

Then he further pepped her:

Chal Hamar Balli Utha Qadam Ki Hitler Ka Uthaee

Get going my prop raise feet such that what Hitler will be counted

But it was to no avail. On most other occasions she immediately responded to these pepping ups and moved with an air of assumed importance to show her *Hitlary* – the Hitler like quality in manner and way. But not now, she had heard Bachchu fix the fare with an accuracy that was akin to the opening and shutting of the logic gate. And she had determined without erring, her lock stock and barrel share of her part of the divide in the earning, and her calculations told her what she should have got in feast, grass, soaked gram and treat, which she had not got, and now was time to get the accounts settled and mischief rewarded with mischief.

She changed her position from a straight one to an oblique one and this time turned her head to aim her shot, and flung the kick at the footboard, banging the footboard with her iron shoes pushing from her hooves with a thud and thump that was the loudest, jolting the cart and she exceeded the usual treatment she gave to the footboard, and in her incessant fury she forgot to count the banging she gave to the footboard.

This exceeded banging of the footboard at a time when she should have shown seriousness to duty and taken to the road with all the passengers seated and settled in their seats and nothing left to do except to move, infuriated Bachchu to the last. He was swelled with rage and started calling her names:

"You disaster, you punk, you horror of a saucy rogue, you muddled fuddled twit, you twist and turn and you show your bum, and you don't move. Now get on with the move you *Phus*."

Now as it happened there was a lady with umbrella standing there close by, waiting undecided to move on to the other side of the road. She had hardly been there less than a minute and no longer, when she suddenly heard some mocking sound coming from the direction of a horse and cart driver, venting his feelings, appearing all verging on to a feigning deliberate scathing directed at her, and as if all the wording in the spoken foul tongue, meant to smudge her person to make her feel fouled up and spoil her good mood she had started with that she had carried so far, but now she was put to face an ugly address to her.

First, she did not mind all the gibberish that that daring horse and cart driver was guttering out, thinking maybe it was not directed at her, but the words 'you fuddled twit' and the bombshell of it all, 'You Phus' and that too with such a force, and with the horse and cart man's head, she could vow definitely tilted in her direction, all that made her convinced that that cocked up rat of a horse and cart driver does mean to direct those ghastly words at her.

She lifted her umbrella that she held in her right hand, and with her short hair wobbling and beating the air and then her shoulder, in fury she pushed herself forward at her highest charge and charged in the direction of Bachchu, and instantly covered the distance between her and Bachchu in a jiffy, and she was at his head and began to lash the umbrella at Bachchu, calling him:

"You crude bum, you stinking rattle brain; you dare open your foul mouth with that gaffe, croaking those stinky words directed at me. You baboonish bellowing goon! You stinking horse and cart of a driver of foul mouth, what you thought I was? I'll show you your worth, for all those ghastly words you have cranked at me, you will pay for it and you will hear about it faster than your rattle brain can think of."

The lady, who was freely lashing Bachchu with umbrella with her extended arm and lashing out words of indeterminate depths, describing the likes and the wit of the Aekkewan as she thought fitted the man, was Lady Councillor in the Town Committee, in the Town Nazim's Office. She never in her life-time had to have that much reason for anger as she was filled with then, at the remarks she had heard passed at her, and she couldn't understand for the life of her, the motive of that cocky horse and cart of a driver to be so glaringly blasting away those unruly wiles all directed at her, and that too, when she was not doing anything so as to even breathe a puff stronger than a lady's puff that might have touched to tickle his skin.

She was standing there minding her business, unable to decide about her move, keeping herself to herself and was ready to swear she had not even looked in his direction, let alone any ticklish thought of throwing any glance at him of any description goaded by any fancy, or doing any smudging of belittling, spear directing them towards him to irradiate him and fling abuses at him of any enormity as he smeared her with, and never she deserved those prickly slants, all flung at her person.

These were the remarks that were to put anyone off the course of normalcy, pushing him or her to the end of the scale of the display of reasoned behaviour weighed down with moderation, and the lady all driven by the utmost of the explosive anger and all pepped up by an urgent tit for tat and impelled to punish the culprit, did exactly that.

The lady was, as it was; known to carry firm belief that 'where leniency was inappropriate, strictness was leniency'. Besides administering the thrashing: as soon as she had entered the council building, went straight to the Nazim and flustered his mind with definite exacerbations, arousing fiery stipulations in the Nazim and filling him with appraisals what that brat of a horse and cart of a driver had said about her and that it amounted to what she said, 'slander' that required straight treatment of injecting sobriety into his unruly wit and thrashing out devilishness off him.

The Nazim who was already averse to any kindness to be shown to the horse and cart drivers for reasons that they had been reported to have recently been violating the rules of good behaviour in stationing the horse and carts in streamline fashion in straight queue one horse and cart behind the other in the waiting roadside queue when queuing for lifting the passengers, and had no obvious sympathy for them. On hearing what he heard from the lady councillor, he took a very grim view of the horse and cart driver's daring act against a lady councillor of consequence, and of her standing. It was already reported to him that the horses' heads swayed in all the four directions, and this had posed danger likely to hurl the passers-by, mostly innocent villagers, and the report was the swinging heads of the horses had pushed them away to another direction and hurled them to fall.

He took a grim view especially, since the reports were, some villagers had also been sufficiently thumped by the horses' muzzles there in the busy market and that there were some feign horses who were wholly of such unpredictable habits. And they exhibited it in the thick of the things in the middle of the town and the horse and cart drivers were reported ignoring the incidents with the innocent villagers, pushed and hurled by their horses.

The Nazim wasted no time and at once sent the case to the Qazi's court for a quick disposal of the case with evident expectations that punishment will be awarded to the culprit in this open and shut case, which will be welcome to him, since it will add to some order emerge on the road. And the most the Nazim was glad about was; out of the punishment, enduring lesson to the horse and cart drivers was to emerge, with salvation towards the pacification of all too an important a lady councillor on the council's panel in his office.

Whereas, as far as Bachchu was concerned, he was bewildered but brave in all that was happening with him. He took all the hits from the lady squarely on his head and on his face. But as far the mare, which so far was stuck holding her ground not intending lifting her feet to move an inch forward, seeing Bachchu being bashed squarely and dealt with without impunity, with strikes and blows all over the head and the face and being thrashed with the fiercest of fury, made a run for life and ran like a ghost with lightning speed in a shot, with all her muscle power in her put in use, hurling her and heaving and snorting with the cart hitched to her and all the passengers on board, and she not seeing where she was going.

And providence had it that the mare just spared knocking down the lady in her furious run for life and the lady escaped and she was not hurt, thanks to the extended arm of the lady while administering the blows. But the close brush of the horse and the cart rim, brushing past the lady, rubbing her clothes in the mare's flight, frightened the life out of Bachchu, who, off course did not know anything of the lady thrashing him was thrashing in anger for an insult she alluded to have been flung on herself.

And he wondered as to what had come upon the lady to be so vehemently beating her umbrella on his undefended head and face and yelling words he little knew about. And he was stunt when he was taken hold of, shoved and pulled by his waist band by the law enforcers and taken to the court of the Qazi on his return voyage and charged for hurling unbecoming phrases and demurring remarks, all in words of rude origin at the person of the Lady, the Town Councillor of the Town Nazim's Office.

The case was presented to the Qazi and the prosecutor had no difficulty in proving that Bachchu was guilty. He told the court of the harassed ladies of his village who suffered harassment almost on daily count from him, which he learnt from the rival horse and cart drivers, some of whom lived in close vicinity where Bachchu lived, and they had actually heard that he calls unknown persons, beckoning them about the ladies of the village by the call 'catch her, catch her' and the ladies were very fearful of any untoward incident that might occur and they were in extreme distress, and at times had to forgo their call of nature and abandon their going to the field.

On hearing all that, the Qazi was convinced that the accused Bachchu was a prone violator of rules and was an offender, harassing the ladies in his village and also the lady of consequence – the Lady Councillor. The Qazi was convinced on these accounts that the accused had committed the offence levied against him of teasing and downsizing the Lady Counsellor by using tricky and punchy unwholesome words normally not spoken in venting one's feelings so openly about another person, using word of 'you Phus'.

But to meet the procedural norms and in observance of the practice at the Qazi courts and to complete the arguments for filling the appendages of justice, the Qazi asked Bachchu.

"Did you say so? You Phus, and all that ...?"

And Bachchu readily said. "Yes sir," and began to say.

"It was to control the ..."

He wanted to tell the court that he was addressing the mare to control her wiles. But before he could say anything further that these words were for his horse, and she needs these words to get her moving when stuck on the road that just that very moment the prosecutor jumped in, thumping the desk and holding him there.

"That would be all, my Lord." Thundered the prosecutor, thumping the desk and holding Bachchu at halt there, and said:

"My lord the case is proved. The accused admits to saying, You Phus, and all that..."

And the Qazi said. "Yes, case proved, guilty as accused."

And the Qazi immediately set out prescribing punishment for Bachchu. The main offence that was levied against Bachchu was of an unrefined, roughened and poking talk that came out from him and had hit the lady to disturb her composure and that he was a cause of unrest to other ladies and the Lady Councillor was badly hit by his talk.

The Qazi nevertheless found that the case of Bachchu was not an easy one, where he could prescribe his oft repeated punishment of putting a fine on the culprit and closing the case and making all satisfied that justice was done by enriching the treasury of the *Sarkar* (government) and letting off the guilty with penalty and warning to be careful in future, like when the horse and cart drivers were dealt with, in the court, when they broke rules of not properly halting their horse and carts on the sides of the roads.

The Qazi determined that it was a more serious case; where a fine for the offence was not the answer. The guilty had to be moulded of his attitude and his habit broken and his brain ruffled, washed and cleaned to disarm him of the ammunition of craggy words he had stored in his mind and the ability he had developed of carrying on in his mind of manufacturing fresh craggy words by exercising his untamed imagination to produce them and fire on the opposite on whom it fitted around there.

The Qazi determined from the case proceedings in the court that all the cragginess in the horse and cart driver was from his deliberations and it had to be put to a hold and infusion of certain refinement had to be homed in, in his mind aimed at its penetration and settling deep in his brain. The Qazi reached to the conclusion that to do all that, his mind had to be pampered with formative ideas, and for this, external aid from a reform society or an institution with an expertise in the behavioural uplift of individuals was needed to be deployed, who had to come to the rescue of the court and do the needful.

After deep thinking the Qazi reached to the conclusion that Bachchu should be sent to a reformation school for a period of training to be taught, refined ways of conversation for improvement in his expression of thought which had to be so tamed such that his mind was not voluntarily or involuntarily under the influence of craggy words of his making that were hitting others with slighting and insinuation concealed in them, ready to ruffle those whom in his eyes he considered a pest.

The Qazi courts in the country of the Nawab gave judgements according to the precepts of the religious beliefs of the accused so that the religious edicts - the articles of the binding faith of a person and the fundamentals of his belief - all those that concerned the accused were honoured by the court. The Qazi therefore asked Bachchu what religion he belonged to?

Bachchu, the horse and cart driver had to submit:

"Sire, I do not know what religion I belong to."

And because the religion of a person was generally taken from the religious followings of the parents, the Qazi asked him.

"What religion your parents belonged to?"

Bachchu who had never seen his parents practice any ritual and rites of any religion inside or outside of his house, or had heard them talk about the wisdom and the beauties of any religion or had heard them discuss the supplementary or the fundamentals of religions which could have shed light on their faith, if they followed one, was unable to answer in the positive as to what religion they followed, and replied to the Qazi:

"Sire, I do not know what religion my parents belonged to." But he added, "I only know of some principles that my mother talked of, who was the last of my parents and she always spoke of these, and they were:

"Eat of what there was to eat that came of your toil. Better go hungry than eat of other's palm. Be contended and remain thankful for what you have. Do not ask for any favours from others. Do not speak of your problems with others. Do not pick a quarrel with others even if you are right. Do not be hasty and..."

The Qazi, who was now learning a great deal about the principal beliefs of the parents of Bachchu, but nothing about the religion they followed, jumped in, just at that last revelation Bachchu was making and halted him just there, holding Bachchu enumerate no further entails into the ethics and the details of the principles taught to him by his parents. The Qazi allowed him add no more, and said in exasperation.

"Yes, yes, they are the universally accepted principles of self-esteemed, but how are they going to help me ascertain your religion. I register you have no religion of any following of your own."

And with those words spoken by him, the Qazi resigned him to pre-judgement lapse, pensively ruminating and deep-down searching in him right thoughts and their implementation to decide of 'what and how' of the judgement, and of the nature of the institution where the accused guilty was to be sent to receive the ruffling of his mind and reformation penetration into his thought process, appropriated to his means and offering bright sequels to help the court.

The Qazi had two places he could send Bachchu to, one a *Pathshala*, the place with teaching in the basics of ethics, with prayer rooms and a garden, where they gave lessons from the Vedas to teach manners in the art of conducting one's life in the tradition of *Gaoo* and *Gita* – love, respect and principles of fine living.

And the other was the Madrassah - the Missionary School with urbanised features, where rigorous training was given in *Aebadat* – the servitude through worship, and *Uboodiat* – the devotion, with submission and love to the progenies of and to the greatest Messenger of God and committal to God servitude and that God was of Oneness.

In this the commonality between the two; was, each taught perfection reached at was evolutionary, and its aspects presented them through stages over the ages through the chosen ones of God. And the theological concepts consisted of were:

For one of them the perfection was reached at through the stages of the *Yugs* – the ages of times, through the *Avatars* – the manifests and the perfection was incomplete yet, and it was not to be achieved in all completeness till after the appearance of the tenth Avtar, who was to appear seated on a white horse at the end of the *Kali Yug*, when he would come with a blazing sword for the final destruction of the evil and the restoration[43] of justice and piety.

And for the other; perfection was complete. The compact absoluteness with concentration of virtues had entered in one theological entity, chosen and approved by God and was done in the open declaration in the assembly of multitude with words *Mun Kunto Maula*[44].... But its edicts had to be protected, and there were Madrassah(s) after Madrassah(s), which all taught: 'there was the T*welfth Hadee* - the last of the deputies of the Prophet Hazrat Mohammad SAWW, who will come to restore and establish righteousness with human grandeur returned using sword Zulfequar that will be by his side and he will have justice and fairness restored in minds and in the realm of the article of faith and implant it to take root

---

[43] It was a referral in their conviction to the appearance of the Twelfth Imam, Hazrat Hujjat Imam Mohammad Mehdi AS. of the House of the Prophet of God Hazrat Mohammad Mustafa SAWW. This Twelfth of the Imams will appear with the Sword Zulfiquar, blazing, and he Ajal Allah Ho Farjahum will enforce peace and justice.

[44] These were words of command which said: *Mun Kunto Maula Fa Haza Aliyan Maula* - whose so ever I am Master, this Ali is his Master, spoken by Prophet Mohammad Mustafa SAWW in his last sermon in this world.

everywhere. The mankind in the wake of it will discover that he AS. will speak one language that will be listened to and understood by all.

And on this occasion dictated by the considerations of economy in travel and logistics in consideration, the Qazi decided to send Bachchu to the Missionary School of the urbanised Madrassah. And the Qazi let the accused off with a minor punishment of three months rigorous schooling at the Madrassah lasting over two hours a day, three days a week.

نہیں مماثلت ہے ویدا اور قر آن میں
مگر طریقت مطہّره ہے انکے ہر فرمان میں
قر آن ایک پیدائش ویدا کئی کئی کہتا ہے
کیسے ادیان یک ہوں جانوں کے دنیا میں
سیّد اطہار حسین

Naheen Mamaslat Haai Veda Aur Quraan Mein
Magar Tareeqat Mutahhara Haai Inkay Her Farman Mein
Quran Aek Paaidaish Veda Kaee Kaee Kahta Haai
Kaaisay Adyan Yak Hoan Janoan Kay Dunya Mein

No similarity there is in Veda and Quran
But observance of outward knowledge in purity is in their each
    edict
Quran says on birth Veda tells several of them
How the religions of souls be one in the world

-: . :-

III

MADRASSAH ON THE HORSE AND CART

X

As Soon as the court order was passed, Bachchu was immediately taken to the *Madrassah*, and he was handed over to the *Modarris* – the teacher giving lessons on morality and the basic in literacy to take charge of Bachchu and the court order was read to the Modarris that read:

"He is to be taught manners in the containment of his thoughts and in the utterances of his words with stress on exercising control such that he does not under any circumstance and by an iota of doubt foils, and speaks a word that was oblique, insinuating an insult towards someone. And that he was so taught that he was not vocal of thoughts giving vent to his personal feelings in a way that was interpreted from his innuendoes that words shooting out from his mouth were uncouth and linguistically of duality in meaning, concealing offending in them, as evidences presented to the court reveal he is capable of doing so, all directed towards his target. These tendencies need uprooted and fineness infused in him. His categorisation for a religion is blank and he is of no Varna – that is he is of no cast."

These were the clearest instructions, giving a complete autopsy of the case, which were issued to the Missionary School by the court, and the court could not be clearer than that. And all that was written in the court order was conveyed to the Missionary School Modarris word by word.

The Missionary School Modarris was all glee that a pupil had arrived at his Madrassah who was of no Varna – belonging to any cast in religion. The Modarris started sharpening his concepts and thoughts and building his plans of conversion strategies to convert the defunct to his way of religion.

Here was a chance for him to bring a pupil devoid of religion to his brand of belief and get himself a place in the paradise in reward, which will be assured after the Godly act he will have performed to have cleaned him up of his fouled up mind and sterilise it and bring him to conversion to his faith and teach him of all those principles that he was taught as novice to believe in by his worthy predecessors, where simplification in belief and idolizing of personalities, with deep ingrained reverence held for the most idolized with vows to loyalties to them was taught. And where virtue in one's self was understood to follow in the wake of the adaptation of this belief and where obedience and submission were driven deep into the pupil with the clobbering of the student's mind to submit to these beliefs, rather than taking to errands to identifying as to where straight virtue was and harbour develop an inquisitive mind that was not wanted. And the student needed no exercise to open his heart and exercise the brain to offer submissions to extraneous thought. Here, the brain was washed clean and heart armoured not to yield to extraneous influence. And it was taught, not to feel of any need to design or venture look into the scrutiny in the anomalies presented by the idolised.

The Modarris had started with his strategies how to convert the wile innocence unmarred by orientations into religion, and hurl him in his smooth fastidious religion killing all the desire of variance in that was to be followed. The Modarris began to work hard on Bachchu from day one, as soon as the found and declared guilty arrived at the Madrassah and the Modarris started his tries to teach Bachchu as much as possible in as little a time as possible, all the related matters of his brand of belief to turn him quickly into an advanced category of a trained devotee after initialising his early convertibility to achieving the end convertibility in as short a time as possible.

But it proved to be a case where the Modarris was plum keen to teach and the pupil was wary and least receptive to assimilate, and one entirely averse to learning a branded and persuasive lesson. Since, for the first time ever in life, Bachchu was made to fold his knees and sit still and listen to the goading sermons on the performing acts of a select number of heroes of pre-set and proactive dispositions and listen to the teacher's created simplified equivalence between all the individualists turned idealized heroes for they happened to have seen the era of the ethos of civility, distinction and of miraculous performance, without choice and accepted as of automation idealized heroes whether their contribution in it to valour was naught.

The Modarris hammered for the recognition of equal superiority status to all of them for having found that era and age and time of mass reversion to civility and for having seen the Supreme Countenance of the Pure of Reverence, 'Certitude of God' (Hazrat Mohammad Mustafa SAWW), the cause of the salvation of the human. Thus, they becoming distinctive to be touching the domains of miraculous performers, and all equal in piety whether or not their contribution in the era of the ethos of the 'Certitude of God' was naught. The Modarris hammered that that was enough qualification, whereby by dint of that virtue they were the touchstone - the Sahabis and for it he clobbered Bachchu's mind that they were carrying a superseding for ingratiation over all the subsequent to follow. And the teacher hammered:

"In affixing the status of men who had seen the supreme countenance of God taught 'Prophet Mohammad Mustafa SAWW', each one was at par in reverence, and the established criteria that each and all qualified for finding equal place after their sequel to death in the paradise for they had embraced the look of the purity full bright face. The teacher meant to say all the companions of the last Prophet SAWW because they had seen the supreme countenance of the Prophet were revered and equal. And he laid stress:

"Stand by the ethics of disallowing scrutiny into the handling of the bygone affairs as naught, and that the superiority of knowledge and valour and spiritual ascendancy and the genesis and the descent of any particular one over any other were of no consequence. And that we were designedly not placed in the time frame to look into it for scrutiny and reform our attitudes."

These were the basics of the teachings that Bachchu was taught and the rule of thumb to follow, in submitting to the binding faith and acceding to the exceeding status of the chosen heroes to enter in his brand of belief. But this lesson from the very beginning did not seem right to Bachchu, since he knew that all horses were not equal and alike; some kicked and bit, and disobeyed, while others were obedient and stood by their Master in help and submission. And he could not think how the idolized heroes, all could be equal in veneration and all firmly arraying and aligning themselves in absolute terms towards the core of the faith without aberration – that was the requirement for veneration.

And Bachchu knew Providence did not make all creation of one likeness; equal in perception and intellect, and this was a questionable ethical flaw in the teaching of the Modarris that Bachchu saw immediately, in allocating equal veneration to all that was not natural. And Bachchu's mind rejected the teachings of the Modarris, finding it illogical and uninteresting, simple as Bachchu was.

The teacher as an innovation in dressing and depiction of manner in teaching, presented his personality in a wound and tugged Safa of a specific pattern on his head, and sat reclined with his elbow resting on a pillow cushion, portraying to teach things related with order and discipline and of precocity in understanding of the affairs of the heaven. And the teacher did all this with an undisguised evidence of concern more to get his reward from the heaven out of his lessons to Bachchu than showing any concern to teach Bachchu anything of worth that aroused skill in the delivery of thoughts and in mellowing and taming his wiles into something that gave nuances to soothing chatters on the road.

Thus, ignoring the requirement that suited the pupil, the Modarris had put his agenda in the fore front, of conversion of Bachchu to his brand of faith and obtaining reward from heaven. But disturbingly he found his pupil proving to be a hard nut, difficult and dismissive at learning anything of detached value in lessons if they were not aligned to invigorate moderation in the wiles of his delivery in communication with his mare.

But the Modarris still aligned him with the powerful fixation in his mind that it was immaterial what barrier was holding Bachchu back from yielding to the teachings and what his thoughts were, whether he wanted to learn what he was taught or not, he continued with his agenda regardless of Bachchu's reservation to yield to his belief. What mattered for him was that he had to press on with his missionary agenda of driving his brand of belief in his head and home it deep down into his brain for securing Paradise, which he saw in the opportunity arising through his lessons to him.

But finding Bachchu that he was not in any way responding to his oriented teachings, he ultimately allowed that Bachchu was a difficult case to be dealt with, laden with the impossibility of letting crack his teaching through the protective shield of the skull isolating his learning skill that resided in his brain. Because nothing that he wanted to teach to Bachchu did sink in his head and all glazed off from it like a beam of light returning diffused and unsuccessful to penetrate through a barrier formed of a polished highly reflective surface. Although the fact remained that beneath the thick crust of Bachchu's skull, lay the finest mesh of the grey matter which was there, untouched and never stroked by any teaching thoughts and was like a virgin field, ready to be ploughed and seed sprinkled in it for miracle to happen and a harvesting bonanza to be reaped.

But the branded teaching of the Modarris were bad seeds and never took roots to bring out shoots from the vast deep fertile and un-ploughed field of Bachchu's mind. The missionary teacher could not stimulate the mind of Bachchu even to the lowest degree of his satisfaction, especially because every now and then and each time in the middle of the lesson, the horse where Bachchu had halted her outside the Madressah was neighing and whinnying and scratching the ground with her feet loudly and when she neighed loudly, isolated of whinnying and scratching, Bachchu responded to her discomfiture with a loud 'Ho'. And to say the least of it, it was as disturbing to the Modarris as a buzzing oversize bee sitting on the tip of someone's sensitive nose, about to pierce its pricking tongue into the mound of the nose and as soon as the voice of the neighing reached to Bachchu it completed its atrocious act and simultaneous with that the loud yelling back of the 'Ho' by Bachchu travelled as a ruckus hitting the unplugged ears of the Modarris to where the mare was, conveying to her wrapped in the 'Ho' - 'Hold on for a bit I'll be coming.'

This 'Ho' of Bachchu and the neighing of the horse disturbed the Modarris's otherwise calm nerves and the proceedings of the class disturbed to the last. He therefore rightly in his mind, thought of a solution and decided after deep thinking to take the whole class out to where the horse was. Because he did not want to waste time and wanted to drive his lesson into Bacchus's brain, beyond what he was entrusted to do, that was his conducting him do more than the actual court assignment. His expanded plan was accelerated teaching, and filling Bachchu's vacant and virgin mind with ideas and notions as went with his brand of belief to win the passport to Paradise, which admittedly he had been trying continuously but so far without any result in his hand.

And the idea of stamping the distinctive impression of his immutable mark on Bachchu's back after his conversion and getting a seat reserved for himself in the Paradise was the sanctimonious lollypop he wanted to grab and eat hurriedly, and the idea was alive and kicking in him to desperation. He as such, charged with the zeal of his undivided missionary duty and his own vision of availing himself to climbing the rungs of the ladder to Paradise through this not an everyday opportunity fallen in his lap plump, invigorated his dedication further and in solution took the whole class out along with all the children to climb and sit on the standing horse and cart, for him to drive the lessons in Bachchu's brain without interference from the horse, and finally bring the devoid of religion into the folds and grasp of the fundamentally active beliefs of his brand of belief of religion.

The Modarris, who had become sufficiently fat and plump, eating all the fancy foods arriving to him from different houses of his pupils that clung to him, making him a fat fellow, dragging himself and Bachchu with him and driving all the children to run to the horse and cart, went and sat with Bachchu in the centre seat of the horse and cart, placing Bachchu facing the horse and the children on the side spaces. Some of them standing with their feet on the foot pedal stepping used to climb on to the horse and cart, and some clung on to the empty luggage rack at the back, poking their heads from behind in the centre space of the horse and cart, and three or four sitting, squeezing themselves on the space of the footboard, taking liberty with the mare with their writing wood-slab, touching, rubbing and resting on the buttocks of the horse.

With that order of the class, some seated, some standing, and as the last-ditch effort to remove the hurdles in his way of achievement of his goal of attaining the Paradise, the Modarris started the lesson to Bachchu in earnest and with the full force of vigour in him.

The horse for the life of her could not see the wisdom of the Modarris that he all along with so many children, his whole Madrassah was planting himself on the Aekka – the horse and cart whose shafts rested on the shoulders of the mare. Then on top of this folly of the Modarris, her keen ears listened to the lessons from the Modarris what he was giving to Bachchu, which her horse sense could tell were highly partisan, pushing the interest of a circle of believers who had tried to bring their clan cult in the prominence, pushing those views which were partisan and innovation, she did not like that dissent being taught to Bachchu and thought the Modarris was branded and his lessons were not formative to making one skilled in exercising intellectual freedom, leaving mind intact and thought left uncontaminated to ascertain and evaluate truth, and there of adopt and absorb the intended philosophy of the religion to lead one form ethical principles for application in life. She therefore, to show her disapproval of the whole thing, gave one and then two and then three highly violent wild jolt and the class and the Modarris were thrown off the cart.

And the Modarris landed with a thump on the floor. It was a thumping fall on the hard patch of ground with a heavy muffling sound suggestive to say some bodily harm to a fattish fellow, and painful to say the Modarris had suffered that brunt in depth. The children were thrown on the ground and they scattered screaming for hurt and some laughing at unusual happening and the discipline of the class went in tatters, completely gone stripped to shatters.

The Modarris, who saw that disarray of discipline, with him thrown on the floor, started to curse the day the mare was born, never letting him continue with lesson. Bachchu immediately rose to his feet and rushed to the Modarris and stood him on his feet. He began to console the Modarris. Bachchu said, "The mare was famous for such odd behaviour and he said, "Some blemish for it goes to her heritage of her English breeding. She was spoiled at the stables of the Elite Englishman in the early days of her breeding". And Bachchu added, "Most of this is, for the reason that the mare is mostly feeling angry because she has not been fed properly. Since for three days in a week sufficient earning is not possible due to her attendance at the Madrassah."

The Modarris saw the relevance of the protest of the mare in a wider context and he straight away sent an admonitory note to the Qazi, saying, "All my efforts to teach Bachchu were being frustrated by the vile acts and doings of the horse. Either it was neighing, disturbing the class, or throwing off the class off the cart". He also let the Qazi know, why the horse had thrown the class off. It was because she was angry since she had nothing to feed herself with, since the day's earning to them was not possible in its adequacy while they were at the Madrassah as the horse and cart was standing idle, not plying on the road.

The Modarris who had long arms, ominously made it clear to the Qazi that he could not accept any disturbance in his missionary duty and knowledge imparting, which was a function that was entrusted to him, he claimed by God. And in imparting the teachings to Bachchu, who was sent to him by the Providence, he said, "All the pricking problems in the way of the teaching must be removed." And so, lightened the Modarris his anger to subside through this letter.

The Qazi after hearing of the episode that had halted execution of his order, immediately ruled that it was Bachchu who was under punishment and needed to go through the reformation and perfection process and attendances to the classes, not the mare. If the mare was not getting stomach full meal on the days when the punishment classes were held, the necessary provision for her meals must be made and provided for, by the Royal Stables with the cost met by the Nawabdom.

The Nawab who was always disposed to reason and was a man of deliberations, with literariness encircling him and who always stood for justice, had no scruples accepting the court findings. The Nawab readily consented to implement the court order of the Qazi and load full of feed and fodder started arriving for the Bachchu's horse.

There was green meadow-grass, oat, husk of barley; overnight soaked gram with a sprinkle of salt and a tinge of olive oil in it with occasional almonds present in the bucket of the gram, and then chunks of Gurd for sweetening the mouth of the mare, all these delicacies started arriving punctually on the appointed days. These were unloaded outside the Madrassah, and suffice to say, there was lavish food in sufficient quantity that started arriving from the Nawabdom. And the mare had never known to have had so good to have eaten that lavish supply of thought filled fancy food for her, all coming to her on the Nawabdom's account and the mare fed and fed with ampleness that she had never fed before.

She ate all those things three days of the week and it was seen to that she was happy. In fact, the food arriving by all measures was so ample that it was more than what was needed for one day and it was clear that after what she could eat in one day, the supply was so exceeded that that one day's quota was going to last longer for another day and it was aimed at so to last longer and keep the mare happy.

In this way eating in abundance and being free of worries made the mare surplus of energy and extremely energetic and she was ready to run at the sound of a whistle with or without the cart hitched to her and with the full load of the passengers to pull, she was ready to heave with agility their load where ever she was to take them.

She now wanted to run faster and with greater heaving power than ever before. But still due to the fact that the mare was not used to a situation where she was left unattended for two hours altogether by her keeper that was Bachchu, she continued to neigh every now and then, and Bachchu each time had to respond with a 'Ho'. And this neigh and Ho continued, and disturbed the class to a point of disruption that was excessive and unfortunate, and this meant in plain language, tingling the chords of dismay and taxing the fair capabilities of the Modarris to the last.

In this situation the Modarris could not teach Bachchu all that he wanted to teach to him in the time frame that he had been given and had at his disposal, and neither could he score the qualifying points for a place in the Paradise and all was a dead loss for the Modarris.

And as the inevitable happens, the time of three months drew to a close and ended and in no cosmology and no influence of angelology could stop it. The assigned time to the Modarris had come to an end and the Modarris had no way but to hurriedly teach Bachchu and make him memorize the urgent lesson:

"If your horse does not move and she kicks and does not pay heed to your spurring and pulling of the reign and the beating of the bridle on the horse and your *Keqhue Keqhueing* fails to move her, you hold yourself still and do not go shouting at her. Do not take aid of expressions arising from your indeterminate depths of expressive power and do not give vent to desire to speak words of impending choice and irresistible languishing that may be interpreted as rough, and derivable to be meaning insinuating as insulting to some. Remain quiet when she is not moving."

Bachchu grasped the lesson and that was easy, and that was. 'Remain quiet when she is not moving', and his term of punishment ended for him and he was sent on to the road to ply his horse and cart all days of the week as ever he wanted. Bachchu was free, and also, he had graduated from the Madrassah.

-: . :-

III

THE ENGLISH LADY OF VIRTUE

XI

Bachchu had successfully completed his punishment of schooling in the realm of quality speaking, he was now sent to resume his normal profession of *Aekkewani* – driving the horse and cart. Bachchu as he understood from what he was taught at the Madrassah was not to say the words. 'You twist, you freak, you don't move, you Phus,' when the horse did not move, or when she went slow, or showed a tendency to be awkward and that he was supposed to remain quiet then. But now after eating the Royal Stable food for three months and not having much work to do, the mare when she had her way, had a tendency to immediately pull and run, turning her run into gallop and lurking in all directions like a hurricane, because she was now full of energy and she was becoming a terror on the road. This was a different situation unknown to Bachchu, and he was not taught at the Madrassah what to say or what not to say in this situation and the words he started to manufacture and that shot out from his mouth at the mare's salvos were:

Aray Kauno Taraf Jaat Haai, Aray Kaaisi Urdi Jaat Haai, Qaboo Mein Naheen Hauway, Aray Mut Urdi Ja, Thum Thum, Ruk Ja Toofan, Aray Tham Tera Satyanas, Thaher Ja Naheen Tori Marammat Karbay. Tham Ja Gori Ghordni.

"Oh, where are you lurking to? Oh, how you flying uncontrollably. Not in any check, oh don't become airborne, stop, stop, you, hurricane. Oh, stop you blight! Stop or I will do your spanking. Stop! You white breed female horse."

Now this last word you white breed, Bachchu often used for the mare because she was bred and broken at the Elite Englishman's stables and this expression sometimes, he also used to bring out in her the English connection for her to perform well, and he used to say that with innocence in mind and only to convey her notional superiority by way of humour. It was needed on occasions when passing remarks at her, which often made the mare look something different and a bit aloof from the local breed - the *Desi* horse types. By this alluding the mare was made to look a bit elevated from those standing alongside her at the horse and cart stand, and this was all in light vein coming off from him to amuse himself and make the mare perform well.

But this expression he used this time was perilous nick. On this occasion when he used these words, there was a lady going there at a fast pace, using her slim heals to spur her movement on the road, followed way behind by her maid, heading to a destination known only to her, but all very pleased with herself as her jostling movement showed itself to anybody. She was going fast minding her own business, till these unruly words of a horse and cart driver reached to her ears, and she never expected to hear what she was hearing. She couldn't believe what was being said by the horse and cart man all appearing related with her frisk movement she was making. Still, she remained in a suspended state of mind, doubting and cheering her disposition and toying with the idea with a glean of hope holding freak possibilities flickering in her mind that they were not meant for her at all, till the last words reverberated in the air and that of 'you blight', you need spanking, and then the thunderbolt of all, 'You breed of White.'

Now this was it, it was a bit too much, and the lady spun turned in the direction of Bachchu and saw an unconcerned blubbering horse and cart driver throwing insinuations, rumbling and rattling his horse and cart and shouting words of tatty descriptions all directed at her, whizzing came and past her and was casting eyes at her. This was just too much and she immediately at the point of screaming yelled at him.

"You stinking horror, you, crackbrain horse and cart of a driver, you blithering baboonish misery, you toad brain crank, you are howling that gibberish against me, I will show you your worth for saying those grisly words for me, I will teach you a lesson, you will pay for it. You toad, you thug, you scoundrel."

And the horse and cart driver least bothered with the blossomy poetic volleys of the lady, continued flinging tatty words of the nature already flung at her and was going strong, and was gone, rumbling those words of ample disgrace.

She noted his outline, built and the general description of his horse and cart outlook and went straight to get the matter sorted out about this shocking and fearful horse and cart driver, the menacing White Hater! She was ready to swear he was a bum. How could he say a thing like that in the very land, very much under control of His Majesty and his rule, where she stood breathing, where was power of the empire's rule, and she by herself a part and parcel of that very Britannia where His Majesty sat on the throne with the sceptre by his side, bless his soul! And that when she had uttered nothing and was going minding her business. Why that slander he spoke, that's was what she wanted to know?

The English lady was Governess of the children of the Nawab and it was known to the *Kotwal* - the Police Commander what her status was. The lady went straight to the Commander's Office, which was very close to where she was struck by those taunting and prickly sacrilege from that saucy horse and cart driver in words of total discomfiture to let her suffer the agony of their sting wholly unjustifiably, and that too just for using the road for which she had the same equal right as that blighter of a horse and cart driver had.

How could he say that! She was never spared the sarcasm of those relentless hard hitting craggy insinuations, bordering on to abusiveness, all shot at her about which any one could pass a verdict that they were an excruciating source of agony to any person of high calibre and position and these coming from a blockhead of a horse and cart driver, who even didn't attire in larger cloth than a *Lungi* – a wrapper cloth, barely covering his private parts. Never mind if she was nearing in closeness to fitting in, in the aggregate description of the meanings of the words he was blabbering.

The English lady was all taken by intense fury and an urgent desire for an immediate tit for tat treatment given to that dreadful man on the spree. She wanted justice served and served then and there, and she every bit putting forward every ounce of her elaborative power and force behind her words, stimulated the Police Commander for a matching action against the scoundrel, and said to the commander.

"Think what he is ready to blabber about a smoothly harmless lady going her way and what mischief he will not play if it was someone, undesirable on the road."

She further said. "This is the kind of man who needs straight and prudent handling in the department of unfriendly punishment."

And she left the Commander's Office, leaving the matter in the hands of the commander hoping for immediate punitive action to follow.

-: . :-

III

THE IMPERIAL THANA AND KOTWALI

XII

It was not a big deal for the Police Commander to straighten a horse and cart driver accused of bereft of civil talk, and whose person was vying at passengers and weighing their fare paying ability and at all the times vexing ladies of composure and consequence. The Commander was already sufficiently worked up by the English Lady's pepping up speech and her syllables of stresses on the slanderous talk of the horse and cart driver so expertly highlighted. He immediately shot order for immediate deputation of a Police Constable to go and collect this unruly horse and cart driver with or without his horse and cart and bring him straight to the Police Station as soon as he is seen at the carriage stand.

The Commander's order was the gospel of the Holy Book and the last word for the Police Station and a duty constable was deputed and run to the stand to collect the horse and cart driver and bring him to the police station. And as soon as Bachchu returned from his trip to the Aekka Stand he was pounced at, and was immediately grabbed by the waist by the most dutiful police constable, and that was a long time since he had left the horse and cart stand, unloading his passengers at their various destination points and loading in and bringing the load of the crop of the passengers to the horse and cart stand, which was the last halt for the Aekka passengers.

The Police Constable whose long wait for Bachchu to show up with his horse and cart, was bringing him to itchy discomfort and making him of jittery nerve, was fuming with anger and breathing fire to say the least, for being late in the prompt production of the wanted man at the Kotwali, and the delay in the prompt production of Bachchu was going to be a blot of infamy on his so far an excellent and utmost proficiency record, and it was going to be a non-efficiency smudge of stain, making his police dexterity marks turned into inefficiency of irremovable smudge on him, turning his unblemished record that he had built and earned over his years of service into non-entity. The Police Constable did not waste any moment to even wait for the passengers to get off from the horse and cart, and he, in a combat like action jumped at Bachchu with a little more of police proficiency than he was trained for during his sweating police training. And with agility greater than that shown on these occasions by the police contingent, firmly held Bachchu grasping him by his waistband, and immediately planted himself on the horse and cart and demanded from Bachchu to drive off to the police station at once, where the Kotwal wanted him in a case at the *Kotwali* - the central Police Station.

The name *Kotwali* and of big *Kotwal* was enough to make the bravest shake and this was only a horse and cart driver with his only very little knowledge of the world around him, and with no insight worth talking of into the intrigues of things that shaped and popped their heads up at the Police Stations and they pounced on ones like of Bachchu, without even their daring make a gesticulation of any provocative or non-provocative nature of imagined rudeness, or suggesting any healthy notional or rational point to the police at the Police Station. They were chastised objects, once in the police station and were *Miskeen,* helpless without visible safety and shuddered and quivered, and always it was found it was best for them not to sit if standing and stand if sitting and not be daring and open their mouths uncalled for.

And Bachchu under the pouncing control of the police constable was not only shaking, he was trembling. And any one even with the most casual perceiving power in him, casting only one glance at Bachchu could see his state which was as if a goat was being taken by a butcher for slaughter. Bachchu was not only shaking, he was pale face and rightly so. It would happen to anyone being taken by the police to the police station in the Land of Seasons and Songs. Bachchu was in the siege of a Police Constable, who still grabbed him by the waist band and was taking him away. With a blank and bewildered mind as to what he had done and why he was called at the Kotwali, he obediently put his horse and cart on the route to the Kotwali as asked for by the ferocious looking Police Constable in early days police uniform which was cut more to show an obedient duty-bound stooge than a countryman of India, with power to beat up and lockup.

Bachchu did not ask the Police Constable, who continued the grab of Bachchu at the waist band, as to what he had done, in case that exacerbates the police ferocity into the unpredictable, already a brooding constable, who looked every inch a mighty brute who was holding his apron from the waist, in case the fury takes over the best of him and he is dealt with fists and blows at once at the spot. And Bachchu drove with his captivator to the police station as meekly as possible.

And every sane person would do that when he is under the pouncing control of a baton wielding Police Constable of the Land of Seasons and Songs, of the days of the imperialist control, especially when the Police Constable was every inch a cocked-up brute, looking for pretexts to land his fists and blows at his prey, and it was an open secret what it meant to be called at the police station! As far as every one's knowledge went the going at the police station was always rough and tough and unidirectional in the flow of non-compensatory body blows and harms.

No sooner than Bachchu was brought to the Kotwali, he was delivered to the Head Constable by the Police Constable, who asked Bachchu what his name was. And as soon as Bachchu's subdued, meek voice came out guiding the Head Constable to the affirmation of the phonetic sound of 'Bachchu'; that was enough to ring the bell. It was the name, on the wanted list that was already with the Head Constable prominently displaying itself on the short list of the names of the unpredictable tongue-lashing horse and cart drivers and the name had now entered the urgent current list since the Governess had lodged complaint with the Police Commander. And it needed no further enumeration. To add fuel to the fire the name had also routed itself recently to the police station from the Qazi court after his court punishment verdict and all information about the tongue-lashing horse and cart driver had landed serially at the desk of the Head Constable and all the complaints had appeared showing the same menace in that name. In this complaint this time he had the surpassing notoriety of subsisting charges to his name of teasing the Governess.

The Head Constable left his urgent entry in the *Rozenamcha*[45] at the spot, there as it was, and sprang to his feet to attend to the more menacing problem and pounced at Bachchu and deposited a hard kick at his shrunk buttock, and snapped the order:

"*Murgha Bunn*" - become a cock. That order was from the annals of the police legendry preliminary punishments, the standard pre-taste of police reform they gave prior to any reason offered to them. The Head Constable was snapping order to Bachchu to set him in a cock like position by kneeling with his bottom up in the air and keep his head down and catch his ears routing his arms from in between his legs to pull his ears downwards and with it his head lower down and bottom up.

This was the artificial position well known to all those who previously had been called by the police at the police station and were rated as crime doers. But Bachchu not being from one of them, did not know what to do and what not to do and how to oblige the Head Constable, and he in his fits of keenness to comply forthwith with the order, started hurriedly crowing, as cocks do – *Kook Rdoon Koon, Kook Rdoon Koon* and that's what he thought he was called for at the police station to do.

This, the Head Constable thought was an open mischief played by the horse and cart driver, in which he seemed to be an expert, and he responded with a hard-swinging kick from the mound of his boot at his undefended buttock that landed there squarely, throwing Bachchu slump forward and Bachchu was sorry to have doctrined that that was what the Head Constable wanted, and the Head Constable snapped:

Makhoal Karta Paya Haai - cuts joke with me.

The Head Constable for his proficiency in the trade of pre- trials of hard criminals was coming from the upper land of Punjab, and none

---

[45] Roznamcha was the police daily entries register of events kept and maintained at the police station. The area of an administrative division in the police jurisdiction falling in the charge of the police station, had all events recorded that took place there as reported, and entry and exit of the police personnel movements from the police station were entered in the register and the Head Constable was all the time aware what was going on around him.

from the south were qualified enough in the thriving police culture of giving kicks and blows as proficiently as they were. And this Head Constable had his distinctions in it.

Bachchu immediately corrected his position after he had the full-fledged flat crash of the boot at his buttock. And the Head Constable grabbed Bachchu's head and pushed it down towards the floor and instructed him to pull head down and raise bottom up and pass hands from in between the feet and said now catch your ears. Once he had put Bachchu in that position - the Murgha position, he gave him another brushing kick at his buttock and shouted at him with a roar and thunder that rumbled the police station.

"Raise that bottom up and stay that way you rogue."

The Head Constable who was the last word in the interpretation of the laws on crime determination and categorising the grades of the offences and was the utmost in the proficiency of crime handling at the police station, gave this first treatment to Bachchu and never asked him anything else, and let him be conditioned by the brunt of the first treatment.

Bachchu with his head down and having been reduced to a cock of a man, saw all the police men passing, toes of the feet first and then the heads turbaned with the Jhabba of the uniform, thought he had been put in that position to look at the policemen and their turn outs and give his opinion on all coming and going like he saw from in between his legs inverted, toe first and their Jhabba next. And Bachchu calculated that there was something seriously wrong and he wanted to know what it was. He therefore asked the Head Constable in as civil a tone as possible.

"*Maeen Baap Hamar Ka Kehray Wastay Murgha Banauwa Hauway*"

My mother and my father, what for have you, me turned into a cock?

Because, Bachchu thought he had been put in that position at the police station to look at the policemen, toe first and head last – reversed and give his opinion on that and he only wanted to verify it in as civil a way as possible.

But this question of 'why and what' was not asked at the police stations in the Land of Seasons and Songs and this was taken by the Head Constable as one raising objection into the procedural set up devised by the police who knew best how to nab mischief, and how to exercise their expertise of crime handling.

This was taken by the Head Constable as an un-abating insult to the police that the question of 'why' was asked at all, and that was a load full of sufficient reason for Bachchu to be upgraded in the brandishing of the treatment of swinging kicks, added with thuds and thumps.

For this, the Head Constable only once looked at the Duty Constable, and that meant authentication to him to be operative on the duty and deliver the treatment. And the hefty Duty Constable who was already edgy and had a bone to pick with Bachchu for keeping him waiting at the Aekka stand, having made him late in the prompt production of the wanted man at the police station did his best what was creditable to the policemen in inventing excelling treatment to be tried on the criminals, and he started in the administration of kicking and giving Bachchu thuds and thumps nonstop in several innovative ways.

And the final kick that the Duty Constable gave was of such a calculated force that it threw Bachchu on the floor and he fell as if celestial gravity had concentrated to disbalance the feet of Bachchu to go up. And Bachchu became a dumping like a turtle turned up, still on the floor with feet up in the air, and his skimpy *Lungi* – the sarong wrapped round him, did not support him cover sufficiently as it ought to have done, and there was nothing left to conceal and all the police men saw what they should not have seen.

This falling over flat on his back was a welcome pause for Bachchu, and the ordeal of he turned into a cock with bottom up and head down, was on hold, and he found it was convenient to be in that state, lying flat with his back resting on the floor as he was. But this was a sight, not even the visionary police men could approvingly look at. And the Head Constable was first to notice the horse and cart driver lying in a ludicrous posture and showing his bared anatomy, and on that is prolonging his disarray, drawing comfort from the position he was in with a spruce of joy stretching across his face. The Head Constable was thrown gorging in shock for seeing him in the millennium of medieval days, when man walked like that.

And as soon as the Head Constable spotted that, that irregularity was choosy, picked by the hijabs man being questioned, he actions bound and with the pick of the words, gushing out from the opening below his curling moustache with his personal fire brand qualities for handling a situation like this developed at various police stations of his postings to perfection, with all the police masteries behind him, yelled at the top of the voice at Bachchu with the fiercest of shout.

"Get on to your feet, you blithering goof of a cock and get to that Murgha position at once you clown, and keep that blabbering mouth shut and keep staying in that Murgha position for as long as not told to stand up on those murky feet, you, cocky goon."

And Bachchu sensing that it was a long order and it meant something in depth and disaster may be round the corner coming to get him fast, quickly lifted his whole self like a shot and climbed on to his feet and turned into the Murgha position at once.

The Head Constable really became for the first time concerned in his duty cycle of police duty that he had met someone of the type who cared too hoots about his crime and was an expert at making things look of little consequence - a something made to look nothing of it.

But because Bachchu's crime was not that of a murderer or that of a thief, but only of a violator of the practice of norms in the social sphere, it merited consideration for leniency by the thinking Head Constable. He could not place his crime to be that very high profiled in the law books of criminology that required giving him bruises deeper than skin. And when the Head Constable saw Bachchu's legs were giving way, and he had enough of the prudent treatment as thought of appropriate for the category of his crime, and his legs were not ready to support the freakish distribution of the weight of his body and his joints were beginning to wobble and he was convincingly ready to slump as a dumping on the floor, the considerate Head Constable passed the order to the Duty Constable: "Stand him up."

When Bachchu as commanded to stand up, straightened his body, his eyes were red shot and defocused. His hair was standing on its roots and bottom was pulled up and his knee joints were ceased to half locked, half opened position and he looked all round a cock he was ordered to be one. The Head Constable looked at his whole form and shape from top to bottom, with an unfathomable inquisitive look and after lengthy scrutiny and a keen survey of him, vented his feeling.

"Foul mouth, gutsy, crude deformed cock, teasing the Governess."

Bachchu had not the foggiest of the idea what the Governess was, and he denied that he had teased any other mare except his horse, and said to the Head Constable.

"Maeen Baap, Hum Nay Kauno Ghordni ka Kuchh Naheen Kaha."

My mother and father, I have not said anything to any ludic horsy.

Bachchu thought it was a matter of another mare that had been teased and that's why he has been called at the police station. And he appropriated the slang Ghordni but that developed the implication that he was calling the Governess Ghordni.

Bachchu was known to be masterly in colloquialism, and all the police thought he directed the gun of colloquial sarcasm towards the Governess directing it at her to slight her and reduce her status to a deluged four-legged creature. Now the word *Ghordni* Bachchu used, was a daily use word, but his history sheet was such that no one was going to accept that he had not used mastery in reducing the status of the Governess. But as for Bachchu it was his daily use slang that Bachchu was conversant with. It was used for a female horse regularly; at best it showed a ridiculous haggard filly and it meant no offence to the filly but if attached to the Governess it was to show a reduction in her status.

And the police men screwed out just that meaning and scored a point against Bachchu they wanted derived and alluded it was used for a lady of merit and of worthiness - a lady of distinction from whom pride flowed. In this situation it was immediately suggestive that

Bachchu is deliberately ridiculing her to the utmost and various police opinions sprang up against Bachchu.

The Head Constable had reports that the horse and cart driver was articulate and acutely subtle at molesting ladies, but this was for himself he had seen him in action. He gazed at Bachchu with a close scrutinising, searching look, focusing his eyes at him and monitoring his face to see if it gave away into something he could draw conclusions from in suspected mischief, because no matter how hardened the criminal was, his scrutinizing pierces betrayed the face and he could always see and read signs he was looking for, especially in the emerging crooks still unproven in the crime domain and he always found something concrete there, for his firm deduction of results from that. But finding nothing concrete there in the Bachchu's face, the Head Constable said in his local western best - the spoken Punjabi, in which he was more comfortable in expressing his concealed feelings than in the ordinary daily lingua franca – the Urdu:

"Makhoal Karda Pia Aiy, Aek Dum Pacca Aiy"

Goes on with his tricks, he is absolutely a hardened offender.

The Duty Constable who had brought Bachchu to the police station, giving the best of his opinion to the Head Constable, said.

"Sahib Jee, Sarda Deeta Aiy Aes Noon Ona Noon"

Sahib Sir he has absolutely clobbered her into rottenness.

And the Day Constable standing there added:

"Sahib Jee Hunrd Yay Ais Tarah Naheen Manda"

Sahib Jee, now, he will not give in like this.

The Day Constable meant this hard nut will not be coming forth to yield by these kicks and thumps and making him a cock. The Day Constable in the best of the police fashion was obliquely suggesting to the Head Constable to think of some other ways to straighten him. Because he and other police men could not think of anything else except that Bachchu was calling the Governess a *'Ghordni'* and this belligerent horse and cart driver they thought was persistently after her to get her down.

The post of the Head Constables was that high in police hierarchy that it was allocated to one of expertise and he never lacking in the grasp of police visionary conclusions, but in this case of conclusive war of wit, the Head Constable was taxed to the last and had to think deep. His rich police blood and police learnedness found answer with pertinence and he said ultimately.

"We shall soon find out all about his trickeries and his silly sallying filibusters he is expert at."

And he said to the Day Constable. "Prepare him to have him taken to the court by the Duty Constable."

The Head Constable who was the educated organ of the police force and the chief asset of the *Kotwali* with his police procedural expertise all stacked behind his years of unblemished record of service, with his police headquarter recognitions bestowing on him the elite title of the *Jamedar Sahib* and he in the picks of the reputations as the police visionary, was also pride fully called *Deewan Sahib* – the keeper of the Police Station. And for the rampant responsibilities he carried on his shoulders, and for his perfections in filling the undecipherable scribbling in his *Rozenamcha* – the jotting down of formularised words per second in Khate Shikastah – the broken letters that required close deciphering and were decipherable only by the class holding the expertise of the like of him and not by the ordinary in education, was also in all ways the mainstay of the police wizards and the Man Mother of Kotwali. He was from the time when deputed to the Kotwali so charged with and that was also his rank and position at the Thana when on deputation to the Thana and his expertise was at the highest.

His imposing boundary of authority of the Thana included under his subjugation a spread of over 5 acres of land - the Thana premises with the constables' barracks and the *Thhanedar* – the *Darogha* and the *Naeb Darogha's,* the Station Officers' residences and the stables for the police horses and male and female jail enclosed areas and cells for temporary halt of criminals and offenders and the vast *Phulwari*(s) – the flower laden plant rows, the armoury and the well-guarded *Mal Khana* – the treasury, with little in it as government's treasure to be guarded. But still prize pieces of confiscated lump of opium, and stolen items of pilfering recovered from the thieves, were guarded day and night, as these had entries in the Rozenamcha. These were dutifully handed over into the charge of the next day Duty Constable.

And it was the Head Constable's interpretation of the sections of the laws and his affixing of the clauses in the building of a case and bracketing an offender of a crime in the category of offence and the categorization of the offender that was absolute, and it helped the judiciary in appropriating the punishment to match to the categorization of the offence he had identified for the punitive.

And with the Head Constable's deducing mind, and his years of expertise behind him to guide the court, left no way the Head Constable could make a mistake, and he categorized Bachchu not for raillery or bunkum but for the class in derisive travesty and sent Bachchu to the Qazi's court charging him with:

"You are going to the Qazi's court to stand trial for what you have said to her in what way you have said to her, what you said to her - the Governess."

And Bachchu was sent to the Qazi's court under escort and the charge sheet sent to the court said:

"He has been at the ladies, let losing his diatribe and flinging foul insinuations at them to belittle them and disturb them - all for no reason, just to ridicule them."

The Qazi finding the horse and cart driver back again on the same charge as before on which already he had sent him for reformation to the Madrassah, took a very grim view of the case. He threw a suspicious glance measuring the man in Bachchu, and stood him there in the court, like a severely contaminated thing, and turned towards the prosecutor for his summary of the case.

The prosecutor was brief and curt and said. "My lord he has said this time. You blight, you uncontrolled beast, you breed of White, oh where are you lurking to, and all that..."

The Qazi asked Bachchu. "Did you say you blight you breed of White and all that...?"

Bachchu, who knew no cunningness but only honesty, mightily said. "Yes Sire," And he spoke. "When I am saying this, it is for bringing her round to her senses."

"That would be all my lord", thundered the prosecutor and said to the Qazi.

"My lord, he most glaringly admits that he said those words and he is even adamant to add more to it for cutting down someone's stature and that admission and the tendency he possesses for a further adding to the molestations of his victim proves his guilt and what he said about the Governess was not a faux pa, but a deliberate scathing of her."

The Qazi said. "Yes, it proves his guilt. Case proved, guilty of offence as accused."

And with Qazi, more than half inclined already to think that the horse and cart driver had done it again and that he was guilty of offence, the proceeding as it went in the court, led Qazi easily into pronouncing Bachchu guilty after he found him by all measures of conceivable truth to be so.

The Qazi however before passing his court order in words precise to speak of the judgement suitable in wordiness and fit in decorum, retired to his chamber to give a thinking break to his mind and produce suitable words to write the punishment, appropriate and befitting that was to keep him away from mischief, which he was continuing to commit without doubt not as faux pa, as the prosecutor said but deliberate feathered insult, and that at the drop of a hat.

It flashed across the mind of the Qazi that he should bar him from plying his horse and cart on the road and send him to work in the fields to do farming at some forlorn place so that he did not have contact with people to get a chance to molest them. The only bother was how will the land be procured and provided to him and the expertise needed for tilling and sowing of the land and other related information on it transferred to him.

This being a long-winded solution although the best in this case to solve the problem, but because of its haul of apparent involvement of logistics inherent in its implementation and the required immense efforts wanted in preparing him to qualification involved for the switch over of the profession of an adamant horse and cart driver on composing rude jests into a docile farmer, he dropped the idea. And then there he did not want any deprivation to the Nawabdom of a carrier vehicle withdrawn from the road. And he thought at length of some other mode of punishment and decided that the best was that he should be allowed to do the horse and cart plying service which was very much wanted by the Nawabdom; but he be ordered to put a gag on his mouth at the moment when his passengers had got seated and all things were ready and he was left with no other step, but only to move with the passengers.

It was reported that this was the time of the journey when he created on the spot grotesque words, manufactured from the mill of his oratorical gibberish and produced lanes of them in ingenuity, not findable anywhere, even in the voluminous, recognised dictionaries in the vaults of the libraries and his words were plain but conveying potent sacrilege of the meanings as he intended, and he flung these on his victims. And the words finding the vulnerable, homed in for molesting them when their ears happened to fall in the purview of their penetrating lethal meanings, hitting their fragilities which he distinctly noticed prior to shooting out the molesting at them. The Qazi therefore diligently formulated the judgement to cover all that aspect of the notoriety.

The Qazi gave his ruling: "The court examined, reviewed and re-reviewed, weighed, and established after deep consideration that the words he – the guilty shot at others, did have a piercing, poking and at the least a two-pronged meaning in them and one of them was of a molesting nature, and has decided the punishment of putting a gag on the mouth of the guilty was an unfettered requirement." And the court order read:

"There shall be two occasions that the horse and cart driver will shut his mouth by gagging himself with a piece of a fair size cloth, such that in its trapping endeavour the cloth will have gone over his mouth leading to the back of his neck where it will be given two knots binding one on top of the other for the gag to remain firm there during all the journey extensive or otherwise, till the horse and cart driver arrived to the end of the journey, the place of the destination for the passengers he was carrying them to. He shall not open the knot during the journey and thereby remove the gag, which shall be removed only at the destination of arrivals. Inspectors at each of the onward going and returning points of the journeys shall remain duty bound to monitor the on and off action of the horse and cart driver for putting on timed gags that will be put on his mouth by him on his own reckoning, prompt at the time of the moving offs with or without the passengers."

-: . :-

III

THE PUBLIC CLAMOUR

XIII

With the court order passed and punishment announced, there was nothing left but its execution and Bachchu was sent back to his horse and cart service and police inspectors were placed in position to monitor his gag on, gag off operation. Bachchu started the timed motions of the voice throttling, speech restrictive court order, which rigorous inspectors were monitoring that the court order was carried out to the letter, which Bachchu did not know why the court order was passed to haunt him when he did nothing. And he always wondered why each time one lady or the other was in his way, like the one running scary like a harassed deer, harried in the village. She ran head on heels and God knows why, when the yelling, 'catch her, catch her' he raised was only directed at the roving horse to be caught in the meadows and not her.

And Bachchu did not know why one lady or the other was shouting at him and people kicking him when he was in his Chhappar, asleep when God knows he was not hurting anybody. And then there was this lady with umbrella beating and breaking her umbrella on him, hitting him as hard as she could when he did no harm to her, and now there was this mysterious punishment given by the Qazi at the instigation of the all too worked up, single minded prosecutor bent on getting a punishment to him. Bachchu wondered and wondered and looked for an answer for these ordeals to his innocent self, and he found none, and he had been lately thinking of such brain bogging questions and trying to find answer.

It was getting late in night. Tonight, his work of passenger lifting and carrying them home had run late in the night, a lot longer than usual. The last train bringing the passengers for lifting them had been

483

late. Bachchu was now returning home. His horse and cart was empty, and freezing wind blew hard and strong and stronger than ever before, and he had to tear through the wind all along his way to home in this weather.

It was cold, very cold. The gusts of freezing wind and the biting cold of the severe winter were freezing the flesh and entering in the marrows of his bones. He heard the crackling of his bones and the cold did not stop hurting him and the mare ran and nothing was bothering her and she kept herself warm and comfortable. She did not feel a freckle of cold, and as for Bachchu, he was shaking with cold like a rope dangling in the blowing wind. The biting wind was freezing every part of him, it was blowing hard and whistling, and his teeth chattered, and he felt numb and frozen and miserable. And he was mentally drowned in gloomy thoughts.

"Oh! How I wish I ran like the mare did, and kept me warm. But if I did that the rocks strewn on the road will knock my feet."

And Bachchu blamed his clumsy feet that were so big and unsafe to let him run on the stone strewn road in the dark. Oh, how he wished he had hooves like the mare did. And he wondered why men couldn't have hooves to run on the roads in the cold dark nights and keep themselves warm like the mare did. And he looked at the scanty twinkling and timid stars in the sky, they were just no help, not throwing enough light from them to light the road and the road was dark. And he wanted to know why they couldn't be bigger to light the road, at least enough to let him see the rocks and stones, and he saw the mare sees in the dark much better and he swore he wanted to be one whole lot like the horse, just the way the mare was, there and then to run on the road like she did, and all such strange thoughts had been coming to Bachchu since he had been gagged and made hermetic.

For keeping the watch and monitoring the performance of the gag on and gag off operation of Bachchu in compliance to the court order, several inspectors were placed on duty and the deputation of the inspectors had meant that the expenses on policing to maintain Law and Order had increased in the Nawabdom. The public had not created any problem of Law and Order and there was no other problem in the Nawabdom, and yet the expenses on the maintenance of Law and Order had increased and for this the police record had suffered. Their impeccable good reputation had got spoiled for the poor statistics they showed in the deployment of increased numbers of police officers as law enforcer vis-à-vis no turmoil. There was no plausible explanation to this misnomer to the police and as to where lay the cause of the increased expenses.

The expenditure on the maintenance of Law and Order had increased spirally uncontrolled to a record high, which had to be met through taxation. The net result was, the tax burden on the public pocket increased to very high figure and the public started to grumble. All this news reached to the Nawab, who did not find it pleasing. He went to the depth of the matter and found that there was one horse and cart driver who had been ordered to gag his mouth and he had to be monitored by the police and the extra deployment of police was increasing the expenditure. The Nawab showed awe and felt curious to see this strange man who was gagged at each marks of the departures of his journey - the arrival and the departure points of the destinations. The Nawab asked for this strange man to be brought to him if possible.

Bachchu was brought to the Nawab, to the very grandeurs of his court in his capital, after lot of coaxing and assurances by the summoning men and the courtiers of the Nawab that no harm will come to him this time against his much reluctance. Bachchu was reluctant and said; when he went to a building of the Nawab, he was beaten and punished there. In one building he was beaten and kicked and in another he was ordered to put a gag on his mouth. "And I am not going to any building of the Nawab." And it was only after lots of persuasion that no harm will come to him this time that Bachchu agreed to go to the Ralah Palace and presented him to the Nawab, but he went there extremely peevish, dreading for the worst, and this created a good impression on the Nawab.

It is in the blood of the Royalties that they want to feel that they are feared and respected, never mind how humane and gracious a particular Royalty was, there was no exception to this doctrine of the factuality of the Royalty expectancies, who are always hankering for awe to be in step with their step. And the natural fear in Bachchu against torture and abuse, created an aura of submission and docility in Bachchu which pleased the Nawab. And the Nawab pleased as he was, to see a deep-down respect shown to him by the man representing a common's attitudinal imperfection; asked him to sit himself down and this was the greatest singular honour that Bachchu was bestowed upon him, ever in the time-honoured pursuit of his horse and cart carriage work to be allowed to sit before someone as high and imposing as the Nawab. And Bachchu sat down in front of the gracious Nawab as gestured by him.

Besides this gesture of kindness, weighed down on Bachchu and pleasant disposition of the Nawab directed at him, there was further to it, Bachchu was asked in an affectionate tone by the Nawab:

"Tell me; what takes upon you that you fling words of disquieting rectitude on the ladies of the Nawabdom, engineering them roll out and thrust on the persons of the ladies of the Nawabdom to their discomfiture?"

Bachchu, who was for the first time exposed to kindness, to sympathetic straight questions, found his mind working like of the young rejuvenated to excellences, ready to exercising philosophic intones of temperament dubbed in sophistication, to pedal philosophic disposition with pervading pageantry stroking him into producing coherent performance. And an ancestral gentleman came out of Bachchu and his faculties awakened to embrace eloquence, and charm subdued his peevishness and he broke the barrier to demonstrative submissions and was rushing to cross all barriers to outspokenness. Bachchu stood on the pedestal of entrusting height to conquer the respect of the Nawab. And he was now ready to outpour hard facts of realities to the Royalty, pampering him to heights and the Nawab all ears ready to listen to him.

And Bachchu like a freshman and even one better from a university of distinction, of standing and creditable records, putting across the best in subdued behaviour and the finest in disciplined talk that could come out of a freshman, spurred by a force unknown, pushing him into an act of performance he had never been through before and had only seen a bit of the likes of that in the acts put forward by his aunt, very neatly and candidly explained to the Nawab that his mare was struck by rigidness at times, imbued with total imbecility and at most times with total petit deluge, and he found the use of set slang when used appropriated to suit to the situation, made her revert to display calm behaviour and the serenity required and expected of her that was all along the requirement was met. And that was the reason for the deployment of his at times untamed verbosity in the slang of the region. Bachchu further appraised the Nawab:

"The words those sprang out of me at the spur of the moment; my mare understood by her precocious talents better, and these did to align her mind, and invigorate her to the display of good behaviour and she turned to behave with moderations, displaying controlled temperament and that was all that was behind the seeming extremes of my words. The slang used was not directed at any other person however precisely they invigorated their thoughts to affixing their connections with the words and the slighting of their persons. These were not meant for them in seeking scoring a hit on them. It was only the requirement that necessitated an address to the mare in the manners of impunity." And Bachchu further added:

"The prosecutor never allowed me to speak and explain, and the verdict of punitive judgement was passed against me on assumptions, and on the summing up of the prosecutor in a hurry."

The Nawab convincingly saw that the horse and cart driver was capable of delivering great speech and was capable of presenting him in his court with such decorum, and the Nawab was very favourably impressed by the performance of Bachchu and was absolutely positive that the vocabulary Bachchu used, necessitated by the requirement imposed on him by the coercions of his mare - his partner in the profession of the passenger carrying work, could not have been so awfully dreadful as to invigorate punishments of the class, he was subjected to.

The Nawab who completely understood the situation and everything related with it that had given rise to impaired justice, an injustice that was leading to problems in his Nawabdom, could not condone that culmination in the injustice. The Nawab was perturbed that justice was miscarried in his Nawabdom at all and it was trampled, and the rights of a human being were quashed and an innocent person was reduced to an inconsequential entity. The Nawab ordered eradication of the injustice done immediately and spoke.

"The injustice had a vehement nature of snowballing; clogging all venues leading to dissuasion of culture and barring all drives to popularising and perpetuating rationality and was the cause of degrading of the humanity at large."

The Nawab said, "The injustice done to an individual in the Nawabdom was already evincing by gathering unseen problems for the Nawabdom, eating up its resources and culminating unrest."

And the good Nawab action bound and without waiting for, and allowing theories in unpredictable succeed and abstract miraculous solutions offer them spear burst through the seam of injustice as a token of gift to him and to his Nawabdom, without making any solicitations for such unexpected solutions to emerge from out of the seams of impossibilities and procure, provide, and fulfil expectancies, and without letting futilities expend efforts on dreams, expecting spectaculars to occur on their own reckonings for the comfort of the Nawabdom, which was not to be its good fortune, started himself to organize a move so that injustice of this nature could never occur again in his Nawabdom. And the nature swung in merriment to pour out the poetic verse to please the Janaan-e Jahan – the dears of the nature:

نفیس جان نفا ست کی راہ پاتی ہے
عصر ہو شب ہو صبح ہو بہار پاتی ہے
عدل کو دوڑ کے گرد ماہ گلے لگائے اب
خدا کی وحدانیت بکھرے خزاں اب جاتی ہے

سیّد اطہار حسین

Nafees Jan Nafasat Ki Raah Pati Haai
Asr Ho Shab Ho Subah Ho Bahar Pati Haai
Adl Ko Daurd Kay Girdmah Galay Lagayay Ab
Khuda Ki Wahdaniyat Bikhray Khezan Ub Jati Haai

The exquisite soul finds the passage to exquisiteness
Be it late afternoon, night, morning, find spring
The full moon runs and embraces the justice
The Oneness of God spreads, the autumn goes now

-: . :-

III

THE CONFERENCE IN
THE NAWABDOM

V

After the presentation of the facts by Bachchu the horse and cart driver, the Nawab issued a *Farman* – a royal decree to the citizens to assemble for a conference in the Nawabdom to hold discussion on the topic of:

'A single person forming a minority may be right and a host of men forming a majority may be wrong'.

The Nawab desired that the attitudes of the people be moulded to accept the fact that truth is not affected by majority opinion. The searching topic of the conference was elucidative of scholasticism which incidentally helped endorse obliquely his own hereditary rule in continuity that one man holding the seat of power and ruling with absolute authority on the singular plea of a vice free rule as his predecessors had presented was rightful to continue with the class of distinctive rule he has to offer in his times.

The Nawab in support of the validity of the subject under discussion was to quote in the conference, with the logical force of truth behind it the powerful verses of the Aayat 103: 1, 2, and 3 from the Book of Guidance – the Holy Quran that said:

1. By the declining day.
2. Man is in loss.
3. Except such who believe and do righteous deeds and between them do the exhorting for truth and the exhorting for patience.

For the understanding of all, the Nawab was to explain what the Sura emphasized was that the majority of men had placed themselves in loss, except a minority that had faith and did good deeds, prompted each other to take to righteousness, and observed patience.

A living victim of the opinion confederacies of majority was grilled, tortured, penalised and punished under the fallacious judgement was to be presented in the conference and the people who though vouched to the divineness of the Sura but changed their conviction to what they believed in their persistency that the majority opinion was always right were to be heralded in to listen to the logic and the anthem of Quran.

The Nawab saw how voluntarily through the notion of absolute correctness of the majority opinion the truth had been side tracked and heralded to an alley leading to a certain cruel deformation of truth. The clenched fist policy of forming prejudged notions in servitude to falsehood, augmented under the belief that power evolving from the majority class holding adherence to their assumed and unspecified commitments to glorification of their evolved idols and to their dicta they dedicated themselves to, bringing it push them in the court of hearing to proposition and persecution that it was absolute, was to be challenged to be delirious to absoluteness vis `a vis the realities, and the attitude was to be corrected.

With their misgivings surrounding them, they were basking in their own tended satisfaction that the extended credibility they apportioned to their belief from the rapture of their mind, burdening their vogue with eulogies that it was idealistic, and the performance of the pneumatic souls did not require weighing in to stand trial by any measure of credibility to the gauge of their yield was to be challenged. And that no idols' performances were above the rigour of the evaluation was to be driven home through the conference.

The coincidence of the majority with feeble wisdom sitting in the driving seat and steering the ship of destiny in a direction to where they preferred it to go, with their unwavering demand of unquestionable submission to their chosen decision, whether rational or not was to be put to regeneration and renewal, and only rationalism was to be evoked. The fastidiousness and all laxities in the illogical reasoning was to be disbanded and ingress into God formulated laws was to be retracted through the resolutions of this conference. Logic and reasoning were to be made concomitant and awakening aroused, and made the guiding and the fundamental principle through which affairs of the individual and of the Nawabdom were to be affixed as a matter of normalcy and as the outcome of this conference.

The Nawab in the conference was to further quote in his address the Aayet 6: 116 of the Holy Quran, throwing light on the pursues of the majority and their whims, and God raising caution against their whims in words:

"(O Prophet) There is the majority in the world that if you go by their whims, they will put you away from the path of God. They pursue only their whims and these people only talk of not much sense."

The Nawab was to drive home that rationality and justice were the hallmark to attaining a balanced elevated society. And it was not the majority opinion that mattered and it was a very important conference.

The bugles were sounded, and the drums were beaten to raise the signature tune from 'Naubat' – alert, to announce that the Nawab was coming out of the palace. In this; the order of the beating of the drum and its sounding on at his entering in the palace was the same as on his leaving the palace, only the melody hidden in the sound of the bugle was different.

The Nawab came out of his palace in the latest steel-top Sedan of dark-black colour, glossy shine, and of chrome plating on the handles, on the body trims and on the bumpers and decorative plates, with chrome rich in the content of chromium, shining to dazzle the eyes. This special car was ordered by the Nawab as soon as these gasoline driven wonders emerged for notice to be taken of them. The Nawab was very much of the contemporary taste, and of a much-heightened gnosis in the recognition to things of choice and equipped with knowledge of the trend that originated in other lands, and he had ordered these cars for his use from the very first batch of these cars built for the Royal Customers.

491

The Nawab believed that when the prosperity kisses the forehead of the fortunate-blessed, and it sways to engulf his exemplary being, and its golden wings take him under its full protective cover, it should be shown off by being exuberant in spending and by shunning thriftiness to a grinding halt. And that would be a sign of showing thanksgiving, and that culture will add to the advancement of the era culture, and to the flourishing of art.

For running these gasolines filled wonders, the Nawab ordered building gasoline pumping station in the Nawabdom and he inaugurated it himself. Of these cars, a pair of them were reserved for the royal use, with one of them carrying foldable top to permit him be seen by his subjects, and there were some others of kinds called general use cars and trucks, which stood at the service of the Nawabdom. And this venture had created, new employment portfolios and job opportunities of drivers to run the cars and trucks and attendant class to run the gasoline station, and all this had become a matter of pleasing consequence for the Nawab.

The royal car of the Nawab was followed by the hosts of the officials of the Nawabdom, in buggies – the carriage drawn by the single horse, and Tanga. Then coaches - the carriages drawn by horses in duals and men walking on foot, riding bicycles, all forming a procession and all proceeding towards the conference venue. The peasantry, aristocracy, judiciary and the state functionaries, all were proceeding to the conference venue as summoned by the Nawab and as their obligation to hear of the Quranic Aayat and attend the conference-address of the sovereign and the Head as in the decree of the royal order.

Special invitation was given to the horse and cart driver, the victim of the lapse of justice on the one hand, and the charge framers - the two ladies of consequence and of distinction on the other hand. And for focusing and heightening attention on the chief invitee – the horse and cart driver as envisaged in the plan, only he was decorated with the rich floral rose garland of special make and length from the bloomed roses that gave out full fragrance, presenting fresh petals. The garland was slipped round the neck of the chief invitee. And the rest of the gathering was not allowed to carry even a tiny petal of the rose on them to let stand out the chief invitee and the elaborate arrangement of the conference was to centre staging and highlighting the victim, who was escorted by the officials of the Nawabdom.

The Nawab took upon himself to display His Highness in a *Sehrangi* - seven colours shedding, shod silk *Sherwani* and a fluffy soft turban, flashed into decoration with a modest size gem of diamond cut to present several facets, all sparking to give an all-round brilliance, and the Nawab entered further in glamour with the brilliance tugged with a rising curving feather holding the diamond under its cover to highlight the grandeur of the Nawab and his Nawabdom of theocracy. And the gentry backed the Nawab by attiring them in their best Sherwani or three-piece suits of the choicest fabrics, with matching floral ties shedding scholasticism and brilliance. And the peasantry showed up in waist cut, and gentry wore the Pagrdi – the turban and donned flowing Dhoti Kurta or the Kurta pyjama.

With all that procedural setting, the conference was a narrative to suggest that the assembly of the educated learned, the aristocracy and the state functionaries, all had failed in their duty. The educated in their learnedness to not stand retaliating against injustice, the aristocracy and the social lords not standing setting instances of perfection to deter injustice. The foundations of justice thus dropped from its pedestal, not arousing fair taste and pursuance of fairness, and the administrators failing in planning and the execution of plausible administrative obligations, lacking to galvanize the rule of law and neglecting to put justice as the centre piece of practice in focus, and all altogether failing to illuminate the society with the light of reasonableness and failing to galvanise it with enrichment of expertise and knowledge. And the contributory inputs that they were to make for creating a hoisted high society was absent.

In these prevailing conditions, the venue of the conference was to tell, alas! All the sophistications all equipped with, and all the obligations they owed to exhibit it, and all the trust placed in them with their allegiance to practice erudition; none had to show of its glamour and all their education had come to no avail to prevail upon and mould the attitudinal change in the majority to devoutness and vitalisation towards *Baqa* – the permanency of goodness and justice, and all their sophistication was lamed, and it was crying at the doorsteps of ignorance and inaction.

The Nawab was of piercing acrimony to all in his speech, and he most eloquently spoke on the subject of truth. He was like an adept candle bearer of evident righteousness who had embarked on nation building. The Nawab said, the thriving societies will huddle their energy to steer towards righteousness away from the wrong and will sort out truth from the falsehood and will agree upon and have consensus on truth, and will discredit values which are without legitimacies of sparkling truth emanating from their behaviour community hundreds of scholars. They will revise edicts and precepts in pursuance by the majority and open their hearts to propositions to change in social and religious precepts as call of progress demanded.

But the Nawab said, "Alas the reverse of the desirous took place in the performing arena of the society and it became apprehensive to adopt goodness and it allowed to be infested with categorical abuses and only showed credit of trickled goodness."

The Nawab bluntly isolated the opportunists, exploiters and the extremists and called them the eternal wrong doers and lamented the performance of others who were permissive of inundating tail butted ugliness in the society and were peddling to strengthen the decline and detaching the society away from virtue.

The Nawab spoke to the audience in plain language to say: "Some among you have failed in the test you were put to, to examine and sieve truth out of the falsehood and you labelled falsehood to be truth and swept truth out of the sight and allowed yourself to be slighted and swayed and erred to land in the pitfall of fallacy and injustice, allowing falsehood pounce on you and make naught of your prevalence in reasoning. You condoned the wrongs done by the quibbling and the scheming individualists and made light of it and discredited yourself denying upon you approaches to uphold the truth."

The Nawab added, "but then the brilliance can never be kept inundated in the haze of falsehood and truth kept submerged and hidden not allowing it showing its spectaculars for the sight of the beholder. It showed its majesty as the crown of glory was placed on the righteous, the pious noble head of the Wali of God Hazrat Ali AS., though a full 25 years late, for triumph to suppress inadequacies that came at Hazrat Ali's ascension to the throne of the Khilafat. The

Prophet of God Hazrat Mohammad Mustafa SAWW to halt any deviation had made it mandatory by his proclamation on an urgent command of God in the Ghadeer-e Khum for Ali to ascend to Khilafat, but Ali was held back on pretence of his youth in age, disregarding his divinity and capability." And injustice shewed as early as that. And the Nawab said. "But, as is the rule the divinity and piety prevail, and it was the nature of truth, it always emerged triumphant."

And the Nawab said: "We are instrumental in gathering here to give recognition to truth and be of service to God to uphold the fundamental rights of the oppressed and wronged in the society. We are reminded of the harmless woman Anna Gelid wrongly called a witch in 1782 (BBC News) in Switzerland and executed for some political gain of the appellant in the tiny Canton of Glarus and now Sep 2007, after her case been continuously examined by the Swiss parliament all through these times, she finally was exonerated on August 27, 2008. After two hundred and twenty-five years, she was served with justice and the stigma on her name of being a witch was removed and thanks to the nature of justice it has shown that the just societies continuously work for justice to prevail."

The Nawab called upon the audience. "Let truth blossom. This will inescapably focus us on our formed beliefs, practices and notions which our virtuous existence desires tampered on the moulding anvil of adulations. Let free discussions and freedom of speech flourish, and assemblies unrestrictive and purposeful held to vent truth-ridden-expositions. Let harmony be the fore play and applied in our discussions, and strength of steel shown in our virtuousness to defend God and the Prophet's words in guidance of rightness, and let nothing may rule our behaviour outside the parameters of normalcy licensing deception overruling decency."

"Let freedom not be demeaned and hampered by the noxious propagandist campaigns. Let history not be made tendentious, and it be unfolded tending truth and discarding pretentiousness and escorting righteousness. Let history be seen not through the monocle of prejudice, but by the magnificence of fairness. Let manifestations of truth and just thoughts for liberalism steer and take-hold of epistemological doctrine, and evolve a society that was just and kind and wholly guided by justness and just practices. And let clamps on speech be lifted to create free institutions to inculcate broadened outlook and bring men on equal footing and develop in them fellow feelings and protect them from diabolism, staggering into the similarities of injustices as administered in likeness to the horse and cart driver, who suffered disorientation and agony at the hands of the miscarriage of justice that declared him guilty, who today stands exonerated."

The Nawab then turned his attention direct to the judiciary and said, "The Qazi's personal limitations which led him detach his faculties from a wholly fair judgement due to his pre-formed opinion he had entered in, made him unreachable to an all-embracing truest possible judgement, leading him extricate a judgement that was to do no credit to the judiciary and to the Nawabdom and was a misnomer to it."

The Nawab pointed out that the judgment the Qazi passed and announced was neither creditable nor laudable, which brought the individual and the state in entanglement and the Nawab lamented that the preformed judgment was not even credulous like the credence given to the General, the shield of the 'Law of Necessity' for him to be shielded by it, who wrenched the fictitious law using force. The case of the horse and cart driver was opposite, and any similarity could not be drawn in the case of the horse and cart driver and the case of the beneficiary General[46] that the lopsided judgement was perceived and passed, and no constraints made to observe pity, remedy and reality.

The Nawab pointed out: "There were generals among generals in the Land of Seasons and Songs who exploited judiciary forcing and enticing them to legalise their usurpation as legitimate action. The Doctrine of Necessity though legalised by Islam; 'that which is otherwise not lawful is made lawful by necessity', but that is God's domain. According to the Greek school of scepticism headed by Pyrrha, the human beings are incapable of passing any judgement about anything. And the human must abide by the law sent by God.

A citation of the medieval justice by the English Cleric and jurist Henry de Bracton died 1267, a defender of feudal aristocracy is

---

[46] General Ziaul Haque, wrenched the Law of Necessity from the judiciary and obtained power to even amend the constitution. And he became an absolute impiety for the society.

plausible to be recalled, but in its adaptation the intention must be only to save life through it from peril. And any excuse to extrude worldly benefit by the General, simply would not wash the General off the guilt of usurpation, who pounced at the capital sneaking in grabbing power and legitimising his dark action. And the judge of the judiciary in the supreme interest of Law of self-preservation announced that the doctrine of the 'law of necessity' was falling within the gambit of the supreme interest of the country and declared the General Zia's abominable takeover, the elixir and the necessity. But the General trampled the entrustment put in him and reviled the constitution equating it to 'a piece of paper' that he can tear. And the judiciary every bit proved they were a spineless vertebra and they must turn their faces to the idealism of the Alvi Justice - Hazrat Ali's justice.

The Nawab announced: "henceforth all Qazi(s) and Judges will take oath at the turn of passing every judgement that they by witnessing justice and just practices and knowing that: The Truest of the Judge was watching their shaping and casting of the judgement, declare on oath that the judgement passed was impassionate, and without any fervour, fear or favour stimulated by any extraneous stimulant. And that the verdict of the judgement was a subordination of God verdict, wholly adhering to the supreme norms of justice."

The Nawab said: "The judgement passed in the first case brought against the horse and cart driver was right to the extent that the intent of the judgement was right, but the outcome of the judgement was flawed and the education that was imparted carried distortion, based on personal interest inhibiting the flourish of academic lessons. And the judgement in the second case against the horse and cart driver was excessive in the recourse of the award of the punishment. The outcome from the first judgement showed that the educational system in the Nawabdom was defective, and the outcome from the second influenced judgement showed that the judicial judgements were sceptical and far from satisfactory."

The Nawab said. "For curing the ill brought about by the first shortcoming, in the execution of the judgement for the correction of the linguistics, I am going to suggest it is due to the teacher hitching him to detachments removed from the duty - building castles in the air to enter in the realm of paradise. I propose reform in education of the grammar of truth in the curriculum to bind intentions to turn to convinced faith essential to galvanise Islam. The concept is, one grand curriculum is devised to cover the education of all the factions that have arisen in Islam and variations dismantled. And the curriculum to be prepared by a panel of religious experts picked, out from the wide spectrum of the factions having nose to smell truth and sieving it from the camouflaging wilderness of claim of truthful produce by the falsehood.

This will collect factuality and clean scholasticism for decorum inherited from all the sources to interweave truth to settle to recognised factuality using the weigh balance of logic, fairness and reason to form the basis for the implementation of the find, as the grand curriculum which now will be accepted by all the factions and the core philosophy of religion to create and propagate general conceptual harmony will have been achieved and will be open to be pursued."

The Nawab continued. "The fabric of the educational curriculum the expertise of the scholars will weave will have the fundamental conflict demolished, lending a concept in teaching which will carry the greatest of force on the delivery of truth and justice, negating deviations from right path and blocking any reversion to the old snuffbox, with conscious effort to dismantle and bar propaganda of falsehood, holding them at bay for ever through the conditioning of the research programme.

The Nawab said. "Let me repeat, the first judgment while correct in intentions to provide benefit of education to the victim, if weighed in the weigh balance of impartial evaluation, made him suffer at the hands of the defective teaching thrust at him, exacerbating wanderings in his mind as to what the truth was. Unsettling settled convictions and letting vulnerability to fallacies hound him. This was all done on the assumption that he had committed an offence which he had not, and it was a judgement wholly one sided that chose to completely ignore the thrashing that the horse and cart driver was subjected to at the hands of the lady thrasher who administered the thrashing in the form of determined blows on the victim's undefended head and face – mostly the face of the horse and cart driver.

And all the thrashing was for an imagined offence from him, ignoring the dignity that abounds an unresisting. And the compensatory benefit of this deliberate thrashing to the horse and cart driver was not allowed by the court. And though the action taken by the lady was entirely based on misinterpretation and fallacy, nevertheless, the lady set herself wholly at thrashing, unmindful of any wrong doing and dauntless of any misguidance perchance taking hold of her, and this aspect of the case by the court was not taken into consideration for providing relief to the victim."

The Nawab continued. "The torture subjected on an innocent person from the sublime court of justice was not condonable, and as a compensatory gesture for the excess committed by the functionary representing the authority of the state, the Nawabdom awards a compensation of one hundred acres of land to the victim from the fertile land stretches of the Nawabdom. Let this be entered in the records books of the land department. It also announces to publish his name in the honours list of the Nawabdom as a relief measure, belated though it is.

And as for the misjudgement of the ladies, which caused the miscarriage of justice, causing tortuous sufferings inflicted on an innocent, the Nawabdom invites the two ladies who lodged the complaint to come forward and offer their apologies for the misunderstanding they allowed them enter in, causing harm to the dignity and the honour of an innocent person, who intended no harm to them, and he unaware that they had taken an offence in the fashion they did from his involuntary exposure to his nurtured linguistic defects which he carried with him, due to an unreachable free for all education system and the Providence's wish manipulating cause in our midst was open to the nature's narrative. The Nawabdom observes, the horse and cart driver − viz Bachchu Yarwah bears no responsibility to cause the arising ferocity emerging in the respectable ladies."

The Nawab weighing the ladies' excessive reaction as the genesis of all the cause, which was due to their uncompromising exposition to his talk and their admission that they were hit by the linguistic defects arising from their linguistic shortfalls that their derivations of the meanings fouled them up and led them to their exceeding reaction, were gracious and surrendered their will to the Nawab, who commanded each party to rise for a compromise to be struck between them, and it be initiated by the ladies. The Nawab proposed the ladies spearhead the apologies for their forgiveness for the imagined offence of the horse and cart driver, and the Nawab's neat mind found further solution in the disputation and said:

"In this regard the victim, the horse and cart driver is also urged to offer his grief for having been a reason, involuntary though it was for causing misunderstanding in the minds of the ladies."

-: . :-

III

THE PRETTY FACE OF THE FORTUNE

XV

The brilliant talk of the Nawab in the conference had its logical effect on the ladies and on Bachchu – the horse and cart driver. Extension of apologies and exchanges of cordialities were made between Bachchu and the ladies. And it was the magnum opus of the Nawab. Through the spectacular event of the conference, the Nawab tidied up the state and the individual affairs. Each of the parties had now a higher tender feeling for the other. And they navigating them through the uncertain waters of doubts and hesitations, finally landed in the lap of volunteerism, and the ladies hit by the syndrome of rescuing an inundated far-gone, sinking in the abyss of the depths of deprivations their mentor, for evolving talent in him, after a short conference between them decided on their roles in glistening the horse and cart driver to make him outshine into sophistications through reform and uplifting, placing him in the investiture of dignity. And they chalked out their portions of contributions in changing his environmental circumstances and the habitation conditions.

One lady putting aside the elitist snob of the credentials of her occupational superiority, volunteered herself to enter into the role of his wife that was if Bachchu accepted and desired so. And the other lady influenced by the instinct of her governess occupancy, decided to provide all the sophistications in coaching, to educating the horse and cart driver for his uplift and grooming. Backed by her English standards, she was the fittest soul for this on taking. And she volunteered herself for the role of the personal coach of Bachchu. And Bachchu, with all his wits about him, exercising full potential of his judgement into enactments, was not insane to have turned down the offers and he most gratefully accepted the offers to become an epitome.

The Qazi available there, immediately solemnized the marriage. And the Qazi felt he had done to retrieve and wrest justice from the clutches of injustice that had held justice in deviance - away from the glorious enactment as dispraised in debacle. And he felt he had duly mellowed injustice and belched out justice from its subduing by the injustice. And thanks to the brilliant talk of the Nawab, it had forced injustice to relinquish justice. And the Qazi said, the Nawab had embathed the injustice and given it to wear the garb of unquestioned justice through his act.

This act of the solemnisation of the marriage between the Lady Councillor and Bachchu was an act of lightening the burden of remorse that the Qazi carried with him. He consciously felt he had not earlier appropriated justice in the measure, right as was to be, and had squandered the great opportunity of showing his great traditionally righteous talent he possessed in the department of administering justice that the squandering away of the opportunity of rendering fair and unquestioned justice and displaying his great meritorious talent unfulfilled was weighing upon him particularly since the time the Nawab had spoken on the subject of justice and had clearly apportioned blame on the judiciary and the justice system.

And thanks to the Providence for putting the good fortune to pursue Bachchu in its tiptoe pursuit that the Qazi was provided the opportunity of lightening his burden of subdued guilt that had permeated through him for its inhabitation in his veins and blood stream, dwindling a careerist's prospects by residing in him, which now found it dislodged from there and was ready to evaporate itself into nothingness and Bachchu was cause to do it and cause to undo it.

In the annals of history, the spectacular was that Bachchu was endowed with a volunteering wife of exacting temperament to nab foul acts, even extending in precaution to include beyond the border-line imperfections in Bachchu to manage his life. And the English Coach was standing to equip him with all the art in the delivery of flowery, altruistic talk and all the deficiencies honking at him, pushing defaults to show their faces of poking slanders obliterated. And where the Modarris had failed, bogged down by his imperfect *Niyat* - the failing intentions of trading approach to get a seat of allocation in the Paradise, the governess had succeeded spurred by her austere of selfless service and desire to wrench for her nothing from out of her service, but just the credit-note from the humanity into the recognition of humanitarianism.

All the philanthropy set to monitor and perfect Bachchu, yielded its honorific, and repeated graces started to flow towards him. Only the short speech effect of the wonderful Nawab was its cause, and the pleasant development of the ladies' offers that had followed the speech that the good fortune took to smartening itself and become the musical clock for Bachchu, and all this became heavenly ado. And the good fortune on its tiptoe pursuit of Bachchu created such consequential sequence in the order of needs and such prizes offered to him on a platter that an aspirant could desire no more. The Nawab had decided to further alleviate the status of Bachchu. He appointed him *Darogha Shahi Astabal* - the Superintendent of the Royal Stables in the Nawabdom.

The Nawab fostered the idea that the duties of the Darogha Stables required a methodical man who understood the language and temperament of the horses and the manners of the stubborn mules. The Nawab felt his vision sharpened by justice had led him come to the door of the right man in Bachchu and he had installed the right man at the right place and had done justice to push away even the whims in problematic issues. Bachchu was to do the breeding of the horses and the mules and do the management of their food and fodder and procure and upkeep the harnesses to make these mules and horses look seemly and besides the upgrading of the carriages, caring and maintaining of the standard of the breeding yards, galvanizing the steeds and their breaking into fine behaving horses and bringing order in the management of the care of the foals and fillies and stallions and mares, and breeding the studs - remedying them of trifling ailments, all was to be taken care of by Bachchu.

Also, there was matching and mating of the beasts for producing cross-breeds of yielding strength for burden carrying and the straightening of the least heeding - the stubborn mules of the Nawabdom. Their training for making them worthy of the army need in eligibility of required competency was to be taken care of by Bachchu. For all this, the Nawab said, Bachchu was the fittest man and he has found the manager.

The mules after they grew into foals in one year, were transferred to the army to carry warfare loads in trains to the battlefields in mountainous terrain. They aided the battle readiness and victory by the army, especially in the hauling of the artillery and carrying the haulages to spots at the enemy position. And the Nawab thought the ceasure of the deterioration entering the standards of perfection in the breeding of the horses and of the mules was an act of onerous, and its confinement was duly transferred into the impeccable hands of Bachchu. But all said, the department of the mules was given to Bachchu more as a gesture of conciliatory measure to pep up his status, rather than a necessity for running the preferences of the Nawab, since of late the Nawab was thinking of plugging the muzzles of the guns and sparing the army of its battlefield warfare duties and deploying them elsewhere.

The indiscriminate slaughter of men, foes, birds, beasts and the ruining of the standing crop, the ploughed fields and the destruction of the pastures was the consequence of the war. It was ambitiousness of enforcing and strengthening the nationalism, which was mutinous to God and it was abhorred by the Nawab and it was the cause of war. The Nawab therefore was thinking of disbanding the army and necessitated by the progressive and the philosophic striving was thinking of turning the army into a divinity approved austere team of Socio-Neo-Faqeers to fill the mission of harnessing the misconceived zealots, following in the footsteps of the Nazim who had raised his team of the Faqeers to even up with the miscreants who were creating havoc in his province. The Nazim's Faqeers were using soothing chants to mellow them. And the Nawab was hoping the army Faqeers might bring out from their *Faqeeri* holdalls, Faqeeri precepts of uniqueness to dislodge vices and inculcate in men affiliations to virtue.

To the Nawab the apprehension from the army was the army's acquired aggressive beguiling fashion moulded of the army custom in the heavy-handed treatment of their adversaries, castigating and hanging those whom they found contrary to their liking for their being too innately wizardly might become more prevalent than desired. Though the Nawab wanted to see they retained their field binocular to mark the murderers and the extremists only and get rid of them who had killed many innocents of the Nawabdom. But it was all along understood by the Nawab that the modus operandi of the army teams of the Faqeers, if they were brought in this vault was going to be different and incomprehensively intricate from that of the Nazism's team of Faqeers, whose modus operandi was call of oneness of God and praise of the Punjatan. But that of the army the Nawab calculated will be foreign to it lurking towards tying up the wizardly.

Therefore, all that enraging fury marked anger, tampered with extreme indiscretion in abruptly throwing surprises at the adversaries and the obnoxiousness shortening of their existence could be accepted at a pinch by the extremist had to be tolerated, if ever he envisaged of not dismantling the army. And the difficulty was his love for the good Generals who were great asset and the Nawab knew he will need them retained intact with their brass caps to hang the miscreants with a little discrete infusion infused in them for their yielding to the general opinion to hang only the deserving - the extremists, turned killers.

For this the Generals were to be made through the aid of the art of subtlety, cladded with change in their conceived notions. Only there was need to administer individualistic treatment General by General to suit to the grandeurs of their individualistically conceived theories, and the deserving for the hanging, arrowed at for their identified action - who considered them exclusive for doing immense creditable work of killing those, who did not see eye to eye with them on their cast-out Sharia they had introduced in their convertibility plan for all to be converted to essentials in belief they decided that seemed total and thorough to them. And they intended taking the overall hold of all the people, disregarding their sublime duty to the committal to God's command in the Aayetul Kursi: *La Aekraha Fiddin* - there is no compulsion in the religion, and where by everyone was free to practice his religion and express his views, but they were least concerned with the largesse of this Aayet and selectively picked commands to suit their notions.

And it was better for the armies laced with intricate weaponries, they thought clever devices, to think that it was not chivalrous to fight the opponent with their devices that were not compatible with the means of the opponent, and it was better they took to sword in one hand and shield in the other. And only unsheathed the sword in the cause of righteousness, and that they thought the sword of reasoned tongue is better than the sword tampered of *Hadeed* – the iron.

But God also wanted to see man progress and make advances in high technological field, in cybernetics, unmanned vehicles and drones but He wanted their use in only to locate the enemies of God and not do mass killings by dropping lethal bombs and firing missiles on peaceful cities.

And in the final dialectics that followed and as the outcome of the Nawab's strategy, the Generals were kept existential by the Nawab for dismantling the killers of the innocent. And the disbanding of the guns and the turning in of the army into a laudable commissioned force of ethics generating Faqeers to raise chants to safeguarding the innocent victims was put on hold and the Generals kept standing for scuttling the killers using their field binoculars to search them out for hanging them as their imperative. And the Nawab entrusted the frisk task of grooming and preparing the mules with fervour to serve the all-intact army. And weighing all the considerations evenly the Generals were thought to be indispensable and lauded and adored.

The army was retained full flung with its flourishes and its colours and Bachchu's post of the Darogha of the Shahi Astabal allowed flourish and he was given a palatial house to live in, with remunerations, commensurate with his status and he was addressed as Yarwah Sahib and his unassuming name of Bachchu was put to oblivion, and without the attachment of Sahib to his name he was not to be addressed. He was no more 'Bachchu' that was in the evolutionary stages of progress and rendering services to Stabil the Khalq – the humanity that was the springboard to cohesion to fame; he had sprung jumped from the thorny field of imputations and landed on the grassy ground of progress, fame and essential service.

And Yarwah Sahib rose to the occasion and gave a Valima Dinner as thanksgiving for his wedding. There was no state clamp on the feast and sumptuous dinner was given by Yarwah Sahib. The state treasury – *Mal Khana* was not shy to give him a helping hand. The vaults of the treasury were opened to give him loan against his new position and against the assets of his lands in the Nawabdom and a great Valima was given. And it was not long before a great friendship developed between the four permanent Queen wives of the Nawab and the new look wife of Yarwah Sahib. And the quatrain of the ladies, and the new look wife of Yarwah Sahib and his English coach received applauds everywhere in the Nawabdom, where they went.

And the conference in the Nawabdom became the turning point in the rehabilitation of justice and reforms. Education was redesigned to free the souls. Research works were started to embrace truth and create learned like of Ayetullahs, and the four season's Land of Seasons and Songs with its charms and its daylong brightness and the pleasant nights, where neither days nor nights, none exceeding the other in any excessiveness in temperament and length as they did where the English Lady came from, presenting an idealistic balance where she was, appealed to the English Lady so much that she never abandoned the land and the providence was kind to her, an English husband sprang up for her and she started a new life in the Land of the Seasons and Songs. And her rewards were the abundances of smiles and the courtesies rushed to her, seeking her out in the Land of Seasons and Songs wherever she went, where the evening breeze blew laden with the fragrance of soil, and the charm of the land in its orthodoxies sought her to appease her. And where law emerged that men with innocent virtues made grade in life. And the sophisticated Poet Sayed Ale Raza Lukhnawi said of the Land of Seasons and Songs:

یوں تو بے تابی میں اس محفل سے اٹھ آنا پڑا
کیا کہیں کیا ہوا جب دل کو سمجھانا پڑا
موت ہی جسکو چھڑا سکتی تھی وہ دل کش دیار
یوں چھٹا ہم سے کہ ہمکو خود ہی چھوڑ آنا پڑا

Yoon Toe Betabi Mein Iss Mahfil Say Oothd Aana Parda
Kya Kahein Kya Hooa Jub Dil Ko Samjhana Parda
Maut Hi Jisko Chhurda Sakti Thhi Woh Dilkash Dayar
Yoon Chhuta Hum Say Ki Humko Khood Hi Choard Aana Parda

Though in anxiety 'had to get up and leave this association
What (I) shall say what happened when the heart had to be consoled
Only the death which could have snatched -
that beautiful surrounding
In this way it got separated from me that (I) had to leave it by myself

-: . :-

III

LAST WORD

XVI

The Land of Seasons and Songs was written for familiarising the Bood-o Baash of the people of India to not knowing India. It endeavours present an idealistic society where justice is of prime importance. The book fills the voids in the rule of law and decency and responds to the mass' need and it endeavours preserve the culture of the sub-continent of India. It was to remind the people of the common heritage of culture evolved out of the imperial orders of different dynasties, which have moulded and tampered the people of the subcontinent to be near to each other. The culture of Pahlay Aap – 'first you Sir' has evolved out of the largess of delight of heart of the people to place the other of his fellow man before him. This courtesy speaks of the efficacy and the uprightness of the people, which must be adhered to in the cultural preserve of altruism of all the countries that make the subcontinent.

The book; The Land of the Seasons and Songs brings the people closer to the Urdu language and presents samples of Urdu literary poets interpreting realities. And what a beautiful country India is for the precept of Rev. Swami Morari Bapu, who says, 'his inner self throbs like Mansoor Hallaj's who said Anal Haque, and Morari Bapu says; Naad-e Aliyan Mazharul Ajaeb Tajadahu Aunan Laka Fin Nawaeb, Kullo Hammin Wa Ghammin Saiyanjalay Be Wilayateka Ya Ali-o, Ya Ali-o, Ya Ali. And I say the following verses to highlight this phenomenon.

گفتار سوامی کرے علی کے پہچاننے کی
دنیا بس نہ کرے ہو خواست گار علی سے علی مل جانے کی
خلافت چھین لی جلدی میں حق سے کارندوں نیں
قباحت گھول دی امّت میں نہ پہچاننے کی

علی تقدیر ہیں دنیا کے راست راہی کی
قدر انسان کے بلاغت کی اور شجاعت کی
ایسا مولا ملا دنیا کو اور اتنا پہلے
کری نہ قدر قباحتیوں نے حصولِ دنیا داری کی

سیّد اطہار حسین

Guftar Swami Karay Ali Kay Pahchannay Ki

Dunya Bus Na Karay Ho Khwst Gar Ali Say Ali Mill Janay Ki

Khilafat Chheen Lee Jaldi Mein Haque Say Karindoan Nein

Qabahat Ghoal Dee Ummat Mein Na Pahchannay Ki

Ali Taqdeer Haain Dunya Kay Rast Rahi Ki

Qadar Insan Kay Balaghat Ki Aur Shujaat Ki

Aaisa Maula Mila Dunya Ko Aur Aetna Pahlay

Kari Na Qadr Qabahatiyoun Nay Husool-e Dunya Dari Ki

Swami Talks of recognising of Ali

The world must not stop be appealing to join Ali

The workers snatched the Caliphate in hurry from the righteous

Dissolved the harm for the Ummat of not to recognise

Ali is fortune of the world of it taking road to rightness

Value of man of eloquence and of valour

Such a Lord Master the world got and so early

The harm doers did not value, did to obtain worldliness

Hazrat Nizami Ganjvi, Hakim Jamal al-Din Abu Mohammad Ilyas was born 1141 AD in Ganja Azerbaijan, died 1209 in Ganja Azerbaijan. He has said the following Masnavi – rhyming verses to spur love in the world:

فلک جُز عشق محرابی ندارد
جہاں بر خاک عشق آبی ندارد
غلامِ عشق شَو خندیزہ ایں است
ہمہ صِحاب دل آں را پیشہ ایں است

Falak Juz Ishq Mahrabi Nadarad
Jahan Bar Khaq, Ishq Aabi Nadarad
Ghulam-e Ishq Shau kandeeshah Een Ast
Hama Sehabdil Aan-ra Pesha Een Ast

The universe without love has no authority to leading
If there is no glowing love there is dust on the world
Who becomes slave of love, he is admired.
This is the profession of all the pious people?

-: . :-